Translation, Script and Orality

Translation, Script and Orality
Becoming a Language of State

Rochelle Pinto

Assistant Editors
Dale Luis Menezes
Mabel Mascarenhas

Orient BlackSwan

TRANSLATION, SCRIPT AND ORALITY: BECOMING A LANGUAGE OF STATE

ORIENT BLACKSWAN PRIVATE LIMITED

Registered Office
3-6-752 Himayatnagar, Hyderabad 500 029, Telangana, India
e-mail: centraloffice@orientblackswan.com

Other Offices
Bengaluru, Chennai, Guwahati, Hyderabad,
Kolkata, Mumbai, New Delhi,
Noida, Patna, Visakhapatnam

First published 2021

ISBN 978-93-5442-004-7

Typeset in
Palatino Linotype 10.5/12.6
by Manmohan Kumar, Delhi

032955

Printed in India at
Akash Press, Delhi 110020

Published by
Orient BlackSwan Private Limited
3-6-752, Himayatnagar Hyderabad 500 029, Telangana, India
e-mail: info@orientblackswan.com

Contents

PART THREE

PART FOUR

To my parents, Rosario and Teofilda Pinto

Preface

Instead of imposing a language on posterity I believe it will be better for us if we leave this problem to be decided by posterity themselves.

[P. T. Chacko (United State of Travancore and Cochin) on 12 September 1949 Constituent Assembly Debates, Vol. IX: 1397–98]

P. T. Chacko's suggestion for the future of language policy in India has been described as a sane voice in the Constituent Assembly debates, a retrospective reaction to the history of state intervention in language use.[1] The history of policy indicates however, that Chacko's views did not prevail. Language policy was so overwhelmingly defined by the presence of the state that even those petitioning for recognition of excluded languages often used statist terms to define them. Over two decades before Goa's integration into the Indian Republic in 1961, literary perspectives on language had begun to converge with the expectations of linguistic nationalism in British- and then independent-India. The consequences of being excluded from modern economies and administration were too severe for the state's linguistic intervention to be ignored. This book is not an account of the debates that contributed to the official recognition of Konkani in 1987 and in 1992, in the Eighth Schedule of the Constitution, a list that determines which languages will be used for official purposes and thereby become the responsibility of the state. Instead, it examines the assumptions about the nature of language itself that are the grounds for official recognition. Konkani was an exemplar of a language that did not meet these criteria. These

[1] Hany Babu M. T., "Breaking the Chaturvarna System of Languages," *Economic and Political Weekly* Vol. 52, Issue No. 23 (2017): 114. The quote by P. T. Chacko has also been sourced from this article.

aberrations from the state model are elaborated in transcriptions and translations and it is in these texts that a language that would eventually meet state criteria and the aspirations of some of its elite was manufactured.

Napoleao Bonaparte, a Konkani text of 1894, is similar to the story *Julus pai tum kiteac chintai? Puta tuca kitem zai?* of 1931 in as far as neither fits current expectations of a translation. Both adapt stories about the lives of Napoleon and Julius Caesar, to comment on contemporary Goa and its history, to assess the political values these historical figures represented, against the situation of ordinary people in Goa.[2] In fact, this strategy of reimagining the lives of historical figures, or, of inserting an account of life in Goa into the biographies of legendary figures did not distinguish between translation and adaptation and was used often in popular writing, even in the early works of the well-known writer V. Varde Valaulikar. As with localised versions of the Ramayana, this could be characterised as a practice of adopting and embedding traditions or genres, unlike modern author-centered conceptions of literature.

Scholarly writing that developed as a parallel to such texts pointed to flaws in popular Konkani print. These flaws were also discussed in popular newspapers, but without assumptions about linguistic corruption, and linguistic history. Formal critiques drew on the authority that the field of comparative philology had acquired across the nineteenth century. This book traces this concern to demonstrate that transcriptions and translations were introduced as a correctional practice to deter the expanding use of popular Konkani. Konkani usage was purged until the language fulfilled philological expectations of a modern vernacular.

In the mid-nineteenth century, Konkani was seen to lack two dimensions, a continuous literature from ancient times, and a sufficiently indigenous script. Literary history hierarchised languages, so that those that were predominantly oral such as Konkani, were seen as deficient in comparison to literary ones. Simultaneously, in the light of the discourse of cultural nationalism, the history of Konkani writing in the Roman script from the sixteenth century on, and subsequently in a multiplicity of scripts, was seen as too diverse, and unstandardised, making for a fragmented literary

---

[2] The book *Napoleao Bonaparte* was advertised in the *O Concanim* of August 5, 1894 without any mention of its author. J.Caetano Francisco De Souza, *Napoleao Bonaparte,* vol. I (Bombay: A.F. Martin & Co., 1914); Caridade Damascino Fernandes, *Julus pai tum kiteac chintai? Puta tuca kitem zai*? (Bombay: Luis Caridade Fernandes, 1931).

culture. Translations were a response to this perception. There are two processes underway in these translations. One is an often-unstated rendition from an oral text to a written one. The other, which is volubly expounded, is the salvaging of devotional texts from the Roman script, valuable as signs of a high devotional tradition, but in a script that nationalist philology found inadequate.

As the hierarchies of colonial comparative philology were absorbed into nationalist discourse, language overwhelmingly came to symbolise political identity. If caste or religious or class lines were sharpened among speakers of the same language, these divides became visible through symbolic differentiation. These tensions were deflected onto aspects of the same language such as script or accents, which came to represent different positions within a cultural conflict. This was a parallel process to the shifting relation between Konkani and other languages such as Marathi, Portuguese, English or Kannada. As a language that was spoken along the western coast, its relation with different states, and with other languages transformed across time, so that a linear history tends to be centred around one state and one set of conflicts.

Through the process of identity formation around the Marathi language and in relation to the state of Maharashtra, there was an unequivocal relegation of Konkani to the status of a dialect of Marathi. In opposition to this, it was proposed that Konkani had the potential to carve out a distinct Saraswat Brahmin identity in Goa in the context of intra-brahmin rivalries along the western coast, by acquiring symbolic capital through the adoption of the Devanagari script (Saldanha 1943).[3] Thus Konkani became the focus of debate as an object of state discourse on issues of education, identity, and caste distinction, and it formally became a language of state about a century later through its association with a script that denoted a majoritarian high culture. The literati's success as it secured exclusive state recognition for Devanagari in Goa in 1987, through the Official Language Act, determined the nature of future debates and structured literary history.

The Devanagari script appeared to be a solution to several issues. It addressed the future of Konkani speakers, promising a unified literature in what was seen as a suitably indigenous script, though few read in it. Its association with Sanskrit gave it symbolic value that allowed it to be used to salvage the past history of writing in the Roman script. This polarisation is however, specific only to the history

[3] See a discussion of V. Varde Valaulikar later in the text.

of Goa and not to the patterns of language use along other points on the western coast. As facets of the language were transformed into symbols of political identity,usages that fell outside the expected boundaries tended to be suppressed in literary histories. Thus Narayan B. Desai emphasises that with the association of Catholics in Goa with the Roman script, the history of printing Christian doctrine in Devanagari and in Marathi along the western coast, among Christian populations who used the local language, tends to be erased (Desai 2002). In the Mangalore region, where Christian devotional texts were always in the Kannada script, there was likewise, no symbolic association with the Roman script which, in at least one instance, was seen as alien (see p. 174). A dominant strand of the history of translation in Konkani, as this book suggests, is the effort to extricate the language itself from its past form and to compensate for its oral and popular tradition.

The history of transcription was a constant process of restoration to the present. In fact, what was underway was a form of translation that involved the production of a language that could be designated as such, an entity to which a history, writing, and a community could be attached. From the perspective of nationalist philology, Konkani did not merely have to be restored from an oral practice, but from the point when it had been alienated from itself, when transcribed into what a majoritarian discourse saw as an alien script. This history reveals again what historians of subcontinental literature have argued; that translation as we understand it today rests on an understanding of language as an object distinct from the self and from other languages. When literary studies adopted this conception of language, the discipline and its associated practices such as translation, became the tools through which language use and literary practice were altered.

References

Desai, Narayan B. 'The Politics of Script: The Case of Konkani (1961–1992),' Goa University, 2002.

Saldanha, Mariano. "Questões de Concani," *Heraldo*, March 14, 1943.

INTRODUCTION

The assumptions of literary history

A catalogue in the British Library in London mentions the *Kisas al-anbiya* (A history of the Saints from Adam), a translation into Konkani by Kazi Kutb al-Din; a rare sign of the presence of Islamic culture in the nineteenth century history of Konkani print.[1] The entry in the catalogue states that it was written in Sindhi characters. Nur Sobers-Khan, lead curator for South Asia at the British library, confirmed that it was written in the Naskh typeface, that the introductory words and the content relied heavily on Arabic and Persian terminology (with possible Sindhi usages, which may explain the initial catalogue description).[2] Published in 1893 from Bombay, the book is possibly the only known copy of a translated Konkani text from this period, in this typeface.[3] Sobers-Khan's approximate summary of the initial lines of the text reads,

---

[1] Kazi Kutb al-Din, *Kisas al-anbiya, A history of the Saints from Adam*, (compiled by Kazi Kutb al-Din in Konkani, and printed in Sindhi characters), Bombay, 1893. Two other catalogue entries exist for this publication: James Fuller Blumhardt, *A Supplementary Catalogue of Marathi and Gujarati Books in the British Museum*. (London: British Museum, 1915), 87, http://dsal.uchicago.edu/bibliographic/bmcatalogs/Z7049.I3B85.pdf. This catalogue entry states that this was 310 pages long and a hundred copies were printed off the Chitra Prabha Press near Nal Bazaar, Ali Char street, Bombay.

[2] I thank Shabnum Tejani for the initial description and help in accessing the text, and Jason Keith Fernandes, Vikhar Ahmed Sayeed, Syed Faisal and Naveed Hassan for help in identifying script and language.

[3] The original entry in the 1915 catalogue as indicated above, suggests this was printed in 'Sindhi characters'. If Sindhi in Nastaliq script is also included in sections of the text, this remains uncorroborated until further examination of the text.

'the author has translated the work into Konkani so that it will be useful to Konkani-speaking Muslims seeking religious guidance [...]he specifically mentions female Muslims (*muslimat*) as the target audience, in addition to Muslim men (*muslimin*). While '*muslimin wa muslimat*' is a Quranic phrase that often gets repeated in Islamic religious discourse, its use here seems to be deliberate, with a view to including female readers in the audience.'[4]

The fact that there are only a few known Konkani texts in this script is not the only reason why it is hard to fit the *Kisas al-anbiya* into a history of translation or into a history of Konkani writing.[5] Literary histories, as critiques of nationalism have demonstrated, did not merely list texts chronologically but used explicit or implicit cultural categories that determined which would be included in national canons of literature.[6] The following sections examine those assumptions of literary histories that positioned Konkani in a hierarchical relation with other languages. This positioning was both a process and a dominant narrative within literary history that would determine how the task of translation was addressed in relation to Konkani.

From the late nineteenth century on, influenced by both philology and nationalism, literary studies linked territories, communities, and languages, to construct linear and continuous histories of language and literature.[7] The eighteenth-century philological model of a tree or a map, through which comparative assessments of languages could be made, subsequently affected various other fields of cultural analysis, such as ethnology and archaeology. Languages were hierarchised in relation to each other, identified with a territory, and the evidence of writing in antiquity endowed some literatures and the contemporary communities associated with them with the valued

---

[4] Correspondence with Dr. Nur Sobers-Khan, formerly Lead Curator for South Asia at the British Library.

[5] Rajend Mesthrie, Sonal Kulkarni-Joshi, and Ruta Paradkar, "Kokni in Cape Town and the Sociolinguistics of Transnationalism," *Language Matters* 48, no. 3 (September 2, 2017): 73–97, https://doi.org/10.1080/10228195.2017.1387168.

[6] G. Aloysius, *Nationalism Without a Nation in India* (Delhi; New York: Oxford University Press, 1998), 151–52.

[7] For an elaboration of the connection between colonial philology, nation formation and contemporary linguistic politics, see Sheldon Pollock, *The Language of the Gods in the World of Men – Sanskrit, Culture, and Power in Premodern India* (Berkeley and Los Angeles: University of California Press, 2006); Andrew Ollett, *Language of the Snakes: Prakrit, Sanskrit, and the Language Order of Premodern India*, 2017; Bernard S. Cohn, *Colonialism and Its Forms of Knowledge – the British in India* (Princeton, NJ: Princeton University Press, 1996), 54–55.

attribute of a long history. The historicity of language (the ability to attach a continuous past to each language) was a fundamental component of modern philological analysis. To such assumptions about language, the legacy of Indology and Orientalism added classicism as a cultural value and held the existence of 'epic' texts as a point of civilisational origin.[8]

The selective literary histories that had emerged because of the philological model also drew on another influential concept; the view of languages as individuated entities, each with a history that implied development over time, from speech to writing, and from simple to complex forms.[9] Ancient languages and texts were linked to contemporary communities. In conjunction with the political structures of nationalism, this positioned Sanskrit and the foundational epics associated with it as a normative beginning for all literary history in India. Nationalist literary organisations transformed such expectations into a dominant cultural model, and a condition for languages to be able to earn official recognition.

Dominant languages in the emerging Indian nation not only provided evidence of literary texts from antiquity, but in fulfillment of the dual expectation that defines the official and commonsensical understanding of literary modernity, also demonstrated their capacity to develop contemporary concepts and usages that would build the nation and the modern citizen. Madhava Prasad elaborates on the consequences of such a linguistic model for minor languages,

> (L)anguage is the first universal, the…element in which humanity inscribes itself and sets off on a journey that will henceforth unfold, not according to the natural cycles, the seasons and seasonal urges, but along the inorganic pathways of history, community and communication…In real political situations where the formation of

---

[8] Vinay Dharwadker, "Orientalism and the Study of Indian Literature," in *Orientalism and the Postcolonial Predicament: Perspectives on South Asia*, ed. Carol A. Breckenridge and Peter van der Veer (New Delhi: OUP, 1994), 158–95; Gauri Viswanathan, *Masks of Conquest: Literary Study and British Rule in India* (Columbia University Press, 1989), 124–25. While Viswanathan discusses a moment in colonial policy when epics failed to meet the requirements of a modern literature and an appropriate pedagogic source, Dharwadker indicates the conjunction of philology and literature in the context of British colonialism and German Indology.

[9] A seminal intervention against the idea of translation as a symmetrical transfer between two languages, was Tejaswini Niranjana's *Siting Translation: History, Post-structuralism and the Colonial Context* (Berkeley: University of California Press, 1992).

> complex social orders such as the nation-state is involved, a sacrifice is necessarily demanded of the speakers of a minor language: keep it for your private needs, but forego the universal dimension, alienate it into the majority language...[10]

Enabled by administrative policy and prevailing linguistic beliefs, literary and linguistic history expelled or marginalised usages that deviated from nationalist prescriptions. The emergence of literary histories that respond to the limits of the linguistic states formed in twentieth century India are an example of how political conceptions are naturalised through practice.

In their self-representations, minor languages were fated to repeat the model, or aspire after a singular conception of (literary) language. Their exponents produced evidence to prove that they belonged within the category of official languages. In light of this quest for parity, Prasad highlights aspects of the notion of equality that is used in relation to languages, which belie the democratic intent associated with its use:

> Some linguists adhere to the normative principle that all languages are "equal", that each is complete in itself and capable of containing within itself all that needs to be contained or expressed. But this theory itself was forged just at that moment when this putative equality was being irrevocably undermined by political developments.[11]

He suggests how this political conception of language simultaneously impinged on speakers:

> While it remains trivially true that a language is just as good as it needs to be for those who speak it, it is also the case that the speakers of certain languages have begun to discern the limits of their language as their worlds become embedded in other encompassing worlds. The experience of the pressure of these limits is arguably one of the defining experiences of modernity.[12]

Likewise, the extraordinary value attributed to antiquity is a condition of linguistic modernity rather than a natural component of literary history. The symbolic and practical consequences for the

---

[10] M. Madhava Prasad, "The Republic of Babel: Language and Political Subjectivity in Free India," in *Theorizing the Present: Essays for Partha Chatterjee*, 2011, 65–81.

[11] Prasad, 71.

[12] ibid.

speakers of languages seen to lack elements of a composite (antiquity and modernisation) linguistic identity has led critics to challenge conventional linguistic histories.[13] It is no longer assumed that a unity of region and ethnicity is a natural attribute of language or that a singular complete history of it exists.[14] Instead, recent histories try to identify defining moments and usages that crystallised conceptions of language, and of literariness, making it possible for others to recover a range of practices that are no longer answerable to a Sanskritised classical beginning.

Negotiating the state model

The People's Linguistic Survey of India by G. N. Devy (founder director of the Bhasha Research and Publication Center) for instance, abjures the search for language families and a developmental history, focusing instead on a, 'snapshot of languages as they are in the early years of the twenty-first century.'[15] It also suggests seeing dialects not as the impoverished remnant of the advanced language or its corruption, but as its repository, 'whose destiny it is to be at the ... interface of an ever-expanding reality, to be the "advance-party" moving towards untapped frontiers of meaning'.[16] The idea of a dialect as 'common currency...with the value of a counterfeit', another formulation of G. N. Devy's, helps illuminate the nature of linguistic expansion outside the limits of conventional literary history.[17]

In 2006, Madhavi Sardesai analysed the changing relationship of diglossia (a situation in which two or more languages or registers

[13] Prasad, "The Republic of Babel: Language and Political Subjectivity in Free India"; Prachi Deshpande, "Scripting the Cultural History of Language: Modi in the Colonial Archive," in *New Cultural Histories of India: Materiality and Practices* (New Delhi: Oxford University Press, 2014), 62–86.

[14] Studies on Konkani now generally attempt to represent all scripts and regions. Rajay Ramesh (Pawar, "Konkani kavitentalen gonyache samaj darshan (1960 te 1990 meren ujavada aayillya devnagritlya Konkani kavitchya sandbhart)," INFLIBNET, 2011, http://shodhganga.inflibnet.ac.in:8080/jspui/handle/10603/14091; Madhavi Sardesai, *A Comparative Linguistic and Cultural Study of Lexical Influences on Konkani* (Goa University, 2006)). Sardesai accounts for different cultures of Konkani between religious communities as well as between oral and written cultures.

[15] *The Being of Bhasha: A General Introduction,* Vol. I, People's Linguistic Survey of India (New Delhi: Orient Blackswan Private Limited, 2014), 14.

[16] ibid., I:16.

[17] ibid.

of a single language are used in a hierarchised or uneven relation to each other within a community), between Marathi and Konkani. This study traced patterns and hierarchies and shifts across time that conventional literary history, which tended to focus on singular languages, had blocked from perception.[18]

Translations such as the *Kisas al-anbiya* alert us to a nineteenth-century facet of Konkani, which, like other languages that circulated among communities of the Indian Ocean was often printed in bi- or tri-lingual texts that had a wider circulation and repertoire of genres, rather than monolingual texts. If as Sobers-Khan suggests, the *Kisas al-anbiya* did in fact particularly mention women, had Konkani in Nastaliq become part of the habitus of devotional reading or recitation in domestic contexts on the western coast of India? The fact that the book was printed in Bombay, along with its Sindhi usages, points to a zone of circulation extending across the Indian Ocean.[19]

From the perspective of linguists and grammarians of the late nineteenth century, this translation into Konkani would have been seen as a mixture of languages. Naoki Sakai however, suggests that the conception of languages as individually distinct entities replicates the political idea of humans as autonomous self-contained units, which underpins the idea of translation as a transfer between two autonomous languages.[20] Instead, viewing translation as a cultural recoding of texts addressed to readers or to a context presumed to be multilingual is better suited to the linguistic cultures of nineteenth-century Konkani print. In contrast to the abstract assumption of monoglot societies, this view does not see multilingualism as a skill of speakers or readers, but as the social existence of languages that are always in contact with each other.

---

[18] Sardesai, "A Comparative Linguistic and Cultural Study of Lexical Influences on Konkani".

[19] Nile Green states that Konkani Muslims from Ratnagiri had become the largest segment of Bombay's Muslim population by the end of the nineteenth century. As an indicative statistic he states that there were 71,000 people from Ratnagiri district registered as residents of Bombay in 1872. The figure had increased to 145,000 by 1901. Middle-class and elite migrants had moved earlier in the century but after the 1860s, according to him, there was a movement of labour into the city. Nile Green, *Bombay Islam: The Religious Economy of the West Indian Ocean,* 1840–1915 (Cambridge University Press, 2011), 183. Sebastian R. Prange, *Monsoon Islam: Trade and Faith on the Medieval Malabar Coast* (Cambridge University Press, 2018).

[20] Naoki Sakai, *Translation and Subjectivity – on "Japan" and Cultural Nationalism* (Minneapolis: University of Minnesota Press, 1997).

The unreflexive or unremarked-on transition between languages that the *Kisas al-anbiya* demonstrates may be seen as an aspect of linguistic existence and literary possibility outside of increasingly audible statist definitions of literature and language. If we assume that this typified most public uses of Konkani until the twentieth century, it helps clarify the moments when the language acquired patronage and became the object of attempts to draw it within the ambit of the state, as exceptions.

With the intention of endowing it with the status that other languages enjoyed, Konkani was objectively named as an individuated language and as one that could impede or ensure the formation of a political community. It was in the early twentieth century, in genres such as newsprint, that the consciousness of a class- and caste-defined community was voiced. However, these concepts only found popular acceptance when they appeared in forms of print that embodied the Konkani habitus in the latter half of the nineteenth century, through which writers addressed readers as familiars, part of a limited community of migrant speakers whose world was made up of known symbols, objects, and value systems. This habitus was always the point of departure from which concerns such as national identity and the vexed question of citizenship could be addressed. It was the condition that allowed statist concerns to be posited in Konkani. In genres such as vocabularies, where a practical need-based exchange between two or three languages, usually within a restricted zone of language use was offered, there seemed to be no perceived limits or barriers to language use, no consciousness that one was a language of state, and the other not.

The overarching concern with philological origins or with conflict over language rights in contemporary times makes invisible the distinctiveness of such bi- or tri-lingual vocabularies. These were produced when the phenomena of migration and affordable print converged, producing Swahili-Gujarati language primers, or Konkani-Swahili vocabularies.[21] The nature of labour exchanges and trade between countries of the Indian Ocean region generated sufficient economic activity to enable such language contact outside

[21] See for instance the twenty-two page *Alīdinā Somajī Līlānī* – A guide to the Swahili language, in Gujarati characters, with English and Gujarati translations. Chiefly for the use of Indians having relations with Zanzibar, Bombay, 1890. Blumhardt, *A Supplementary Catalogue of Marathi and Gujarati Books in the British Museum*, 9, or the *Vocabulário Português-Guzerate* by L(a)xmanbhai T. Baia. Pedro Bir M. F. C., *A Handbook of the English, Hindustani, Konkani, Swahili Languages* (Nairobi: Uganda Railway Press, 1902).

state-driven linguistic use, suddenly bringing languages into legible contact with each other. The following sections present some pertinent discussions of how oral forms were positioned in relation to writing and literature.

Orality and origin

This discussion of orality indicates that the axes along which minor languages deviate from dominant conceptions of literature overwhelmingly structure their history. Thus, Walter Ong's account of the culture of orality asserts that the concept of 'oral literature' empties the oral of everything other than its difference from the written and defines it from within the terms of the written.[22] Primary orality, or an oral culture in which the dominance of literacy is absent, no longer exists, he states. However, his discussion of the attributes of oral texts helps us recognize their persistence through the transition between oral cultures and literary writing.[23] Ong's depiction of writing as 'imperialist activity' is pertinent for oral cultures such as Konkani. Konkani's misfit with the categories of dominant philology drew from the fact that its oral culture was studied by and large as a supplement to those elements of Konkani writing that met the expectations of literary history. Commentaries on Konkani translation as stated in the preface, have a strained tenor because there are at least two kinds of translation being effected; one is a continuous but invisible translation from an oral culture to a written one, and another is the recuperation of Konkani writing from its problematic early modern history, a discomfort that in contrast, is explicitly voiced.

Sheldon Pollock's comprehensive account of Sanskrit in the first century of the Common Era illuminates how it implicates languages whose early modern existence was predominantly oral in India, or how it impacts 'the continuum of patois that constitutes language'.[24]

---

[22] Walter J. Ong, *Orality and Literacy – The Technologizing of the Word* (London and New York: Routledge, 2002), 11. A critique of Bakhtin's privileging of the folk within literary history echoes this view of the tendency of writing 'to assimilate other things to itself'. Classical anthropology in this view represents the difference of oral cultures from the perspective of writing when it privileges the non-European as the trace of the cultural truth. Roberto González Echevarría, *Myth and Archive: A Theory of Latin American Narrative* (Cambridge: Cambridge Univ. Press, 1990), 9.

[23] Ong, 11.

[24] Pollock, *The Language of the Gods in the World of Men – Sanskrit, Culture, and Power in Premodern India*, 24.

Pollock recognises Sanskrit's exclusive self-designation as a written and literary language, as an act of power ('(O)ne thing that could not be *kāvya* was the purely oral').[25] He also points out that this was accomplished though the Sanskrit literary realm never objectively defined or enforced its implied limits.[26] This elaboration of Sanskrit literarisation (the transition to literary use within the history of a language) emphasises that language acquired cognitive definition and objective identity, or, was recognised as a language, only at the moment of writing, and through the production of texts.[27]

The hegemonic effect of Sanskritic self-representation is also highlighted in Andrew Ollett's work on Prakrit, a medium of courtly literature used across the first century of the Common Era. Ollett points out that the philological model anticipates that the distinctive nature of a language emerges either when we trace its difference from a prior stage of its existence, or the extent of its derivation from Sanskrit.[28] In fact, he argues, this tells us little about the relation of Prakrit with either Sanskrit, or with vernacular languages. The place of Prakrit in literary history, he emphasises, can be understood by examining the relations between literary conventions in various languages, rather than assuming that it is origin or language hierarchies that illuminate its existence. This highlights the fact that the customary focus on origin does not merely draw on modern philology, but extends a familiar convention through which literary texts validated themselves by indicating the antiquity and continuity of the tradition to which they belonged.[29]

Pollock cites instances of Sanskrit writing that referenced the realm of the oral. He suggests for example, that the Ramayana framed 'its own orality in a way that would be impossible in a preliterate world...'[30] In another instance, it appears the oral was refigured within the realm of literary writing, as in his depiction of the *Bṛhatkathā*, which 'existed less as an actual text than as a conceptual category signifying the *Volksgeist*, the Great Repository of Folk Narratives, which may indeed be the source of its entry into the literary language taxonomy.'[31]

---

[25] ibid., 3.

[26] Pollock, 12.

[27] Pollock, 4, 23.Pollock's assertion that oral languages '... existed in oral prehistory but only in a phenomenological rather than a conceptual sense, as "Language" or language continua rather than as defined languages', suggests itself as a description of the existence of Konkani prior to the sixteenth century.

[28] Ollett, *Language of the Snakes*, 20.

[29] ibid.

[30] Pollock, 13.

[31] Pollock, 92.

The hegemony of the Sanskritic model reinforced by modern philology made other markers of literary difference unrecognisable and marginal. The notion of an oral realm progressively displaced by writing and then by literary writing was naturalised. However, as Ollett's work suggests, the binaries of literary and non-literary, or orality and writing, or even cosmopolitan and vernacular, do not reveal the status of Prakrit as a codification of literary practice. This attention to the universalised teleology of language as firstly, writing (literization – a term Sheldon Pollock uses to mark 'the development of a written form of the vernacular') and then literature (literarization) also helps understand the knotted discourse around the literary history of Konkani.[32]

Philology as a condition of translation

Modern philology depicted language as an object that could be analysed across historical time and as an index to categorise peoples and race. This shaped the notion of translation as an exchange between autonomous language communities, a notion that was universalised but also contested. One of the grounds on which it was contested was that the characteristics attributed to communities and individuals, of being autonomous or monolingual and distinct from each other, often inappropriately referenced modern European contexts.

One of the earliest studies to indicate how these conceptions drew on ideas about language rather than actual historical processes was Tejaswini Niranjana's *Siting Translation* in 1992.[33] In colonial contexts, the idea of the indigenous as distinct communities and as a cultural category extended such concepts into practice and worked as an internal limit or a cultural boundary. This demarcation of communities of language speakers continues to frame our writing of literary history. Aamir Mufti draws attention to how this concept, 'set the stage for the elaboration of contradictions between national and non-national social imaginaries in the subcontinent, in particular between the Indic complex and the Indo-Persian ecumene…'.[34] In other words, it problematised or repressed literary

[32] Pollock 25, 27.

[33] *Siting Translation* questioned the assumptions concerning modern subjectivities associated with language.

[34] Aamir R. Mufti, "Orientalism and the Institution of World Literatures," *Critical Inquiry* 36, no. 3 (March 1, 2010): 475, https://doi.org/10.1086/653408.

and cultural spheres of circulation that were not modeled around the idea of a singular culture, and for which national boundaries were irrelevant.

Mufti and Rashmi Bhatnagar insist on the importance of eighteenth-century philology as the primary impetus for the spatial and temporal organisation of colonial languages in relation to European ones. In her account of the creation of Hindi through the language textbook *Premsagar* produced in 1810 in Fort William College in colonial Calcutta, she argues that colonial languages were seen to represent the past of European languages, while the social context of their writers and their literature represented a phase within world history, usually the past of Europe.[35] When these concepts were directed within the Indian subcontinent, the effect was a 'linguistic purge', of 'geographically identified outsiders', demarcating the boundaries of the Hindi language that could be included as one's own and that which lay outside that boundary.[36] Similar acts of disciplining continued, Bhatnagar suggests, until the invention of the 'linguistic indigenous', identified with the influential linguist, George A. Grierson.[37] Mufti alerts us to the 'mutual interdependence between…secular-national and Hindu-religious formations', insisting that a modular 'secularised' notion of a national literature merely repeated the exclusions of the religious model, with the 'indigenous as facilitator of the authenticity of tradition'.[38]

These assumptions continue to influence contemporary work as Prachi Deshpande suggests in relation to Marathi. She observes that, 'the gap between synchronic/structuralist linguistics and critical, contingent histories of literary culture' is 'filled, and overdetermined, by immediate political contexts, with languages as sites of recovering community or national pasts.'[39] Even histories resistant to the pursuit of purity, she argues, in an important observation, commit the contemporary language activist-scholar to the search for the authentically *deshi*, or the cultural core of a language.

---

[35] R. D. Bhatnagar, "Premsagar (1810) and Orientalist Narratives of the 'Invention' of Modern Hindi," *Boundary 2*, 39, no. 2 (January 1, 2012): 77. https://doi.org/10.1215/01903659-1597898.

[36] ibid.

[37] ibid., 78.

[38] Mufti, 474–75.

[39] Prachi Deshpande, "A Classical Past for a Modern Language: Historicizing Marathi" (November 2, 2017).

The unexplored philology of sixteenth-century translation

In light of the dual demand that contemporary languages should demonstrate both, a literary past, as well as the capacity for modern innovation towards the national future, Konkani has the unforgivable history of having simultaneously acquired distinction as a written and literary language, through the mediation of missionaries, and in the Roman script. Comments by Thomas Stephens, the first Jesuit to produce a doctrinal text in Konkani, suggested that the language was a simpler usage among brahmins, but not the customary 'pure Marathi' that was used to read the Puranas.[40] Since the aim was to expand the numbers of Christians who could understand the Catechisms they produced, a number of Konkani texts emerged at this point.[41] The absence of prior texts written entirely in Konkani makes missionary publications, such as the *Doutrina Christam* by Thomas Stephens and others, the first full texts in the language. Irrespective of the discomfort they would cause mid-twentieth century linguists, as doctrine that was modelled on European or local popular and authoritative treatises, these new publications acquired cultural authority.

This did not go unrecognised when language became pivotal to the assertion of political borders and community identity, though in intervening centuries, Portuguese as a language of literary print had replaced Konkani. From the 1850s onward, one section of the literati hoped to extend to Konkani the status of European and Indian vernaculars. In the late nineteenth century, its potential as a marker of regional Goan Hindu identity was elaborated, and it was recovered, but only when it had been rendered into the Devanagari script.[42] For the most radical proponents of Marathi in the twentieth century, however, Konkani remained the language that should never have been named.[43] What the nature of the 'simple language of the brahmins' was in the sixteenth century is as yet unclear, as histories of state formation in Maharashtra and Goa enmeshed the 'pre-history' of Konkani in bitter debates over its status as a dialect to Marathi.

---

[40] Ananya Chakravarti, "Between Bhakti and Pietà: Untangling Emotion in Marāṭhī Christian Poetry," *History of Religions* 56, no. 4 (2017): 365–87.

[41] ibid.

[42] Mariano Saldanha, "Questões de Concani," *Heraldo*, March 14, 1943.

[43] Anant Kakba Priolkar, *The Printing Press in India: Its Beginnings and Early Development, Being a Quatercentenary Commemoration Study of the Advent of Printing in India 1556* (Marathi Samshodhana Mandala, 1958). Priolkar never referred to it as anything other than the 'brahmin dialect'.

The delinking of language from a formulaic history helps foreground the moments when Konkani transformed as it acquired and lost patronage from state and church. Accounts of early missionaries help us gauge its changing relation both to Marathi and to Portuguese and to English. When versions of the Konkani Ramayana and the Mahabharata were discovered in the late twentieth century as sixteenth-century recitations that had been transcribed in the Roman script by missionaries, it consolidated the inclusion of the language within literary history. It also implied however, that that history was constitutively corrupted by its agents and by the Roman script.

The language used in the Mahabharata and Ramayana had to be salvaged from its script and restored to the moment when it was transcribed, a moment as yet 'untouched' by colonial influence. From the perspective of dominant histories, the point when it was literized was also the point when it was alienated from itself, not because of the loss of its oral existence, but, as indicated in the preface, because it had been translated into an alien script, via speakers of Portuguese.

'Multiliteralism' or literary production in multiple scripts

In contrast to the approaches outlined above, in 2011, the Konkani Department at Goa University hosted a lecture by a scholar of Navayati literature.[44] Navayati is said to be an amalgamation of Persian, Arabic, Marathi, and Sanskrit, with a preponderance of Konkani, and is spoken and written by a community of Muslims in Bhatkal and areas of coastal Karnataka. Both the *Kisas al-anbiya* of 1893 and Navayati offer a view of Konkani as a coastal language, one that has been in translation/transaction with other languages via commerce and devotion for centuries. This does not imply the absence of hierarchy that may be perceived for instance, between Arabic and Konkani as devotional languages or different dialects of Konkani.

In another instance, Narayan B. Desai uses the term 'multiliteralism' to try to capture the phenomenon of literary production in Konkani

---

[44] Seminar on the Navayat Konkani Muslim Community: Bhashik Ani Sanskritik Asmitai, Konkani Department, University of Goa in Association with Goa Konkani Akademi, 2011, https://www.youtube.com/watch?v=bob3IIiee5Y contributed by Dr. Nandkumar Kamat.

down the western coast of India in different scripts in his thesis, 'Politics Of Script: The Case Of Konkani (1961–1992)'.[45] Desai's study, which is alert to how caste interests are involved in the writing and representation of the language, traces discourses around transcription/translation that dispel the idea of a single authentic and original culture. The formation of linguistic states in India in the mid-twentieth century impelled assertions from those whose spheres of influence were threatened. The two moments of colonial linguistic surveys and state formation are significant for areas that fell within the direct jurisdiction of British India, though this scarcely diminished their impact on Goa and other Konkani speaking territories. This history however, needs to be layered with conceptions of language and cultural difference that operated within Portuguese colonialism.

In as far as we have written evidence for it, the process of translations of and into Konkani began in the sixteenth century under the Christianising imperative to produce suitable literature. This event that was violent and led to the flight or expulsion of some local populations, is one of the reasons usually cited for the creation of Konkani-speaking communities down the western coast. It is possible however, as alternate histories of the Navayati and other groups in coastal Karnataka indicate, that trade rivalries, agricultural conditions, and economic necessity were also factors prior to the Portuguese rule that caused the spread of Konkani-speaking communities into the region of Goa and across the western coast.[46] Until recently as Jason Keith Fernandes has emphasised, the relative invisibility of cultural influences linked to the Islamic presence in Goa was due to the historiographic reliance on Portuguese texts. Produced in the aftermath of conquest, the diminished presence of the Muslim or Islamicate (pertaining to culture) influence in these texts was a sign of the victory of the Portuguese that converged, centuries later, with the Indian nationalist minoritisation of cultures

[45] Narayan B. Desai, *Politics of Script: The Case of Konkani (1961–1992)* (Goa University, 2002). http://library.unigoa.ac.in:8081/xmlui/handle/123456789/380.

[46] K. G. Vasantamadhava, "A Few Observations on Cochin Museum Copper Plate No. 8 Dated Saka 1603 i.e. 1681 – a Study in Relation to Konkana Brahmana Settlements in Gove, Coastal Karnataka and Kerala," *Purabhilekh-Puratatva: Journal of the Directorate of Archives, Archaeology and Museum*, Goa II, no. 2 (December 2001): 92. This source for instance, claims that the Cochin brahmins repeat a legend of migration caused by an attack of Alauddin Khilji of 1294, but that neither the date nor other particulars to the migration story can be corroborated.

that were seen as inauthentic.[47] This observation seems relevant in light of a census of languages conducted in Goa at the time of its annexation by India, in which Urdu was listed as fourth among spoken language, after Portuguese.[48]

Outside of Goa, Konkani-speaking communities existed as linguistic minorities without a central claim on the state, and they employed a range of languages for trade, and for pedagogic and devotional purposes, though expectedly, Konkani was perhaps least frequently used as a language of state administration. Producing a coherent narrative about translation in Konkani implies an engagement with this history, even when that history (as is the case with this introduction), tends to be structured around contemporary linguistic states such as that of Goa.

On being a minor language

There are many ways in which languages are designated as minor ones. A factor that leaps to mind, but is in fact not a criterion, is the number of speakers who claim it as their spoken language in the official census.[49] In the case of Konkani, both the websites of the Government of India census of 2011 and that of the Central Institute of Indian Languages, Mysore, lists over two million speakers,

[47] Jason Keith Fernandes, "Indo-Portuguese Art and the Space of the Islamicate," in *Parmal*, vol. 7 (Goa: Goa Heritage Action Group, 2008), 42; Jason Keith Fernandes, "Rethinking Origin Myths in Goa," *O Heraldo*, April 17, 2015, https://www.heraldgoa.in/Edit/Opinions/Rethinking-origin-myths-in-Goa/87380.html. The selective nature of Portuguese representations of history was first noted by Sanjay Subrahmanyam.

[48] Oscar Pereira, "Present Day Administration in Goa – a Reflection of Past Legacies," in *Goa and Portugal: Their Cultural Links*, ed. Charles J. Borges and Helmut Feldmann (Concept Publishing Company, 1997), 81.

[49] The official term in India is linguistic minorities or minority languages, but studies on these indicate that the official definition does not apply to any single group: 'The Supreme Court of India, in 1958, presented a parameter for defining a minority language as "the language of the minority community" (which is defined as a community numerically less than 50 per cent). However, this parameter is not applicable at the national level because "there is no linguistic group in India which can claim the majority status" (Chaklader 1981, 14).' Rajeshwari Pandharipande, "Minority Matters: Issues in Minority Languages in India," *JMS: International Journal on Multicultural Societies* 4, no. 2 (2002): 3. Pandharipande systematically invalidates official categories as none of them can be sustained for any state. See also Braj B. Kachru, Yamuna Kachru, and S. N. Sridhar, *Language in South Asia* (Cambridge: Cambridge University Press, 2008).

where Kannada has over 43 million speakers and Marathi over 82 million.[50] However, the fact that in 1960, 84.3 per cent of people in Goa reported it as their language, discounts it from being the language of a minority as it was numerically significant within state political boundaries. From the perspective of the *People's Linguistic Survey of India,* which grapples with the fact that data about several spoken languages in India is either not collected or not released, Konkani is far from being a minor language. There are literary texts in the language, it is recognised as the official language by a state, and more recently has been backed by private capital to promote its presence.[51]

The official definition of a minor language in India is dispersed across various entities and commissions.[52] A report on a workshop on linguistic minorities held at Mysore in 2006 emphasised that the absence of a numerical majority of speakers and written texts is only one factor in the identification of minority languages. Affiliation to powerful institutions or groups, or a diminished 'functional load', implying contexts such as literary or scientific or legal ones in which a language was not used, had to be taken into account when determining its position, and the responsibilities of government to its speakers (Sachdeva 2006).[53]

Numerically minor languages, because they were often spoken in areas already associated with major languages, are also identified with a struggle for state recognition. Yet Sanskrit, with only about 24,821 speakers who returned it as their mother tongue (an increase from 14,135 in 2001), does not need a social movement

---

[50] http://censusindia.gov.in/2011Census/C-16_25062018_NEW.pdf. Accessed March 3, 2019. Comparative figures for 2001 are available at:http://www.censusindia.gov.in/Census_Data_2001/Census_Data_Online/Language/Statement1.aspx, http://www.ciil-lisindia.net/konkani/konkani.html

[51] http://vishwakonkani.org

[52] 'The office of the Commissioner for Linguistic Minorities was set up in July, 1957 in pursuance of Article 350B of the Constitution, which came into existence as a result of the Constitution (Seventh Amendment) Act, 1956, consequent to the recommendations of the States Reorganization Commission.' http://www.minorityaffairs.gov.in/sites/default/files/rti-Chapter2.0.pdf, accessed September 16, 2018

[53] Rajesh Sachdeva, "A Report of the Workshop on Linguistic Minorities" (Mysore: Government of India, National Commission for Religious and Linguistic Minorities, Ministry of Minority Affairs in collaboration with Central Institute of Indian Languages, Ministry of Human Resource Development, March 27, 2006), http://www.ciil.org/Download/Linguisticminoritiesreport.pdf.

or a linguistic state to earn it official recognition.[54] In comparison, many languages that have less than 10,000 speakers are not listed on official websites.

The unproblematic inclusion of Sanskrit in the Eighth Schedule may be compared with the figure of over two lakh people who claimed English as their spoken language. For different reasons, English is the official language of state in various states as well as a subsidiary official language of the Government of India, but is not included in the Eighth Schedule.[55] Thus the manner in which the political cultures of each language intersected with the perspectives of the colonial state, and with the post-1947 one, determine whether they are assigned the role of official languages, minor languages, or are erased altogether.[56] In contrast to English, for instance, Portuguese had no official status after the annexation of Goa, though it was both the spoken and written language of the elite for centuries and was the primary language of administration. Sociolinguists have thus generated a range of terms to attempt to grasp at the different kinds of power associated with language, particularly after the formation of the linguistic states in the mid-twentieth century, rather than the deceptive term 'minor'.[57]

However, we see a different use of the term minor in a recent book on literature in modern Kerala, which discusses how lower-caste representations in the nineteenth century, had similarities with

---

[54] Afonso Botelho, "Primary Education and Language in Goa," 2002, 215, http://203.200.22.249:8080/jspui/handle/123456789/9129. Conversely, Botelho cites the case of Urdu in Jammu and Kashmir, which is not the majority language nor is English in Nagaland.

[55] http://www.rajbhasha.nic.in/en/official-languages-act-1963. Accessed on March 8, 2019.

[56] Linguistic studies however, offer more sensitive categories by which to indicate the different status of languages in varying contexts, based on the domains across which they are used, the autonomy or power they have in these domains etc. Rajeshwari Pandharipande, "Minority Matters: Issues in Minority Languages in India."

[57] Udaya Narayana Singh, "Multiscriptality in South Asia and Language Development," *International Journal of the Sociology of Language* 2001, no. 150 (2006): 61–74, https://doi.org/10.1515/ijsl.2001.036; Rajeshwari Pandharipande, "Minority Matters: Issues in Minority Languages in India"; Nishaant Choksi, "Scripting the Border: Script Practices and Territorial Imagination among Santali Speakers in Eastern India," *International Journal of the Sociology of Language*, no. 227 (May 2014), http://www.degruyter.com/view/j/ijsl.2014.2014.issue-227/ijsl-2013-0087/ijsl-2013-0087.xml?format=INT.

upper-caste Hindu idioms.[58] Conventionally, such a phenomenon has produced two kinds of interpretations; one that views this as an emulation of upper-caste practices to enhance social status, the other, as a means to appropriate brahminical practices to serve different groups. However, the author, Udaya Kumar points to the innovativeness of turning the figure of Siva into an Ezhava, and draws on Deleuze's argument, 'that minor literature works by denuding a major language and making it stutter', to convey the effect of this play with different traditions.[59] The use of the term minor here does not denote a different language, but describes a mode of incubation within a dominant tradition that repositions it within cultural practice.

In the more familiar context of linguistic states and language/dialect hierarchies in relation to Assam, Manjeet Baruah states, '(T)here is a clear need to make a shift from the analytical farce in the criterion of language as determinant of region, widely followed in modern Indian regional literary studies'.[60] The attempt to match geographical territory to language to create a particular linguistic or literary region carries many accompanying assumptions about history, religion and, as the case of Assam will indicate, space and geography. Thus, different aspects of the cultural life of an area become visible, because the dominance of a single-language state model brings together differing attributes in a vortex of conflict. What such attributes might be however differs, depending on the cultural traditions in each region. Baruah speaks of how the standardisation of the Assamese language altered the cultural significance of the *buranji*, the chronicles of Ahom nobility:

> Kamrupi language and *buranji* narrative became dialects and relics of the past respectively, whilst modern Assamese 'standard' appropriated (or re-created?) a narrative which was new to itself, but had earlier been textually related to the Kamrupi language, now reduced to a 'dialect'.[61]

As a result of the state need for standardisation, aspects of orality and performance that would localise narratives like the *Mahabharata*

---

[58] Udaya Kumar, *Writing the First Person: Literature, History and Autobiography in Modern Kerala*, First edition (Ranikhet: Permanent Black, 2016).
[59] ibid., 61
[60] Manjeet Baruah, "Assamese Language, Narrative and the Making of the North East Frontier of India: Beyond Regional Indian Literary Studies," *Modern Asian Studies*, March 2013, 680.
[61] Baruah, 658–60.

were diminished in preference for the idea of authenticity associated with printed versions of these texts.

The quote above identifies aspects close to the experience of Konkani speakers, as well as the more general consequence of standardisation and print that has affected languages across the subcontinent. It should be noted though that far greater transformations occurred in the way the area of the Brahmaputra valley was spatially reoriented politically, as a sub-continental frontier north-east of Bengal. Cultural representations from this time on made historical origin and geographical place fixed attributes, as opposed to other representations of the valley as a region of flux, migration and settlement of populations from different regions. Baruah says, 'While in the Ahom *buranjis*, the people and space from Myanmar up to the valley was the present', in the emerging cultural identity of standardised Assamese, 'this relation had changed into the past or history for the valley, while the present came to be located in the valley's *historical* relation with the Gangetic culture.'[62] These markers of time and space were not separate from, but a composite part of the broad set of notions that affected linguistic and literary production.

Thus we see that administrative imaginaries impinged differently on each cultural and literary practice. Oppositions of hill and plain, savage and civilised, Gangetic and south-east Asian traditions created polarisations, that in literary practice appeared as a shift from 'hybrid-texts' (involving manuscript and performance) to 'mono-texts', or, a shift from cultural practices to writing, the hierarchisation of languages and dialects, and anxiety over the question of indigenousness.[63]

As Baruah emphasises, it was not that readers would not understand the diversity of languages had they been represented in print, but that the production of literature in itself was a practice that transformed the relation between languages. The place of a minor language therefore, need not be defined by a conflict between two autonomous languages (Marathi/Konkani) or between a language and a dialect, but by the process through which a form of a language becomes dominant. Baruah suggests how literature itself would define the experience of becoming a minor language by positioning one form as a dialect in relation to a dominant language in a novel. If we were to analyse the history of dialect in Goa against standard writing or dominant spoken Konkani, then

---

[62] ibid., 660.
[63] ibid., 662.

Konkani would be positioned as a dominant language with a distinct caste association.[64]

This indicates that those who represent languages that are minor in one particular context are not necessarily culturally or politically marginalised. Those who advocated Konkani in Devanagari for instance, would be seen as both culturally and politically dominant in the state of Goa. This range of variables indicates that what is in fact constant about modern language use, is the push to administer and create a model of a language that represented a singular identity, and a limited cultural boundary – a dominant language in one script that would homogenise state identities.[65] An effect of this model, dominant since the nineteenth century, is to think of and experience variations in language use as oppositions. One such opposition is the experience of being a minor language or literary practice in relation to an official standard. Thus, Bodhisattva Kar states, '(T)he language and the dialects, the standard and the deviants, the mainstream and the margins, are neither prehistorical residues nor technical aberrations but constitutive conditions of development and metropolitan knowledge,' or, a template for the 'infinite reproducibility' of the oppositions discussed above.[66]

Konkani is discussed in relation to minor languages because of its history of association with the state, the official literary body Sahitya Akademi, and with many other cultural and official institutions. Its acceptance into these structures has led to the reproduction of attributes of dominance that alert us to the need to see such positions as structured phenomena that keep producing reactions to a set of conditions, rather than viewing a language as a historically finite entity.

In a discussion of Kodava, a minor language in Karnataka, Sowmya Dechamma indicates that while Kannada is a dominant state language, Kodava is in a dominant position in relation to languages such as Are-Bhashe, Kodava-Mapale, Erava and

---

[64] For a representation that refers to Gauddo as a people and language in uncritically anthropological terms, and which discusses Gawdi as a dialect of Konkani, in itself represented as a dialect of Marathi, see A.M. Ghatage, *Gawdi, A Survey of Marathi Dialects, VIII* (Bombay: The Maharashtra State Board for Literature and Culture, 1972).

[65] See Choksi, "Scripting the Border: Script Practices and Territorial Imagination among Santali Speakers in Eastern India," *International Journal of the Sociology of Language* for a clear description of state formation.

[66] Bodhisattva Kar, "'Tongue Has No Bone,'" *Studies in History* 24, no. 1 (February 1, 2008): 76, https://doi.org/10.1177/025764300702400102.

Kuruba.[67] She asserts that when an oral language is represented in a written script, even when, as in the case of Kodava, the intention is to intervene in state policy and linguistic politics, the result is the creation of a normalised form. Language analysts understand this to mean a tendency to replicate the 'central fiction' of a single language for a single territory. It is identities and power structures that get translated in the process, she asserts, and the script bears 'the burden of hegemony of the minority within the minority', she says, encapsulating a central aspect of the history of Konkani.[68] Most significantly, she cites Michael Cronin, who asserts that the place of minority languages within translation studies will be to point to the 'world of continuous relational adjustments' that is the nature of our linguistic existence.[69]

The Roman/Latin script in other histories

To return to the question of script, the Kannada and Malayalam scripts, in which Konkani is also written, particularly the Kannada script, which has the maximum number of readers, (but in a linguistic state where Konkani does not have official recognition) are not seen to have failed the test of indigenousness. Other literary cultures that use the Roman script are those of the Khasi language, various languages of Naga tribal groups, Santali and Mizo. Khasi and Mizo are Non-Scheduled languages, that is, they are not official languages of state and some languages of Naga tribal groups appear neither in the Eighth Schedule nor on the Non-Scheduled list.

Khasi initially appeared in print in the Bengali script in 1816, as a translation of the Gospel of Matthew by the Serampore Baptist Mission, but subsequently, the Welsh Baptist Mission represented by Thomas Jones developed the Roman script for the language, suggesting that it was better suited to its structure of consonants.[70]

[67] Sowmya Dechamma, "Scripting Language, Scripting Translation," in *Textual Travels: Theory and Practice of Translation in India*, ed. Mini Chandran and Suchitra Mathur (Routledge, 2015), 112–29.

[68] ibid., 125.

[69] ibid., 126.

[70] Monier Williams, ed., *Original Papers Illustrating the History of the Application of the Roman Alphabet to the Languages of India* (London: Longman, Brown, Green, Longmans, and Roberts, 1859), https://catalyst.library.jhu.edu/catalog/bib_2886222. See Monier Williams' two texts reproducing correspondence that debates the transcription and production of Indian language texts in the Roman script. Tilottama Misra states, 'though there were 11 major Khasi dialects, it was the Ka Ktien Sohra, the spoken language of the Cherra region, that acquired

Ao and Mizo were also written in Roman.[71] In these contexts, if language becomes a contested symbol, it is over orthography and versions of the Roman script rather than the script itself.[72] Studies that are critical of the suppression or displacement of existing belief systems by Christianity do not express the sustained discomfort with the Roman script voiced in relation to Goa, suggesting that it is only when a composite nationalist majoritarian cultural model is the norm, that deviations from it become criteria for exclusion.[73] However, the development of Ol Chiki to replace the Devanagari, Brahmi and Roman scripts in which Santali is written, indicates the need for a cultural assertion against prior dominant scripts, and an account of the opposition to the use of Roman for the Bodo language suggests that script is and can become a sign for contested nationalities in these areas as well.[74]

Making Konkani a language of state

A state-centric history of translation in Konkani therefore, does not reflect the historical occurrence or use of the language, but selectively reorganizes that history to privilege aspects that match the cultural symbolism of the state. The separation of languages

recognition as the dialect chosen for the printed books in Khasi because it was the language chosen by the Welsh missionaries who adopted the Roman script for the Khasi language and published Christian and other literature in that script.' In relation to Mizo, she states that it was the Lusei dialect that was selected for literary production. Tilottama Misra, "Speaking, Writing and Coming of the Print Culture in Northeast India," in *Emerging Literatures From North-East India: The Dynamics of Culture, Society and Identity*, ed. Margaret Ch Zama, First edition (Thousand Oaks, California: SAGE India, 2013), 19.

[71] Misra, 20.

[72] Meenaxi Barkataki-Ruscheweyh, "Fractured Christianity amongst the Tangsa in Northeast India—Bible Language Politics and the Charm of Ecstatic Experiences," *South Asia: Journal of South Asian Studies* 41, no. 1 (January 2, 2018): 218, https://doi.org/10.1080/00856401.2018.1400728.

[73] For a history that resists a teleological nationalist model, see Joy 1969– Pachuau, *The Camera as Witness: A Social History of Mizoram, Northeast India*, n.d., https://catalyst.library.jhu.edu/catalog/bib_7461784.

[74] M. S. Prabhakar, "The Politics of a Script: Demand for Acceptance of Roman Script for Bodo Language," *Economic and Political Weekly* 9, no. 51 (1974): 2097–2102. The contestation over Ol Chiki andRoman for Santali has however, become the object of dispute in public discourse as the Roman script is seen to represent Christian Santals. https://www.telegraphindia.com/1170904/jsp/jharkhand/story_170637.jsp. Accessed on August 29, 2018.

from dialects and the assumed symmetrical link between ethnicity and state is a framing strategy and official norm for what languages should be, rather than a description of their given state.

Nishaant Choksi's study of script practices among Santali speakers is a useful point of reference as Choksi similarly pulls away from the borders of linguistic states to account for a different territorial imagination among the Santals.[75] While Santali scripts similarly do not belong within any one state boundary, the literature does evoke a territorial imagination to which Santals can belong, with or without a modern state.

As a quick contrast, while Konkani eventually gained recognition as an official language in Goa in 1987, it does not have a unified territorial imagination that is linked to a single state. Language activists of the late twentieth century therefore attempted to forge a symbol and vehicle of high cultural acquisition around the Devanagari script in the hope that a single script and the ideal of a unified high culture would draw in all writers and readers, but this particular movement acquired a strong Saraswat Brahmin identity that extended down the western coast. Therefore, as another point of contrast to Santali, while Konkani has rarely had state patronage prior to official recognition, it has had the backing of powerful castes for half a century.

After the annexation of Goa, with the ruling party proposing a merger with Maharashtra, the question of the official language of state hung in balance until a popular referendum settled the question.[76] With Portuguese as the primary administrative language through the centuries of Portuguese rule, supporters of Konkani had to reconstruct a public position for the language. The question of the sudden delegitimisation of Portuguese after 1961 and its impact requires a separate study.

While the history of Konkani is variable enough, it has to be mentioned that a parallel world of Marathi writing reveals the interests of different sections of Goan society, particularly after the mid- to late-eighteenth century when the New Conquest districts

---

[75] "Scripting the Border: Script Practices and Territorial Imagination among Santali Speakers in Eastern India," *International Journal of the Sociology of Language*. Accessed on April 18, 2015, http://www.degruyter.com/view/j/ijsl.2014.2014.issue-227/ijsl-2013-0087/ijsl-2013-0087.xml. I thank Prathama Banerjee for her suggestions with regard to this source.

[76] Parag D. Parobo, *India's First Democratic Revolution: Dayanand Bandodkar and the Rise of the Bahujan in Goa*, First edition (Orient Blackswan Private Limited, 2015).

in the eastern part of Goa were acquired from former rulers. The relation of Marathi to Konkani varied quite sharply from the end of the nineteenth to the twentieth century, as did the claim of different caste groups over Marathi itself. Histories of Konkani in the Kannada script likewise, would uncover a different relation to Tulu, Kannada, Kodava, and languages that do not have official status. Konkani, and the western coast in fact, requires a literary and linguistic history that traces the relations between languages across contexts, whether devotional or administrative, or literary rather than focusing only on those representations in which language is posited as a self-contained and singular entity.[77]

This volume includes excerpts and essays in multiple scripts of Konkani with the exception of Malayalam and Naskh, with the idea of revealing how the questions of translation differ. The public reception of a text in each script as though it were intended for a separate community is distinctive enough for us to treat the transcription of texts from one script to another as a translation, as this anthology does. Despite the attempt to move against the constrictions of a singular state- or script-divided history, this account is framed predominantly by the experience of translation in the context of Goa.

This book is structured as a two-part long essay divided into chapters. The first part examines how nineteenth century concerns shaped the writing of histories of the sixteenth century. It also indicates the approaches suggested in recent work for the study of the sixteenth-century encounter with conversion and colonialism. It traces the impact of the mid-twentieth century discovery of the sixteenth century Ramayana and Mahabharata on how the language was perceived.

Part II traces nineteenth-century concerns with different genres and fields of writing and the resolutions of cultural anxieties through the adoption of the Devanagari script. These sections are interspersed with excerpts from the introductions and prefaces to transcribed/translated texts that are historically significant or difficult to access. Part III starts with a short note by Mabel Mascarenhas on translations in the Kannada script, though this is not a full history of the issue in the context of Mangalore and other centres of Konkani literary production.

Following this section, in Part IV, critical essays in Konkani (also in various scripts) have been included as well as essays in Portuguese,

[77] Dechamma, 2015.

the language in which much critical work was produced until the integration of Goa in 1961. The section contains essays which discuss the choices of script made by early European missionaries and offer significant analyses of how the conflicts over script structure political identity. They also examine facets of cultural life that are revealed and transformed through translation, whether the cultural distance between languages, the uses of confession manuals, questions of dialect and language learning.

The original orthography and format choices in excerpts and essays, including in some cases, the elision or use of accents in early printed texts, has been retained to preserve fidelity to the source text. Translations into English, unless otherwise specified, are mine.

PART ONE

I

Transliteration as Translation

The Ramayana and the Mahabharata as Sixteenth-century Texts

The earliest available written Konkani Mahabharata and Ramayana are codices transliterated by missionaries from recitations by narrators whose identity remains ambiguous. Among other kinds of devotional literature, these were a cultural resource for doctrinal texts and vocabularies produced in the sixteenth and seventeenth centuries. These transliterations (the rewriting of a text choosing the closest possible letters from another language to match the sound of the original language) in the Roman script are believed to have more than one narrator as their source and have received much attention in literary histories (Miranda 2011).[1] Their discovery in a library in Portugal, and their gradual acquisition stretched over decades.[2]

---

[1] Rocky V. Miranda says that stanzas 245–50 of Codex number 773 are said to contain the pseudonym of Xamaraja, from Quelossim, Salcete, Goa. Xama's name is not found in any of the remaining poems covering 436 pages of the Codex though other names occur. According to Miranda, the codices 771 and 772 are in Konkani prose. Codice 771 carries tales from the Mahabharata, while 772 has those from the Ramayana. While the *Adiparva* and *Hauzadvazachi Katha* are in both codices, there is no mention of Xama as the writer of these.

[2] This history, taken from Fr. A. Noronha's preface to Lourdino Rodrigues' edition of the Mahabharata, is retold in text after text and reveals a chain of contact between names associated with the history of literature in Goa. These codices are said to have been discovered by Sanskrit teacher and literary critic Mariano Saldanha who informed the historian A K. Priolkar, who obtained the microfilm of the *Shri Krishna Charitra* – the Marathi codex no. 773. The archivist and author Panduronga S. S. Pissurlenkar then copied one of Xama's poems and Fr. Graciano Morais included one of these texts in his Konkani grammar. But,

Between 1945 and 1950, the Sanskrit and Konkani teacher Mariano Saldanha did two things that were historically significant for the literary history of Konkani. He brought out the second edition of the *Doutrina Cristã*, (the first extant printed text in Konkani) a book of Christian doctrine written by the English Jesuit, Thomas Stephens (1549–1619) and published in 1622. The other significant act was his discovery in 1950, of the codices (a manuscript in book form) that began to feature in literary histories as the earliest signs of a written literary tradition for Konkani. Literary history began to apportion different values and meanings to these texts. Editions of the codices as well as the *Doutrina* began to be printed from this moment on by prominent scholars. However, within histories of Konkani writing, the codices containing the Ramayana and Mahabharata displaced the early doctrinal texts, many of which had emerged only in the seventeenth century.[3] It was as though these codices provided a more appropriate beginning to a literary history of a language that was in peril of being deemed unfit to meet modern expectations.

By the mid-twentieth century the different scripts in use for different languages in Goa had come to represent sharply polarised identities. The strictures of linguistic nationalism foregrounded the introduction of the Roman script for Konkani writing by Portuguese missionaries as an aberration. This became a criterion that qualified the enthusiasm with which these twentieth-century discoveries were received into literary history. As Sowmya Dechamma (2015) has stated in relation to Kodava literization (or the attainment of literacy as Sheldon Pollock describes this moment in the history of a language), script was isolated from other aspects of language to bear the 'burden of hegemony' over the question of cultural identity. The Roman script, in which Konkani continues to be written, became an index of cultural inauthenticity only in the late nineteenth century. The chapters in this section provide a brief overview of the complexity of cultural translation involved in the production of missionary literature in seventeenth-century Goa. Though these years saw considerable physical and epistemic violence accompanying the process of translation, languages and cultures were not seen as fundamentally different and alien from each other. Subsequent sections indicate how the Roman script became an impermeable barrier in the translation of texts, a

---

according to Noronha it was only after 1961, when the Sanskritist and scholar José Pereira emphasised the significance of these manuscripts that Fr. Antonio Pereira had them photocopied and brought to Goa.

[3] The first printing press in Goa was established in 1556.

phenomenon that may be read in the wider context of philological influence outlined earlier.

The Christian ecumenical imperative of producing literature in local languages across the world saw the reworking of devotional and poetic practices and of language use. Konkani usage altered both within a sub-continental context, as well as in relation to doctrinal texts being produced in languages of Latin America and other parts of the world, though most early popular devotional material was produced in Marathi. From the sixteenth century on, whether through transliteration and transcription from oral narratives to Roman script (as with the Mahabharata and Ramayana) or in continuous transaction with Portuguese, Latin and Marathi, Konkani became a language of doctrinal instruction.

Christian ecumenism as context for translation

Recent approaches to Christian missionary literature in colonial contexts have examined how texts, genres and practices of reading could be appropriated and transformed by colonial subjects to produce meanings that were resistant to received ones.[4] One of the most effective accounts of how a missionary text, John Bunyan's *Pilgrim's Progress,* traversed 'a transnational landscape' is Isabel Hofmeyr's *The Portable Bunyan* (2004). Hofmeyr displaces the idea of a fixed original significance that gave the text its place on the English national canon. Instead, she argues how translation enabled the misreading and reinterpretation of missionary texts as objects and as practices. Her book traces theories of translation ('every text with the "right" message was translatable') that were particular to Protestant evangelism. It suggests that these were transformed by the realities of linguistic contexts and the need to negotiate between a 'first-language' convert and a 'second-language' missionary, or with shared ideas of the book as a magical object (ibid., 13). By touching on the book as an object, on practices of reading, or on notions of sin as elements that would determine the course of translation, Hofmeyr helps chart what a study of translation across a Christian conceptual universe could entail.

Similarly, Hephzibah Israel (2004, 11–12) comments on her approach to the translations of the Bible into Tamil:

[4] For a critical reading of translation studies see the introduction to Hephzibah Israel, *Religious Transactions in Colonial South India: Language, Translation, and the Making of Protestant Identity* (New York: Palgrave Macmillan, 2011).

> I realize this focus on Bible translation may appear to contribute further to the scholarly bias that has viewed non-Western Christianity through textually-oriented lenses based on belief and doctrine rather than practice...However, rather than move away from textual focus, my aim is to study precisely how the Bible has been constructed as "scripture" for Tamils; how translation processes…make visible the non-textual discourses that seek to construct religious power; and finally, examine how Protestant Tamils challenge or appropriate particular translations by mobilizing "popular" forms of Christian devotion and practices.

Israel reminds us that claims about the existence of the Syriac Bible from the third or fourth century of the Common Era requires us to see Christianity as a cultural idiom outside the colonial context. In fact the anticipation that Eastern Christianity could be made compatible within a unified church was one of the contexts through which difference was encountered.

Vicente L. Rafael's account (1993, xviii) of the translation of Christian texts into Tagalog in the context of colonialism in the Philippines asks,

> How did the Tagalogs respond to the conjunction between translation and conversion? …Can we understand Tagalog translation… in relation to native idioms of exchange and reciprocity which shape notions of social hierarchy? How did their concepts of reciprocity in particular, *utangnaloob* and *hiya* ("debt of gratitude" and "shame") differ from the ideas of indebtedness and hierarchy, expressed in such Catholic practices as prayer, and in the politico-legal injunctions found in the Law of the Indies?

A recent comparative account of missionary literature in seventeenth-century Brazil and India indicates how writing and orality were important elements of anthropological hierarchies that led missionaries to privilege writing (Chakravarti 2018). Within cultures of writing, missionary writers, transcribers, and translators made diverse linguistic, theological, and formal choices. While the Mahabharata, Ramayana and other texts were transcribed in Roman Konkani or Marathi, forms such as the *Doutrina Christã* of 1622 were composed in Konkani. The *Discurso sobre a vinda de Jesu,* or the *Kristapurana* of 1616 as it came to be called, composed in the Marathi *ovi* metre associated with the saint Eknath, drew on the form of the *Purana* and was written in the Roman script (Priolkar 1958).

Alexander Henn's reading of the popular Marathi *Kristapurana* by the English Jesuit Thomas Stephens details the multiplicity of local terms for goddesses and for concepts that were absorbed in the effort to make Christian concepts portable (2014). The prevailing understanding that 'gentile' belief systems were a corruption of the true religion, or one from which the truth had to be extracted, was a corollary to seeing the other as an inferior but proximate version of the self. Differences had to be overcome, but were mapped along degrees of possible distance and proximity from the self rather than constituting a contrary pole of otherness (ibid.) If Stephens' *Kristapurana* embedded Christian concepts within prevalent devotional concepts and figures to make the unfamiliar familiar, Henn asserts that 'the stated major goal' of other versions of the *Puranas* produced at the time, 'by contrast, is to refute and disempower the principles and forces of what it calls the *Conconni Ponni,* that is, the beliefs and practices of the Konkan people' (ibid., 74). Yet he also emphasises, as indicated earlier, that 'the most striking feature of the text is how conceptually similar and theoretically inherent to the Self it presents this Other. Nothing of the *Conconni Ponni,* it seems, is really different or altogether new to the Christian author; all is just in reversed order…' (ibid., 78).

Ananya Chakravarti's elaboration of localised spatial references in the *Kristapurana,* its metric form and linguistic choices, indicates the text's embeddedness in the particular history of the Salcete district of Goa and the participation of informants in the construction of the text. This implies the need for an analysis that leans less on a differentiation of local and foreign cultural elements than an account of the symbolic effect of such composite texts. In relation to the first book of the *Kristapurana,* the 'Adi Puranna', which is a version of the Old Testament, she examines the resonances between puranic cosmogonies and genealogies and Old Testament ones.

She indicates that the depiction of local deities responded to prevailing hierarchies between brahmin and non-brahmin deities, and traces how the meanings attached to symbols sacred to Hindu rituals were reversed through their incorporation into the text (Chakravarti 2018, 207–11). The production of texts not only contested *Conconni Ponni,* as Henn points out, but also inserted itself into some of the heterodox or less dominant devotional practices, thereby permeating the caste structure and forms of cultural assertion (Chakravarti 2017, 365–87). Such analysis is crucial to the understanding of various cultural phenomena and the repetition of motifs from these texts that are visible in the nineteenth and twentieth centuries.

Konkani and Marathi

The distribution of the labour of exegesis between Konkani and Marathi suggests a repositioning of Konkani within the world of devotional literature. Chakravarti's work (2018, 201) would suggest that this process produced a 'workaday Kōṅkaṅi catechism and grammar as pastoral aids', while the *Kristapurana* was in 'the high poetic language of the region, Marāṭhī, in the *ovī* metre.' While the catechism, the *Doutrina Christam em Lingua Bramana Canarim* of 1622 in Konkani was intended for use as everyday doctrine by the same Jesuit author, the mastery of Marathi literary forms was evidently seen as a necessary task for the success of mission literature. The ambiguity arising from the use of terms such as *Bramana marastta* for the Marathi associated with brahmins, as well as *Lingua Bramana Canarim* to denote Konkani spoken by brahmins acted as an impetus for scholars in the nineteenth century to claim the *Kristapurana* and other works as Konkani texts, in the hope of extending the antiquity and prestige of the Konkani language (ibid., 201, 203). Historians of Konkani have furnished inscriptions and usages that appeared even before the sixteenth century in texts that were predominantly in other languages, as evidence that Konkani was a written language (Gomes 1997, 1999, 2000). However, there is no evidence of an entire text, whether a record or any other kind of official document in Konkani, which suggests that that these inscriptions were what Sheldon Pollock would term as the 'pre-history of literization'.[5] Unlike the time lag that separated literization or writing, from literarization (or the 'attainment of literature') in other languages, the moment when Konkani was used as a primary language in a literary text is also when it was simultaneously designated as a language.[6]

Chakravarti's comments on the linguistic world of Salcete, the location of Thomas Stephens' activity, helps illuminate some of the anxieties and strategies of the Konkani language campaigns of later centuries. Her account is neither restricted to the opposition between high and low usages, nor to a polarisation of the oral and written. Not only was the dialogic form of the *Kristapurana* suited to its function as a catechism, she argues, it was also familiar in the context of the Purāna. Recitation, oral performance and listening were dramatised within the *Kristapurana* as Chakravarti indicates,

[5] Sheldon Pollock, *The Language of the Gods in the World of Men – Sanskrit, Culture, and Power in Premodern India* (Berkeley and Los Angeles: University of California Press, 2006), 292.

[6] ibid., 287.

drawing on and altering the 'trope of *phalaśruti*, or the fruit acquired through listening…' (Chakravarti 2018, 207).

Outside of the domain of conversion and devotional literature, as Chakravarti comments, 'one could reasonably expect to find Kōṅkaṅi, Marāṭhī, and Portuguese, and quite possibly Kannaḍā, Sanskrit, and Persian; moreover, the area had been subject to three different polities of three different faiths...' reminding us that the realms of account and record-keeping could include other languages and practices (ibid., 209). Since Konkani did not become a written language of administration until some centuries later, a large number of concepts that were worked upon in Portuguese, Latin, Marathi and Konkani were related to the domain of devotion and religion and associated economic questions such as the question of land administration. The mutual status of these languages would transform across the centuries to include English in the nineteenth century as a defining language in the sphere of Konkani reading and print. The twentieth-century perception that the Roman script had introduced a cultural rupture justifies treating the transliterations shaped by that understanding, as translations. Chakravarti's analysis indicates however, that transcriptions/translations or adaptations that precede the nineteenth century did not carry these meanings even if the language that she primarily examines was Marathi.

Signs, languages, and bodies in the translation of Christianity

Among the approaches discussed above, Henn, Rafael, and Israel argue against treating translation as a sign of syncretism, a term commonly used in the context of conversion and translation. The discussion of syncretism indicates how language use intersected relations of power in the sixteenth century, and how differently cultural nationalism of the twentieth century viewed this question. These arguments have two dominant strands, one which suggests that we pay more attention to the nature of power structures supporting these transformations, while the other emphasises that the idea of syncretism presumes a division between the religious and a neutral ground of signification from which syncretism may be perceived. As an instance of the first strand, in the context of the Philippines, Rafael (1993, 5–6) asserts, 'Christianity set the rules of a colonial enterprise while maintaining a position above those rules. It also sought to define the boundaries of native culture while at the same time claiming an attachment to an origin outside those boundaries.' Chakravarti's comparative account of mission work in Brazil, speaks of a 'strictly controlled Christian civility', indicating the different relations through which texts circulated in imperial contexts other than Goa (2018, 177). Rafael (1993, 7) argues that translation limited the boundaries of resistance, while offering a vocabulary for the same: 'Conceived dialectically, conversion requires one's submission to and incorporation of the language and logic of Christianity as the condition of possibility for defining and subsequently overcoming one's prior state of subordination, whether to a pagan past, a colonial overlord, or the local elite.'

As an instance of the second contention with the idea of syncretism, Henn (2014, 18) points out that it often presumes a prior separation of the religious from the secular, whereas both the semiotic status and bodily enactment of religious signs indicates there was no third ground of signification for the synthesis of opposition. A significant observation in this regard is made by Županov(2001; 2005) who traced the strategy of accommodation by Jesuits in south India such as Roberto de Nobili who adapted formal Sanskritic practices in order to draw on the status enjoyed by upper castes. Such work embeds translation in both bodily and textual practice. The example of de Nobili indicates the inventiveness and strategising of missions on the ground, which received ambivalent responses from their parent Church. Županov suggests that the persistence of caste and ritual practices among new Christians even after conversion led Nobili and other missionaries to propose the categories of civility and religion, which would allow them to accept new Christians, despite their adherence to earlier structures. The concept of *adiaphora*, which signified elements that Christianity did not need to prohibit as it was indifferent to them, allowed missionaries to elide those practices that could not be removed, and to focus instead on a separate realm of the religious, which alone had to be monitored for the intrusion of erroneous beliefs (Xavier and Županov 2015, 153; Županov 1996, 1201–23). Županov suggests that this separation may have been the origin of what eventually became a routine distinction between culture and religion.

This is further complicated by Chakravarti's assertion (2018, 226) that the hierarchisation of oral and written cultures implied that 'civility could not exist in the realm of orality; thus *accommodatio*, as a form of cultural practice, was limited to the literate world.' Thus, while language and its relation to signs and objects was the focus of study among early missionaries, it was not a neutral, autonomous object through which to negotiate colonial difference. Instead, it was one entity among the bodies, icons and existential concerns that Henn and Županov detail in their study of texts produced in the encounter between missionaries and the subcontinent.

These are some of the possible frameworks for understanding the early translation history of Konkani. Its complexity explains why the twentieth-century desire for a unitary language, script and identity in fact led to a series of repetitive ruptures in the areas where there was a misfit between linguistic usage and political demand. From a position in the present where identities are defended by demonstrating an allegiance to script or language, allowing for these complex connotations of translation to enter the field of literary history is challenging. We are required for instance, to stretch the limits of historical understanding when we read Chakravarti's description of the burial of a Christian woman in Salcete. The funeral rites, according to an account by a Jesuit, were explained to the deceased's two sons who attended the funeral; the one a convert to Christianity, the other Hindu (2013, 523). These points of cultural transition and encounter require us to suspend contemporary identity compartments to be able to imagine the transformations through which these figures from the past lived. These bereaved sons, moving as the accidental subjects of history are, seem to demand that we understand this moment as a cultural translation resulting from missionary projects and state power, but without seeing these only as institutional forces. Instead this burial indicates that it was the language of grief, of family, and of belonging that was also reworked. Rather than hurriedly burying a past that we are not allowed to own, it is possible to find interpretive positions that allow it to disturb the sharp divides of the present.

II

Script as an Indice of Political Distinction

By the time Konkani acquired Official Language status in Goa in 1987, the only state where it has official recognition, its script had become a symbol of cultural differentiation within literary and political spheres, not only in Goa, but in every state with Konkani-speaking communities (Desai 2002). These crystallisations of identity extended to all the scripts in which the language is written, and are articulated in relation to Devanagari (the only officially-recognised script of Konkani), as the apical sign of authenticity. While we may find arguments in contemporary Goa that associate particular groups such as Catholics or Hindus with a language or script, the realities of their political interests and of their linguistic worlds were not as neatly divided, as some detailed accounts of the period indicate (Pereira 2013, 124). In fact it needs to be emphasised that language remains a volatile symbol for the articulation of class aspiration, economic access, caste inequities and religious polarisation and the claims made for any aspect of any given language are far from stable or static across time.

Pereira also details the pre-integration (1961) tussle over language in Bombay, where the Portuguese/Marathi/Konkani conflict of the nineteenth-century was redirected towards the imperative of having Konkani identified as the language of state. This campaign was directed as much towards the Indian state that was likely to assume power, as within the Goan society itself. In the nineteenth century, the upper-caste Hindu public claim for Marathi was a political and pedagogic stance, as also a movement that recuperated a cultural tradition in Marathi.[1]

[1] While the cultural tradition may have been contested and variable, a majority of Hindus were familiar with Marathi as a language of devotion. Many Hindus were also lettered in Marathi.

A strand of the political campaign explicitly countered the possibility of official recognition of Konkani, which, as a claim on the state, was identified with Catholics. Konkani, though a widely *spoken* language, was not used in any form of public writing, aside from lay doctrinal use, but a few prominent individuals had begun to speak of it as the neglected vernacular tongue of Goa (da Cunha Rivara 1858).

By the time of the integration into India in 1961 however, long-standing intra-brahmin tensions between the Saraswats and the Deshasth, Karhade and Chitpavan brahmins who were reluctant to extend parity of status to the Saraswats, had led to the adoption of Konkani in Devanagari as the distinguishing mark of Saraswat brahmins against other brahmins, particularly in Maharashtra (Deshpande 2010, 29–58). Thus, Pereira concludes (2013, 94), 'there was a situation of language conflict in Bombay wherein the older generation was pro Marathi and the younger one, especially upper-caste Hindus were advocates of Konkani.' State formation in Maharashtra and expansionist linguistic geographies of Marathi supplemented an anti-Konkani stance (Naregal 2001). Pereira's thesis indicates how a strategy of this vociferous campaign was to exert pressure on the Sahitya Akademi to oppose the recognition of Konkani.[2]

Language without a state, script without a readership

If Konkani was a language without a state, Devanagari in the mid-twentieth century was a script with scarcely any readership. Pereira (2013, 124) paraphrases the prominent writer Ravindra Kelekar: 'Tracing the history of Konkani Shri Kelekar informs (sic) that when they started to write in 1945, there were only 10–15 Devanagari books and 1000 Konkani books in Roman script. He adds that the process of making Konkani a literary language began since then.'

[2] Pereira's thesis notes that after the Sahitya Akademi acceptance of Konkani as a literary language in the year 1976, literary and cultural activities began to be conducted in Konkani. The first award was presented to Ravindra Kelekar for his work in the Devanagari script. The Sahitya Akademi winners of 1979 and 1980 also used the Devanagari script. Hence, according to the author, the Akademi presumed that Devanagari was the script for Konkani. After questions were raised about the choice of script, the Akademi directed the question to an Advisory Board. The Advisory Board which included Antonio Pereira from Goa, P. J. Saldanha from Mangalore, N. Purushottam Mallya from Kerala and Fr. William D'Silva from Karnataka, met in Goa in 1981. This decision of the Advisory Board was accepted by the Executive Council of the Sahitya Akademi.

Several Konkani conferences have asserted that the maximum numbers of readers in Konkani are to be found for works in the Kannada script, while Devanagari has had to forge its readership from the time it came to symbolise a politico-cultural claim on the state (Rodrigues 2013).

The campaign around Konkani in Devanagari has been interpreted, in part, as the symbolic claim of Saraswat brahmins (both Hindu and Catholic) over Konkani; a phenomenon through which the future nation of Goa could be claimed as a distinct entity from Maharashtra and Maharashtrian brahmins. For Catholic upper castes whose identity had begun to be problematised under hegemonic nationalist definitions of cultural tradition, the sign of indigeneity and markers of Indianness attached to Devanagari guaranteed belonging within a high culture other than Portuguese. Desai (2002, 184, 194) emphasises that the campaign for Devanagari was sustained by a section of brahmins from the Kanara and Kerala areas where Konkani was otherwise written in other scripts.

This swiftly transforming map of linguistic relations indicates that the political quest for a composite identity, whether during the nineteenth-century search for a vernacular, or the twentieth-century thrust towards regional identity and state formation, in fact made it impossible to speak of Konkani as a composite entity. It ensured that from the mid-nineteenth century on, one would have to identify which particular configuration of caste, script, religion, or state were assumed when one spoke of Konkani in the public realm. Further, these configurations transformed every three or four decades, as the brief sketch of linguistic relations described earlier indicates. Caste status concerns between various groups of brahmins on the western coast are not as often verbalised in Portuguese print (as opposed to Marathi print or oral practice) as are religious or class divides, but they existed nonetheless as determining factors, providing patronage or oppositional force depending on the moment and issue at stake. Despite public rhetoric that would seek simple religious divides, the solidarities of caste as well as a democratic if paternalist desire to ensure that those writing in the Roman script were participants in a national high culture, meant that there was Catholic support for Devanagari. Among the Catholic literati, this was accompanied by the conviction that Devanagari was scientifically and culturally appropriate for Konkani, at least in the initial phases of the campaign (Pereira 2013). Devanagari was also offered as a via media to make literature in one script available to other Konkani readers, thereby expanding the readership and therefore the commercial viability of Konkani print.

The test of nationalism

From the 1940s on, discussions around the question of Konkani literature began to approximate linguistic nationalism, carving out a history, a people, and a literature for the language. Though the particulars of the would-be nation were unclear (would it be Goa, India, or was it nationalism built around a people caught between states), this was viewed as politically appropriate activity, since to aspire for recognition from a nationalist high culture is a necessary condition for inclusion within it.

A brief article written by an editor of a Konkani daily, Uday Bhembre (2014), lists significant milestones that would mark the public and formal recognition of Konkani; the first Konkani Parishad held in 1939 in Karwar, the Konkani broadcasts from 1956 by All India Radio and the meetings of the Konkani Parishad, the eighth session of which was held in Margao in 1962, a year after Goa's annexation.[3] In 1963, the Goa government accepted Konkani as a medium of instruction in schools. The opinion poll of 1967 around the question of a merger with Maharashtra also saw the consolidation of public opinion in favour of Konkani.

While the Catholic literati from the early twentieth century had begun a public exercise of critique and correction of popular Konkani, the support for the language around the time of integration has to be seen in context of an assertion against the proposed merger with Maharashtra (Parobo 2015). In contrast to the popular Konkani publications of the late nineteenth and early twentieth century therefore, the Konkani Parishads were signs of institutional backing for Konkani from dominant sections of society which would eventually force recognition of the language on the state.

Research on the different phases of the language movement emphasises that linguistic nationalism was an abstraction that allowed cultural symbols to be carved out as a claim to a regional sphere of dominance and a representative addition to a national

---

[3] The Konkani Bhasha Mandal was founded by M. M. Shanbag in 1939 in Karwar. Armando Menezes presided over the third Konkani conference at which V. V. Valaulikar gave a lecture. This was held in 1942 in Bombay. Menezes started the Konkani Samaj the same year in Karnatak College in Dharwar. The Konkani Sahitya Samiti began in 1944 in Bombay. Radio Goa began broadcasts in Konkani in 1945, and All India Radio began Konkani programming in 1952 according to K. V. Gulvadi, from Bombay. The Konkani Cultural Association was set up in 1965. The Konkani Bhasha Prachar Sabha in Cochin began a campaign in 1966 to secure official recognitiion for the language. See Shanbhag 1970.

culture. Jason Keith Fernandes (2013, 110) emphasises that the establishment of Konkani Parishads followed the pattern of a movement for the recognition of Kannada:

> Similarly the Saraswat Parishad also moved the location of its conferences, being one way to attract the interest of those who could not afford to travel to a single fixed location. What should be also stressed is that these strategies, as well as the forms that the conferences would take, were also drawn from the patterns of the early Indian National Congress, and other national public interest associations that formed civil society, both in the colonial period, and later the post-colonial period.

Madhavi Sardesai's (2006, 64) work tracing diglossia in different usages and phases of Konkani elaborates the national vision of the initial Parishads, which sought a territorial form and expansionist unity:

> The Konkani state envisaged by this movement stretched beyond the boundaries of present-day Goa which is only a territory that was under Portuguese dominion. For the proper development of the Konkani language and the Konkani people through their language, the Konkani movement must mobilise itself towards Samyukta Goem "United Goa" comprising of Goa plus the adjoining Sindhudurg and Karwar districts respectively, of Maharashtra and Karnataka.

Desai, who notes how Konkani successfully propelled itself within half a century into being considered a state language, with only forty per cent of the total number of speakers residing in Goa, also details (2015, 80) the vision for expanding state boundaries to encompass territories with a concentration of Konkani speakers:

> In a proposal for the Vishal Gomantak (Large Goa) suggested during the decade following liberation there was a suggestion to include the following: Goa, three talukas of Karwar district (Haliyal, Supa, Karwar) from Karnataka, four talukas of Ratnagiri district (Kudal, Sawantwadi, Vengurla, Malwan) and Chandgad taluka in Kolhapur district in Maharashtra, two talukas in Belgaum district (Belgaum and Khanapur) with the estimated population of around twenty lacs, the minimum size for an autonomous state, as recommended by the Morarka Commission. But the GPCC President Purushottam Kakodkar and the UGP leadership were against such an idea.

Such imaginings indicate that the territorial aspirations for linguistic nationalism were firstly, impossible in the face of more muscular nationalisms in neighbouring Maharashtra, and occasionally extra-territorial, given that the cultural imaginaries that could unite Konkani speakers could be based on caste, or a combination of ritual and territorial allegiance that did not have identical boundaries. Language became the overburdened sign through which difference was both suppressed and articulated.

III

Other Ramayanas and Mahabharatas

In 1975, the year the Sahitya Akademi recognised Konkani as a literary language, the litterateur Suniti Kumar Chatterji made an inaugural speech at the tenth session of the Konkani Sahitya Parishad, detailing the reasons why Konkani deserved to have recognition as an independent language. His address to the Konkani Sahitya Parishad was in the context of a campaign to invite personages who were visible in national fora to support the claim for recognition. Chatterji's address was unambiguously clear about what a language community needed to bolster the demand for recognition, as these were evidently uncontested norms in literary circles at the time.

His address began with Sanskrit couplets translated into English, that adapted the migration myth of brahmins to Goa to bolster the idea of an original culture of brahmin settlers, damaged by the Portuguese who also however left a Christianised culture. In this way, Chatterji conceded the presence of a significant Christian culture with its own textual practices represented by upper-caste Catholics. An argument about language devolved from these premises: to be recognised as an independent language, Chatterji suggested, Konkani would have to showcase its roots in a high culture, and should eventually work towards one script, preferably Devanagari (though this was not always Chatterji's position regarding the choice of script).[1] As a modern Indian language, Konkani lacked

---

[1] Udaya Narayana Singh (2001, 72) suggests that Chatterji at one point also advocated the Roman script as a single unifying mechanism for the nation. Dennis Kurzon (2010, 68–69) has an account of both the nineteenth century discussion over Romanisation, and Chatterji's proposed system. Chatterji, according to him, cites two pre-Independence meetings when the proposal for Romanisation was considered: 'At the All-Parties Conference in Calcutta in 1927 (under the auspices of the Indian National Congress), a Sindhi and Bengali proposal to write Hindustani

'full translations of the *Ramayana, Mahabharata,* the *Bhagavata* and some other *Puranas* – correct and authoritative versions in prose' (1974, 19). Chatterji mentioned the retrieved codices containing the Mahabharata. Konkani according to him also needed translations of the Bible and early Christian texts to indicate its lineage in a high Christian culture. In the absence of these, he said, Konkani lagged behind other modern languages.

In 1969, Suniti Kumar Chatterji (1890–1977) was elected President of the Sahitya Akademi of India and President of the International Phonetic Association. He was also President of the Asiatic Society, Calcutta. He edited and published over fifty cultural and linguistic studies in Bengali, English and Hindi.

The following excerpt is an address by Suniti Kumar Chatterji in his capacity as President of the Sahitya Akademi to the All India Konkani Sahitya Parishad in 1974, in Panjim. Chatterji's presence was an indication of support for the recognition of Konkani as a literary language. The speech he delivered therefore, addressed the possibility of including Konkani in the list of languages recognised by the Akademi. In the course of his speech, Chatterji included Sanskrit verses transcribed in the Roman script and translated into English, retelling a popularised legend of Parashurama that was favoured by brahmins about the origin of Goa, including in it an account of the arrival of the Portuguese, and the birth of Konkani. The speech itself exhorts Goans to produce appropriate translations of the Mahabharata and Ramayana if they desired that Konkani be included in the national mainstream. The excerpt reveals the link between the recognition of Konkani as a literary language and the agenda for translation that accompanied it.

Excerpt 1
Courtesy State Central Library, Panjim
Suniti Kumar Chatterji, *Inauguration Speech by Suniti Kumar Chatterji, All-India Konkani Sahitya Parishad Tenth Session,* (Panaji, Goa: Udai Bhembro, General Secretary, 1974), pp. 4–19.

गोमन्ते स्थापितो देशः सह्याद्री-चरणे नवः
कुले च पाश्चिमाम्भोधेः परशुराम-विष्णुना ।।१।।

(1) Gomante sthāpito deśaḥ Sahyâdri-caraṇe navaḥ,
kule ca Paścimâmbhodheḥ Paraśurāma-Viṣnunā ॥1॥

---

in Roman was rejected, and at the All Bengal University and College Teachers Conference held in Faridpur in 1934, a proposal to write Bengali and other Indian vernaculars in Roman was likewise rejected by a thirty two to twenty five vote.'

At the foot of the Sahyadri Mountains (Western
Ghats), in Gomanta, a new land, washed by
the Western Ocean (the Arabian Sea), was
established by Vishnu as Parasurama (1)

दौहित्री संस्कृतस्यासौ वाक् कोङ्कणीति विश्रुता।
ओजस्विनी मधु-स्त्रावा अत्रैव प्रकटाऽभवत्।।२।।

(2) dauhitrī Samskrtasyâsau vāk Koṅkaṇī'ti viśrutā।
ojasvinī madhu-srāvā atraiva prakaṭâ'bhavat ॥2॥

The language known as Konkani, a grand-
-daughter of Sanskrit, full of vigour, flowing
with honey, came to take form here (2)

पुण्य देशेऽत्र गोमन्ते विप्रा वेदविदां वरा: ।
सारस्वत-कुलोद्भू तास्तधान्ये चार्य धार्मिण: ।।३।।

(3) punye deśe'tra Gomante viprā Veda-vidāṃ varaḥ।
Sārasvata-kulôdbhū tathânye cârya-dharmiṇaḥ ॥3॥

In this holy land of Gomanta, Brahmans,
The best among those who knew the Vedas,
Born in the Saraswat clan, and others follo-
wing the Aryan or Hindu religion, (3)

असृजन नूतनं राष्ट्रम् आर्य-द्रमिड-कोल्लका:।
मङ्गेश: शान्तदुर्गा च तैस्तत्र वै प्रतिष्ठिता: ।।
श्रीविष्णुश्च तथा चान्ये देवर्षि-नृपपुङ्गवा: ।।४।।

(4) asrjan nūtanam rāṣṭram Ārya-Dramiḍa-Kollakāḥ।
Mangêśah Sānta-durgā ca tais tatra vai pratīṣṭhitah ॥
Śrīr Visnuś ca tathā cânye DevaRṣi-Nṛpa-puṇgavāh ॥4॥

-Namely, Aryans, Dravidians, and Kollas
(or Nishadas), created a new state, where
they established (shrines of) Mangesha (Siva),
Santa-Durga (Uma), Sri and Vishnu, and of
other Gods, Sages and Heroic Kings (4)

तत्: कलियुगे घोरेऽभवद् वै फिरङ्ग-शासनम्।
गोमन्ते यै: समानीतो धर्मो येसू-समीरितम्।।
देवे भक्ति र्नरे प्रीती र्यत्र वै मौलिको नय: ।।५।।

(5) tataḥ Kali-yuge ghore' bhūd vai Phiraṇga-śasanam ।
Gomante yais sam-anīto dharmo Yesū-samīritah ॥
Deve bhaktir Nare prītir yatra vai mauliko nayah ॥5॥

Then in this terrible Iron Age, there came
the rule of the land by the Phiranga (Ferin-
ghee or Portuguese) people. They brought
to Gomanta the religion preached by Yesu
(Jesus Christ), of which the basic principles
were Faith in God and Love for Man. (5)

एवं गोमन्तके राज्ये भारतनीति-वर्धनी।
संस्कृति र्नुतना जाता कोड्कणीं वाचमाश्रिता।।६।।

(6) evam Gomantake rājye Bhārata-nīti-vardhanī ।
samskṛitir nutana jātā Konkaṇīm vācam aśrita ॥6॥

In this way in the state of Gomanta (Goa),
A new culture was born with the Konkani language
as its vehicle. (6)

कोड्कणीं वै समाश्रित्य आर्य-ख्रिस्तान-मुस्लीमा: ।
श्रेयसं राष्ट्रिकं सर्वेऽलभन्त प्रेयसं तथा।।७।।

(7) Konkaṇīm vai samāśritya Ārya-Khristāna-Muslimāh ।
śreyasaṃ rāṣṭrikam sarve' labhanta preyasam tathā ॥7॥

Aryans (= Hindus), Christians and Muslims,
through this Konkani speech, acquired all
that was beneficient and pleasant in the state (7)

भारतीय-महाजातेर्भाषेयं लब्ध-गौरवा।
भुवि यातु प्रतिष्ठांवै विद्या-ज्ञान-प्रदायिनी।।८।।

(8) Bharatīya Mahajāter bhāṣêyam labdha-gauravā ।
bhuvi yātu pratiṣṭham vai vidyā-jñāna pradāyinī ॥8॥

This Speech of the Great Nation of India,
now restored to its glory, may once again
be established in the world, bringing. Arts
and Science for all (8)

शुभेयं परिषद् गोय्यां कोड्कणीं-वाक्-प्रपालिनी।
विश्व-जने भवेद्द हृदया शक्ति-प्रदा च भारते।।९।।

(9) Śubhêyam Pariṣad Goyyām Konkaṇī-vāk-prapālinī ।
viśva-jane bhavedd hṛdyā śakti-pradā ca Bhārate ॥9॥

May this auspicious assembly, seeking to develop the Konkani language, bring joy to the heart of all men, and give strength to India (9)

मैत्री विश्व-जने येषाम् भूषिताये धिया श्रिया।
गोमन्त-कोङ्कणा: सर्वे विजयन्तां सदा भुवि।।१०।।

(10) Maitri viśva-jane yesām, bhūsitā ye dhiyā sriyā ।
Gomanta-Konkaṇāh sarve vijayantam sadā bhuvi ॥10॥

They have friendship for all, they are endowed with Intelligence and with Grace; may the Gomanta-Konkani people always be triumphant in the World. (10)

It is for me a privilege, and a happiness to come to Goa for the second time, to participate in this **Tenth All-India Konkani Sahitya Parishad**, which is of momentous importance particularly now for the Konkani-speaking people of Gomantaka, of Goa and the Western sea-board of India. This Parishad will help them to recover their lost sense of identity and their forgotten *locus standi* among the different communities of the great Indian Nation, our *Bharatiya Mahajati.* The recovery of the Identity of the Goan and Konkani people in their historic evolution in their language and culture and in their special stance (whether as Hindus or Christians) among the various "language-communities" of India, will be of very great value in the fullest Integration of India. A knowledge and appreciation of what the Konkani-speaking citizens of lndia (even when they had lost this knowledge, for the time being, "under the compulsion of events in history") have contributed to the growth of Indian civilisation and culture, will give an added sense of power and pride, and hope and endeavour to the lndian people in their path of progress in the domains of material and economic well-being, of mental and intellectual advancement, and of spiritual aspiration and realisation as well.

Konkani, which by its own right should be recognised as one of the major languages of lndia, has for the last few centuries been under a cloud. The Konkani people, particular1y the Hindu Saraswats and the Christians, have been since the 16th century and again during the 19th and 20th, in the forefront of Indian peoples, through their glorious intellectual and cultural attainments and their successful commercial and industrial enterprises, side by side with their invaluable services in preserving the ancient literary heritage of India in Sanskrit and in bringing to India the Latin culture of Portuguese Christianity. The people of North India have to confess to their shame that they know so little of the Konkanis (and the Dravidian speaking Tuluvas, the people of Madhvacharya) living by the Western Sea. Till now living under four different administrations and dominated everywhere by speakers of other languages who were better known to the outside world, the Konkanis (although conscious of their linguistic and social existence as a distinct and separate bloc of people) acquiesced in being lumped together with Marathi speakers in Maharashtra, as Goans in Portuguese-ruled Goa (where the Christianized people under the umbrage of the Roman Catholic Church had kept up some vestiges of their Konkani linguistic heritage, but where, owing to religious intolerance of a section of the Portuguese Christians, the Hindu Goans became virtually a suppressed people), and in Mysore (now Karnataka) they joined the local majority people the Kannadigas in accepting the Kannada language and script outside of their domestic circle; and the same thing took place in the case of the Konkanis who settled in Kerala, where they adopted Malayalam although they kept up Konkani....

...

I had occasion to go to Europe for the first time in 1919 as a Government of India scholar for studying Linguistics in London. ... As I was interested in Phonetics, I started on board our steamer taking down phonetic transcriptions of the *Story of the North Wind and the Sun* in the script of the *International Phonetic Association* from the dictations of my fellow students during the voyage. There was a student from Mangalore in South Kanara district in Karnataka (it was the old Madras Presidency in those days). He was K. N. Kudva, who later came back from England after passing the Indian Civil Service Examination, and served with distinction as an I. C. S. Officer for many years before he passed away. Kudva told me he belonged to Madras Presidency, but his language was Konkani, an Aryan language allied to Bengali and Hindi. I knew that of course, but I knew nothing about Konkani excepting that it was "a dialect of Marathi", and was spoken by the *Konkanastha Brahmans* of Maharashtra, while a debased form of it was current among the Christians of Portuguese Goa. Kudva did not know much about the connexion of Konkani with Marathi – but he thought Konkani had its own independent character as a language. He kindly translated the story into Konkani for me, and read it to enable me to take down a transcription. But I never published it and I left it at that, that Konkani was a form of Marathi, knowing nothing about the Konkan speaking people along the sea-coast from Bombay to Cochin, and of their place in Indian society. That was in 1919.

It was only in 1971 when I first visited Manipal, Udipi, and other places in South Kanara, and after I visited Goa for the first time in 1972, that I made a great discovery for myself – the character and place of the Konkani people, small in number, neglected by others and even by themselves, but unique in their contributions to Indian progress. It was a discovery about the Konkani-speaking people as a whole, whether of Ratnagiri or Goa, of Bombay or Poona, of Mangalore or Cochin, or of Bangalore or Madras, or whether they were Christians or Hindus (as Saraswats or the ordinary Hindu masses). I came also to discover how there was absolutely no *Linguism* in Karnataka where Kannadigas, Tuluvas, Kodagus and Tamilians lived with Maharashtrians, Konkanis, Luso-Indians, and Anglo-Indians in perfect harmony, without fighting over their languages, as we often see today in some of the states of North India. Then when I saw what Dr. Tonse Madhav Ananta Pai was doing all his life (he is now nearing 80), I was filled with wonder and admiration.... Another great people of India slowly came within my ken – I should say, flashed within my perception before I could study the whole thing, – and I was all the richer in my mind for that.

We have all heard about these eminent Konkanis, without knowing much or even anything about their Konkani heritage and background....

...

And it is strange that such a gifted people as the Konkanis, particularly the Saraswat Brahmans and the intellectual *élite* among Konkani-speaking Christians of Goa and Mangalore, should remain almost unknown to the rest of India, and should be forced to sail under false colours. The *All-India Saraswat Directory and who's who* as projected by the *Samyukta Saraswat* Monthly of Bombay, if completed, will be a great help in making the Konkani people know something about itself through the achievements of one of its most important sections....

The Konkanis, even orthodox Saraswats, are singularly free from caste prejudices, and can easily mix with other groups, even to the extent of intermarrying with them. Another and perhaps more obvious reason is that there is no Konkani-speaking state to have the label of *Konkani* ready made for them. Goa is the only area where live perhaps one half of the Konkani speakers in the whole of India today; and in all the Konkanis are not a large population, perhaps not more than 2 millions – in Maharashtra, in Goa, in Karnataka and in Kerala, and in other parts of India and a Konkani population of some 8 lakhs is concentrated as a majority community only in Goa, forming over 95% and more of the people of the *new State of Goa* (which was erstwhile Portuguese India). Nowhere do they form more than 10 to 15% of the population in the areas where they live. Prof. S. M. Katre, our authority on the history of Konkani as a language, gave it as his considered view that Konkani was an independent language, side by side with Marathi and Gujarati as the two other main languages of the Western Sea-board; and Konkani is emphatically not a dialect of Marathi, as many Maharashtrians (as well as some Konkani speakers themselves) declare or think it to be. But he thinks that although Konkani is certainly to be developed as a Modern Indian literary Language, and encouraged in every way, there is *no case for a Konkani-speaking State*. But here an exception is to be made – in the case of Goa. Goa is one of the component and distinct states of the Indian Union, with its own government, and Goa has given to Konkani as the majority language its place of honour as the real and native official language of the State, side by side with English, with Portuguese, and with Marathi and Hindi as and when desired. We have the State of Manipur in the eastern – most border of India, with its bare one million of people, with some 6 to 7 lakhs of Manipuri-speaking. And yet Manipuri has a rich literature, and has been given the status of an independent administrative language, besides being the language of higher education in the College stage. The advance made by the Manipuri people in their language and literature and their intense love for it has been responsible for this – the comparative smallness of the population was outweighed by other considerations. So too in the State of Goa Konkani is both *de facto* and *de jure* an Official language of the State, and here this great language can be secure in having a home of its own. With the contribution of the Konkani people to Indian life becoming more and more known to and acknowledged by the rest of India, and their language receiving once again a greater attention from them, Konkani, it is hoped, will ere long be established in its proper niche in the Hall of Indian Languages. It has already been given a recognition in the Census Report for 1971 – not as a mere dialect of some other language. Its case has been placed before the *Sahitya Akademi* – the National Academy of Letters where it is receiving sympathetic consideration on being presented by representative and responsible organizations and personalities from all over the Konkani area, and including both Hindus and Christians. The representative institutions like the *Konkani Obheas Kendr* and the *Konkani Bhasha Mandal* of Goa, and the *Konkani Bhasha Prachar Sabha* of Cochin, and other similar institutions, with the support of the Government of Goa, besides some publishing houses in Goa (using both Devanagari and Roman) and Bombay and Mangalore, and other places, are seeking to rehabilitate Konkani by bringing out both literature of information and literature of power in the language.

There are still some problems in the full development of Konkani. These I am sure will be discussed by the present *all-India Konkani Sahitya Parishad*, and a solution should be found out, if such a solution is required. They are mentioned below *seriatim*.

(1) The question of Script. Want of a single script has certainly been a drag in the full development of the language. Four scripts are still in use for Konkani-the Devanagari, the Roman, the Kannada and the Malayalam. It is fortunate that Konkani speakers are generally agreed that there should be a revival and use of only Devanagari for Konkani, as Devanagari was alone used as the proper script of Konkani (as e.g. in a Konkani document from Cochin reproduced in Devanagari characters dated 1557 Saka = 1665 A.D. which has reproduced in facsimile from Amsterdam in 1678 A.D. in Van Rheede's *Hortus Indicus Malabarianus*) and the consensus of opinion among Goan Christians, who have preserved the Konkani language in the Roman script for these nearly four centuries, and have a flourishing Roman Konkani literature, is that for integration with the rest of India, ultimately the language should have one script – only the Devanagari, the Roman being kept up for some time without seeking abruptly to remove it. That is, Konkani, in the interests of the Roman Catholic Christians of Goa and South Kanara and other places, should be allowed to continue as a *Bilitteral Language*, like the great Hindustani speech of North India using both the Devanagari (for its Hindi style) and the Perso-Arabic (for its Urdu style). Many years ago a *Konkani Script Committee* for Christians in Goa honoured me by asking my views and my advice as to what should be done in this matter, and taking note of the religious and cultural interests of the Christian Konkanis of Goa. I suggested that bilitteralism will be the only satisfactory solution for the present. And I was glad to see that there was an agreement with this view, though at that time it was not thought feasible to switch on to Devanagari.

The use of Kannada and Malayalam scripts is bound to be restricted, and with Devanagari spreading more and more, and the Roman continuing. But no time limit should be given, as it will smack of compulsion. In this way, there will be no problem of script for Konkani. A number of other Indian languages (as well as languages outside India) are still in the same situation of bilitteralism or multi-litteralism, and so we need not break heart over Konkani: e, g. Indian languages like Hindustani (Perso-Arabic, Devanagari, and some Roman); Sindhi (Perso- Arabic, occasionally Gurmukhi, and now also Devanagari); Kashmiri (Perso – Arabic, Sarada, Devanagari and some Roman); Maithili of North Bihar (Old Maithili or Tirahutiya, now being revived, and Devanagari); Manipuri (Bengali-Assamese, and Old Manipuri now being sought to be revived, besides Roman and Devanagari); and Santali as current in Bengal, Orissa, Bihar and Assam (Bengali, Oriya, and Devanagari scripts, besides Roman, and a brand-new alphabet called the "Ol-script", rather complicated though on the Roman model); and Mundari (Roman and Devanagari). We can mention also the case of the Yugoslavs, with Serbo-Croat as their language with two scripts officially recognized-the Cyrillic as used by the Greek Orthodox Christians and the Roman by the Roman Catholic Christians). And the great German language uses two scripts side by side, the Gothic or German Black Letter and the Roman.

Until a kind of *Indo·Roman Script* is accepted and established *for all Indian languages, beginning with Sanskrit,* Konkani may advantageously be written in Devanagari, to be in line with most of the Indian languages as they are now, Devanagari being the most widely used Indian script.

(2) Dialects in Konkani. It has been said in disparagement of Konkani that it is not a single speech – it has a number of dialects, which are generally mutually – intelligible but some times some of the words, forms and locutions in a dialect are not universally understood. Unfortunately owing to the disruption of the Gomantak State by the Portuguese conquest of Goa in 1510 and subsequent happenings, the Konkani speaking people had largely to become refugees in Karnataka and then in Kerala and they had to come under the umbrage of other languages and were deprived of the binding and unifying force of a common literary form. George Abraham Grierson, Sten Konow, and Jules Bloch have written on the dialects of Konkani, but he has treated them all as forms of one language. All the dialects go back to a Common or Single Old Konkani of the centuries before 1000 A.D. Dr. Jose Pereira in his valuable work on the Development of Konkani as a Literary Language (1965) has given a *history of Konkani Literature,* and he thinks there was a period of undivided Konkani as a literary language of both prose and poetry down to the 16th century. From this paper, and from Manohar Sardessai's *Concept of the Unity of India in Konkani Literature* (as in "Essays on Konkani Language and Literature in honour of Professor Armando Menezes", Dharwar, 1970)

we see that already in the first part of the 16th century Krishnadas Sharma (sic) had written in Konkani *Ramayana* and *Mahabharata* and *Purana* stories like *Ashvamadhu*, *Krishnacharita* and *Raghunathvamsachi Katha*. The great unifying works for Indian languages and literatures, the *Ramayana*, the *Mahabharata*, and the *Bhagavata Purana* had already come to Konkani, in evidently a common linguistic and literary heritage of Gomantaka.

But a gradual split of Konkani gradually took place, with the suppression of Konkani by fanatical priests in Goa, by the use in literature side by side of five forms of Konkani, by the beginning of the 18th century, which Jose Pereira enumerates as (1) *Saxtte* (=*Sasti*), (2) *Karwari*, (3) *Barhdexi* (*Barhdesi*), (4) *Manglluri* (*Mangaluri*), and (5) *Antruze*, a dialect to the North of Goa. These dialects did not break up the language, but each dialect specialised in a particular c1ass or type of literary composition, which have all been described by Pereira. The situation seems to have been like what we see in Ancient Greek, when all the various dialects (like Ionic, Attic, Aeolic, Doric, and in later times the Koiné) which could all be used in a literature which maintained its unity inspite of dialects. lt is heartening to see that often the makers of a Modern Konkani literature have come to the rescue of Konkani, like V. R. Varde Valavalikar (popularly known as *Shenoi Goembab*), and a modern phase of Konkani is well under way. Further, Konkani speakers both Hindu and Christians have manifested a pride in their language, and the Roman Catholic Church particularly is anxious to bring about a complete unity of speech for the Catholic church service so that differences between Konkani of Goa and that of Mangalore are resolved. They have taken up this work seriously, and the results have been successful.

The same sort of thing is happening in *Himachal Pradesh* which has declared for *Pahade* as its State Language. But this Pahade is not a single speech, – it is split up into about a dozen dialects, of which *Mandeali* the dialect of Mandē, is spoken by the largest number. The intellectuals and the literary élite of Himachal Pradesh have started their new State or Official Language on a Mandeali basis, permitting full use of all other Pahadē dialects, as they are all more or lesss mutually intelligible; and Hindi is still in the offing.

So it would seem that the matter of dialectal divergences is no real problem for Konkani, and the use of various dialect forms will help to bring about the variety and richness of Modern Konkani diction, and the evaluation of a Standard Konkani of prose binding all the dialects will be a matter of course.

(3) The modern literature or Konkani is growing, thanks to the galaxy of writers at the present day who are coming up, both

Christian and Hindu, following the lead of Valavalikar and a few pioneers who dedicated themselves to the revival of Konkani. But there is lack of earlier printed editions or what may be called Early or Medieval *Konkani classics* – of the few that survived, e. g. the 'writings of Krishnadas Sharma (sic). Outstanding Christian classics in Konkani which have a literary or cultural appeal for all Konkani-speakers should be brought out in Devanagari, as they are already available in Roman. All specimens of Konkani as in the inscriptions (with the oldest one going back to the Gupta period – as it is believed) and letters and other documents also should be published in a *Corpus of Old Konkani* prior to the Portuguese advent. And a representative, critically edited Collection of the best Konkani folk poetry, Saraswat and other Hindu, as well as Christian, is a desideratum.

(4) In the study of the philosophy of the Vedanta and in the formulation of any special school or interpretation of the Vedanta, it has been considered proper to prepare commentaries in Sanskrit of the three basic groups of texts on the Vedanta-the *Prasthana-trayas* as they are called. These are (i) the *Sruti-Prasthana* or the Vedas, and particularly the old and authoritative Upanishads, (ii) the *Smriti-Prasthana* or the *Gita* from the *Mahabharata*, and the (iii) *Nyaya-Prasthana*, or the Vedanta-sutras of Badarayana. Without these commentaries, no school of Vedanta can be given any status or recognition. So too, for European languages with Christian cultures in their background, translations of the Bible are a *sinequa non* – the entire Christian Scriptures as in both the *Old Testament* and the *New*. Konkani I believe has (sic) already has that, thanks to the Roman Catholic Church. But Konkani, as a modern Indian language, still lacks full translations of the *Ramayana*, the *Mahabharata*, and the *Bhagavata* and some other *Puranas* – correct and authoritative versions in prose. Herein, Konkani is still lagging behind most of her sisters and cousins like Bengali, Hindi, Marathi, Gujarati and Oriya, and even the great Dravidian languages: and it has been mentioned, even as a language of the Tibeto-Burman family which is now within the orbit of the Hindu religion and philosophy, like Manipuri, spoken only by some 7 lacks of people, has its versions of these great books.

Societies for the Development of Literature in Konkani should seriously take the matter in hand, and there should be established through the joint efforts of all lovers of their mother tongue among Konkanis who believe in their Indian heritage of Sanskrit literature a most precious possession a Society for translating and publishing in Konkani our great classics like the *Ramayana*, the *Mahabharata*, some of the oldest and most important *Puranas*, the complete works of Kalidasa, Pali texts like the *Dhammapada* the *Sutta-nipata* and a few others, and, of course, to start with, selections from the Vedas, and at least the 12 oldest Upanishads. When all this translation work is achieved and published, then alone there will be a tremendous accession of self – respect and power among all Konkanis – particularly the Saraswats who have been the custodians of the Sastras and of all Sanskrit literature for so many centuries. Muslim Konkanis similarly should endow their mother-tongue with a translation of the Quran, and of some of the most human Sufi c1assics from Arabic and Persian.

I am afraid as an old man of 84, in his senility, I have been rather garrulously inclined, and have already bored you. I must now stop, but I give you my best wishes for the success of the Parishad, and for the rehabilitation, with all glory of your beautiful speech of Gomanta, with its rightful place among the Modern Languages of India.

Jivatu Konkani Jayatu Ca!

Printed at D. M. Nadkarni & Sons, Margao, Goa and published by Udai Bhembro, General Secretary, 10th session, Akhil Bharatiya Konkani Sahitya Parishad, Panaji, Goa

Before the codices

Versions of the Mahabharata and Ramayana that were produced before the sixteenth-century Konkani codices became available seem much freer to innovate, modify and choose source texts. Though the Devanagari script was seen to represent a nationalised culture, its legitimacy was not seamlessly extended to the language. Texts written in the script were however, unburdened by interpretations that by and large, cast the history of writing in the Roman script as one of linguistic degradation. The combination of philological nationalism and state recognition meant that the value attached to Devanagari allowed Konkani to participate in the present and transact with other languages without having to explain the past. Prior to state recognition, Valaulikar for instance, did have to labour to produce a non-Sanskritised idiom and combat the arguments that had extended through the first half of the twentieth century, that the language was a dialect of Marathi. The issue of the kind of dialect and morphological choices made in officially-circulated Devanagari and the question of readability is not addressed here.

The effort to recover Konkani renditions of the Ramayana whether as 'correct and authoritative versions' or as folk forms is evident in various proceedings of the Konkani Sahitya Sabha. In fact the attention to folk forms, even if this resulted in the co-opting of the folk as a symbol of sub-nationalism, indicates considerable investment prior to Chatterji's recommendations. Among folk forms, one can find mention of the *Godde Ramayana* of Kochi, of stories around events related to Sita's life, and the Ramayana Ranmale that is performed during the Shigmo festival in Goa (Gomes 1990, 141–48).[2]

The *Raghu Ramayana*, a Konkani version of the Ramayana written in the Malayalam script by G. Kamalammal was published initially in seven parts between 1930 and 1940 and published as a complete work in the Devanagari script in 1981.[3] Manohar Rai Sardessai, whose *A History of Konkani Literature* continues to be the most comprehensive overview of translation in Konkani across scripts, mentions that the source for the *Raghu Ramayana* was not the *Valmiki Ramayana* but the *Adhyatma Ramayana* in Malayalam. Twentieth-century translations that emerged before the appearance of the codices tend to reference a prior text. In 1966, R. V. Pandit's tales from the Ramayana and Mahabharata were produced specifically for school children, under the aegis of the Konkani Bhasha Mandal with Manohar Rai Sardessai. The *Geet Ramayana*, a prose and verse translation of the Marathi work of G. D. Madgulkar was produced by B. V. Baliga in the Kannada script.

In 1976, Shree Sitaram Prakashana in Goa published Shripad Raghunath Desai's *Yakshaprasna*, a translation of four chapters of the Sanskrit *Vanaparvan* of the Mahabharata for children. According to Desai, the Konkani he used was influenced by the tenor of the language favoured by the Gomantak Press in Bombay.[4] The Gomantak Press was associated with Shenoi Goembab, as the writer V. Varde Valaulikar in popularly known, a proponent of Konkani at the turn of the century, well known for his acerbic ridicule of the predilection for Sanskritising contemporary languages.

---

[2] The Godde Ramayana, written in the Malayalam script in Konkani on palm leaves was published by the Konkani Language Institute in Cochin.

[3] Manohar Rai Sardessai, "Konkani: Writers And Writing," *Indian Literature* 25, no. 6 (November 1, 1982): 118–24, https://doi.org/10.2307/23330238.

[4] Shripad Raghunath Desai, "Konkani: Quality and Quantity," *Indian Literature* 21, no. 6, Language and Literature Survey 1976–77 (n.d.): 213.

Ravindra Kelekar's *Konkani Mahabharat*, published in 1987 in two parts, was a synoptic narrative called a 'transcreation' by him. His version has been received as a 'rational' rendition of the text. Kiran Budkuley (2013) for instance has the following to say about it:

> Born of exhaustive research and thoughtful interpretation, *Mahabharata: Ek Anusarjan* displays simple, chaste, home-grown Konkani idiom. While Kelekar admits fidelity to Bhandarker's (sic) authenticated version, his 'cleansed and scrubbed tale' brooks no irrational or divine aspect of theme or character to go (sic) without comment.

In 1989, Mahabaleshwar Sardesai produced a Mahabharata for children in Devanagari verse, published by the Seva Samiti, which had set up a school in 1934. With the growing opinion that children should be instructed in the 'mother tongue', the school began instruction in Konkani from 1940. Subsequently, a press was set up and in the 70s and 80s Konkani publications were produced, some of which won Sahitya Akademi awards. The preface to Sardesai's text, written by Damodar Narsinh Naik two years after Konkani was given official language status in the Devanagari script, declared that Konkani had become the 'Rajbhasa'. Aside from the children's Mahabharata, Mahabaleshwar Sardesai also published a Konkani Ramayana, and Aesop's fables.

Shenoi Goembab is the pen name of Vaman Rogunath Varde Valaulikar (1877–1946), who produced much of his work in the early decades of the twentieth century. He is one of the earliest proponents of Konkani to urge that its speakers recognise it as the 'mother-tongue' of Goa instead of Marathi. Though Goembab wrote numerous books and articles, the ones on Konkani were singularly directed towards proving that it was a distinct language with its own literary tradition. In the context of Bombay where he lived, this was an assertion against the dominance of Marathi. Goembab's translation in prose, Shri Bhogvontalem Git, *comprising selections from the* Bhagavad Gita *was completed in 1935, but published in 1959. In his articles and his many satirical books, Goembab's singular exhortation to Goans was to shun a Sanskritised Konkani and to use simple prose that was likely to draw people to the language.*

Shri Bhogvontalem Git *was printed at the Gomantak Press in Bombay in 1959. The press was associated with Goembab's campaign for a non-Sanskritised Konkani in the Devanagari script, as a means to combat what he saw as the cultural dominance of Marathi. The text carries prefatory notes by the Konkani poet Kashinath Shridhar Naik and the celebrated Kannada poet, M. Govinda Pai. K. S. Naik supported Valaulikar's publications through the length of his working life and his introduction reveals his proximity and involvement in the pattern of Valaulikar's thought and work. In order to arrive at a satisfactory idiom for his text, he states, Valaulikar had analysed debates over interpretations across various editions of the Gita, and had begun to compare similarities between Vedic dharma and religions such as Islam and Christianity as he wanted his text to be written in a simple idiom like popular English translations of the Bible.*

As a sign that the use of the Devanagari script to write Konkani also involved some uncertainty, Naik describes Valaulikar's deliberations over what would be the right scheme of orthography to write Konkani in Devanagari. Valaulikar altered the orthography of words according to what he thought was the right usage and felt he had to study the roots of words or would not be able to achieve the simplicity and purity that he desired in his work. Both Goembab and Naik were of the view that Devanagari was the right script for Konkani. In the production of the text, according to him, Goembab had helped bring Konkani closer to the status of Marathi. A thousand copies of the book were printed.

Goembab had assumed that his concerns about language would be addressed after he had completed a basic translation of the text, but realised that the issues were interlinked. Naik was then editor of the first Devanagari Konkani paper, the Novem Goem*, a task he had to set aside to assist Valaulikar. Despite three revisions of the text, Goembab did not entirely achieve the perfection of language he had sought, he stated. The inclusion of an address by Govind Pai, an award-winning Kannada poet, indicates that there was a continuing conversation and unity of purpose among Konkani speakers along the coast. Some of this work was an explicit celebration of the cultural repertoire of Konkani Brahmins. Pai cited other (published and unpublished) translations to Konkani from South and North Canara. He thanked K. S. Naik for allowing him to write the preface in his own idiom and not the standard Naik had created along with Valaulikar through the Gomantak Press.*

Excerpt 2
Courtesy State Central Library, Panjim
Shantaram Varde Valaulikar ed., *Samagra Shenoi Goembab*, Khand iv, *Shri Bhogvontalem Git, – vol. 2 Collected Literature of Shenoi Goembab*, (Goa: Goa Konkani Akademi, 2003), pp. 175–184

संपादप्याली दोन उतरां

संवसारांत आनी आमच्या भारत देसांतूय तरेकतरा जायते धर्म पातळ्ळ्यात. तांतूंत आमचो वेदिक धर्म चड पुर्विल्लो. वेद आनी उपनिषदां हे ताचे मुखेल ग्रंथ. ह्या ग्रंथांचे सार म्हळ्यार 'श्रीमदभगवदगीता.' विस्तारान ल्हान पणून म्हत्वान म्हान अश्या ह्या अप्रूप ग्रंथाचीं सगळ्या हिन्दी आनी येवरोपीय भासांनी एकापरस अदीक भाशांतरां जाल्यांत. पणून आमचे कोंकणींत - तिगेले खाशेले देवनगरी लिपींत - मेकळें अशें भाशांतर ऐकूय जावंक नासलें. तें आज 'श्रीभगवंताले गीत' ह्या नांवान भायर सरता.

हें भाशांतर जाल्लें पळोवचें अशी म्हाका उमळशीक लागल्यार आज कशींय ४०/४५ वर्सां जालीं. काळजांतले हेच ओडीन, १९२७ वर्सा हांवें शणै गोंयबाबांची पैलीवैली भेट घेतली. पणून ह्या ना त्या कारणान तें काम फुडें पडत गेलें. अखेरेक, १९३५ वर्सा तांणी हें भाशांतर करून तें तीन खेपो निवळायलें. फुडें, ह्या भाशांतरावांगडाच ताची फोडणिशी बरोवन, गीतेचे शिकोवणेचो सार-गाबो वाचप्यांक दिल्यार बरें जायत अशें येवजून, तांणी त्या कामाक हात घालो. कारण, गिता म्हळ्यार हजारानी वर्सांनी आनी हजारांनी ऋषिंनी जल्मवेर बसून केल्ले चिंतणेचे सार आसा. संवसार म्हळ्यार कितें, तो आपशींच जाला कि कोणें घडला, आपशींच जाल्यार कसो, घडला जाल्यार कोणें, तो घट्टलो कसो आसा, तो खैं रावता, संवसारांत मनीस जल्माक येता कित्याक आनी मरता कित्याक, मरण म्हळ्यार कितें, मरतरीच मनीस वा ताचो आत्मो खैं वेता, तो सासणाचो कि खिणयाळो, मनशाचे फाटीक कर्म म्हळ्यार करणी कित्याक लागल्या, ताचेपासून सुख-दुख कित्याक भोगता, तीं ताका मेल्या उप्रांतूय भोगचीं पट्टात कि नात, पातक म्हळ्यार कितें, पुण्यताय म्हळ्यार कितें, तीं कोणें निर्मिलीं, तांची बादा मनशाक जावचें कारण कितें, तें खैंसून आयलें, हांतूंतल्यान कशें सुटचें आनी सासणाचें सुखी कशें जावचें-बी तरेकतरा प्रस्नांनी विचारी मनशाचो जीव काथलावता आनी ताका नाका-पुरो जाता. ताका मागीर कितेंच गोड लागना. तो सुखाक आंवडेना. दुखाक कांवचेना. कितलींय आडमेळीं आयलीं जाल्यारूय तो तान-भूक विसरून रात-दीस त्या प्रस्नांचे फाटल्यान धांवता. असल्या म्हळ्यार ह्या प्रस्नांची तड पळोवंक नेटान वावुरिल्ल्या आनी अखेरेक मनाची मोटी थंडाय जोडिल्ल्या आमगेल्या पुर्वज ऋषिंनी, त्या संबंदाचे आपणाले अणभव आनी विचार, वेद-उपनिषदां-बी ग्रंथांनी बरोवन दवल्ल्यात. ‘श्रीमदभगवदगीता’ म्हळ्यार त्या विचारांचो रोस न्हय, - आपरोस. देखून तो पोसो भरून निखटो ताळ्यांत रकोवन उपकारना. तो थोडो-थोडो तळटार घेवन, जिबेन चाटून, ताची ल्हवु-ल्हवु रूच घेवंक जाय. पणून मूळ गितेनूच हेकाम जायना; तें, उतराक उतर दवरून करूं नज जाल्ल्या भाशांतरान कशें जायत? देखून तांतूंतली दरएकली म्हणणी फोडून-विस्कून, ओपारी-देखी दिवन उकती करची पट्टा. ते भाशेन तांणी ती करपाचें थारायलें. हे खातीर तांणी वेगळ्या-वेगळ्या काळांत आनी थळांत उजवाडा आयिल्ल्यो गिता पुंजावन त्यो वाचून काडल्यो आनी तांतूंतल्या वेगळ्या-वेगळ्या पाठांचो बारकायेन अभ्यास केलो.[१] गितेंत आयिल्ल्या अदीक-अर्थी उतरांचो कोश घडून, वेगळ्या वेगळ्या विदवानांनी केल्ले तांचे तरेकतरा अर्थ उठावन काडले. गितेचेर, पुर्विल्ल्या-अर्विल्ल्या आनी भायल्या-भितल्ल्या विदवानांनी बरैल्ल्यो फोडणीश्यो वाचून, तांगेल्या सम आनी आड मतांची वळेरी बरोवन काडली. वेदीक धर्माचे मुखेल ग्रंथ आनी ताच्या धर्मीक खांद्यांच्या वेगळ्या-वेगळ्या मुखेल आचार्यांनी आप-आपणालेल्या मताभाशेन केल्ले तांचे वेगळे-वेगळे अर्थ आनी फोडणीश्यो वाचून काडल्यो.[२] येसू क्रिस्ताची जीण आनी क्रिस्तांव धर्माचें बिब्ल, म्हम्मुदाची जीण आनी इस्लाम धर्माचें कुराण, तशेच तालमूद-बी हेर धर्माचे

[१] ह्या ‘दोन अतुरां’ चेअखेरेकपुवूर्ण दिल्या ती पळयात.

मुखेल ग्रंथ, तांची भाशांतरां आनी फोडणीश्यो वाचल्यो. त्या धर्माचे आनी वेदीक धर्माचे शिकोवणेंतलीं सारकेपणा आनी तीं नासल्यार तांचीं कारणां सोदून-येवजून काडलीं. हे भाशेन, आगळें-उणें अडेशीं-तीनशीं पानांचे आयतें एकठावन जातकूच तांणी आपणाल्या गिते-भाशांतराक कसलेच भावनेची बादा जावची न्हंय हे खातीर, आपणालें मन आनी मेंदू हांचो सोद घेतलो आनी तांचेर आपल्या[3]-पेल्या कसल्याय मत्तांची पुटां चडिल्लीं आसल्यार बारकायेन सांसपून पळोवन तीं काडून उडैलीं. हे भाशेन, आपणाली नदर शुद्ध, सत्त्वीक, आनी उजू करून आनी योगभारीत जावन तांणी हें भाशांतर चौथे खेपेक निवळावंक घेतलें. हें भाशांतर बिब्लाच्या इंग्रजी अणकाराभाशेन सादें, सोंपें आनी नितळ जावचें अशी तांची इत्सा आसली. पणून जेन्ना ही निवळावणी सव्या अध्यायांतल्या इकराव्या शिळोकाचेर पावली तेन्ना त्यांच्या मुखार एक नवीच अडचण आयली. ती म्हळ्यार उतरांच्या रूपांची. तीं थारावपांत आपणाली कसलीय तरी चूक जाता अशें तांकां दिसलें. ती सोदून काडचे खातीर तांणी दाखै, पळै, सोडै हीं उतरां फुडलीं रूपां दा**खौं**क, प**ळौं**क, सो**डा**क अशीं जावचे बदला दा**खोवं**क, प**ळोवं**क, सो**डोवं**क अशीं जातात म्हणपाचे समजलें. तशेंच तांणी 'न्हंय' हें क्रियापद फोडून पळैलें. त्या वेळार, ताचेवैली नाखया उच्चाराची कुरु (ं) गाळून उडोवंक जाय, म्हळ्यार तें **'न्हंय'** हाचे बदला **'न्हय'** अशें बरोवंक जाय अशें तांकां दिसलें.[5] म्हणटकूच हेच भाशेन दरएकल्या उतराचो आनी तांतूंतल्या मूळ धातुचो सोद घेवन तांचो खोल अभ्यास केल्याबगर आपणाल्या गिते-भाशांतराक येवंक जाय तितली नितळसाण येवची ना आनी तें जाय तितलें शुद्ध जावचें ना म्हणपाचे तांकां उकतें दिसलें. भाशेच्या अभ्यासाचें हें काम थारायल्ल्या भितल्लेंच एक आसलेंय जाल्यार, तें गितेच्या भाशांतरा उपरांत हातांत घेवपाचो तांचो आदलो बेत आसलो. तो तांकां बदलचो पदलो आनी गीतेचें भाशांतर बऱ्यांतलें बरें जावचें हेखातीर, तें कडेक दवरून, भाशेच्या शास्त्रीक अभ्यासाक हात घालचो पडलो. हें म्हाका समजलें तेन्ना हांव पेंचांत पडलों. कारनत्या वेळार, म्हळ्यार १९३७त म्हज्या हातांत 'नवें गोंय' आसलें. ताका आंकपट्टे नवें खाण जाय जातालें आनी ताची पुर्वण करपाचो सगळो भार एकट्या शणै गोंयबाबांचेर पट्टालो. पणून म्हाका व्याक्रणाची भूक लागल्ली आनी गितेच्या भाशांतराचे तानेन म्हजो जीव व्हर्सतालो.[6] देखून, तीं दोनूय कामां जाता तितले बेगीन जावचीं हे खातीर मोट्या कश्टान हांवें 'नवें गोंय'

---

[2] ह्यो फोडणिश्यो सुमार पंदरा-वीस आसात.

[3] देव-धर्म, न्याय-नीत आनी संवसार ह्या संबंदान खासा शणै गौंयबाबांलीं मत्तां वेगळे तरेचीं आसलीं. ((१) गोमन्तोपनिषत्, दूसरें खंड, मुंबै, १९३९, पानां ३४०-४१. (२) पुण्यात्मो राम कामती, मुंबै, १९३९, पानां १-२. (३) कोंकणी विद्यार्थ्यांक, मुंबै, १९५८, पान ३७.) तीं गीतेंतल्या त्या संबंदाच्या मत्तांक जमसारकीं नासलीं.

[4] कोंकणिची व्याकरणी बांदावळ, मुंबै, १९४९, पानां ११०-१२.

[5] बांदावळ, पान १५९.

[6] "... गितेसारक्या ग्रंथाच्या भाशांतराचो चंद्रहार कोंकणिच्या गळ्यांत अजून घालपाचो आसा... तिचें व्याक्रण घडपाचें आसा... तिचो कोश करपाचो आसा..." पुण्यात्मो राम कामती, 'उजवाडावप्याली दोन अतुरां,' पान १५.

थांबोवचो निर्णय घेतलो. पणून हो संवसार मोटो विचित्रांचो आसा. तो केन्ना कोणाक कसो भाजून काडीत हें समजना. तशें पळैल्यार, शणै गोंयबाबांनी आपणाल्या खाशेल्या संवसाराचो चिंता-हुस्को सोडिल्लो आनी ताच्यो उखला-डवरी काळाचेर सोंपोवन तांणी कोंकणी संवसाराक वेंग मारिल्ली. ताची दशा पळोवन तांचो जीव आकूळ-पिकूळ जातालो. देखून, तो जाता तितलो सरी करून हुस्क्या-मेकळें जावचें अशें तांणी थारयल्लें. ते म्हातारे जाल्ले; पणून तांगेली लिखणी ऐन तरणेपणान शिंवशिंवताली. आदीं ते, हे वाचूंक जाय, तें वाचूंक जाय अशें म्हणटाले. पणून आतां तागेलें सगळें वाचप सोंपल्लें, आनी मनां-मेंदूंत सांठावल्लें बरोवंक तांगेली लिखणी फुरफुरताली. तांची प्रकृत बरी नासली; ती भौन भौन तांका धोंगशिताली. जाल्यारुय, तिका चेपून, आंगांत आशी-नाशिल्लें बळगें एकठावन, नवो धर्म थापण्या देवदूतावरी,[७] मोट्या हावेसान ते त्या कामाक लागल्ले. त्या कामाचेर तांचो कितलो मोग आशिल्लो आनी ते खातीर तांणी आपणाल्यो सगळयो संवसारीक आशा-मनिशा आनी वान्सा मारून, कितलें खर तप केल्लें हें हांवे सांगपाची गरज ना. त्या बळग्याच्या नेटार उश्यासरीं पाविल्ल्या मर्णाक लेगीत “थांब, म्हजें काम अजून सोपूंक ना” अशे सांगून ताका ते धिस्पटायतले आसले. ह्या वेळार तांकां एक-दोनूच वर्सा थंडायेचीं गेल्लीं जाल्यार एकटे कोंकणींतूनच न्हय तर संवसार-साहित्यान आनीक एका भोव बऱ्या ग्रंथाची भर पड्टली आसली. पणून घटीत वेगळें आसलें. ते भाशेन ताणें आपणाक जाय तसेंच करून शणै गोंयबाबाली अेन म्हत्वाच्या वावराचीं दोन-तीन वर्सां खाल्ल्यानं, ‘कोंकणिची व्याकरणी बांदावळ’च अर्दकुटी उल्ली[८] अशे न्हय तर गितेचे फोडणीशेवांगडाच ह्या भाशांताराची निखटी निवळावणीय जैंचे थै रावन विचारी संवसाराचे मोल करू नज इतलें लुस्कान जालें. हें पळोवन जीव चुरचुरता. पणून आतां ताका उपाय ना.

हे भाशेन, हें ‘श्रीभगवंताले गीत’ जशें म्हज्या हाताक लागलें तशें वाचप्यांमुखार येता. हे भाशांतर शणै गोंयबाबांनी तीन खेपो निवळायल्ले अशें वैर म्हळां. पणून तीं तीनूय निवळावपां एकेच तालकेचेर जाल्ल्यान, तातूंत कांय जाग्यांर ओळीक ओळ दसून, उतरांत उतरां आनी अक्षरांत अक्षरां घुसपल्ल्यांत. ह्या कारणान, आनी म्हज्या अजाणपणान आनी घळयेपणान, ताचे हे छापी तालकेंत जायत्यो चुको उल्ल्यात. तशेंच, हांतूंत मूळ गितेंतले शिळोक दिवंक जाय आसले; पणून ते दिवंक नात. हे खातीर हांव मखलासी मागतां आनी शणै गोंयबाबाअसलो समान-धर्मी आनी समान-सबावी म्हा-आत्मो फुडें सरून, हें चड गरजेचें आनी भोवच म्हत्वाचें पुस्तक निवळावन, फावो-जाल्ले फोडणीशेसैत वाचप्यांक दितलो अशी आस्त धरतां.

---

[७] देवदूत म्हळ्यार देवान धाडिळ्ळो, देवाची सांगणी घेवन आयिळ्ळो भोव बरो आत्मो.

[८] ‘कोंकणिचे व्याकरणी बांदावळीं’त, १८१ व्या पानार, “कोंकणी लोकांले पूवर्ज (त्यत्) हें अुतर जायतें अुपकारायताले अशें दिसता. ह्या संबंदाची फोडणिशी फुडें येतली” अशें म्हळां. पणून ती तातूंत आयिळ्ळी दिसना. देखून हेंय पुस्तक अदर्कुटें अुळ्ळे अशें म्हणचें पड्टा.

ह्या पुस्तकाचे प्रस्तावनकार भौमान्य राजकवी मंजेश्वर गोविंदबाब पै हांची 'शणै गोंयबाबाले बरपावळि'च्या वाचप्यांक हांवें वळख करून दिवपाची गरज ना. तांगेले जायते इतिहासीक सोद शणै गोंयबाबांनी मान्य केल्यात.[९] हाचेवरसून ते पैल्या पांवड्याचे इतिहास-सोदपी आसात म्हणपाचें उकतें दिसता. तांकां बावीस भासो येतात. इतिहासाच्या मळार तांणी जायते मुळावे सोद लायल्यात. तांणी काय खेळ रचल्यात; आप-जिणे-कथा बरैल्या. ह्या भायर ते निजाचेच कवी आसात. श्रीकृष्ण परमात्म्याचेर भकतीन थबथबल्लें तांणी एक लांब-गीत रचलां. तशेंच बुद्ध भगवान, क्रिस्त स्वामी आनी गांधी म्हात्मे हांगेल्या जिणेंतल्या दुखाळ प्रसंगांचेर, काकुतीन उपाट भरिल्लीं तीन कथा-गितां तांणी रचल्यांत. तांगेली ल्हान-व्हड कवनांय जायतीं आसात. तीं सगळीं रोसाळ आनी म्होंवाळ जाल्यांत. लोकांच्या तोंडांत तीं रात-दीस घोळटात. हे भाशेन, तांणी केल्ले कानडी साअित्याचे भारीभरकूम सेवेन तुश्टल्ल्या थैंच्या मद्रास सरकारान १९४८ वर्सा तांकां 'आस्थान-कवी' म्हळ्यार राजकवी ही उंच पदवी दिली. कानडी-साअित्य-संवसारांत असली पदवी मेळैतलेतेच तेच पैले आनी एकलेच आसात. हाचे वरसून, तांणी केल्ली कानडी साअित्याची सेवा कितली मुळावी आसा आनी ती कितली तोला-मोलाची जाल्या तें उकतें दिसता.

हे सेवेन भारावल्ले कानडी-साअित्य-परिशदेन, आपणाले १९५० वर्सा मुंबै भरिल्ले ३४वे बसकेचो येजमानकेचो पाट तांकां दिलो.[१०] पणून तो मान आपणयताना आपूण कोंकणो आसां आनी आपणाली आवै-भास कोंकणी आसा हें, आडखळनासतना खणखणीत ताळ्यान सांगूंक ते विसल्ले - भियेले नात. राजकवी गोविंदबाब पै हांचो जल्म आनी तांगेले सगळें मुळावें-ताळावें शिकप, तांगेल्या आज्या-पणज्यांभाशेनूच, हेर भासांच्या चेपणातळा सांपडल्ल्या कोंकणाच्या दक्षीण मुलखांत आनी परक्या भासांत जालें, जाल्यारूय आपूण कोंकणो आसां, हें ते विसल्ले नात. हांतूंतूच तांगेलें सगळें तेज सांठवलां. तांगेले कान कोंकणी हें उतर आयकनाफुडें फुलतात आनी तांगेलो आत्मो -

आसूनी खैं खैं तरी आमी, मायी!
आमचीं हृदयां सदां तुजे पायीं!
तुजेंच न्हय गे हें हाड-मास?-
तुजेवीण खैंची आमची दूद-भास?[११]

अशें विचारून भुरकुटून किटकिटूंक लागता! हें पळोवन खातकुतल्यो जातात. हे भाशेन, आवैभुंयेच्या आनी आवै-भाशेच्या मोगांत अखंडपणान

[९] (१) गोंयकारांची गोंयाभायली वसणूक, पैलें खंड, मुंबै, १९२८, पानां १४३, १४४, १४८; (२) 'कांही मराठी लेख,' पैलो वांटो, मुंबै, १९४५, पानां १८७, १९९.

[१०] *Bharat Jyoti*, Bombay, dated 24th December 1950, Vol. 13, No. 10, page III, Story of the Asthana-Kavi.

[११] 'साद', संपादपी डॉ. अेच. ओ. मास्कारेंज्यस, मुंबै, १९५०, पैलें वर्स, तिसरो आंक, पान १३.

पेंवन आपलेपणाच्या तेजान लखलखण्या व्हडांत-व्हड कानडी साअित्य-सुर्याची प्रस्तावन कोंकणी साअित्य-समराटांच्या ह्या पुस्तकाक दिवंक मेळ्ळी हे हांव म्हजें मोटें भाग्य समजतां.

निमाणें, कोंकणीं लोकांक आवै-भाशेचो मग आतांचेकूय अदीक रुजचो आनी ते भाशेचे सेवेक तांणी चड अगत्यवादान लागचें ह्या हेतून, ह्या पुस्तकाच्यो एक हजार प्रती कोंकणिचो प्रसाद म्हणु वांटपाच्यो थारायला. ते भाशेन तो हेत तडीक वचूं अशें मागून हांव हीं दोन उतरां सोंपैतां.

गोमन्तक छापखानो
मुंबै - ४
ता. २८-१-१९५९

का. श्री. नायक

पुर्वण
शणै गोंयबाबांल्या सोदपा-वावराची एक पत

शणै गोंयबाबांक गितेचे इतिहासीक बसकेचो आनी तांतूंतल्या एक-दोन शिळोकांचो दुबाव येतालो. तांतूंतलो एक दुबाव, जाय-जाल्लो आधार मेळून खरो कसो जालो ह्या संबंदाची गजाल सकला दिल्या. तिचेवरसून, तांगेले इतिहासीक सोद कितले मुळावे आनी घट-गुंड्या बुनियादीचेर आधारिल्ले आसात तें वाचप्यांक दिसतलें:

गितेच्या इकराव्या अध्यायांत श्रीकृष्ण संवसाररूप दाखैताल; तें पळोवन तो भिता आनी श्रीकृष्णाक विनैता: "माथ्यार मुकूट घाल्लो आनी हातांत गदा आनी चक्र आशिल्लो असो आदले भाशेनूच तुका पळोवंक हांव सोदतां. अगा हजार भुजाच्यां, संवसारांचे रुप घेतिल्ल्या देवा तूं त्याच रुपाचो **चार भुजांचो** जा" (११-४६). ही ताची मागणी मान्य करून, श्रीकृष्ण आपणाल्या मुदलच्या रूपान दिसता. त्यावेळार, अर्जुन म्हणटा: "श्रीकृष्णा, तुगेलें हें माणकुले मनीसरूप पळोवन, आतां म्हगेलें मन थारावले आनी हांव धेयभानार आयलों" (११-५१). हाचेवरसून, ह्या वेळार श्रीकृष्णान आपणालें संवसाररूप पालोवन दाखैल्लें रूप मनशाचें आसून मनशाक चार हात नासतात हें कोणाकूच सांगूंक नाका. तरी आसतना एकाद्रे श्रीकृष्णाकूच तितले हात आशिल्ले जाल्यार तांतूंतल्या फकत दोन हातांत गदा आनी चक्र हीं दोन आवतां दिवन, ताचे उरिल्ले दोन हात, 'महाभारत'कार वा गिताकार रिते दवरचो नासलो; पणून वैर दिल्ल्या पैल्या शिळोकांत तशें करूंक ना. हाचेवरसून त्या शिळोकांतल्या मुदलच्या खऱ्या उतरांची उखला-दवर जाल्ली आसूंक जाय वा तो शिळोकूच गितेंत कोणेंय अडेचो शिरकटायल्लो आसुंक जाय असो शणै गोंयबाबांक दुबाव आयलो. कारण असल्या 'चमत्कारां'चेर तांचो विस्वास नासलो. वेदीक धर्म, तागेल्या खाशेल्याच घरांत सकलां पडून, आनी थैं हेर धर्म किल्लून वा भायल्यान येवन मातून आमची वाट लागूंक, सगळ्यांत वैलें आनी पैलें

कारण असले 'चमत्कार' आसून ते आमी आतां ना करूंक जाय. कारण असल्या 'चमत्कारां'नी खऱ्या गिन्यान्याक बाद येता आनी तो उखलून धरतल्यांची वाट लागता, हांतूंत दुबाव ना. पणून चिकित्सायेन भरिल्ल्या ह्या विसाव्या शेंकड्यांतूय संपादिल्ल्या कै टिळकांल्या 'गीतारहस्य' ह्या ग्रथांतलेगीत तोच पाठ घोळैला.[१] देखून, त्या शिळोकाची फोडणिशी करपाक शणै गोंयबाब अनमनताले. अखेरेक, जायतो सोद करतकूच, गितेची एक वेगळी प्रत तांच्या हाताक लागली. तांतूंत वैर दिल्ल्या पैल्या शिळोकांत "**चतु**र्भुजेन" **(चार** भुजांचो) हाचे बदला "भुज**द्वयेन" (दोन** भुजांचो**)** असो पाठ तांकां मेळ्ळो.[२] म्हणटकूच मुदलचो, गितकाराच्या हातचो, खरेलो शुद्ध पाठ 'भुजद्वयेन' होच आसा हांतूंत दुबाव उरना. पणून ते भाशेन, ह्या पुस्तकांत बदल करूंक ते पावले नात आनी हांवेंय तो केलो ना, हे खातीर वाचप्यानी मखलासी करची.

प्रस्तावन

- राजकवी गोविंदबाब पै

म्हजे मान्य मित्र, मुबैंच्या गोमंतक छापखान्याचे धनी श्री काशिनाथ श्रीधर नायकांनी तांचेर म्हजे मित्रवर्य श्रीश्री[१] शणै गोंयबाबांनी केल्ल्या, 'श्रीमद्भग्वदगीता' ह्या ग्रंथाच्या कोंकणी भाशांताराक हांवें एकी प्रस्तावन बरोवका म्हणु म्हाका बरप धाडलां. शणै गोंयबाबांनी कोणाक 'कोंकणीचे अशोक' म्हळा कि त्या व्हड मनश्यांलो निरोपु नाकारच्याक म्हजें मन आयकना. देखून ह्या कामाक हांवे हातु लावका जालो.

ही प्रस्तावन तम गितेकच न्हय, परंत शणैल्या गितेच्या कोंकणी भाशांतराक मात. जाल्ल्यान, शुरवेर आमची आवैभास जी कोंकणी हिच्या संबंदान आनी शणैनी तिका वैर हाडपाक केल्ल्या सेवेच्या संबंदान हीं दोनि-दोनी चि - उतरां सांगतां.

हिंवाळ्यांत कितले कि जंतू न्हिदोन पडतात आनी गिमांत पुना सशक्त जागे जातात खै. तशीच आतां जागेल्या आमची कोंकणी. कोंकणी ही तिजी भैणभास जी मराठी हिचेपरस कितलि फाटली म्हणून शासनांत मराठी कै कितले पूर्वांसून तंथै दिश्टी पडचीं कोंकणी शब्दांसूनय कळता. तशेंच इसवी १२९०त रचन जाल्ल्या आनी मराठीचें आद्य काव्य म्हणोन घेवच्या श्री'ज्ञानेश्वरीं'त वावुल्ल्यां कितले कि कोंकणी शब्दांसूनय समजता, इत्यादी. जाल्यार, आदले कान कशें मागल्या शिंगांत निपून वेतात, तशें वेळु मुखार सरतां आमची कोंकणी मागशी-मागशी पडली आनी दीसु सांजेतांच उजवाडु कशें घर-घरच्या दिव्यांत मात रावता, तशें ती उलवणेंत मात उरली. शिवाय, म्हाका तम अशें दिसता कि ती साअित्यांत अद्याप पावली ना. - न्हय, न्हय, पैर ची पैर थांय ती पावन आशिल्ली. पणून थोडेच वर्सां फाटीं,

---

[१] श्रीमद्भगवद्रीतारहस्य अथवा कर्मयोग शास्त्र, तृतीय मुद्रण, पुणें, शक १८४० (सन १९१८) पान ७७१.

जेदना शणै गोंयबाबान तांची कोंकणीची ती वज्रलेखणी हातांत उबारली, घे! तेदना सुटली कोंकणीची ती शेंकडे लांब साडे साती, फाटी सरले तिजे ते हिंवाळ्याचे दीस आनी तांच्या फाटो फाटी तिज्यांत फुलेच्या लागलो आतांचो हो नवो वसंतु!

हेंच दुसऱ्या भाशेन सांगूं जाल्यार, म्हाका आस्ता आसा कि, आमचे शणै गोंयबाब हे कोंकणी भाशेक वैर काडपी 'म्हाआचार्य',[२] मात न्हय, ते आतांच्या बरपी कोंकणीचे - आतांच्या कोंकणी साअित्यांचे - बापूय व्हय. हें चूक आसों ना आसों, पणून हें मत म्हजें थीर मत. तांची कोंकणी म्हळ्यार आमचें कुळार - गोंयची निप्पट दुदभास, तिजें नितळ दूद. म्हज्या कोंकणीत जाल्यार परक्या दुदकार्न्याले दूद जायतें मेळनू ती भौ उदकळ जाल्या. देखून म्हजे कोंकणीक आनी तांचे कोंकणीक रात-फालें. अशें जाण जावनूय हांव तांच्या गितेक खैच्या हातान प्रस्तावन बरोवं? नज, तांच्या ह्या भांगराच्या सोराक म्हजो पितळीचो आंकडो लागोवच्याक नज म्हणु म्हजें मन दचकून, एक दोन फावटीं मागसार-मुखार जूंय घेवपाक लागलें खरेंच. परंत तेदना म्हज्या उगडासाक आयली, श्रीरामान सेतु बांदैताना ल्हानशे एकि चानि येन आंब्याचो एकु सुको कातो हाण्णु तांतूत घालपाची सेवा केली म्हणून, म्हज्या भुरगेपणांत आयकिल्ली एकि काणी. सै म्हाका देवु पावलो म्हळें आनी देखून हें कोंकणी गितादेविचें मंदिर उक्तें करतना म्हजीं हीं चार आबोलीं उंबरारी दवरतां.

जगाच्या त्या त्या भाशेच्या म्हा-बराप्यांल्या शैलींत जे जे कितले सदगुण आसूंक जाय, - देखीक, नितळपण, दादलेंपण, गोडसाण, गोमटाय, इत्यादि - ते तें सगळेय भरपूर आसात शणै गोंयबाबांल्या कोंकणीत. तितलें च न्हय, फांत्यावैल्या आदल्या कोंब्याच्या सादावरी तांची कोंकणी कोंकणी-जगाक जागोवंक फाव जाली. हो आनीक एकु सदगुणु तिजांत आसा. अशी तांणी आपणाल्या बरापावळींत फुडल्या साअित्याक कोंकणी भास भांगारान घडोवन दिली. तांच्या कोंकणी गितेक हीच म्हजी प्रस्तावन...

कोंकणींत शणै गोंयबाबांले हें पैलें एकिची भाशांतर मात न्हय, आनीक यीं तीनि पुणि वेगळीं भाशांतारा आसात अशें दिसता.

(१) ईसवी १९१४च्या आसपास म्हजे व्हडले भैणीचे घोव, आमच्या दक्षिण कानडा जिल्ल्यांतल्या मुल्की गांवचे सुप्रख्यात कानडी कवी, नाटककार आनी गाणार श्रीश्री बंगलेकार नारायण कामत (१८७२-१९१८) हांणी 'साकी' म्हणु मराठींत जें एक प्रसिद्ध गीत आसा तांतूंत रचिल्ले कोंकणी भाशांतर. हें आतांच कानडी लिपींत मंगळूरांत छाप जालां.

---

[२] किरीटिन चक्रहस्तमिछामि त्वां द्रष्टुमहं तथैव। ततेनैव रूपेण **भुजद्वयेन** सहस्रबाहो भव विश्र्वमूतें ||४६|| श्रीभगवद्गीता, edited by राजवैध जीवराम कालिदास शास्त्री, रसशाला औषधाश्रम, गोंडळ, काठियावाड, विक्रम संवत् १९९३ (क्रि.स. १९३७), पान १०७. ह्मा गिता-ग्रंथाक जोडिल्ल्या Introduction, पान ११ वेल्यान, १२३५ **संवतांत (क्रि. सन १९७९त**) बरैल्लया आनी सुरते मेळिल्लया हाताळ्यावरसून तो छापला आनी त्या हाताळ्यांत **हरीवंशूय आसा** म्हणपाचें समजता.

बंगालींत भायर पडीलल्या मनशाच्या नांवाआर्दी दोन श्री लायतात, ती रीत हांगा अुपकारायल्या.

(२) उत्तर कानडा जिल्ल्याचे सुप्रसिद्ध संस्कृत विद्वान आनी बीनकार श्रीश्री मंगेश राव तेलंग (१९७९-१९४९) हांगेलेय पद्यांत बांदिल्ले कोंकणी भाशांतर आसा. हें हांवे आज पर्यंत पळेल्लें ना.

(३) म्हजे मित्र, आमच्या दक्षिण कानडाचे श्री रामचंद्र कृष्ण प्रभु, हे एकि फावटी म्हाका सांगताले कि तांचे मित्र श्री बाळकृष्ण भगवंतशर्णे वा बाकिबाब बोरकार नांवाचे एक सुप्रसिद्ध कवी, जे आतां पुण्यांत आसात खैं, ते गीतेचें कोंकणी भाशांतर पद्यरूपान करताले. तें दोनि वर्सांच्या पूर्वी आपणें पळैतना, तांतून दोनि अध्याय जावनु तिसऱ्या अध्यायाचें भाशांतर चलतालें म्हणून.

ही नंतां आनीय चडेती कोंकणी भाशांतारां आसात कि नात, हाव नेण....

मंजेश्वर
ता: ५-११-१९५५

गोविंद पैं

THE CODICES AS ORIGINALS – CONFRONTING THE PAST

Unlike the versions of the Mahabharata mentioned above, in translations that drew on the codices as a source, the question of the appropriateness of language itself was of compelling interest. The value attributed to antiquity ensured the codices a significant place within literary history, but only as oral texts whose transition into writing was never complete. They were valuable as evidence of pre-sixteenth century Konkani that remained to be restored and transmitted to the present when the changes introduced by its mediation as writing were removed. In 1988, Lourdino Rodrigues' rendering of the codice Mahabharata in the Roman and Devanagari scripts as separate texts, was impelled by a desire to restore a usage that was free from incorrect grammatical loans from other languages, and to produce an ordered and corrected version of the recovered codices that were otherwise difficult to read, (and whose pages were not in order), leading to misapprehensions about the extent of the texts transcribed.

His preface and introduction asserted that the revised edition of the first section of the Mahabharata was undertaken to expose readers to the Konkani language, 'unadulterated' by Portuguese, Marathi or Latin usages (1988, XIII).[5] The significance of producing a text in 'true'

[5] According to Fr. Noronha's introduction to Rodrigues' text, between 1560 to 1670, various Jesuit priests had compiled vocabularies of which at least six sets

Konkani, one that could be said to have had a regular grammar before it was submerged by interactions with other languages is evident in Rodrigues' analysis of the linguistic elements of Konkani grammar. This was especially with regard to solecisms that had evidently 'been appropriated by many educated Goans without reflecting that it amounts to a gross violation of a simple grammatical rule… the infraction of which cannot be tolerated even to (sic) the illiterate people' (1988, XVIII). The Devanagari version of Rodrigues's text was edited by Pratap Naik and published in 1990 (Miranda 2011, 8). The belief that Konkani had a better defined grammar than Marathi prior to the sixteenth century, and the comparison between the writing of the educated and the speech of the illiterate, suggested to these translators the existence of either a mediating group of scribes or a written text, between those reciting the Mahabharata, and its eventual rendering in the Roman script (ibid., 9).

Though he was to alter his position on this later, in his own rendering of the codices in 1990, Pratap Naik (1990, 204) seems to assert that the scientifically appropriate script for a spoken language was Devanagari, and states that Rodrigues should have used the Devanagari, Modi or the Kannada script, while emphasising that Konkani had drawn usages from other written languages such as Kannada and Farsi-Arabic, as well as grammatical constructions from Marathi. The resistance to the Roman script in Naik's work seems to combine a desire for a script that was not associated with a colonial power and a belief that Devanagari offered the right convergence of sound and spelling, which would help regularise Konkani. According to this rationale, it was the attempt by the missionaries to render this spoken early Konkani in scripts not suited to it (Roman) that had produced errors noted by the scholars who had studied the texts, including Rodrigues.[6]

---

exist in Goa, 'each of them being an enlarged version of the previous one, which are intimately connected with the Konkani codices nos. 771 and 772, that are also Jesuit works. The written sources of these vocabularies are the said codices, so that to understand the meanings of the words contained in the stories of these codices the said vocabularies are not only very useful but often essential, as many vocables of these stories are not found in the existing Konkani, Marathi and Hindi dictionaries,' pp. XXI–XXII.

[6] Naik, *Solavya Shekdyatale Konkani Mahabharat*, x, xiii, xxx.

A BEGINNING FOR LITERARY HISTORY-RENDERING ROMAN KONKANI ALIEN

Olivinho Gomes's Ramayana (Gomes was among those who worked for the gradual copying and transportation of the originals), published in 1996 by the Goa University Press in Devanagari may be included among these attempts to place the recovered manuscripts at the beginning of a written history of Konkani.

Most critiques that privileged Devanagari foregrounded ways in which the Roman script was phonetically inadequate, resulting in orthographic errors. This consensus, which, if articulated differently may have been unproblematic, helped to relegate the popular print of the nineteenth century which was also in the Roman script to a low tradition that could not be owned within the regional literary canon. Konkani in Devanagari became an index of cultural distinction and transliterating texts was an intermediary process that allowed them entry into the bibliographies of Indian literature. The implicit cultural dispossession of those who wrote in Roman and the underlying privileging of particular dialects such as Antruzi were not as yet commented on in public discourse.

The following images are samples from the codices of which the District Archives of Braga, Portugal once had the only copy. From the time reproductions of these began to be available in Goa, they were inserted into its literary history and were reprinted. Each reprint indicates the shift in the significance attached to establishing the antiquity of Konkani and how best these texts should be recuperated for a contemporary audience. While other editions of the Mahabharata and Ramayana therefore assume a master text or folk versions that are universally available, the codices provided a beginning for the written literary life of the language. The status of the Mahabharata and Ramayana as classical epics is also significant as it implied that the literary history of Konkani could fit the mould of majoritarian nationalism.

Excerpt 3
Courtesy State Central Library, Panjim
Images from the codices containing the Konkani *Mahabharata* in Roman characters

---

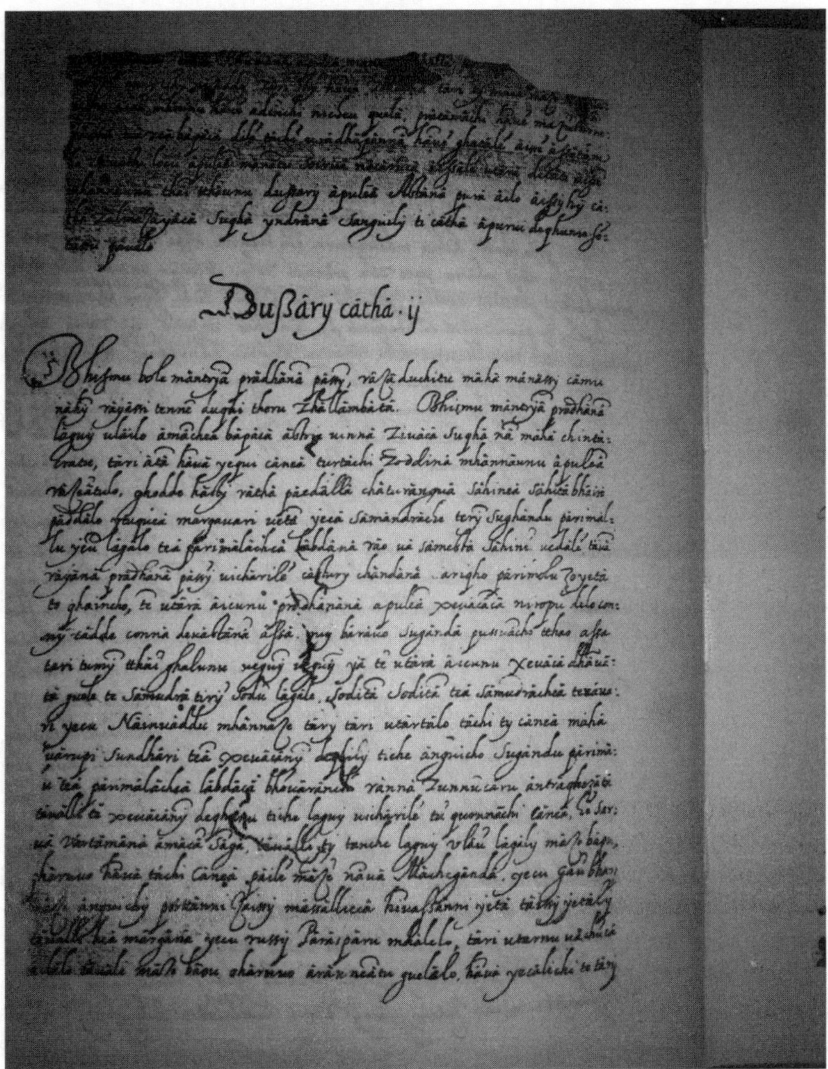

Dußâry câthâ · ij

Olivinho Gomes' *Konkani Manasagangotri* published in 2000 was a comprehensive account of pre-eighteenth century writing with excerpts from early texts rendered in Devanagari. It began with a philological history contesting the idea that Konkani had no written literature, and provided an account of writing that did not exclude script or genre. It ended with the dwindling of Konkani print at the end of the seventeenth century as a result of the numerous injunctions against the language (and against print) from both

Church and State. The popular literature in Konkani of the late nineteenth and early twentieth century therefore does not find a place in this account, or in other accounts that unify the histories of Konkani in Roman, Devanagari, Kannada and Malayalam scripts. In part, this may have been because a majority of texts were printed in Bombay and surviving copies are scattered among predominantly western libraries, especially, the British Library, London.

Gomes' account of the Konkani Ramayana, sections of which were transcribed in the codices 771 and 772, suggests how Ramayana stories were embedded, as was customary, in the geography of Goa (2000, 24). Gomes speaks for instance of the abduction of Ram (2000, 25) 'while a child, from his native Ayodhya and his arrival in Goa, where he meets with the *gaunkars* (village elders) of the villages of Majorda, Utorda, Chicolna etc.'

Rocky Miranda's *The Old Konkani Bharata*

Rocky V. Miranda's introductory volume to *The Old Konkani Bharata*, the most recent and painstaking scholarly edition of the Konkani codices, provides a linguistic rationale by which to date various usages of the language. He divides these three periods: the Middle Indo-Aryan period, a period prior to the Indo-Aryan, indicated by borrowings from Sanskrit, and the Old Konkani used in the *Bharata* (2011, 3).

This revised *Bharata* by Miranda provides a fresh account of the history of language use in and around the year 1600. Miranda suggests that the name 'Vishnudas Nama', which features in the Konkani *Bharata* is a homage-like reference, as was customary, to the author of a Marathi *Bharata* that was known at the time, and does not refer to the creator of the version recorded by the Portuguese (2011, 12–14). The Konkani *Bharata*, draws on the prior Marathi one, but also has several deviations from it, according to him. A more likely source or tradition for the codices, he says, are the number of Kannada innovations in the folk version of the *Bharata*, innovations which can be seen in the Konkani version as well. Miranda's deliberation over the choices of script and dialect when editing this text confirms that the focus of all new editions and translations tends to be the production of language itself.

Translating within the language

Most translations are a convergence of two elements: the findings of fresh historical research, the reception of which is sometimes (though not in the case of Miranda) overwhelmingly shaped by contemporary linguistic-political positions on the question of script.[7] The object is not to produce versions or aspects of the *Bharata*, but to see the text as a vehicle for the restoration of the Konkani language itself. Latinisms and Portuguese derivations and the script are gradually pared away as editions of these texts are brought closer to the standard of the present to restore them to a 'non-Christian' or non-Western tradition.

As stated earlier, this is not Miranda's own approach to the text. Miranda's decisions about the treatment of elements from Sanskrit and Marathi indicate his interest in recovering the historical relationship between the languages, rather than in rewriting the text as a singular movement towards a 'pure' Konkani. For instance he notes that the *Bharata* is written in Konkani prose interspersed with Marathi verse in *ovi* form or in Sanskrit verse, and indicates that this may have been a convention of the time, rather than suggesting that any of the languages be purged from the text (ibid., 28–31). He draws our attention to the nature of prayer in instances in the *Bharata* where appellants confess sins, and on occasion acknowledge that they are sinners and ask for forgiveness for selfishness and other trespasses. This relationship to God and to sin is closer to Christian doctrine, and cannot be traced in the Sanskrit or Marathi *Bharata*s. Likewise he points out that the ringing of temple bells in some passages to summon worshippers must have drawn from the customary use of Church bells to summon the faithful (ibid., 35–38). The entry of these Christianised ideas of divinity and of worship along with local usages, he suggests, distinguishes the Konkani *Bharata*. In an interesting development to this relocation of the sixteenth century *Bharata*, Miranda also mentions an anonymous text that could have been a revised version of Diogo Ribeiro's *Vocabulario da Lingoa Canarim* (a Konkani-Portuguese and Portuguese-Konkani vocabulary) of 1626 in which quotations from the *Bharata* can be traced (ibid., 18).[8]

---

[7] Miranda's (2011, xii) explicit decisions in favour of 'the dialect of the Gowda Saraswat Brahmans of South Kanara district' and 'Goan Standard Konkani' or Devanagari seem to be an extension of dominant stances on language rather than an explicit rejection of alternatives. His choices seem to have been made in anticipation of a likely readership in those scripts and registers for this text.

[8] There is no certainty however, over the date of this copy of the *Vocabulario*, which implies that while early missionary texts did draw from the *Bharata* as a source, this particular copy of the *Vocabulário* may be preceded by one without references to the *Bharata*.

Rocky Miranda's PhD thesis on the Synchronic and Historical Phonology of Six Konkani Dialects was completed in 1971. He also authored 'The Assimilation of Dravidian loans to Konkani morphological and phonological Patterns', for the Indo-Iranian Journal *in 1977, and 'Caste, Religion and Dialect Differentiation in the Konkani area' in the* International Journal of the Sociology of Language *in 1978, among various other publications in the field of linguistics.*

The Old Konkani Bharata, *published in 2011 by the Central Institute for Indian Languages, Mysore, is the most meticulous consideration to date of the transliterated codices from the sixteenth century, containing the Konkani Ramayana and Mahabharata. This edition is a translation into the South Kanara Saraswat Konkani in the Kannada script, and a Devanagari edition has been published by Asmitai Pratishthan in Goa. It provides a comparative examination of the possible influences on the orally recounted Mahabharata.*

In the 'Preface', Miranda traces his attempts to find versions of the Mahabharata that were influences on the Konkani version. He argues that Kannada folk versions may have been a source for the Konkani transliteration. He also suggests that Jaimini's Asvamedha may have been a source for the Konkani Asvamedhaparva, and that Visnudas Nama's Marathi Bharata and the Kannada Janapada Mahabharata were likely sources.

Excerpt 4
Courtesy Central Institute of Indian Languages, Mysore
Rocky V. Miranda, ed., *The Old Konkani Bharata*, (Mysore: Central Institute of Indian Languages, 2011), pp. ix–xiii, 1–6, 7–17, 18, 28–34, 35–40.

Excerpted from the Preface

...

At the end of several stories in the Konkani Bhārata there is the name of Viṣṇudās Nāmā (Uisttnnudâssu Nâmâ) who is said to have told these stories to the listeners. This gave the impression that the author of the Konkani Bhārata was this Viṣṇudās Nāmā. However, while I was reading a history of Marathi literature (Deshpande 1969) I learned that Viṣṇudās Nāmā was a well-known Marathi poet and that he had written a Bhārata in Marathi. It was, therefore, reasonable to suspect that the Konkani Bhārata was based on this Marathi Bhārata...Later, I came across an earlier article of Professor Pissurlenkar on the same subject (Pissurlenkar 1956). From these articles, I learned that Professor Pissurlenkar had examined the Konkani Bhārata in Braga in 1954. He claimed in his articles that the Konkani Bhārata was just a translation of Viṣṇudās Nāmā's Marathi Bhārata. However, even … a cursory examination of the available parvas of Viṣṇudās Nāmā's Marathi Bhārata makes this claim untenable. Although the Konkani Bhārata is based on Viṣṇudās Nāmā's Marathi Bhārata, there are major deviations from Viṣṇudās Nāmā's Bhārata in this work…

I came across two parvas of Viṣṇudās Nāmā's Marathi Bhārata (Virātāparva and Karṇaparva) in Braga codex 773 which includes several Marathi works in verse. Then I came across Professor M. R. Joshi's editions of Viṣṇudās Nāmā's Nalopakhyana (Joshi 1970–71) in which he gave details regarding the location of Viṣṇudās Nāmā's Marathi Bhārata parvas. From this information, I was able to locate two versions of the Ādiparva of Vishnudas Nāmā's Marathi Bhārata at Marathi Samshodhan Mandal, Mumbai. However, I was not successful in locating any of the other parvas in Goa, Mumbai, and Pune in the libraries mentioned by Dr. Joshi…I was particularly interested in those parvas of Vishnudas Nāmā's Marathi Bhārata that corresponded to the parvas found in the Konkani Bhārata. Therefore, I copied from Dr. Joshi's collection of manuscripts of Viṣṇudās Nāmā's Sabhāparva, Udyogaparva, Bhīṣmaparva, Droṇ aparva, Gadāparva, and Suśuptiparva.

The Konkani Bhārata has a few Sanskrit verses which are in very corrupt Sanskrit. In these verses, the language is ungrammatical and the lines are not in accordance with the rules of metre. I needed help in reconstructing their correct forms… I was able to find five of the fourteen Sanskrit verses in the subhāṣitasangrahas. I still needed help with the other nine verses. Dr. Jagannath was kind enough to reconstruct for me these verses according to correct Sanskrit grammar and metrical rules…

In order to compare the Konkani Bhārata with the Sanskrit Mahābhārata, … I used the Mahābhārata edition of the Gita Press Gorakhpur, which has a Hindi translation.

…

I wanted to convert these references to those of the Bhandarkar Oriental Research Institute (BORI) edition of the Mahābhārata.…

I was intrigued by the fact that the Aśvamedhaparva of the Konkani Bhārata bore hardly any resemblance to the Āśvamedhikaparva of the Sanskrit Mahābhārata. Then I learned about Jaimini's work called Aśvamedha from the preface to the Asvamedhika-parva in the BORI edition. The editor of the Āśvamedhikaparva has given a complete summary of Jaimini's version in his preface. From this, it became clear that the Aśvamedhaparva of the Konkani Bhārata was based on Jaimini. My thanks are due to my wife, Pushpa

Bobde, who suggested that I examine the Marathi works found in a maṭh in her village, Gowdagere, and see if there were any that were relevant to my research. I soon learned that the ... people in the village were planning to cast all these old Marathi works into the Gowdagere lake since no one was around there now who could read these works as they were in the Nagari script. I hastened to the village before these precious works were consigned to a watery grave. On examining these works, I found that they were mostly Old Marathi works in verse (ovi metre) printed in the nineteenth century which included the Mahābhārata stories such as Pāṇḍavapratāpa and Kathākalpataru (see, respectively, Śrīdhara 1868 and Krṣṇayājñavalki, no date). Among the works at the math, there was even a printed version of one parva of Viṣṇudās Nāmā's Marathi Bhārata: Svargārohaṇaparva. The Konkani Bhārata, however, does not have any parvas from the Mahābhārata after the Gadāparva except for Aśvamedhaparva. Jaimini's Aśvamedha appears to have had a very influential position in the Marathi area. In Marathi works like Pāṇḍavapratāpa and Kathākalpataru which include the Mahābhārata story, although the general account is based on the standard Sanskrit Mahābhārata, the Aśvamedhaparva stories are based not on the standard work but on Jaimini's Aśvamedha. I found among the works at the math also a Marathi version of Jaimini's Aśvamedha (Śrīdhara 1894).

...

(A)n article by C.N. Ramachandran ... made me aware that among the innovations in various versions of the Mahābhārata in Gujarat and Karṇataka some were common to the Konkani Bhārata.... I was looking for a Kannada Janapada Mahābhārata edited by P.K. Rajaśekhara in 2004 which was mentioned by C.N. Ramachandran.... A number of innovations in this Kannada folk version of the Mahābhārata were in the Konkani Bhārata as well...

... I had decided to use the Karṇataka Saraswat dialect of Konkani in the Karṇataka edition since I could expect the maximum number of readers for this work from among the speakers of this dialect.... I went to Manipal to see Mr. Shantaram Baliga, editor of the Konkani monthly Panchkadayi which is published in this dialect.... I was delighted when Mr. Baliga kindly agreed to do the translation himself.... I should also thank him for going over the portions of the text which I translated into Karṇataka Saraswat Konkani and for making corrections there. The Karṇataka Saraswat dialect has a number of regional and social variants. The dialect used here is that of the Gowda Saraswat Brahmans of South Kanara district...

...When I got interested in editing the Konkani Bhārata, I was in the process of editing another Old Konkani work, Diogo Ribeiro's Konkani Vocabulario compiled in 1626 – just the Konkani-Portuguese part of this Dictionary. When I examined the Konkani Bhārata, I felt that it would make more sense for me to first work on the Konkani Bhārata and then go back to the dictionary project since the dictionary has lots of vocabulary from the Konkani Bhārata and even entire quotations in some of its versions. These can offer a deeper insight into the Old Konkani vocabulary and aid my editing of Diogo Ribeiro's Vocabulario.

In the first chapter, Miranda continues to explore various theories that have a bearing on the historiography of the Bharata. *He suggests that an older version of the Kannada script may have been in use at the time the Portuguese first encountered Konkani. He also indicates that the prevailing custom at the time may have been to write prose in Konkani and verse in Marathi, and not, as later linguists assumed, that Konkani was the spoken vernacular to Marathi's written script.*

Miranda's argument addresses many facets of what is customarily assumed to be a single source and a single author for the Konkani text. Based on contemporary and historical linguistic analysis across Konkani-speaking communities who migrated at different points in time, Miranda draws conclusions about the kind of Konkani the missionaries encountered and the changes brought about through transliteration.

---

p. 1–6

I. The Old Konkani Bhārata

...

1. Old Konkani Writings

Adequate documentation is available for Old Konkani only from around 1600. The only works composed by native speakers of Konkani are found in manuscripts preserved at the University of Minho Library in Braga, Portugal. ...These appear to have been narrated by native speakers of Konkani but transcribed in Roman script by the Portuguese missionaries....

However, the missionaries have mentioned that Konkani had its own native script at that time which they did not use. The author of an anonymous Portuguese-Konkani dictionary (Anon. 3) found in Biblioteca Nacional, Lisbon, has given some specimens of this native script at the end of his dictionary. It is clear that this script is an older version of the Kannada script. In his well-known work Janua Indica (Archamone, no date), Ignazio Archamone has made a systematic comparison of the two scripts used by Konkani and Marathi. These happen to be Kannada (an older version) and Nagari respectively.

There is only one extant Konkani work that was composed in the Kannada script. It is Amador de Santana's Flos Sanctorum, a manuscript of which is found at Bibliothèque Nationale, Paris (See Santana, no date).

...

2. Orthography

As mentioned earlier, among the extant Konkani works, all except one (Santana, no date) has been written in the Roman script. The missionaries used Portuguese orthographic conventions to a large extent. Thus, for instance, *s* is represented by *ss* intervocalically and *s* is represented by *x*.

...

In preparing a systematic Roman transcription for Konkani, the missionaries made some interesting innovations. They had to devise letters to represent Old Konkani sounds not found in Portuguese.

...

Double letters are written to indicate not gemination but retroflection. Thus, *tt, tth, dd, ddh, nn,* and *ll* are used to represent [ṭ], [ṭh], [ḍ], [ḍh], [ṇ], and [ḷ] respectively. If the missionaries used double consonant letters to indicate retroflection, how did they represent geminates? They had no representation for geminates and there is reason to conclude that they needed to represent them as there weren't any geminates in Konkani at the time it came to be written in Roman transcription. The geminates in Konkani from various sources must have undergone degemination in Goa by 1600. These geminates would have been present when the Portuguese conquered Goa since the Southern Konkani Saraswats (that is, those Saraswats who moved out of Goa soon after the Portuguese arrived and settled in coastal Karnataka and Kerala) have still preserved these geminates in certain environments. These Saraswats left Goa because of religious persecution and they would have left long before 1600. Bardes Christians who left Goa around 1700 or after and settled in Karṇataka have not preserved the old geminates.

...

Modern Konkani dialects like the Goan Standard dialect and the Karṇataka Christian dialect have geminates in many such native words which have resulted from later gemination as well as from recent Sanskrit borrowings.

The missionaries in Goa must be given credit for evolving a remarkably systematic Roman transcription for the Konkani language over 150 years before Sir William Jones and other Sanskritists evolved a systematic Roman transcription for Sanskrit and other Indian languages. It should be noted that the eighteenth century Sanskritists had a good model in devising a systematic Roman transcription. This model was the Nagari script and other Indian scripts which were used in writing Sanskrit in a very systematic fashion. The English writers who had no access to such a model wrote Hindi and other Indian languages in the Roman script in a chaotic manner even in the late eighteenth century. See, for example, the transcription of Hindustani words by Hadley (1772)...

Unlike the eighteenth-century Sanskritists, the Goa missionaries had no good model before them in devising their Roman transcription around 1600. As far as we know, they did not study Sanskrit documents in Nagari or other scripts. The native Konkani scholars that would have narrated to them Rāmayāna and Mahābhārata had a good background in Marathi. However, looking at the Sanskrit aphorisms they introduced in their narration of the Mahābhārata, it appears that their knowledge of Sanskrit was quite deficient.... We do not know how far the ... missionaries were familiar with the Marathi writings in the Nagari script. In any case, the irregularities in the Marathi or Konkani spellings of the time did not affect the missionary Roman transcription. They went by what they heard: they noticed no contrast between short and long *i* and *u* non-finally and therefore they did not make that distinction there. However, they noticed that the Konkani speakers made a distinction between short and long *i* and *u* in the word-final position.... So they tried to represent that in their transcription. Also, they noticed no distinction between *kh, ks,*and ṣ. All three letters representing the etymological *kh, kṣ* and ṣ were pronounced [kh]. So, they uniformly wrote *kh* in this case. However, the irregularity in representing the unaspirated and aspirated consonants is found in the missionary transcription just as much as in the native writings.

Miranda (pp. 6–10) compares twentieth-century editions of the codices, many of which were prepared without access to the originals, and reproduced errors in number and order that been introduced when the first copies were made. He provides a detailed account of the disordering of the leaves of the codices when they were stamped with modern numerals.

---

3. Manuscripts

There are two Old Konkani manuscripts in Roman script in Braga, Portugal, at the University of Minho Library (formerly Braga District Library): Codex 771 (C. 771) and Codex 772 (C. 772). C. 772 has the Mahābhārata (767 pages), an incomplete version of a story from the

Rāmayāna (59 pages), and a couple of minor stories. In the case of the Mahābhārata, the title of the entire work does not appear at the beginning but it is referred to as Bhārata in several places. The titles of the individual parvas are given. It has ten parvas:

Ādiparva, Sabhāparva, Araṇyaparva, Virāṭaparva, Bhīṣmaparva, Droṇaparva, Karṇaparva, Salyaparva, Gadāparva, and Aśvamedhaparva. In addition, there is a second copy of Bhīṣmaparva in it which is incomplete. The major item in C. 771 is Rāmayāna (268 pages). But it has also got some parts of the Bhārata such as Ādiparva (162 pages) and an incomplete version of one story from the Aśvamedhaparva called Hamsadhvaja's story (a little over 15 pages), and some minor stories. In addition, there is a third manuscript at the University of Minho library, codex 773 (C. 773. See Śyāmā, no date), which contains several Marathi works in verse. The Marathi material in this codex is also in the Roman script.

Each parva of the Konkani Bhārata has two or more stories (kathās) which are more like chapters than stories: Ādiparva has eighteen stories, Bhīṣmaparva and Aśvamedhaparva have ten stories each, Sabhāparva and Araṇyaparva have seven stories each, Virāṭaparva and Droṇaparva have five stories each, Gadāparva has three stories, Karṇaparva and Sályaparva have two stories each. Altogether, the Konkani Bhārata has sixty-nine stories....

Because so many pages are out of order in this material, one gets the impression that many stories of the Konkani Bhārata are incomplete. However, when the pages are arranged in the right order we can recover all stories in all parvas in complete form at least in one copy...although short gaps are found in some parts which appear to be due to the scribe missing parts of the material as he copied it from elsewhere... There are also numbering errors in the original manuscripts. I have examined in this connection only those portions of the codices which contain the Konkani Bhārata stories.

...

4. Previous Work

Rodrigues (1987) and Nayak (1990) edited the Ādiparva from C. 771 and C. 772.

...

Since they had access only to copies made from the copies of the codices at Xavier Centre, the codex numbers are interchanged in their references as well. Soon after Fr. Antonio Pereira brought copies of the Braga codices to Xavier Center of Historical Research, Rodrigues had a copy of these made for himself. He was able to decipher the Ādiparva portion of the Bhārata in C. 771 and C. 772. He prepared one version of the Ādiparva in the Roman script and another in Nagari script.... However, instead of preserving the Old Konkani spellings, Rodrigues has modernized the spellings in his Roman version. Thus, for example, the very first sentence of the Ādiparva *Astânapura nânua nagara* appears there as *Astnapur nanv nogor*.... Rodrigues informed me that the person that gave financial support for the publication of this work in Roman script wanted him to publish the work in modern Konkani spellings.

Rodrigues gave the Nagari version to Fr. Pratap Nayak of Thomas Stephens Konknni Kendr who published it with certain modifications in 1990. Rodrigues was displeased with some of the modifications made by Nayak in the Nagari spellings adopted by him. Original *râze* 'kingdom' and yogue 'suitable', for example, were transcribed as राज्य and योग्य by Rodrigues but Nayak changed them to राजे and योगे. Rodrigues objected to this because he felt that writing राजे and योगे would make these words have the same final vowel as words like भले 'good' M PL DIR and माते 'mother' F SG OBL. In fact, neither राजे and योगे nor राज्य and योग्य are the correct representations of the words in question. A satisfactory solution to this problem is available in the codices themselves. In careful writing, the scribes write not *râze* and *yogue* but *râzĕ* and *yoguĕ*. They use *e* with the short vowel mark above *(ĕ)* in order to distinguish it from the *e* as in *bhale* and *mâte*. In Old Konkani (as well as in Old Marathi), after a palatal consonant, the vowel *a* changed into *e* in the non-final position but into ĕ in the final position. Thus, for example, the name of the god Yama is written as *Yemu*. In this process, the preceding *y* appears to get deleted after another consonant other than *r*. Thus, Sanskrit *kārya* is written as *câryĕ* or *câriyĕ* but *rājya* and *yogya* are written as *râzĕ* and *yoguĕ*. Occasionally, the scribes write *râzia* and *satia* as well in accordance with Sanskrit spellings. (Note that *i* represented *i* as well as *y* at that time). Even in modern languages like Konkani and Hindi, words written as *rājya* and *yogya* are pronounced as [rājjĕ] and [yōggĕ] or [rājjI] and [yōggI]. In other words, such words end in a geminate consonant followed by a short *e* or *i* in actual pronunciation. So, there is good reason to believe that the spellings used in the codices like *râze* and *yoguĕ* were phonetic spellings and accurate. Nayak was aware that the scribes wrote *râzĕ* and *yoguĕ* with e in final position, at least in careful writing. However, he says that he did not indicate the short vowel as there is no mark for short e (ĕ) in the Nagari script (Nayak 1990: xiii). It is worth noting that in the Marathi Ādiparva of Viṣṇudās Nāmā's Bhārata, *rājya* and *kārya* are written as राज्ये and कार्ये.

Rodrigues (1987) has presented two important hypotheses about the Konkani Bhārata in his introduction. One hypothesis is that of the two versions of the Ādiparva (C. 771 version and C 772 version), the one in C. 771 is a rough copy whereas the one available In C. 772 is a fair copy. The other hypothesis is that someone orally narrated the stories and someone else (the priests) took them down. Nayak (1990) has accepted these although he does not agree with some of Rodrigues's other claims.

...

If one examines the two versions of the Ādiparva, the Ādiparva version in C. 771 clearly has the look of a rough copy since someone has struck off many items there and made many alterations. However, I think it was intended to be a fair copy by the original scribes. It is clear from the handwriting that someone other than the original scribes made most of the alterations in it and gave it the look of a rough copy. The Ādiparva of C. 771 was originally prepared by two scribes of which the first one makes very few spelling mistakes. There are more mistakes in the pages prepared by the second scribe. Both the scribes have made other types of mistakes some of which have been corrected by the person who made the alterations. He has not attempted to correct spelling mistakes. In fact, he is himself quite poor at Konkani spellings. Although a few of the alterations are indeed corrections of errors, many are not. Some of the alterations are Konkani replacements for Marathi items. I counted the number of alterations in the first three stories. There are about sixty alterations here. Only about eight of these are corrections of outright grammatical or lexical errors. Many alterations involve rewording or elimination of redundant elements. About a dozen are replacements of Marathi elements by Konkani equivalents. For example, the Marathi forms *hounu* 'becoming', *zâta* 'while going', *zaunu* 'going', *manuxeâssi* 'to man', and *râzeâssi* 'to the kingdom' are replaced by *zâunv, uetâ', uachunu, manuxeâca,* and *râzeâca* respectively. ...

The Ādiparva of C. 772 is obviously a copy of the altered version of the Ādiparva from C. 771. Almost all the alterations made in the 771 version have been incorporated in the 772 version. It looks quite neat since no one has made any alterations there. Although the Ādiparva in C. 772 was meant to be a fair copy of the version in C. 771, it was prepared by an incompetent scribe whose spellings, especially in the beginning stories, are chaotic. The most common spelling error is the interchange of *a* and *â*. Consider, for example, the following three sentences from C. 772:

C. 772, p. 1r (1): *Ho putru mâcâ tu' bhiquecâ̲ dy. A̲mâ'chea̲ râzĕâcâ̲ râoza̲ita. Tâ̲'ua tinne' râya̲che hâty' ta̲ca̲ bhiquecâ̲ dilo mhonnu Bhismu na'uâ̲ ttheile'.*

[="Give me this son as alms. He could be the king for our kingdom."
Then, as she gave him into the king's hands as alms, he was given the name Bhīṣma.]

These three sentences in C. 772 contain 14 errors involving the interchange of *a* and *â*. The incorrect letters are underlined. There are many such errors involving the interchange of a and *â* elsewhere in C. 772. Now examine the same two sentences In C. 771:

C. 771, p. 147r (285): *"Ho putru mâcâ tu' bhiqueca dy. ^Ama'cheâ râzeâca râo zâita."*
Ta'ua tinne' râyâche hâty' tâcâ bhiqueca dilo mhonnu Bhismu nâ'ua ttheile'.

The sentences from C. 771 are free from the interchange of *a* and *â* errors. For this reason, in preparing the present edition, the Ādiparva text of C. 771 has been used instead of the version from C. 772.

In the following sections (pp. 10–17), through a discussion of excerpts and variations in the Mahabharata stories, Miranda establishes that the Marathi Bharata was a source for the Konkani one, and contained variations that are seen in the regions of Gujarat and Karnataka as well.

---

5. The Authors and Storytellers

In the standard Sanskrit Mahābhārata, which is said to be the work of Krṣṇadvaipāyana Vyāsa, Vyāsa's pupil Vaiśampāyana relates the story of Mahābhārata to Arjuna's great-grandson Janamejaya. The storyteller is Vaiśampāyana in six parvas of the Konkani Bhārata.... However, in the Ādiparva of the Konkani Bhārata the storyteller is said to be Súkendra (called Sukha Indra), Vyāsa's son and pupil. In the Aśvamedhaparva, the storyteller's name is not given. However the Aśvamedhaparva in the Konkani Bhārata is not from Vyāsa's Mahābhārata. In the Marathi-Konkani area, in stories from the Mahābhārata, the Aśvamedhaparva is usually not from Vyāsa, but from Jaimini. In C. 773 (Xeâmâ, no date), we come across a work called Dharmâchâ Asvamedhu: Tâmbradhuazâchy cathâ (Nâmâ, Pâtthacu, no date (a)), which is clearly based on Jaimini's work. Pāṭhaku Nāmā's Aśvamedhaparva or parts of it are also available at Bharat Itihas Samshodhak Mandai (Nāmā, Pāṭ haku, no date (b)). In later Marathi works like Pāndavapratāpa, (Srīdhara 1712) although the other parts of the Mahābhārata account are based on Vyāsa, the Aśvamedhaparva is based on Jaimini. This is also true of the Marathi work Kathākalpataru (Krṣṇayājñavalki, no date) which contains stories from Mahābhārata in addition to other stories.

Jaimini is said to have composed his own Mahābhārata but only the Aśvamedha in that work is now available. It has very little in common with Vyāsa's Aśvamedhaparva. He is said to have been Vyāsa's pupil. However, Jaimini's Aśvamedha is suspected to be a much later work in which case its author could not have a disciple of the author of the standard Mahābhārata in Sanskrit. In Jaimini's Aśvamedha, Jaimini himself relates the story to King Janamejaya. Although the Aśvamedhaparva in the Konkani Bhārata is based on Jaimini, Jaimini's name does not appear in it.

In Droṇaparva, the name of the person relating the story to Janamejaya is given as Chângu Niurutidâssu, or Niurutidâssu. We are told at the end of all five stories of Droṇaparva ... that Niurutidâssu tells the story to Janamejaya. In Karṇaparva, the storyteller's name is given as Chângu who is said to relate the story to the Kṣatriya king, presumably Janamejaya. It is not clear who this Chângu or Chângu Niurutidâssu is.

At the end of two of the ten parvas (Ādiparva and Araṇyaparva), we are told that the account is based on Skandapurana.

6. The Immediate Source: Viṣṇudāsdās Nāmā's Marathi Bhārata and Other Accounts

In many of the stories of the Konkani Bhāratas, after giving the name of the storyteller who tells the Mahābhārata story to King Janamejaya, the name of the person who tells the same story or presents its ṭīkā (= interpretation) to other people is given as Nāmā (written Nâmâ). For example,

Sabhāparva, at the end of story 3: *Hechi cathechy tticâ Uisttnnudâssu Nâmâ samestâ sruteâ'ca sângata.*

[=Viṣṇudāsdās Nāmā tells the ṭīkā of this same story to all listeners.]

Virāṭaparva, at the end of story 5: *Hichi cathâ mrutaloquy' Prâ'cho xerannâgatu Nâmâ sângata.*

[= Nāmā who has taken refuge in God tells this same story in the world of mortals.]

Usually, his name is given as *Visttnnudâssu* Nâmâ. Several times, he is referred to as *Prâ'cho (Paramesporâcho) Xerannagâtu* Nâmâ (Nāmā, who has taken refuge in God). Once, he is called *Nâmadevu.* Among the sixty-nine stories, Nāmā's name is found at the end of twenty-two stories: Virāṭaparva, story 5, Bhīṣmaparva, stories 1–8 & 10, Gadāparva 1–2, Aśvamedhaparva 1–10.

Who does Nāmā tell his stories to? In several stories we are told that he is telling his story to Kṣatriya kings or to listeners who are Kṣatriya kings. In a few cases, we are told that he is telling the story to all.

Considering that Nāmā's name appears at the end of so many stories, one might assume that this work was composed by someone called Nāmā in Konkani. That is what I had imagined as well. However, one day, while reading a work on the history of Old Marathi literature, I came across a section in it on Nāmadeva and Viṣṇudās Nāmā (Deshpande 1969: 100–102) which naturally aroused my curiosity. Nāmadeva is a famous Marathi poet. Sometimes, he calls himself Viṣṇudās Nāmā because he considers himself a devotee of Viṣṇu. However, Deshpande points out that there are several poets in Marathi literature that have called themselves *Viṣṇudās* and more than one among them has called himself Viṣṇudās Nāmā. One of these Viṣṇudās Nāmās is known to have written a Mahābhārata which is also called Bhārata. There are also several poets who call themselves *Nāmā*. For example, C. 773 (Xeâmâ, no date) has works by three different Nāmās: Viṣṇudās Nāmā, Pāṭhaku Nāmā and Simpā Nāmā. In the case of some works, the author's name is given simply as Nāmā, but it is difficult to determine which of the Nāmās wrote them.

I came across two of Viṣṇudās Nāmā's Marathi Bhārataparvas (Virāṭaparva and Karṇaparva) In C. 773 from Braga (Xeâmâ, no date). In addition to these two Bhārataparvas, there are also other works by this Viṣṇudās Nāmā in the same codex such as Prelâda charitra (Prahlāda caritra), Harichandra purânna cathâ (Hariścandra purāna kathā) and Suqhadeua … charitra cathâ (Sukhadeva caritra kathā). Later, I came across another work of Viṣṇudās Nāmā, Nalopākhyāna (Joshi 1971–72). In its introduction, the editor has given information on where the manuscripts of Viṣṇudās Nāmā's Marathi Bhārataparvas are found. One of the places mentioned there is Marathi Samshodhan Mandal, Mumbai, where two manuscripts of the Ādiparva of Viṣṇudās Nāmā's Marathi Bhārata are found.

Even on examining the two parvas of Viṣṇudās Nāmā's Marathi Bhārata from the Braga Codex 773 (Virāṭaparva and Karṇaparva), it was clear that the Konkani Bhārata was based on Viṣṇudās Nāmā's Marathi Bhārata. From the other parvas that became available later, it is further confirmed that the Konkani Bhārata is based on Viṣṇudās Nāmā's Marathi Bhārata. The authors of the Konkani Bhārata have not mentioned their own names. They have mentioned only the name of the Marathi poet Viṣṇudās Nāmā at the end of so many stories. This is their public acknowledgement that their work is based on Viṣṇudās Nāmā's work.

I was earlier under the impression that nobody in Goa was aware that the Viṣṇudās Nāmā mentioned in the Konkani Bhārata was a Marathi poet and that the Konkani work was based on his Marathi work. Rodrigues and Nayak appeared not to be aware of this fact.

Then, I came across articles of Pissurlenkar who had examined the Braga manuscripts as early as 1954 (see Pissurlenkar 1956, 1969). These make it clear that he already knew that the Konkani Bhārata was based on Viṣṇudās Nāmā's Marathi Bhārata. Pissurlenkar has claimed that the Konkani work found in the Braga codices is just a translation of the work of the Marathi poet Viṣṇudās Nāmā. Even after a cursory examination of the Konkani Bhārata and the parvas of Viṣṇudās Nāmā's Marathi Bhārata that have become available, it can be concluded that the Konkani Bhārata is not a mere translation of the Marathi work. There are numerous deviations in the Konkani Bhārata from Viṣṇudās Nāmā's Marathi Bhārata.

...

6. In VNBh, It is Droṇa that breaks Abhimanyu's bow and eventually kills him with Brahmaśakti (VNBh Droṇa 3.90, 99–100). In the KBh, it is Karṇa who cuts off the string of Abhimanyu's bow from behind. Then he cuts off his right arm and Duryodhana cuts off his left arm. Others shoot arrows at Abhimanyu's chest and kill him. (KBhDroṇa p. 346r (67)).
7. In the KBh, Droṇa decides to meditate on Síva on his final night and offer Duryodhana a boon from Síva so that he can be impervious to any attack by the Pāṇḍavas. He tells Duryodhana to come to him after midnight to receive his blessing (KBhDroṇa p. 363v, (714)). When Kṛṣṇa hears about this, he stealthily takes Arjuna to Droṇa and makes him fall at Droṇa's feet just at the time Duryodhana is expected to come for his blessing. Droṇa's eyes are shut. He assumes that it is Duryodhana and blesses Arjuna, "May you be victorious over your enemies. No weapon or arrow will touch you. No one will be able to kill you." (KBhDroṇa p. 364r-365v (715–18)). This episode is not found in VNBh.
8. In VNBh, when Droṇa hears that his son has been killed, his spirit leaves his body and goes to Yamapurī in order to find out whether his son has reached there. Yama tells Droṇa that his son is a ciranjīvī and, therefore, no one could have killed him (VNBh Droṇa 7.106). Then Droṇa's spirit returns to the battlefield. In the KBh, Droṇa's spirit goes to the seashore where his son was performing penance. When he finds him safe there, he returns to the battlefield (KBhDroṇa p. 373v (734)).

...

Interestingly, one of the deviations found in the Konkani Bhārata is also found in another work. The story of Droṇa's spirit entering the body of a dead buffalo after Droṇa's body is destroyed is not in Viṣṇudās Nāmā's Marathi Bhārata, but it is found in another Marathi work included in Braga Codex 773: Gneânadeu (No date).

Where did the innovations in Viṣṇudās Nāmā's Marathi Bhārata, Gneânadeu's work, and also other innovations in the Konkani Bhārata come from? These authors are likely to have gathered most of them from the oral or written accounts current in the region. Some of these innovations are found not only in the Konkani-Marathi area but in a larger area that includes Gujarat in the north and Karṇataka in the south. Ramachandran 2009 has discussed several folk versions of the Mahābhārata including the Bhil Bhārata of northern Gujarat and two folk versions of the Mahābhārata from Karṇataka. These contain several innovations found in the Konkani Bhārata and Viṣṇudās Nāmā's Marathi Bhārata:

1. In all three folk versions, one or both sons of Satyavati suspect an illicit relationship between their mother and Bhīṣma or Vyāsa. When they realize that their suspicions are groundless, they are full of remorse and commit self-immolation (Ramachandran 2009: 334, 340). A version of this incident is found even in Kumaravyāsa's Mahābhārata in Kannada (Ramachandran 2009: 348). This episode is found both in the KBh and in vNBh. In the KBh, only Satyavatī's first son by Śāntanu, Citrāngadā, suspects such a relationship between her and a strange man that visits her at night. He later discovers that the strange man is Vyāsa, Satyavatī's son by the rsi Parāśara (KBh Ādi (C. 771) p. 149rv (289–90)). In VNBh, both sons of Satyavatī suspect such a relationship between Satyavatī and Bhīṣma (VNBh Ādi (2) 15.72–74). There is no such episode in the Sanskrit Mahābhārata.
2. In all three folk versions, Kṛṣṇa has animosity towards his nephew Abhimanyu and wishes to destroy him. During the Kuruksetra war, he arranges things in such a way that Abhimanyu has to die (Ramachandran 2009: 334 339) Note the same incident in the KBh (KBh Droṇa p. 331 v (652), 336r (661)). In the Sanskrit Mahābārata Kṛṣṇa has no animosity towards his nephew and he does not plot to get him killed.

...

In the Kannada work Janapada Mahābhārata, when Dharma loses everything in the

game of dice and wins back everything (Ramachandran 2009: 334) Note that in both the KBh and VNBh, Draupadī wins and liberates her husbands. However Śakuni comes and stops her from continuing the game. (KBh Sabhā p. 97v-98r (192–93), VNBh Sabhā 7: 578). In the Sanskrit Mahābhārata, Draupadī has nothing to do with Duryodhana. She is able to liberate her husbands because of a boon given to her by Dhrtarāstra.

Among these folk versions mentioned by Ramachandran, I have had access only to Janapada Mahābārata (Rājaśekhara 2004). In this work I noticed other innovations whichclosely resemble those found both in the KBh and in VNBh or to those found in one of them.

...

3. According to the Sanskrit Mahābhārata, and also according to Viṣṇudās Nāmā's account, it is King Śāntanu that meets Sugandhā (Satyavatī) first and is smitten with her fragrance. For a king to fall in love with a boatman's daughter and to desire to marry her is understandable. But, in the Konkani Bhārata, it is Bhīṣma that meets Sugandhā and arranges her marriage with his father (c. 771, p. 147v- 148v (286–288)). He does not first inform his father about it and obtain his approval. It appears highly inappropriate for a king's son to arrange his father's marriage in this fashion with a boatman's daughter however fragrant she may be.

4. Sugandhā starts relating her own story in the first person (C. 77, p. 148r (287)) but after a while there is an abrupt shift and the narrator continues the story. ...

5. The arrangement of Sugandhā's marriage with King Śāntanu is called (*gandharuiuhão (gandharvavivāha)* which does not make sense since King Śāntanu was not even present there (C. 771, p. 148v (288)) at that time. It is an arranged marriage in the Konkani Bhārata. It is possible that the narrator was thinking of Śāntanu's earlier marriage with Gangā which was a gandharvavivāha, at least according to Viṣṇudās Nāmā.

...

There are inconsistencies in the other stories as well. Some of these inconsistencies appear to be due to the fact that different parts of the Bhārata were narrated by different persons...

We are referring to these narrators of the Konkani Bhārata as the authors of the Konkani Bhārata. They must have narrated the stories of the Konkani Bhārata chiefly on the basis of Viṣṇudās Nāmā's Marathi Bhārata. Scholars who have examined the prose style and also the errors in the Konkani Bhārata have concluded that these stories must have been related orally by someone and taken down by some other person or persons in the Roman script (Rodrigues 1987: xvi. Nayak 1990: vii, Sardesai 2006: 73–91). The narrators had to be Konkani persons who had a knowledge of Marathi literature but the scribes that took down the narration must have been missionaries who had already acquired a good knowledge of Konkani vocabulary and who could take down Konkani material in Roman script in accordance with orthographic conventions which they had themselves already fixed. What they originally took down has certainly not come down to us in codices 771 and 772. What has come down to us in these codices appears to be fair copies prepared by various scribes of what was originally written down. The abrupt gaps found in several stories could have come only from omissions made by scribes while copying from some other written material... It is clear from the handwriting that several scribes were involved in the preparation of these codices.

The influence of the Christian religion is clearly discernible in certain passages of the Konkani Bhārata. The narrators and any other Konkani persons who were involved in the preparation of the work might have been Christian converts…

In the following section (pp. 17–18), Rocky Miranda discusses the ambiguity regarding the dating of the Bharata, *and whether the absence of Portuguese words suggests that the text hailed from a period prior to the arrival of the Portuguese. Against this he suggests that many Old Konkani texts do not contain a single Portuguese word and that their absence does not signify the antiquity of the texts which were recited and copied by scribes. The Konkani transliteration in turn may have been the source for subsequent texts produced by missionaries. Miranda notes that one version of a text reputed to be influenced by the* Bharata, *Diogo Ribeiro's seventeenth century Portuguese vocabulary carries quotations from the* Bharata *but has no date, while the 1626 version does not include any quotations.*

---

8. The Date of Viṣṇudās Nāmā and his Marathi Bhārata

There is much uncertainty regarding the date of Viṣṇudās Nāmā and that of his Marathi Bhārata. According to Deshpande (1969: 101) the Viṣṇudās Nāmā who wrote the Mahābhārata … lived in the fifteenth century and wrote his Mahābhārata around 1428 (Saka 1350). He is said to have written all eighteen parvas of the Mahābhārata. According to Joshi (1971–72);' Viṣṇudās Nāmā's period is 1338–1410 (Joshi 1971–72: 5, 7). In his opinion, Pāṭhak Nāmā, who wrote Aśvamedhaparva, wrote his work after he came to know of Viṣṇudās Nāmā's work on the Mahābhārata. Pāṭhak Nāmā is said to have lived in the first half of the fifteenth century (Joshi 1971–72: 5). However, others estimate that Viṣṇudās Nāmā lived in the second half of the sixteenth century (See Khanolkar 1977: 348–350). According to Joshi (1971–72: 6), Viṣṇudās Nāmā lived in Paṇḍharpur.

9. The Date of the Konkani Bhārata

The Konkani material in the Braga codices was probably prepared circa 1600. It could have been prepared only after the advent of the European missionaries who wanted to look at these works in the Roman script. The first missionaries who took a special interest in the study of Konkani and Marathi and later composed works in these languages were Thomas Stephens and Diogo Ribeiro. Stephens arrived in Goa in 1579 and Ribeiro in 1580. It is reasonable to assume that the Braga codices were prepared some years after these missionaries arrived in Goa.

Quotations from the Konkani Bhārata are found in a Konkani-Portuguese dictionary manuscript (Anon. (4). No date.) which appears to be a revised version of the original Konkani-Portuguese dictionary prepared by Diogo Ribeiro. Therefore, the Konkani Bhārata must have been prepared before this version of Ribeiro's dictionary. Unfortunately, the author's name and date of compilation are not given in this version of Ribeiro's dictionary. One version of Ribeiro's Konkani-Portuguese dictionary bears the author's name and the date: 1626. This one, however, has no quotations from the Konkani Bhārata.

Two Konkani Bhārata quotations found under the lexical entries *Agra* 'tip' and ^*Amanguelo* 'ours' from the anonymous revised version of Ribeiro's dictionary are given below. The compiler of the dictionary does not say where the quotations are from. He has made some minor modifications in the wording and spellings contained in these quotations.

Agra [= Tip.] *Hie suuecheâ agrâka zetuquy mâty lâgatâ tituky bhumi nede'*, [= 'I will not give as much earth as sticks to the tip of this needle'.] This is Duryodhana's statement to Krṣṇa regarding his decision not to give any part of the kingdom to the Pāṇḍavas. See C. 772, p. 276v (542): *He suuecheâ agrâca zetuquy mâty lâgatâ, tetuquy bhumi nedem.*

...

In the following section (pp. 26–33), Miranda discusses the appearance of Marathi and Sanskrit in the codices and what we may deduce about their usage at the time. He notes that the verses are either in Marathi or in Sanskrit, and that there are about fourteen Sanskrit verses that are not part of a central narrative.

---

12. Alteration in Names

The names in the Konkani Bhārata are altered in many cases. The Sanskrit versions of the names are given here in parentheses.... The alterations are not the result of scribal errors but must reflect the way these were actually pronounced. In general, the alterations here match those found in Viṣṇudās Nāmā's Marathi Bhārata.

Many of the alterations are in accordance with the phonological pattern of Old Konkani. It should be noted, however, that we are generally dealing here with the pronunciation of Sanskrit loans in

Old Konkani rather than the natural evolution of Sanskrit words in Old Konkani.

...

Some of the names have become unrecognizable because of various alterations: for instance, *Quissiâ (Keśī), Sancarassenu (Saṅkarsana), Sudâmâ (Sudhanvā) Sudfraxenâ (Sudeṣṇā, Suqhassenu (Suṣeṇa).*

Although such alterations in names match those in Viṣṇudās Nāmā's work and in other works of the same period, there are some minor differences. For example, Pradyumna's name is given as *Padminu* in the Konkani Bhārata and as *Pradminu* in the Marathi works...Some names found in the Konkani Bhārata are entirely different from their counterparts in Sanskrit works. Thus, King Śāntanu's second wife's name is given as *Sugandhā* and not as *Satyavatī.* Bakāsura's name is given as *Tonddiyo* (= Big Mouth). He is *Tondiyaā* in Viṣṇudās Nāmā's Marathi Bhārata...

...

13. Marathi Elements

According to the conventions of those times, whatever is found in the Konkani Bhārata in verse is not in Konkani. It is either in Marathi or Sanskrit. Among the sixty-nine stories of the Konkani Bhārata, forty-six begin with an ovi, a popular Marathi metrical form of four lines in which the second and the third lines or the first three lines usually rhyme with one another. The rhyming lines must end with the same consonant-vowel sequence. However, one of the rhyming lines may end in an oral vowel and another in a nasal vowel, or one may end in a short vowel and another in a long vowel. As long as the two vowels are otherwise of the same quality, the rhyming condition is satisfied. For example,

Bhismu bole mantriâ'-pradhânâ' pâssi' [=Bhīṣma says to the ministers]
râzâ duchitu mâhâ mânasi' [= The king is very depressed in his mind]
câmu nâhi' râyâssi [= The king has no desire]
tenne'duqhy zhallambatâ [= Thus he is very sad and suffering.]

...

Sometimes, the ovi is followed by its meaning in Konkani.

Even in the Konkani prose, Marathi elements do appear. A number of feminine nouns ending in – *y* [ī] take the Marathi plural ending – *â* [ā] instead of the Konkani plural ending –*o*. For example,

C. 771, p. 206r (391): *hâttauattiâ* 'a small market' pl.

...

In C.771 Ādiparva,many but not all Marathi elements used by the original scribes have been replaced with Konkani equivalents by another person at a later stage.

...

14. Sanskrit Elements

There are fourteen Sanskrit verses in the Konkani Bhārata. Although they are all referred to as 'sillocas' in the Konkani Bhārata, not all of them are ślokas. In fact, twelve of them are ślokas or anustubhs, one a śārdūlavikrīḍita, and one a sragdharā. Of these fourteen verses, two occur twice.

These Sanskrit verses are very corrupt, full of incorrect Sanskrit forms. The number and order of the syllables also are not in accordance with the metre. ...I came across the correct forms for five of the ślokas in subhāsitasangrahas.

...

For the most part, these Sanskrit verses are aphorisms uttered by some character or other to stress some point. They are not part of the narrative.

...

The only other Sanskrit material found in the Konkani Bhārata is something Dharma was supposed to say but since he would not say it, Kr̥ṣṇa says it for him. In the Droṇaparva, in an attempt to dishearten Droṇa and make him drop his weapons, Kr̥ṣṇa tells Dharma to declare that Aśvatthāmā has been killed. Kr̥ṣṇa knows that Droṇa is likely to take this statement seriously if Dharma makes it because Dharma always speaks the truth. When Kr̥ṣṇa asks Dharma to speak, Dharma says only *ka*. At that point, Kr̥ṣṇa cries aloud that Aśvatthāmā has been killed and blows his conch. What he says is given as follows in corrupt form, as elsewhere. The last word cannot be identified.

c. 772, p. 373v (734): *Asuastamâ [Aśvatthāmā] hâto [hato] asuauânaro*

...

15. Latin and Portuguese Glosses

There are marginal glosses in Latin in C. 772 in Ādiparva, Sabhāparva, and Araṇyaparva. Many of them are translations of some Konkani words, phrases or sentences in the body of the text. However, they are usually not precise translations. The Konkani phrases or sentences in the body of the text for which the glosses are provided are not explicitly indicated but it is usually easy to identify them. In some instances, these marginal glosses are just an explanation or interpretation of what is described in the body of the text...

...

C. 771 also has many Portuguese glosses. The Portuguese meaning is usually given above the Konkani words.

...

In the following section (pp. 35–40), Miranda cites instances where Christian concepts of God and practices of worship appear in the Bharata, suggesting to him that those reciting or transcribing may have been converts to Christianity who were familiar with the Mahabharata and Ramayana, or that the missionaries transcribing the texts introduced concepts and elements that seem to draw from a Christian framework.

Miranda's elucidation of each process involved in producing this written text; recitation, morphology, transliteration, transcription, prior sources, and prior religious concepts, does away with the idea of one original text or a singular cultural source. His research indicates that the process of reciting and writing is distributed across many persons, and many textual sources, leading us to think of this text as one that was received through the coming together of a range of historical factors, some accidental, and some more determined by the cultural practices of the time.

---

18. Christian Influence

When we examine the prayers that we come across in the Bhārata, we find that the person who prays usually acknowledges in his prayer that he is a sinner and asks God to forgive the sins he commits every day.

The Pāṇḍavas are described praying in this fashion before they eat:

C. 771, p. 218r (409): "^*Aga, he sateua'tâ Paramesparâ, âmy' dissâca ânny râtrica mellunu tuzeuari sahassru aparâdu caritâu'. To itucoi â'macâ' bhagassi.*"

Aissy prârthanâ carunu zeuannâca samasta pancaty baissale.

[= "O true lord! We commit a thousand offences against you day and night. Forgive us all." Having prayed thus, they sat down to eat.]

...

Here is a prayer said by the Pāṇḍavas and Kauravas:

...

[= "O omnipotent. lord! Creator of heaven, this mortal world, and hell! We are all sinners.We commit a thousand sins each day and night. We do not speak the truth in our [selfish] interest. Because of our selfishness,we give trouble and pain to others. We commit such several offences. Forgive us all these trespasses. Do not give us bad inclinations. Make us (our tongue) remember you and your devotion each and everyday."]

...

Such prayers are found in the Konkani Bhārata but not in the Sanskrit Mahābhārata or in Viṣṇudās Nāmā's Marathi Bhārata. They would look more proper in a book of Christian doctrine. Sin and penance are important concepts in Hinduism as well but there is no total preoccupation with sin and penance in Hindu prayers. When a typical character in the Sanskrit Mahābhārata prays to any god, he is not likely to be concerned with the forgiveness of his sins. He is likely to request from the deity he is praying to a potent weapon with which he could vanquish his foes.

Also, addressing god as *sateua'tâ Paramesparâ* [= true lord] as in the first two prayers in this section and as *Âgâ suâmiyâ, sarua hucumadhârâ, sarga, mrutu, pâtllicheâ rachannârâ!* [= 0 lord, omnipotent, creator of heaven, earth, and the netherworld], as in the third prayer given in this section, is noteworthy. According to the articles of the Christian faith, a Christian must believe concerning God that he is the one true lord who is omnipotent and the creator of heaven and earth. See Credo: *Satemânitâ, Paramesparâ, bâpâ, sarua hucumadârâ, suargui'cheâ uâ prathumicheâ rachannârâca* (Stephens 1622, Chapter 6). [= I believe in God, the omnipotent father, creator of heaven and earth].

Even more in the Christian style is the confession of sins in the Konkani Bhārata.

Note Bhīṣma's confession of his sins to Vidura the day before he is going to fall in the battle.

C. 772, p. 322r (633): Bhīṣma confesses his sins before Vidura after praying thus,

"Âgâsuâmiâ, hânua aparâdhy. Zituquy' papa' hânue' zânnatâ queliâinti ty[ty'] tu' mâcâ bhagassi.

[= 0 lord! I am a sinner. Forgive me the trespasses that I have knowingly committed.]

...

According to Hindu practices, in order to become free from sin, one might bathe in a holy river like the Gangā, listen to religious stories, make pilgrimages, give donations to Brahmans, or perform japa (repetition of the name of a deity). Confession is not a Hindu practice.

In the following passage, the ringing of temple bells to remind the faithful to come to the temple is also noteworthy.

c. 772, p. 275v (540): *Ytuqueâ madhe' phânte' zâlem. Nagarântu Prâ'chio murty deullântu âssilialio thai' ghântto uâzilio. To xebdu, âycunu ze Prâ'che bhagtyuanchalla te utthunu ueguy' ueguy' âile' [âile]. Âpule' nite carma sârnu, sarua aparaâdy mhonnu, namascâru carunu âpule tthâi' baissale. Ytuqueâ madhem brâmhannâna purânna sânguile'.*

[= By then it was dawn. Bells rang where there were idols of the Lord in the temples. On hearing that sound, the devotees of the Lord got up and came. Completing their daily routine and saying 'We are all sinners' they bowed and sat down in their places. The Brahman read the purāna.]

There is yet another instance where the temple bells are rung to remind the faithful to say their routine prayers at home:

c. 772, p. 227v (445): *Phânteâri ze-ze tthâi' Paramesparâche nâ'uy' murty sthâpileâti, te deully' ghântto uazliio [uâzilio]. To sabdu âicunu ze bhagta âssati; te ubatthunu Paramesparâche' chintana caru' lâgale.*

[= At dawn, wherever images have been established in the name of God, in those temples, the bells rang. On hearing that sound, those that were devotees of God got up and started contemplation of God.]

It should be noted that it is in a church that they ring bells in order to remind the pious people to come to the church and attend mass or some other religious ceremony. The same church bells are also rung in a different fashion to remind the people to say their routine prayers at home. Take, for instance, the angelus bell. The bells in a temple do not have such ... functions. The bells in a church are large and their loud sound can be heard in the surrounding area whereas the bells used in a Hindu temple are small. A Hindu priest preforming a puja might ring a bell during the ceremony (somewhat like the little bell used in a church during certain ceremonies). But this little bell cannot be heard outside the temple and therefore it cannot play a role in calling the faithful to come to the temple. Often a slightly larger bell hangs elsewhere in the temple which the visitor may ring one or more times. This bell, again, does not play any role in calling devotees to the temple or in reminding them to say their prayers at home.

The narrators of the Konkani Bhārata stories might have interpolated the above passages in their narrative because they were Christian converts although they were learned men conversant with Hindu treatises like Rāmāyana and Mahābhārata. We cannot rule out the possibility that the missionary scribes engaged in writing down the narration also had a hand in the introduction of the passages that show Christian influence.

The narrators of the Konkani Bhārata, being Christian converts, or the missionaries that took down the narration, were responsible for yet another characteristic of the Konkani Bhārata. In works like the Bhārata, it is customary for the author or authors to invoke deities like Gaṇeśa or Sarasvatī at the beginning. For instance, one comes across such invocations at the beginning of every parva of Viṣṇudās Nāmā's Marathi Bhārata. However, such invocations are conspicuous by their absence in the Konkani Bhārata. On the other hand, there are frequent references in the Konkani Bhārata to one supreme deity who is referred to as Paramesparu (< Skt. parameśvara = the supreme lord). Hindus give this appellation to one of their chief gods such as Viṣṇu or Śiva. However, Christian missionaries adopted this appellation for their concept of God in their translation of Christian doctrine. Also, the term for Viṣṇu's abode, Vaikuṇṭha, was adopted by them to refer to the Christian concept of heaven. It is also interesting that, in the Konkani Bhārata, there are many references to statues of God but not to statues of gods.

19. Other Influences of the Authors' Times and Locale on the Konkani Nāmā

The authors I am referring to are Viṣṇudās Nāmā and the anonymous narrators of the Konkani Bhārata.

The characters in the Sanskrit Mahābhārata have the privilege of visiting live gods but the only references that are found there to their visiting temples and statues of gods are believed to be later interpolations (See Karve 1991, p. 194, footnote). However, temples and statues play a significant role in the Konkani Bhārata. There are kings like Vicitravīrya who devote themselves to building temples and installing statues of God in them (C. 771, p. 151 r (293)). We see Vyāsa meditating in a temple when he is getting ready to make King Vicitravīryas wives pregnant by his mere glance (C. 771, p. 151 v (294)). Gāndhārī goes into a temple to recite a mantra in order to have a son (C. 771, p. 156v (304)). Arjuna is advised by holy men to visit statues of God all over the earth in connection with his penance (C. 771, 222v (418)). Accordingly, Arjuna visits many temples and worships many statues during his penitential pilgrimage (C. 771, p. 223r (419)). Krṣṇa advises his older brother Balabhadra to go and worship statues of God during his pilgrimage for the expiation of his sin of brahmahatyā (C. 772, p. 280r (549)). We have already noted that when bells ring in the temples, devotees start praying at home or come to the temple to listen to readings from the ... purānas (C. 772, p. 275v (540)).

The characters of the Mahābhārata in Sanskrit do not communicate with one another through letters, but the characters of the Konkani Bhārata do so routinely. There are over fifty references to letter writing in the Konkani Bhārata.

...

In the Konkani Bhārata, letters are written not only by humans but also by gods, rāksasas, gandharvas, and vānaras. Even Yamadūtas keep written records.

There is no reference to the use of betel leaves in the standard Sanskrit Mahābhārata. In the Konkani Bhārata, Duryodhana offers betel leaves to anyone who has been entrusted with an important or challenging task by him. This practice, however, must be a lot older. In Jaimini's Aśvamedha, we come across Krṣṇa offering a vītaka (a betel-leaf roll with areca nut, etc.) to any warrior who would go and fight the daitya king Anuśālva. Krṣṇa's son Pradyumna accepts it. Later, Krṣṇa offers another vītaka to anyone who would accompany Pradyumna...It is safe to assume that although Jaimini's Aśvamedha might have been written many centuries after the standard Mahābhārata, it would have been nevertheless written many centuries before Viṣṇudās Nāmā's Marathi Bhārata and the Konkani Bhārata.

It is interesting that the kings that interact with the Pāṇḍavas and the Kauravas are ... mostly from areas close to Goa and Maharashtra: Marâtte (Maharashtrian), Guzara (Gujarati), Telunga (Telugu), Cânadde (of Karṇataka). The only ones mentioned from elsewhere are Conozy and Gouddy.

Among the materials used by Duryodhana in building the lac palace where he planned to burn down the Pāṇḍavas, there are items like lac, oil, wax, and dârû. The word dârû (dārū) comes from Persian. It means 'alcohol' and also gunpowder...If dârû refers to 'gunpowder' here, it is the most blatant anachronism in the Konkani Bhārata.

...

20. General Observations

In this chapter, we have had to dwell among other things on certain flaws of the Old Konkani Bhārata but it must be stressed that it is nevertheless the finest piece of work among Old Konkani writings. After all, the Mahābhārata has a fascinating story to tell... Later writers like Viṣṇudās Nāmā have introduced numerous innovations in the story which make the story even more dramatic. More importantly, they have eliminated the many long and dull appendages that are found in the Sanskrit Mahābhārata.

PART TWO

IV

The *Doutrina* and the Quest for a True Language

A trilogy of texts

The following section traces nineteenth-century concerns about the derivations and adaptations of the *Doutrina Christam*, composed in Konkani by Thomas Stephens in 1622. The *Doutrina* as a sixteenth-century genre emerged as a response to the spread of Protestantism, shifting the task of religious instruction of both children and adults from the family to the Church.[1] While versions of such catechisms circulated without formal approval, including some that were printed in Goa, those issued after the Council of Trent (which extended from 1545–1563), had to carry licences of approval. Approved versions such as the *Catecismo Romano* and the 1597 version by the Jesuit Roberto Belarmino became models for later translations, but the one of 1566 by Marcos Jorge and Inácio Martins had the widest circulation in the Portuguese colonies in the form of translations into Tamil (1597), Japanese (1592) and Konkani.[2]

The *Doutrina* embodied an attempt to contain the degree of variation in the translation of Christianity across cultures. An account of early *Doutrina* mentions that synoptic versions called *cartinhas*, which included an alphabet, were dispatched in large numbers on early voyages to the colonies. These were intended to facilitate language learning.[3] The same account notes how later translations, without the alphabet were inevitably embedded in local practices

---

[1] Maria Cândida Drumond Mendes Barros, 'Notas sobre os catecismos em línguas vernáculas das colônias portuguesas (séculos XVI–XVII)', *Iberoromania*, Vol. 57, 1, 2003, pp. 27–63.

[2] ibid, p. 1.

[3] ibid, p. 11.

of spirituality, in which music, musical instruments, performance contexts and words invoked different meaning systems, indicating that the *Doutrina* was part of ritual or oral and written practice rather than an autonomous text. The system of licencing was an attempt to monitor necessary deviations from what was a model rather than a fixed text.

The composition in Konkani by Thomas Stephens, is said to have found acceptance among readers soon after its publication.[4] An article that compares two seventeenth- and eighteenth-century *Doutrina* used for proselytisation among the Tupi in Brazil remarks that the initial activity of the Jesuits in the New World rested on a trilogy of textual genres; the *Doutrina*, a grammar, and a vocabulary, a trilogy that can be traced among the early publications in Goa as well.[5]

A different conception of cultural influence drove the production of the trilogy than the one governing the mastery of popular indigenous devotional genres such as the Purana, which produced works like the Marathi *Kristapurana* of 1616, also by Thomas Stephens. Through texts such as the *Kristapurana*, prevalent beliefs might be modified or overturned, and Christian concepts introduced to increase receptivity or convergence with current beliefs. The reason

---

[4] Stephens' *Doutrina* is said to have followed the lost *Doutrina* of Andre Vaz of 1556, and Francis Xavier's *Doutrina* in Portuguese in 1557 as well as a version of the Marcos Jorge *Doctrina* in 1614. See Joseph Velinkar, "Translations of Portuguese Texts into Konkani and Konkani Compositions into Portuguese with Educational Influence on Literature and Art and the Transfer of Technology," in *History of Mathematical Sciences Portugal and East Asia III: The Jesuits, the Padroado and East Asian Science* (1552-1773) / (Singapore; World Scientific, c2008.),177. According to A. Pereira, *The Makers of Konkani Literature* (Goa: Xaverian Press, Pilar, Goa, 1982). Diogo Ribeiro, a Jesuit assigned to the College of Rachol in Goa printed his own *Declaração da Doutrina Christam*, which he stated (in the complete title), was based on the work of Cardinal Bellarmine, in 1634.

[5] Ruth Monserrat, Mota, and Cândida Barros, "Comparação entre dois diálogos de Doutrina Jesuíticos Tupi: João Filipe Bettendorff (1687) e José Vidigal (1740). The texts referred to are: *Compendio da doutrina christam na Lingua Portugueza & Brasilica* by João Filipe Bettendorff of 1687, and a manuscript *Doutrina* in Tupi, in dialogic form, identified as such by José Vidigal and adopted for pastoral use in 1740. Ruth Monserrat, Jaqueline Mota, and Cândida Barros, "Comparação entre dois Diálogos de Doutrina Jesuíticos Tupi: João Filipe Bettendorff (1687) e José Vidigal (1740)," XIII *Jornadas Internacionais Sobre as Missões Jesuíticas*, no. Simpósio 3. Línguas indígenas no período Jesuítico e Pós-Jesuítico: História e Sociedade, accessed February 12, 2014, http://repositorio.museu-goeldi.br/jspui/bitstream/123456789/523/1/evento_Bettendorf_versao%20editor.pdf.

for the switch from the written language of devotion and worship, Marathi, to the literisation in the *Doutrina*, of a predominantly spoken language, Konkani is not yet clear, but late sixteenth-century directives on language issued by Church councils held in Goa, advocate compositions in local languages to prevent a slide back to non-Christian practices among new converts.[6]

Interpretations of colonial encounters of this period draw attention to the transformation of sixteenth-century ethnological frameworks when 'the world was a concatenation of singularities bound mostly by the notion of a unitary Creation', to seventeenth-century conceptions of Brazil and India as imperial outposts of an empire with Portugal at the centre (Chakravarti 2018, 22). This was a time when Europeans 'had to learn the…symbolic structures of local cultures', many of which were internalised (ibid., 17). The trilogy of doctrine, vocabulary and grammar may be seen as one among a range of strategies that were adopted 'in the face of the manifest failure of coercion' (ibid., 23).

Aside from using indigenous forms as a model, or attempting to produce a uniform translation of one text across different cultures, Maria Leonor Carvalhão Buescu and Cláudio Costa Pinheiro (1992) indicate how Latin and Portuguese as well as classical Roman usages were positioned as a universal standard that other languages might approximate (2009, 41). Dictionaries, vocabularies, and grammars implicitly adopted this standard to equate or assimilate terms and words emanating from African, Latin American, and Asian contexts. Pinheiro reminds us of the simultaneity of intellectual influence, when he states that the first grammar of the Portuguese language appeared in 1536, followed closely by grammars of Tamil, Tupi, Chinese, and Japanese. According to Manohar Rai Sardessai (2000, 42), Thomas Stephens' grammar of Konkani, the *Arte da Lingoa Canarim* published in Goa in 1640, was modelled on a Latin grammar. Sardessai also describes the *Vocabulario da Lingoa Canarim* by Diogo Ribeiro, of 1626, as a translation. The second volume, he states, 'reveals that it is an enlarged version of a dictionary compiled by some Jesuit priests from Salsette' (ibid., 45). With 14,000 entries and

[6] '(T)he fourth Provincial Council in 1592 was distressed that the practices of 'witchcraft, divination, superstitions', and the 'bad habits and perverse education' which Goans received when they were Hindus persisted after their baptism; it advocated, as an antidote, more translations of catechisms into Konkani.' Rochelle Pinto, *Between Empires: Print and Politics in Goa* (New Delhi: Oxford University Press India, 2007), 84, 93.

422 pages, the dictionary provides Konkani words in the Roman script, followed by their translation into Portuguese, and, is also structured as a Latin grammar (ibid., 45-46).[7]

Sardessai elaborates (ibid., 46) on the kind of Konkani used by Diogo Ribeiro in his *Vocabulário*:

> Besides throwing significant light on the state of Konkani language of the seventeenth century Fr Ribeiro's vocabulary also reveals the existence of loanwords from Sanskrit, Kannada, Persian and Arabic, some of which are no longer in current usage in Konkani. It may be noted that the Konkani of the Vocabulario shows a marked influence of Kannada. Many ... Kannada vocables are no longer in use in Goa's Konkani dialects which goes to prove that Konkani had already borrowed a number of Kannada words.

Olivinho Gomes (1997) and Rocky Miranda (2011) both mention the work of two Franciscan Friars, Amador de Santana's *Flos Sanctorum* composed in the Kannada (or Kandvi) script, as translated from the Latin and printed in 1607; and the *Symbolum Fide*, said to be translated from the work of Cardinal Bellarmine by Joao de São Mathias. From a survey of a number of texts across these two centuries, Miranda concludes that Konkani tended to be used for prose and Marathi for verse. Fr. Antonio de Saldanha's *Sancto Antonichi Acharya*, (The Miracles of St. Anthony) based on the life of St. Anthony of Padua and published in 1655, was in two parts, the first in Konkani prose, and the second part in Marathi ovi verse.[8] Sardessai (2000, 52) notes, '(i)t contains a rich vocabulary mainly drawn from 'tatsama' words. It does not betray any influence of Portuguese lexicon or Latin syntax.' Sanskritic influence is not the only feature of the text, which also coins occasional words by combining Portuguese words and Konkani vocables (ibid., 53). The use of the coconut plant as a symbol and metaphor of division of being in the Trinity, or of the different elements of the fish are another sign, according to him, of the creation of new symbolic culture

---

[7] A recent edition of this work is Toru Maruyama, ed., *Vocabulario da lingoa canarim feito pellos Padres da Companhia de Jesus que residem na christandade de Salcete e novamente acressentado com varios modos de fallar pello Padre Diogo Ribeiro da mesma Companhia, anno 1626* (Nagoya, Japan: Dept. of Japanese Studies, Nanzan University, 2005).

[8] The ovi was a popular oral metre used in texts composed in Old Marathi such as the *Jnanesvari*, and usually comprised three rhymed lines of uniform length and one unrhymed line. For a discussion of ovi see Christian Lee Novetzke, *The Quotidian Revolution: Vernacularization, Religion, and the Premodern Public Sphere in India* (Columbia University Press, 2016), 222.

within the Konkani language (ibid., 55). With reference to Stephens' *Doutrina*, Sardessai stated (ibid., 40), '(I)n this Catechism we see an attempt to use Hindu religious terms to express the teaching of Christian Doctrine. It will be seen that in the course of time these terms will be slowly replaced by Portuguese ones. For example, you have in this Catechism Sanskrit tatsam words like, 'Xanti, Sodoivi, Xeronna, Omrut.'

The seventeenth century, which saw the emergence of the first few Konkani grammars and Church edicts favouring Konkani, is also marked by dwindling production in the language, and the emergence of edicts against the spoken language. In 1684, the Viceroy prohibited the use of Konkani altogether and printing itself was formally banned from 1754 to 1821 in Goa (Pinto 2007, 84-85). As a result, the literary historian and linguist José Pereira (1971, 3) argued, the efforts of those who had composed the first grammars and works in standard Konkani did not form a basis for continuous development into a medium for written literary texts. According to him, the grammars and vocabularies produced by missionaries helped standardise a written form of the language in which Goans and Portuguese wrote catechisms, confessionals, and theological treatises and translated religious texts (ibid.). He subsequently traces a breakdown into isolated dialects of the standard, once the decree of 1684 banning Konkani was issued. Literary production according to him was dispersed among dialects of Konkani whose speakers worked in isolation from each other. In another work on Goa's literary history, Pereira remarked that writers 'have had to write in their language as if it had never been written in before; one is always coming across assertions that a particular writer is Konkani's first.'[9] This is one of the initial theses about how missionary intervention developed a repertoire for Konkani, which colonial policy itself subsequently shattered. Most literary histories trace a narrative of decline after this moment, though Pereira's thesis has never been substantially examined in the context of linguistic theories about the development of the language.

Educating the parish

By 1945, when the scholar of Sanskrit and Konkani, Mariano Saldanha published his edition of Stephens' 1622 text as the *Doutrina Cristã em língua Concani*, the lack of homogeneity in versions of

[9] Pinto, *Between Empires*, 85.

catechisms circulating among lay Catholics was a concern within the Catholic church.[10] Popular catechisms in Konkani present a situation of structured encounter between the clergy and lay populations, in which sections of the clergy were likely to have been familiar with elements of Latin and Portuguese. The *Doutrina Christam* of 1622 was a point of reference and a prototype of a genre, but it reverberates in these discussions as a corrective touchstone for Konkani. Typically, catechisms would contain orations, the sacraments, commandments, and distinctively, questions and responses in the form of a dialogue, which communicated basic tenets of belief. Across the following sections, the distinction between popular and formal linguistic approaches to devotional texts is not easy to sustain with regard to the texts themselves, as writers sought to produce popular genres informed by linguistic analysis. Popular writers were also receptive to suggestions regarding script and orthography. It is therefore in the commentaries and articles about these texts that a category of the popular acquires definitioin.

The early missionary apprehension regarding the absorption of sacred concepts from other religions through language and genre was replaced by concern over whether the fidelity of Konkani words to concepts had been sustained across a period when doctrine was customarily, orally transmitted. Nineteenth and early twentieth-century editions would suggest that the question of an original (literised) language or a received standard was never fixed, and a need persisted among local churches for re-editions that were both faithful, sanctioned, and could be understood (Pinto 1961).[11] Mariano Saldanha mentions various *Doutrina* published by lay Catholics from 1820 on, in Portuguese and in Konkani (1945, 25).[12]

Popular prayer manuals that were likely to have contained elements of the *Doutrina* were printed in Bombay prior to 1873 and

---

[10] In 1857 Joaquim Heliodoro da Cunha had reprinted Stephens' grammar of Konkani written in Portuguese, along with a few sections from the *Kristapurana*.

[11] Padre Francisco Xavier Pinto, *Catecismo da Arquidiocese de Goa em Concani, Edição da Arquidiocese* (Cidade de Goa: Tipografia Popular, 1961). Notes in the book suggest a 1943 edition, and another smaller version of this text appeared in 1948.

[12] *Compêndio da Doutrina Cristã em língua portuguesa e Goana,* printed in Bombay by Manuel da Cruz, in 1820, and *Manual de Devoções e Doutrina Cristã,* printed in Bombay in 1848. There is also mention of a *Doutrina* without a date, printed in Goa, and the *Manual da Missa e da Confissão* (containing a *Doutrina*) by Miguel Vicente d'Abreu, Nova Goa, Imprensa Nacional, 1860. Other catalogues also mention a *Catecismo da Doutrina Christã em Concanim* (Nova Goa, Imprensa Nacional, 1901).

in Mangalore from 1882.[13] In 1890, Jose Benjamin Rodrigues wrote the *Catecismo da Doutrina Christa* while Eduardo Jose Bruno de Souza published two catechisms in 1897 and 1899. De Souza also published a translation of rites for the dead in 1894. His work is unlikely to have elicited any complaints from critics for he was among those who urged the improvement and restoration of Konkani to a literary standard.[14] A catechism in Devanagari that finds mention in some texts is likely to be the *Kristanv Dotorn ani Catecism* of 1898, published from Sholapur at the Anandvrat Chapkhanyat by J. O. Pires, while a publication of the same name in Roman characters is said to have emerged in 1894.[15]

A *Catecismo da Doutrina Christã* of 1915 claimed that an earlier edition was free of errors, but had introduced some changes in oral prayers. The hesitation over including new terms stemmed from a reluctance to introduce words that were alien to those who would use the book in daily prayer. It also revealed that anxiety over the assumed impoverished status of Konkani extended to doubts over its ability to maintain a stable relation of word to concept. The editor explained,

> In the first place, our aim is not to introduce any one mode of speaking and writing concanim, but only to provide the means by which, the rudiments of Faith can be taught by the best mode possible to those who do not understand Portuguese…we saw…what great divergences existed, that were difficult to reconcile with respect to certain words, phrases and modes of concanim…what secure criteria did we have to follow?[16]

Driven above all by religious interest 'that in us should prevail over all others'; the writer was compelled to,

---

[13] Five other texts published between 1873 and 1878 are mentioned in J. F.Blumhardt, *Catalogue of the Library of the India Office*, Vol. 2; Pt. 5, 1908, 105. http://archive.org/details/in.ernet.dli.2015.536312.

[14] See Madhavi Sardesai, 'A Comparative Linguistic and Cultural Study of Lexical Influences on Konkani', Goa University, Taleigao, 2006, pp. 22–225, for an account of the discussion of popular Konkani in Bruno de Souza's novel, *Kristãv Ghorabo.*

[15] An incomplete *Doutrina* in Devanagari may be found at the Thomas Stephens' Konkani Kendra, and the Sholapur *Doutrina* in the British Library, London. The catalogue of Marathi printed texts in the British Library lists the 1894 *Doutrina* in Roman.

[16] *Catecismo da Doutrina Christa em Concanim,* Third edition (Nova Goa: Pereira and Andrade Livraria Editora, 1915, 5.

> lament more than anyone else the current state of concanim, that we would wish to see cultivated on par with the most beautiful Portuguese language; but being forced to accept things as they are, what is important is to employ great diligence to avert a situation in which the (we repeat, lamentable) corruption of the language jeopardises the teaching of the Faith.[17]

Despite repeated recommendations to the effect, he emphasised, children in the parish schools rarely knew the Portuguese catechism when knowledge of it would have been useful, to the extent of providing a corrective influence to errors that arose out of their reading in Konkani.[18]

Popular devotional texts and how to correct them

Presses set up by English and German missionary groups simultaneously produced Konkani texts in the Kannada script. In 1841, the Basel Mission Press or the German Evangelical Mission Press was set up in Balmatta, Mangalore. The first books produced were translations of Bible stories and other texts into Kannada and a Tulu translation of the Gospel of Matthew.[19] By the 1870s, versions of scriptural narratives began to appear in Konkani.[20] The number of presses working in this region, such as the Codialbail Press, installed in Mangalore by Jesuits in 1882, as well as the number of titles in Konkani soon exceeded those in the Roman script. Devotional texts

---

[17] ibid., 6.

[18] All such publications carried an Imprimatur, indicating they had been scrutinised and permitted to be published by the Archbishop, as is evident from the second edition of the *Devocionario em Concanim* of 1927 by B. M. Mascarenhas. The title page of this edition contained a reference to the *Doutrina Christam*, the liturgy of the mass in Portuguese and Konkani, a preparation for confession and communion in Konkani, a litany to the Virgin Mary and St. Francis Xavier in Latin and Konkani and the hymn, *Rigló Jesu*, among others. (*Devocionario em Concanim*, B.M. Mascarenhas, Bombay, B.X. Furtado, 1927). I thank Derrick D'Costa for this contribution.

[19] Reinhard Wendt, *An Indian to the Indians?: On the Initial Failure and the Posthumous Success of the Missionary Ferdinand Kittel* (1832–1903) (Otto Harrassowitz Verlag, 2006), 234.

[20] A. C Burnell, ed., *The Parables of the Sower, Etc.* St. Matth. XIII, 1-35. Translated from the Vulgate into the Konkani Spoken by the Roman Catholics of South Canara [by P. Noronha]. With an Introductory Note on this Dialect [Signed: A. B., i.e. A. C. Burnell]., trans. Pio Noronha (Mangalore: Basel Mission Press, 1872).

such as the *Stabat Mater* were printed in 1855 in Goa in the Roman script as well as songs, proverbs, and hymnbooks, intended for wider consumption.[21]

Popular devotional literature also began to emerge and it is likely that the circulation of these texts was seen to have interfered with the desired consistency in the relationship between word and concept. Translations that enjoyed the widest circulation narrated the path to canonisation and the miracles of favoured saints. The lives of St. Isabel, St. Anthony and Our Lady of Lourdes for instance, were extremely popular.

Articles written in the *O Heraldo* of the 1910s by Christovam Pinto (a public servant who lived in Lisbon until his return to India in 1912) are an early acknowledgement of such popular devotional print, and the beginning of a public critique. Two later articles, '*A Romanização e a Desnacionalização de Concani*' and '*A Desnacionalização pelo Concani*', in the *O Heraldo* of 1917 indicate how philology and language could be seen as foundational to political identity, or in the case of the non-elite Catholics of Goa, a liability. Many years before T. B. Cunha's famed excoriating account of how Goan Catholics were denationalised, *Denationalisation of Goans* (Bombay: Goa Congress Committee, 1944)), Pinto's articles indicate that the Roman script was viewed as politically destructive. He noted that while the *Doutrina* survived among those who could read in the Roman script, it had passed from generation to generation because it had been learned by rote with some alteration and adulteration of its words.[22] In defense of Devanagari, he believed that printed devotional material survived, not only in Goa, Bombay, Pune and Belgaum where Devanagari was the indigenous alphabet, but also in Karnataka and Mangalore, where, among Konkani-speaking Christians, devotional material was printed in the script of that land, as they did not know the 'original' script of Konkani. In Goa, the Balbodh script was familiar to Hindus as well as to those Christians who had frequented the national Lyceum of Panjim, the seminary of Rachol, or Marathi classes in Bombay, he stated.[23] He made special reference to the material published in Devanagari by J. O. Pires from Karachi and by D. F. Dantas from Sawantwadi. A transliteration into Devanagari

[21] Miguel Vicente de Abreu, *Stabat Mater e outras orações em Concanim* (Nova Goa: Imprensa Nacional, 1855).

[22] Christovam Pinto, "A Cultura de Concani,"*O Heraldo*, September 16, 1915, No. 2, 157 edition.

[23] Christovam Pinto, "O Concani e a sua Romanização," *O Heraldo*, October 7, 1915.

had also been attempted by the Barão de Cumbarjua and was given to Pinto in manuscript form so that it could be made public.[24]

Pinto said that he was often asked by readers how a culture could progress without the basic books of language and literature of the kind available in British India whether in 'Aryan or Dravidian languages'.[25] Sixty years ago, he emphasised, British India lagged behind Goa with respect to the state of educational material. Some translations of legal codes made the knowledge of 'Hindu law' (*legislação hindu*) available, and the indigenous population had sacred poems elaborated in Sanskrit and in Pali, which were however, exclusive to brahmins. It was the zeal of those among the English who believed in public instruction in his view, that resulted in the promotion of indigenous culture, with the intent of spreading national education, and transformed literary production in recent years.[26]

Transliteration, according to him, was not intended as a language of composition, but was an intermediary tool that had served English and European Orientalists and Egyptologists like William Jones to record oral histories and narratives.[27] Once indigenous languages had been mastered, scholars preferred to read in the original scripts as the Roman script, he claimed, could not replace an alphabet that had fifty-two letters. Konkani in the Roman script, in this account, could not be used to transliterate anything effectively other than colloquial Konkani and prayers for daily devotion. In comparison, those writing in the Kannada script had a flourishing literary universe. Not only could Pinto claim that J.O. Pires, the Barão de Cumbarjua and Gerson da Cunha supported the use of the Devanagari script, but he had received a letter from the linguist and his close friend, Msgr. Sebastião Rodolfo Dalgado stating that knowledge of Devanagari was indispensable for the acquisition of Konkani.

Thus, the contemporary spurt of printed texts in Roman in Bombay did not constitute cultural progress, but quite the contrary. 'Through the romanised system, though it is through the artifice of transliteration, the culture, if it can be called that, restricts itself to the narrow circle of the christians of Goa who speak concani, which is, as is recognised by all, very adulterated…'[28] Instead, by

---

[24] ibid. Pinto acknowledged the catechism in the Roman script by the late parish priest, Pe. José Benjamin Rodrigues of Mapusa. Pe. Rodrigues taught Marathi in the seminary of Rachol, and therefore could not be ranked among the unlearned.

[25] Christovam Pinto, "O Concani e a sua Romanização," *O Heraldo*, October 7, 1915.

[26] ibid.

[27] ibid.

[28] ibid.

adopting the vernacular alphabet, Christian Goans would be able to participate in the general culture of all the populations of the Konkan from Ratnagiri to Mangalore in the south and if there were greater efforts made to standardise the language, Konkani speakers could begin to approach what he saw as the 'grand indigenous intellectual movement' in British India.

The following is an incomplete three-page long introduction in Portuguese written in 1901 by the Patriarca das Índias Orientais (including Goa and Daman), Archbishop D. Matheus de Oliveira Xavier, to a doctrinal text in Konkani produced for daily prayer. The introduction to the Konkani catechism mentions an edition of 1910 produced through consultation with a range of priests at the Rachol seminary in Goa. The new version which was produced by comparing a Portuguese edition and an old Konkani edition was said to be free of errors, but with some changes in oral prayers, which might cause hesitation among lay Catholics accustomed to the earlier version. Those framing it had taken care, said the Archbishop, to ensure that it was in accordance with a prior manuscript that had been ratified by a Canon Mello.

Excerpt 5
Courtesy Thomas Stephens' Konkani Kendra, Porvorim.
Archbishop D. Matheus de Oliveira Xavier (Patriarcha das Índias Orientaeis), 'Introduction', *Catecismo da Doutrina Christa em Concanim*, third edition, (Nova Goa: Pereira e Andrade Livraria, 1915)

A quem lêr

Estando esgotada a edição anterior do *Catecismo da Doutrina Christã em concani,* saida dos prelas da Imprensa Nacional em 1901 e publicada com liçenca do finado Patriarcha D. António Sebastião Valencia de saudissima memoria, publicamos esta nova reformada com autorisação de S. Exa. O Sr. D. Matheus, Patriarcha das Indias Orientaeis, esperando do publico o mesmo apoio que a anterior teve.

Pereira e Andrade

Excerpted from the incomplete introduction by Archbishop D. Matheus de Oliveira Xavier (Patriarca das Índias Orientais), pp. iv–vi

'... Recorremos portanto ao expediente de formar pouco a pouco juízo dos defeitos e qualidades da obra por meio da informação e da contradição; e assim sob a Nossa presidencia reunimos juntas de sacerdotes competentes, nas quaes se discutiu com liberdade a material comparando entre si os textos do catecismo nas duas línguas não perdendo de vista a versão concanim tradicional; além de obtermos as apreciações de muitos outros eclesiásticos de dentro e fora de Goa. Nas juntas também se examinaram e cotejaram as formulas do Credo e Actos seguidas nas differentes parochias e missões, achando-se muitas differenças e variantes. Não esquecemos enfim fazer verificar, que o catecismo impresso concorda com o manuscripto julgado em termos de ser dado ao uso dos fiéis pelo Cónego Mello.

De exame tam instructivo e minucioso tiraram-se as seguintes conclusões principaes:

1. A nova versão está immune de erros doutrinaes; apresenta apenas um lapso ou equivoco acerca da qualidade da dor para obter o perdão dos peccados fora da confissão, de facil correcção por outros lugares, onde se ensina sem ambiguidade a verdadeira doutrina.
2. Nas orações communs, especialmente no Credo, introduziu alterações e mudanças que podem trazer embaraço aos fieis costumados as formulas da versão antiga.

...

3. Para exprimir as verdades, certas pessoas e cousas da religião, empregou termos novos, alguns porventura mais proprios que os antigos, mas tendo o inconveniente de poderem causar extranhesa.

A vista do que, sempre na persuasão de ser conveniente a introducção gradual d'um unico texto concanim, resolvemos mandar reformar a edição do que foi coordenado pelo presbytero José Benjamin Rodrigues, já fallecido ha muito, e fazer outra edição, na qual se restabeleceu a forma usual das preces communs, (Padre Nosso, Ave Maria, Credo, Salve Rainha e Confissão) adoptando-se entre as variantes a que melhor pareceu, e se eliminaram os termos novos que realmente podessem causar extranhesa. D'este trabalho encarregamos o Conego Penitenciario da Nossa Sé Mt. Revd. Pedro Remígio das Mercês Barreto, que o executou, quanto podemos apreciar com intelligencia e summo cuidado, ficando tambem com o encargo de dirigir a impressão da edição nova, afim de sahir possivelmente perfeita.

Afora as ditas modificações e outras de menor importancia, não ordenamos se reformasse a linguagem do catecismo. Em primeiro logar o Nosso fim não e introduzir este ou aquelle modo de falar e escrever o concanim, mas sim providenciar, até onde de Nós depender, para que se ensinem do melhor modo possível os rudimentos da Fé aos que não entendem o portuguez. Em segundo logar no decurso do exame, a que procedemos, vimos ainda melhor ... que profundas divergencias, difficeis de conciliar, existem a respeito de certas palavras, phrases e conceitos de concanim. Na escolha pois de estylo e linguagem que criterio seguro haviamos de seguir? Que regra adoptariamos por autoridade, que não houvesse de ser contradictada? Pelo summo interesse da religião, que em Nós deve dominar todos os outros, lamentamos mais que ninguem o estado actual do concanim, que quiseramos ver cultivado a par da bellissima lingua portugueza; mas tendo de forçosamente acceitar as cousas como são, o que a que importa é empregar summa diligencia para obstar a corrupção (lamentavel repetimos) da lingua prejudique o ensino da Fé.

É este nova edição do catecismo concanim revista e reformada nos limites do exposto, que hoje approvamos, mandando a seja a unica adoptada na escolar de catechese do Seminario de Rachol e escolas parochiaes, excluida a anterior, juntamente com o catecismo portuguez extrahido do da diocese da Madeira por Nossa ordem. Não obstante repetidas recommendações Nossas e de Nossos Predecessores, raro é que os meninos das escolas parochiaes saibam o catecismo em portuguez, quando este conhecimento é-lhes evidentemente muito util, mesmo para completaro ensin o emconcanim e corregir quaesquer defeitos, que d'elle possam provir.

Exortamos os Revd[os] Parochos a tornar effectivosos Nossos mandados, ajudando com pastoral paciencia os mestres de capella a ler e explicar este catecismo…

V

Two Systems of Transliteration

Dalgado and the Influential Orientalists

In a publication of 1881, *The Koṅkaṇî Language and Literature*, Gerson da Cunha stated,

'(T)he best prose piece in Koṅkaṅî is the Lord's Prayer, which is also available for comparison with the other languages of its own and other groups. The Lord's Prayer in Koṅkaṅî, published in the *Propaganda Fide's Oratio Dominica*, Rome 1870, along with other translations in 250 languages…is both grammatically and prosodiacally incorrect. I append below the prayer, as it is now said, in juxtaposition to its Latin equivalent, romanized according to the system in vogue amongst the majority of Orientalists'.

The Lord's Prayer in multiple languages was printed in versions of the *Oratio Dominica* from at least the sixteenth century on. In correcting the version of Konkani that had appeared in 1870, Gerson da Cunha inaugurated yet another intervention in the writing of Konkani – the adoption of the transliteration system of the British Orientalists.[1]

Gerson da Cunha (1844–1900) was a member of the Bombay Branch of the Royal Asiatic Society. He published books on medicine, history, numismatics,

---

[1] The Lord's Prayer in 250 languages and 180 forms of writing, *Oratio Dominica in CCL. Lingvas Versa* et CLXXX Charactervm Formis; Vel Nostratibvs Vel Peregrinis Expressa Cvrante Petro Marietti. Eqvite Typographo Pontificio Socio Administro Typographei s. Consilii de Propaganda Fide, ed. Pietro Marietti (Romae, 1870).

archaeology, linguistics, and literary history. Some of his publications are, The Origin of Bombay, *published in 1900 by the Bombay Branch of the Royal Asiatic Society, a* Memoir on the History of the Tooth-relic of Ceylon, *published by W. Thacker, London, 1875,* Notes on the History of Chaul and The Sahyâdri-Khanda of the Skanda Purana: A Mythological, Historical and Geographical Account of Western India, *both published by Thacker, Vining and Co. in Bombay in 1877. His* The Koṅkaṇî Language and Literature *of 1881, printed in Bombay at the Govt. Central Press marks an early phase in the efforts of Catholic elites to propagate a distinct history and identity for Konkani.*

The two excerpts from da Cunha's texts, an image from the Horticus Malabaricus, *and 'The Lord's Prayer' are appendices that precede his book,* The Koṅkaṇî Language and Literature. *The first is a reproduction of a note signed by three Brahmans, Ranga Botto, Vinaique Pandito, and Apu Botto (names reproduced in accordance with Portuguese orthography), who are said to have assisted in Van Rheede's compilation of the Hortus Indicus Malabaricus. It constitutes an early sample of Konkani writing that was translated into Latin and has been reproduced in the 1881 edition of the text. The second is a rendition of 'The Lord's Prayer' that was translated into multiple languages at various points in time by the Catholic Church. Dissatisfied with the most recently available translation, da Cunha undertakes his own. Accompanying it is a facsimile of the version that da Cunha rejects.*

Excerpt 6

J. Gerson da Cunha, Appendices A and B, excerpt from *The Koṅkaṇî Language and Literature*, 1881, pp. 43–45

43

APPENDIX A.

The following is the Testimonial in the Koṅkaṇî language and modified Devanâgarî characters, signed by three Brâhmaṇs, and published in the Preface to the first volume of *Hortus Indicus Malabaricus* by H. Van Rheede, Amsterdam edition of 1678, with its accompanying Latin translation.

स्वस्तिश्री शालिवाहनशक १५९७ राक्षससंवत्सर चैत्रबहुल १० को
श्री राजपाटणी बैसिके रंग भट्ट तथा विनायक पंडित आपु भट्ट तेगवैद्य
तानिं कोचिन्चा कुमदोर आंढ्रिकि फांडे त्यावगनिरोपान ह्या मलबारदेशा
तु आस्तिले ओषधमात्र वृक्षवालि झाडरवंड ओळखतेल्या मनुष्याकनु
स्नागोदेऊनु तेते गांवांतु पेट्टवून तिनिं वारवद आणवून त्यात्या झाडांचे फुल
फूल पान बीज समस्तात्यान्यातुतुकाळावरि सपादून तिंतीचि तारिली त्यातुप
रांत आमिं आमगेल्या वैद्यग्रंथाचानि घेटाजमाणी त्यांत्या ओषधाचे गुण
वाऊनु मतानजोजो गुण आमका कळ्ळेलो तोवान्यां आरवदांची नावं पळ्ळेउनु
आजिदानि वर्षंसकान्ति साजे आमिं लागिरावूनु हालिकुस पादून दिला तेल
टिक अब्राह्मणुंचाकनज अब्राह्मणु आंमि आमचीं निसाणि कर्णु दिली
ते सत्यब्राह्मणु मानु वेंजर इदखणु नागरब नपानद्द बरवूनु दिली श्रीः

रंग भट्टु

विनायकपंडित

आपु वी आप

HOC EST.

AB anno millesimo quingentesimo nonagesimo septimo dicto á Bramanis *Palivanapaco* (qui apud nos est annus 1674) : usque ad decimum Aprilis anni dicti *Requeçao* (qui apud nos est Annus 1675). Ego RANGA BOTTO, VINAIQUE PANDITO & APU BOTTO, omnes tres de Natione & Religione Bramanas & Gymnoso-

B 1079—6 *

44

phistæ antiqui in districtu *Cochinensi* per mandatum Nobilis D. Henrici á Rheede, Commendatoris terrarum Malabaricarum & Civitatis *Cochinensis*, curavimus per servos nostros qui notitiam arborum, plantarum, herbarum & convolvulorum habebant, eas ex terra Malabarica cum suis floribus, fructibus & seminibus ad Civitatem prædictam, ut delinearentur & describerentur, adferri, quarum nomina scripta sunt in libro nostro vocato *Manhaningattnâm*, in quo etiam continentur virtutes & vires earum Medicinales, & præter hasce eis addidimus quod diuturna nostra experientia & magno labore ac sudore de iis didicimus & observavimus, & ut hic liber perficeretur, laboravimus per spatium duorum ferme annorum, ita ut omnis & quilibet, qui eum lecturus & visurus est, ei possit adhibere fidem quam ipse fuisset daturus, si res in ea scriptas ipsemet fuisset expertus; juramus itaque secundùm consuetudinem nostram, quod omne in eo contentum verum sit; in cujus rei fidem fecimus præsentes chartas quas propriis manibus nostris subscripsimus. Datum in Civitate *Cochinensi* vigesimo die Aprilis anni millesimi sexcentesimi septuagesimi quinti.

RANGA-BOTTO, VINAIQUE PANDITO,
APU BOTTO.

Traductum ex lingua Bramanum per subscriptum
VINAIQUE PANDITO
in linguam Lusitanicam, *&* *ex lingua* Lusitanica
in Latinam *per me*
CHRISTIANUM HERMAN de DONEP,
Secretarium Civilem Civitatis *Cochinensis*.

45

APPENDIX B.

The best prose piece in Koṅkaṇî is the Lord's prayer, which is also available for comparison with the other languages of its own and other groups. The Lord's prayer in Koṅkaṇî, published in the *Propaganda Fide's Oratio Dominica*, Rome 1870, along with other translations in 250 languages, at page 218, under the heading of *Oratio Dominica, Kanarice*, Dialecto Goana, is both grammatically and prosodiacally incorrect. I append below the prayer, as it is now said, in juxtaposition to its Latin equivalent, romanized according to the system in vogue amongst the majority of Orientalists.

The Lord's prayer is, indeed, far more suitable, as a standard of comparison, for translation into different languages than the Parables of the Sower, &c. (St. Matthew, xiii. 1—35); although the latter is seven times at least as long as the prayer. The parables were, moreover, translated into Koṅkaṇî, and published at Mangalore by the Basel Mission in 1872, this being the passage selected by H. H. Prince Bonaparte for giving specimens of the dialects of Europe.

Pater noster, qui es in cælis:	Âmchya Bapâ, tum sorgâr assai;
Sanctificetur nomen tuum:	Tugem nam hoḍ zaum:
Adveniat regnum tuum:	Tugem râj amkam heum:
Fiat voluntas tua, sicut in cælo et in terra.	Tugî khośi zośi sorgâr zatâ tośi sounsârant zaum.
Panem nostrum quotidianum da nobis hodie:	Anim amchó dispoṭhó guirâs az amkâm dî:
Et dimitte nobis debita nostra,	Anim amchim pâtkam bogośi,
Sicut et nos dimittimus debitoribus nostris.	Zośi amim amcher chukleleamku bogośitaum.
Et ne nos inducas in tentationem.	Anim amkâm thauṇieṇ poḍum dium nakâ.
Sed libera nos a malo. Amen.	Puṇ amcher sorvoi vaiṭ vigu hetâ tem nivâr. Amen.

(As a point of comparison: An excerpt from *The Lord's Prayer in 250 Languages and 180 Forms of Writing,* (1870) 1975, p. xxix. Accessed from archive.org—http://archive.org/details/TheLordsPrayerIn250Languages/page/n89/mode/2up?q=marratice—public domain Mark 1.0)

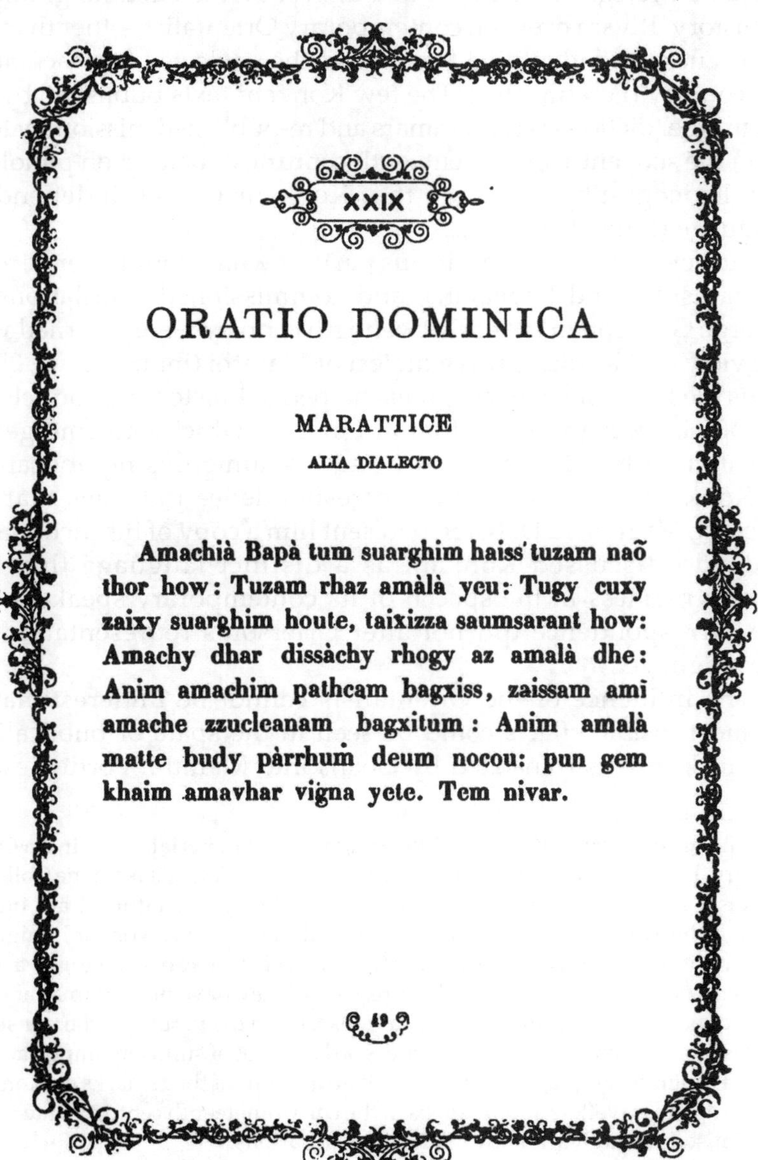

XXIX

ORATIO DOMINICA

MARATTICE

ALIA DIALECTO

Amachià Bapà tum suarghim haiss'tuzam naõ thor how: Tuzam rhaz amàlà yeu: Tugy cuxy zaixy suarghim houte, taixizza saumsarant how: Amachy dhar dissàchy rhogy az amalà dhe: Anim amachim pathcam bagxiss, zaissam ami amache zzucleanam bagxitum: Anim amalà matte budy pàrrhum deum nocou: pun gem khaim amavhar vigna yete. Tem nivar.

49

An essay on Konkani by J. H. da Cunha Rivara, the Secretary to the Governor General, customarily marks the beginning of a public discussion over the question of a vernacular. By 1858 when his seminal essay on the Konkani language was published, linguistic studies produced under the English colonial administration in India had relegated Konkani to a dialect that needed no grammar or history. Rivara drew on contemporary Orientalists other than the Portuguese and identified Konkani as the neglected 'vernacular' of the country (Pereira 1971). The few Konkani texts published by the Goan elite (dictionaries, grammars and re-published missionary texts from the sixteenth and seventeenth centuries) focused on philology and lexicography, to argue that Konkani was an independent language (Pinto 2007, 224).

Surveys conducted in various parts of what would later become Maharashtra and Karnataka, and commissioned translations by George Grierson in the early twentieth century were returned with the view that Konkani was a dialect of Marathi (ibid., 223–24, 252).[2] Thus the *Linguistic Survey of India* helped to bolster vigorous claims for official recognition of Marathi in Goa, which had emerged in the aftermath of Rivara's essay and his numerous republications of Konkani texts; Grierson's correspondence indicates that the linguist, Msgr. S. R. Dalgado had sent him a copy of his dictionary.[3] Dalgado discussed Konkani as a distinct language that had lost its richness in the speech of its contemporary speakers, but the correspondence did not alter Grierson's representations of the language.

The influence of the Orientalists cannot be underestimated. Its most visible effects could be seen in the spate of publications of Sanskrit texts translated by Goans into Marathi, Portuguese or

---

[2] See *Linguistic Survey of India*, #9196, uncatalogued material, 1901, India Office Library, London. A letter from the Mamlatdar of Pen, A.G. Tilak, to the Collector of Nasik said, 'I have further to report that with all my efforts I am unable to give the Konkani version of the Prodigal Son's story. Konkani language as such is nothing different from Marathi...the Konkanis have got a very limited vocabulary of words and expressions. They have no grammar and are consequently unable to express various ideas. From the perusal of the translated words, you will come to know that the words are not of sufficient importance to form a separate language.' See Pereira for an account of the remarks on Konkani by European travellers and linguists in the early nineteenth century which were legitimised through academic and state institutions.

[3] Ibid. The introduction to Dalgado's Konkani-Portuguese dictionary also references the correspondence.

English.[4] The literary and linguistic histories produced at this time either combated Konkani in preference for Marathi, or tried to install Konkani anew as the object of literary studies.

The most significant body of work that was produced at the turn of the century however is that of the ecclesiast Msgr. Sebastião Rodolfo Dalgado (1893) who wrote over fifteen texts of grammar, glossaries, studies of creoles and dialects developed through the influence of Portuguese, dictionaries, and translations. Dalgado's approach to the revival, correction and restoration of Konkani reproduced the preference for Sanskrit as a source language and favoured the elimination of words of Arabic and Persian origin.[5] Despite this, Dalgado's texts demonstrate a dual impetus: in his declared position on etymology and philology, he saw Portuguese, Arabic, and Persian as non-indigenous imports; a view that was bolstered by this time by the work of William Jones, Max Müeller, and Dalgado's own correspondence with Grierson.

In the detailed discussions of the source of words, his stance seemed to vary, exploring instead how borrowings were mutual between languages, how they were not consistent or unilinear, and how the absorption of these, once they had entered into everyday use, enriched the language— not just Konkani, but also Portuguese. This approach, that suggested how European languages had also been transformed, seems to contrast with the definitive pronouncements on the superiority of Sanskrit as the only correct source language that should be used to restore Konkani to its purity (Dalgado 1893).[6] He emphasised instead the 'procreative elasticity of language and the persistent cooperative actions of

---

[4] Angelo de Gubernatis, *Savitri: An Indian Dramatic Idyll,* trans. J. Gerson da Cunha, Bombay: Ranina's Union Press, 1882. da Cunha had encountered the text through Angelo de Gubernatis' Italian translation and through Schlegel's critiques in French. See Filipa Lowndes Vicente, *Other Orientalisms: India Between Florence and Bombay, 1860–1900* (Orient Blackswan, 2012).

[5] This position is also repeated in a grammar of Konkani in the Kannada script. J. O. Pires' *Konkani Bhasheche Laghu Vyakaran* of 1907, which stated that the language would need to draw words from Sanskrit if it was to be taken to the level of Bengali.

[6] The introduction stated that 'having noticed similarities with Sanskrit – not just in scientific or religious terminology…, but in words and phrases in daily and domestic use..., 'Dalgado had written the dictionary to provide it to those who wanted a 'complete dictionary of a language so obscured, and altogether deserving of a better fate, as much for its intrinsic merit, as for being a unique rational and viable vehicle of popular instruction, particularly religious.'

man' that could produce innumerable words from diverse sources (ibid., xviii).[7]

The other pole of Dalgado's linguistic work was the insistence on Devanagari as the right script and Konkani as the language that was the only possible rational choice if popular instruction had to be promoted. His work in particular advocated the Jonesian system of transliteration as it was based on Sanskrit, and in comparison said that the early missionaries who had produced Konkani texts and Romanised versions of Konkani did not distinguish between different kinds of consonants and vowels (ibid., xii).[8]

A footnote to this analysis declared that not all Romanisation was transliteration because the sixteenth-century system represented the letter, while the Jonesian tried to reproduce the sound (ibid., xii).[9] The distinction made here was between the Romanisation of the early years of Portuguese colonial rule and the eighteenth-century German and English Orientalists. Dalgado also said that the tendency to see the Konkani of early doctrinal texts as a language that was between Konkani and Marathi was a perspective favoured by missionaries who considered it erroneously as the vulgar dialect of Goa (ibid., xiv).[10] To judge a language by this erroneous yardstick, said Dalgado, was 'to stretch it out on the bed of Procustes (sic) or to have it shod in another's shoes, making vices of its virtues thereby, and finding defects in its perfections.'[11]

---

[7] In other sections, p. xvii for instance, Dalgado would also say that Konkani, as with other Indo-Aryan languages did not have sufficient conceptual terms and that the dictionary used neologisms drawn from Sanskrit. On p. xx he stated that 'it would not make sense to exclude words that have been drawn from Portuguese entirely since they constitute almost a tenth of the vocabulary and it would horribly mangle the language, depriving it of a vast repertory' that was already in use. He also states on p. xxi that a work likes this may seem unnecessary in the case of languages with a large corpus of classical literature, but in the case of Konkani, 'an etymology is the unique and rational means to restore a language'.

[8] The preference for the Jonesian system since it was derived from Sanskrit, as opposed to the system of Lepsius, was also supported by Max Mueller.

[9] This is footnote 13 in the 1893 edition. Dalgado's view is echoed by most linguists such as Sardessai and Rocky Miranda who see the sixteenth century transliteration as systematic, but without differentiations between types of consonants that later methods would introduce.

[10] The footnote to this adds that this is also the opinion of Suriagy Anand Rau, Maffei, Pires and Murphy.

[11] Dalgado also suggested that a 'small philological examination of the old catechisms evidences its pronounced tendency towards Sanskritism. If it is a question of analogy, such analogy may be found also between Portuguese and Spanish, between Marathi and Gujarati.' p. xiv.

The potential impact of linguistic choices on nation formation is just one political situation to which both Dalgado and Mariano Saldanha (whose work is discussed below) responded. Their work accompanied and enabled the Catholic Church's response to this developing context by emerging as a patron of the Konkani language. In fact, Saldanha indicated in his introduction to the *Doutrina Christã*, that as Konkani had no pedagogic or official presence, were it not for the instruction received in catechism classes etc., the Konkani-speaking population would have had no semi-formal encounter with the written word. An additional influence was the Padroado-Propaganda conflict that divided the clergy within the Catholic Church. Though the cultural consequences of this conflict have yet to be sufficiently explored, it is known that this structural divide within the Catholic Church, had become the vehicle for the discussion of hierarchies of race, caste and language that defined the local church. It is possible therefore, that both Dalgado's and Saldanha's opposition to words of Persian or Hindustani origin were not an extension of majoritarian nationalism, but an indirect rejection of the anti-Portuguese thrust of the Propaganda mission, particularly in British-ruled territories. The adherence to Portuguese, Sanskrit and Konkani may well have been an attempt to champion a particular cultural heritage against its dissolution within the larger sphere of Catholic practice influenced by priests of the Propaganda Fide. Though it inevitably took the form of a distanced paternalism, these circumstances make it evident that this section of the elite did act strategically to respond to the changing political climate of the time.

Mariano Saldanha's *Doutrina Cristã* – the Konkani original and its corruption

In his introduction to the 1945 edition of the *Doutrina Christã* Mariano Saldanha (1945, 27) said that the language of Stephen's text, 'could be called Luso-concani', though he perhaps used the term to denote a cultural rather than a linguistic hybridity as later comments would suggest since it was the same book used by metropolitan Christians that was refurbished by the Jesuit Thomas Stephens, and 'offered to the Lusitanian metropolis of Eastern Christianity' or, Goa. For Saldanha, the simultaneity of textual production meant that it was this and not a Portuguese text that was the 'original' language text. He regretted that though it was from this text that generations of 'concani christians' drew their infant recitations, these were 'perpetuated not in the original which is today completely unknown, but by oral transmission more or less altered and reproduced in manuals whose authors are often in total ignorance of the revered name of the one who left the precious legacy.' (ibid., 27–28).[12]

He cited Dalgado, who said that the newer Konkani catechisms presented so many variations and rectifications to prosody, and glosses on abstruse terminology, that they were 'reproductions of oral formulations, deformed over time and not a re-edition of the old texts.' (ibid., 51). Saldanha's meticulously argued history mentions the existence of a Marathi *Doutrina* and a manuscript in Kannada characters in the form of a dialogue between Guru and 'Xixya', both of which he suggests are adaptations of Stephens *Doutrina*. He also cites a manuscript edition in France in both 'Canarim de Goa' and Portuguese, and an older manuscript from 1788 that he suggests is in 'Concanised' Marathi (ibid., 28-29). The evidence of these and other translations said Saldanha, was taken by the author of the eighteenth century *Oriente Conquistado* to be a sign of the greater popularity of Stephens' *Doutrina* over the earlier one by St. Francis Xavier.

However, the sense of Konkani as a language that had declined as it grew closer to the present was so acute, that Saldanha upheld the *Doutrina* as a sign that even foreigners were able to produce a text from within the resources of the language in the seventeenth century, without recourse to foreign words. He contrasted this to the language in the contemporary, which even when written by indigenous writers was lexically impoverished and saturated with foreign words (ibid., 33).

The sharpest criticism of recent editions is in section IV of the text, which traces errors that resulted in entirely different words and meanings, including some changes that Saldanha demonstrated, made no sense. He said that errors had only been produced in those

---

[12] Saldanha's text begins with a description of the continuing life of these early catechisms and *devocionários*, which, 'in a more or less modified form, continue till today to nourish faith and popular piety; its doctrine and its hymns and orations ... are still recited today and sung ...in shrines and in families, where the popular feasts of Sant'Ana, of Senhora do Monte, of Piedade and others, afforded the devotees the opportunity of tempering their devotion with ancient melodies of litanies and chants....' He cites the *Oriente Conquistado* (*Carta de Lourenço Peres, de Goa,* 17 Dez 1563 in *Cartas do Japão, Índia, etc., na Academia das Ciências, vol III.*) and other published letters of early Jesuits to say that students from the earliest colleges set up by the Jesuits used to sing the doctrine and recite it to their families and children. . Mariano Saldanha, ed., *Doutrina Cristã em língua concani por Tomás Estêvão* (Lisboa: Agência Geral das Colonias, 1945, 2).

Doutrina that were edited by indigenous speakers and this saddening state of affairs had to be rectified by issuing an authorised *Doutrina* afresh (ibid., 45). Saldanha offered his work as a fulfillment of this need, a salvaging of this early text that a language with scarce literary resources could not afford to lose; a text according to him, from which all others flowed (ibid., 48).[13] He noted however, that it was not his intention to restore the hieratic and antiquated Konkani of Stephens' text, in contravention of the natural evolution of the Konkani language. It would instead be a mixture of those usages that were preferable and had greater semantic value in the present and those that were so erroneous that they had to be replaced with recourse to the original.

Translating back as the way forward

The translation 'back' to different versions of Konkani was thus the way forward, particularly for children who did not learn Konkani in school. Even in the case of twentieth-century priests who cited a preference for the Portuguese text as the original, it was a preference for true and stable words for concepts that was being expressed rather than the idea of the Portuguese *Doutrina* as the source of authentic meaning.

Saldanha identifies three ways in which the early missionaries dealt with the relationship between words and concepts across languages: the first was to introduce Portuguese words where there seemed to be no equivalences, and the Portuguese terms were then habilitated into local pronunciation, as in the case of *bautism, resper, mis,* etc. The second was to find words that were so far from everyday use that they were closer to Sanskrit, and if they had entered into everyday usage, it was due to the missionaries who drew them into Christian signification. The final form of accommodation was to draw words that had definite usages in Hindu devotional practices into Christian usage, a strategy, said Saldanha, that 'scandalized listening christians, for whom it was a

---

[13] He qualified this lament by saying that not all alterations were necessarily corruptions and for this reason, the *Doutrina* had to be recovered through a comparison that he had carried out between texts of 1932, 1936 and 1941, issued by the Diocese of Bombay, Goa and Mangalore. Saldanha lists ten other *Doutrina* most of which were published between 1883 and 1921, of which at least five were in Konkani. (Saldanha, *Doutrina Cristã em língua concani* por Tomás Estêvão, 48).

profanation to apply names of pagan divinities and cults to their religion and God' (ibid., 34).[14]

Aware of this discomfort, Saldanha states, Diogo Ribeiro in his *Declaração* (a later version of the *Doutrina*) glosses the use of the word *Vaicuntha* (translated as paradise of Vishnu), arguing for its common usage among both common people and those who would well understand the provenance of the word. 'With the approval of the Holy Office', otherwise known for prohibiting texts that violated the laws of the Inquisition, 'the word that was formerly profane, was sanctified', said Ribeiro (ibid., 35).Yet after all, said Saldanha, Diogo Ribeiro himself always used *paraíso* (paradise) rather than *Vaicuntha* sensing perhaps that the latter could not capture the Christian sense of the word. In popular usage therefore, *Vaicuntha, deulla* and *guru* gave way to *suarga, igroz* and *padre*; the last two denoting a return to the option of adapting Portuguese words to Konkani usage (ibid., 36).

Different kinds of failure

Such concerns continued into the 1980s, but the ways in which each writer identified the problem with Konkani was different. For instance, the sense of the dispersal of the genius of the language that José Pereira mentions is different from Dalgado's late-nineteenth century critique of the form of transliteration used in early doctrinal texts as compared to the eighteenth-century Jonesian system. This in turn is different from both Dalgado's and Saldanha's mid- to late-twentieth century concern that the oral transmission of early doctrine had deviated sufficiently from the original texts, to introduce errors that were perpetuated when the corrupt oral form was rendered in print. The question of an original language or of the provenance of Konkani words and the preference for some source languages over others were facets of attempts to identify reasons for linguistic degradation and ways to overcome it. However, each of these approaches had different consequences for the reception of popular writing, and for the position the literati would adopt within nationalist linguistic forums and institutions.

An interest in linguistic rigour and standardisation as a foundation for literary production was not problematic in itself, especially when the impetus was to secure cultural and economic mobility. When attached to assumptions about the inadequate indigenousness of the

[14] *deulla* (temple) – *a igreja;* guru (priest) – o padre; *Vaicuntha* (paradise of Vishnu) – *o paraíso; Yamacundda* – o inferno)

Roman script, however, it resulted in formulations such as Cristovão Pinto's, which warned of the 'denationalisation' that occurred through a corrupted Roman script. From this perspective, there was an unquestioned association of Devanagari with indigenousness. A recent and significant discussion of the nature of philological debates around Marathi reveals that the question of the vernacular and its representation even within the sphere of Marathi writing was never a settled one, finding a different locus of authenticity from time to time.[15] However, the idea that the Roman script was non-indigenous was such a firmly-held belief, that it allowed for the rejection of popular Konkani to be represented as an objective failure that could be laid at the door of its less educated writers and speakers. All these arguments tended to be linked together in the works of the Goan literati.

Sebastião Rodolfo Dalgado (1855–1922) was a doctor in Canon and Civil law as well as a Sanskritist. His Hitopadesa *of 1897 was published by J. Bastos from Lisbon. In 1916,* História de Nala e Damaianti-episódio de Mahabharata *was published from Coimbra. Aside from his publications on Indo-Portuguese dialects in Daman and in Sri Lanka, Dalgado produced a number of texts on Konkani, such as the* Florilégio dos Provérbios Concani, *Coimbra, 1922,* Bouquet of Konkani Proverbs, *a* Gramática de Língua Concani *in 1922, the* Influência do Vocabulário Português em Línguas Asiáticas, *Coimbra, 1913, and the* Glossário Luso-Asiático, *Coimbra, 1919.*

The Diccionario Konkani-Portuguez-Philologico-Etymologico composto no alphabet Devanâgarî com a Translitteração segundo o systema Jonesiano *published in 1893 on the Indu-Prakash press in Bombay, was written in Devanagari with a transliteration into the Roman script following the Jonesian system. It is noteworthy that the book carried the official approval of the Bishop of Damão (Daman), also officiating as the Archbispo Primaz and Patriarcha das India's Orientaes.*

Dalgado stated that the tendency to see the Konkani of early doctrinal texts, as a language that was between Konkani and Marathi, was a perspective favoured by missionaries who considered it erroneously as the vulgar dialect of Goa. As Dalgado explained the choices he made while compiling this dictionary, his analysis of the kind of Konkani used in different missionary texts are of interest. Likewise, the impulse to remedy the lexically-impoverished popular idiom while trying to ensure that the dictionary was accessible to Konkani-speakers provides an interesting discussion of a range of available literature and linguistic theory.

The initial sections, until page xii, offer a rationale for the preference for Devanagari as an appropriate script. Dalgado's comparative and linguistically-

[15] Prachi Deshpande, *A Classical Past for a Modern Language: Historicizing Marathi* (November 2, 2017).

informed approach helps locate the sound values of Konkani consonants and vowels within a range of Indian and European languages. Latter sections of this introduction explain the choices he made when compiling the dictionary, and these sections not only reveal his assessment of early Konkani writing, but provide an account of the relationship between Konkani, Sanskrit and other languages such as Marathi and Gujarati. Dalgado's approach privileges Sanskirit as a primary language as a measure for comparisons and argues against seeing Marathi as anterior to Konkani.

Dalgado also noted the need to tap into those areas where the language was most productive, as with proverbs, in the case of Konkani. He asserted that being aware of almost all contemporary popular production in Konkani, his concern with everyday usage meant that his linguistic choices were directed towards ensuring that the language would see a proliferation in the number of words that could be generated.

Excerpt 7
Sebastião Rodolfo Dalgado, excerpt from the 'Introducção', *Diccionario Komkaṇî-Portuguez: Philologico-Etymologico composto no Alphabeto Devanâgarî com a translitteração segundo o Systema Jonesiano*, pp. ix–xxvi. Accessed from archive.org—archive.org/details/diccionariokomk00dalggoog/mode/2up.

INTRODUCÇÃO

No decurso do meu estudo do sanskríto, a que me tenho dedicado nas horas vagas desde que voltei d'Europa como missionario ultramarino, ha mais de oito annos, notei muitos pontos de analogia entre esta lingua e o idioma fallado em Gôa, hoje geralmente conhecido com o nome de *komkaṇî* ou concaní. E esta affinidade não se limitava á terminologia scientifica ou religiosa e á phraseologia elevada, mas se extendia á vocabulos e phrases de uso quotidiano e domestico, á construcção grammatical, ás declinações e conjugações.

Originou-se d'aqui em mim o desejo de indicar em um pequeno opusculo os principaes pontos de contacto entre uma e outra lingua, para que espiritos atilados com melhor estudo e mais vagar elaborassem um diccionario completo da lingua tão descurada, e todavia digna de melhor sorte, assim pelo seu merito intrinseco, como por ser o unico vehiculo racional e viavel da instrucção popular, especialmente religiosa.

Considerando porem mais pausadamente e tendo em vista a apathia que predomina em similhante materia, julguei dever eu mesmo me incumbir desse trabalho, que, sem ser um *thesaurus linguæ,* não tivesse nada a invejar á maioria das outras línguas indianas, pelo menos nas linhas geraes [(1)].

Surgiam porém muitas difficuldades para, levar a effeito o meu projecto e me fizeram mais d'uma vez sentir o peso da empresa....

p. x

A primeira e principal versava sobre a *logographia* do *komkaṇî.* A lingua no seu presente estado consiste mórmente na linguagem colloquial. A sua litteratura existente é quasi exclusivamente religiosa, posterior á dominação portugueza. Os antigos auctores que estudaram o *komkanî* denominado então, impropriamente, língua brahmana ou canarina, pelo maratha, e alguns pelo sanskrito, escreveram as suas obras no alphabeto romano com certo systema uniforme e quasi etymologico, se bem que nem sempre correcto, representando os sons peculiares por lettras dobradas ou italicas, sem estremar comtudo as vogaes longas das breves. Posteriormente foram dados á estampa alguns livros e folhetos sem nenhum methodo e até sem distincção das consoantes dentaes ecerebraes e dos sons aspirados e inaspirados, causando assim grandes embaraços para a sua corrente leitura e exacta intelligencia. Ultimamente foram inventados ou formulados alguns methodos mais ou menos imperfeitos ou complicados, que podem tera sua utilidade parcial sob o ponto de vista phonetico ou pratico.

Mas o *komkaṇî,* á guisa das outras línguas neo-aryanas, ou gauríanas, como as chama o professor Hoernle, devia ter tido alphabeto proprio ou indiano. Qual teria sido ? Não se sabe com certeza. Dizem que ha alguns livros antigos das communidades agricolas escriptos em caracteres canarís[(2)]. Mas isto se explica facilmente por razões de dominação, commercio e visinhança.

O canarí, posto que tenha os mesmos sons e o mesmo numero de lettras que o maratha e mais duas vogaes, e possa fielmente, e talvez melhor, representar o *komkaṇî,* pertence á familia dravidíana, e a

[1] "Mas antes de nos accusarem dessa ousadia," dizia Cunha Rivara em 1859 (na sua Prefação á Grammatica da Lingua Concaní, escripta por um missionario italiano) "accusem-se primeiro a si proprios de incrivel negligencia aquelles, que podendo e devendo cultivar a sua lingua materna, obram tanto pelo contrario, que não só não promovem o seu estudo, mas por um phenomeno singular entre as nações policiadas totalmente e desprezam, e a abandonam á corrupção da cega barbaridade." E d'alli para cá não tem havido notavel mudança, a não ser a publicação de alguns periodicos na lingua vernacula.

[2] J. Gerson da Cunha, *The Koṅkaṇî Language and Literature,* p. 41. – Suriagy Ananda Rau, *Grammatica da Lingua Maratha,* p. xxii do Prefacio.

lingua de Gôa é evidentemente do ramo aryano(3). O seu alphabeto, portanto, devia ser o devanâgarî, como o é das outras línguas irmãs, com alguma diversidade da configuração de lettras(4).

p. xi

Na ignorancia pois do primitivo alphabeto do komkaṇî, julguei que devia adoptar o maratha *bâlabodha*,que pouco differe do devanâgarî propriamente dito, em que são impressos os livros do sanskrito na presidencia de Bengala e na Europa; e isto pelas seguintes razões: 1.ª porque ha muita gente que já o sabe; 2.ª porque n'elle são impressos os livros sanskritos na presidencia de Bombaim; 3.ª porque facilita o estudo demaratha aos que o não têem, bem assim o de guzerathe(5).

O alphabeto devanâgarî, tal como é usado no sanskrito, tem tão sómente um som para cada lettra, no que consiste a sua principal perfeição. No komkaṇi, porém, ha quatro consoantes com dois sons bem distinctos e diversos: च , *cha* e *tsa,* छ, *chha* e *tsha,* ज, *ja* e *za,* झ, *jha* e *zha.* Mas este inconveniente se nota tambem n'outros idiomas neo-aryanos, com a differença que no *komkaṇî* os sons são subordinados a certas regras fixas e faceis, expendidas no proprio logar, e as excepções

---

[3] O alphabeto da lingua tamul, que é a principal entre as dravidianas, tendo só trinta symbolos proprios e mais quatro adoptados do sanskrito não pode assumir a paternidade do da canarí, que é inteiramente talhado pela norma do devanâgarî.-"The Konkani language was formerly written with the language called Bālbōdha or Nāgar; sometimes it was written with the Modi Alphabet, which is the Mahrāṭṭi Alphabet. Now the Kanarese Alphabet is generally used, and although it does not express all Konkani sounds, yet it is better adopted for this than the Latin Alphabet." Angelus Maffei, *A Konkani Grammar*,p. 1

[4] E é neste alphabeto que apparece um attestado passado por tres brahmanes de Cochim na lingua de Gôa sobre o *Hortus Indicus Malabaricus* de H. Van Rheede, impresso em Amsterdam em 1678; bem como os nomes das plantas de que trata a mesma obra.-"The Indian Alphabet is a marvellous and magnificent phenomenon quite unrivalled in the world...This Alphabet represents a symmetrical combination of symbols, designed by skilled Grammarians to indicate various shades of sounds, and is grouped in scientific order. The hand of a Brahmanical Scholar, dealing with a highly polished Language is detected here."Robert Cust, *Linguistic and Oriental Essays*, Second Series p. 27.

[5] E' na verdade estranhavel que não se tenha dado nenhuma importancia até hoje em Gôa, não obstante a facilidade da acquisição, ao conhecimento da lingua e litteratura sanskrita, nem o governo se tenha compenetrado daconveniencia da creação de uma cadeira, para o seu ensino, em quanto no mundo civilisado o seu estudo anda actualmente quasi a par do da grega e da latina. (*Cfr.* Max Müller, India, *what can it teach us?* Lecture I).

são pouquissimas[(6)]. As linguas europeas tambem, não exceptuando até a latina, têem *c* e *g* com dois sons. Não achei, portanto, necessario, e mesmo pensei mal cabido, excogitar novos signaes graphicos para estremar os dois sons, como fez o padre Maffei, sem embargo de admittir que o alphabeto maratha é o proprio da lingua[(7)].

Alem disto, a lingua de Gôa tem dois sons peculiares, que não se acham em nenhuma outra língua indiana([8]). Taes são os de ए *e* e *o* abertos[(9)]. E' verdade que no canarí ha lettras especiaes para designer assim o *e* e ऑ*o* longos, como breves. Egualmente, alguns idiomas neo-aryanos, como bengalí, o sindhí, o orya, têem o *e* e *o* breves, se bem que a sua occurrencia seja muito rara, sem lettras peculiares para os caracterisar[(10)] Mas ha muita differença, como é obvio, ainda que ás vezes se confunda no uso, entre o som breve e aberto.

p. xii

Posto que seja da natureza do alphabeto perfeito que cada lettra de que se compõe represente uma é unica voz simples da sua respectiva lingua, como o é, por exemplo, no sanskrito, todavia na actualidade não se encontra quasi nenhuma lingua viva, cujas lettras, pelo menos vogaes; não tenham mais de um som. Entre as linguas europeas o italiano leva as lampas na correspondencia dos seus sons e symbolos. Mas o proprio italiano tem o *e* e *o* abertos e fechados sem nenhuma regra geral que os distingua. Relativamente perfeito será pois o alphabeto que tiver regras breves, faceis e invariaveis para marcar a diversa phonese de cada lettra. O Koṁkaṇî não é uma excepção ao principio universal. Tem porém a vantagem de designar, sem criar confusão, quaes os casos em que as referidas vogaes têem o som aberto. Julguei por isso superfluo inventar mais dois caracteres para o denotar.

Mas a maioria dos que fallam Koṁkaṇî não conhecendo ao presente os caracteres marathas, tornava-se necessario represental-o, e podem ser pelo alphabeto romano, mais conhecido. Ha varios systemas

---

[6] *Vid.* Ganpotráo H. Navalkar, *The Student's Marathi Grammar,* p. 5. – Suriagy *opere ci.* pp. 17 e 18.

[7] *A Konkani-English Dictionary,* pp. 6 e 8.-A *Konkani Grammar,* p.1.

[8] Apprehende o padre Maffei, na sua citada grammatica, que as vogaes do Koṁkaṇi têem quatro, cinco e até seis sons diversos, o que, a ser verdade, seria phenomenal na linguistica oriental.

[9] No Sanskrito estas vogaes são sempre longas.

[10] *The Journal of the Royal Asiatic Society of Great Britain and Ireland,* col. 11, p. 296. – J. F. Browne, *A Bengali Primer·,* p. 8. – 0 singhalí, ou chingali, que commummente os philologos classificam entre os sanskritoides tem quatro sons de *e* com outros tantos caracteres, mas nenhum destes é aberto. *Cfr.* C. Chounavel, *A Grammar of the Sinhalese Language,* pp. xi. e 2 Rev. C. Alves, *The Sinhalese Hand-Book,* p. xi.

de *romanisação,* e podem ser inventados sem grande difficuldade muitos outros. Qual devia adoptar? Bem ponderado o assumpto, achei preferivel o da romanisação translitteral de Sir William Jones, muito superior ao do professor Lepsius, posto que fosse excogitado primariamente para a transcripção do Sanskrito :1.º porque é commummente seguido pelos orientalistas ainda na romanisação das linguas vernaculas; 2.ºporque é mais simples e mais em harmonia com o alphabeto devanâgarî; 3.º porque facilita o estudo do sanskrito, que alem de ser a língua das linguas, na phrase de Max Müller, é para ó Koṁkaṇî o que o latim é para o portuguez ou italiano(11).

Optado uma vez o systema jonesiano para a translitteração do Koṁ kaṇi como subordinado ao alphabeto devanâgarî, decididamente superior ao latino, empenhei-me em applical-o sem nenhuma modificação, que longe de simplificar embaraçaria a escripturação e a leitura, e destruiria aquella perfeita consononcia que deve existir entre um e outro alphabeto, para que

p. xiii

a transliteração sorta o seu desejado effeito(12). Assim, não distingui por signaes, o que aliás seria facil, o som dento-palatal de च *cha* e ज *ja,* nem *o* aberto de ए *e* e ओ *o.* Dei porém as regras e notei as excepções. Nem mesmo supprimi, como se costuma fazer no maratha e outros idiomas congeneres, o *a* final, que é sempre mudo, e o medio, que o fosse, pela simples razio, que tal lettra estava inherente á consoante devanâgarî(13). Não ha comtudo nenhum incoveniente

---

11 "I naturely decided to follow that system which was so modestly put forth by Sir William Jones in the first volume of the 'Asiatic Researches' and has since, with slight modifications, not always improvements, been adopted by "the greatest Oriental scholars in India, England, and the Continent....In "reading that essay, written about eighty years ago, one is surprised to see how well its author was acquainted with all that is really essential either in the physiological analysis or in the philological definition of alphabet...The points on which I differ from Sir W. Jones are of very small consequence. They arise from habit rather that from principle....I am glad to find that in the second edition of his 'Standard Alphabet' Professor Lepsius bas acknowledged the practical superiority of the system of Sir W. Jones in several important points, and I think he will find that his own system may be still further improved." 'Max Müller, *Science of the Language*, vol. II, p.178, edição de 1899.

12 Não é verdade, como suppõe Phillipe Neri Pires na sua *Grammatica Maratha,* que o polysono alphabeto inglez é a base deste systema, que tem pornorma o latino.

13 Releva muito não confundir a translitteração e a romanisação, que se distinguem como a especie do genero. Nem toda a romanisação é translitteração: esta representa a lettra, aquella o som. A symbolisação caracteristica dos dois sons de *ch* e *j* poderia ser romanisação, mas não translitteração.

em seguir o uso geral, especialmente quando se escrever só nos caracteres romanos[(14)].

Não ha duvida que tomando o portuguez como prototypo parecera a muitos diffuso e embaraçoso o presente systema de translitteração. Por exemplo, poder-se-hia substituir a nasal ṁ por um til sobre a vogal precedente[(15)], e omittir a constante distincção de ई e ऊ longos sem affectar o som, como se faz na escripta *moḍî.*

Mas uma lingua oriental não tem de se guiar por nenhuma lingua europea. O koṁkaṇî deve ser escripto no proprio alphabeto devanâgarî (ou análogo, canarí); e quando for necessario romanisal-o, deve-se seguir um tal systema que é já adoptado de commum acordo para a lingua-mãe e outras vernaculas, para conservar com manifesta utilidade pratica as relações da familia[(16)].

De resto, quando se trata de reduzir á systema a escripturação d'uma lingua que ainda está na infancia ou na renascença, e nem mesmo é definida nas linhas geraes, o que se requer sobre tudo não é a economia de umas poucas lettras ou signaes diacriticos, mas sim a clareza, a distincção, a regularidade e a uniformidade no seu conjuncto.

p. xiv

Verdade é que muitas vezes difficuldades typographicas de imprensas ordinarias podem demandar a modificação ou alteração de certos caracteres e signaes orthographicos. Mas isto, longe de ser uma perfeição real, não passa d'uma mera necessidade adventicia e ephemera, que tambem pode variar de imprensa para imprensa. Para obviar esses incovenientes têem sido propostos varios planos de alphabeto commum, nenhum delles generalisado, sendo mais recommendavel pela sua simplicidade e clareza o do professor Max Müller, que todavia não o segue[(17)].

---

14 Applicando ao *Padre Nosso* este systema abreviado com a supressão de *a* mudo e simplificado com a omissão do accento sobre *i* e *u* longos, teremos a sua escripta concebida do seguinte modo: *Âmchyâ Bâpâ tuṁ sorgâr âsây, tujeṁ nâṁv thor jâṁv, tujeṁ râj âmkâṁ yevuṁ, tuji ...*

15 Mas então dever-se-hia ou supprimir o accento circumflexo ou combinal-o com o til por um typo apropriado.

16 "The idea of substituting a modified Roman Character bristling with dots, accents, and italics, may be relegated to the Greek Kalends."-Cust, *op. cit.* p. 417.-"If we write Konkani with Kanarese or Mahrāṭṭi letters, many things will be settled by themselves, *i.e.* only by writing in a more suitable Alphabet, especially if we prefer the Mahrāṭṭi or Sanskrit; because with Kanarese something would remain still doubtful." Maffei, *A Koṇkani Grammar*.

17 *Science of Language. – Survey of Language,* edição of 1855.

Fixado o alphabeto e o systema da translitteração, a outra difficuldade versava sobre a organisação do *vocabulario.* O *koṁkaṇî,* como e sabido, tem passado por varias phases historicas, e anda fraccionado na sua uniformidade não só pelas provincias, mas até pelas aldeas e classes. Não chegaram ainda ao acordo os eruditos em classificar a linguagem dos *purâṇas* christãos, querendo uns que seja o *koṁkaṇî* normal, de que o presente é a corrupção levada ao extremo; opinando outros que é o mixto do sanskrito, maratha e *koṁkaṇî;* e mantendo mais alguns, talvez com melhor razão, que é o maratha do Konkão, tendo cá e lá uns resaibos do *koṁkaṇî* propriamente dito[(18)]. A prosa dos livros antigos tambem differe immenso da língua que actualmente se falla, não só na phraseologia, mas ainda na morphologia, parecendo occupar um logar medio entre o *koṁkaṇi* e o maratha, por que estudaram os missionarios a lingua de Gôa, considerando-a erradamente seu dialecto vulgar[(19)].

Alem disto, cada provincia, cada localidade tem seus idiotismos, suas peculiaridades linguisticas. Nas Novas Conquistas, em Savantvadi, no districto de Ratnagiri, a língua se resente do maratha. No Canará do norte e do sul importa em grande escala do canarí, tulú e hindustaní. Salcete (de Gôa) tem muitas suas especialidades. O concelho das Ilhas está muito aportuguezado. Ajunte-se a isto o distinctivo phraseologico de varias classes ou castas, e conceber-se-ha claramente quão intrincado será

p. xv

o trabalho de apurar, sem ferir susceptibilidades egoisticas, a verdadeira forma e a exacta pronuncia no meio de tantas cambiantes[(20)].

---

[18] Dr. Gerson da Cunha, *op. cit.* p. 29.-Suriagy Rau, *Diccionario Maratha-Portuguez,* no prefacio. – *Grammatica da Lingua Concani* do padre T.Estevão, editada por Rivara, p. ccxxxiv.

[19] Desta opinião são tambem Suriagy, Pires, Murphy, padre Maffei, devotado cultor do *koṁkaṇî.* Ora analysando a lingua por similhante padrão, nada mais consentaneo com a razão do que extendel-a no leite de Procustes ou calçal-a com cothurnos alheios, apodando de vicios as suas virtudes e de defeitos as suas perfeições. Os effeitos desse processo são patentes, e um catecismo ultimamente composto, se bem que de grande merito *in se,* os torna bem salientes. Um pequeno exame philologico dos antigos catecismos evidencia a sua pronunciada tendencia para o sanskritismo. Se é questão de analogia, tal analogia se dá tambem entre o portuguez e o hespanhol, entre o maratha e o guzerathe. "Mas se deben consultar gramaticas, diz Hervas *(Catalogo,* tom. 1 p. 65) para conocer su carecter proprio por medio de su artificio grammatical."

[20] Diz a proposito o missionario italiano na sua citada Grammatica (p. 144). "'A 2.ª difficuldade a hum estrangeiro é a diversidade de muitas vozes e de muitas

Procurando ser sobranceiro a todos os preconceitos e tratar do assumpto com a devida imparcialidade, tomei como o ponto de partida a lingua tal como é ao presente fallada na provincial de Bardez, que na opinião geral a conserva melhor, notando no proprio logar os termos exclusiva ou principalmente usados n'outras partes. E como o meu decidido empenho era fazer um diccionario pronunciadamente etymologico(21) e sanskritisar quanto possivel a lingua, no que julgava consistir a sua pureza e perfeição, tomei por norma considerar como mais puro o vocabulo que mais se approximasse da sua origem typica, e caracterisar as suas variações phoneticas como corrupções ou abreviações, posto que algumas destas tenham a sua razão de ser pelo processo genesetico dos idiomas prakritos, que tambem têem a sua lei similhante á de Grimm. Assim, applicando este methodo, dei *udika* (agua) como corrupção de *udaka,* que é como se vê no sanskrito; preferi *dâra* (porta) a *dera,* porque temos, na lingua-mãe *dvâra,* que perdendo pela regra um dos elementos da lettra composta se reduz a *dâra;* marquei *akamâna* (affronta) e *śeguṇa* (virtude) como aberrações de *apamâna* e *suguna;* puz *askata* (fraco) e *śakata* (força) como barbarismos de aśakta e *śakti.*

Não quero porém pretender com isto que notei minuciosamente todas as variantes verbaes, o que seria fastidioso e improficuo, mas sim as mais importantes e communs e taes que se poderiam classificar como formas justificaveis nos idiomas vernaculos.

Não podia, com tudo, desprezar totalmente a litteratura puranica e antiga, que contem um grande thesouro de vocabulos muito uteis, e necessarios até, quando se tratar de restaurar devidamente a lingua e banir o abuso de lusitanismos, que muitas vezes não se coadunam com o seu genio oriental. Introduzi varias vozes extrahidas principalmente do Purana do

p. xvi

padre Estevão, que é *facile princeps* no seu genero, e é inteiramente vasado nos moldes dos poemas marathas de Dnyânobâ e de

---

frases, que ha entre as diversas tribus; pois quasi cada tribu, como tem os seus diversos modos no vestir, comer, e outros usos da vida, assim tambem os tem na falia. A 3.ª difficuldade é a diversidade, que se acha em diversas regiões de Concanã no uso de muitas frases e palavras, que em huma parte usão, em outra não; em huma parte usão em um sentido, em outras em outro."

21 O systema phonetico é bom e desejaval (e condiz com a indole das linguas indianas), quando se conheça a exacta phonologia da loquela. Mas quando os tympanos, e ás vezes a lingua, são embotados a ponto de não distinguir o som de varias lettras, tal systema confundirá necessariamente varias vozes bem distinctas. Cumpre pois conhecer primeiro a orthophonia da lingua e depois regular a sua orthographia phonetica.

Muktesvar; e umas poucas do Purana do padre Francisco Vaz de Guimarães, se bem que nãotenha tanto valor como o outro, nem sirva para o estudo da lingua, por sermenos classico e estar recheado de arabismos e iranismos. Escolhi de preferencia os termos *tadbhâvas,* que exprimem a forma litteraria e representam os *tatsamas* ou corrupções do sanskrito em voga na linguagem colloquial, e os que são importados da religião brahminica para designer os da christã, sem occasionar nenhuma censura ou reparo[(22)].

Em quanto á prosa antiga, por maiores diligencias que empreguei, só pude ter á mão umas poucas obras. D'entre essas prestei mais attenção ao *Jardim dos Pregadores* do padre Miguel d'Almeida, impresso em 1658, e delle extrahi a maior parte dos vocabulos dados como antigos, porque era pela sua naturesa destinada para o povo, que o devia facilmente entender, não obstante a sua pronunciada tendencia para o marathismo, assim na estructura syntaxica, como no aspecto morphologico. Ajuntei mais algumas tiradas da Grammatica do padre Estevão e d'um velho diccionario manuscripto Portuguez – *koṁkaṇî,* provavelmente o dos jesuitas[(23)].

Pelo que toca aos termos poeticos, quasi todos se referem aos hymnos e canticos religiosos, alguns dos quaes de subido valor litterario e linguistico colligidos em um opusculo pelo meu particular amigo, P.[e] Lucio Francisco Vas, de Orlim, que me ministrou tambem varias outros materiaes.

Sendo o *koṁkaṇî,* como actualmente é fallado, muito deficiente em vocabulos genuinos para exprimir varios conceitos e para corresponder ao diccionario Portuguez-koṁkaṇî, que estou elaborando, tive de importar muitos neologismos, mórmente do sanskrito, que na terminologia está para os idiomas indianos ainda do grupo tureniano, na mesma razão como o grego para as linguas europeas, tendo demais a vantagem de serem de facil intelligencia os elementos constitutivos dos termos[(24)].

---

[22] "Amongst the numerous terms of the Hindú religion and theology Christian preachers and translators will recognize several as correspondent to the terms of the true faith and competent to convey their import." Molesworth, *A Dictionary, Maratha and English,* p. xx.

[23] Dos livros modernos não me escapou quasi nenhum, quer seja cathecismo, devocionario, ou manual quer seja vocabulario, historia ou fabula.

[24] Every person acquainted with the spoken speech of India knows perfectly well that its elevation to the dignity and usefulness of written speech has depended, and must still depend upon its borrowing largely from its parent or kindred source, that no man who is ignorant of Arabic or Sanskrit can write Hindustani or Bengali with elegance or purity, or precision." H. H Wilson, *Asiatic Journal, vol.* xix, p. 15.

p. xvii

O poderio portuguez exerceu grande influxo e deixou rastos indeleveis nas principaes linguas da India. Com a nova civilisação entraram novos vocabulos para significar objectos até então desconhecidos ou pouco vulgarisados. Adoptaram-se tambem muitas palavras portuguezas, quando não faltavam as suas correspondentes vernaculas, ou podiam sem difficuldade ser cunhadas com os proprios elementos. Geralmente os lexicographos ou omittem a maior parte d'esses vocabulos por não serem classicos ou germanos, ou os dão como provenientes d'outro idioma indiano.

O *koṁkaṇî* occupa, como era de esperar, um logar proeminente na apropriação do portuguez. Um decimo, e talvez maia, da linguagem conversacional consta de palavras portuguezas ou derivadas das portuguezas. Como devia proceder a seu respeito na coordenação do diccionario ? Omittil-as totalmente, como fez um auctor[(25)], seria esphacelar horrivelmente a lingua privando-a do vasto repertorio que está na bocca de toda a gente. Introduzir todos os termos, muitos dos quaes são usados sem nenhuma necessidade, ou por mal cabido alarde ou por reprehensivel ignorancia doproprio idioma materno, seria avolumar consideravelmente o diccionario e avultar o seu preço (o que possivelmente devia procurar evitar para o tornar accessivel ao povo), e sobretudo seria desfigurar e desnaturalisar a obra com elementos exoticos, que não lhe augmentariam o merecimento.

Era necessario, portanto seguir uma via intermedia. Admitti: 1.º todas as vozes que, além do *koṁkaṇî,* eram usadas em uma ou mais linguas orientaes, por ser indicio seguro da necessidade ou conveniencia de taes vozes[(26)]; 2.º todos os vocabulos de tal modo naturalisados que andam na bocca de todos, sem até se atinar na sua proveniencia, adoptados ou para marcar uma linha divisoria entre os christãos e os hindús, ou por não se achar o termo vernaculo adequado, ou por não ser commummente conhecido, ou para evitar o incommodo de o cunhar[(27)]; 3.º muitas palavras

---

[25] Ignacio Xavier de Souza Rodrigues, *Diccionario Concani-Portuguez*. Escaparam-lhe todavia algumas palavras, como : cruz, cavouqueiro, esquadro, leilão, teima, tijolo

[26] Ha porém varios vocabulos adoptados n'outras linguas indianas quo não têem cabimento na de Gôa ; taes como, no maratha : armada, barquinha, tronco (cadeia), jogar por jogo; no singhalí: atalaia, assucar, avano, balde, bastão, burro, caldeirão, canastra, leito, lençol, sarampo, tacho, trigo, etc. ; no bengalí: habito, quintal; no hindustaní: carabina, compasso, pão, prego; no tamul: almondega, estante, sotaina, trave.

[27] Taes são : pai, tio, irmão, mana, cunhado, padrinho, madrinha, afilhado, vigario, sermão, padeiro, pedreiro, cavouqueiro, arma, arame, purga, pegão, etc;

que são mais usadas do que as suas respectivas vernaculas[28]; 4.º mais algumas

p. xviii

inteiramente desnecessarias, para mostrar que a lingua tem muitas para a representar e que só o culpavel desleixo ou o pedantismo as podia empregar([29]). Exclui porém muitos vocabulos que não eram geralmente usados pelo povo, bem assim os ecclesiasticos, os administrativos, os forenses, os militares e os de varias artes e officios.

Formado assim o plano dos materiaes, restava dar-lhes a devida disposição e conveniente forma, tendo principalmente em vista e clareza, a concisão e a similaridade com o portuguez.

...

p. xix

Como tive em mira abranger o maior numero possivel de vocabulos portuguezes, para que não se julgasse que faltavam os seus correlativos no *komkaṇi,* for necessario introduzir muitos synonymos, que aliás pareceriam escusados. Evitei porém, ainda com o risco de ser obscuro algumas vezes extiradas definições e descripções e até phrases longas.

Sobre tudo, dei muita importancia á phraseologia idiomatica da lingua, em que consiste a sua principal belleza e opulencia[31]. O que se exprimiria em portuguez por um simples verbo ou substantivo verbal, em *komkaṇi* de ordinario se enuncia com o nome auxiliado de verbos, taes como: fazer, ser, pôr tirar, dar, deixar, tocar, bater, quebrar, pegar. Se bem que introduzi uma grande copia de similhantes phrases, omittindo as que admittem a traducção litteral, não tenho comtudo a presumpção de ter esgotado amateria.

Espero que não parecerá estranha a inserção de taes phrases nos nomes,em quanto que nas línguas europeas são postas nos verbos, assim porque osverbos que entram na sua composição são mui poucos, como porque, segundo a índole da lingua, os verbos concluem a phrase. Achei por isso mais congruente expol-as, bem como as maximas e os proverbios, na palavra inicial salvo quando esta seja uma particula ou voz incidental.

---

[28] Taes são : cantar, rezar, acabar, tempo, calor, feitiço, etc.

[29] Omitti comtudo dar os correspondentes de alguns vocabulos portuguezes, pois que isto propriamente relata ao segundo volume.

[31] Para se convencer desta asserção basta referir-se aos seguintes artigos: *âṁka, kâna, hâlîja, ghara, jîbha, jîra, ḍolo, takalî, toṁḍa, dâṁta, nâṁva, path, pâṁya, poṭa, mana, raga, lajja, vâta, hâta.*

Em certos casos obvios tão sómente indiquei no fim doa significados, á imitação de Molesworth, os verbos que de preferencia se empregam nouso do vocabulo e ordinariamente não se comformam com os portuguezes.

p. xx

E' facil a formação de similhantes phrases, que não têem nada de peculiar.

Os adagios e os proverbios constituem o repertorio em que se acham conglobadas a philosophia e a erudição d'um povo, e por onde se afere com exactidão a natureza e o grau da sua civilisação. Quem os conhece mais e applica melhor do que o commum da gente passa por sabio e douto. A prova escorada n'um proverbio não reconhece refutação que não se funde n'outro proverbio de maior ou egual peso e acceitação. O oriente prima notoriamente neste genero de litteratura, como attestam o *Paṁchataṁtra* e o *Hitopadeśa*[32].

O *koṁkaṇî* possue um sem numero delles e de todos os matizes. Muitos se baseam n'um facto historico ou fabuloso *(kahâṇî)*, e não se percebem sem o conhecimento da sua origem. Uns são communs a diversos povos, outros peculiares ao de Gôa ; uns são a traducção dos portuguezes, e outros têem data recente. Alguns devem soar chulos ou obscenos aos ouvidos da educação europea. Ha muitos que não têem os seus equivalentes nas linguas d'Europa. Ha alguns que são obscuros ou indefinidos e sujeitos a varias interpretações e versões.

Escolhi os mais salientes e usuaes, dei os seus correspondentes, equivalentes ou approximados em portuguez, latim ou alguma outra língua europea, e quando não me occorreram, traduzi-os ora livremente, ora litteralmente, sem entrar nas suas explanações.

Assim como os homens, as palavras tambem têem a sua biographia, ás vezes muito interressante e curiosa, sem o cabal conhecimento da qual a existencia e mesmo o conceito de algumas dellas seria um mysterio linguistico. O *koṁkaṇî* se gloria de possuir muitas deste jaez, cuja noção, ainda que succinta, concorre poderosamente para apreciar o valor philologico da lingua. Eu porém me limitei só a umas poucas, mais usuaes, dando em notas a sua composição, e historia[33].

---

[32] "Beyond all valuation are the Proverbs and the Phrases appearing in the dictionary. Not only do they serve as examples and authorities for the senses given, and this service is exceeding great, but they declare the people declare more than could many volumes of description-their manners and customs, sentiments and judgments and modes of reasoning and thinking." Molesworth.

[33] Vid. *ajarâvara, aṁtashkaraṇa karavalî, kalâraṁta, chuḍedâna, tinasâna donapâra, purāṇa, biramata, madhyâhna, lâbha, sâ*, etc.

As preposições e as particulas, os prefixos e os suffixos, uns derivados do sanskrito, alguns communs ao maratha e outros privativos do *koṁkaṇî,* que entram largamente na estructura da lingua e demonstram irrefragavelmente a sua procedencia e indole constituem um fecundo nucleo, que pela propria elasticidade procreativa e pela persistente acção cooperadora do homem pode produzir um semnumero de vocabulos analogos e até diversos com cunho nacional, supprindo desta arte a sua apparente deficiencia.

p. xxi

E' por isso indispensavel a clara intelligencia da sua natureza, da sua significação original e primaria e dos seus usos e applicações. Tratei pois detalhadamente destas vozes, bem como de algumas locuções com variadas *nuances* de sentidos, explicando por extenso a sua composição e virtude productiva e illustrando com muitos exemplos o seu emprego[(34)].

A etymologia foi, como já mencionei, o que me induziu a elaborar o presente diccionario, que concebido no modesto plano, directamente tendente a mostrar a origem dos principaes vocabulos do *koṁkaṇi* e a sua analogia com a irmã primogenita da familia indo-europea, foi assumindo gradualmente as actuaes proporções, sem comtudo, mesmo com dar um appendice, ter eu o desvanecimento de haver abrangido todo o vocabulario.

Parecerá talvez á primeira vista trabalho inteiramente improficuo o investigar donde uma palavra vem e qual a sua genealogia, por quanto para todos os fins praticos basta saber o que é, qual a sua natureza e potencialidade significativa. Ora isto poderá ser verdade, se se trata de uma lingua que, como a latina ou a portugueza, está já organisada e definida em todas as suas partes, e possue uma vasta litteratura classica sobre variados ramos de artes e sciencias, e diccionarios de auctoridade incontestavel, compilados sobre bases seguras e incontrovertiveis. Não acontece porém o mesmo,quando é mister recompor uma lingua desorganisada com os seus elementos em parte olvidados, em parte desfigurados e em parte estropeados, e com os auxílios externos razoavelmente reclamados, e reconduzil-a ao seu pristino estado de perfeição, de que mostra inequivocos vislumbres no meio das brumas que a obumbram. Então a etymologia longe de ser um assumpto de vã erudição, toma-se uma

---

[34] Taes são d'entre outros : *a, apa, ara, âṁta, ud, upa, ku, cha, chera, cho, jâya, jâyato, dur, najo, naya, nâ, nâkû, nis, paṇa, pra, prati, phâvuṁka, be, ya, re, vi, sara, sâṇa,* su, so, *sva.*

necessidade impreterivel e o unico meio racional e efficaz para a methodica restauração da lingua. Eis como: 1.º determina a exacta estrutura do vocabulo, e, por conseguinte, a sua correlativa phonese, evitando assim muitas homonymias apparentes, que provem da sua ignorancia(35); 2.º precísa a sua significação original e primaria e suggere as modificações secundarias compativeis com o conceito radical(36); 3.º define quaes termos são organicos e quaes exoticos, quaes classicos e quaes vulgares, no que consiste exclusivamente a differença especifica de muitos

p. xxii

synonymos(37); 4.º aponta a norma de formar phrases com elementos identicos ou analogos, como se pode verificar com uma ligeira referencia ao diccionario(38).

Acresce a isto uma razão extrinseca, não de pequeno peso nas actuaes circunstancias, e vem a ser : que não uma algaravia, um *jargon sans raison d'être*, como o sestro de ridiculisar ás vezes inculca, a lingua que ostenta tão illustre, prosapia, e mesmo nos andrajos em que filhos desnaturados a deixaram, timbra de ser digna filha de tão nobre mãe, de que recebeu por legitima partilha, e não a titulo de emprestimo ou esmola, a selecta porção de vocabulos que constituem o *substractum* dos mais cultos membros da familia aryana. Muitas palavras (taes como : pai, mãe, padre, hora, seringa) que tomâmos por portuguezas, partiram nos tempos prehistoricos das ribanceiras do Indo, passaram na sua excursão cosmopolita para a Pelasgia e Ausonia, e devassando a Lusitania voltaram com novo trage para a Âryavârtta. E quando os polidos romanos diziam: *Deus; tu; non; frater, gener, socera, nepos; ignis, aura; dies, hiems; cor, pens, dens, donum; novus; duo, tres, septem, novem*, etc. não faziam mais do que repetir as nossas dicções de casa : *Deva, tûm* ; *nâ; bhâva, jâṁ*

---

[35] D'onde procede que ouvidos embotados não distinguem entre *gado, godo, ghado* e *ghoḍo*, entre *garo* e *goro, âṁgâcho* e *hâṁgacho, bâta* e *bhâta, âda* e *hâḍa, vaḍa* e *vhaḍa* ou *hoḍa*.

[36] D'aqui se percebe porque muitas vozes da procedencia sanskrita se prestam, por uma progressão natural e scientifica, a numerosas accepções, que n'outras linguas têem vocabulos especiaes.

[37] Isto dá a razão de varios polyonomos, como, por exemplo: *dishṭa e nadara, nâda e âvâja, apamâna* e *bemâna, grâsa* e *gâṁsa, patí e ghora, patîna* e *bâila, putra* ou *pûta* e *chedo, krodha* e *kîṁva, pâna* e *kholo, anna* e *khâṇa, dagdakashṭa* e *ghâsa hûsa.*

[38] Deve-se porem observar que alguns compostos, que são dados como de origem sanskrita, são de formação moderna, como o é a terminologia grega com os materiaes suppridos pela lingua classica.

vaya, sâsû, nâtû; âga, vâreṁ; disa, hiṁva; harḍeṁ, pâṁya, dâṁta; dâna; navo; dona, tína, sâta, nava[39] E quem não ficará admirado de ver que *hydro* é o nosso *udaka, metro* o nosso *mejapa* e *siringa* o nosso *śiṁga?*

Guiado pois pelo principio etymologico, tive de modificar mais d'uma vez a escripta de alguns vocabulos, quando posteriormente descobri a sua origem, como tambem de alterar os significados, mórmente sendo abstractos e genericos, que antes havia adduzido por meras conjuncturas. Donde é claro que as palavras que não vão escudadas pela sua origem são sujeitas a correcções quer phoneticas, quer significativas.

O processo que observei nesta materia foi o seguinte: percorri attentamente os diccionarios sanskritos de Monier Williams e Vaman Apte, o maratha de Molesworth, que tomei por *standard work,* o guzerathe de L. G. Patell, o hindustaní de T. Craven, o canarí de W. Reeve, o tamul de P. Percival, e o vocabulario singhalí de C. Alves, e notei todos os termos que se me afiguraram appropriados pelo *koṁkaṇi* d'alguma destas línguas.

p. xxiii

Quando porém não foi possivel descortinar, depois de muito descutir, a paternidade de certas que não tenham visos de ser *deśajas* ou aboriginaes, segui a ordem inversa:: conjecturei o seu sentido, e recorri aos diccionarios: ingles-sanskrito de Apte, inglez-maratha de Candy,inglez-hindustaní de Craven, e inglez-bengalí-hindustaní de P. S. D'Rosario. E se fui feliz em muitos casos, trabalhei baldadamente em não poucos.

O sanskrito, como era natural, prendeu-me mais attenção, por consideral-o mãe da lingua. Tive por isso o cuidado de notar as mais leves differenças de uma vogal ou consoante. Em quanto aos nomes, dei geralmente a forma crua *(crude form),* e em quanto aos verbos, a forma crua ou a base. Puz no fim entre parentheses o correlativo vocabulo latino, com o intuito de mostrar, não que a língua latina é filha da sanskrita, como a portugueza ou a italiana é d'aquella, mas que ambas são irmãs e têem origem commum na linguagem aryana *prevedica,* como é commumente admittido agora pelos cultores da philologia comparada. Não fui todavia muito diligente nesta particularidade, nem entrou ella no meu plano original; apontei tão sómente os mais salientes, que, sem grande applicação da lei de Grimm, por si só denotavam a sua similaridade[40].

---

[39] Vid. व्युत्पत्तीप्रदीप (*Vyutpatipradîpa*) de Govind Shankar Bâpat, *in fin.*

[40] No one supposes any longer that Sanskrit was the common source of Greek, Latin, and Anglo-Saxon...To speak the same language constitutes a closer union

Ao sanskrito segue o maratha, que se approxima tanto do *koṁkaṇî* que muitos auctores o têem por seu ascendente immediato, e com o qual eu mesmo tenha talvez condescendido mais do que devia, adoptando vozes e phrases omittiveis. Cumpre porem advertir: 1.º que não apontei differenças terminacionaes e ligeiras cambiantes; 2.º que varias palavras dadas como marathas occorrem no hindustani, no tamul, no canarí, para não fallar do guzerathe; 3.º que muitas destas são attribuiveis ao sanskrito, posto que tenham passado por grande decadencia phonetica; 4.º que algumas dellas podiam provir da *bâlabhâshâ* ou prakrita antiga directamente para *koṁkaṇi,* sem intermedio do maratha; 5.º que mais algumas, especialmente as que são marcadas pelos lexicographos como usadas no Konkão, podiam ser passado do *koṁkaṇi* para o maratha[41]; 6.ºque muitas são evidentemente accessões modernas, ás vezes desnecessarias; 7.º que as imitativas ou onomatopieas podiam ser inventadas pelos konkonasthas independentemente do Maratha, no qual não poucas dellas têem significação diversa;

p. xxiv

8.º que finalmente muitos vocabulos poeticos, litterarios, desusados ou antiquados n'aquella lingua, são usuaes e vulgares na de Gôa. Donde se vê que em muitos casos não é a origem, mas a simples coexistencia que é indicada por taes palavras.

Pelo que respeita aos outros idiomas, deprehende-se claramente que o seu contingente, em grande parte perfeitamente dispensavel, leva o sello de enxertia moderna, se exceptuarmos talvez o hindustani, devida ás mesmas causas que introduziram elementos heterogeneos em varias linguas do mundo civilisado[42].

D'aqui concluo resumidamente; por inducçao, sem assentar estiradas theorias, nem aventar alambicadas hypotheses: 1.º que a língua *koṁkaṇî* e aryana e inflexiva e não dravidiana ou agglutinativa; 2.º que se assemelha muito á *bâlabhâshâ;* 3.⁰ que dista menos do sanskrito no organismo grammatical e no vocabulario do que o maratha; 4.º que não é dialecto ou corrupção do maratha;

---

than to have drunk the same milk, and Sanskrit, the ancient language of India, is substantially the same language as Greek, Latin and Anglo-Saxon. Max Müller, *India,* pp. 21 e 27.

[41] "From a compilation, made and kindly lent by Mr. Reid of the Civil Service we obtained, for our first edition, several Konkaṇi words." Molesworth

[42] O contingente do canarí representa effectivamente uma parcella mui pequena, e tambem insignificante, se exceptuarmos *tâṁtîṁ, duḍû, badî, barauṁka* com seus derivados, *bhâṁgâra, madhavaḷa* e mais uns poucos. O mesmo se pode dizer com maior razão do tamul.

5.º que se approxima mais do maratha antigo, que por seu turno se approxima mais da *bâlabhâshâ,* do que do moderno; 6.º que se avisinha muito na sua estructura phonetica das linguas gaurianas do norte, mórmente do bengali; 7.º que representa com muita probabilidade a lingua *sarasvatî,* que os orientalistas tomam por extincta, sendo os emigrantes de Trihotra ou Tirhut que a introduziram no Konkão[(43)].

Depois disto, acho excusado analysar mais detidamente as fontes da lingua, as phases porque passou, a litteratura que produziu e o futuro que espera, o que tambem alongaria muito esta introducção, que já de si é assaz estirada. Nem faltam livros que forneçam alguns dados interessantes sobre estes pontos, que não estão ainda satisfactoriamente desenvolvidos[(44)].

p. xxv

'Tendo expendido minuciosamente a razão de ser do diccionario nos seus variados aspectos, no qual consumi tres annos de insanos labores, cumpre-me agora declarar que não nutro a pretenção de o considerar como obra perfeita, que satisfaça cabalmente o seu *desideratum,* nem era de esperar outra coisa attenta a sua natureza e o plano que me tracei na sua composição. Nem me abalançaria a dal-o á estampa tão cedo, sem o limar mais pausadamente, sé não fossem os conselhos em contrario de pessoas que me mereciam muita consideração. Ter-me-hão, naturalmente, escapado alguns vocabulos usuaes, além dos obscenos que omitti d'adrede, alguns significados, algumas phrases. Notar-se-ha talvez que alguns significados não correspondem exactamente ou que são mal applicados, ou que podiam ser substituídos pôr outros mais expressivos e classicos. Mas isto se pode dizer de muitos outros diccionarios deste genero, compostos nas circumstancias mais favoraveis com melhores materiáes e mais efficaz collaboração.

...

---

[43] गोमंतकीयभाषाहीबहुतकरूनप्राचीनसरस्वतीभाषेचेंरूपांतरहोऊनझालेलीअसावी, असेंदिसतें. प्राचीनबालभाषेशीहिचेंसाम्यपुष्कळआहे. आणिसांप्रतचीमराठीभाषाहीबालभाषेपासूनचआलेली असल्यामुळेंयादोहोंचाबराचनिकटसंबंधआहे. तशांतपुनःहीभाषामराठीच्यासंन्निधअसल्यामुळें सांप्रतप्रायःमराठीच्याअनुषंगानेचवाटतेअसेंम्हणण्यासकांहीबाधनाहीं. ... कित्येक (शब्द) जुन्या मराठीग्रंथांमध्येहीआढळतात. ...उच्चरादिकांच्यासंबंधानेतिचेंबंगालीभाषेशींबरेंचसादृश्यआहे. 'अ' यास्वराचाउच्चारबंगालीतज्याप्रमाणेंकांहीसा 'ओ' यास्वरासारखाहोतो. बंगालीलोकांमध्ये 'बाबू' असाजोप्रतिष्ठितशब्दआहे, त्याचाचअपभ्रंश 'बाब्' असागोमंतकीतयेतो. Ramchandra Gunjikar, सरस्वतीमंडळ, (Sarasavatîmadala). Vid. सह्याद्रीखण्ड (Sahyâdrikhamda), ed do Dr. Cunha, p. 305.

[44] *The Konkaṇî Language and Litterature, já citado. – Ensaio Critico pelo* editor da Grammatica do padre Estevão, Cunha Rivara, que bem merece da lingua pelo muito que se empenhou pelo seu estudo e cultura.

E mesmo no seu presente estado não sahíria o diccionario, se não recebesse valiosa cooperação e poderoso incentivo. Muitos amigos fizeram me suggestões de grande alcance ; alguns franquearam os livros de que podiam dispor, vantagem importante á vista da sua penuria no mercado. O meu irmão, Dr. Daniel Gelasio Dalgado, ministrou-me os nomes botanicos e animou-me muito para proseguir no trabalho[45]. O meu primo, padre Manuel Antonio Dias, coadjuvou-me constantemente quasi desde o princípio, e ultimamente se encarregou da revisão em Bombaim. O meu *pandit* de sanskrito, Ramchandra Sabnis, de Savantvadi, ajudou-me muito nas investigações etymologicas pelo tempo que residi naquelle estado. O sr. barão de Pernem deu gostosamente um valioso subsidio pecuniario.

Consigno pois aqui meus agradecimentos a todos os que me prestaram seu concurso directo ou indirecto.

Em conclusão, seja-me permittido emittir uma opinião, que tambem involve os meus ardentes votos. Sendo as linguas o melhor espelho do espírito humano, na judiciosa phrase de Leibniz, e o conhecimento da materna o ponto de partida para o rapido e proficiente estudo das forasteiras e de varias disciplinas, o *kointkaṇî* não tem razão de ser na sua actual condição de decadencia e desorganisação, nem faz honra, nem aproveita aos que a fallam.

p. xxvi

Então de duas uma: ou tem de ser descartada, como um fato velho irremendavel, e substituida por outra melhor, ou tem de ser restaurada, não a esmo e a capricho de cada qual, mas methodica e scientificamente.

Ora extinguir a lingua d'um povo essencialmente conservador e tradicionalista não é tarefa que entre no calculo do homem, demanda um esforço quasi sobrehumano. Já foi tentado esse expediente draconico sob melhores auspicios e com meios que se acharam mais conducentes, mas nada se conseguiu.

Cumpre pois erguel-a do abatimento em que jaz e aperfeiçoal-a com todos os recursos que a philologia subministra. Nada mais congruente e adequado para esse fim do que a creação d'uma cadeira de *kointkaṇî*, no Lyceu de Nova-Gôa e d'outra no seminario de Rachol, e a sua adopção como baseda instrucção nas escholas primarias e parochiaes. E serão bem dignos da eterna gratidão popular os que o fizerem em pró da lingua, de que se pode dizer com muita propriedade amoldando os versos de Camões:

E na lingua como quando se imagina,

---

[45] Não me foi possivel ter a nomenclatura de aves e peixes.

Com pouco corrupção se crê que é a *aryana*.

E se comtudo algum pessimista julgar que a presente obra não terá a dita de produzir nenhum effeito pratico e que é baldado o trabalho de quem a elaborou, considere-a pelo menos como um modesto monumento levantado para a memoria da sua lingua materna por um seu humilde cultor.

Honovar, 14 de setembro de 1893.

S. R. Dalgado

Mariano Saldanha (1878–1975) was professor of Marathi at the Lyceum in Panjim until 1929 when he assumed the Chair of Sanskrit in Lisbon upon the death of Mgr. Sebstião Rodolfo Dalgado. Among Mariano Saldanha's several publications are Meghaduta ou a Mensagem dum Exilado, *Nova Goa, 1926,* As Investigações de um Gramático, *Lisbon, 1933, and* A língua concani, as suas conferências e a acção portuguesa na sua cultura, *Bastora, 1954. Among the better known of his works is the* Doutrina Cristã em Língua Concani, *the second edition of the text by Thomas Stephens, S. J., first printed in Rachol in 1622.*

This second edition of 1945 carried a lengthy introduction with notes and a glossary and was published by the Divisão de Publicações e Biblioteca Agência Geral das Colónias, Lisboa. The introduction is among the best-researched and annotated pieces of writing on an early Konkani text. It includes a historical context for the emergence of the Doutrina, placing it alongside similar works by Franciscans, and recommendations from the Church Councils. It has a brief account of the life and work of Thomas Stephens, a linguistic analysis of the work, and a comparison with contemporary Doutrina, foregrounding what he saw as a linguistic corruption of Konkani in twentieth century productions of the Doutrina.

The introductory pages provide a detailed bibliographic history of the first catechisms and confessionals to emerge from the press in Goa, including those that weren't known at the time, as well as republications or versions of doctrinal texts said to have been published in the eighteenth century, but of which, at the time he wrote, were not extant and were rarely mentioned in bibliographies. Saldanha also discusses the ambiguity over the term 'canarese' when applied to varying versions of Konkani, Kannada or Marathi and asserts that the Doutrina was written in Konkani.

Saldanha privileged particular linguistic sources and texts as those that would bestow recognition on Konkani as the language of Goa. However, according to the Catholic literary elite who wrote predominantly in Portuguese, efforts like Saldanha's were thwarted by what they saw as the corrupted colloquialisms of popular Konkani that were unusable for literary work. The excerpts from Saldanha's introduction indicate the points at which he thought mistranslations and misinterpretations had occurred because of the decline in Konkani usage. He therefore upheld the Konkani of the missionary period as the right standard to which Konkani ought to be restored, and for which his predecessor in the field, Msgr. Dalgado among others had worked.

The following is an excerpt from Saldanha's discussion of extant manuscripts and copies and of the circulation of the Doutrina. He states for instance that one could call it a 'luso-concani' text since parts of it were a close rendition of the catechism in the text used to teach Christianity in the metropole, but it also created sections that had been reproduced in later versions and that passed into the oral devotional practice of the land.

Saldanha asserted that the Doutrina survives as an oral tradition in the recitations of prayers that passed down the generations among people who may not have known the name of the first translator of the text. The initial pages of the excerpt, from 27–33, are an emphatic rebuttal of the early ambiguous term 'canarim', used by various missionaries to refer to Konkani, as well as to other languages along the western coast and hinterland, and specifically, to Thomas Stephens' Doutrina.

Excerpt 8
Mariano Saldanha, *Doutrina Cristã em língua concani*, por Tomás Estêvão, S. J., Impressa em Rachol (Goa) em 1622. Segunda edição, facsimilada, com Introdução, Notas e Glossário por Mariano Saldanha (Divisão de Publicações e Biblioteca Agência Geral das Colónias, Lisboa MCMXLV), pp. 27–39, 45–51.

Assim pois a *Doutrina* de Estêvão bem se pode chamar luso-concani, porquanto o mesmo livro por onde se ensinava a doutrina à cristandade da metrópole lusitana foi vertido, quási com as mesmas preguntas e respostas, por êsse primeiro ou dos primeiros concanistas europeus e oferecido à lusa metrópole da cristandade oriental. É por êle que gerações sucessivas de cristãos concanis vêem balbuciando as suas primeiras orações na infância e as derradeiras preces de boa morte, perpetuadas aquelas não no original, hoje completamente desconhecido, mas por transmissão oral mais ... ou menos alterada e reproduzidas em manuais, cujos autores talvez ignorem de todo o saüdoso nome de quem legou a preciosa herança.

III

Particularidades lingüísticas

23 – *Linguagam e vocabulário*: A *Doutrina* de Estêvão, sendo o livro impresso mais antigo que possuímos em Concani, é um documento altamente apreciável para o estudo tanto do texto primitivo da doutrina como da língua nos séculos XVI e XVII.

As expressões «língua brámana canarim», em que o autor a diz ter escrito, ou simplesmente «língua brámana» ou ainda «canarim», empregadas pelo Visitador e pelos Inquisidores nas respectivas licenças, não designavam na época – ao contrário do que alguns supõem na Europa – o canarês, que é a língua do Canará, do grupo dravídico, mas sim o vernáculo de Goa, o concani, que aliás nada tem com aquêle, nem é dravidico, pois é de origem sanscrítica e irmão de marata; e como tal pertence ao grupo lingüístico indo-europeu.

Canarim é a lusitanização de Kan*a*ddí, que para todo o Mundo designa o natural do Canará (Kan*a*ddá) e a sua língua, isto é, o *canarês*. Os antigos portugueses, porém, aplicaram-na ao princípio a todos os naturais, cristãos e hindus, de Goa e ao seu idioma, que aliás são estranhos ao Canará; e ao depois a limitaram só aos cristãos, chamando os outros *gentios* ou pagãos, ... como se uns e outros não fôssem da mesma terra, o Concão; e o êrro foi por todos carinhosamente abraçado e perpetuado, ainda depois de ser reconhecido como tal. O mesmo fizeram chamando *hindustane* ao marata e *língua brámana* tanto ao sânscrito como ao concani, e incluindo sob a designação de o *malabar* o tamul e o malaialão. Já aliás o *Catecismo*, citado no § 5, diziam os seus autores nativos, em 1554, que era composto em «tâmul» e não em malabar e, contudo, continuou-se quási sempre a confundir tudo sob o nome de «malabar».

Mas os principais responsáveis por essa trapalhada tôda não são tanto os seculares, que não se dedicavam ao estudo das línguas locais, quanto os próprios missionários, que, lidando com o povo e estudando e cultivando as suas línguas, bem sabiam os seus nomes apropriados e as suas diferenças; e não obstante, longe de imporem, com a autoridade da sua competência, as designações correctas, repudiando as falsas, preferiram adoptar e perpetuar o êrro popular, gerado mais pelo descuido do que pela ignorância. Entre os escritores ... da Companhia pretende-se desculpar êsses descuidos, alegando que ao tempo era natural a hesitação e a impropriedade nos têrmos, por não estarem ainda bem estudados e classificados os vernáculos, cousa que, aliás, não era absolutamente indispensável para se saber o nome duma língua, que geralmente é dado pelos naturais e não pelos estrangeiros. Ora a nenhum filho de Goa teriam os missionários ouvido chamar à sua língua «canarim» ou simplesmente «brámana», como se só em Goa houvesse brâmanes. Esta língua, designada entre os cultos por *concnni*, era vulgarmente conhecida por *Goenchi bhás* (língua de Goa), ou simplesmente por *Govi*, o goense, como o português é a língua de Por tugal; os europeus não tinham, portanto, que escogitar nomes para a sua designação; mas, como estavam fortemente imbuídos da errada noção de Goa ficar situada no Canará e de ter sido colonizada por canareses, apegaram-se à falsa designação, que ainda continua.

É por isso necessário frizar com tôda a ênfase:

A Doutrina de *Tomás Estêvão é escrita, não em canarês, língua do Canará, mas no concani de Goa: assim como o seu Purana é composto em marata e não em hindustane, nem em concani, nem em canarês, como se tem escrito.*

24 – Neste livro, como nos outros da época, os seus autores, apesar de estrangeiros, provaram que se podia manejar a língua, ainda para o uso literário, dentro dos recursos do seu próprio vocabulário, sem importações europeias desnecessárias, em contraste com a linguagem actual até escrita dos próprios naturais, tão empobrecida no seu léxico, saturado de vocábulos estranhos.

Havia, porém, um problema em que devia ter esbarrado a acção catequística dêsses missionários: ex- ... primir em vernáculo certas idéias e factos que, sendo desconhecidos ou diferentes nas religiões indianas, eram desprovidos de vocábulo apropriado. Remediaram, porém, a deficiência de três maneiras: a) O primeiro espediente, mais pronto e fácil, foi aproveitar os próprios vocábulos portugueses, que depois se adaptaram à fonética popular, tais como *miss, Ispirt-Sant, bautizm, cum'sar, Pascã, resper* (*receber* em casamento); b) em segundo lugar lançaram mão de certas palavras, indianas na forma, mas tão estranhas na língua, que, ou foram por êles cunhadas com o auxílio de sânscrito, ou se já existiam, a êles devem a sua vulgarização no significado cristão, tais foram «yectaru» (comunicação dos santos}, «s*a*d*a*iv*a*» (bem-aventurado), «*a*lp*a*bh*a*j*a*n*a*l» (temperança), yec*a*bh*a*ct*a* (jejum), «pottarlhu» (gula, etc. [(1)]; c) e finalmente adoptaram vocábulos bem conhecidos e correntes da própria religião hindú para designar pessoas e cousas mais ou menos idênticas do cristianismo, como «deull*a*» (templo), guru (sacerdote), «Vaicuntth*a*» (paraíso de Vixnnú), «Yam*a*-cundd*a*» (região de Yam*a*, o deus da morte), para exprimirem, respectivamente, a igreja, o padre, o paraíso, o inferno, etc.

25 – Os vocábulos desta última classe escandalizavam, ao que parece, os ouvidos cristãos, para quem era profanação aplicar à sua religião e Deus nomes de divindades e cultos pagãos. Foi por isso que o Padre Diogo Ribeiro, no prólogo da sua Declaração ... (§ 10), achou dever justificar o emprêgo da palavra «V*a*incutth*a*» (como êles escreviam), com o seguinte arrazoado:

«Sabida cousa é... que as vozes e palavras... só aquilo significam que os homens quiseram significassem...Digo isto... por razão desta palavra (V*a*incutth*a*) de que uso...a qual em língua canarim entre os

---

[1] Muitos destes vocábulos, já hoje correntes entre os cristãos maratas, se acham agora registados nos respectivos dicionários modernos. *Sadaiva* não foi inventado pelos missionários, porquanto se vê empregado no sentido de afortunado no poema marata Dnyanesvari e num provérbio «S*a*d*a*ivachi d*a*xi' anni N*a*radevacha palav lagava» . Mas foi por eles vulgarizado com o novo significado de bem-aventurança cristã.

gentios significa o seu paraíso dêles, em que moram seus pagodes (deuses); porém já hoje na mesma língua entre os cristãos se toma e se entende pelo nosso paraíso de glória e bem-aventurança... e assim neste sentido se usa já comumente da dita, não só entre os cristãos rudes, mas também entre os que se bem entendem. Esta é a Rezão por que o Padre Tomás Estêvão, Religioso da nossa Companhia, usou dela muitas vezes não só na sua *Puranna* – recebida de todos com tanta aceitação – mas ainda na sua cartilha de doutrina cristã, também impressa com aprovação da mesa do Santo Ofício e Revedores, com que a dita palavra, sendo dantes profana, ficou santificada».

E contudo o próprio Diogo Ribeiro emprega quási sempre *paraíso*, parecendo que «V*a*incuttha» não logrou captar simpatia cristã, tendo sido logo substituído por «su*a*rga»; o mesmo sucedeu com deull*a* e *guru*, que foram retiradas em benefício de *igroz* e *padri*. «Bh*a*incutth*a*» (com *bh*) é ainda usado, mas é só para designar o paraíso de Adão, como em «Bh*a*incutthantlem ph*a*ll*a*», o fruto do paraíso terrestre, porque é composto do ... sânscrito *Bhumi*-concani *bhuim*=terra e «V*a*icunttha»= paraíso, dando «Bhumi-V*a*icuntth*a*» – «Bhaincuttha».

26 – *Sistema ortográfico*: Os jesuítas, apesar de comporem obras em concani e em marata línguas que com grande proveito aprendiam no seu Colégio de Salsete [(1)] como o demonstram essas obras,

---

[1] «Ao Colégio de Salsete se aplicaram êste ano (1576) oito irmãos moralistas ao estudo da língua Canarina (concani), tão necessária para a cultura dos cristãos e conversão dos gentios. Ordenou o Padre Visitador (Alexandre Valignano) que os desocupassem de qualquer outro ministério, que não falassem entre si senão a língua da terra; e o Padre Reitor era exactíssimo em fazer observar esta ordem: que todos os dias praticassem com os naturais a certas horas determinadas, que aprendessem a ler e escrever nos próprios carateres do país; e com estas diligências...dentro em seis meses souberam escrever e falar na língua canarim perfeitamente; e indo o Padre Visitador a Salsete, o receberam no refeitório com orações no mesmo idioma e saíram logo a publico a pregar aos naturais, que por uma parte ficaram contentissimos de se ver providos de tantos Mestres e tão idóneos...Um seu poeta celebrou êste benefício com versos tão elegantes, que os começaram a cantar publicamente não só os cristãos mas também os gentios», *Or. Conquist.*, tomo 2°, pág. 108.

Convém notar, porém, um facto não registado por nenhum cronista jesuíta; Antes de 1576, um filho de Goa, estudante de Teologia, ensinou no Colégio de S. Paulo de Goa, desde 1563, o concani a alguns Irmãos por uma *Arte* por êle próprio organizada. Foi êste, portanto, o primeiro ensino de Concani aos europeus, êle o primeiro professor e a sua Arte a primeira gramática da língua; e os alunos "estavam aproveitados para poderem tratar com a gente da terra". (Vide Carta do Irmão Lourenço Peres, de 7 de Outubro de 1563).

nunca possuiram nas suas tipografias de Goa tipo vernáculo, cuja complicada estrutura dificultava a sua preparação, vendo-se por isso obrigados a imprimir as suas composições em caracteres romanos.

Outro motivo, além deste, haveria para a romanização: é que, no intuito de desviar os neo-cristãos da literatura hindú, tida por inconveniente para a moral cristã, era-lhes proïbido freqüentar as escolas pagãs e todo o ensino missionário ao indígena era limitado à instrução europeia, banindo-se por completo o estudo do próprio vernáculo; de modo que, logo na segunda geração dos convertidos, difícilmente se encontraria quem estudasse ou pudesse ler as suas próprias línguas nos caracteres nativos, orientação em grande parte defeituosa, que vem sendo perpetuada até hoje sòmente entre os cristãos de Goa e é única em tôda a India e em todo o Mundo.

Para adaptar pois, os caracteres romanos à fonética ... indiana, tiveram os missionários de recorrer a certas convenções, que, sendo nos manuscritos um tanto variadas, nos impressos, naturalmente por imposição tipográfica, são uniformes. Jgnora-se quem tenha sido o seu autor; e se já estavam em uso ao tempo de Estêvão, é possivel que êste lhes tenha dado a devida regularidade, porquanto na sua Gramática escreve: «Aquêles (europeus) que nestas partes estudam a língua da terra, não a escrevem comumente senão na nossa letra (a romana) e para isto se fazer com a perfeição devida pareceu necessário dar as advertências seguintes». Com estas advertências ou regras talvez tenha facilitado a escrita, tanto que «os que sabem nossa letra mais fàcilmente escrevem e lêem por ela, do que costumam os escrivães da terra pola sua», como êle diz. [(1)]

Neste sistema tôdas as letras têem o som que lhes corresponde em português; e as convenções especiais, salva uma ou outra excepção (como o *a* itálico representando o *a* breve do alfabeto indiano) são as mesmas que vêem sendo geralmente observadas ainda hoje entre os cristãos de Goa, a quem por isso não deveria surgir sensível dificuldade na leitura; mas são precisamente os que mais embaraçados se verão na leitura apropriada dêsse *a* itálico, tão profusamente empregado ... no texto. Não conhecendo em geral nenhum alfabeto indiano, desconhecem a existência e o valor dessa vogal, que na escrita (mas nem sempre na fala) confundem com *o* e a representam sempre por esta vogal, escrevendo, por exemplo, *Pormespôr*, o que os missionários escrupulosamente transliteravam em P*a*ramesp*a*r*a*, segundo a escrita indiana.

---

[1] T. Estêvão – *Arte da Lingoa Canarin*, pág. 1.

27 – Para facilitar, pois, a leitura dêsse *a* itálico, pode-se estabelecer, de um modo geral, as seguintes regras, aliás desnecessárias a quem saiba ler o alfabeto indiano:

1) Esse *a*, quando não é mudo, tem *quási* o som de *o*, aberto ou fechado. No *Vocabulário* que acompanha esta *Doutrina* representamos esta letra por dois símbolos: *ȯ*, com um ponto por cima, quando é aberto, como em pat*aca* = patóc, e ö, com dois pontos, quando é fechado, v. g. «P*a*r*a*mesp*a*ru» = Pörömespöru [1].

2) O *a* itálico final é quási sempre mudo na fala e na prosa, v. g. «b*a*ss*a*ta», pronunciado bȯssȯt. Exceptuam-se os Presentes antiquados «assa» (está), «naza».(não pode), «s*aca*» (pode), pronunciados *a*ssö (ou *a*ss*a* entre os cristãos), nȯzȯ, sȯcȯ; e a 3.ª pessoa do Imperfeito habitual do Indicativo, como «aica» (ouvia), «vacha» (ia), que se pronunciam aicȯ e vȯchȯ [2]

Sôbre a sua pronúncia na poesia, vide adiante o § 28.

...

IV

As «Doutrinas» modernas e a sua comparação com a de Tomás Estêvão.

30 – Como já se disse (§ 12), desde o século XIX vieram aparecendo produções catequísticas da autoria de filhos de Goa; e é hoje grande o número de manuais que expõem a doutrina. cuja redacção na parte comum é a mesma de Estêvão, com a modernização ou suposta correcção de alguns vocábulos, tentativa que às vezes tem sido infeliz e descabida.

Com efeito, pelo decorrer do tempo, a pobreza gradual da língua, permanecida inculta, tornou muitas expressões incompreensíveis por obsoletas ou adulteradas, tendo sido modernamente substituídas e com razão, por outras mais em uso, como *crupa bharity*, substituída por *curpen bharlelê*; *Matê* (que se pronunciava *Matie*, ó barro), por *Mayê*, etc. Mas outras que não podiam ser eliminadas por estarem já cristalizadas na linguagem religiosa, tẽem dado lugar a verdadeiras adulterações intoleráveis, tornando o texto baixo e incorrecto, além de desvirtuado no sentido. A estas

---

[1] Êstes símbolos são adoptados pela Comissão de Concani, de Bombaim, mas com certas restrições, que aqui não foram seguidas, para evitar confusões.

[2] Em alguns Mss. da época vê-se o *a* final breve representado por *â* quando acentuado; v. G. aic*â* – aic*ó*, ouvi vós. Estêvão porém recomenda para todo o *a* breve só a, marcando-o com um ponto por baixo quando acentuado. Mas nem a sua Gramática, nem nenhuma obra saída da Tipografia de Rachol segue estas convenções, talvez por deficiência tipográfica.

desfigurações não teem escapado os próprios autores modernos, cujo esfôrço, aliás louvável, para a emenda nem sempre tem sido acertado. Assim, *dayally caranniyo*, obras de misericórdia, que na bôca popular estava cor- ... rompido em *divalleo cornneo* (*divalleo* é o plural de *divally*, uma festividade hindú), foi emendado para *devaleo cornneo*, obras divinas. *Xarannam yetaum*, que se pronuncia sòrnaitaum (da Salvé Raínha), modificaram em sörv örnitam, que não é nada. E assim se lê também *görb sambavlo*, Ele (Jesus) concebeu, *cuxint zolmolo*, nasceu no ventre, etc.; mantiveram erros populares, como *upordés* por *upôdés*, e assim muitos mais, como se verá nas notas.

Esta corrida desenfreada para o abismo da corrupção lingüística, que nunca se viu em nenhum autor concani de procedência europeia, manifesta-se hoje – é triste confessá-lo – só em escritos dos próprios nativos, cujo vernáculo é esta língua; e exige sem demora, para o bem da língua e da catequese, o entrave de um documento autorizado, como é o próprio original, para se não continuarem a tentar reformas à toa.

31 – É para corresponder a esta necessidade que se faz a presente reedição, que visa especialmente a dois objectivos principais: a) fornecer aos estudiosos da língua, salvando-o da ruína e desaparecimento, o seu mais antigo monumento literário impresso, de entre os existentes, datado de mais de três séculos, e cuja perda, além de irremediável, seria muito lamentável para uma língua de tão escassa literatura; b) e habilitar a catequese a restaurar, até certo ponto, a sua deturpada doutrina em concani, oferecendo-lhe a própria fonte original de que derivam todos os textos modernos; e a obstar ao mesmo tempo a novas adulterações, que já aparecem em formação.

Deve-se notar, porém, que nem tôdas as alterações actualmente em uso constituem corrupção, havendo até ... algumas preferíveis à expressão do autor, Tornava-se, por isso, indispensável comparar, com o de Estêvão, os textos modernos autorizados e indicar nestes tôdas as divergências, quer as que devam ser eliminadas como incorrectas, quer as que podem ser mantidas como correctas e preferíveis. É o que se procurou efectivar por meio de notas que acompanham os capítulos, tarefa ingrata por melindres naturais, mas imposta pelo bem da língua e mesmo da religião. Este confronto, porém, teve de se limitar só às orações e à doutrina comum a todos os manuais, visto que a parte explicativa ou catequística própriamente dita, variando em cada manual e diferindo da de Estêvão, foi excluída como insusceptível de comparação e estranha ao nosso caso, embora também carecesse, e muito, de correcção na sua linguagem.

32 – Para êste estudo comparativo recorremos aos três manuais de doutrina últimamente aprovados pela respectiva autoridade para

as dioceses de Goa, de Damão (incluindo Bombaim), hoje extinta, e a de Mangalore, isto é, para tôdas as três dioceses onde se faz uso de língua e doutrina concanis. São os seguintes:

I – Pustoc Cristãu Dotirnichem. 3.ª edição 1936. (Para Goa).

II – Catecismo da Doutrina Cristã em concani, 1932. (Para Bombaim).

III – Cristanv Dotorn – Cardinal Gasparrichea «Catholic Cathekismak» sari zaun; Mãgllur Diocezi passun boroil'lo (sic); Codialb*a*il Press, Mangalore, 1941 (anónimo); em caracteres canareses.

...

Por motivos óbvios não damos os nomes dos autores das duas primeiras publicações, que nas nossas *Notas* à *Doutrina* designamos genèricamente por *Gs.*, isto é (de autores) *Goeses.*

Foram ainda consultadas, entre outras, as obras seguintes:

IV-Tomás Estêvão – Purana Cristão. 4.ª edição, por J. L. Saldanha, Mangalore, 1907.

V – Diogo Ribeiro S. J. – *Declaração da Doutrina Christã,* Rachol, 1632.

VI – Angelus F. X. Maffei S. J. – Trechos selectos da Bíblia em Concani, na sua *Concani Grammar,* Mangalore, 1882.

VII – *Lenkranchi pòhili pothi,* em marata, de Bombay Tract Society, 1893 (Protestante).

VIII – Eduardo de Sousa, *Doutrina em Concani,* Bombaim, 1897.

IX – *Catholik Dharmasambhandhim Praxnnottaravali va Prarthanam;* Catecismo em marata pelo bispo Leo Meurin S. J. e aprovado para as dioceses de Bombaim e Puna; 8.ª edição, 1915.

X – Resumo do mesmo, aprovado para a extinta diocese portuguesa de Damão.

XI – Remígio António Lôbo – *Manual da Missa, Confissão e Comunhão em Português e Concani,* Bombaim, 1921.

XII – Padre Ludovico da Caridade Ferrão – *Livrinho de Cânticos. Hinos, Ladaínhas,* etc. Mangalore, 1897. (Com a aprovação do prelado de Mangalore).

...

XIII – G. O. Pires – Cristanv Dotón ani Catisism (em caracteres maratas), Sholapur, 1894.

33 – Do confronto dos três manuais aprovados se reconhece com lástima maior deficiência literária nos dois catecismos que devem a sua autoria a filhos de Goa e dêstes dois o que mais carece de revisão é precisamente aquêle que um decreto eclesiástico «manda servir de texto no ensino e explicação da doutrina», segundo informa o mesmo livrinho. Por maior que seja a nossa consideração pelos ilustres autores, não nos foi possível deixar de indicar, pelo menos por amor à língua, essas deficiências que a desfiguram.

Não sendo o concani objecto de ensino primário nem de cultura, é só no catecismo e na linguagem religiosa que a infância encontra a primeira e quási única oportunidade de aprender a dição mais correcta e literária e o vocabulário mais acima do vulgar. Se êste e aquela forem errôneas, a sua assimilação reflectir-se-á mais tarde na sua linguagem. Pois agora até esta única fonte, que restava ao povo para aprender a forma literária do seu vernáculo, está sendo involuntàriamente deturpada com grave prejuízo da infância (e não menos de outras idades), a quem seria mau serviço deixar-se ensinar a falar e escrever o concani do modo como está redigido um dêsses manuais, especialmente na sua parte explicativa, em cuja apreciação, porém, não podemos entrar, como já se disse, por ser matéria estranha ou diferente da de Estêvão.

Não se imagine porém – convém notá-lo-que se pretende restaurar ou encarecer cegamente e em tudo o texto hierático ou a linguagem, um tanto antiquada, de ... Estevão, contrariando a evolução natural do concani. Pelo contrário, em relação aos catecismos modernos, procurou-se indicar as suas expressões que fôssem toleráveis e até preferíveis às do original, como já se disse, ao mesmo tempo que se apontavam outras, que, mesmo na fase actual da língua, fôssem manifestamente incorrectas e impróprias para a cultura literária e para o ensino da infância.

Da ortografia missionária [(1)] é fácil prever que, não obstante os esclarecimentos já ministrados, algum embaraço não deixará de causar mesmo a muitos cultores e defensores dedicados da língua que desconheçam qualquer alfabeto indiano e não tenham paciência de poucos minutos para se inteirarem daquela ortografia. Estes exclamarão com certeza enfadados, como às vezes se ouve: «Nem se pode lêr; isso não é concani». E no entanto o livro foi bem lido e a sua linguagem com preendida por aqueles para quem foi expressamente escrito; e a linguagem religiosa moderna, herdada daqueles tempos, não difere muito daquela.

Em todo o caso, já agora não subsiste motivo para lamentar – como há 40 anos o fazia o insigne e laborioso concanista, Monsenhor Dalgado – que por des-conhecimento do texto primitivo não se podesse comentar o catecismo concani, rectificando as

---

[1] Desta ortografia diz o orientalista inglés, Dr. A. C. Burnell: «O seu (de Estêvão) sistema de transcrição era baseado exclusivamente no alfabeto português, mas é muito mais perfeito do que os sistemas defendidos 200 anos depois em Calcutá» (pelos ingleses). Burnell – *Specimens of S. Indian Dialects*, n.º 1. Admitindo mesmo que não seja tanto assim, não há dúvida que é suficientemente perfeito para os fins práticos a que se destinava.

suas numerosas variantes. Pois a nova edição do antigo texto original de T. Estêvão e mais o comentário linguístico – em notas ... e glossário – que o acompanha, embora não tão extenso como era para desejar, habilitarão em grande parte os futuros catecismos a deixarem de ser, como até aqui, simples «reprodução das fórmulas orais, deformadas pelo tempo» e reformadas por meras suposições [1]

[1] Monsenhor R. Dalgado: Dic. Português-Konkani, pag. XI.

VI

Popular Literature, Dictionaries and Histories

In their well-intentioned insistence that Konkani as it was used was unfit as a vehicle for literary use, the litterateurs failed to recognise or support a vibrant field of Konkani production.The popular texts produced in Bombay, Karachi and elsewhere saw several genres emerging at once, though literary histories continued to point to an absence of writing, barring José Pereira's histories of literary Konkani (1973, 27–46). Despite the relentless criticism in commentaries on popular Konkani, the continuing intellectual investment by the elite in the language is evident; it perhaps sprang from a fear that the language restricted the community's ability to generate or acquire usages that were not already familiar.

The appearance of a wide range of genres in popular Konkani, given that it had a small readership, however, demands a more complex analysis than a rebuttal of elite concerns. Basil Bernstein's distinction between the 'restricted linguistic code' of lower-class English dialects in Britain and the 'elaborated linguistic code' of others is also cited by Walter Ong in his discussion of the culture of orality (Ong 2002, 103). Ong elaborates that the restricted code is sufficiently expressive in contexts shared by speaker and listener. When dealing with the unfamiliar, he asserts, a more elaborate code is needed. This characterisation of the restricted code as oral in origin, and therefore 'close to the human lifeworld', helps illuminate aspects of popular Konkani translation and the elite response to it (Ong 2002, 42-43).

The cookbook as a vocabulary

We could consider Pedro Dias' *The Goan Cook's Guide* of 1894 an act of translation, as it combined the form of the vocabulary with that of the cookbook; an interesting departure from the first vocabularies produced by missionaries. *The Goan Cook's Guide* was probably a valuable companion to cooks employed on ships, in clubs, restaurants, bars and homes in Bombay and elsewhere. Its select vocabulary in English, French, Hindustani and Konkani, along with interest tables, salary charts, glossaries and menus would allow Goan cooks to gain a grip on exactly those words, measures and meanings they would need in the course of their daily work. Recipes in Konkani for the Half-pay Pudding, Conservative Pudding, Nurse Hannah's Pudding and Mysterious Pudding were therefore translations of culturally distinctive objects and processes across languages.

If the Konkani language was overtly referred to in this book or others that are similar in their creation of a translatable language, it was to claim it and own it as a familiar object from the past that would anchor the migrant's journey towards different things and meanings. Such claims can be found in the introductions and prefaces and advertisements for the publications themselves. They have been included as part of translation discourse because they represent a distinct approach that spoke of language as a marker of identity, but not an identity that was national or territorial, save as a terrain for nostalgia. The term *amchi bhas* (literally, our speech/language), often the only term used to denote Konkani, summoned a language and a community of familiarity, with a similar past. The texts examined here were so distinctively for Catholic Goans, that demarcating a religious boundary was unnecessary. The fact that this was in Roman Konkani already signified that boundary.

The recipes in João Manuel de Souza's *The Goan Barman's Guide* (1909) carried titles in English but recipes in Konkani for the Byculla Cocktail, Cholera Cocktail, Corpse Reviver, India Cocktail, Stars and Stripes, and American lemonade. If such texts spoke of Konkani as a sign of the advancement of the community, it was an advancement that was different from the idea of linguistic improvement that a lettered high-cultural perspective would imply. Bi- and tri-lingual Konkani dictionaries of the second half of the nineteenth century for instance, did not signify the development of an objective interest in the language, but the entry, finally, of its speakers into economies that required a rapid formalisation of their linguistic and literary skills and into the conceptual innovations that that experience would bring. The contact with numerous languages and work situations across British and Portuguese colonies required an acquaintance with cosmopolitan cultures. Printed texts served this need, but their linguistic code continued to extend an oral worldview and the moral and cultural universe of the rural parish. Ong remarks (2002, 45), '(F)or an oral culture learning or knowing means achieving close, empathetic, communal identification with the known... Writing separates the knower from the known and thus sets up conditions for 'objectivity', in the sense of personal disengagement or distancing'. Konkani print enabled and contained the encounter with the unfamiliar by restricting the horizon of moral and cosmological reference to a rural Catholic worldview. Viewing this as a process of translation from an oral worldview to print helps explain the participation of readers across caste in the production and reception of these texts.

Ong notes the tendency to situational rather than categorical thinking in oral cultures that do not demonstrate the context-free or autonomous written discourse detached from the author (ibid., 47). Thus it was primarily for speakers of Portuguese that systematic grammars and cross-referenced vocabularies or etymologies for Konkani were produced. In contrast, vocabularies that appeared in Konkani carried a sense of immediacy, and conveyed the impression of being a direct response to an encounter with unfamiliar cultures, rather than embodying a disinterested perspective from which the language was studied. When Ong states, '(O)ral cultures of course have no dictionaries and few semantic discrepancies', or '(A)n oral culture has no vehicle as neutral as a list', it encapsulates the defining characteristics of popular dictionaries, and is a far more effective characterisation of what constituted the popular at this point in time, than reverting to the social origins of their users as an explanation (ibid., 42, 46).

Vocabularies and dictionaries

The dictionaries, vocabularies, and devotional texts that were published in the 1860s and 1870s preceded and paralleled Dalgado's work. At least thirty vocabularies, grammars and language primers were produced from the end of the nineteenth century to the 1940s, largely in the Roman script, with a few in the Devanagari and Kannada scripts. Ramcandra Poroba Launda's *Vokabulario Popular* in Portuguese, Konkani, Marathi and English, (published in Goa in 1916) and D. F. Dantas' *Konkani Bhasecem Laguvyakaran* (published in Sawantwadi in 1910) were both in the Devanagari script.[1]

[1] K. C. Dutt, *National Bibliography of Indian Literature: 1901–1980 – Comprising Dogri, Konkani, Maithili, Manipuri, Nepali, Rajasthani* v. 5, 25–26, Accessed May 2, 2015, http://www.eurobuch.com/buch/isbn/8172010575.html.

The *Vocabulário Inglez, Portuguez e Concanim* of 1873 by Paulo Maria Homem was intended for children and printed in Bombay. In 1878, D. F. X. Dias and Munshi Nur Mohammed Khan jointly produced a *Vocabulary in Five Languages* in English, Portuguese, Konkani, Marathi and Urdu from Satara, on the Bodha Sudhaka Press, priced at 2 *annas*. It carried entries for numbers, collective nouns, trees, clothes, and 'things pertaining to the Universe and land'. The preface to the *Manual de Tres Mil Vocabulos* of 1892, in Portuguese, Konkani, English, and French, claimed that it was a response to requests, 'since so many of our compatriots have emigrated in such large numbers to British India, where the principal languages are English and Hindustani,' and since many who 'wanted to study Portuguese and Konkani...could not find a book which could guide them in these languages' (Pinto 2007, 232). In this relatively tiny print market, it is worth noting that the book ran to five editions, with the fifth edition printed in 1937. Since Kenyans were 'daily brought into greater contact with Europeans Indians and Goans' in British East Africa, P. M. Fernandes Costa Bir's publication of 1902 *The English, Hindustani, Konkani, Swahili Vocabulary* from Nairobi sought to address the need for familiarity with Swahili. In contrast, in Kerala, grammars and language primers in Konkani appeared largely to supplement the symbolic support for the unification of Konkani writing in Devanagari.[2]

Shakespeare in summary

The voice propagating cultural improvement in these texts, or the suggestion that reading the plays of Shakespeare in translation would help raise the lot of Konkani speakers was neither abstract nor removed by class or anonymity. An adaptation of Shakespeare's *Winter's Tale, Innocente Hermione vo Dubavi Leontes* by the prolific writer Sebastião Gabriel D'Souza (who went by the pen-name Karachiwalla) in 1926, did not acknowledge the source of the adaptation, but dwelt, instead, on the need to stoke an interest in cultivating the language among readers.[3] Most of these translations were in fact summaries of the plot, frequently interpreting the actions of main protagonists from a localised moral framework, such as

---

[2] See Rava 1975 and1977, both printed in Devanagari, referenced in Dutt, 25–26.

[3] Karachiwalla translated Shakespeare's *Merchant of Venice, As You Like It,* and *Hamlet* into Konkani and presented them in Bombay (Fernandes 2010, 136).

Twelfth Night vo dogam bou boinam zoullim, which was written by Douglas F. X. Fernandes In 1911.

In 1912, V. Varde Valaulikar wrote and published *Gore Bailecho Callo Ghov*, an adaptation of Shakespeare's *Othello*. He also adapted *The Tragedy of Hamlet* to *Rajput Hamlet ani Bapaichem Bhut* and *A Comedy of Errors* as *Zunvllea Bhavancho Ghuspa-Gondoll* in 1914. The significance of Ong's observation, that 'writing makes possible increasingly articulate introspectivity' even as it enables object-like visual descriptions of an exterior world is never more apparent than in the tenor of Konkani employed in Valaulikar's texts (2002, 103). Though Valaulikar's texts would become emblematic of Konkani print in Devanagari as used by an elite stratum of the upper castes, the force of his rhetoric was directed against the pretensions of Marathi high culture, particularly when employed by Goans. They therefore, not only explicitly espoused simple Konkani as a political stance but could scarcely do any thing other than participate in the existing culture of the language. This implies the appearance of a similar polemical and familiar tone of address that characterised works in the Roman script, in which Valaulikar initially wrote. His translations of Shakespeare and his polemics about language were lengthier than contemporary popular works, indicating a readership familiar with longer texts and thematic elaboration. They did not differ significantly however, from the simple extractions of plot and moral observations of counterparts in the Roman script.

Rags to riches: *Bertholdo* and the *Mysteries of Bombay*[4]

Translations from popular European novels and plays were common to both a Portuguese and Konkani readership. For instance, the rags-to-riches story of *Bertholdo* was a seventeenth-century Italian opera and subsequently a novel based in Verona, about a man who rose in the Italian court through his own sagacity. In 1889, an English translation was produced in Bombay, and sold simultaneously in Goa. A serialised translation in Konkani appeared in 1890 in the first Konkani journal, the *Udêtechê Salok*. Two other Konkani versions, *Bertholdachi Contha* and *Bertholdoanim techy Ojapanchi Choturai* appeared in the first decade of the twentieth century.[5] *Berthold anim*

[4] This section is drawn from Pinto 2007, 240–41.

[5] Advertisements in the newspapers *O Luso-Concanim* in 1901, and in the *O Goano*, on June 13, 1908.

Albion Patxai Verona Xaracho, advertised as a comic opera, and the tale of the success of a simple peasant who transcended his social origins,was performed at the Empire Theatre in 1916.[6]

Other literary preferences among Konkani writers were stories about the demise of monarchies and aristocracies. These enacted and legitimised the rise of protagonists through individual effort delinked from circumstances of birth as in the case of S. G. D'Sousa's *Faust eoc dublo istudant.* The publicity for the text cited G. W. Reynolds' English adaptation of 1847 as a source.[7]

Adaptations enabled other kinds of mobility. J. L. Lobo's *Mysteries of Bombay* (1924) in Konkani, which also probably drew its title from G. W. Reynold's series, *Mysteries of London,*[8] was a fantastic tale that depicted the criminal world of Bombay, represented in the image on the front cover in costumes meant to depict Pathan, Goan, Italian, Muslim, Hindu, and Parsi criminals. The detective novel, even without an identifiable source, was a supple genre, amenable to exploring the temporalities and spaces of urban life through adaptation.[9]

The history of Goa was also refigured through such adaptations. Texts such as Dumas' *Chateau d'If, A History of Charlemagne* were scarcely recognisable from original texts save for the titles and names of protagonists.[10] These served as a canvas for the creation of an ancient past, for ample descriptions of the Goan landscape, for the detailing of wedding rituals and medical practices and a critical didactic commentary on both the imagined past and contemporary

---

[6] An English translation emerged in Bombay in 1903. *Bertholde or Wonderful Sallies of Wit being the Adventures of a Peasant…,* Mrs Radhabai Atmaram Sagoon trans. (Bombay: Tatva-Vivechaka Press, 1903). See *O Goano,* 4 March 1916.

[7] Another edition was issued in 1883 as quoted in Pinto, Between Empires, 241.

[8] G. W. M. Reynolds's *The Mysteries of London* was written from 1844 to 1856, 'for a newly literate lower-class readership', according to Trefor Thomas' introduction to the 1996 edition. Priya Joshi's *In Another Country* has a detailed analysis of the reception of Reynolds Mysteries. The text was available in Bombay contemporaneously.

[9] C. M. Pinto's detective novel *Gupit Pulisechi Cannim, ani Bomboichi gupit sociedade choram-crimidoranchi* (Stories of the Secret Police and Bombay's Secret Society of Thieves and Criminals), sometimes reads as a gratuitous naming and use of the roads of south Bombay and the milieu of the growing middle class. An adaptation of the *Adventures of Sherlock Holmes* by Alex A. Pais was published in the Kannada script in Mangalore in 1919.

[10] In 1908 *Carlos Magnacho tiatr* was staged by Douglas Comic Opera. See *O Goano* of October 17, 1908. Sebastiao Salvador de Jesus Dias, *History of Emperor Charles the Great,* (Bombay, 1892). *Carlos Magno,* the play, was performed in the 1890s. Based on the life of Charlemagne, it was translated into both Portuguese and Konkani.

reality that formed the bulk of the narrative. Horacio Lobo's Konkani rendering of the first Canto of *Os Lusíadas* drew on the sixteenth-century epic poem in Portuguese, composed partly when the poet Luis de Camões was imprisoned in Goa. The book was published in Bombay at the Goa Times Press in 1931. This was several decades prior to Olivinho J. F. Gomes' translation of the entire epic, as *Luzitayonn* in Konkani in 2003.[11]

Stories and histories

The distinction between stories and histories in Konkani texts of this time was blurred, irrespective of the genre from which they were translated. By the end of the nineteenth century, the distinction between history texts and other genres of writing was consolidated among the literati who were on the boards of Education or on state library committees, but novels, whether in Konkani or Portuguese, still drew much from history as a form, using it as a convention for truth telling within novels. The titles of books sometimes overtly suggested that they were fictional narratives as with *Conta Portuguez Revolusavanchi* (Stories of the Portuguese Revolution), or *Custobha,* named after a leader of a peasant rebellion in Goa. *Istor Portuguez Indiechi* (A Story of Portuguese India), referred directly to events in recent history, but the word '*istor*' could carry connotations of a fictional narrative as well as a non-fictional account.[12]

---

[11] Dutt, National Bibliography of Indian Literature, 25–26.

[12] Advertisements for these plays can be found in *A Luz,* 14 January 1900, and *O Goano,* 4 March 1916. *A Luz,* 4 March, 1916. An adaptation of a tale from the *Arabian Nights,* titled *Teg Gossai, Razamche put anim panch ostoreo Baghdad xaracho* by S. G. D'Souza or Karachiwalla was published in 1915. In 1917, the Konkani adaptations *Aladin and Magic Lantern* and *Robinson Cruzoe* were advertised. In 1910, F. X. Douglas Fernandes wrote *Ali Baba anim Challis Chor,* followed by another version in 1962, by Felicio Cardozo. *Alladin ani Tacho Ojeapancho Divo,* and *Ali Baba ani challis chor* were performed in the 1890s. See *Soth Uloi,* January 12, 1957. In 1926, Mariano D'souza adapted Henry Sienkiewicz' *Quo Vadis* to Konkani in the Roman script. Rafael Fernandes' *When the Curtain Rises,* a study of the *tiatr,* popular theatre in Goa, lists translations published by *tiatrists.* In the early twentieth century, the prolific João Agostinho translated *Dongui Voiz,* a one-act farce by Molière, performed in 1931, and *Teg Zann Tubbokar,* based on Dumas' *The Three Musketeers.* An abbreviated translation, *Cavalleiro Dom Quixote de La Mancha ani escudeiro Sancho Panza* was produced by J. Caetano Francisco de Souza in 1917. As quoted in Fernandes, *When the Curtains Rise – Understanding Goa's Vibrant Konkani Theatre,* 72, 101.

Shenoi Goembab is the pen name of Vaman Rogunath Varde Valaulikar (1877-1946), whose works were pivotal to producing and championing a Konkani idiom that would be found acceptable by the literary and caste elite of Goa. Among other texts, Valaulikar translated Mogache Lagn *of 1913 from Molière's* Le Medecin Malgrè Lui, *reprinted by the Gomantak Xapkhanno in 1938.* Konknni Bhashechem Zoit, *a text emphasising the validity of the language, carried the attestation by three brahmins of Malabar, appended by Van Rheede to his* Horticus Malabaricus, *that Gerson da Cunha had also reproduced in his book on Konkani (appended in section III).* Jhilba Rano *of 1950 was a Konkani adaptation from the Arabian Nights set during the time of the Kadambas of Goa.*

In the preface, Kashinath Sridhar Naik recalls that in 1913, the first time the play was published, though Goan Hindus spoke Konkani in everyday settings, it was not used in literary or other kinds of formal writing. In fact, he claims, when the first edition was published, and Goembab wanted to advertise it in a well-known Goan Marathi weekly, the editor hesitatingly permitted a Konkani advertisement only after the same ad was carried in a Marathi paper in Bombay. Twenty-four years later, Naik states, by the time the second edition appeared, there was greater recognition for Konkani. He emphasises however that Marathi was the only language that carried authority for people in public and political discourse and they resorted to it often. According to him, prior to Konkani acquiring its status through publications like Valaulikar's, its speakers made efforts to distance themselves from their heritage and erase it. In a telling commentary on caste relations between Goans and Maharashtrians, he said that the Saraswats would not reveal that they were Saraswaṭs, but would say they were Marathi brahmins. At the time of writing however, he said they were ready to defend Goa and Konkani if these were stigmatised. Public speeches and plays were being produced in Konkani and the self-hatred of yore had diminished. As a mark of the status the language had achieved, he commented that even the swami of the Chitrapur math bestowed his blessings in Konkani. Naik also commented on four treatises brought out by a Konkani Samiti on the propagation of Konkani.

Ramchandra Shankar Nayak who wrote a preface to this edition, was a professor at Escola Normal in Panjim, and helped stage the play there. Nayak reported that people pointed out that all the characters used the brahmin dialect and wanted to know why they should read it. Nayak stated that he thought Shenoi Goembab had deliberately chosen to adopt this dialect and defended Goembab, saying that his version of Konkani was filled with idioms, phrases, and metaphors; that whatever the differences with him, his diligent work was valuable and the authority and command he had on the language was immense.

Excerpt 9
Courtesy State Central Library, Panjim
Kashinath Shridhar Naik, 'चोवीस वर्सांनी', in V. Varde Valaulikar, मोगाच्या लग्ना tr. from Moliere's *Le Médecin malgré lui*, Shantaram Varde Valaulikar ed., *Samagra Shenoi Goembab*, 2003, pp. 3–7.

चोवीस वर्सांनी

'मोगाच्या लग्ना'ची ही दुसरी खेप. पैली खेप १९१३ वर्सा भायर सरिल्ली. तिका आज बद्द दोन तपां म्हळ्यार चोवीस वर्सां जालीं. इतल्या काळांत, कोंकणी भाशेच्या संवसारांत जायतो बदल जाला.

चोवीस वर्सांफाटी, गोंयचे हिंदू आजचे सारकेच घरा-दारांत जरी कोंकणी भास उलैताले, तरी तिका बरपाक्षरी मान दिंवक तयार नासले. तिका ते आवै-भास म्हणनासले आनी जायते जाण तिका 'हेंगाडी' म्हणून चाळैताले. ते भाशेंत कितेंय बरौचें व छापचें म्हळ्यार व्हडली पिसाय कशी तांकां दिसताली. इतलेंच न्हंय, तर तें एक दशा-होगडावणें काम अशें ते समजातले. 'मोगाचे लग्न' नवेंच भायर सल्लें म्हणपाची कोंकणी जाहिरात घेंवक गोंयचें ते-वेळचें एक मराठी साताळें जायतें अनमनलें खैं. पुस्तकाची जाहिरात कोंकणी भाशेंत दिवप म्हळ्यार, ताका मोटें पातक दिसलें जांवयें. परंत तेंच पातक मराठणांतल्या एका पत्रान करतकूच, गोंयच्या पत्राक चिके धीर येवन ताणे ती जाहिरात छापली खैं! गोंयच्या बरपाक्षरी हिंदूंक त्या वेलार मराठी देखिची आनी धिगयेची कितली गरज लागताली ताची ही एक पत म्हणूंक जाय. आजूय ही दशा सामकीच निवळ्ळया अशें म्हणूं नज. गोंयकरांक आपलो खाशेलो मेंदू उशाताळा घालून मराठी मेंदूने वावुरची वजूच जाल्याश दिसता. अजुनूय इल्ल्याइल्ल्या कुस्कुटावण्या कामांत लेगीत मराठी काजूल्याच्या उजवाडा बगर तांचे पावल फुडें पडना. मराठीचे ते इतले बंदे जाल्यात कि मराठी पत्रांनी कितेंय छापून आयल्याबगर तांकां तें खरें-शेंच दिसना. हालींच, दोन-तीन वर्सां फाटीं, आमका मुंबै येवचें आसलें. गाडी म्हारग देखून मडगांवच्यान मोटारीन पणजे वाचून वापोरार चडपाचें आमी थारायलें. परंत मदल्या बोरयेच्या सांकवाक काय नखानामी जाल्ल्यान, ताचेवेल्यान मोटारी वचूंक दिनात अशें आमी आयकलें. हाचें खरेंपण काडूंक, मडगांवच्या एका विद्‌वान इष्टाक विचारतकूच आमकां जाप मेळ्ळी, "हय, 'ज्ञानप्रकाशां'त तशें आयलां; म्हणटकूच तें खरें आसूंक जाय!" ही जाली गोंयां आशिल्ल्या हिंदूंची गजाल.

भायर पाविल्ल्या हिंदूंची चलणूक जाल्यार सामकीच आत्महीणपणाची जाल्ली. गोंया आसताना, घरांत आनी चार-चौगांत कोंकणींत उलौंक जे लजनासलें, तेच भायर पावतकूच सामके धरिल्ल्या-बांदिल्ल्यावरी जाताले. आपली भास परक्या लोकांनी आयकल्यार आपणाक ते हांसचे नात मू? ते आपणाक पिशे म्हणचे नात मू? अशें तांकां दिसतालें. मुंबैसारक्या शारांत दोग कोंकणे मनीस एकठांय जाल्यार कोंकणींत उलौंक लजातालें खैं. ते एकमेकांकडेन इंग्लेजींत नाजाल्यार मराठींत उलैताले हें तर जालेंच, परंत बिराडाक वेतकूच बायलां-भुरग्यांकडेन लेगीत मराठीत येसाय मारतले! तांकां आपणालें पवित्र जल्म-भुंयेच्या नांवाचीय लज दिसताली. आपूण कोंकणे आनी गोंयकार म्हणून सांगूक तांकां उणेपण दिसतालें. आपले चलणुकेक गोंयकारपणाचो वास लेगीत येवचो न्हंय म्हणून ते जतनाय घेतालें. त्याखातीर ते आपली रीत-रवीस सांडटाले, व्हडविकेचो इतिहास चेपणा घालताले आनी आपली जातूय फापशीताले. आपलें कोंकणपण लिपून 'गोंयाभायलो' दिसूंक ते तांकत तितले वावुरताले. एकादया बामणाक जात सांगची पडल्यार, तो आपूण 'महाराष्ट्र सारस्वत' आनी 'गौड सारस्वत'

म्हणून सांगतालो. हेर जातीय बामणांली आत्महीनपणाची उणाक देख घेवन आपून 'मराठे' म्हणून सांगताले!

ही दशा ह्या चोवीस वर्सांत जायती निवळ्ळया. खासा गोंयां तशेंच गोंयाभायर, गोंयच्या हिंदूंक आपले भुंयेची आनी भाशेची आतां आदलेवरी लज दिसना. त्या दोंतूयं जायतें सत्व आस म्हणपाचें गिन्यान तांकां आयलां. गोंयाची कोणेय कसली बिर्मत घेतल्यार तांचें शिसल रोखडें उसळटा आनी ते ताका मोट्या किंवाट्यान फापसून बुडडून उडैतात. कोंकणी भाशेकूय ते भौमानाचे नदरेन पळेतात. गोंयच्या राजकर्णी सभांनी पुर्तुगेज भाशे वांगडा कोंकणी भाशेंत जायते जाण उलौपां करतात आनी परक्या भासांच्या घांसान घुस्मटून उस्तरीं घालौंचे बदला, खाशेले भाशेंत मेकळ्या आनी खणखणीत ताळ्यान आपणाली म्हणणी धा-जाणांच्या कानार घालतात. कांय जाण ते भाशेंत कवनां करतात, खेळ रचतात आनी माचयेचेर करून दाखैतात. मराठीच्या कांय अभिमान्यांकडसून कोंकणी भास चिड्डून उडौंक तरेकतरा उपाय चल्ल्या आसतानाय, ती भास आपूण आपल्या घरा-दाराची यजमान्न म्हणून गोंयां माथें वैर उबारूंक लागल्या, ही अभिमानाची गजाल म्हणूंक जाय.

भायर पाविल्ल्या हिंदूंचे आत्माहीणपण दिसानदीस जायतें उणें जायत चल्लां. तांकां आपली चूक समजल्या. 'गोंयाभायलो' जावपांत तांकां आतां व्हडपण दिसना. आवै-भास सोडली आनी रीत-रवीस सांडली म्हणून कोणूच वैल्या पांवड्यार चडलो-सो जायना, हें तांकां कळूंक लागलां. लाभ-लुस्कान पळेनासताना आनी बरें-वायट येवजिनासताना दोळे धांपून परक्यांचो अणकार करतल्याक 'रानवट' समजतात आनी दीस-रात खोंटो घेवच्यो पट्टात हाचो तांकां उपाट अणभव आयला. तांचो अभिमान जागो जाला. ते आतां आवै-भाशेचे सेवक पोट-तिडकेन लागल्यात. **तें आपल्या सभांनी कोंकणींत उलैतात. कोंकणींत बरैतात. व्होवळीक-पत्रां कोंकणींत धाड्टात. ते हाती आनी छापी नेमाळीं कोंकणींत काड्टात. कोंकणी खेळ बरौन ते मोट्या आट्यपाट्यान माचयेर हाडून आपले समारंभ सोबैतात. चित्रापूर मठाच्या स्वामींसारके व्हड-व्हडलें विद्वान आनी अधिकारी पुरुश असल्या उत्सवांनी मुजरत येवन कोंकणींत उलौपां करतात आनी आशीर्वाद दितात.** हे भाशेन, ज्या मुंबै शारांत काय वर्सांफाटीं आपलेच मजगत कोंकणींत निखटें उलौंकूय जे लजेताले ते थैं आज आपणालो जायतो वेव्हार ते भाशेंत करूंक लागल्यात.

मराठी लोकांच्याय मनांत कोंकणी भाषेसंबंधान मान आनी आदर वियेंवक लागला. ती भास वैर सरता म्हळ्यारह्या आदीं तांकां चड वायट दिसतालें. मराठीची ती सर्तदार कशी ते लेखताले. तिणे माथें उबाल्ल्यार मराठीचे हातपांय आंवळून तिचे सत्तेचो आवांठ उणावतलो अशें ते समजाताले. कोंकणी भाशेची सेवा करतल्यांक ते 'सवत सुभा' घट्टात म्हणून दुशण लायताले. तांकां ते 'निर्बुद्ध' म्हणटाले आनी जे आत्मघातके कोंकणी आवै-भांशेक जिवी हुलपावन तिचे मसुंडेर मराठीचो चौरंग मांडूंक सोदतात तांकां ते 'सुबुद्ध' म्हणून तांची फाट थापट्टाले. कोंकणी भास तांकत तितली कुस्कुटावचे खातीर तिका ते भास हें उतर लावचे बदला 'मराठीची बोली' म्हणटाले. ते दीस आतां फाटीं पडले. कोंकणीचे दिसांदीस चट्टें तेज आनी बळगें पळौवन, उपाय ना जावन, वोगीच वायटपण कित्याक म्हणून, मराठाणांतले कांय समजीक लोक आंता वेगळ्याच सुरान उलौंक लागल्यात. उदाहरणांक, मराठणांताले 'कोंकणी-

अहिराणी समिती'न तिचे संबंधान येवजणी करून हालींच जे चार सिद्धांत काडल्यात तांतूंतलो दुसरो आनी चौथो सिद्धांत ध्यानांत घे-सारको आस. दुसऱ्या सिद्धांतांत समिती म्हणटा कि 'कोंकणदेगेवेल्या सगळ्या भासांभितर दक्षिण कोंकणांतले भांशेक '**कोंकणी**' हे नांव पुर्विल्ल्या काळापासून घोळटा. देखून तेंच नांव ते भाशेक दिवचें. कोंकणदेगेवेल्यो हेर भासो उत्तर कोंकणी कशो लेखच्यो; नाजाल्यार, तांचीं जीं जातिंचीं आनी गांवांचीं नांवां चलतात तींच चलचीं." चौथ्या सिद्धांतांत, **कोंकणी भाशेंत सरस्पत घडूंक हुशार कोंकणी भासकारांक समितीन मोटे तोखणायेन बुद्द दिल्या.***

कोंकणीचे दशेंत घडून आइल्लो हो घसघशीत बदल तिच्या भाग्यवंत फुडारासंबंधान इल्लोय दुभाव उरूंक दिना. तिका हे दीस येवंक तिगेलीं जीं भुरगीं वावुल्ल्यांत तांतूंत 'मोगा'चें आंग जायते आस म्हणपाचें सांगूंक नाका. 'मोगाच्या लग्ना'ची पैली खेप सल्ल्यार जायते दीस जाले. ताचेखातीर मागणेर मागणी येवन भौनभौन पर्थावची पट्टाली. देखून दुसरी खेप काडची थारायली आनी छापून्य जाली; पुण प्रस्तावानेबगर, तीं उजवाडा हाडची म्हळ्यार जिवार आयलें. खासा आमकां प्रस्तावना नाशिल्ले पुस्तक हातांत घेतकूच, धनयाक विचाल्ल्याबगर ताच्या घरांत रिगिल्ल्यावरी दिसता. देखून आमी मोटे चिंतेंत पडल्यों. 'मोगाच्या लग्ना'ची प्रस्तावना म्हळ्यार 'व्होवळीक्'च ती! ती सांगतले पुरोयत तसल्याच अधिकाराचे विद्वान जायत. गोंयां पुरोयत जायते आसत खरे; परंत तांतूंतले चडशे मराठ-संस्कृत पंडित! आयकतल्यांक आनी वाचतल्यांक समजना तसलो 'वदतो व्याघात' करून ते मेकले जाठात आनिम मराठी पत्रानी अपले फोटोचे ब्लैक, मुजरत करून धाडून, ते केन्ना छापून येतात हाची वाट पळेतात. गोंयच्या हितायपरस तांकां आपल्या नांवाचो सुमाराभायर वसवस सुटला. सगळे मराठाणभर आपल्या नांवाचो जागर जावचो इतलोच तांचो हावेस! मराठणाभायर आनीक संवसार आस हें नकळत. गोंयच्या ह्या 'पंडितां'च्यो कसल्योच खबरी दिवच्यो न्हंयत, अशें मराठणांतल्या सगळ्या पत्रांनी थारायल्यार, जायत्या जाणांची तोंडां धरतलीं, हातांतल्यो लिखण्यो गळून पट्टल्यो, त्यांच्यो संस्थो वाऱ्यार उबतल्यो आनी त्यांच्यो सगळयो 'चळवळी' वळवळून मरतल्यो, हांतूंत निखालूस दुभाव ना.

पुणेंचे पत्रावळीवेले 'सुबुद्द' उतराचे गोटे वेंचच्या नादांत आपुण कसली भिकार भास बरौन उजवाडा हाट्टांत हाची येवजणी लेगीत करपाची तांक त्यांच्या मेंदूक ना. ते आपलीं उलौपां आनी बरपां जडजड संस्कृत उतरांनी भरून चिपळूणकार-सावरकारां सारक्या मराठीच्या 'अफझुलखानां'कूय गिराण लायतात आनी आपली मराठी गिनान्याची भाटी चंवाठयार फोडून घाणी-गुट्टाणी घालतात! "मराठी भास आस देखून आमी वेपार उद्योग करून पोट भरतांत; 'हिंदू' म्हणून घेतांत आनी 'हिंदुधर्मा'चो अभिमान धरतांत; तेंच ती भास नाशिल्ली जाल्यार - आमी इतले बाबत आनी अबर्गत आसत कि - आमकां वेपार-उद्योग करूंक कळचो नासलो, आमी उपासांनी वळवळटल्यों असल्यो, आमचो धर्म विसरतल्यों असल्यो, आमकां रामायण - भारत - भागवत बी ग्रंथ वाचूंक मेळचे नासले, आमचे काले आनी शिगमे उरतले आसले, आमची रोमटां जैंचे थैं थप्प जातलीं आसलीं, आमचीं घुमटां आनी म्हादळीं फुट्टलीं आसलीं. आमी धर्मा-भायरे, संस्कृताये-भायरे, आनी अभिमाना-भायरे जावन ना-नपश्यात जातल्यों आसल्यों. मराठी भास गोंयां आस देखून माणसुकी.

हिंदू धर्माबगर मराठी भास वांचत आनी वाडत; परंत गोंयचो हिंदू धर्म मात मराठी नासल्यार अर्द खीण उदक घोंटूंक पावचो ना. तो फुक करून जीव सांडटलो आनी एकल्या गोंयाकूच न्हंय, तर सगळ्या हिंदुस्तानाक सुतक धरचे पड्टलें!" म्हणपाच्यो, निजाच्या भैंकऱ्याक लेगीत सोबानाशिल्ल्यो होवयो ते गातात. असलीं जीव नाशिल्लीं रडकुरीं उलौपां छापून मराठाणभर ते वाट्टांत आनी आपले वंगदा आपले कुळवंत आनी कर्तृत्वी भुंयेचो उंच लोकिक वाऱ्यार उबैतात! तांगेले हे अपेशी करणेन, फडक्या-भाणशिऱ्याच्या 'प्रवासी' सारक्या बोंदराचेर ज्या नाखाट्यान ते किंवाट्टात तो नाखाटो ते आपल्याच हातांनी कापून शिंबरे जातात! परंत हें तांच्या ध्यानांत येना. तांचे सामखार हारसो धल्ल्यारूय तांतूंत ते पळेनात! इतलें मराठीचें तांकां पिशें लागलां. कोंकणींत बरैल्यार आपल्या खोल गिनान्याचो दिवो सासणाचो पेटत रावन ताचो उजवाड सगळ्याक सारको बरो पडचो ना आनी आपणाक कोण वळखुचो ना अशेंय कांय जाणांक दिसता. तांकां आपले बुद्दिच्या उजवाडाक गोंय आनी हेर कोंकण सामकें ल्हान आनी अशीर 'आकुंचित क्षेत्र!' दिसता. असले 'पंडित' 'मोगाच्या लग्ना'ची व्होवळीक सांगूंक कित्याक उपकारतात? आमी येवज-येवज-येवजिलें. निमाणें, घस्स करून आमच्या म्हऱ्यांत एक म्हूर्त उबी रावली. ही म्हूर्त म्हळ्यार पणजेच्या 'इस्कोल नोर्माला'चे विद्वान प्रोफेसोर **भौमानेस्त बाब रामचंद्र शंकर नायक**. मराठी आनी पुर्तुगेज भासांनी भौ बरें उलौंक आनी येत आसतानाय, आपली आवै भाशेची तांकां इल्लीय अळशीक दिसना. इतलेंच न्हय, तर ते भाशेंत ते सोबीत बरी सरस्पत घट्टात, म्हणपाचें तांगेलो 'चवथीचो चंद्र' सांगता. गोंयच्या हिंदू आनी क्रिस्तांव विद्वानांत हो एक अपवादूच म्हणूंक जाय. 'व्होवळीक' सांगूंक आमी तांचेकडेन विनंती घाली आनी ताणी ती सटकरून मान्य केली. कोंकणींत प्रस्तावना बरैल्यार आपूण उजवाडा येवचो ना हें जाण जावनूच न्हय, तर दक्षणेची लेगीत कुस्कूट आस्त नासताना, ताणी आपलो मोलादीक वेळ खर्चून, खोल येवजणेन भरिल्ली सुंदर बरी प्रस्तावना बरौन दिली. खरेले विद्वान आनी खरेले पंडीत म्हणटात ते अशेच आसतात. विद्येखातीर तांगेली विद्या. ते दुडवांक आनी मानाक वसवसनात. ह्या गुणाखातीर प्रोफेसोर नायकांची कितली तोखणाय करची आनी कितले उपकार मानचे तें आमकां समजना.

पणजेच्या 'उनियांव आकादेमीका'च्या भुरग्यांनी हो खेळ करून दाखैलो आनी प्रो. नायकांचे मदेवर्तेन ह्या खेळाच्या देखावांचे तीन फोटे मेळ्ळे. हे भाशेन, ध्याना-मनांत नासताना, हें पुस्तक सगळेच वाटेन सुंदर तरेन वाचप्यांच्या हातांत पड्टा; ताका ते फावो जाल्लो येवकार दिवन 'मोगाच्या लग्ना' भाशेनूच 'गोंयकाराचो मुंबैकार', 'कोंकणी भाषेचे जैत' आनी 'वसणूक' ह्या नव्या खेपांची वाट पळेतल्या पुस्तकांक हात घालूंक आमकां पालव दितले, अशी आस्त आस.

गोमंतक छापखानो
गिरगांव, मुंबै, १९३८

उजवाडापी

VII

The Test of Konkani in Newsprint

In 1946, a government publication addressed to the *gaunkars* (land rights-holders in each village) of Taleigao was a sign of the changing status of Konkani, as it was issued in three languages — in Portuguese, in Konkani (in both Devanagari and Roman), and in English. The *Princípios duma reforma agrária – discurso proferido por Sua Exa.o Governador Geral no dia 22 de setembro de 1946* (Principles of agrarian reform - a discussion proffered by his excellency the Governor General on the day of September 22nd, 1946) urged that agricultural workers be given rights in the village *comunidades*, which were ordinarily hereditarily appointed councils for the administration of village land.[1] While this exhortation would move against the interests of some powerful castes, it was also an acknowledgement of the amplitude of the campaign identifying Konkani (in two scripts) as the vernacular language of Goa, and the changing status of English.

The 1940s seem to mark a definitive shift within discussions and translations of Konkani, towards nationalist discourse and the anticipation of institutional structures. While the assumptions of linguistic nationalism became hegemonic from the mid-nineteenth century, it was in the mid-twentieth century that literary and language societies lent institutional authority to the idea of Konkani as a marker of identity. A sign of this was Evagrio Jorge's translation into Konkani of T. B. Cunha's conflicted tract on cultural nationalism, *Denationalisation of Goans* as *Goenkaranchem Dhesboxtteponn* (Shanbhag 1970, 57).[2] These texts are visceral in their

---

[1] *Comunidade de Goa – Princípios duma reforma agraria – discurso proferido por sua exa. O governador Geral no dia* 22 de setembro de 1946. Edição de Estatística e Informação. This was a government bulletin issued in Goa in 1946.

[2] The Konkani text was published from Bombay by António Fernandes in 1944. Jorge also translated Mikhail Nikolaevich Alekseyev's *Karyukha,* as *Porki*

excoriation of cultural symbols, signaling sharp polarisations over issues of identity. In another instance, across two articles in the *O Heraldo* in March 1943, Mariano Saldanha combated an accusation made by *Um Gôes Hîndu* (a pen-name, 'A Hindu Goan') in the *Ultramar* of 1940, that da Cunha Rivara (the Portuguese official who initiated a campaign in favour of Konkani) was a *maratófobo* (anti-Marathi). Saldanha's defence indicates how overwrought the opposition between Marathi and Konkani as a symbol of rivalry between Hindus and Catholics had become, alongside the struggle among Catholics over the nature of Konkani. His defense of Rivara leaned on Valaulikar's mocking belittling of the Saraswat affinity to Marathi. Valaulikar had used verbally aggressive idioms to displace Marathi from its position of a literary language in relation to Konkani. In ridiculing Marathi as a borrowed symbol of cultural identity, Valaulikar, according to Saldanha, had compared its use to the chewing of pre-masticated words, on which speakers had bestowed the title of the mother tongue: '*Tannem fokot morattheanchim uxttem utram tondant ghalloun, apli dudh bhas mhoratthi mhonun…*'; the analogy with '*uxttem*', or food that had been tasted by another as a source of pollution turned a quintessentially brahminical idiom for disgust into the equally recognisable political tool of shaming to prod a sub-group of brahmins into forming a distinct identity. In his own ironic parody of the anti-Konkani stance, Saldanha called on another hierarchical relationship central to Goan society when he said that those who were annoyed with the imposition of Konkani probably thought that, 'impure and corrupt…Konkani which ought to have considered herself as the humble *mundkkarn* [the proverbially oppressed tenant farmer], of Marathi, had proclaimed herself the independent *bhatkarn* (landlady)…'.[3]

A recent text (Parobo 2015) highlights the significance of the victory of a Bahujan party, the Maharashtrawadi Gomantak Party, in the elections to the state government in Goa soon after the annexation. A prominent component of its anti-Saraswat cultural agenda was the promotion of Marathi. There is much to be explored in the electorate's decisive vote for the MGP and its rejection of the symbols of its cultural agenda. Newsprint that preceded the annexation of Goa in 1961 reveals some of the social dimensions

---

Bhasanchem Rakasan, and is said to have translated Vimala Devi's *Monção* into Konkani and serialised the latter in *Uzvadd*. Quoted in Dutt, National Bibliography of Indian Literature, 25.

[3] Mariano Saldanha, 'Questões de Concani', *Heraldo*, March 14, 16, 1943.

to questions of translation and script and indicate the immediate contexts of reception.

The context of the Roman script among Mangloreans is quite different. The first Konkani monthly *Konkni Dirven* was published in the Kannada script, in 1912. The *Dirvem* had lay editors, unlike the *Rakno*, a national weekly that emerged in 1938, and had the backing of the church (Vas 2007, 26). Both the *Konkni Dirvem* and the *Rakno* began to devote column space to the discussion of the mother tongue, script, and language through the discourse of shame (strongly associated, by Goans and Mangloreans, with the experience of speaking Konkani when in the company of dominant language speakers).[4] In 1944, questions of orthography and grammar were extensively discussed in the *Rakno*, as a route to standardisation and towards a common script:

> In 1945 an article 'Roman Script for Konkani' says, "It is a thousand pities that our veteran Konkani lover Jerome A. Saldanha has turned against our Kanarese Konkani script and that he has adopted (sic) foreign script for the publication of the proceedings of the Konkani Literary Society in the '*Rakno*' and '*Mangalore*'...We certainly do not expect the westerners, no, not even our Goan co-religionists to read our Konkani writings in an alien script but we are depriving tens of thousands of our poor illiterate village friends from reading the proceedings of the Konkani Literary Society" (2007, 142).[5]

In contrast to Konkani in Goa, therefore, which was represented as lacking literary production, Konkani writing in the Kannada script denoted an already popular realm of circulation. The following sections trace some of the debates over language in the Portuguese and Konkani papers between the 1940s and 1960s.

Vauraddeancho Ixtt and everyday Konkani

When newspapers in Goa addressed Konkani as a problem in the 1950s, it was to avert the embarrassment of seeing a language that had popular acceptance unprepared to shoulder the weight of

---

[4] In her thesis (2007, 127–28) Vas states that in the article 'Mathe Konkni Bhashecho Shinn', 'Pascal Lasrado expresses how Konkani Matha is humiliated by using foreign or English words in place of Konkani. In the *Konkni Dirven* of 1923 a series of articles were published with the title *Amche Mai Bhashechi Abhivriddhi* (Development of our mother tongue)'. For an elaboration of this context, also see the excerpts from Narayan B. Desai's thesis.

[5] As cited in Celine Vas, 'The Contribution of Christian Missionaries to Journalism in Karnataka', Mangalagangothri, 2007, p. 142.

being a state language. It is therefore refreshing to read the articles of Pe. Conceição M. Rodrigues in the *Vauraddeancho Ixtt* as he took issue with the gentry's project of improvement, and its prominent advocate, Pedro Correia Afonso, an engaged and satirical critic of popular Konkani in the 1950s. The *Vauraddeancho Ixtt* (Workers' Friend) was a weekly published in Roman Konkani in 1933 by the Society of the Missionaries of St. Francis Xavier, known as the Pilar Society in Goa. It addressed issues of language, caste, and later, land and fishing rights (Noronha 2008, 185). One of Pe. Rodrigues' articles talked of the shame and ridicule to which Konkani speakers used to be subjected. His approval of the interest displayed by the cultivated people of Goa in the language was not without irony.[6] To illustrate the impracticality of some of the suggestions offered by the lettered, Rodrigues asserted that the task at hand was to work with what people currently spoke, 'and not what they spoke at the time of the conquest or 50 years after; nor that which they could or should have spoken, but purely simply that which they currently think and speak.'[7]

He asked whether anyone had ever suggested that the Portuguese revert to the language used by historical figures in the past, such as D. Diniz or that of the sixteenth century chronicler, João de Barros or the poet Camões, as a means of linguistic improvement, when even the language of the Romantics sounded antiquated a mere century later. From the time of Dalgado's turn-of-the-century linguistic studies, various critics, whether they were priests editing new editions of the *Doutrina* or the scholar Mariano Saldanha, had taken issue with the inclusion of suffixes, prefixes, words and prepositions from other languages, particularly Portuguese, in the speech and writing of Catholic Goans.[8]

Pe. Rodrigues was as concerned with uniformity and orthography, but akin to the solutions proposed by the Konkani newspaper *Porjecho Adar* earlier in the century, he urged that writers steer clear of both pedantry and puritanism. He applauded a decision to introduce Konkani in the first three levels of primary school but proposed the

[6] 'A lingua da nossa terra e a lingua que o povo fala', February 3, 1951 *Vauraddeancho Ixtt*. This was written in response to an article by Afonso on January 26, 1951 in *A Vida*.

[7] Ibid.

[8] To this Rodrigues replied that it scarcely mattered if the same word did not exist in other Aryan languages, as Konkani was without doubt a living language and would only be worsened by strange borrowings. 'Pelo Concani', February 10, 1951 *Vauraddeancho Ixtt*.

appointment of a commission composed of people such as journalists and writers who actually employed the language. This was without doubt a reference to the gentrified interest in the language exemplified by the formation of the League of Catholic Writers in Konkani, which wanted to produce improving literature for the working population of Goans, particularly those in Bombay. The paternalistic zeal often visible in the unmistakable enthusiasm with which the Lusophone elite took to the improvement of Konkani, had led to the formation of the Church-backed *Liga dos Escritores Católicos em Concani* (League of Catholic Writers in Konkani) in Margao in 1950. The League set itself the task of producing and circulating Catholic literature, 'among the popular class, to conserve the faith', and to foster the 'development of piety…and honest recreation in the clubs'.[9] It aimed to improve, disseminate, and regularise Konkani writing. Translations of books included the 'well known books of St. Afonso de Ligório, S. Francisco de Sales', and the 'brief lives of saints, which all domestic libraries should have.'[10] Plans for improving literature involved translations of short stories and novels, brief apologetic literature, Dominican missals, manuals for the holy week and possibly a Reader's Digest in the form of a Catholic Digest, aside from theatrical pieces.

Not one to back down in the face of Rodrigues' critique, which challenged the authority of those who had no proximity to the language, Correia Afonso took on the priest in a feisty article that drew on a quote from a long passage on the jackfruit by Varde Valaulikar, who if anything, was known for his rhetoric against Sanskritisation and other pretensions of the learned in favour of everyday Konkani.[11] The piece, which was substantiated with quotes from Dalgado, ended with Correia Afonso saying that he drew his authority to speak on Konkani from his knowledge of popular speech and because he was a vernacular writer and a linguist.

Newspapers such as *A Vida*, and the *O Heraldo*, and the *Vauraddeancho Ixtt* give us a glimpse of the institutional and individual activities that tried to clarify a space for the Konkani language at a time when independence from the British colonial state had just been secured, or was imminent, affecting Goan populations in Bombay and elsewhere. Pedro Correia Afonso's praise for the language used by the Konkani

---

[9] Aprovação do Venerando Prelado aos Estatutos da Liga dos Escritores Católicos em Concani (Margao, 1951), 3–4.

[10] ibid.

[11] Pedro Correia Afonso, 'Problemas do Concani – mais comentários', August 7, 1957, *A Vida*.

Bhasha Mandal, and for Dalgado, brought together scholarship and advocacy that had emerged in the first half of the twentieth century.

To be or not to be

However when Correia Afonso took issue with the Konkani words for 'church', and for 'soul', because they had been incorrectly translated from the Latin to the Portuguese and then adapted to Konkani, he had begun a battle with words that had become second nature in the context of Christian devotion. Such critiques must have weighed heavily (if they were read) on a population of writers and readers who in any case had only just begun to see institutional recognition for the language, and we may gauge how rigorously the critique was undertaken, from the inordinate column space devoted to whether '*vortouta*', the verb 'to be', should or should not be used in the present indicative in Konkani.[12] Correia Afonso cited various respected writers whose sentences implied the verb instead of using it, a grammatically correct practice, according to him, and he therefore advocated that the word '*vortouta*' was surplus to the language.

The issue may not have been one of a simple divide between popular and formal writing, if we follow the account of these public disputes over verb forms in Sanches de Souza's articles in *A Vida* in 1957. De Souza emphasises the consequences of not having a simple and publicly accepted standard for writing, which he suggested was offered by Mariano Saldanha, and initiated by Janin Rangel in Goa. Persuasive proof of this argument was the popularity of João Agostinho Fernandes' play *Kunbi Jaki* of 1934, which he claimed, continued to be read over the years, and was written in an idiom not very different from Saldanha's. Likewise, João Luis Carvalho's satirical *Dha Mandament*, of 1927, representing the needs of Goan migrants in Bombay, was popular according to him, because it was in an idiom that was widely understood. The choice of these texts is significant, as they did not represent genres or themes that were distant from the lives of popular readers.[13] In contrast, he said, Joaquim António

[12] As a sub-theme in a long running series called 'Problemas do Concani', see 'Quem Introduziu o 'Vortota?' February 15, 1958, *A Vida*, 'Lições dum lindo hino Marial', of March 26, 1958, and 'Comentário a uma gramática', July 16, 1957, *A Vida*.

[13] Sanches de Souza, 'Problemas do Concani', Part II, September 14, 1957, *A Vida*. De Souza provides an account of the exchange between Balcrishna Borcar and Mariano Saldanha on the same issue.

Fernandes, who taught Konkani at the Diocesan Seminary in Parel, had brought out the primers *Poilem Pustok* and *Dusrem Pustok* edited by the União Indiana and used by the Instituto Indo-Português in Bombay to teach Konkani, but these were so complicated they could scarcely be understood by those who wanted to learn the language.[14] Similarly, he claimed, the Rev. Ayres Fernandes in Bombay, editor of the journal *Udentechem Noketr* had followed in Fernandes' footsteps and had adopted a rigorous method for a vocabulary that was largely made up of imports from regional Indian languages. 'And do you know what the results of these efforts were?' asked de Souza. The Diocese of Bombay had to sell the press on which the journal was printed because the number of subscribers had fallen from 5000 to 400, and the book *Vangel*, by the same professor Fernandes had to be shut away in cupboards and libraries because there were no buyers for it.

A Vida and the *Vauraddeancho Ixtt* were not the only sources of contradictory views over how Konkani was to be written. De Souza (1957) recalled that in the three-member commission appointed to discuss Konkani orthography, comprising Ramchandra Naique of the Escola Normal, Mariano Saldanha and Joaquim António Fernandes, each had a different direction for the writing of Konkani, with Naique advocating Devanagari. Simultaneously, the Konkani Bhasha Mandal agitated for the recognition of Konkani as a regional language with the government of Bombay and that of Goa. Mariano Saldanha's advocacy of the Roman script was opposed by representatives from Ratnagiri, Karwar, Mangalore and Sawantwadi at a meeting of the Konkani Bhasha Mandal, a sign that such organisations could influence state policy, which was always feared for the practices it might exclude, when it decided on a particular framework for language use and pedagogy.[15]

One of the more unusual accounts among these is the two-part series, '*O Culto do Concani*' in *A Vida* of October 1957. A. J. de Heredia retold the story of migration of the Navayati community, whose origin, as a frequently-cited colonial history of Mysore claimed, could be traced to the House of Hashem from where they, along with their slaves, set out in flight from persecution.[16] Their language,

---

[14] The Konkani primers are also mentioned in the cited article.

[15] Sanches de Souza, 'Problemas do Concani', September 24, September 26, and October 15, 1957, *A Vida*.

[16] One stream of migrants is said to have halted their journey at Cape Comorim, to formed the Nubis community, while the other stream settled and married into families of the western coast. A. J. de Heredia, 'O Culto do Concani', *A Vida*, October 17, 1957. The article was an excerpt from the proceedings of the 7th Congresso Provincial held in Goa.

a variety of Konkani, found a place according to him in the census of 1911. Heredia linked this narrative with the legendary one of the Saraswat brahmins, a rare coevalness in the narrative of migration of both groups to the western coast.

Valaulikar and the possibilities of Devanagari

The writer Propercia Correia Afonso waxed eloquent about the revival of folk forms and children's tales by Xantabay (Shantabai) Valaulikar and Varde Valaulikar in her review of an issue of *Nove Goem*, a quarterly published by Valaulikar in 1937.This approach signaled the shift of sections of the Catholic elite towards the idea of linguistic authenticity that figures like Valaulikar were well placed to substantiate. As an upper-caste urbanised advocate of a popular idiom for Konkani, Valaulikar's attentiveness to folk and children's literature demonstrated that Konkani possessed two dimensions associated with the idea of a vernacular, which resonated with the contemporary European valorisation of the folk as the cornerstone of national culture. Propercia Correia Afonso was self-confessedly persuaded to consider Devanagari as the script through which Goans could recover the language of their infancy, linked to the restoration of a civilisational legacy through the folk. Valaulikar's volatile interventions published from Bombay and Goa were a corollary to asserting that the Hindu brahmins, the Shenoys, were not subordinate to the Marathas or to other brahmins of the western coast and was a mocking exhortation to the Goan Hindus to assert an independent identity by acknowledging Konkani as their mother tongue.[17] An effect of this position was a partial defence of Goan Catholics and their self-identification as Konkani speakers against disparaging references to them in Marathi.

The category of the popular after Valaulikar

The numerous books written by Valaulikar in both the Roman and Devanagari script were retellings of the history of Goa, translations of Shakespearean plays, modern plays, and language primers among other genres. The oeuvre of a single individual represented

[17] As other contributions represent Valaulikar's work, he is not discussed at great length in this section.

what a literary shift to another script would entail, and is in fact, a parallel to the realm of popular writing in Roman Konkani. Minor languages typically strain to produce the entire panoply of genres and functions attributed to dominant languages, as a mode of entry into the order of official languages. From the nineteenth century on, scientificity (grammars and dictionaries), literariness, authenticity (folk forms), and classicism (Sanskritic or any texts of antiquity) were essential attributes of a modern language. Valaulikar individually produced this range of genres, but it was not language as a composite entity, but the demonstrated potential of the Devanagari script that that made Konkani appear as a viable sign of Goan Hindu identity. The realm of popular publishing in Roman had also produced this range of writing, but rather than being recognised for having furnished a literary field in the register of the popular, it was seen as an uncontrolled unfurling of the language in texts imprinted with colloquial usages seen to have been miscegenated with other languages and grammatical structures inappropriate to Konkani. Of particular interest in this context, is Madhavi Sardesai's account of Valaulikar's influence on the writer Joaquim Antonio Fernandes (1889–1975), the author of the *Konknni Nad-Xastr* of 1972 in the Roman script, and a Konkani language teacher in the Diocesan seminary of Parel from 1936.[18] Sardesai suggested that Valaulikar's insistence on the popular register in Devanagari found resonance with Fernandes, who is said to have regularised the Roman script. This indicates that Valaulikar's tradition cannot be restricted to or contained solely by the subsequent dominance of Devanagari. Sardesai highlights the approach preferred by both twentieth century writers to draw on the resources of contemporary spoken Konkani, even when it included non-indigenous words and terms, and to resist the import of unfamiliar terms even if they were from indigenous languages, if they were distant from customary usage. Thus Sardesai's work reveals a strand common to a few writers across the century, to work for the standardisation of Konkani while remaining as close as possible to what was familiar to readers of popular texts.

The shadow of linguistic nationalism disallowed recognition of popular genres that were in the nature of cultural tools; texts that imparted information, such as vocabularies and dictionaries, but also

---

[18] Madhavi Sardesai, 'A Comparative Linguistic and Cultural Study of Lexical Influences on Konkani', Goa University, Taleigao, 2006, p. 245-248

letter-writing manuals, speech templates for weddings, dance tips, or guides to secret signs that could be used when conducting an urban romance, that allowed those formerly restricted to certain social realms to circulate in unfamiliar ones. Such texts that enabled minor languages to expand and proliferate into the present were a contrast to those that demonstrated a link with high literary traditions of the past. Curiously, Valaulikar's translations of Shakespeare, adapted to Goan cosmographies, do not vary greatly from popular histories produced in Roman, but it was his ability to furnish literary writing in Devanagari that was a sign that Konkani could be a bearer of high culture.

Cultural authenticity had been so closely linked with territory and with a demonstrable pure past, that despite being a fairly recent innovation, through its association with pre- and post-independence Indian linguistic through its, Devanagari seemed to reverberate with indigenousness. This is one of the arguments that determined the turn of the Catholic elite towards Devanagari as the sign that would secure Konkani a place in the contemporary, equipping it to receive and participate in contemporary knowledge production and simultaneously endow it with a respectable origin.[19]

Mariano Saldanha in *A Vida*

Across March and April 1961, the zeal for improvement acquired a punitive tone in the work of Mariano Saldanha who wrote four articles in the Portuguese newspaper *A Vida*. These elaborated an astringent review of *Eka Otmiachi Konta*, a Konkani translation of the autobiography of St. Thérèse of Lisieux, who died at the end of the nineteenth century, and was canonised in the early twentieth.[20] Saldanha's ire with the kind of Konkani used began with the title itself. His analysis of each word tried to demonstrate that the careless transliteration of contemporary spoken Konkani was not faithful to the grammar of the language. Contemporary loanwords from other languages did not follow the logic of absorption and adaptation that Konkani in prior centuries had, and were spelled in an ad hoc manner, he stated. For example, he pointed out that while Fr. Sylvester Menezes' translation of *The Imitation of Christ*

[19] Propercia Correia Afonso, 'Vidas, lições de Vida', November 5, 21, 25, and December 12, 1957, *A Vida*

[20] 'Bibliografia Konkani – Eka Otmiachi Conta', *A Vida*, 11 and 13 April 1961.

or *Kristacho Patthlav* in Manglorean Konkani, was in keeping with modified Latin usages and Konkani usages, the same text in the Goan Konkani translation followed a Portuguese grammatical order, and was titled *Pattlau Christacho.*[21]

The third section of the review expressed annoyance at the loanwords from Indian languages that had never been used customarily in Konkani, even though substantive numbers of prior imports had been naturalised over the centuries. The sudden change, he claimed, was a result of the tussle between the Padroado and the Propaganda, a dispute over jurisdiction and control of Catholic populations, between the Portuguese church orders and the Vatican instituted Propaganda. The tensions inherent to the relationship between the priests and parishes under the authority of the Vatican and the Portuguese orders were exacerbated in the nineteenth century. The opposition had become the ground for the expression of various social conflicts particular to the situation, such as the race, caste and class hierarchies within the clergy. Linguistic preferences for words from non-Portuguese languages were one way to signal opposition. According to Saldanha, the purge of words used by Padroado priests in prior translations of Konkani texts, led to their replacement with alternatives, regardless of the fact that this would interrupt traditions and associations already in place.[22] Saldanha also took issue with the religious journal *Dor Moinneache Rotti.* He argued that Goans never used the word *rotti,* which was probably used to indigenise Christian symbolism around bread. *Bhakri* was the word commonly used. He surmised that since the journal was started in Karachi, perhaps it had borrowed the term from local usage there. What is startling however is the vehemence with which Saldanha affirms that Sanskrit and Portuguese had elevated the language to a level, and that Konkani therefore owed them some allegiance rather than the prosaic borrowings from Arabic or Urdu. In this he echoed Dalgado's declaration that Arabic and Persian were not native to Konkani in its original form.[23]

---

[21] 'Bibliografia Konkani – Eka Otmiachi Conta', *A Vida,* No. 6537, April 4, 1961.

[22] 'Bibliografia Konkani – Eka Otmiachi Conta', *A Vida,* No 6546, April 11, 1961.

[23] *A Vida,* March 24, 1961, p. 4. In 1961, a Konkani translation of the Gospel of St. Mathew was produced by the Archbishop of the Patriarchal See in Goa, funded by the League of Catholic Writers in Concani and was mentioned in the proceedings of the League.

Pe. Conceicao M. Rodrigues (1912–1984) was associated with the Pilar Society, particularly its revival in 1939. He edited the newspaper Vaurradeancho Ixtt *(Friend of the Workers) at the time the following articles were published: 'A lingua da nossa terra e a lingua que o povo fala', February 3, 1951, and 'Pelo Concani', February 10, 1951. The articles defend the popular usage of Konkani against criticism by the literati.*

These articles were a response to the series of articles titled, 'Problemas do Concani' by Pedro Correia Afonso in the Portuguese newspaper published from Goa, A Vida, *specifically an article that appeared on January 26, 1951. Rodrigues recalled that the Konkani language used to be associated with a lack of education, and was ignored, ridiculed and forgotten or its speakers feigned a lack of memory, betraying a marked inferiority complex.*

He affirmed that the task at hand was to engage with the idiom in which people currently spoke instead of advocating methods and linguistic schemes of the past, which were entirely at odds with the speech of those who had kept the language alive. Against the rigidity of uniformity proposed by some critics, he asserted that it was the diversity and peculiarity of regional tone and social divisions that constituted the beauty of the idiom of the language and gave it its variety and charm. Rodrigues was however, quite adamant about the singularity of language and opposed the idea that dialects of Konkani had a distinct identity.

He quoted Pe. Saldanha from the paper Anglo-Lusitano, *who said that loan words from other languages should not be considered a disadvantage, for if English and Portuguese were purged of their foreign loan-words, they would be unrecognizable and incomprehensible to their speakers. Against the 'pedants and purists' therefore, Rodrigues exemplified a stance that advocated the 'way followed by all living languages', which was to borrow and adapt within measure. He noted that a fifth of all Portuguese words had been borrowed from other languages.*

As with many writers who opposed critiques that contained an element of disdain or contempt, he did however, agree on the urgent need to regularize the orthography, phonetics, morphology and syntax, but through mechanisms that worked with rather than against the current usage.

Courtesy State Central Library, Panjim.
Pe. Conceição M. Rodrigues, 'A lingua da nossa terra e a lingua que o povo fala', February 3, 1951 and 'Pelo Concani', February 10, 1951, *Vauraddeancho Ixtt*.

XIX N° 5
ıçao Semanal
PELA CENSURA

Director:—*Pe. João Francisco Fernandes*
Proprietario:—*Pe Arsenio Lucio Fernandes*
Administrador:—*Pe. Mariano Pereira.* S. F. X.

Á Lingua da nossa terra é a lingua que o povo fala

Vem isto a propósito do interessante artigo—*A lingua que o povo fala*—do nosso ilustre amigo e distinto homem de letras Sr. Pedro Correia Afonso, publicado na edição de 26 de Janeiro de " A Vida ".

Antes de esclarecimentos que se nos pedem sobre as afirmações que fizemos a respeito de unificação ou, melhor, uniformização da nossa língua, não podemos deixar de exprimir a satisfação que sentimos no íntimo da alma, a ver que o concani, a língua da nossa linda terra, a língua das nossas queridas mães, não é já um tema indigno da gente culta, uma língua, cujo conhecimento e sobretudo a fala correcta, importe vergonha e revele analfabetismo, e que por isso deva ser ignorada, ridicularizada, esquecida, ou ao menos fingido o seu esquecimento.

cando o termo *fala* da nossa tese, dizíamos que a língua é aquela que o povo presentemente fala e não o que falou nos tempos da conquista ou 50 anos atrás; nem o que podia ou devia ter falado, mas pura e simplesmente o que hoje correntemente pensa e fala.

A este propósito pergunta-nos o ilustre articulista:

—1) " E' aquela definição do concani peculiar à língua de Goa ? "

—2) " Não são o marata, o inglês, o francês, o português, a língua que o povo fala ?"

3) " E no entanto, são estas línguas *uniformes* ou *unificadas*, seja por um processo natural, seja por um processo artificial de imposições, por decreto ou lei ? "

E prosseguindo, conclui :

(contd.)

Tudo isso traía com certeza se não mais, ou um baixo nível intelectual que não sabe apreciar devidamente os valores, ou abastardamento do carácter, ou ambas as coisas por junto, resultando sempre em um vincado complexo de inferioridade.

Aquele grande concanófilo, Cunha Rivara, ria-se de tais ridículos canecos que se envergonhavam, no seu tempo, de falar ou comprender concani e punham o seu timbre em falá-lo mal.

Mas felizmente hoje não é assim. Hoje mesmo, dentre os periódicos que o correio despejou sobre a nossa banca, tres—" *Heraldo*, " " *Anglo-Lusitano*" e " *Ave Maria*" —ocupam-se do concani em extensos artigos.

***

Vamos agora aos esclarecimentos. Na edição de 20 do próximo findo, nós afirmamos que a *Língua concani é aquela que o povo fala*. E restringindo este princípio um pouco geral, diziamos: *não é naturalmente qualquer porção do povo; mas a parte principal, quer geográfica, quer política quer sobretudo cultural e literàriamente*. E expli-

4) " O que faz a beleza dos idiomas e dá às línguas a variedade que faz o seu encanto é precisamente, a diversidade dos tons regionais, as peculiaridades dos agrupamentos profissionais. "

A divisão em parágrafos e os números são nossos. Respondemos lacònicamente, para não ocuparmos muito espaço, a cada uma das preguntas.

1) Especìficamente a denifição dada aplica-se a qualquer língua; individualmente cabe só à língua concani ou à língua da nossa terra. Esse *povo* que fala, naturalmente, é o povo desta terra.

—2) O marata correcto, o "inglês inglês" o português de lei, são naturalmente—o que os respectivos povos—a sua *pars potior*—falam presentemente.

—3) 'A terceira pregunta temos a responder afirmativamente. As línguas (e não os seus dialectos) invocadas, são todas elas unificadas e uniformizadas, quer por processos naturais quer sobretudo por processos artificiais.

4) Uma cousa é língua, o idioma dum país, outra cousa são os dialectos, os provincianismos, os regionalismos.

A língua num país é única, com a sua ortografia, fonética, morfologia e síntaxe únicas; mas os dialectos, podem ser muitos, como sucede em Portugal, onde a Língua portuguesa é única desde Portugal às Províncias Ultramarinas, mas os dialectos e regionalismos são muitos. Os nossos indianismos por exemplo que não fo.

(*Continua na 4a. página*)

VAURADDEANCHO IXTT—4 3 de Fevereiro de 1951

A Lingua da nossa terra é a lingua que o povo fala

(Continuação da 1a. página)

ram legitimados, não são português de lei, não são português correcto, assim como não o é o bundo da Africa.

Os dialectos estão para a Língua, na mesma razão em que os filhos ilegítimos e espúrios estão para os legítimos, ou as medidas falsas para a medida padrão.

Assim como não se podem tolerar medidas falsas, assim em boa sociedade não podem ser tolerados os dialectos ou regionalismos. Ninguém, já se vê, tolhe a liberdade de os usar na sua propria casa, e só para os seus proprios negócios.

O uso do calão, e da gíria são considerados como defeitos da linguagem, em todas as literaturas.

A beleza duma língua, parece que está na maior perfeição da sua qualidade essencial e constitutiva que é a de ser meio de comunicação. Quanto mais fàcilmente é compreendida e quanto mais prestável e fácil é de ser aprendida e caracterizada, tanto mais bela e perfeita é uma língua.

Quem pode ouvir, por exemplo, sem sentir dor dos nervos, este trecho, duma fala regional minhota e outros queijandos:

Olá...Ora antão muito bôs dias ou muito bouas noutes. Sim...Porque eu cá na cedade, nem sei bem a cantas ando, porque não m'intendo lá muito bem c'os relojos.

Pois é berdade: e cá estou de borta das minhas biajes às capitais. Custou-me mas sempre chiguei.

Ora eu, como nunca tinha fazido biajes, arrezorbi noitro dia ir até às Lisbouas ber o meu primo Zé Cangalho, que está a serbir numa loje de panos.

xxx

Toda a língua viva evolui-se duma geração a outra, sobretudo antes de ser cristalizada em determinadas fórmas de cânones gramaticais autoritativamente impostos por um elemento unificante.

E' comparar a língua portuguesa do tempo de D. Diniz com o português actual.

Mesmo hoje em dia quem se atreve a escrever como Joao de Barros ou Camões?

Até a forma de escrever da época pre-romântica já parece antiquada e nenhum escritor de nome é capaz de tomá-la por modelo.

Hoje mesmo lemos no "Anglo-Lusitano" este trecho do Rev. Pe. Saldanha, s.j. que perfeitamente traduz a nossa idea neste ponto, porisso preferimos a sua prosa à nossa.

Nor do I consider it a disgrace that we have developed our own Concani or Govani, which we have enriched with words from Portuguese and English. After all, English is the richest language in the world precisely because it has drawn largely from many languages, Latin and French, and Anglo-Saxon. The pedants and purists tried to "purify" the language by cutting down all words that were not of Anglo-Saxon origin. Thus they wanted to say, "again bite of inwit" for "conscience." Such ridiculous attempts were laughed out of court by Messrs. F. G. Fowler, and H. W. Fowler, the compilers of the concise Oxford Dictionary, by pointing out that "again bite of inwit" might be good Anglo-Saxon, but very bad English, and that conscience though a word lifted bodily out of the Latin "conscientia" was good current English.

Adoptar por motivo razoável novas formas, baptizando-as com todos os legítimos ritos da nossa Língua, não é nenhum empobrecimento nem degenerescência, é processo seguido por todas as línguas vivas.

Se examinarmos a língua portuguesa, veremos que perto de uma quinta parte das palavras, registadas nos seus dicionários, são de origem diversa do latim de que ela se origina.

(contd.)

Segundo o cômputo feito no prefácio do *Dicionário Etimológico* de Antenor Nascentes, sobre 100.000 vocábulos portugueses de uso geral, 81.000 são de origem latina, 10.000 de origem grega; importados de outras línguas europeias, 2.000; de línguas asiáticas, 950; de línguas americanas, cerca de 100; africanas, 47; oceânicas, 37. (Vide Lições Elementares de Liter. Port. por Júlio J. Martins.)

Não é portanto de admirar que o concani, que não teve literatura abundante, e que por tantos anos foi esquecido, tivesse de recorrer a outras línguas em contínuo uso, sobretudo o português, para formar o seu léxico.

O que o povo faz, seja por facilidade ou em obediência à lei de menor esforço, não é vício, nem defeito, nem crescimentos anormais para serem amputados

O desenvolvimento anormal ou anomalias orgânicas são raras em comparação ao todo; não são gerais e duradouras, passando por hereditariedade de geração a geração. Se fossem tais já seriam normais relativamente a tais povos, e não havia razão para preocupações ou intervenções cirúrgicas.

Ninguém pensa que são doenças ou desenvolvimentos teratológicos os montões adiposos que se acumulam em certas regiões dos corpos [illegible]

Voltaremos ao assunto.

, XIX N° 6
caÇao Semanal
PELA CENSURA

Director:—*Pe. João Francisco Fernandes*
Proprietario:—*Pe Arsenio Lucio Fernandes*
Administrador:—*Pe. Mariano. Pereira.* S. F. X.

PELO CONCANI

Não podemos deixar de aceitar que alguns sacerdotes, sobretudo aqueles que estavam habituados a falar português desde a infância, falem um concani polvilhado de muitos termos portugueses que o geral do povo não usa para exprimir a mesma idea.

Porisso nós desde o princípio, pensadamente, dissemos que a língua-modelo será não a de todo e qualquer indivíduo, mas do povo em geral, da maioria, dos que sobretudo pensam e falam *habitualmente* o concani.

Concordamos também que certo séctor da sociedade para fazerem alarde da sua ilustração portuguesa ou inglesa, metem muitos termos dessas línguas; mas isso felizmente não sucede com o grosso da população.

Sempre há dois extremos que é preciso evitar: o pedantismo e puritanismo dum lado, que não são capazes da aceitar nenhum termo da origem estrangeira; nem o *snobismo* e crioulismo que por capricho e vaidade pretendem dar brilho à sua frase e fa- com o pronome relativo *que*. Entendem que tal construção é um barbarismo, de origem estrangeira.

Razão em que se fundam, é talvez a ausência desse pronome na linguagem vulgar, e nas línguas irmãs arianas.

A linguagem vulgar, que as mais das vezes, é simples e concreta, assemelha-se à linguagem das crianças em que quase falta a subordinação. Mas isto não sucede com a linguagem erudita, instrumento das mais altas abstrações e subtilezas do pensamento humano.

Não se quer dizer que não se possa prescindir-se desse pronome; mas esta possibilidade não é razão suficiente para se eliminar um direito adquirido com posse de tão longa dura. A argumentar-se assim, podia-se eliminar também esse pronome da língua portuguesa; porque perfeitamente se pode prescindir desse uso.

Mas não se encontra esse pronome nas línguas afins!

(contd.)

zer alarde da sua erudição, empregando termos de línguas estranhas que aprenderam, em detrimento da nossa.

Tornamos a insistir portanto que é preciso antes de mais uniformizar a nossa língua, a sua ortografia, a sua fonética, a sua morfologia, a sua sintaxe.

Neste problema primordial estão compreendidos todos os outros problemas, como o de depuração da língua de excrescências desnecessárias; porque uma vez consagrado e canonizado um padrão, outras variantes ou modos de construção ficarão espúrios ou relegados à classe de dialectos, giria etc., que podem continuar à vontade, mas nas falas intergrupais.

Com a introdução do concani como língua veicular nas primeiras três classes, como foi aprovado na reunião dos professores da I. Primária, terá o concani a ganhar muito e o Governo terá prestado um excelente serviço aos naturais desta Província Ultramarina.

Mas antes de pôr em execução essa acertada medida, é conveniente que o Governo nomeie uma comissão para uniformizar a língua, composta de pessoas que realmente a cultivam como são os jornalistas e escritores em concani.

O Pronome relativo "Que" em conçani

Alguns acham que é contra o génio da língua a construção de frases Que importa. O concani não é dialecto dessas línguas; ele tem a sua morfologia e sintaxe bem diferentes, evoluidas numas circunstâncias mui diversas doutras.

De resto não sabemos até que ponto seja verdadeira a instância supra de que não se usa o pronome relativo nas línguas afins. Podemos citar muitos textos quer em marata quer em sanscrito com emprego dêsse pronome.

xxx

Como já dissemos, e tornamos a repetir. O concani é língua viva, ela não pode escapar-se à lei de evolução, à lei de endosmose e oxosmose, a de dar e de receber, e não só na esfera do léxico, mas também da gramática. A evolução é integral, não se restringe só ao léxico, mas estende-se também à sintaxe, como sucedeu com a língua portuguesa.

Ora o concani de contínuo contacto com o português e inglês, sendo estas línguas quase veiculares da maior parte do cabedal literário dos que a escrevem, não admira que elas tenham feito uma tremenda e profunda impressão neles.

Lemos com muito prazer o que a este respeito escreveu o Rev. Pe. Elias de Souza no *Aitarachem Vachop.*

Mas sempre convém guardar um meio termo. Não convém abusar desse modo de construção, que pa-

(*Continua na 4a. página*)

(*Continuação da 1a. Página*)

rece deselegante; nem convém condenar os que para maior clareza o usam, com sobriedade.

Simplificaçao da ortografia

Segundo o nosso modo de ver os caracteres romanos perfeitamente são suficientes para representar todos os sons da nossa língua.

Mas para a maior facilidade e para a pôr ao alcance das massas, é preciso que a sua escrita seja simples.

A escrita simples é aquela que mais corresponde ao som sem muitas convenções; que se dispensa de sinais diacríticos e de caracteres especiais; que evita erros aos que a escrevem, por ser estandardizada.

Segundo este critério é preciso desprezar certas modulações e meios tons imperceptíveis ou difíceis de se notarem, a uma grande maioria dos que a falam.

Assim é mister eliminar:

1.° Todos os *hagas* aspirados mediais, que são difíceis de se perceberem, e os salcetanos e uma grande parte dos Bardezanos não usam.

2.° Eliminar a distinção entre *us* breves e longos, como também entre *os* breves e longos. E' assim por diante.

Pedro Correia Afonso (1892–1965) served in the Serviços Agrícolas e Florestais of the government in Goa, and is known for his studies on agricultural development. The column 'Problemas do Concani' in the newspaper A Vida *had various contributors, and the most frequent among them was Pedro Correia Afonso. He regularly took issue with various publications of the time, from printed grammars, public speeches and the regular usage of spoken Konkani. He supported the prescriptions made by the prominent writers Valaulikar and Dalgado for the formulation of norms for written Konkani and opposed what he saw as unnecessary and erroneous grammatical and lexical usages. The article 'Uma singular tradução', criticised a translation from the Bible and noted errors in the understanding and transmission of words from Latin and Portuguese. The focus of his attention tended to be devotional material whose usages had been naturalised among Catholic Konkani speakers. Some articles in these columns implied that the task of arresting the continued dissemination of errors in these oral and written traditions was the responsibility of educated priests.*

Courtesy State Central Library, Panjim.
Pedro Correia Afonso 'Problemas do Concani – Uma singular tradução' April 4, 1957 and 'mais comentários', August 7, 1957, *A Vida*.

Problemas do concani

Uma singular tradução

por PEDRO CORREIA AFONSO

Há uns vinte anos escrevendo ao "Heraldo dos Domingos" a propósito dum Auto de Natal em concani encenado no Cine-Teatro Nacional por um grupo de amadores de Aldonã, dizia eu que a prova das qualidades artísticas dum tradutor da Bíblia estava na forma e geito com que conseguisse transpor para concani o *Magnificat* e outros hinos e antifonas do mesmo sublime tom. Todos os hinos a Maria que exornam o ofício divino oferecem ao poeta tradutor as mesmas oportunidades,

Foi assim na certeza de poder saborear um bom bocado, que comecei a ler a tradução do *Ave Maris Stella* em verso concani que se publica no último número do "Aitarachem Vachop".

Muitos a terão lido e terão ficado sossobrados como eu fiquei ao ler que a segunda linha *Dei Mater Alma* foi traduzida — até sinto arrepios ao reproduzi-lo, tão enorme é a enormidade— por *Avoi O m·a Devachea.*

Justos Ceus ! Anda por ali à solta um pretendente a poeta em concani que pensa que *alma* em latim é um substantivo a significar o mesmo que *alma* em português, e, portanto, de ser traduzido em concani por *Otmó !* Maria é Mãe e Alma de Deus !

Vá que não vá a ignorância do latim, embora seja inexplicável dada a categoria do ilustre pretendente a poeta concani. Mas vir dizer solenemente, num jornal de propaganda da doutrina católica em vernàculo e leitura dos domingos para os leigos, que Maria é *Alma de Deus é,* sôbre fenomenal disparate, uma grosseira heresia !

Como não caiu esta enormidade sob os olhos vigilantes do Revmo. Redactor de "Aitarachem Vachop" ? E como passou indiferentemente sôbre ela o Mt.° Revd.° Censor Eclesiàstico ?

Não conhecer o significado do adjectivo *alma* aplicado naqueles Versos à Mãe de Deus é já ignorância demais mas inventar um novo atributo de Maria, de tão revolucionária categoria, ultrapassa os limites ...

preocupado com a notavelmente exdruxu a ideia de que *Alma* em latim é o mesmo que *Alma* em português, qualquer dicionário diria ao ilustre poeta concani que *almo, alma* significa "que cria, que alimenta. Bom, benigno. Venerável".

O hino *Alma Redemptoris Mater* foi traduzido para inglês por grandes sumidades. Newman transpôs estas palavras em "*Kindly* Mother of the Redeemer". J. Wallace traduziu: "*Sweet* Mother of Our Saviour blest".

Identicamente, em concani podíamos escolher os mais variados termos poeticos para traduzir *alma.*

Dalgado que preparou o seu Dicionário P rtuguês-Concani expressamente para ajudar os padres a compôr os seus sermões e traduções não se esqueceu, ele que naturalmente lia com inteligência e sentimento o seu Ofício Divino, que os padres topariam com frequência com o adjectivo *almo, alma.* Deu assim os seus significados:

"*Almo—Vagounno, ballgonno; povitr, bhagevont, vondvont; kolyini, prosonn, upkari, hitkar*".

Reparem como Dalgado, assim como Cândido de Figueredo (acima) dividiu os vocábulos em grupos. O primeiro grupo de Dalgado corresponde ao primeiro grupo de C. de F. : "que cria, que alimenta", visto que *vagounno* e *ballgonno* traduzem o mimo, o desvelo com que as mães tratam os seus filhos. O terceiro grupo não tem correspondência em português. Significa propício, favorecedor, beneficiador.

Para o nosso caso, é o segundo grupo que interessa, correspondendo, tanto por tanto, ao segundo grupo do dicionário português.

Para uso vulgar *povitr* chegava e sobejava : *Devachi Povitr Avoi.*

Mas o vocábulo *vondvont* tem um peculiar sentido poético muito aproveitável na versificação, pois significa adorável, venerável, venerando, reverendo. Deriva de *vondon* - culto, adoração; reverência, homenagem.

* * *

(contd.)

E' interessante que o adjectivo *Almus, alma, almum* ocorre em não poucos hinos e antifonas que os padres recitam ou entoam todos os dias, segundo as estações do ano. Temos além do *Ave Maria Stella, Dei Mater Alma*, a antifona *Alma Redemptoris Mater*. Temos ainda o cântico *Te Mater Alma Numinis*. No hino "Inviolata", lê-se o verso "*O Mater Alma Christi Carissimi*".

Ap icado a Jesus lemos no hino *O' Gloriosa Virginum* as palavras "*Quod Heva tristis abstulit Tu reddis almo germine*" — "O que Eva nos tirou com triste dano, tu nos dás no teu Filho Soberano".

Aplicado ao Espírito Santo não poucos hinos concluem com as linhas "*Cum Patre et almo Spiritu sit sempiterna gloria*".

O autor da tradução teria sempre vivido na ingenua persuasão, ao cantar ou recitar estes hinos, que eles proclamam mais uma glória de Maria, ignorada por Santo Afonso Maria de Ligório – Maria, Alma de Deus?

* * *

Se ali tivesse o espírito já

Na mesma tradução encontramos a frase *Virgo Singularis* traduzida em "Eklich Tum ge Ankvari".

Decididamente o esforço que o ilustre poeta fez, está a sair bastante infeliz. Ficamos sabendo que nesta singela e significativa poesia cristã em latim, velha de séculos, exprimindo a devoção marial de todas as idades, a palavra *singularis* está no sentido numérico de *uma só*. Maria é para o tradutor a *única Virgem!*

Numa tradução portuguesa do Ofício Pequeno de Nossa Senhora encontro esta boa versão: "Virgem inimitável".

Quem possua, na verdade e com naturalidade, um sentido poético e saiba sentir no ouvido cultivado a música das palavras, encontra em concani as mais suaves variantes para exprimir esta idea muito singela e terna que aquelas palavras significam: "Virgem Sem Par".

E' caso para a Autoridade Eclesiástica mandar expungir das páginas do jornal católico, de tão larga circulação entre leigos nem sempre possuidores de devida cultura cristã, aqueles singularíssimos versos em concani...

Administração de

A VIDA

Desde hoje todos os recibos para os assinantes, facturas e recibos para anunciantes e nas repartições publicas serão assinados pelo signatário.

Os que devem das assinaturas ou anuncios e desejam efectuar o pagamento voluntário devem também fazê-lo nas mãos do signatário, na Administração do jornal, das 10½ às 12 horas.

Margão, 4 de Abril de 1957.

Pela Administração,
Pedro Correia Afonso

Problemas do concani

Mais comentários

por PEDRO CORREIA AFONSO

Porque eu afirmei no meu artigo "Comentário a uma Gramática" que "é uma regra elementar do concani que o verbo *ser* se não emprega no presente do indicativo", pregunta me o sr. Pe. Crescencio Monteiro, contestando o, onde é que eu encontrei essa regra elementar, subentendendo-se, provavelmente, em que Gramatica.

Recordando-me de que há uns anos punha-se numa canção de cinema o dilema pungente que assim se exprime em inglês:

Which came first
the chicken or the egg,
the egg or the chicken,
the chicken or the egg...

eu ouso perguntar ao sr. Pe. Monteiro—o que é veio primeiro: a língua ou a gramática... a gramática ou a língua? Em outras palavras, as Gramáticas decretam as formulas da fala da gente ou apenas constatam e codificam aquelas formulas? O sr. Pe. Crescêncio Monteiro nunca diz "Eu *remo* as minhas culpas fazendo penitência" porque há por aí muitas Gramáticas que o *ensinam* ou, pelo contrário, as Gramáticas apenas *constatam* que é uma regra geral da língua portuguesa não se empregar o verbo *remir* senão nas flexões verbais em que entre um *i*?

Há apenas duas maneiras *científicas* de saber se aquilo que eu afirmei é de facto uma regra geral ou não é: verificar primeiro se na usança vulgar, assim como em português se não diz "eu remo os meus pecados", também se não emprega em concani o verbo *ser* no presente indicativo; e, segundo,--buscar as necessárias abonações nas obras de escritores reconhecidos pela sua vernaculidade.

Que a minha afirmação passa o primeiro *test* nem preciso demonstrá lo. O sr. Pe. Crescêncio Monteiro atenda à sua própria fala quando não se encontra no púlpito a desparar sobre a cabeça dos ouvintes o seu tiroteio de *vortovtas*, atenda às conversas dos companheiros de viagem em um camião ou *ferry boat*, ande pelos mercados e feiras e pelos campos e o verifique rá. Não é só questão de o povo não empregar o verbo *vortvotá*. Não emprega verbo nenhum, como apontei no meu artigo.

gramant hachi namna. Dinvchole Babumamalya porsant durga-degek vónnkun ho ubo ravla khoro; poront soglli bhitol'li petth ani bhayle petthemeren hacho dhôm-dhôm. Haka zolma yevn kitlim vorsam zalim tim sangum nozot. Poront zannem tachem bhikonn ruzvonn ghal'lem tya monxachi punnyatay motti khori. Ab'ba! Koslo tor ponnôs ho! Hachi tokhnnay kitli mhonnun kortolo! Sogllya Gõyam poilemvoilem dabonn tem haka. Sravonn mhoino laglyaruch ho futtunk arômb zata. Kartik mhoino yeta mhonnsor, ponnosuch ponnos! Sokoilem mull dhorun voile tengxemeren, khandya-khandyanim ox'xe kuchkhuchit ponnos. Pan koslem tem dixtti poddna. Ponnôs ponnun kedo, il loso, mannkuloch. Ponnsul mul'lyar chôdd borem. Mottayen vhodd'yaxá nal'laeden zayt. Dhong pong nikhalus na. Vantkulli gudd'ddi koxemxem. Vanoyen borem. Bhitôr soglle ghorech ghore. Nazuk bore Champin koxexe. Char kosli ti nach. Ghoro zalyar hollddduvem sotmyachem bhangar. Mhonvan thopthopit. Giber dovorina fuddem virgollun udok. Pot tant pautocuch bomblemeren thonddây. Bhikonn tori kedem? il'lenxem kukulem. Mavui mannkuli mutth koxi. Hya ponnsak dabonn zoxem sogllyam adim futt'tta toxim tachim ponnsulãy sogllyam adim piktat ani sogllyam adim ulgotat".

Teve de ser longa a transcrição porque não queria perder a sua unidade e estragar a delícia do leitor. O trecho vem, porém, para exemplicar a regra que apontei e o Pe. Crescêncio Monteiro contesta. Não tenho dedos de mão bastantes para contar as frases sem verbo. Valaulicar não despensou o verbo *ser* no presente do indicativo para fazer estilo. Despensou porque assim é que se exprime em concani.

Não se trata de não empregar o verbo *vortovta* isto é outro assunto - trata-se do facto de, como regra geral, o verbo *ser*, em concani, não se empregar no presente do indicativo.

De modo que, se as Gramáticas que o Pe. Crescêncio Monteiro leu e conhece nada dizem a respeito desta regra, então a única coisa que me resta dizer é que as tais gramáticas é que são deficientes.

(contd.)

Vamos pois ao segundo.

Por encontrar mais à mão cito primeiro umas frases do necrologio do meu Pai publicado em 1937 na revista "Novem Gõy". Neste trecho fala-se, por acaso, de *uma* pessoa no plural. Era esta, entre nos, uma regra geral de cortesia, mas hoje só a usam os indus:

"He vidvan ani kortutvi Gõyche put, Marsache 27 ver sanjevella, 78 vorsanche pirayer, Bannavle bhayr poddle. Zatin bamônn. Tanchi ghorvèdd vidvanachi... Tangelem kuttumb mottem..."

Tres frases sem o verbo *ser* no presente do indicativo. O Pe. Crescêncio provávelmente diria "*Tageli famil motti vortovia*" (a sua família é numerosa).

Em seguida transcrevo um mimoso trecho de Valaulicar. E' do seu conto "Babumamalo ponnôs":

"Ponnôs zalyar ponnôs. Toslo ponnôs ho nhoy. Sogllya Bhot

Mas deve haver pelo menos uma Gramática em que tal regra se deve achar mencionada. Não a li mas estou em apostar que a deve constatar. Refiro-me à gramática ainda inedita de Monsenhor Dalgado.

Não pode deixar de te-la mencionado na Gramática o grande concanista que a julgou tão importante que até a registou no seu *Dicionário Português-Concani*.

Sob a rúbrica *ser*, depois de dar os seus diversos significados em concani, Dalgado que escreveu o Dicionário expressamente para ensinamento dos padres,— que, afinal, compulsando o mesmo Dicionário, inventaram o *vortovta* ! - diz o seguinte:

"Omite-se geralmente este verbo no presente do indicativo; ex: *hanv boro*, eu sou bom; *te vayt*, êles são maus; *hem khorem noy*

isso não é verdade".

E mais em baixo, para explicar outra regra que não vem aqui ao caso: "este livro é de Pedro, *hem pustck Pedruchem*; é homem de ciência, *vidyecho monis*.

Se o sr. Pe. Crescêncio Monteiro quer por força uma *autoridade* —creio que a de Dalgado e a dos autores, cujos passos citei em abonação, chega e sobeja.

Aí tem, pois, o sr. Pe. Crescêncio Monteiro a resposta à sua pergunta: "Onde teria o autor encontrado essa regra elementar ?"

—Na usança popular.

—Na prática dos bons escritores vernáculos.

—Na lição mestra do Pe. Dalgado.

Mariano Saldanha (1878–1975) was professor of Marathi at the Lyceum in Panjim until 1929 when he assumed the Chair of Sanskrit in Lisbon. An earlier section of this book carries an excerpt from Saldanha's significant work, the second edition of the Doutrina Cristã em Língua Concani, *by Thomas Stephens, S. J., first printed in Rachol in 1622.*

Saldanha published at least twelve articles on the state of Konkani literature in newspapers and periodicals in Goa from the 1930s to the 1960s. The excerpted articles, a polemical critique of the written Konkani of Catholic Goans, appeared in a series titled 'Eka Otmiachi Konta', published in A Vida *of 1961. Saldanha examined what was a Konkani version rendition of an excerpt from a French biography of Sta. Teresinha do Menino Jesus.*

On March 24, A Vida *published the first part of Saldanha's account of the decadence of Konkani in modern times. Saldanha's sarcasm is unrelenting as he noted that Catholics had no engagement with the texts produced by Hindu Goans in Devanagari, or by Manglorean Catholics in the Kannada script. He commented that it was only in Goa that people wrote their own vernacular as though it were a badly assimilated foreign language. Against the idea that the process of decadence had begun when European priests introduced the Roman script, he asserted that they had transliterated the language with care and fruitfully introduced new terms from other languages. These were sufficient, he said, and Konkani had no need for the recent imports from Hindustani.*

Saldanha stated that while non-elite uses of the language may not be concerned with inconsistent spellings and usages, no language had developed based on colloquial and popular speech alone. The concern expressed in the articles was that inconsistencies had grown to dominate Konkani writing even among priests and within devotional texts. In the issue of April 13, 1961, in A Vida, *Saldanha declared that as soon as some 'concanists' from Goa got hold of a word from Hindustani, they held steadfast onto it and foisted it on the Konkani language at the first opportunity in an effort to 'purify' it. Saldanha also emphasises that while some words from Portuguese and English had been assimilated into everyday use by all sections of society, recent borrowings from Arabic or Persian (via Urdu), were unwelcome and alien to Goa.*

Mariano Saldanha, 'Eka Otmiachi Konta', March 24, 1961, *A Vida*.

BIBLIOGRAFIA CONCANI

Eka Otmiachi Konta

"Sogllo (1) sonvsar mozo môg kortolo".
S. Teresiuha do Men. Jesus.

"Beatam me dicent omnes generationes".
Virgem Maria

"Phuddã socolloiquy sonchoti
Aponneassi sodoivi mhonnoti
Sorvã tthaim".
T. Estevão, in PURANNA

"Tea nimitim sorvoi rochona Tuca xeronno
yeunu nomoscaru coritati".
J. de Pedrosa—SOLILOQUIOS

"Maria optimam partem elegit, quae non auferetur ab ea".
Cristo, in S. Lucas.

"Morieno borova nivaddu quela,
Utomu bhagu venchila,
Zo tiyessi doivem zoddola,
Ta covonnem no caddava".
T. Estevão, in PURANNA.

"Morieno maha utomu vantto venchunu caddilo".
M. d'Almeida —SERMÕES

"Christãovandô, aica tumi
equê chitim eantha Saibinnichi :
....

"Asguim equê bijiaxim bolum lagolim,
choza korunxim apulê manim :
hi Socori distê suorguinchi,
nahim dixê duninchi".
Do PURANNA, de Bombaim

Acetalização desta quadra :
"Sogllim (2) apnnam bhitori mhonnum lagolim;
ojapo korunu apulê monim :
Hi Choc (o) ri dista Suorguinchi,
Disoaam matui prutuvinchi."

"Give me the strength lightly to bear my joys and sorrows ;
And give me the strength to surrender my strength to thy will with love."
R. Tagore—GITANJALI

"Jim suk dukkam (sic) hanvem bhogchim assoti,
tim hoguralên sohon kor (1) xi maka takot di ;
Ani meji (sic) sogli xokti Tujea itchê sarki zaunu,
hanvem bhoktin Tuka somorponn kor (1) xi maka samórthya di."

Da Versão do GITANJALI, em concani de Carvar, por **Govind Poi**

(contd.)

I Generalidades

Editada por um sócio ilustre da Ordem dos Carmelitas Descálços, de Margão, veio à publicidade, vertida em concani, esta autobiografia de "Santa Terezina (sic) do Menino Jesus", biografia cujo título original não é dado, nem a edição utilizada, ao contrário do que se costuma e se deve fazer nas traduções com proveito de quem se interesse por dados bibliográficos. E' verdade que o rev. editor informa que a Santa deixou escrita uma pustoca intitulada ***Eka Otmiachi Konta*** (***Eca Otmiachi*** (sic) ***Konta*** (sic), ***hem nanv hia*** (sic) ***pustokachem ...***" Mas, perdão. Esse é o nome da tradução concani e não do livro original, que foi escrito em francês.

Não me toca apreciar a essência do livro, que é de carácter religioso, mas ùnicamente a sua apresentação linguística; e essa infilizmente, a começar pelo título, deixa muito a desejar, não obstante a cooperação de alguns clérigos mencionados no Prefácio e talvez versados no manejo da língua.

E' forçoso porém reconhecer que a cultura de concani entre os cristãos de Goa se acha ainda—e *sempre se há de achar* — nas suas "primeiras tentativas"; e pouco sucesso obtêem os que se esforçam por escrever com alguma correcção, devido isso tudo a várias causas, duas das quais são a falta do estudo apropriado da língua e a carência de publicações competentes que sirvam de modelo. Mas revistas e livros redigidos com a devida correcção da autoria quer de hindús quer de cristãos extragoeses, há-os em razoável número para quem os saiba aproveitar; mas, escritos como são em caracteres maratas ou nos canareses, não são accessíveis aos nossos cristãos em geral, que a essas "garatujas dos gentios" ***afddonant*** fogem delas. Merecem por isso as suas produções não crítica severa, mas a devida compreensão e complacência. O que porém não se pode deixar de extranhar é a sem-cerimónia com que os mesmos, confiados nos seus supostos estudos, feitos sem base nem guia, ostentam, ainda em casos correntes e triviais e até na ortografia, erros incríveis, que fàcilmente podiam evitar consultando algum dicionário ou pelo menos algum hindú da vizinhança.

A isto queria o autor destas linhas limitar a sua opinião, superficialmente exposta para não entrar em pormenores desagradáveis, tanto mais que, cônscio da sua própria insuficiência, reconhece que "fácil é criticar, mas difícil praticar". O livro porém tanto pelo seu assunto, como pela po

(contd.)

pularidade e simpatia de que goza a sua heroína, é destinado à grande divulgação e a ser lido e relido com avidez e piedoso interesse ; e o rev. editor também recomenda : ***ekuch pavtti*** (*-tthi*) ***vachun dadoxi*** (*dha-*) ***zanv*** (***zaum***) ***naka Portun, portun vach***"; "não se contente com uma só leitura ; leia-o repetidas vezes" (3) E' natural por isso que a sua linguagem, ortografia e redacção, assim repetidamente saboreadas com grandes ***anvddés, khotkhotés*** e ***amurkhé hanxés*** (expressões muito favoritas do tradutor) sejam consciente ou inconscientemente assimiladas e imitadas como modelo. E' para prevenir contra esta influência que infelizmente me compete, a bem da língua, sublinhar algumas das deficiências mais importantes e aproveitar essas oportunidades para discutir e aclarar algumas questões de interesse aos meus colegas concanófilos.

*

Não consta da página fachada o nome do tradutor (nem o ano da impressão, que, segundo certa moda tipográfica, é preciso ir buscar nas trazeiras do livro). Mas um rápido relance de vista na mesma página denuncia imediatamente ser obra de algum

VIDA-INTER

América

Em uma mensagem ao Congresso dos EUA, o Presidente Kennedy propõe a redução do auxílio militar ao estrangeiro, com aumento da ajuda económica, em que se gastará uma verba total de 7.000 milhões de dólares. Haverá só uma agencia reguladora e o auxílio irá de preferencia aos países que tenham condições para promoverem o seu próprio progresso social e politico. O fim disto não é uma campanha anti-comunista. Esse plano visa ao desenvolvimento simultaneo da economia e da democracia. Kennedy apela para que os outros países progressivos do Mundo também cooperem neste esforço gigantesco. O auxílio será dado em empréstimos pagáveis em dólares pelo limite máximo de 50 anos, com juros fracos ou mesmo sem eles. O plano foi elogiado tanto por congressistas republicanos como por democráticos.

Em Nova Delhi, Averrel Harriman também se referiu ao plano, dando os seus detalhes e afirmando que em questões internacionais

(contd.)

diatamente ser obra de algum cristão de Goa. Só nós em geral possuimos o particular condão de escrever o nosso próprio vernáculo a modo de quem escreve em lingua estrangeira mal assimilada.

Entre parênteses: Ocorre me a propósito a lembrança do seguinte trecho copiado, se não me engano, da revista *Sad* em 1953: ***Europeu padrimnim portuguez ani inglez bhassanvori konknni borounchi rit ghalun dil'lean tiji vatt laglea, ti sbaddlea*** — "desde que padres europeus introduziram a prática de escrever o concani pelo estilo português e inglês, ficou a lingua degenerada, corrupta". Pois nada disso é verdade. Conheço a literatura quase toda desses padris existente em Goa e na Europa, dentro e fora do território português e posso atestar que, se há algum concani dos cristãos escrito com menos incorrecção possível, sem nada de estilo europeu, mas genuinamente indígena é precisamente aquele que nos legaram os antigos missionários europeus, os únicos que, apezar de estrangeiros, assimilaram admiràvelmente, ao contrário da nossa incrível inaptidão moderna, o génio, a gramática e o vocabulário nativo, suprindo a insuficiência deste para as necessidade da nova religião com importações, quer portuguesas quer sanscríticas e maratas, mas nunca da lingua hindustane ou urdu (árabe-persa) como os actuais concanistas tanto se regalam em fazer. Os poucos vocábulos urdus por eles usados já estavam no seu tempo goanizados.

E é precisamente por causa dessa correcção linguística por parte de estrangeiros que alguns indianos, principalmente hindus, suspeitam, e é muito provável e natural, que nessa tarefa tenham os padris recebido valioso auxílio dos seus convertidos de castas superiores. A decadência do concani escrito é exclusivamente devida aos próprios goeses cristãos, pois só principiou a manifestar-se justamente depois da retirada desses padris europeus após a extinção das ordens religiosas; foi quando, na segunda metade do século XIX, os goeses, aliás com o ideal digno de todo o louvor e gratidão, começaram em Bombaim a editar publicações vernáculas na generalidade muito deficientes, porquanto, como verdadeiros cristãos de Goa, vivendo embora quase toda a vida entre os maratas e dedicando-se à cultura do concani, nunca procuraram, como ainda hoje não procuram, aprender marata, que tão útil lhes teria sido para a assimilação do génio e estilo dos idiomas indianos e portanto de concani. E o pior tem sido no presente século em que certos escritores, ingènuamente confiados nos seus "estudos especializados", pretendem ousadamente consertar, restaurar, depurar etc. o vernáculo e só o desconsertam ainda mais com as novidades obtidas nas suas locubrações, tais como *vhoirlo, baherlo, teaka, saheb, xahanno, nahann,* ***pisaiponn*** e outras ***pisaiponnans*** anti-concanis desse quilate.

Abril 1960.

Mariano Saldanha

(*Continua*)

Notas :

1) Vão aqui transcritas, mesmo com o risco de enfado, algumas das passagens que a leitura da presente publicação me fez lembrar pela similaridade dos conceitos. Acompanhem nas traduções antigas para se apreciar o sabor das duas linguagens. O sabor métrico só poderá ser apreciado por quem saiba ler poesia indiana à maneira indiana, guardando melòdicamente a sua cadência prosódica, cadência que absolutamente falta nas actuais composições poéticas dos cristãos e mesmo nas antigas por estes *corrigidas*, isto é, estragadas. Vi nestes dias transcrito num artigo de jornal um fragmento dos hinos da Sra. do Monte. Como era um cristão que o fazia, suspeitou-se logo que devia estar errado, e estava de facto; errado na ortografia, errado nos vocábulos, na rima, na prosódia...

2) *Sogllim*... todas as religiosas do convento, quando para lá entrou, ainda aos três anos de idade, a futura Mãi de Deus.

3) *Vach (tum)*: O emprego da 2a. pessoa do singular, especialmente por parte de um autor dirigindo-se aos seus leitores não é aprovado pela ética indiana. V. Valaulikar até entendia que da gramática devia ser eliminada essa pessoa no singular, que todavia serve para invocar seres celestiais, como em *Tum sorgar assai, Tum sodoiv* etc.

Mariano Saldanha, 'Eka Otmiachi Konta', April 4, 1961, *A Vida*.

Bibliografia concani

Eca Otmiachi Konta

(Continuação do no. 6530)

"Arjund, dusrea kitear mon lainastatanam
sodinch zo mozo ugddas korta
tea monxeak hanv mellunk sompo".
Bhagvad-Gita, trad. de Vam. Valaulikar.

II Exame da fachada

Entrando na apreciação do livro:

Logo na primeira linha da fachada lê-se: "Sta. Terezina (sic) do Men. Jesus". Mas em português e portanto em concani creio que geralmente se diz Terezinha, forma mais popular e carinhosa do povo português, embora em ambos os casos o sufixo seja o mesmo.

Objectar-se-á talvez que o concani não possui o fonema ou som português de *nh*, nem os alfabetos indianos letra que o represente. Primeiramente os goeses, pelo contacto íntimo de 4 séculos com a língua portuguesa, já adquiriram, há muito tempo, esse som — e vergonha seria o contrário — e o pronunciam com toda a correcção e facilidade; pode não o ter assimilado a plebe, mas a sua fala não é modelo nem autoridade em nenhuma língua. A classe média mesmo não instruida sabe dizê-lo e até conhece aqui mais *Inacinhos* e *Marianinhas* do que há em Portugal. E o próprio livro em questão, na sua extranha incoerência, enquanto nuns passos diz Terezinha e Terezina nos títulos das estampas escreve sempre Terezinh. Como, segundo informa o rev. editor, muitas foram as mãos clericais que na redacção do livro intervieram, procederam certamente segundo o Evangelho e as mãos esquerdas não trataram de saber o que as direitas teriam feito; daí talvez essa constante e máticos recomenda expressamente respeitá-la porque "assim é a pronuncia dos naturais". Hoje porém quem ignora essa pronuncia dos naturais são os próprios naturais. Ou talvez não seja bem a ignorância, mas consequência dos tais "estudos especializados", que em má hora vieram perturbar a evolução natural da língua.

Konta: O sânscrito *kotha* é adoptado tal qual por todos os vernáculos, ao menos na escrita, e mesmo em concani o é por todos os hindús e pelos cristãos extra-goeses que eu saiba. E' verdade que o Puran de Bombaim escreve *kontha*, *Christãovandó* e outros plebeismos; mas foi escrito no século de 600, em que toda aquela região era povoada por kollis, agoris, bonddaris e outras castas inferiores, que falavam o marata degenerado; e eram — segundo escreveu um jesuita — bons agricultores e possorcares, mas não serviam para aprender latim, que se lhes ensinava nos colégios de Baçaim e de Karanjá, perto de Bombaim. Contudo eles ainda escreviam *kontha* (com *th*); quem perdeu esse *h* fazendo *konta*, somos nós, os latinistas de Goa, talvez porque o latim popular *contare* não tem *h*. De resto *konta* com nasalização não é nada corrução. Está dentro das normas formativas de alguns vernáculos. O que porém sucede é que mesmo entre nós ela é usada em sentido depreciativo, como em *tachió konta aikun amchem pott bhoro-nam*, "ouvindo as suas lérias não ganhamos pão nem férias", e "lérias" são "patranhas com que se pretende iludir a boa-fé dout'em". *Eka Otmeachi Konta* seria portanto as "patranhas duma Alma", o que

VIDA-INTE

Mensagem Papal pela Páscoa

Sua Santidade o Papa João XXIII, falando ante-ontem a 250.000 pessoas reunidas na Praça de São Pedro, disse da violência e injustiça que entristecem o seu coração e condenou a atitude dos que aterrorizam pelos seus actos os que amam a paz e a justiça. O Sumo Pontífice apelou para que todos honrem a Glória e triunfo de Nosso Senhor e terminou por desejar uma Páscoa felíz e abençoada para todo o Mundo, em 16 línguas, incluindo o russo, dando por fim a Benção Apostólica *urbi et orbi*. A ceri mónia foi transmitida pela rádio e televisão.

Outras mensagens

O Arcebispo anglicano de Cantuária, Dr. Fisher, frisa mais uma vez, na sua mensagem pela Páscoa, a necessidade da unidade cristã e o de York, Dr. Ramsey, que sucederá a Dr. Fisher em Junho, declara que os homens, brancos e pretos, devem olhar uns para os outros à luz da Páscoa e o *apartheid* desaparecerá.

Paz pelo desarmamento

Tem havido demonstrações a favor de proibição das armas nucleares e desarmamento total em vários países, incluindo EUA e Inglaterra, participando nelas milhares de pessoas.

Argélia

Um porta-voz do departamento norte-americano de Estado exprimiu ante-ontem a esperança de que as propostas negociações franco argelinas começarão em 7 conforme o plano, e serão bem sucedidas.

(contd.)

Os Chefes argelinos, porém, tornaram claro que eles só tomarão parte nessas negociações se a França desistir de negociar com aborrecida falta de uniformidade ortográfica até no nome da própria heroina do livro !

Finalmente, se os alfabetos indianos não possuem símbolo apropriado a esse som, tratará de o ter aquele, que for adaptado ao concani, pois não é a língua que se há de adaptar ao alfabeto.

Otmiachi Konta : é o título do livro. Há duas formas temáticas diferentes ; e em *ia* vg. *doro*, cordão, *doreak*, *kolokoleak*, *rupem-peak*; em *ea* vg : *tutio tiak*, *doria* (em Salsete *dorio*), mar, *doriak*. *rupia piak* ; pois o presente tradutor, seguindo a nova moda, escreve ambos os temas da mesma forma — em *ia* ; de modo que *rupiacho duddu* (pg 55) tanto pode ser moeda de rupia, como de *rupem* prata, a assim *doriak* tanto serve para *doro*, como para *doria*, *ghoddiank* é datívo igualmente de *ghodde*, cavalos, e de *ghoddió*, éguas, e portanto em vez de *borea otmeak* escreve *boria otmiak*. Mas o *i* de *ia* obriga a fechar a vogal anterior como em *doriak* ao mar e por isso *otmiak* também deviamos pronunciar *ótmiak*, o que é incorrecto; ao passo o *e* de *ea*, sendo aberto, mantém também a abertura da vogal anterior, como em *doreak*, *otmeak*. Em conclusão, devia ser *otmeachi* e não *otmiachi*.

Esta diferença entre *ia* e *ea* era sempre observada pelos antigos missionários e um dos seus graviria dar razão a um leitor, que, ao restituir-me o livro, classificou-o de "Patranhas infantis". O carácter do livro e da sua autora exigia a forma mais nobre e literária—*Kotha*.

Descendo ao longo da fachada, ainda temos esta frase : *Fransez bhaxen thaun Konknne bhaxen utrailam Moddgonvchiam Karmelitas Deskalsos hannim* ". Ainda bem que aqui escreve *bhaxen* (*bh*), quando no texto é quase sempre *baxén* (*ba*), mas *bhaxén* é caso instrumental, que não quadra para o caso, nem se adapta bem à posposição ablatival *thaun*: devia ser *bhaxent thaun* (ablativo locatival) ou melbor *fransez bhaxentlem* (outra forma de abl. locatival). O conhecido escritor concani de Mangalur, rev. Pe. Silvester Meneses no seu *Kristacho Patthlav* (Imitação de Cristo em caracteres canareses, diz muito bem : *latia bhaxê thaun*, vertido do latim ... em que *bhaxê* é apenas o tema, que admite todas as posposições ; e essa frase está idiomática, apezar de o autor não ser de Goa, ou, melbor, justamente por não ser de Goa, *Latia* é forma muito usada em Mangalur. E a propósito : um cristão de Goa também traduziu o mesmo livrinho, mas marcou-o logo com o *trade mark* do *digitus Christiano-Goanensis*, denominando-o *Patthlav Christacho*, por ser esta a ordem em português e em inglês.

Konknne bhaxen : *Konknni* tem duas declinações : Nós dizemos *eké konknnê bailên*, uma mulher hindu, *ekê konknni bailên* uma mulher do Concão e *konknni moratthi*, *bengali bhaxent* e não *konnknné*, *moratthé*, *bengalê bhaxent*.

Moddgonvchiam : A palavra é *Moddganv* (aldeia do *motth*, prácrito *moddh*) cujo *a* na linguagem coloquial se abrevia em *o*, mas na escrita todos (não cristãos de Goa) conservam esse *a*. E é por isso que em português deu *Margão*, *Belgão* e não *Margonv*, *Belgonv*...Num conto publicado por um hindu na revista *Avoi*, de Malvane, e intitulado *Vonvllam-Vas*, lê-se *Moddganvchea xallentlem xikxonn* ... *Moddganvchea xallek Mei mhoineachi roja*...

Hannim : O tema do pronome *ho* no plural é *ham*, e portanto *hankam hancho hamnnim*, e não *hannim*, como escrevem muitos, até hindus ; e não deve ter o traço de união com *Descalços*, porque são palavras separadas. A frase inteira podia ter outra ordem melhor, como esta : *Tem* (*jivit*) *fransez bhaxentlem Moddganvche* (e não *Moddgonvchiam*) *Karmelitas Descalsos hamnnim konknni bhaxent utrailam*).

Abril 1960.

Mariano Saldanha

(*Continua*)

Mariano Saldanha, 'Eka Otmiachi Konta', April 13, 1961, *A Vida*.

Bibliografia concani

Eka Otmiachi Conta

(Conclusão do no. 6537)

III Exame do interior

"Hanvem boroilan tem polleun kanvuch ojiap (ojap) zatam"... S. Teresinha do Men. Jesus.

A observação do interior deste monumento literário oferece um campo vastíssimo para comentos. Vai-se por isso resumir em grupos gerais algumas das considerações mais importantes.

a) *Aspiração das inaspiradas*, como em *dhatt, bhag* (felicidade) *dhoria, ghodd*, (ramo de bananas) *vhoir, bhosunk, ghelolo*... em vez de *datt, bag* (jardim) *doria, godd* (doce) e assim as outras que não devem ter *h*.

b) *Inaspiração das aspiradas* vg: *oi, noi, ozar, gam, baxen, uni burgeponn*... em vez *hoi, nhoi, hozar, bhaxen, vhoni, bhurgeponn*... E assim também a cerebralização das dentais e vice-versa, isto é, *dd, tt*, em vez de *d,t* e vice-versa.

Estas confusões, características nas publicações da maior parte dos cristãos de Goa, têm sido a causa da ideia errónea que alguns estudiosos têm feito da nossa fonética e um professor eminente de Paris estranhava que entre todos os idiomas só o concani tivesse uma fonética diferente e contrária à evolução dos actuais vernáculos.

romano) *Sáib* vg. *Sáib ghella*, e assim *lhan, nhann, lhuv, lharam, mhataro* ... Agora, porém, alguns concanistas, especialmente clérigos, no seu empenho de reformar, consertar e depurar a língua, descobriram que se deve escrever *Saheb, mahataro, nahann, hallu* ...e como isso não é correcto, está sendo abraçado por quase todos.

Tanto o *sáib* conc. como o *saheb* dos maratas provem do árabe *sahib*, em que o *h*, sendo intervocálico, ou deve passar para a primeira consoante (dando shaib), como nos árabes *mohina-mhoino, bahir-bhair* ou deve emudecer, como em *tahan-tan* (séde) *kahanni kanni* e não *than, khanni*, que são outras palavras diferentes. Mas em *sahib* a primeira consoante é a sibilante *s*, que já é de si aspirada e não aceita mais aspiração, e portanto o *h* tem de emudecer, deixando a palavra reduzida a *sáib*, com o ditongo *ái* (que não existe no nagárico) acentuado na primeira vogal por ser mais forte do que a segunda, dando *sáib* e assim se escrevia. Agora *saheb* está bem em títulos nobiliárquicos maratas, como Rau Saheb Dexmukh, Rau Saheb X. Colaço (de Mangalur).

Nahann vem do sânscrito *snana*, cujo *s* inicial foi, já no prácrito, assimilado pelo *n* seguinte, dando *nnhanna*, e como o concani não usa *nn* no começo da palavra, ficou esta reduzida a *nhann*.

Hallu (*ho*[illegible]), que se vê no livro, também não tem razão, embora talvez assim digam em Salsete. O sânscrito *loghu* deu no prácrito *lohu*, donde o concani *lhov* ou *lhuv*. Os maratas porém inverteram a ordem das consoantes e fizeram *hollu*.

Igorz Matha: *matha* é *marata*, em conc. *matho* significando *cume* vg *Ghantthacho matho*. O que o autor quer dizer é *mata* sem *h*, nominativo de *mátar*, latim *mater*.

Os antigos missionários escreviam *igrez*, que deu *igroz*, como *freguês-fergoz*, o antigo *ingrez-ingroz*. *Igroz* deu o tema *igorge*, pelas mesmas razões fonológicas por que *visrot* deu *visorta*. Deste tema *igorje* fizeram especialmente em Salsete, *igorz*, que não é tão correcto como *igroz*. *Igorz* também daria *igroz*, como *gorz-goroz*.

Mariano Saldanha

(Continua)

(contd.)

Foi preciso convencê-lo a não tomar como exemplo e autoridade os nossos escritos, porquanto os cristãos de Goa pronunciam bem, mas, por falta de instrução alfabética, representam mal a sua própria pronúncia dificultando assim a leitura e compreensão. Achou curioso que houvesse semelhante fenómeno!

c) *Má divisão silábica* no fim das linhas e em todas as páginas, como *sopun-am, khat-ir, xik-osta xedd-ianche, ghoddd-ot, sorg-inchio*... Nem uma criança de instrução primária faria semelhante divisão que ao menos os tipógrafos podiam ter corrigido.

d) Expressões anti-idiomáticas: *konn porim, konn bhaxen*; *konn* em nominativo e *porim, bhaxen* em instrumental; devia ser *konna bhaxen*... *Apleak*: *Aplo* é adjectivo genetival de *apunn*, cujo dativo é *apnnak* e assim *apnnacho* e não *apleacho*, mas é o falar de Salsete. Sempre se disse e se escreveu *sonvsar*, pronúncia que já vem do sânscrito, e é seguida por todos os vernáculos, incluindo o concani, em que ninguém diz *sonsar*, a não ser talvez em Salsete.

bariksann...o sufixo *sann* junta-se aos adjectivos de gosto, como *góddsann, tiksann* e aos de côr vg *dhovsann, kallsann*. com *barik, motto*, diz se *barkai, mottai*.

titleim, kiteim, tacheim...devia ser *titlem i, kitem-i, tachem i, oxem-i*.

pisaiponn. O sufixo *ponn* junta-se aos substantivos e adjectivos concretos para os tornar abstratos, como *bhurgeponn, boreponn*. *Pisai* já é um subst. abstrato, de *pisso* e não aceita mais *ponn*; etc. etc.

*

Vocabulos com *h*: Sempre se disse e se escreveu em Goa (em

Falando ante-ontem a jornalistas, o Presidente Charles De Gaulle da França apelou para que os nacionalistas argelinos negociem com o seu país, nada dizendo, porém, sobre a questão da participação nas conversações do Movimento Nacional Argelino, grupo que é considerado um satélite da potência colonial pelo Governo Provisório da Argélia, que se recusou a tomar parte nas negociações designadas para 7 do corrente em Evian depois de o Ministro para a Argélia, M. Joxe, ter anunciado que esse grupo também participaria nelas. De Gaulle declarou que a França não deseja manter a Argélia, ou qualquer outro território que se oponha a isso, sob a sua administração. Se a Argélia se decidir a separar da França, cessará o auxílio francês aquele país, os franceses residentes lá serão convidados a ir para a França e os argelinos residentes na França serão expulsos. Se ao contrário a Argélia resolver continuar a sua associação com a França, o auxílio francês continuará, mas só sob garantias de cooperação entre argelinos e moslems e de existência de bases francesas na Argélia. Logo que a guerra na Argélia cesse, todos os prisioneiros serão postos em liberdade.

Rússia

Há notícias desencontradas sobre o envio dum homem ao Espaço pela Rússia. Segundo o Prof. André Kuzuietzov, esse envio é provável num futuro próximo. Mas o órgão comunista britânico *Daily Worker* afirma que um homem foi já enviado na Rússia ao Espaço e regressou vivo, estando porém a sofrer das consequências da viagem.

Em Jerusalém, o agente do Ministério Público no julgamento de Adolfo Eichman, antigo Coronel da Gestapo, acusou-o de crimes contra Israel e contra a Humanidade e outros. As acusações feitas tornam-no merecedor da pena de morte por enforcamento. A defesa alega que o réu foi trazido à força da Argentina e que ele está a ser julgado por um país inexistente quando da prática dos crimes de que é acusado. Levanta além disso suspeição de parcialidade contra os juízes do Tribunal que o está a julgar.

O Dr. Konrad Adenauer, Chanceler da Alemanha Ocidental, comentando ante-ontem esse julgamento, fez votos por que toda a verdade seja lá revelada e a causa da Justiça servida, acrescentando que o nazismo já deixou de existir na Alemanha.

Laos

Um porta voz americano declarou ante-ontem que a demora na resposta soviética à Inglaterra sobre a questão de cessação de fogo em Laos pode levar a uma situação muito séria. Acrescentou que aumentou o fornecimento de armas soviéticas às forças esquerdistas daquele país e, interpelado sobre se o mesmo se dá com o auxílio americano às forças governamentais, respondeu: Um tanto.

De Londres, porém dizem que se espera dentro de dias um acordo anglo soviético sobre a solução do problema laonense.

A Inglaterra propôs datas fixas tanto para a cessação de fogo como para a Conferência Internacional proposta.

Congo

As autoridades da ONU enviaram esforços para a cidade de Kabalo, onde houve recentemente um

Mariano Saldanha, 'Eka Otmiachi Konta', April 14, 1961, *A Vida*.

Bibliografia concani

Eka Otmiachi Conta

(Conclusão do no. de ontem)

Importação de vocábulos extranhos: Habituados ao emprego de palavras portuguesas ou inglês s, alguns concanistas de Goa, quando apanham um vocábulo da religião hindu ou da língua hindustane, agarram se a ele e o impingem logo na primeira oportunidade a fim de "depurar" a língua. No presente livro, entre outras depurações, vê-se usado *môtt* por convento e abadia; dantes, dizendo-se *igroz devull*, *lôgn*, *kazar* sabia-se a que templo e a que religião se referia, agora dizendo-se *devllant gela* não se percebe se foi à igreja, ao pagode ou à mesquita, do mesmo modo *lôgn zalam* pode agora ser tanto dos cristãos, como dos hindus ou maometanos. Não importa, com tanto que se apresente como última novidade, um termo usado com nova significação. Assim faziam os missionários protestantes e mesmo os católicos não portugueses, que tanto para adular os seus convertidos, como por aversão ao Padroado português, seu rival, expulsaram dos antigos catecismos vernáculos dos nossos missionários as palavras *bautism*, *padri*, *igrez*, *sacrament*, *profet*, *altar*... substituindo-as respectivamente por *dnyan snan*, *guru*, *devull devadravya*, *duradruxtti*, *devará*...e mais palavreado trovejante do sânscrito. E os nossos clérigos, que adoptam *devull*, *lôgn* ... porque não hão de chamar *bhôtt* ao padre e *horidâs* ao pregador? cismo, traduzindo o "pão nosso" substituira *grâsu* por *bhakri*, fui amàvelmente informado (o que muito agradeço) :de que não foi *bhakri* que ele empregara, mas sim *rotti*, o que foi ainda pior do que *bhakor* ou *bhakri*, porque além de não ser palavra vernácula de Goa, nem tem a nobreza genealógica que tem o *bhakhor*, porquanto este—segundo a etimologia dos maratas—provém do sânscrito *bhas-kara* (o que faz luz) isto é, o sol, nome dado por causa da sua configuração circular, enquanto que uma outra apa como a lua, mais delicada e mais apreciada seria chamada *sandon* de *chandnem*, lua; note-se que é apenas uma etimologia popular. Mas o *rotti* não tem nada disso. *Rotti*, *nasto*, *mosko*, *bichannem*, *xiddi*, *torkari* são mimos da *Mumboichi bhas*, que em G a entram como parte do *samonn* dos emigrantes e com eles se vão embora sem conseguirem criar raizes no solo linguístico do país.

Mais : clérigos de Goa publicam ou publicavam em Carachi a revista religiosa *Dor Mhuiniachi Rotti*, muito divulgada nos nossos lares cristãos. Pois creio que não há de haver em Goa uma só leitora (sem ser emigrante, é claro) que como dona de casa tenha na sua mesa substituido pe'o forasteiro *rotti* os seus tradicionais e populares *unddo* e *bhakri*. Ainda mais : Há poucos anos clérigos de Mangalur fundaram lá a

(contd.)

Do hindustane importado pelos nossos emigrantes o tradutor serve-se, entre outras palavras, de *rotti* pão ou apa, *torkari* hortaliça, *xiddi* escada e até de um composto híbrido *xiddi ani corrimão*. Palavras como *iskad*, *verdur* (hortaliça) figuram no concani desde séculos ; já estão por tanto enraizadas na língua e tão generalizadas, que até as curumbinas de Loutulim empregam *verdur* nos seus ingénuos *versos* de *pitthans* e *bensanvans*, como no seguinte :

> "*Yerdura bhitor yerduru*
> *Konkonno dudhi xirextlu* ; (1)
> *Toso Bab ámcho Inturu*
> *Novream bhitori girestu.*"

E diga-se agora se há o direito de expulsar um vocábulo português concanizado durante séculos e usado até pelas últimas camadas sociais do país para ser substituido por outro de origem árabe, estranho em Goa, apezar de usado pelos emigrantes. A este respeito há que notar o seguinte e afirmá-lo com toda a ênfase : Goa tem o direito e dever de adoptar e manter as adoptadas — antes palavras das línguas portuguesa ou inglesa, a quem deve o seu progresso e elevação social, do que as das línguas árabe e persa (urdus) a quem pouco ou nada deve. Agora os emigrantes sim, esses têm de assimilar algum palavreado hindustane para viverem naquelas terras onde ganham o seu *rotti* cotidiano.

*

Adenda et corrigenda : Tendo eu escrito, há meses, em *A Vida* que um clérigo goês no seu cate- Instituição do Pão de S. António, a que chamaram *S. Antonicho Grásu*. Em Goa e pelo visto clérigos que tivessem aspirado uma pitada dos ares de Bombaim teriam logo preferido a designação de *S. Antonichi Rotti*. E note-se que em Mangalur não é estranha a palavra *rotti* ou *rontti*, como vi escrito e como o atesta o dicionário de Maffei; contudo, para uso literário e nobre a classe ilustrada preferiu o poético *grásu*, vocábulo que os implantadores do cristianismo extrairam em Goa da rica mina sanscrítica e dignificaram enxertando-o na sua Doutrina; e foi o clero goês que nos tempos do Padroado o divulgou por toda a área de concani, desde Malvane e Sauntvari até Carvar, Mangalur e Calicute; pois hoje são os próprios sucessores do mesmo clero que na sua própria terra o enjeitam para afagarem o prosaico *rotti* dos mussulmanos !

Basta. Pela categoria da autora, do assunto e dos reverendos tradutores e editores, este livro podia ter constituído uma contribuição valiosa para a faminta língua e literatura concani; mas não foi feliz, e admiração seria se o fosse. Como *solatium miseris*, só pode consolar-se com ter inúmeros sócios em quase todas as obras produzidas na mesma literatura por nós, cristãos de Goa.

Maio 1960.

Mariano Saldanha

---

(1) Ouve-se também dizerem *xiresco* (fresco) ; mas *xirextlu* (excelente) rima melhor com *girestu*. *Inturu* é *Ventura*.

In the late twentieth century, the impact of the Sahitya Akademi can be seen in the formation of a national secularised canon that can act as a compelling universalising script for inclusion through conformity and homogenisation.[24] With reference to the Goa Konkani Akademi's support of translation activities such as Ravindra Kelekar's adaptation of the Mahabharata, Narayan B. Desai (2002, 158) states,

> This or the earlier translations of *Yakshaprashna* and *Raghuvansho* of Kalidasa from Sanskrit to Konkani..., translations of the *Bhagavad Gita* both in prose and in verse were claimed as the proof of competency of the language to express the rich ancient Indian thought and ideas, in the line of Shenoi Goembab's *Gomantopanishat*. All this shaped the common standard of Konkani in Devanagari, for Goa, and also prepared a base for staking claims to the 'national' status.[25]

The Navjivan Trust in its mission to make the works of M. K. Gandhi available in as many languages as possible, subsidised the Konkani translation of Gandhi's autobiography, *Satyache prayog va atmakatha* by Gurunath S. Kelekar in 2010. One could argue that the Goa Konkani Akademi extended this translation map, as it published Ravindra Kelekar's *Ami Taankan Manshant Haadle* from Gujarati in 1990, and Harishchandra Nagvenkar's *Shejari* from Kannada. *Aesop's Fables* and the *Bhagavad Gita* were rendered over and over into Konkani, with the Gita being produced in the Kannada and Devanagari scripts.[26] Suresh Amonkar's *Shree Bhagwantan Gaeellem Geet* of 2002 lists ten of the translations he traced between Valaulikar's edition of 1959 and 2002. Among these were one from Cochin and

---

[24] Among translations from Rabindranath Tagore's oeuvre are *Pandurang Bhangi's Chitrangada Bidai Obishap,* and B. B. Borkar's *Sanjeevani* in verse. Rabindranath Tagore, *Chitrangada,* trans. *Pandurang Bhangi* (Panaji: Rajahans Vitarana, 1990). *Fulachem Mol, Paris Mani* and *Ghovacho Labh* are other translations by Borkar of Tagore's work into Konkani. Raghunath Desai, "Konkani: Quality and Quantity."

[25] Desai, 'Politics of Script: The Case of Konkani (1961–1992), 158.

[26] In 1941, Mangesrao Telang wrote a mid-twentieth century version of the Bhagavad Gita in Konkani, as did B. N. Kamath. V. V. Valaulikar's 1959 edition in Konkani prose, *Bhagavantalem Geet* often finds mention in literary histories of Goa, as does Borkar's 'transcreation' of 1960, both in Devanagari. In 1976, Bakibab Borkar, who translated texts from a number of languages from the mid-century, also produced Dharmanand Kosambi's Marathi text, *Bhagwan Buddha* in Konkani.

one from Calicut.[27] Amonkar's corpus of translations symbolises the effort to expand the category of the national-secular to incorporate texts from various spiritual and religious traditions. His translations of the *Dhammapada* in 1997 from Pali into Konkani, *Shree Bhagwantan Gaeellem Geet* mentioned above, the *Tirukkural* in 2004, the *Rosall Konkani Jnaneshwari* from Marathi in 2009, the Gospel of St. John, *Sant Juvamvan Pramanem Jezu Kristachem Xubhvartman,* in 2009, the *Japuji Saheeb* on the teachings of Guru Gobind Singh in 2008, and the Jataka tales and *Zencho Distavo* and a Devanagari version of the *Kristapurana,* are driven by the desire to demonstrate the potential of Konkani in Devanagari to absorb and incorporate a cultural range that would otherwise be received in other languages of translation.[28]

The Sahitya Akademi's journal *Indian Literature* and other reviews periodically summarised translation histories in each language. In the 1980s, these accounts were framed by references to the ongoing language movements. The Akademi's own position on script has however been marked by a relatively rigid adherence to the official script.

Venchik Lok-Kannio, a collection of folk-tales (not a translation) by folklorist Jayanti Naik, was rendered into Romi by Felicio Cardozo for publication by the Goa Konkani Akademi. Cardozo is listed as *lipyantor* in the book credits, an unusual and necessary modification to the appellation of translator or adaptor. The language movement expectedly propelled increased translations across scripts and interest groups. Many organisations supporting the production of work in the Kannada and Malayalam scripts were initially as concerned as state organisations with replicating the national literary canon; whereas in the case of inter-script transliterations, a regional canon seems to be emerging with the intention of producing a united readership for Konkani writing.[29]

Translations that have occurred in fact from Konkani in Kannada script to Devanagari or vice versa, as in the case of Melvyn Rodrigues and R. V. Pandit, or from the Kannada to Romi, are a sign of the convergences within the literary world of Konkani. An understanding of the different impetuses and moments that generated translations of the *Doutrina* or the Mahabharata for example, across all active scripts, could not be achieved in this anthology, evident in the

---

[27] Suresh G. Amonkar, *Shree Bhagwantan Gaile Geet* (Mapusa: Geeta Prasar, 2002).

[28] Suresh G. Amonkar, *Zencho Distavo* (Mapusa: Geeta Prasar, 2013).

[29] Olivinho Gomes, "Konkani Scene: Flowering of a Crop," *Indian Literature* 31, no. 6 (128) (November 1, 1988): 48.

absence of a discussion of translation from or into the Malayalam script, but it is hoped that this has contributed to detailing some of the contexts that frame histories of transliterations and their resonances and meanings.

Translations into English are prompted by the impetus to make canonical works in Konkani available to a notionally national readership, as in the case of Damodar Mauzo and Pundalik Naik, two prominent Konkani litterateurs who continue to be translated into English.[30] Aside from English, translations are directed to dominant Indian languages, and to languages in proximity to Konkani.[31] An extension of this is the effort to make fiction based in Goa and written in English available in Konkani, and perhaps assist in language learning.[32]

In contrast to the initial set of organisations set up after 1987 when Konkani was declared the official language of Goa (along with Marathi), the Dalgado Konknni Akademi has focused on Konkani literature in the Romi script as it is called in Konkani, and to address the relative absence of formal backing for the script. Awards and award ceremonies instituted by different Konkani organisations down the western coast stand as a counter and sometimes supplement to the institution of the Sahitya Akademi, though a vigorous discourse continues among these organisations. Some approaches replicated the state model of transforming language (and history) into symbols of sovereign cultures. Other approaches retained the character of the movements they had emerged from, and developed agenda that were recognizably responses to questions that the movement had raised, such as that of cultural dispossession. Organizations could combine these approaches and sometimes changed their positions, but their overarching character could be deciphered from the symbolism they favoured. In Goa for instance, the Goa Konkani Akademi, the Dalgado Konknni

---

[30] Manohar Shetty, *Ferry Crossing: Short Stories from Goa* (Penguin Books, 1998). Sacheen Pai Raikar translated *Theresa's Man* by Damodar Mauzo and *When an Ass Mounts a Cow* by Pundalik Naik was translated by Vidya Pai.

[31] The Institute Menezes Braganza in 2009 undertook a translation of stories from Konkani to Hindi, with Budkuley and M. Surlakar as translators. In 1991, *Karmelin* by Damodar Mauzo was translated by Narayan Shejwalker into Hindi, by S. M. Krishna Rao into Kannada and later by Vidya Pai into English. *Konkani Katha Sangraha*, compiled by Chandrakant Keni was translated into Kannada by S. M. Krishna Rao, K. Budkuley and M. Surlakar (eds). *Katha Darpan: Konkani Kahaniyan Hindi Mein* (Hindi). Goa: Institute Menezes Branganza, 2009.

[32] Anita Pinto, *Espi Mãy Porot Xirkoli... Ani Gõycheo Her Kannio*, trans. Isidore Dantas and Pandirarinath Lotlikar, First edition (Goa, 1556, 2012).

Akademi, Goenkarancho Daiz, and the Thomas Stephens' Konknni Kendr, each have quite a distinct character and agenda.

In Mangalore, while some institutions consolidated a pan-Konkani identity around the sign of Devanagari, they also provided new sources of patronage to writers who dissipated the dominance of Devanagari. Mandd Sobhann, set up in 1986, and presented itself at the time as a non-conformist cultural programme rather than an institution, thwarting the cultural conservatism of the Mangalorean Catholic milieu as well as challenging the dominance of Devanagari by producing performance and musical forms that combine various traditions.[33] As a predominantly musical endeavour initiated by the writer Chafra D'Costa (Charles Francis D'costa) and other members with roots in trade unionism, the organisation used performance to counter cultural divides and to generate new performance traditions. In 2001, the platform inaugurated Kalaangann, a cultural centre in Mangalore. Organisations in Mangalore have harnessed private capital and support from diasporic communities for their activities. With the development of digital technology, dictionaries, and a script converter, translations and Wikipedia projects have rapidly created viable avenues of circulation.[34]

Visible symbols of these are the World Konkani Conventions, the first of which was held in Mangalore in 1995. A significant element of its mandate was the establishment of a World Konkani Centre, which was fulfilled with the inauguration of the Centre in 2009. Under the leadership of the Konkani writer and activist Basti Vaman Shenoy, the various organisations that support the activities of the Centre include business people and its various programmes have been inaugurated by state Chief Ministers and other politically prominent figures. These attributes, including the investments and interests of diasporic communities, have led to the reproduction of normative cultural symbols as a mark of achievement, redefining the position of Konkani.

Despite the insistence on the separation of the spheres of Devanagari and Roman writing and readers, the works that have been translated in parts over the last decade indicate the possibility of an audience and of a number of translators who have diverse reading and writing skills. Non-governmental Konkani organisations and the advances in digital technology have therefore done more

---

[33] http://www.manddsobhann.org/mandd-sobhann/the-birth, Accessed October 22, 2018.

[34] http://www.konkanidictionary.com, http://konkanverter.com/sample-page/, Accessed October 22, 2018.

than governments to produce readers who can read in more than one script.[35]

Online blogs, groups and lists such as the Goa Book Club have created avenues for circulation, critical discussion and publicity for translated material.[36] While blogs, newspapers and smaller publishing houses have allowed for a discourse on caste and cultural dominance to appear, there is no singular script or language that has been selected over others to assert the recovery of marginalised cultural groups. Current debates over the medium of instruction in schools for instance, indicates another field of conflict in which cultural and economic access, communal politics, cultural prestige and caste concerns converge over the question of language, indicating the different positions from which language and script claims are made.

A noteworthy reconsideration of Konkani as a contemporary language of translation was Madhavi Sardesai's thesis, which characterised prior centuries as a time when Konkani was an 'active translator' of languages, to the late twentieth century when, according to her, it had become a passive consumer of readymade Marathi translations.'[37] Sardesai's work, which included literary writing, kinship terms and oral usages among predominantly women informants, noticeably avoided pejorative judgments about usages that are not dominant. Though some questions of power are not foregrounded, she illuminated the nature of difference in Konkani writing across time and social divisions through linguistic rather than social categories, enabling a comparison with other

---

[35] https://www.sahapedia.org/tags/konkani-1, https://blog.wikimedia.org/2015/07/15/konkani-wikipedia-goes-live/

[36] In 2013, two short stories were translated from Konkani by Augusto Pinto; 'Bhivkure' by Vincy Quadros and 'The Barren Wife', by Evagrio Jorge. Pinto's translation was first published in the *Navhind Times* of Saturday, 10 September, 2012. The story 'Vanzud' which has been translated as 'The Barren Wife' was published in '*Swatantra Goyantli Konkani Katha*' (Konkani Stories from Free Goa 1962–1976). A N. Mhambro's short story, 'Vithu loses his Key' was translated by José Lourenco from Konkani (available on http://www.konkanistories.blogspot.in/.Adv). John Fernandes' compilation of the folk songs of the Christian Gawdas, *Goencho Mull Avaz* was published in Devanagari, with an excerpt translated by Augusto Pinto.This was published in the *Navhind Times*' Panorama' of August 11, 2013 as 'Gawda Maand: A Phoenix like rise from iconoclastic ashes'.

[37] Sardesai's comment was made in the context of her analysis of the now defunct Devanagari newspaper, *Sunaparant*. Madhavi Sardesai, 'A Comparative Linguistic and Cultural Study of Lexical Influences on Konkani', Goa University, Taleigao, 2006, p. 129.

languages. This differs markedly from the organising principle of much literary history, in which difference from the standard or ideal was represented through criticism rather than analysis. Over the last two decades, the discourse around Konkani is no longer preoccupied with compensation for its supposed lack but has to contend with the changed symbolism it has acquired in the context of pedagogy and economic opportunity, and the assertion of disprivileged castes. A recent counter to the literary historiography on Konkani is Fr. Pratap Naik's essay, 'Official Languages of Goa'. Against the effort to endow the language with evidence of usage and antiquity, Naik argued that this preoccupation had compelled the appearance of histories carrying evidence of various scripts and languages that were claimed as early Konkani.[38] Against this, he asserts that Konkani was a spoken language, forced to manifest evidence of its use in writing in response to the pressure to become a nation-like vernacular.

[38] Fr. (Dr.) Pratap Naik, S.J., "Official Languages of Goa," *Goa Today*, November 2013, 12–14.

PART THREE

A Brief History of Translations into Konkani in the Kannada Script

Mabel Mascarenhas with contributions from Anil Pinto
(All translations in this section are by Mabel Mascarenhas)

The Kannada script is predominantly used to write Konkani in the region of coastal Karnataka and Devanagari if used, is in the north Karnataka region. The question of which script and what form of script is appropriate for the writing and translation of Konkani continues to be contentious. Among those who write in the Kannada script, William R. da Silva's adaptations are drawn from spoken Konkani as well as written resources of the past. The emphasis however, is not on the recovery of an ideal or classical form that is removed from the spoken form of the present – a distinct departure from other scholarly engagements with the language.

Spiritual and religious publications

Popular religious publications and grammatical texts were among the earliest texts to be printed. Among early translations was one by an unnamed 'a Jesuit priest', who translated *Novea Testamentaco mukhya sangati*, published from Mangalore, Codialbail press, 1903. The Church and the clergy continue to play a dominant role in the production of Christian religious texts. As with Konkani in Romi (Roman or Latin) script, the publication of vocabularies and popular devotional texts coincided with the emergence of a popular print market for Konkani in the Kannada script.

Fr. Raymond Mascarenhas' translated *Amcha Somi Jezu Kristhacho Novo Thesthamenth* (*Our Lord Jesus Christ's New Testament*) from the Latin Vulgate and published works such as *Jezuchem Lhaan Pul* or *Little*

Flower of Jesus in 1923, *Mariyecha Payamlaagim* or *At the Feet of Mother Mary* in 1954, *Mariyecho Patlav* or *Following Mother Mary* in 1955.

Novea Purgatarinthlya Athmyancho Mhaynoya Mhaynyachem Bhakthiponn November (The Month of Souls in Purgatory or Prayers of November Month) is a translation from English by Fr. Louis Bothel in 1927. D.J. Albuquerque and S. J. Poi published the *English Konkani Vocabulary* in Kannada script in the 1930s.[1]

The Goichi Sevadharmik Samiti or the Diocesan Liturgical Commission took upon itself the task to produce a translation of the Bible, in 1974, following the decision of Vatican II to have liturgical material in local languages. In the case of Christian doctrine, the close link between reading and daily practice and prayer ensures that the circulation of these texts to date continues to be authorised or not, by the Church. When producing doctrinal texts, the Church was not only concerned about the accuracy or fidelity of words and concepts, but also that the language should be familiar to readers, and the two questions were posed as one when trying to arrive at appropriate linguistic usages for doctrinal texts. The introduction to these texts therefore addresses both questions as one – the question of their use and popular acceptance, linked to the question of which language they are in, or rather, which version of the language.

William R. da Silva completed the first translation of the entire Bible into Konkani and had it published in the Kannada script in 1997. It was however refused the imprimatur by the Church in Mangalore and circulates as a private version. Da Silva has championed the use of lay Konkani and emphasised the significance of gender in relation to language. His version of the Bible according to him has incorporated both these. It also draws on early versions and languages such as Greek, Hebrew, Aramaic and Latin rather than translations from modern languages such as English and French. Fr. William B. Barboza (1945–) also translated the Old Testament into Konkani. His translation of the complete Bible, *Povitr Bible* in

---

[1] *Dev Spirith Santhamchem Bakthipann* is a translated copy of prayers from English by Felix Paul Noronha and published by Rev. Fr. John T.S. Rodrigues in 1950. *Pavithr Rozarik Betayllo October Mahino* or Month of October, dedicated to the queen of Holy Rosary was translated into Konkani from Latin by Fr. J.B. Polese. *Bethlehemache Vater* is a translation by Lena Martis (1960) of *Christmas and the Saints* by Hertha Pauli. Rev. Sylvester F. Menezes translated *The Sunday Missal* in 1962. *Velnkannichea Bhalaikechye Mayek Novenachim Magnnim* (Novena prayers to the Mother of Good Health of Velankanni) was translated by Fr. J.S. Crasta. *Apokalipsacho Ho Kaall* is a translation by V.J.P. Saldanha of *This Apocalyptic Age* by Robert Bergin. *Jezu Kithyak?* is a translation by Navin Kulshekar of Rajendra Prabhu's *Why Jesus*.

Konkani, is accepted as the official Bible translation of the Mangalore Diocese. His *Povithr Pusthak Porno Sollo, Bhag I* (The Holy Book, Old Testament, Section I) was published in 1995.

William Madtha was a linguist who worked in the Department of Kannada at Karnatak University, Dharwad, and was a former president of the All-India Konkani Parishad. He authored *The Christian Konkani of South Kanara: a Linguistic Analysis* in 1984, contributed '*Konkani bhaase mattu saahitya*' to the *Kannada Viswakoosa,* and has published various linguistic studies of Konkani such as 'Comprehensive Konkani Dictionary: Lexicographical Methodology.' In his essay 'Bhashanthar: Bhashevyjnanik Siddhanth' (Translation: Linguistic Theory), Madtha emphasises that translation needs to be responsive to geographical, temporal and social factors. If Mangalorean, Goan, and Kerala Konkani are language dialects, then ancient, middle and present Konkani variations are temporal. In the same way Kudmi, Saraswat, Christian and Navayat Konkani are social variations. These language variations should be seen as significant, according to him, and care taken to retain cultural markers while gauging whether translated words are familiar within a particular culture.

Madtha dwells on the fact that cultural concepts are difficult to translate. When there is a wide gap between the culture and language formation of the original and the target language, he states, *abhhashantharikarann* happens. One must sometimes retain original words in order to preserve a feel of those aspects of the culture of original language. Other difficulties include availability of multiple word meanings, difference in norms of collocation, differences in sentence constructions and so on.

Fr. Pratap Naik who writes in both Devanagari and Kannada scripts and has translated and transliterated between scripts, is a prominent language activist and developed the institution, Thomas Stephens' Konkani Kendra in Goa. His essay '*Bhashantharachim Thathvamani Kala*' (Principles of Translation and Art) which explores various facets of translation points out that in the Mangalore diocese when English prayers were translated into Konkani, the translator did not pay much attention to grammar, and hence, while the words were in Konkani, they were shaped around the grammatical structure of the English language. In contrast, in Goa, while English sentences were translated into Konkani one could see the influence of Marathi grammatical structure. The Marathi language and culture have a significant influence on the Hindu population and many even today regard Marathi as the cultural medium of the Hindus, states Naik. When a translation maintains the essence while changes in form, style and presentation are creatively incorporated we term this an adaptation. He points to Shenoi Goembab's translation of the *Bhagavad Gita* in prose, which cannot be sung like the Sanskrit work. Essence according to him is of prime importance unlike form and style.

Konkninth Annkar Sahith by Francis D'Cunha refers to Pratap Naik's essay *'Bhashantharachim Thathvamani Kala'* which listed different types of translations such as *Anuvaad, Bhavanuvad, Saransh, Rupanthar* and *Spashtyanthar*. He classifies translations into Konkani into three areas: translation of religious writings, translation of creative prose literature and translation of poetry.He mentions the names of a few prominent translators of prose such as Shenoi Goembab, Ravindra Kelekar, Manohar Rai Sardessai, Olivinho Gomes, William da Silva, V.J.P Saldhanha, J.B Moraes, A. X. Patrao, and Melvyn Rodrigues among others. William da Silva, William Barboza, Edward Noronha, J.B. Moraes, Cyril G. Sequeira, Maurice D'sa, Francis D'cunha himself and H. Raghavendra Rao are also prominent translators of poetry into Konkani.

Among religious writings, he mentions the translations of the liturgy, the Bible and the achievements of Sylvester Menezes. Highlighting the importance of translation of liturgy and other religious texts including Bible, D'cunha claims that it has impacted reading and writing (even praying) in Konkani by children. He also points out that through translations of religious texts Konkani language has been enriched with translations from Latin, English and Sanskrit. Through translations, some Portuguese words as well as words of Sanskritic and Dravidian origin have been absorbed into Konkani.

Rev. Sylvester F. Menezes translated the four gospels into Konkani in 1957 in the Kannada script. He is the founder editor of *Raknno* (1889-1967) and wrote several biographies of saints, prayer books, and translated the New Testament into Konkani.[2]

Menezes stated that his aim was to avoid foreign terms, not just from the Portuguese language but also of Dravidian origin. Hence the use of Konkani terms as *khallem, soop, sheth, mallo* or *dongor* in place of the more common angann, thaddpen, gado, thott, or guddo. He compared the entire text with the Marathi version of the Gospels by Pandita Ramabai and the more recent *Harmony of the Gospels in*

---

[2] He published *Our Lady of Lourdes* in 1922, *Francis of Assisi* in 1924, *Mariyecho Jhelo* or *Garland of Mother Mary* in 1938, *Pornno Sollo* or *The Old Testament* in 1947, *Fatimacho Thallo* or *The Voice of Fatima* in 1948, *Piyus Baravo* or *Pope Pius the 12th* in 1949.

Goan Konkani (*Amcho Soddvondar*) by Joaquim Antonio Fernandes, apart from frequent references to translations in Kannada and Tulu.

Rev. Victor A Pinto (1934-), a scripture translator and professor, translated the complete New Testament *Povitr Pustak* into Konkani in 1979. He also translated the psalms[3] into Konkani in 1988.

Transliterations between scripts

V. J. P. Saldanha or Khadap as he is popularly known, is among the most prominent and prolific Konkani writers in the Kannada script and along with Cha. Fra. is known for his social critique and satire. His work distances itself from the orthodoxies of both Church, state, and the more embedded community practices. The introduction to his novel *Saiba Bhogos* indicates that Khadap authored at least fifty literary works and essay collections and helped begin and sustain several Kannada periodicals. It reveals that the Konkani literary community in Karnataka inserted itself into histories of the language differently, as it takes the Inquisition in Goa as a point of departure to begin a history of migration from Goa down the western coast. Histories of language and community are therefore intertwined. Unlike histories of Konkani written from the perspective of the history of Goa, those narrated by speakers of Manglorean Konkani, feature the expulsion of Christians by Tipu as a significant event, along with the fact of having to leave the region of Goa after the arrival of the Portuguese.

The history of sixteenth century missionary textual production in Goa therefore does not have the same resonance. Khadap's book carries a reproduction of a note signed by three Brahmans from the Konkan region, Ranga Botto, Vinaique Pandito, Apu Botto, who are said to have assisted Van Rheede's compilation of the *Hortus Indicus Malabaricus*. Following Garcia d'Orta's *Colóquios dos simples e drogas da Índia,* Van Rheede's text is one of the better known botanical texts sourced from the sub-continent. While the same facsimile is reproduced in Gerson da Cunha's 1881 text, this one emphasises that the botanical samples were sourced from Kerala.

The recognition of Konkani as a language in Karnataka is referenced among Christians against the history of persecution and migration. Many of Khadap's novels revisit this theme. The introduction to *Saiba Bhogos* mentions appeals made to the Konkani Sahitya Akademi

[3] https://openmybag123.wordpress.com/2011/12/04/the-history-of-the-bible-translation-in-konkani/

for the recognition of Konkani in Karnataka as well. As with Cha. Fra. D'Costa, the appearance of Khadap's novels in Devanagari is perceived as the entry of Konkani in the Kannada script onto an officially recognised literary platform. Unlike their counterparts among Devanagari users from Kerala or Goa, Cha. Fra. and Khadap have become canonical through their distance from cultural authority. This excerpt has been included in this section as it is an index of the symbolism of the Devanagari script in the region of Mangalore.

The transliteration of the much translated poet of Goan origin, R. V. Pandit's *Dorya Gazota,* by Swami Supriya (Fr. C. C. A. Pai, S. J.) explicitly offered the text as a contribution to the advancement of Konkani. The transliteration was directed towards creating a popular literature and world of readers in the Devanagari and Kannada scripts, following recognition of the language by the Sahitya Akademi. In order for Konkani texts to transcend the pedagogical genres of proverbs and dictionaries, R. V, Pandit's poems were intended to build a corpus of pleasurable literature. This is apart from the fact of R. V. Pandit's prolific output and translation into English. The use of both scripts indicates that this text is not only intended for those reading in the Kannada script, but that the text itself represents a bridge between scripts and readerships. Mabel Saldanha and William D' Silva attempted a transliteration of Ravindra Kelekar's '*Thullashee*' in 1977. A transliteration from Devanagari to Kannada script, of poems written by Dinakar Desai was published by Kudla Anand Shanbagh in 2007. Bonaventure Peter Fernandes' novel *Tichea Morna Uprant* written in Romi transcribed into the Kannada script by Fr. Pratap Naik S. J. Yesvanta Palekar has transliterated *Don thembe dukham,* which was published in Goa, Sahitya Prakasan, in 1977.

Among translations and transliterations from Kannada to Devanagari are the fifth edition of Khadap's *Devachem Kurpen,* which was published in Devanagari in 1995 by Rego and Sons. Shivram Karanth's Kannada text was translated as *Matyecho Mog* by Yeshwant Sadanand Palekar in 1994. U.R. Ananthamurthy's acclaimed Kannada novel *Samskara* was translated into Konkani by Vincent Alva, popularly known by his pen name, Vincy Pamboor. Alva writes in three languages: English, Kannada and Konkani. S. L. Bhyrappa's *Daatu* in Kannada was translated as *Sheem Hupatana* by Alka Sinai Assoldekar in 2007. Suryanath U. Kamath's Kannada novel *Eesi Jayisidavaru* was translated by Sandhya R. Shevgoor as *Tapasvini* in 2005. *Chirasmarane,* a Kannada novel by Niranjana appeared as *Saxvilo Ugdas* by Vitty in 2008. M. N. Prabhu translated fifty Kannada Poems of S.R. Ekkundi, into English as *The Bakula Blossoms* and later into Konkani as *Bakula Kusuma.*

In a foreword to a translation of Na. de Souza's story from Kannada to Konkani, William R. da Silva emphasised the lack of sponsorship and the challenge posed by the script. He opined that the original Konkani spoken by the Mangalorean Christians had been corrupted over the years as Kannada sounds and words had replaced it.

Other language translations

J.B. Moraes was a journalist and a prominent Konkani writer and translator (1933-2014). Of the eleven books he authored, some are in Devanagari and the others in Kannada script. His collection of poems, *Navi Vokal* was published in 1922. His first novel, *Koshedan Kelli Khoon* won an award from the Goa Konkani Bhasha Mandal in 1980. His second collection of poems, *Bitarlen Tufan* published in 1984, won the Sahitya Akademy Award in 1985. Other noted awards include Maharastra Gourav Puraskar in 1990, and the Daiji Dubai Award in 2005. His translations into Konkani include Shakespeare's *Romeo and Juliet* published in 1954, a novel, *Ontya Nashillem Sopann* in 1975, *Kannada Sahityacho Itihas* in 1989 and Shivaram Karanth's novel *Chomana Dudi*.

In 2001, he translated B. A. Sanadi's Kannada poems as *Novem Poinn* or *Navem Payna*, which was published from Kumta, Karnataka, by Prakash L. Prabhu. Moraes spoke about the difficulty of translating poetry, which ran the danger of losing the original essence of a poem in a literal translation and of losing a hold on its original form if it is freed of the author's intentions.

Parvo was translated from English by P. J. D'souza in 1913 and published from Mangalore. *Nilsim Bhagda,* an adaptation of the adventures of Sherlock Holmes was written by Alex A. Pais in 1919 and published from Mangalore. Kasargodu Chinna, former chairman of the Karnataka Konkani Sahitya Akademi, translated several plays into Konkani. *Ganti* is Konkani translation of a Bengali play, while *Eklo Anneklo* is a translation from Malayalam, *Karmadheena* from Kannada and *Ailo re Ailo* from Russian.

Eulalia Alvares translated Shakespeare's *Othello* in Konkani in 1965. *Petanathllem Thonn* (1969) adapted the novel *Lucius Flavius* written by Joseph Stellman S. J.

Thakazhi Sivasankara Pillai's Malayalam novel *Cemmiin* was translated into Konkani as *Sungttan* by William R. da Silva in 1995. *Kantyancho Khuris* is a Konkani translation by M. P. Rodrigues of the story *Exiled* written by Joseph Spillman. Rev. Fr. Edward Murphy's

English novel *The Scarlet Lily* is translated into Konkani titled *Mogachi Rani* by Rev. Fr. Dheeratha Prabhu in 1961.

Bangle Narayana Kamath (1872–1918) was a prolific playwright and stage actor in Kannada and has to his credit plays such as *'Prahlada Charithra'*, *'Dhruva Charithra'*, *'Parvathparinaya'* and *'Draupadivasthraharana'* among others. He translated the *Bhagavad Gita* into Konkani as *'Githamritha Sakii.'* Mulki Narasingarao published it in 1921. B.V. Baliga, a noted Konkani activist and writer, and founder editor of the Konkani magazine 'Panchakadayi', produced an interpretation of *'Srimad Bhagawadgeeta'* in simple Konkani verse in 1984.

K. N. Rao Dandeli translated the *bhajana*s of Purandara Dasa into Konkani as *Purandaradasali Bhajana* in 2000. Shri Madvadiraja's *Shrilakshmishobhane Padaani Kanni* was translated into Konkani by Venkatraya Shanbhogue Koderi in 2012. This work was explicitly directed to women and was an attempt to explain Madhva philosophy.

Adaptations from English

C. F. D'Costa (1931–1992) or Cha. Fra. as he is known, was a prominent playwright and satirist from Karnataka who in 1951 became the editor of the Konkani periodical *Poinnari.* He is also associated with other Konkani periodicals such as *Zag-mag, Vixal Konkonn, Udev,* and was the founder of *Jivit.* In 1955, he published his first play, *Sobit Sounsar,* followed by *Sunne Mazor Hasta,* which was transliterated into Devanagari, *Tomato, Vishenticho Bhav* and *Tornem Tornem Mornem,* which was also transliterated. He wrote approximately twenty-five plays altogether and received a Sahitya Akademi award in 1986 for his anthology of poems, *Sonshyache Kan.* His works have been translated into English, Konkani, Marathi, and Malayalam

Cha. Fra. adapted three plays from English to local situations, in different times and historical contexts. The anglicised versions of names replaced by ones familiar to the region and to the pronunciation of rural Konkani, and cultural practices such as local funeral rituals were built into the play. *Mankddacho Pai* is a translation of a play adaption by Lois N. Parker of W. W. Jacob's short story 'The Monkey's Paw' written in 1901. It is evident that Cha. Fra. translated this story as an experiment in Karnataka.[4]

[4] "Works-of-Cha-Fra-A-Study-UGC-Project-Report-by-Anil-Pinto-2008.pdf – File Shared from Box," 53, accessed May 14, 2015, https://app.box.com/shared/03vo57f5t5.

His *Shirigundi Shimaon* is an adaptation of Shakespeare's *Timon of Athens*. Cha. Fra.'s plays normally have a three-act structure, but *Shirigundi Shimaon* set in mid-nineteenth century Mangalore, has a five-act structure in keeping with Shakespeare's play.[5] Cha. Fra.'s next play *Ankwar Mesthrim* was translated and performed in Tulu as *Harishchandra Mastr* and *Satya Panade*. *Dakther Dusman* is an adaptation of Henrik Ibsen's *An Enemy of the People*.

The introduction to the translation of *Sunne Mazor Hasta* by Hema Naik emphasises its significance within the corpus of Konkani works in the Devanagari script, in which texts from Goa have a greater representation. Fr. Pratap Naik and Fr. Mathew Almeida of the Thomas Stephens's Konkani Kendra who transliterated the text mention the institutional backing of Goa Konkani Akademi. *Tornem Tornem Mornem* was published in 1989 by Thomas Stephens' Konkani Kendra in the Devanagari script.

Currently a number of organisations and websites exist to promote the publication of Konkani texts and to support the work of translation and exchange in various scripts. Konkani Bhas Ani Samskriti Prathistan is one such organisation that encourages translation and transliteration.[6] Konkani Language and Cultural Foundation promotes translation into Konkani in Kannada script.[7] Such conferences and trans-national organisations have effectively provided an alternative to the Sahitya Akademi's role in publishing, circulation and bestowing social recognition through awards for literary and linguistic work, though the dominant discourse on language tends to follow nationalistic models that valorise high cultural models.

Diasporic communities of Konkani speakers have been a source of funding and a sone for the circulation of texts. The Kuwait Konkani Kendra for instance, supported the publication of Fr. Pratap Naik's Adi Parva.[8]

The following texts are examples of some of the prominent figures whose works have defined the field of translation in Konkani in the Kannada script.

---

[5] ibid., 31.

[6] http://www.thehindu.com/todays-paper/tp-national/tp-karnataka/Konkani-flavour-in-other-languages-too/article14863800.ece

[7] The three-day workshop they organised titled Konkani Kannada Anuvada Karyagara is an example. http://vishwakonkani.org/workshop-on-kannada-translation-of-konkani-short-stories-report/

[8] Pratap Naik, *Solavya Shekdyatale Konkani Mahabharat: Aadi Paro* (Panaji: Tomas Stevens Konkani Kendra, 1990).

Manohar Rai Sardessai (1925–2006) was an accomplished poet in Konkani and French. He wrote in these languages as well as in English and Marathi. His collection of poems, Pissolim *(Butterflies) won a Sahitya Akademi award in 1980. He was actively involved in the movement promoting Konkani from the 1940s on and was the initial editor of a project to write a Konkani encyclopedia. His writings have been translated into French, Kannada, Marathi and Gujarati.*

The excerpt from his A History of Konkani Literature *published by Sahitya Akademi in the year 2000 is a brief account of the history of translation into Konkani in Kerala. Sardessai does not specify the script into which these texts were translated though both Devanagari and Malayalam were used. The history of Konkani publications in Kerala argues that the first book published by the Konkani Bhasha Prachar Sabha was an effort to record folklore that existed until then as oral tradition. As a compilation of songs, moral precepts and the history of relations with Goa, the* Konkani Lok Geet *of 1975 appears to have been the representation of a community's existence within Kerala. This was followed, he states, by two books of proverbs, one published in 1978, and the other in 1985 by the Kerala Konkani Academy. Interestingly, while Sardessai notes that prominent litterateurs Payyanur Ramesh Pai and P. G. Kamath were concerned with ensuring that the latter publication,* Konkani Mhanuyam Soru *contained uniform spellings, he adds that this may have been detrimental to the nature of the language of proverbs, collected over the preceding half century, the time it took for the book to emerge.*

In 1989, the folk Konkani version of the Valmiki Ramayana 'used for the stage art, Godde', found in 64 palm-leaf scripts and in the Malayalam script was published by the editor of the Konkani Language Institute, Professor R. K. Rao. The discovery of the Godde Ramayana *helped in the production of literary histories that aimed to represent a unified Konkani culture.*

This essay was first published in A History of Konkani Literature, from 1500 to 1992, *Sahitya Akademi, 2000.*

(13) Translation :

Translations play an important role in the development of any language and literature. They enhance the power of expression of a language, enrich its vocabulary, broaden its vistas, energise it with new ideas and images.

In Kerala, we have two translations of Bhagavad Gita. The first one having the original along with a free prose translation in Konkani by N. Lakshmi Narayana Bhat, the cheif priest of Kochi, Tirumala Temple: It has been published in 1978. This is also the first translation of the Gita to be published in Kerala Konkani. The second is by Indrakant Vasudev Shenai, in prose version only, and published by the Konkani Vidya Pith, Kochi in 1981.

K. Ananth Bhat has translated the select ten verses of the famous Hindi poet Surdas and the book 'Sur Bhajan Mala' (1979) has been published in both Devanagari and Kannada scripts, by Sri Venkateswara publicaitons, Mangalore. This has also the importance of being the only translation of Surdas in Konkani.

'Ek Swapnaco Arthu' (1980) is the Konkani version of the puranic episode in which, Ashtavakra is the hero. The translator is Sudas Shenai and the publishers Konkani Vidya Pith, Kochi. This also has the significance of being the only one of its kind in Konkani of Kerala, at least. The Vidyapith also published 'Goddi Goddi Kannio' [(1981) [sweet stories] a translation of 'Majedar Kahaniyam' by the Hindi writer, Sudarshan Sinha' Chakra'. The translator is Indrakant Vasudev Shenai. "The translation is at once clear and simple, and children of all ages will surely like them". This book also is unique as far as Kerala Konkani is concerned.

In 1981, Konkani Bhasha Prachar Sabha in Kochi, came forward to publish a word for word translation, of 'Srimad Devadasa Stotram, by K. Purushattam Pai, a Sanskrit scholar.

'Jnyan Pana' (Psalm of Wisdom) is a time tested work of Poonthanan Nampootiri, the great Malayalam poet of the 16-17th centuries A. D. Dr. M. R. Panikkar, a physician of Kerala, had translated the work into English and published in 1979. Based on this English version, N. Purushottam Mallya translated it into Konkani to be published by Prof. Visvanath Mallya of Kochi translate the English and Hindi children's stories eight in number. The book 'Kanijain Zhelo' (1984) has been published by the Kerala Konkani Academy. It is a highly devotional sanskrit poem.

'Sri Krshna Karnamrit' by the sage Leelasuka. The first 101 stanzas are published by Dr. P. B. Janardhan (1921) with a scholarly introduction and commentary.,Konkani prose version and English verse translation are done by Janardhan himself. The Konkani verse translation is by the poet Sarat Chandra Shenai. (1953).

Swami Ranganathananda, head of the Ramakrishna Math, Hyderabad is a great orator and writes fluently on spiritual themes. His discourses in India and abroad, His books are famous for their

316 A History of Konkani Literature

synthesising effect of science and spirituality. 'Eternal Values for a Changing Society' is a famous book of his. 'An Introduction to the study of Girls' and related essays have been translated into Konkani by P. G. Kamath and published by the Kerala Konkani Academy in 1978. This book fills a void in Konkani literature, hence its importance.

Sahitya Akademi, New Delhi, is publishing the histories of the literatures, of the twenty two languages recognized by it and also their translations in the other twenty one languages. As a part of this project, Prof. R. K. Rao has translated the History of the Malayalam Literature into Konkani (1988). The translator has chosen to give the verse quotations in Malayalam, in their transliterated Devanagari script, and their the sum and substance.

Takezhi Sivasankera Pillai is a world famous novelist and short-story writer of Malayalam. His novel, 'Rantidangazhi' (Two Measures), is typical of his writings. This has many translations in languages Indian and foreign. Prof. Rao has translated the book into Konkani, with the title, 'Don' Dangati Bhat' (1989). It reminds one of its Hindi translations 'Do Ser Dhan'.

The first psychological novel in Bengal is 'Chokher Bali'. by RâbindraNath Tagore. This has been fully translated into Konkani, unlike the English and Malayalam translations, from the Bengali original in the Devanagari script, by N. N. Anandan and published by the Sahitya Akademi in 1989.

(14) Miscellaneous

In a multilingual nation like India, it is imperative on the part of every citizen to learn as many languages as possible for the smooth functioning of the Indian society. And for this learning, materials like self-instructors, bilingual vocabularies, grammars, etc, related to languages akin to them are necessary for all language-groups. These days, many authors and publishers have come forward. The name of Prof. R.K. Rao the Director of the Konkani language Institute, (President, All India Konkani Sahitya Parishad, (1990-'92) comes foremost on the Kerala Konkani scene. A teacher of Hindi, and also of Urdu, by profession, he had ample experience and more than enough occasions, to train students in the learning process of languages, foreign to them. This can very well be experienced in the case of the series of Konkani self-instructors published by him for the use of Hindi, English and Malayalam speakers. His Konkani Vyakaran (1977) deserves a special mention. Another attempt was that of Indrakant Vasudev Shenai, founder-director of the Konkani Vidyapith, as part of the syllabi for the examinaitons conducted by the Vidyapith. The two parts of Konkani Parichay (1980) were conceived as text-books for students appearing for the examinations. Hence, they had limitations of their own. It is quite natural, that Prof. Rao's experiment excelled those of Shenai who lacked such training and experience, which Prof. Rao had.

His Holiness Srimad Sudheendra Tirtha Swamiji of Sri. Kashi Mutt Samsthan, is in the habit of giving discourses in Konkani, whenever there is a gathering of disciples. They very ofter have the form of parables. Hundreds of them have been recorded by some ardent devotees and disciples. Payyanur Ramesh Pai has collected and edited them and published under the banner of Kerala Konkani Academi, with the title, Saropadesahe Kaniyo' (1989). The imprtance of this book rests on the fact that it is the only book of this type and in Konkani in Kerala.

• • •

Rev. Sylvester F. Menezes (1894–1968) translated the four gospels into Konkani in 1957 in the Kannada script. He is also the founder editor of Rakno *(1889–1967). He has written several biographies of saints, prayer books, and has translated the New Testament into Konkani. He published* Our Lady of Lourdes *in 1922,* Francis of Assisi *in 1924,* Mariyecho Jhelo *or* Garland of Mother Mary *in 1938,* Pornno Sollo *or* The Old Testament *in 1947,* Fatimacho Thallo *or* The Voice of Fatima *in 1948,* Piyus Baravo *or* Pope Pius the 12th *in 1949. The Encylopaedia of Indian Literature mentions that he produced the Passion Hymn in 146 verses, a Daily Missal in Konkani, and a Konkani-English dictionary.*

His translator's note in English to the Konkani translation of The Holy Gospel of Jesus Christ *(1958) emphasises the inadequacy of the Konkani language.*

> *It was felt that though a translation from the Greek would be more ideal from the scholars point of view, a translation from the Vulgate was a more practical need, especially for use in liturgy...It was decided that our Konkani version should be based upon the Confraternity version, itself the fruit of the labours of some thirty eminent Biblical scholars in England and America...*
>
> *Though based on the Confraternity edition the present work does not adhere to it in every detail. In places where a different rendering from other versions was deemed preferable this latter has been adopted. In doing this we are specially indebted to the recent rendering of the Gospels from the original Greek into modern American English... (Translator's Note)*
>
> *The writer is at pains, while being true to the original to also be intelligible to the average reader, nay more to give him a readable text, with due regard to the dignity of diction demanded by the nature of the subject. In this connection it must be said that the poverty of the Konkani language and its present peculiar transitional stage have proved a real difficulty.*
>
> *Konkani has several dialects but as yet it has not one literary language. The aim of the present writer has been to eschew as far as possible all foreign terms, not only of Portuguese but also of Dravidian origin. Hence the use of such pure Konkani terms as* khallem, soop, sheth, mallo, dongor *etc. in place of the more common* angann, thaddpen, gado, thott, guddo *etc.*

He has besides, compared the entire text with the Marathi version of the Gospels *by Pandita Ramabai and the more recent* Harmony of the Gospels *in Goan Konkani (Amcho Soddvondar) by Joaquim Antonio Fernandes, not to mention frequent references to translations in Kannada and Tulu.*

In an introduction to another translation of the Holy Gospel of Jesus Christ titled Jezu Kristacho Povithr Vangel *he explains how in order to benefit high school students, the Gospel story has been divided into different chapters and titles and reiterates what other Konkani translators of the Bible say about the translation process, 'while being faithful to the original meaning of the Gospel, alongside, the aim of making it easy to understand and clear to read has been kept before our eyes. Apart from Latin, the translations in English, Marathi and Kannada which are translated from Greek and Latin original works have been read line by line ..." (Translated from Konkani).*

ಪ್ರಸ್ತಾವನ್

ಪವಿತ್ರ್ ಪುಸ್ತಕ್ ಜಾವ್ನಾಸಾ ದೆವಾಚೆಂಚ್ ಉತಾರ್; ಪವಿತ್ರ್ ಅತ್ಮ್ಯಾಚಾ ಪ್ರತ್ಯೇಕ್ ದೇವ್-ಪ್ರಕಾಸಾಖಾಲ್ ವಿವಿಧ್ ಗ್ರಂಥ್-ಕರ್ತಾಂನಿ ವಿವಿಧ್ ಕಾಳಾರ್ ಲಿಖ್ಲ್ಲೆಂ ತಸಲೆಂ. ಜೆಜು ಕ್ರಿಸ್ತಾ ಆದಿಂ ಬರಯಿಲ್ಲ್ಯಾ ಗ್ರಂಥಾಂಚಾ ಸಂಗ್ರಹಾಕ್ ಪರ್ನೊ ಸೊಲ್ಲೊ ಮ್ಹಣ್ತಾತ್; ಜೆಜು ಕ್ರಿಸ್ತಾ ಉಪ್ರಾಂತ್ಲ್ಯಾಕ್ ನವೊ ಸೊಲ್ಲೊ ಮ್ಹಣ್ತಾತ್. ನವ್ಯಾ ಸೊಲ್ಲ್ಯಾಂತ್ 27 ಪವಿತ್ರ್ ಗ್ರಂಥ್ ಆಟಾಪ್ಲ್ಯಾತ್. ತ್ಯಾಂ ಪಯ್ಕಿ ಚಡ್ ಪ್ರಸಿದ್ಧ್ ಚಾರ್ ವಾಂಜೆಲ್. ಸೊಡ್ವಣ್ದಾರ್ ಜೆಜು ಕ್ರಿಸ್ತಾಚ್ಯೆ ಜಿಣಿಯೆಚೊ ಆನಿ ಶಿಕವ್ಣೆಚೊ ಸಂಕ್ಷೆಪ್ ಹ್ಯಾ ವಾಂಜೆಲಾಂನಿ ಬರವ್ನ್ ಆಸಾ.

ವಾಂಜೆಲ್ ಮ್ಹಳ್ಳ್ಯಾ ಗ್ರೀಕ್ ಭಾಷೆಚಾ ಸಬ್ದಾಕ್ 'ಬರಿ ಖಬಾರ್' ಮ್ಹಣ್ ಅರ್ಥ್ ಜಾತಾ. ದೆವಾಚಾ ಪುತಾನ್ ಸಂಸಾರಾಕ್ ಹಾಡ್ಲ್ಲಿ ಸೊಡ್ವಣೆಚಿ ಬರಿ ಖಬಾರ್ ವಾಂಜೆಲಾಂತ್ ಆಟಾಪ್ಲ್ಯಾ. ವಾಂಜೆಲ್ ರಚ್ಲ್ಲ್ಯಾಂ ಗ್ರಂಥ್-ಕರ್ತಾಂಕ್ 'ವಾಂಜೆಲಿಸ್ತ್' ಮ್ಹಣ್ ನಾಂವ್. ವಾಂಜೆಲಿಸ್ತ್ ಚೊವ್ಗ್ ಆಸ್ಚೆ: ಮಾತೆವ್, ಮಾರ್ಕ್, ಲೂಕ್ ಆನಿ ಜುವಾಂವ್. ತ್ಯಾಂ ಪಯ್ಕಿ ಪಯ್ಲೊ ಆನಿ ನಿಮಾಣೊ ಸೊಮಿಯಾಚೆ ಆಪೊಸ್ತಲ್ ಜಾವ್ನಾಸ್ಲ್ಲೆ.

ಪರ್ನ್ಯಾ ಸೊಲ್ಲ್ಯಾಂತ್ ಎಜೇಕಿಎಲ್ ಪ್ರವಾದಿನ್ ದೆಖ್ಲ್ಲ್ಯಾ ದೃಷ್ಟಾವಾಂತ್ ಚಾರ್ ನವ್ಯಾ ಪ್ರಾಣಿಂಚೊ ಪ್ರಸ್ತಾಪ್ ಆಸಾ: ಮನಿಸ್, ಸಿಂಹ್, ಬೋಯ್ಲ್ ಆನಿ ಗರುಡ್. ಹ್ಯೊ ಚಾರ್ ಪ್ರಾಣಿ ಚೊವ್ಗಾಂ ವಾಂಜೆಲಿಸ್ತಾಚೆಂ ರುಪ್ಕಾರ್ ಮ್ಹಣ್ ಸಾಧಾರ್ಣ್ ಅಭಿಪ್ರಾಯ್. ಸಾಂ. ಮಾತೆವ್ ಆಪ್ಲ್ಯಾ ವಾಂಜೆಲಾಚ್ಯೆ ಸುರ್ವೆರ್ ಕ್ರಿಸ್ತಾಚಿ ವಂಶಾವಳ್ ದಿತಾ ಆನಿ ಉಪ್ರಾಂತ್ ತಾಚೊ ಮನ್ಸ್ತಾ-ಸ್ವಭಾವ್ ಆನಿ ರಾಯಾಳ್ ವ್ಹಡ್ವಿಕ್ ವರ್ನಿತಾ ದೆಕುನ್ 'ಮನಿಸ್' ತಾಚೊ ರುಪ್ಕಾರ್ ಮ್ಹಣ್ ಧರ್ಲಾ. ಸಾಂ ಮಾರ್ಕ್ ಆಪ್ಲೊ ವಾಂಜೆಲ್ 'ಅರಣ್ಯಾಂತ್ಲ್ಯಾ ತಾಳ್ಯಾ' ವಿಷ್ಯಾಂತ್ ಸಾಂಗೊನ್ ಸುರು ಕರ್ತಾ: ದೆಕುನ್ ಸಿಂಹ್ ತಾಚೊ ರುಪ್ಕಾರ್. ಸಾಂ ಲೂಕ್ ಆಪ್ಲ್ಯಾ ವಾಂಜೆಲಾಚ್ಯೆ ಸುರ್ವೆರ್ ಯಾಜಕ್ ಜಾಕರಿಚಾ ಯಜ್ಞಾ ವಿಷ್ಯಾಂತ್ ಬರಯ್ತಾ; ದೆಕುನ್ ಯಜ್ಞ್ ಜಾವ್ನ್ ಭೆಟಂವ್ಚೊ ಪಾಡೊ ಯಾ ಬೋಯ್ಲ್ ತಾಚೊ ರುಪ್ಕಾರ್, ಶೆಕಿಂ ಸಾಂ ಜುವಾಂವ್ಚೊ ರುಪ್ಕಾರ್ ಜಾವ್ನಾಸಾ ಗರುಡ್; ಕಿತ್ಯಾಕ್ ತಾಚೊ ವಾಂಜೆಲ್ ಆರಂಭ್ ಕರ್ತಾನಾಂಚ್ ಗರುಡಾಬರಿ ತೊ ಉಂಚಾರ್ ಉಬೊನ್ ವೆತಾ ಆನಿ ಜೆಜು ಕ್ರಿಸ್ತಾಚೊ ದೈವಿಕ್ ಆರಂಭ್ ಆನಿ ಸ್ವಭಾವ್ ವರ್ಣುಂಕ್ ಲಾಗ್ತಾ.

ಪಯ್ಲ್ಯಾ ತೀನ್ ವಾಂಜೆಲಾಂಕ್ 'ಸಿನೊಪ್ತಿಕ್' ವಾಂಜೆಲ್ ಮ್ಹಣ್ತಾತ್. ತಾಂಚಿ ತಿನಾಂಯ್ಚಿ ಮಾಂಡ್ಣಿ ಎಕಾ ಥರಾಚಿ, ಸಾದಿ ಆನಿ ಸಂಪಿ. ತೆಗ್ಯಿ ಜಣ್ ಪಯ್ಲೆಂ ಸೊಡ್ವಣ್ದಾರಾಚಾ ಮುನಿಯಾರ್ಪಣಾಚಿ ತಯಾರಾಯ್ ಸಾಂಗ್ತಾತ್: ದುಸ್ರೆಂ ಗಾಲಿಲೆಯಾಂತ್ ತಾಚೆಂ ಮುನಿಯಾರ್ಪಣ್ ವರ್ಣಿತಾತ್; ತಿಸ್ರೆಂ, ಗಾಲಿಲೆಯಾ ಥಾವ್ನ್ ಜೆರುಜಲ್ಯಾಕ್ ತಾಚೆಂ ಪಯ್ಣ್; ಆನಿ ಚೊವ್ತೆಂ, ಜೆರುಜಲ್ಯಾಂತ್ ತಾಚೊ ಪಾಶಾಂವ್, ಮರಣ್ ಆನಿ ಪುನರ್-ಜಿವಂತ್ಪಣ್. ಪುಣ್ ಸಾಂ. ಜುವಾಂವ್ನ್ ನಿಮಾಣೊ ಬರಯಿಲ್ಲೊ ಚೊವ್ತೊ ವಾಂಜೆಲ್ ದುಸ್ರ್ಯೆಚ್ ಮಾಂಡಾವಳಿಚೊ. ಪಯ್ಲ್ಯಾ ತಿನಾಂತ್ ನಾತ್ಲ್ಲ್ಯೊ ಸಬಾರ್ ಸಂಗ್ತಿ ಹ್ಯಾ ಚೊವ್ತ್ಯಾ ವಾಂಜೆಲಾಂತ್ ವಾಚುಂಕ್ ಮೆಳ್ತಾತ್.

* * *

ಪವಿತ್ರ್ ಪುಸ್ತಕ್ ನೆಣಾ ಜಾಂವ್ಚೆಂ ಮ್ಹಳ್ಯಾರ್ ಜೆಜು ಕ್ರಿಸ್ತಾಕ್‌ಚ್ ನೆಣಾ ಜಾಂವ್ಚೆಂ ಮ್ಹಣ್ ಸಾಂ ಜೆರೊಮ್ ಆಮ್ಕಾಂ ಸಾಂಗ್ತಾ. ಹರ್ಯೆಕಾ ಕ್ರಿಸ್ತಾಂವಾನ್ ಕ್ರಿಸ್ತಾಚಿ ವಳಕ್ ಕರ್ಚಿ ಗರ್ಜ್. ಹ್ಯಾ ಪಾಸತ್ ಕ್ರಿಸ್ತಾಚಿ ಜಿಣಿ ಆನಿ ಶಿಕವ್ಣ್ ಆಟಾಪ್ಲೆಲೊ ಪವಿತ್ರ್ ವಾಂಜೆಲ್ ತಾಣೆಂ ವಾಚಿಜಯ್; ವಾಚಿಜಯ್ ಮಾತ್ರ್ ನಹಿಂ, ವಾಂಜೆಲಾಚಾ ಉತ್ರಾಂಚೊ ತಾಣೆಂ ನಿಹಾಳ್ ಕರಿಜಯ್ ಆನಿ ತಾಚ್ಯೆ ಶಿಕವ್ಣೆ ಪರ್ಮಾಣೆ ಆಪ್ಲಿ ಜಿಣಿ ಮಾಂಡುನ್ ಹಾಡಿಜಯ್. ದೆಕುನ್ ಪವಿತ್ರ್ ಸಭಾ ಆಪ್ಲ್ಯಾಂ ಭುರ್ಗ್ಯಾಂನಿ ಪವಿತ್ರ್ ಪುಸ್ತಕ್ ಚಡ್ ಕರ್ನ್ ವಾಂಜೆಲ್, ತವಳ್ ತವಳ್ ವಾಚಿಜಯ್ ಮ್ಹಣ್ ಒತ್ತಾಯೆನ್ ಸಾಂಗ್ತಾ ಆನಿ ಭಾವಾರ್ಥ್ಯಾಂನಿ ದಿಸ್ಪಡ್ತೆಂ ತೊ ವಾಚುಂಕ್ ಉತ್ತೇಜನ್ ದಿತಾ.

ಪವಿತ್ರ್ ಪುಸ್ತಕಾಚೆಂ ವಾಚಾಪ್ ಹೆರಾಂ ಬುಕಾಂಚಾ ವಾಚ್ಪಾಬರಿ ಜಾಯ್ನಾಯೆ. ಕಥೆಚ್ಯೆ ಯಾ ಶೈಲೆಚ್ಯೆ ಸೊಭಾಯೆ ಖಾತಿರ್ ವಾಂಜೆಲ್ ವಾಚ್ಚೊ ನಹಿಂ. ಶೈಲೆಚಿ ತಿತ್ಲಿ ವಿಶೇಸ್ ಸೊಭಾಯ್ ತಾಂತುಂ ಮೆಳ್ಚಿ ನಾ. ವಾಂಜೆಲ್ ಆಮಿ ವಾಚ್ಚೊ ತಾಂತುಂ ಆಟಾಪುನ್ ಆಸ್ಚಾ ಅತಿ ಉತ್ತೀಮ್ ಶಿಕವ್ಣೆ ಪಾಸತ್. ಪುಣ್ ಹಿ ಶಿಕವ್ಣ್ ವಯ್ರ್‌ಚ್ ನಿಶೆವ್ನ್ ಆಸಾನಾ. ಬಗಾರ್ ಮೊತಿಯಾಂಬರಿ ಗುಂಡಾಯೆಂತ್ ತಿ ಮೆಳ್ತಾ. ಹ್ಯಾ ಖಾತಿರ್, ಪವಿತ್ರ್ ಪುಸ್ತಕ್ ವಾಚುನ್‌ಂಚ್ ವೆಚೆಂ ನಹಿಂ, ಬಗಾರ್ ಥೊಡೆಂ ಥೊಡೆಂಚ್ ವಾಚುನ್, ವಾಚ್‌ಲ್ಲ್ಯಾಚೊ ಅರ್ಥ್ ಕರ್ನ್, ಸಮ್ಜಾಲ್ಲೆಂ ಸತ್ ಮತಿಂತ್ ನಿಹಾಳ್ನ್ ಆನಿ ಆಟವ್ನ್, ವಾಚ್ಪಾ ಥಾವ್ನ್ ಆತ್ಮಿಕ್ ಆದಾಯ್ ಲಾಭಾ ಸಾರ್ಕ್ಯೆ ರಿತಿರ್ ತೆಂ ವಾಚಿಜಯ್.

ಹ್ಯಾ ಸಂಬಂಧಿಂ ಆಧುನಿಕ್ ಕಾಳಾರ್ ಪವಿತ್ರ್ ಸಭೆನ್ ಕಥೊಲಿಕಾಂಕ್ ಪ್ರತ್ಯೇಕ್ ಬೂದ್‌ಬಾಳ್ ಸಾಂಗ್‌ಲ್ಲಿ ಆಸಾ. ಭವ್ತಿಕ್ಪಣಾಚೆಂ ವಾರೆಂ ಸಗ್ಳ್ಯಾನ್‌ಂಚ್ ವಿಸ್ತಾರೊನ್, ಕ್ರಿಸ್ತಾಂವ್ ಭಾವಾರ್ಥಾಕ್ ಮೋಸ್ ಚಡೊನ್ ಆಯಿಲ್ಲ್ಯಾ ಹ್ಯಾ ದಿಸಾಂನಿ ಕಥೊಲಿಕಾಂನಿ ಪವಿತ್ರ್ ವಾಂಜೆಲಾಚಿ ಗುಂಡಾಯೆಚಿ ಸಮ್ಜಣಿ ಜೊಡುಂಕ್ ಜಾಯ್ ಮ್ಹಣ್ ಪಾಪ್‌ಸಾಯ್ಬ್ ಆಮ್ಕಾಂ ಸಾಂಗ್ತಾತ್. ಪಾಪ್‌ಸಾಯ್ಬ್ ಪಿಯುಸ್ ಬಾರಾವೊ, ಆಮೇರಿಕಾಚಾ ಭಿಸ್ಪಾಂಕ್ ತಾಣೆಂ ಬರಯಿಲ್ಲ್ಯಾ ಎಕಾ ಪತ್ರಾಂತ್, ಆಮ್ಚ್ಯಾ ಕಾಳಾರ್ ಕ್ಲೆರಿಕಾಂಚಾ ಆಪೊಸ್ತಲಾದಿಕ್ ಲಾಯಿಕಾಂನಿ ದೀಜಯ್ ಜಾಲ್ಲ್ಯಾ ಸಹಕಾರಾ ವಿಷ್ಯಾಂತ್ ಉಲಯ್ತಾನಾ, ಕಥೊಲಿಕ್ ಸಾಧನಾಚಾ ತರ್ನಾಟ್ಯಾಂನಿ ಸಮರ್ಥ್ ವಿಷ್ಯಾಂತ್ಲಿ ಚಡ್ ಗುಂಡಾಯೆಚಿ ಸಮ್ಜಣಿ ಜೋಡ್ನ್ ಘೆಂವ್ಚಿ ಗರ್ಜ್ ದಾಕವ್ನ್ ದಿತಾ. ಹ್ಯಾ ಇರಾದ್ಯಾನ್ ಆಟ್ ಯಾ ಧಾ ಜಣಾಂನಿ ಮೆಳೊನ್, 'ಸ್ಟಡಿ ಸರ್ಕಲ್' ಆಸಾ ಕರ್ನ್ ಶಾಸ್ತ್ರಿಕ್ ವಿಷಯ್ ವಾಚಿಜಯ್ ಆನಿ ತರ್ಕ್ ಕರಿಜಯ್, ಆನಿ ಅಶೆಂ ನೆಣಾರ್ಯಾಂಕ್ ಶಿಕಂವ್ಚ್ಯಾ, ವಿರೋಧ್ ಉಲಯ್ತೆಲ್ಯಾಂಕ್ ಸಮ್ಜಾಶಿ ಕರ್ಚ್ಯಾ ಆನಿ ಬರ್ಯಾ ಮನಾಚಾಂಕ್ ಕುಮೊಕ್ ದಿಂವ್ಚ್ಯಾ ಕಾಮಾಕ್ ತರ್ಬೆತ್ ಜಾಯ್ಜಯ್ ಮ್ಹಣ್ ಸಾಂಗ್ತಾ.

ಪವಿತ್ರ್ ವಾಂಜೆಲಾಂಚೆಂ ಹೆಂ ಭಾಷಾಂತ್ರ್ ತಯಾರ್ ಕರ್ತಾನಾ ವಯ್ರ್ ಸಾಂಗ್‌ಲ್ಲೊ ಉದ್ಧೇಶ್ ಮತಿಂತ್ ದವರ್ಲಾ. 'ಸ್ಟಡಿ ಸರ್ಕಲಾಂಕ್' ಮಾತ್ರ್ ನಹಿಂ, ಹೈಸ್ಕೂಲಾಚಾಂ ಸರ್ವ್ ವಿದ್ಯಾರ್ಥಿಂಕ್ ಉಪ್ಕಾರಾಶೆಂ ವಾಂಜೆಲಾಚಿ ಕಥಾ ವಿಂಗಡ್ ವಿಂಗಡ್ ಅಧ್ಯಾಯಾಂ ಆನಿ ಶಿರೋನಾಂವಾಂಖಾಲ್ ವಿಭಾಗ್ಲಿಲ್ಯಾ. ತ್ಯಾ ಶಿವಾಯ್, ತಪ್ಶೀಲ್ ಷರೆ ಬರಯ್ಲ್ಯಾತ್ ಆನಿ ಪುರಾವಣೆಂತ್ ಹೆರ್ ಚಡಿತ್ ಸಮ್ಜಣಿ ದಿಲ್ಯಾ. ವಾಂಜೆಲಾಚಿ ಕಥಾ ವಾಚುನ್ ಯೆತಾನಾ ಥಂಯ್ ಥಂಯ್ ಲ್ಹಾನ್‌ಶಿಂ ನೆಕೆತ್ರಾಂ (*) ಪಳೆಂವ್ಕ್ ಮೆಳ್ತೆಲಿಂ. ತೆಂ ನೆಕೆತ್ರ್ ಆಸ್ಚಾ ಉತ್ರಾಕ್ ಯಾ ವಿಷಯಾಕ್ ಪುಸ್ತಕಾಚ್ಯೆ ಅಖೇರಿಕ್ ಷರೊ ಮೆಳ್ತಲೊ ಮ್ಹಣ್ ಸಮ್ಜಾಜಯ್.

* * *

ಹ್ಯಾ ಭಾಷಾಂತ್ರಾಚೆಂ ಕಾಮ್ ಸುರು ಕರ್ನ್ ಲಗ್ಭಗ್ ಪಂಚ್ವೀಸ್ ವರ್ಸಾಂ ಜಾತಾತ್. ಕಿತ್ಲೆ ಪಾವ್ಟಿಂ ಮ್ಹಣ್ ನಾ ತೆಂ ತಿದ್ವಿಲಾಂ ಆನಿ ಪರ್ತ್ಯಾನ್ ಪರ್ತ್ಯಾನ್ ಬರಯ್ಲಾಂ. ವಾಂಜೆಲಾಚಾ ಮೂಳ್–ಉತ್ರಾಂಕ್ ವಿಶ್ವಾಸ್ ಸಾಂಬಾಳ್ತಾನಾ, ಸಾಂಗಾತಾಚ್ ಸಮ್ಜೊಂಕ್

ಸುಲಭ್ ಜಾಯ್ಜಯ್ ಆನಿ ವಾಚುಂಕ್ ಸುಢಾಳ್ ಜಾಯ್ಜಯ್ ಮ್ಹಳ್ಳೊ ಉದ್ದೇಶ್ ದೊಳ್ಯಾಂ ಮುಖಾರ್ ದವರ್ಲಾ. ಲಾತಿನ್ ಶಿವಾಯ್, ಗ್ರೀಕ್ ಆನಿ ಲಾತಿನ್ ಮೂಳ್-ವಾಂಜೆಲಾಂಚೊ ತರ್ಜುಮೊ ದಿಂವ್ಚಾ ಇಂಗ್ಲಿಷ್, ಮರಾಠಿ, ಕನ್ನಡ ಇತ್ಯಾದಿ ಭಾಷಾಂತ್ರಾಚೆಂ ವಾಕ್ಯಾನ್ ವಾಕ್ಯ್, ವಾಚುನ್ ತಜ್ವೀಜ್ ಕೆಲಾಂ. ತರಿಪುಣ್ ಹ್ಯಾ ಭಾಷಾಂತ್ರಾಂತ್ ಸಬಾರ್ ಊಣ್ ಆಸ್ತೆಲೆ ಮ್ಹಳ್ಳೆಂ ಬರಯ್ಣಾರಾಕ್ ಖಂಡಿತ್ ಭೊಗ್ತಾ. ಛಾಪ್ಯಾಚಿ ಪ್ರತಿ ಪುನರ್ ವಾಚ್ತಾನಾ ಸಬಾರ್ ಕಡೆನ್ ಬದ್ಲಾವಣ್ ಕರ್ಯೆತಿ ಮ್ಹಣ್ ತಾಕಾ ದಿಸ್ಲಾಂ. ಜಾಣಾರಿ ವಾಚ್ಪಿ ಹ್ಯಾ ವಿಷ್ಯಾಂತ್ ಕಾಂಯ್ ಸೂಚನಾಂ ದಿತಿತ್ ಜಾಲ್ಯಾರ್ ತಾಂಚೊ ವ್ಹಡ್ ಉಪ್ಕಾರ್ ಜಾತೊ.

* * *

ಶೆಕಿಂ, ಇತ್ಲ್ಯಾಂ ವರ್ಸಾಂಚಿ ಹಿ ವಾಂವ್ಟ್ ಪರ್ಗಟ್ ಕರುಂಕ್ ಕಿತೆಂ ಉಪಾವ್ ಕರ್ಚೊಗಿ ಮ್ಹಣ್ ದೊಳೆ ವಾಠಾರ್ನ್ ಆಸ್ತಾನಾ, ಉದಾರ್ ಮನಾಚಾ ಆಮ್ಚಾ ಭಿಸ್ಪಾನ್, ಆತಾಂ ದೆವಾದಿನ್ ಬೆಸಿಲ್ ಪೆರಿಸಾನ್, ಹೆ ಚಾರ್‌ಯಿ ವಾಂಜೆಲ್ ದಿಯೆಸೆಜಿಚಾ ಖುಸ್ತಾರ್ ಪರ್ಗಟ್ ಕರ್ನ್, ಭೋವ್ ಉಣ್ಯಾ ಮೋಲಾಕ್ ವಿಕುಂಕ್ ಮುಖಾರ್ ಸರ್‌ಲ್ಲ್ಯೆ ಖಾತಿರ್, ತಾಚೊ ಉಪ್ಕಾರ್ ಬಾವುಡ್ಲಲೊ ತಿತ್ಲೊ ಪಾವಾಸೊನಾ. ತಾಚ್ಯೆ ದಿಯೆಸೆಜಿಚಾ ಹರ್ಯೆಕಾ ಕುಟುಂಬಾಂತ್ ವಾಂಜೆಲಾಚಿ ಏಕ್ ಪ್ರತಿ ಆಸಾಜಯ್ ಮ್ಹಳ್ಳೊ ತಾಚೊ ಅತ್ರೆಗ್ ಸುಫಳ್ ಜಾಂವ್ದಿ ಮ್ಹಳ್ಳೆಂ ಆಮ್ಚೆಂ ಮಾಗ್ಣೆ. ತ್ಯಾ ವರ್ವಿಂ ಆಮ್ಚಿ ಸಮರ್ಥ್ ಥಿರ್ ಜಾಂವ್ದಿ, ಕಿತ್ಯಾಕ್ ಸಾಂ ಪಿಯುಸ್ ಧಾವ್ಯಾನ್ ಸಾಂಗ್ಚಾ ಪರ್ಮಾಣೆ: "ವಾಂಜೆಲ್ ಆಮಿ ಕಿತ್ಲೊ ಚಡ್ ವಾಚ್ತಾಂವ್‌ಗೀ, ತಿತ್ಲೊ ಚಡ್ ಘಟ್ ಜಾತಾ ಆಮ್ಚೊ ಭಾವಾರ್ಥ್."

ಭಾಷಾಂತ್ರ್-ಕರ್ತ್.

ಪೆಂತೆಕೊಸ್ತ್,
1958.

V. J. P. Saldanha or Khadap as he is popularly known, is a prolific writer in the Kannada script and along with Cha. Fra. is known for his social critique and satire. His work distances itself from the orthodoxies of Church, state, and the more embedded community practices. The introduction to the novel Saiba Bhogos *suggests that Khadap authored at least fifty literary works and essay collections and helped begin and sustain several Kannada periodicals.*

The introduction reveals the different location of the Konkani literary community in Karnataka, as stated earlier, which takes the Inquisition in Goa as a point of departure to begin a history of migration from Goa down the western coast. The history of sixteenth century missionary textual production in Goa therefore does not have quite the same significance, particularly for sections of the Christian community that instead marks its persecution by Tipu Sultan in popular accounts, as a significant political event for the formation of community memory. Many of Khadap's novels revisit this theme. The appearance of Khadap's novel in Devanagari is perceived as the entry of Konkani in the Kannada script onto an officially shared literary platform. The introduction mentions appeals made to the Konkani Sahitya Akademi.

As stated earlier, the last page in this text reproduced a note signed by three Brahmans, Ranga Botto, Vinaique Pandito, Apu Botto, who are said to have assisted Van Rheede's compilation of the Hortus Indicus Malabaricus, *which after Garca d'Orta's* Colóquios dos simples e drogas da Índia *is one of the better known botanical texts sourced from the subcontinent. While the same facsimile is reproduced in Gerson da Cunha's 1881 text, the one appended to* Saiba Bhogos *emphasised that the botanical samples were sourced from Kerala.*

प्रकाशकालीं उतरां

मंगळूरांत कोंकणीं साहित्य निर्मितीक आनी प्रसाराक बुन्याद घालेले लेखक, कांदबरीकार, कवीं पयकी एकलो महान कोंकणीं साहिती विजेपी सल्डान्हा. कन्नड भाषेंत निरंतर कादंबरी रचनं केलेल्या डॉ शिवराम कारंत, अनकृ., त.रा.सू हांगेले वरीची कोंकणीं भाषेंतूय कथा, कादंबरी, नाटक सृष्टी केल्लेल्या पयकी विजेपी - 'खडाप' एकलो. तागेले लिखणे ताकून ५० वयर कथा, कादंबरी, कवन व्हाळून येवन, कोंकणीं साहित्य क्षेत्रांत एक विशेस क्रांती जावच्याक कारण जालें.

गोयांत १७ व्या शतमानांत पोर्तुगेज आडळ्तेदारांनी इन्क्विजीशन कानून हाणू कोंकणीं लोकावयर केलेले अन्याय, हिंसा कार्य आनी ताजे निमित्तानआमगेले म्हालघड्यांनी कोंकणीं जणालें गोंय सोणू, केनरा आनी तेनकाक, न्हेशिल्ल्या आंगवल्यारी धांवोन येवचे तशी जालें. त्या काळाचे चारित्रिक विषय आपण्याले सृजनशील बरपान कोंकणीं साहित्यांत हाडून एक दाकलो केललो पयलो महान ससाहिती वि.जे.पी. सल्डान्हा - 'खडाप' ते. महान कादंबरीकाराल्यो कन्नड लिपींत आशिल्ल्यो साहित्य कृत्यो देवनागरी

लिपींत लिप्यांतर करका म्हळ्ळेली इच्छा आमकां विश्व कोंकणीं साहित्य अकाडेमीक खूब वरस ताकून आशिल्ली. तें योजन हातांत घेंवचें प्रयतनूय शुरुवात जालेलें. आज त्या योजनाची पयली लिप्यांतर साहित्य कृती 'सायबा भोगोस' आतां लिप्यांतर जावन प्रकाशन जातची आसा.

ह्या लिप्यांतर वावराचें सक्कडय श्रेय फामाद कोंकणीं कवी, कविता ट्रस्टचे अध्यक्ष मानेस्त मेलवीन रोड्रिगस आनी तांची पतीण एवरेल रोड्रिगस हांका फावो जाता. मानेस्त मेलवीन बाबान पुस्तक लिप्यांतर करून परगट जांवचें मेरेन सर्व वावराची जवाबदारी हातांत घेवन निरंतर काम केलां. मेल्वीन बाबाला प्रेतनान 'सायबा भोगोस' पुस्तक सुंदर वाचप्यांगेल्या हातांत पांवच्या तशें जालां.

खडापालें 'सायबा भोगोस' पुस्तक कन्नड लिपी ताकून देवनागरींत लिप्यांतर करच्यांक आनी उजवाडवच्याक कबूली दिलेल्या दि.वि.जे.पी. सल्डान्हालो पूत रॅनसम सल्डान्हा हांकां देव बरें कोरों आनी 'सायबा भोगोस' पुस्तक सोभीत जावन छापून दिलेले ब्रिलियंट प्रिंटर्स, बेंगळूर हांकां आनी पुस्तकाचो फोर चित्राल्लया श्री रघू अपारा हांकांय देव बरें कोरों.

कर्नाटकांत फायस जालेल्यो कन्नड लिंपिंतुल्यो अत्युत्तम कोंकणीं कादंबरी, मटव्यो काणयो, कविता झेलो इत्यादी कृत्यो देवनागरीक लिप्यांतर करून देशाच्या गोंय, केरळ, महाराष्ट्र राज्यांनी रावपी कोंकणीं साहित्य मोगींक पावोंवच्या उद्देशान विश्व कोंकणीं केंद्र आनी विश्व कोंकणीं साहित्य अकाडेमीन लिप्यांतर योजना मांडून हाडलां आनी मुखारय हें प्रेतन मुखार वेतलें. कोंकणीं साहित्यीक आनी वाचपी लोकं हें प्रेतन स्वागत करतले असो म्हाका विश्वास आसा.

ह्या वावराक कर्नाटक सरकाराचें अनुदान लाभलां अशें कळोवच्याक संतोस जाता. हो विश्व कोंकणी साहित्य अकाडेमीक अभिमानाचो विषय जावन आसा. देव बरें कोरों.

विश्व कोंकणीं केंद्र
कोंकणी गांव, शक्तीनगर
मंगळूर

बस्ती वामन शेणै
अध्यक्ष, कोंकणी भास आनी संस्कृती प्रतिष्टान
तारीक: आगोस्त १५, २०१३

दुसऱ्या छाप्याक प्रस्तावन

आमच्या पुरवजां पयकी सबार जण, आपलें पेट भिछाणे घेवन, व तेंय नासतां, गोंय आपलें मूळपीठ सांडून तेनकाक आयल्ले आनी तांतले चडावात जण मंगळुरा भोंवारी केनरांत रावले म्हणच्याक पुरावे आसात. तांणी तशें येंवच्याक कारणां सबार आसल्ली - दुखोळ, पेस्त पिडा (जी मुख्य जावन, सांतीस्सीम त्रिंदादीच्या 'लागोवा' तळ्यांत मरोन कुसल्ल्या हस्तिच्या मोड्या थावन प्रारंभ जाल्ली म्हणतात) आनी 'इनक्विजिसांव', इत्यादी, हांचे पयकी, इनक्विजिसांव संस्थांचे ख्यास्तेचो प्रस्ताप हे काण्येचो एक मुल्या फातर.

भावाड्ताचे बचावे खातीर - धर्म भृष्ठता नास करच्या बऱ्या इराद्यान हो संस्थो इस्पानियांत (स्पेयन) आनी पुडतुगलांत (प्रमुख कॅथॉलिक राष्ट्रांनी) स्थापन केल्लो. तवळ रायांकय कॅथॉलिक सभेच्या फुडाऱ्यांनी नेमक करचें आसल्ले. देकुन राया राणीयांकय हे 'धारमीक कोडती'चेर पुरतो अधिकार नातल्लो. म्हणतच, संस्थोच सद्द्याक दुष्ठो आनी क्रूर जालो. मुळावो ईरादो भंगलो. बळाधीक गवर्नारांच्या आनी स्वार्थी आनी अतिरेकी आनी कपटी थोड्या पाद्री मुखेलिंच्या हातांत, धर्माच्या नांवान लूट, क्रूर हिंसा, अन्याय, फारीकपण आनी लाभाडपण चडोन समडतिची आनी समाजिची वीदवाव्ळ जाली. १५६० इसवेंत, दोम गस्पार दे लियांव पिरेरा, गोंयचो प्रथम आर्च बिशप जावन येतच गोंयातंय 'इनक्विजिसांव' प्रारंभ जालें - क्रमेण तेंच 'धारमीक फरंगी पिडेचें' व्हड खेस्तांव जालें. (केनरांतलें सिज्म, केनरा क्रिस्तावांची बंधड - हीं खरगां उपरांतली).

"सायबा भोगोस!" काणी प्रारंभ जावच्या वेळार (१६६१) गोयांत इनक्विजिसांवाक पुरती १०० वरसां भरल्लीं! पुडतुगेजांचो प्रभाव चिक्के निंवोंक लागल्लो जाल्यारय, धारमीक कोडतींचो रुबार्ब देंवोंकनातल्लो. आमचे समाजेक तर, भोव सुरवेर लागल्ले ग्राच्चार ते!

'सायबा भोगोस' ही कथा लिखिशें प्रच्योदन दीवन, 'राकणो' पत्रार उपरांत प्रगट केल्ल्या मा. मार्क वाल्डर हांकां हो लेखक ऋणी. आनी आतां दुसरो छापो जावन प्रगट करूंक मुखार सरल्ल्या रेगो एँड सन्स, बेंगळूर हांकांय म्हजे धन्यवाद.

- खडाप

~~~
~~~

A collection of short stories, Khel ani her katha *by Yashwant Chittal was translated from Kannada into Konkani by Melvyn Rodrigues in 1986. Melvyn Rodrigues is a prolific poet and essayist and a recipient of a Sahitya Akademi award in 2011 for his collection of poems,* Prakriticho Paas. *Some poems from the collection have been translated into Punjabi. He has at least six other published books, among which are a novel, a collection of essays and collections of poetry. He is associated with various Konkani associations and is the founder of 'Zage Kavi' and 'Kavita Trust'; co-founder of Mandd Sobhann, founder member of Daiji Dubai and the editor of www.konkanipoetry.com.*

William R. da Silva in his introduction to this publication speaks of the deterioration of Konkani language and literature. He suggests that the translation of both popular and canonical literature from other languages would have a rejuvenating effect on Konkani.

ವಾಚ್ಪ್ಯಾಂಲಾಗೀ ಸಂವಾದ್

ಕೊಂಕಣೀ ಲೊಕಾಚೇ ಪ್ರಜ್ಣೇಂತ್ ಏಕ್ ನವೀ ಸಂಧೀ ಆಯಿಲ್ಲೇ ಪರಿಸ್ಥಿತೀಂತ್ 'ಕೊಂಕಣೀ ಸಾಹಿತ್ಯ ಕಲಾ ಸಮಿತೀ' ಉಬ್ಜಲ್ಲೀ; ಆನೀ ತಿಚೊ ವಾವ್ರ್ ಬರ್ಯಾ ಮನಾಚ್ಯಾ ಕೊಂಕಣೀ ಮ್ಹಾಜಣಾಂ ಮುಖಾರ್ ದವ್ರೂಂಕ್ 'ಪ್ರಗತೀ ಪ್ರಕಾಶನ್' ಉಬ್ಜಲ್ಲೆಂ. ಏಕ್ ಖಿಣ್ ವರ್ಸಾಂ ಸುಂಕುಡ್ಡ್ಯಾಚೇ ನೀದ್ ಕಾಡ್ಲ್ಯಾ ಉಪ್ರಾಂತ್ ಆಪ್ಲೇ ನಿದೇಚೇ ಪೊತೀ ಫುಟವ್ನ್ ಪಾಕಾಟೆ ಉಸವ್ನ್ ಪಿಸೊಳೇ ಉಬೊಣೆಕ್ ಭಾಯ್ರ್ ಸರ್ಲ್ಯಾಂತ್ – ಹೀ ಸಮಿತಿ ಆನಿ ಹೆಂ ಪ್ರಕಾಶನ್. ಕೊಂಕಣೀ ಲೋಕ್ ಶಿಂಪಡ್‌ಲ್ಲೇಕಡೇ ತೀಂ ಪಾವ್ತಲೀಂ ಜಾಲ್ಯಾರ್ ತುಮ್ಚೊ ಯೆವ್ಕಾರ್ ಆಮ್ಕಾಂ ಯೇಂವ್.

ಕೊಂಕಣೀ ಲೊಕಾಚ್ಯಾ ಆನೀ ಭಾಶೇಚ್ಯಾ ಕುಳಾರಾ, ಮ್ಹಣ್ಜೇ ಗೊಯಾಂತ್, ಏಕ್ ನವೀ ಘುಂವ್ಡೀ ಆಯ್ಲ್ಯಾ. ಪುರ್ತುಗೆಜಾಂಚ್ಯಾ ವಸಾಹತು ಬಂಧನಾಂತ್ಲೆಂ ಸುಟೊನ್ ಅಜಾದ್ ಜಾಲ್ಲೆಂ ಗೊಂಯ್ ತ್ಯಾ ಸ್ವಾಧೀಕ್ ಉಗ್ಡಾಸಾಚೇಂ ಪಂಚ್ವೀಸ್ ವರ್ಸಾಂ ಸಂಭ್ರಮಾನ್ ಚಲಯ್ತಾ – ದಶೆಂಬ್ರಾಚೇ ಎಕುಣಿಸಾವೇರ್, ಹೊ ಸಂವಾದ್ ಬರಂವ್ಚ್ಯಾ ದಿಸಾ. ಪುಣ್ ನಾಜುಕಾಯೇನ್ ಚೊಯ್ಲ್ಯಾರ್, ಗೊಂಯ್ ಏಕ್ ರಾಜ್ ಜಾಂವ್ಚೆಂ ಆನೀ ಕೊಂಕಣೀ ಭಾಶೇಕ್ ರಾಜ್‌ಭಾಸ್ ಜಾವ್ನ್ ಮಾನ್ಯತಾಯ್ ಮೆಳ್ಚೀ ಹ್ಯಾ ಸಪ್ಣಾಂಚೆಂ ಶೀಡ್ ಪಿಂಜ್ಲಾಂ ಆನೀ ಭಾಸಾವ್ಣೇಚ್ಯಾ ಉತ್ರಾಂಚೊ ಪೂಲ್ ಮಡ್ಲಾ. ಪಣ್ಜೇಚೊ ಸಾಂಕೇವ್ ಪಡ್‌ಲ್ಲೇಬರೀ. ತಾಚೇ ಬದ್ಲಾಕ್ 'ಮರಾಠೀಪಣಾಂ' ಚಡ್ಲ್ಯಾಂತ್. ದೆಖೊನ್ ಪುಂಡಲೀಕ ನಾಯಕ್, ಫಾಂಕಿವಂತ್ ಕೊಂಕಣೀ ಬರವ್ಪೀ, ಉಲವ್ಪೀ ಆನೀ ನಾಟಕಿಸ್ತ್, ಹಾಚ್ಯಾ ಫುಡಾರ್ಪಣಾಖಾಲ್ 'ಕೊಂಕಣೀ ಪರ್ಜೆಚೊ ಆವಾಜ್' ಉಠ್ಲಾ. ತೊ ಮಜ್ಭೂತ್ ಉರೊಂ ಆನೀ ಭಾಸಾವ್ಣ್ಯಾಂನೀ ಉರ್‌ಲ್ಲೊ ಫುಡಾರ್ ಕರ್ನ್ಯಾಂನಿ ಜ್ಯಾರೀ ಕರೂಂಕ್ ಪಾವೊಂ. ಹೀ ಆಮ್ಚಿ ಅಭಿಲಾಷಾ.

ಪುಣ್ ಕೊಂಕಣೀ ಭಾಸ್ ಆನೀ ತಿಚೆಂ ಸಾಹಿತ್ಯ್ – ಹೀಂ ದೋನ್‌ಯೀ ಫುಂಗರ್ಲ್ಯಾಂತ್; ದುಧಾಧಾರೇವೀಣ್ ಸುಕ್ಲ್ಯಾಂತ್; ತೀಂ ಆಕುಡ್ಚೇ ಪಯ್ಲೆಂ ಭಾಯ್ಲ್ಯಾ ಸಾಹಿತ್ಯಾಚ್ಯಾ ವೀರ್ಯಾನ್ ಭರವ್ನ್ ತೀಂ ಪರತ್ ಫಳಾಧೀಕ್ ಕರ್ಚೀ ಆಶಾ ಆಮ್ಕಾಂ ಆಸ್‌ಲ್ಲ್ಯಾನ್ ಆಮಿ ಭಾಯ್ಲ್ಯಾ ಭಾಸಾಂತ್ಲೆಂ ಉಂಚ್ಲೆಂ– ಲೊಕಾ ಮೊಗಾಳ್ ಜಾಲ್ಲೆಂ ತಶೆಂಚ್ ಪುರಸ್ಕಾರ್ ಮೆಳ್‌ಲ್ಲೆಂ– ಸಾಹಿತ್ಯ್ ಕೊಂಕಣೀಂತ್ ತರ್ಜುಮೊ ಕರ್ಚ್ಯಾ ಕಾಮಾಕ್ ಘಾಲಾ. ಕೊಂಕಣೀಚೇ ಮೂಳ್ ಕಾಲೆತೀ ಹಲಕ್ ಜಾಂವ್ಚೀ ನ್ಹಯ್; ತಶೆಂ ಮ್ಹಣ್ ಭಿತರ್ಲೆಂ

ರಗೇತ್ ಅಶಕ್ತ್ ಜಾವ್ನ್ ಹಾಡ್ಲೆ ಸಾಹಿತ್ಯ್ ಆಲ್ಬೆಂ, ನಿಳಾ ನಾತ್ಲ್ಲೆಂ ಜಾಂವ್ಚೆಂಯಿಯೊ ನ್ಹಯ್ ಮ್ಹಣ್ ಹೊ ಮೊಗಾಚೊ ವಾವ್ರ್ ಆರಂಭ್ ಕೆಲಾ. ಭಿತರ್ಲೇ ಸಕ್ತೀನ್ ಆನಿ ಭಾಯ್ಲ್ಯಾ ವೀರ್ಯಾನ್ ಕೊಂಕಣೀ ಭಾಸ್ ಆನೀ ಸಾಹಿತ್ಯ್ ಪರೇತ್ ಜಿವಾಳೂನ್ ಯೆಂವ್ಚೆಂ ಆಮ್ಕಾಂ ಜಾಯ್.

ಸಾಳಕಾಚೊ, ರಾಕ್ಣ್ಯಾಚೊ, ಪುನವಾಚೊ ಆನೀ ಹೆರಾಂಚೊ ವಾವ್ರ್ ಚಲೊಂ; ತಾಂಚೆ ಬರಾಬರ್– ಪುಣ್ ತಾಂಚೇ ಪರೇಸ್ ಮೆಕ್ಳೊ– ಪ್ರಗತೀಚೊ ವಾವ್ರ್‌ಯಿ ಉಬೊ ರಾವೊಂ ಮ್ಹಣ್ ಆಮಿೊ ಹೆಂ ಪ್ರಕಾಶನ್ ಜಿವಾಳಾಂವ್ಕ್ ಮನ್ ಕೆಲಾಂ. ಆದ್ಲ್ಯಾ ದಶಕಾಂತ್ ಚಾ. ಫ್ರಾ. ದ ಕೊಸ್ತಾಚೊ 'ಸುಣೆ ಮಾಜರ್ ಹಾಸ್ತಾ' ನಾಟಕ್ ಜೆ. ಬಿ. ಮೊರಾಯಿಸಾಚ್ಯೋ 'ನವೀ ವ್ಹಕಲ್' ಕವಿತಾ, ಚಂದ್ರಕಾಂತ್ ಕೇಣೀಚೇ 'ಎಕ್ಲೊ ಎಕ್ಸುರೊ' ನವಲ್–ಕಥಾ ಆನೀ ರವೀಂದ್ರಬಾಬ್ ಕೇಳೇಕಾರಾಚೀ 'ತುಳಶೀ' ನವಲಿಕಾ ಆಮಿೊ ಉಜ್ವಾಡಾ ಹಾಡ್ಲ್ಲೀಂ. ಹ್ಯಾ ದಶಕಾಂತ್ ಕಾನಡೀ, ಮರಾಠೀ, ಮಲೆಯಾಳಮ್, ಹಿಂದೀ, ರಶಿಯನ್ ಇತ್ಯಾದೀ ಭಾಸಾಂತ್ಲೆಂ ಸಾಹಿತ್ಯ್– ಚಡಾವತ್ ಮಟ್ವ್ಯಾ ಕಾಣಿಯೊ ಆನೀ ಕಾದಂಬರೀ– ಆಮಿೊ ಉಜ್ವಾಡಾ ಹಾಡ್ಟಲ್ಯಾಂವ್. ಹೇ ವಾಟೇರ್ ಪಯ್ಲೊ ಸಂಗ್ರಹ್ ಯಶವಂತ ಚಿತ್ತಾಲಾಚ್ಯೊ 'ಖೆಳ್ ಆನೀ ಹೆರ್ ಕಥಾ' ಮ್ಹಳ್ಳೆಂ ಪುಸ್ತಕ್ ದಶೆಂಬ್ರಾಚೇ ಎಕುಣೀಸ್ ತಾರಿಖೇರ್ ಉಜ್ವಾಡಾ ಯೆತಾ. ಗೊಯಾಂತ್ ಉರ್‌ಲ್ಲ್ಯಾ ಕೊಂಕಣೀ ಪರ್ಜೆಚ್ಯಾ ಆವಾಜಾ ಬರಾಬರ್ ಹ್ಯಾ ಕಾಣಿಯಾಂಚೊ ಆವಾಜ್‌ಯಿ ಉಠೊನ್ ಕೊಂಕಣೀ ಮಟ್ವ್ಯಾ ಕಾಣಿಯಾಂಚ್ಯಾ ಸಾಹಿತ್ಯ್ ಮಳಾರ್ ನವೀ ಜಾಗ್ವಣ್, ನವೆಂ ಚೇತನ್, ನವೊ ದಿಷ್ಟಾವೊ ಆನೀ ನವೆಂ ಶಕೂನ್ ಜಾಂವ್.

ಶ್ರೀ ಯಶವಂತ ಚಿತ್ತಾಲಾನ್ ಬರಯಿಲ್ಲೀ ಪಯ್ಲಿ ಮಟ್ವೀ ಕಥಾ 'ಬೊಮ್ಮಿಯ ಹುಲ್ಲು ಹೊರೆ'; 1949 ಇಸ್ವೆಂತ್ ತೀ ಕಥಾ ಉಜ್ವಾಡಾ ಆಯಿಲ್ಲೀ. ತೇ ಕಥೇ ಬರಾಬರ್ ಸುರೂ ಜಾಲ್ಲೊ ಕಾನಡೀ ಸಾಹಿತ್ಯಾಚೊ ಝುರೊ ಅಜೂನ್ ಸುಕನಾಸ್ತಾನಾ ವ್ಹಾಳ್ಕಾ. ಮಟ್ವೀ ಕಥಾ ಆಪ್ಲೆಂ ಮೂಳ್ ಮಾಧ್ಯಮ್ ಜಾವ್ನ್ ಘೆವ್ನ್, ಹೆರ್ ಕಾನಡೀ ಬರವ್ಪ್ಯಾಂಚ್ಯಾ ಸಂಪ್ರದಾಯಾಂತ್ ಬರಂವ್ಕ್ ಸುರೂ ಕೆಲ್ಲೊ ಶ್ರೀ ಚಿತ್ತಾಲ ಆತಾಂ ಪಾಂಚ್ ಮಟ್ವ್ಯಾ ಕಾಣಿಯಾಂಚೆ ಸಂಗ್ರಹ್ ಆನೀ ತೀನ್ ಕಾದಂಬರೀ ಕಾನಡೀ ಲೊಕಾಕ್ ದೀಂವ್ಕ್ ಪಾವ್ಲಾ. 'ಸಂದರ್ಶನ' (1957), 'ಆಬೋಲೀನ' (1960), 'ಆಟ' (1968), 'ಕತೆಯಾದಳು ಹುಡುಗಿ' (1979), 'ಬೇನ್ಯಾ' (1982)– ದೆ ತಾಚ್ಯಾ ಕಾಣಿಯಾಂಚೆ ಪಾಂಚ್ ಸಂಗ್ರಹ್. ಆಯ್ಲೆವಾರ್ 'ಚಿತ್ತಾಲರ ಕಥೆಗಳು' (1983) ಮ್ಹಳ್ಳೊ ವಿಂಚ್ಣಾರ್ ಕಾಣಿಯಾಂಚೊ ಸಂಗ್ರಹ್ ಉಜ್ವಾಡಾ ಆಯ್ಲಾ. ತಾಚ್ಯೊ ಕಾದಂಬರೀ: 'ಮೂರು ದಾರಿಗಳು' (1964), 'ಶಿಕಾರಿ' (1979) ಆನೀ 'ಛೇದ' (1985). ಮುಖಾವಯ್ಲಿಂ ಕಸಲೀಂಚ್ ಶಕುನಾಂ ನಾಸ್ತಾನಾ ಕಾರವಾರಾಂತ್ ಬಾಡ ಮ್ಹಳ್ಳೇಕಡೇ 'ಬೊಮ್ಮಿಯ ಹುಲ್ಲು ಹೊರೆ' ಬರವ್ನ್ ಕಾಡ್ನ್ ಕಥಾಕಾರ್ ಜಾಲ್ಲೊ ಶ್ರೀ ಚಿತ್ತಾಲ ಉತ್ತೇರ್ ಕಾನಡಾ ಜಿಲ್ಲ್ಯಾಂತ್ಲ್ಯಾ ಗೋಕರ್ಣಾಚೇ ಹನೇಹಳ್ಳೇಚೊ. ಬೊಂಬಯ್ತ್, ಇಜ್ನೆರ್ ಜಾವ್ನ್, ಎಕಾ ನಾಂವಾಡ್ದೀಕ್ ಸಂಸ್ಥ್ಯಾಂತ್ ಉಂಚ್ಲ್ಯಾ ಹುದ್ದ್ಯಾರ್ ವಾವುರ್ತಾ. ಉತ್ತೇರ್ ಕಾನಡಾ ಜಿಲ್ಲೊ, ಪುಣ್ ಪ್ರತ್ಯೇಕ್ ಕರೂನ್ ತಾಚಿ ಹನೇಹಳ್ಳಿ, ತಾಚ್ಯಾ ಕಾಣಿಯಾಂನೀ ಪರೇತ್ ಪರೇತ್ ರುಪೇತೇ ಆಸಾತ್. ತಶೆಂಚ್ ತಾಣೆ ಚಲಯಿಲ್ಲೆಂ 'ಆಮ್ಚೇ ಭಿತರ್ಲ್ಯಾ ಮನ್ಶ್ಯಾಕ್ ಸೊಧ್ಚೆಂ' ಪ್ರಯತ್ನ್ ತಾಚ್ಯಾ ಕಾಣಿಯಾಂಕ್ ಏಕ್ ಗುಂಡಾಯ್ ದಿತಾತ್. ತಾಂತು ದೆವ್‌ಲ್ಲ್ಯಾಂಕ್ ಮನ್ಶ್ಯಾಂ ಮಧ್ಲ್ಯಾ ಸಂಬಂಧಾಚೊ, ತಾಂಚೇ ಪರಿಸ್ಥಿತೀಚೊ, ಸಂಸ್ಕಾರಾಂಚೊ ಆನೀ ತಾಂಚ್ಯಾ ನಾಗರೀಕಪಣಾಚೊ ಆಂಗ್ ಶಿರ್ಶಿರಾಂವ್ಚೊ ಅನ್ಭವ್ ಜಾತಾ. ತಾಚ್ಯಾ 'ಕತೆಯಾದಳು ಹುಡುಗಿ' (1979) ಸಂಗ್ರಹಾಕ್ 1980 ಇಸ್ವೇಂತ್ ಕರ್ನಾಟಕ ಸಾಹಿತ್ಯ ಅಕಾದೆಮಿಚೊ ಬಹುಮಾನ್ ಆನೀ 1983 ಇಸ್ವೇಂತ್ (ಭಾರತೀಯ) ಸಾಹಿತ್ಯ ಅಕಾದೆಮಿಚೊ ಬಹುಮಾನ್ ಮೆಳ್ಳ್ಯಾ ಮ್ಹಣ್ಟಚ್ ತಾಚ್ಯಾ ಕಾಣಿಯಾಂಕ್ ದುಸ್ರೆಂ ಪ್ರಸ್ತಾವನ್ ಗರೇಜ್ ನಾ.

ಹೊ ಆಟ್ ಕಾಣಿಯಾಂಚೊ ಕೊಂಕಣೀ ತರ್ಜುಮೊ, 'ಆಯ್ದ ಕಥೆಗಳು' (1976) ಮ್ಹಣ್ ಕಾನಡೀ ಭಾಷೇನ್ ಕೆಲ್ಲ್ಯಾ ಸಂಗ್ರಹಾಚೊ. ಏಕ್ ಚಳ್ವೇಳ್ ಆನೀ ಏಕ್ ಉಮೆದ್

ಜಾವ್ನ್ ಕೊಂಕಣೀ ವಾಚ್ಪ್ಯಾಂಕ್ ದಿಲಾ. ಕಾನಡೀ ಲಿಪಿನ್ ಕೊಂಕಣೀ ಸಾಹಿತ್ಯ್ ರಚ್ತೇಲ್ಯಾಂಕ್ ತೊ ಏಕ್ ಮಾಪ್ ಯಾ ಪ್ರಮಾಣ್ ಜಾಯ್ನಾ ಜಾಲ್ಯಾರ್ ಚಿಂತಾ ನಾ; ಏಕ್ ಉಮೇದ್ ಜಾಲ್ಯಾರ್ ಪುರೊ; ಆನೀ 'ಬಂಧನ್' ಕಾಣಿಯೆಚ್ಯಾ ಬರ್ಮಾಚಾರೀಕ್ ಆಪ್ಲ್ಯಾ ಭೊಗ್ಣಾಂಚ್ಯಾ ಕಳ್ವಳಾಂಚ್ಯಾ ಘರಾಂತ್ ದಾರ್ ಉಘಡ್ಟಾನಾ ಮುಖಾಮುಖೀ ಜಾಲ್ಲೇ ದೇವಿಬರೀ, ಏಕ್ ಸಾಹಿತ್ಯಾಚೇ ತಶೆಂಚ್ ಸಾಹಿತ್ಯಾಂತ್ ಆಟಾಪ್ಲ್ಯಾ ಭೊಗ್ಣಾಂಚ್ಯಾ ಮಾಟಾಚೇ ಮುಖಾಮುಖೀ ಜಾಂವ್, ಅನ್ಭವ್ ಜಾಂವ್ ಆನೀ ನವೊ ಬಾಂಧ್ ಜಾಂವ್.

ಮಂಗಳೂರ, ದ.ಕ.
ದಶೆಂಬರ 19, 1986

ವಿಲ್ಯಮ್ ದ ಸಿಲ್ವ

Na D'Souza's story Mog mat pavana (ani her katha) *was translated from Kannada into Konkani by Melvyn Rodrigues in 1987 and published by the Konkani Sahitya Kala Samiti, Mangalore. Na D' Souza or Norbert D'Souza is a Kannada writer and the President of the 80th Kannada Sahitya Sammelana held at Madikeri in January 2014. He has been recognised for his contribution to Kannada literature with the Karnataka Sahithya and Central Sahitya Akademi awards. He has written more than forty novels, many short stories, plays and literature for children. His well-known works include* Kadina Benki, Dweepa, Mulugadeya Oorige Bandavaru, Swargada Baagilalli Naraka, Hosa Kathegalu, *and* Giliye Oh Giliye, Devarige Dikku *and* Tabbali Mattu Bhootada Eduru Betala.

In his foreword to the text, William R. da Silva discusses two difficult aspects of book publishing in Konkani: lack of sponsors and the script. He states that the script writing style has changed and not the language itself. Instead, the written language has been brought close to the spoken language and its pronunciation. He feels that the original Konkani spoken by the Mangalorean Christians has been corrupted over the years as Kannada sounds and words replaced it.

ವಾಚಪ್ಯಾಂಲಾಗೀ ಸಂವಾದ

ಹೆ ಪುಸ್ತೇಕ್ ತುಮಕಾಂ ದಿತಾನಾ ಹ್ಯಾ ವರಸಾಕ್ ಆಮೊ ಭಾಸಾಯಲ್ಲೀಂ ಕನೀಶ್ಟ ತೀನ ಪುಸ್ತಕಾಂ ತುಮಚ್ಯಾ ಹಾತಾರ್ ಘಾಲ್ಲೇಬರೀ ಜಾಲೀಂ. ಆಮಕಾಂ ತೇರ್ ರು. 200.00 ದೀವ್ನ್ ಜಾಂವಚೆ ಸರಸಾಂದೆ ದೋನ್ ಹಜಾರಭರ್ ಮೆಳಲ್ಲೆ, ತೆದನಾ ವರಸಾಕ್ ಚಾರ್ ಪುಸ್ತಕಾಂ ದೀಂವ್ಕ ಅವಕಾಸ್ ಮೆಳಟೊ. ಪುಣ್ ಚಾಲೂ ವರಸಾಂತ್ ತಿತಲೆಂ ವದಗೋನ್ ಆಯಲೆಂ ನಾ ಆಮಕಾಂ, ಫುಡಲ್ಯಾ ವರಸಾಂತ್ ತರೇಯ್ ಜಾತಲೆಂ ಮ್ಹಣ್ ಭರವಸತಾಂವ್. ಹೀಂ ಪುಸ್ತಕಾಂ ಹೆರಾಂಕ್ ಫುಂಕ್ಯಾಕ್ ವಾಚೂಂಕ್ ದಿಂವಚೆಂ ಕಾಮ್ ಕರತಲ್ಯಾಂವರವೀಂ ಆಮಚೆ ಸರಸಾಂದೆ ಬಹುಶಾ ಚಡಚೆನಾ'ತ್.

ಆನಏಕ್ ಆಡಕಳ್ ಮ್ಹಳ್ಯಾರ್ ಲಿಪೀರುಪಾಚೀ. ಸಾದೊ ವಾಚಪೀ 'ಕೊಂಕಣೀ ಆವಾಜ, ಕಾನಡಿ ಲಿಪೀ' ಮ್ಹಳ್ಳ್ಯಾ ತತ್ವಾ ಪರಮಾಣೆ ವಾಚ್ ಮ್ಹಳ್ಯಾರ್ ಸಮಜಣೇನ್ ವಾಚತಾ ಆನೀ ಆಪಲೀ ಆದಲೀ ಸವೇಯ್ ಮೊಡಟಾ. ಹೇ ವಾಟೇರ್ ಆಮಕಾಂ ಆಡಕಳಟಾತ್ ಅರ್ದುಕುರೆಂ ಕೊಂಕಣೀ ಶಿಕೇಪ್ ಆಸಲ್ಲೆ, ಆಪೂಣ್ ಏಕ್ ವ್ಹಡ್ ಬರಪೀ ಮ್ಹಣ್ ಲೆಕತಲೆ ಆನೀ ಕೊಂಕಣೀ ವಾಚೂಂಕ್ ಯಾ ಮೊಲಾಕ್ ಘೆಂವ್ಕ ನಾಕಾಜಾಲ್ಲೆ ನಿಬಾಂಕಾರ್. ತಾಂಕಾಂ ಸಮಜಂವಚೀ ತಾಂಕ್ ಆಮಕಾಂ ನಾ; ಯಾ ತೀ ಫುಡಾರಾಂತ್ ಯೇತ್ ಮ್ಹಳ್ಳೊ ಭರವಸೊಯ್ ನಾ.

ಆಮೊ ಕೆಲ್ಲ್ಯಾ ಲಿಪೀಸುದಾರಣಾಚ್ಯಾ ವಾವರಾಬಾಬತೀನ್ ಏಕ್ ಅಭಿಪ್ರಾಯ್ ಅಸೊ ಆಸಾ: ಆದೀಂ ಆಮೊ ಕೊಂಕಣೀ ಬರೇವ್ನ ಆಸಲ್ಲ್ಯಾಂವ್. ಆತಾಂ ಪುರಾ 'ಕನ್ನಡ' ಕರತಾತ್. ಅಶೆಂ ಉಲಯತಲ್ಯಾಂಕ್ ಖರೇಪಣೀ ಕೊಂಕಣೀ ಆವಾಜ್ ಕಿತಲೆ ಆಸಾತ್, ಕೊಂಕಣೀ ಸರ ಕಿತಲೆ ಆಸಾತ್, ಕೊಂಕಣೀ ವೆಂಜನಾಂ ಕಿತಲೀಂ ಆಸಾತ್ ಮ್ಹಣ್ ಖಬೇರ್ ನಾ. ವಾಕ್ಯಾಂಚೀಂ ರುಪಾಂ ಕಸಲೀಂ ಮ್ಹಳ್ಳೀಯ್ ಖಬೇರ್ ನಾ. ಕನ್ನಡ ಯಾ ಕಾನಡೀ ಭಾಶೇಚೀ ಮ್ಹೂರ್ ತಾಚೇಪಯಲೆಂ ನಾ. ತಸಲೆ ಜೇಣ್ 'ಹೆ ಸಾರಕೆಂ, ತೆಂ ಚೂಕ್' ಮ್ಹಣಚೆಂ ಧಯ್ರ ಘೆತಾತ್. ಹೆಂ ನೆಣಾರಪಣ್ ಉಗತ್ಯಾ ಪ್ರದರ್ಶನಾಕ್ ಘಾಲಚೆಂ ಪೊಕೇಳ್ ಧಯ್ರ್. ಹಾಚೇಪಾಟಲ್ಯಾನ್ ಶಿಕೇಪ್ ನಾ, ಸಂಶೋಧನ್ ನಾ,

ಯಾ ಪ್ರಯೋಗ ಕರಚೆಂ ಬರೆಂ ಮನೇಯ್ ನಾ. ಖರೇಪಣೀ ಸಾಂಗಚೆಂಜಾಲ್ಯಾರ್ ಆಮಿೊ ಲಿಪೀ ಬರಂವಚೀ ರೀತ್ ಬದಲಿಲ್ಯಾ ಶಿವಾಯ್ ಭಾಸ್ ಬದಲೂಂಕ್ ನಾ. ಬರಪಾಂತಲೀ ಭಾಸ್ ತೋಂಡಭಾಶೇಕ್ ಆನೀ ತಿಚ್ಯಾ ಉಚ್ಚಾರಾಂಕ್ ಲಾಗೀಂ ಹಾಡಲ್ಯಾ. ಮಂಗಳುರೀ ಕೊಂಕಣೀ ಯಾ ಮಂ.ಕ್ರೀ ಕೊಂಕಣೀ ಆಪಲೆ ಮುಳಾವೆ ಆವಾಜ್ ಪುರಾಯ್ ಬದಲೂಂಕ್ ಪಾವಲ್ಯಾ. ತಾಂಚ್ಯಾ ಜಾಗ್ಯಾರ್ ಕಾನಡೀ ಆವಾಜ್ ಆನೀ ಸಬ್ದ್ ಘೆತಲ್ಯಾತ್. ಅಶೆಂ ಘಡನಾಯೆ. ಮಂಗಳುರಾಂತಲೀ ಭಾಸ್ ಆನೀ ಹೆರ್ ಪ್ರದೇಶಾಂತಲೀ ಭಾಸ್ ಏಕರೂಪೀ ನ್ಹಯ್. ಕೊಂಕಣೀಚ್ಯಾ ಏಕರೂಪೀ ಫುಡಾರಾಕ್ ಆಮಿೊ ಕೆಲ್ಲೀ ತಬದೀಲ್ ಭೋವ್ ಉಪಕಾರಾಚೀ ಜಾತಲೀ. ಪಾಂಚ್–ಸ ವರಸಾಂಭಿತೇರ್ ಆಮಿೊ ಸಬಾರ್ ಕೊಂಕಣೀಚೀಂ ರುಪಾಂ ಉಲಯತಲ್ಯಾಂವ್ ತರೇಯ್ ಏಕೇಚ್ ರೂಪ ವಾಚತಲ್ಯಾಂವ್ ಆನೀ ಬರಯತಲ್ಯಾಂವ್. ತಿತ್ತೂನ್ ಪಾವನಾತಲ್ಯಾರೇಯ್ ತಸಲೆಂ ಏಕರೂಪ್ ಮಾನೂನ್ ತರೇಯ್ ಘೆತಲ್ಯಾಂವ್!

ಅಸಲೇಕಡೇ, ಆಮಕಾಂ ಏಕರೂಪ ಜಾಯ್. ಆಮಕಾಂ, ಗೊಯಾಂಕ್, ಬೊಂಬಯ್ಕ್, ಕೊಚ್ಚೀಕ್ ಏಕವೇಟ್ ಜಾಯ್ ಮ್ಹಣಟಲೆ ಆಸಾತ್. ಏಕ್ ಕಾಶಟೀ ಜಾಯ್ ಮ್ಹಣಟಲ್ಯಾಂನೀ ಹಜಾರ ಮುಂಜಿನಾಡೆ ಜಾಯ್ ಮ್ಹಣಚೆಂ ತರೇಯ್ ಕಶೆಂ? ಖಂಯಚೀಂ ಹಾಡಟಲೆ ಪೊಂತಾಂ ನಾಡ್ಯಾಂಕ್ ಖೊವಂವ್ಕ? ತಶೆಂ ಮ್ಹಣಟೇಚ್ ಆಮಿೊ ಬದಲೂಂಕೇಚ್ ಜಾಯ್.

ಆಮಿೊ ಜಾಲ್ಯಾರೇಯ್ ಸಗಳೆ ಬದಲೋಂಕನಾಂವ್. ಇಲ್ಲೆಇಲ್ಲೆಚ್ ಬದಲೋಂಕ ಲಾಗಲ್ಯಾಂವ್. ಪ್ರಮಾಣರೂಪ ನಾತಲ್ಲೇಕಡೇ ಆದಲೆಂ ಮ್ಹಣ್ ನಾ, ಸವಯೇಚೆಂ ಮ್ಹಣ್ ನಾ; ಸಗಳೆಂ ಮೊಗಾಚೆಂ ಆನೀ ಆಶೇಚೆಂ ಆನೀ ತಾಚೇರ್ ಬಾಂದೂನ್ ಹಾಡಲ್ಲೆಂ ಮ್ಹಣ್ ಬದಲೇಪ್ ಸುರೂ ಕೆಲಾಂ. ಬರ್‍ಯಾ ಮನಾನ್ ತುಮಿೊಯ್ ಬರಾಬರ್ ಯೆಂವಚೆಂ ಆನೀ ಸಾರಕೆಂ ನ್ಹಯ್ ಆಸಲ್ಲೆಂ ತಿದವೂನ್ ಏಕರೂಪ್ ಜೊಡೂಂಕ್ ಹಾತಾಂತ್ ಹಾತ್ ಘಾಲಚೆ. ತುಮಕಾಂ ತಶೆಂ ಕರೂಂಕ್ ನಾಕಾ ತರ್ ಆಮಚೇ ವಾಟೇವಯಲೆ ಅಲೇಕ್ ರಾಂವಚೆಂ. ಆಡಕಳಚೆಂ ನ್ಹಯ್.

ಉಲಂವಚೀ ರೀತ ಕಶೀ?

ಸಂಸಾರಾಂತಲ್ಯೋ ಸಕಡ್ ಭಾಸೋ ಉಲೇಂವ್ಕ ಶಿಕಯತಾತ್, ಆನೀ ವಾಚೂಂಕ್ ಶಿಕಯತಾತ್, ಆನೀ ಬರಂವ್ಕೇಯ್ ಶಿಕಯತಾತ್. ಪುಣ್ ತಶೆಂ ಕೊಂಕಣೀಕ್ ನಾಕಾ ಮ್ಹಣಟಾತ್! ಆಮಚೀ ನ್ಹಯಗೀ ತೀ ಮುಳಾನ್ ಆನೀ ಸಂಯಬಾನ್? ಆಮಚೀ ಭಾಸ್, ಆವೇಯ್ ಭಾಸ್. ತಿಣೆಂ ನಾಗಡೀ ಆಸಚೆಂ, ಕುಡಕೆ ನ್ಹೆಸಚೆಂ ಆನೀ ಘರಾಭಿತೇರ್ ಉರಚೆಂ– ಭಾಯ್ರ ಆಮಕಾಂ "ಚೆಡೀ ಯಾ ಚೆಡಯೋ" ಆಸಾತ್, ಅಶೀ ಚಲತಾ ಆಮಚೀ ಜೀಣ್! ತ್ಯಾ ಭಾಯ್ರ, ಆಮಚೀ ಭಾಸ್ ಮ್ಹಳ್ಯಾರ್ "ಆಮಚೀ": ಕ್ರಿಸ್ತಾವಾಂಚೀ ಆನಿ ಕೊಂಕಣ್ಯಾಂಚೀ, ಕ್ರಿಸ್ತಾವಾಂ ಮಧೆಂ ಪಾದರೀಂಚೀ; ಬಾಮಣಾಂಚೀ; ಚಾರಡ್ಯಾಂಚೀ, ಗಾವಡ್ಯಾಂಚೀ, ಸುದರಾಂಚೀ; ಯೆಣೆಚೀ ಆನೀ ತೆಣೆಚೀ; "ಆಮಚೀ" ಮಂಗುಳುರೀ ಮಿಜಾಸಕೇಚೀ ಆನೀ ತಾಂಚೀ, "ಉಡತೀ", "ಧಡಬಡೀ", "ವೊಡತೀ" ಆನೀ "ಕಸಲೀ ಹಾಬಾ" ಮ್ಹಣ್ ಉದ್ಗಾರ್ ಹಾಡಂವಚೀ; ಆಮಚ್ಯಾ ಚೆಡ್ಯಾ–ಚೆಡವಾಂಕ್ ಭರಲ್ಲೇ ಪ್ರಾಯೇಚೀ ಗಳೀ ಸೊದತಾನಾ, "ತೋಂಡ ಸೊಡಟಾನಾ ಕಳ್ಳೆಂ; ತೀಂ ಫಸ್ಟ್; ತೀಂ ಸೆಕೆಂಡ್; ತೀಂ ಕಾಟ್" ಮ್ಹಣ್ ಸಾಂಗೋಂಕ್ ಉಪಕಾರಚೀ; ಸರವೆಂಟ್ ಸಂಸ್ಕೃತೀ ಸಾಂಬಾಳೂನ್ ದವರೂಂಕ್, ಆನಿ ವೇರ್ಗ ಬಾಂದಚೀ. ದುಸರೀ ಕಸಲೀಯ್ ಆಸಾ? ದಯಾ ಕರೂನ್ ತುಮಿೊ ಸಾಂಗಾ; ಹಾಂವ್ ನೆಣಾಂ.

ಬರಪಾಚೀ ರೀತ್

ಬರಪಾಚೀ ರೀತಿ ಬದಲ್ಲ್ಯಾ ಆಮಚ್ಯಾ ಪುಸ್ತಕಾಂನೀ. ಕಶೀ ಮ್ಹಣಟಾತ್? ಎಕೇ ಶಿಸ್ತೇನ್. ಆತಾಂ, ಸುರವೇರ್, ಆಮಿೊ ವ್ಯಂಜನಾಂನೀ ಮಾತ್ ಗಾಂಟಾಯಿಲ್ಲೀಂ ಉತರಾಂ ಸೊಡೇವ್ನ್ ತಾಂಕಾಂ 'ಮೊನೊ' 'ಆ' ಆನೀ 'ಅ' ಚೆಂ ದೀಗರೂಪ್ 'ಅೀ'

ಉಪಯೋಗಾಂತ್ ಹಾಡಲಾಂ. ದಾಕಲ್ಯಾಕ್: ದಾಕ್ಲೊ ಯಾ ದಾಖ್ಲೊ ಮ್ಹಣ್ ಬರಂವಚೀಂ ಉತರಾಂ, ಯಾ ಉತ್ರಾಂ ಸೊಧ್ತಾ, ಕಾಡ್ತಾ ಮ್ಹಣ್ ಬರಂವಚೀಂ ಉತರಾಂ, 'ದಾಕಲೊ', 'ಉತರ್', 'ಉತರಾಂ', 'ಸೊದತಾ', 'ಕಾಡಟಾ' ಮ್ಹಣ್ ಬರಯಲ್ಯಾಂತ್. ಅಶೀಂ ಸಕೇಡ್ ಉತರಾಂ. ಎಕಾ ಸಬದಾಚ್ಯಾ ದುಸರ್ಯಾ ಆನೀ ಚವತ್ಯಾ ಜಾಗ್ಯಾರ್ ಯೆಂವಚೀಂ ಅಕ್ಷರಾಂ ಕೊಂಕಣೀ ಮೊನ್ಯಾ ಆವಾಜಾಕ್ ಸರೀ ಜಾವ್ನ್ ಬದಲೀಲ್ಯಾಂತ್. ತಶೆಂಚ್ ಸಬದಾಆಕೇರೀಕ್; ಅಪರೂಪ್.

ಇತಲೆಂ ತುಮಿ ಮಾನೂನ್ ಘೆತಾತ್ ತೇರ್, ತುಮಚೆಂ ವಾಚೇಪ್ ಆನೀ ಬರೇಪ್ ಬದಲತಲೆಂ; ಬರ್ಯಾ ಆನೀ ಎಕವಟಾಚ್ಯಾ ಫುಡಾರಾಕ್ ಬದಲತಲೆಂ ಆನೀ ಉಲೇವ್ಪ, ತೊಂಡಾರೇಚ್, ತುಮಚೇ ಸುವಾದೀನ್ ಉರತಲೆಂ.

ಬರೆಂ ಮಾಗೋನ್,

ಮಂಗಳೂರ, ದ.ಕ. **ವಿಲ್ಯಮ ದ ಸಿಲ್ವ**
01–11–1987

Konkninth Annkar Sahith *by Francis D'Cunha was published by Karnataka Konkani Sahitya Academy, Mangalore in 2004. D'Cunha emphasises that translation increases the social and cultural familiarity between people of different languages.*

He classifies translations into Konkani into three areas: translation of religious writings, translation of creative prose literature and translation of poetry. Among religious writings he mentions the translations of religious texts, the liturgy, achievements of Sylvester Menezes, translation of the Bible and other religious literature. The prominent translators of prose include Ravindra Kelekar, William da Silva, V.J.P Saldhanha, J.B Moraes, A. X. Patrao, and Melwyn Rodrigues among others. William Barboza, Edward Noronha, J.B. Moraes, Cyril G. Sequeira, Maurice D'sa, Francis D'Cunha and H. Raghavendra Rao are the prominent translators of poetry into Konkani.

ಕೊಂಕ್ಣಿಂತ್ ಅಣ್ಕಾರ್ ಸಾಹಿತ್

ಫ್ರಾನ್ಸಿಸ್ ಡಿಕುನ್ಹಾ
ಭಾಶೆಕ್ ಅಣ್ಕಾರಾಚಿ ಗರ್ಜ್

ಭಾಶೆಚೆಂ ಕುಳಾರ್–ಸಂಸ್ಕೃತಿ

ಮನ್ಶಾಚಾ ವಿಶಿಷ್ಟ್ ಗುಣಾಂ ಪೈಕಿ ಭಾಸ್‌ಯೀ ಏಕ್. ಆಪ್ಣಾಚೆಂ ಭಗ್ಣಾಂ ಸಗ್ಳಿಂ ಹೆರಾಂಕ್ ಬರ್‍ಯೆ ರಿತಿನ್ ಕಳಂವ್ಕ್ ಮನ್ಶ್ಯಾನ್ ಕರ್‍ಚ್ಯಾ ಪ್ರೇತನಾ ವರ್‍ವಿಂ ಭಾಸ್ ಉದೆಲಿ. ಉಲವ್ಣ್ಯೆಕ್ ಆನಿ ಉಚಾರ್‍ಚೆಕ್ ಭಾಸ್ ವಾಪರ್‍ತಾಂವ್. ಹ್ಯಾ ಪಾಸತ್ ನಮುನ್ಯಾವಾರ್ ಆವಾಜ್ ಘಡ್ಲ್ಯಾತ್ ಆನಿ ಸಬ್ದ್, ಉತ್ರಾಂ ಉದೆಲ್ಯಾಂತ್.

ಉಲಯಿಲ್ಲೆಂ ಉತಾರ್ ಜಗವ್ನ್ ದವರುಂಕ್ ಘುರ್‍ತ್ ರಚ್ಲೆ. ಅಶೆಂ ಲಿಪಿ ಜಾಲಿ. ಉಲವ್ಣ್ಯೆ ಸಂಗಿಂ ಬರಾಪ್‌ಯೀ ಮೆಳೊನ್ ಭಾಸ್ ಜಾಲಿ. ಆಜ್ ಸಂಸಾರಾಂತ್ ಹಜಾರೊಂ ಭಾಸೊ ಆಸಾತ್. ತಾಂಚಾಕೀ ಥೊಡ್ಯಾ ಉಣ್ಯಾ ಸಂಖ್ಯಾನ್ ಲಿಪಿಯೊ ಆಸಾತ್. ಕೊಂಕ್ಣಿ ಭಾಸ್, ರೋಮಿ, ಕಾನಡಿ ಆನಿ ದೇವ್‌ನಾಗರಿ ಲಿಪಿಂನಿ ಬರಯ್ತಾತ್.

ಭಾಸ್ ಸಂಸ್ಕೃತೆಚಾ ಶ್ಥೆತಾಂತ್ ವಾಡ್ತಾ. ತ್ಯಾ ಶ್ಥೆತಾ ಥಾವ್ನ್ ಸಾರೆಂ, ವಾರೆಂ, ಬರೆಂ ಪೂರಾ ಜೊಡ್ತಾ. ಹರ್‍ಯೆಕೆ ಸಂಸ್ಕೃತೆಂತ್ ಆಸ್ಚೆ ಭಾಶೆಂತ್ ಉತ್ರಾಂನಿ ವಾಕ್ಯಾಂಚೆ ಬಾಂದಾವಳಿಂನಿ ಆನಿ ಹೆರ್ ಜಾಯ್ತ್ಯಾ ಸಂಗ್ತಿಂನಿ ಆಪ್ಲೆಂಚ್ ಖಾಶೆಲೆಂಪಣ್ ವ ವಿಶಿಷ್ಟತಾ ಆಸ್ತಾ. ಎಕಾ ಕೊಂಕ್ಣಿ ಭಾಶಿಕಾಕ್ ಆನಿ ಕಾನಡಿ ಭಾಶಿಕಾಕ್ ಉಲವ್ಣ್ಯೆ ರಿತಿನ್‌ಚ್ ಪಾರ್‍ಕುಂಕ್ ಜಾತಾ. ಇಂಗ್ಲಿಷ್ ವಾಕ್ಯಾಂಚಿ ಬಾಂಧಾವಳ್– ವ್ಯಾಕರಣ್, ಕೊಂಕ್ಣಿ ಭಾಷೆಕ್ ತಾಳ್ ಪಡಾನಾ. 'ಚಾ ನಾ' ಮ್ಹಳ್ಳೆಂ 'Tea no' ಮ್ಹಣ್ ಬರಂವ್ಕ್ ಜಾಯ್ನಾ. ವೆವೆಗ್ಳ್ಯೊ ಭಾಸೊ ಉಲಂವ್ಚ್ಯಾ ವ್ಯಕ್ತಿಂಚೆ ಸಂಬಂಧಿತ್ ಆಟ್‌ನೇಟ್ ವೆವೆಗ್ಳೆ ಬಸೊನ್ ಯೆತಾತ್.

ಎಕೆಚ್ಚ್ ಭಾಶೆ ಭಿತರ್‌ಯೀ ಹ್ಯೆ ಖಾಶೆಲೆಪಣಾಂತ್ ಜಾಯ್ತೊ ಫರಕ್ ಆಸ್ತಾ. ಮಂಗ್ಳುರಿ ಕ್ರಿಸ್ತಾಂವಾಂನಿ, ಸಾರಸ್ವತ್ ಕೊಂಕ್ಣ್ಯಾಂನಿ ಆನಿ ಗೊಂಯ್ಚ್ಯಾ ಕೊಂಕ್ಣಿ ಲೊಕಾನ್ ಉಲಂವ್ಚೆ ಭಾಶೆಚಿ ಬೊಲಿ ಆನಿ ತಾಳೊ (ಧಾಟಿ) ವೆವೆಗ್ಳ್ಯೊ ಆಯ್ಕೊಂಕ್ ಮೆಳ್ತಾತ್. ತ್ಯಾ ಶಿವಾಯ್ ಸಬ್ದಾಂಚೊ ಅರ್ಥ್‌ಯೀ ಬದಲ್ತಾ. ಕೊಡ್ಯಾಳ್‌ಗಾರಾಂನಿ ಆನಿ ಕೆನರಾಚಾ ಲೊಕಾನ್ ವಾಪರ್‍ಚ್ಯಾ 'ಪಾಂಯ್' ಸಬ್ದಾಚಾ ಅರ್ಥಾಂತ್ ಕಿತ್ಲೊ ಅಂತರ್ ಆಸಾ. ಕೊಡ್ಯಾಳ್‌ಗಾರಾಂಕ್ ಪಾಂಯ್ ಮ್ಹಳ್ಯಾರ್, ಚಲೊಂಕ್ ವಾಪರ್‍ಚ್ಯೊ ವಿಸ್ವೊ (Legs). ಕೆನರಾಂತ್ಲ್ಯೆ ಕೊಂಕ್ಣಿ ಲೊಕಾಕ್ ಹೊಚ್ಚ್ ಸಬ್ದ್ – 'ಬಾಪುಯ್' (Father) ಮ್ಹಳ್ಳೊ ಅರ್ಥ್ ದಿತಾ.

ಕೊಡ್ಯಾಳ್‌ಗಾರಾಂಕ್‌ಚ್ಚ್ 'ಬಾಬ್' ಥೊಡ್ಯಾಂಕ್ 'ಬಾಪುಯ್' ತರ್ ಆನಿ ಥೊಡ್ಯಾಂಕ್ 'ವ್ಹಡ್ ಭಾವ್' ಜಾವ್ನ್ ಅರ್ಥ್ ದಿತಾ. ಭಾಸ್ ಏಕ್ ತರೀ ಅರ್ಥ್ ಸಮುದಾಯ್ ವ ಸಂಸ್ಕೃತೆ ಥಾವ್ನ್ ಉದೆತಾತ್. ಹೆ ವೆವೆಗ್ಳೆ ಆಸ್ತಿತ್.

ಭಾಸ್, ಉಲಂವ್ಕ್ ವ ಕಳಂವ್ಕ್ ವಾಪರ್ಚೆಂ ಮಾಧ್ಯಮ್. ತಿತ್ಲೆಂಚ್ ನ್ಹಯ್, 'ತಾಕಾ ಭಾಸ್ ನಾ' ವ 'ತಾಕಾ ಭಾಸ್ ಶಿಕಯ್ತಾಂ' ಮ್ಹಣ್ತಾನಾ ಆಮಿ ಕಿತೆಂ ಸಮ್ಜಾತಾಂವ್? ಭಾಸ್ ರೀತ್–ನೀತ್ ಆಟಾಪ್ತಾ. ಗರ್ಜೆಚೆಂ ಗ್ಯಾನ್ ಜಾಣಾ ಜಾಂವ್ಚೆಂ ಗರ್ಜ್ ಆಸ್ತಾ. ಏಕ್ ಭಾಸ್ ಉಲಯ್ತೆಲ್ಯಾಂಕ್ ತಾಚೆಚ್ಚ್ ರೀತ್–ನೀತ್ ವ ಜಿಣ್ಯೆ ಶೈಲಿ ಆಸ್ತಾ. ದೆಕುನ್ ಭಾಶೆ ದ್ವಾರಿಂ ಪ್ರಾದೇಶಿಕತಾ ಆನಿ ಸಂಸ್ಕೃತಿ ಅರ್ಥ್ ಜಾತಾ.

ಭಾಶೆಂಕ್ ಆಪ್ಲೆಂಚ್ ಖಾಶೆಲೆಂ ಸಾಹಿತ್ ಆಸಾ. ಗಾಂವಾಂತ್ ಲೊಕಾನ್ ಆಪ್ಲ್ಯಾ ಅನ್ಭವಾನ್ ಆನಿ ಸಮ್ಜಣೆನ್ ಘಡ್ಲೆಲ್ಯೊ ಸಾಂಗ್ಣ್ಯೊ, ಕಾಣಿಯೊ, ಪದಾಂ, ಭಜನಾಂ, ಗಾದಿಯೊ, ವೊವಿಯೊ ತೊಂಡಾ ಥಾವ್ನ್ ತೊಂಡಾಕ್, ಗಿನ್ಯಾನಾ ಥಾವ್ನ್ ಗಿನ್ಯಾನಾಕ್ ವ್ಹಚೊನ್ ದಾಯ್ಜ್ ಜಾವ್ನ್ ರುತಾ ಜಾಲ್ಲ್ಯೊ. ಹಾಕಾ 'ಲೋಕ್‌ವೇದ್' (Folklore) ಮ್ಹಣ್ ವೊಲಾಯ್ಲಾಂ.

ತ್ಯಾ ಶಿವಾಯ್ ತಿ ಭಾಸ್ ಉಲಯ್ತೆಲ್ಯಾಂ ಥೊಡ್ಯಾಂನಿ ಆಪ್ಲ್ಯೆ ದೆಣ್ಯಾಸಕ್ತೆನ್ ಕಾವ್ಯಾಂ, ಪದಾಂ ರಚ್ಲ್ಯಾಂತ್. ಕಾಣಿಯೊ ಕಾದಂಬರಿ ಘಡ್ಲ್ಯಾತ್. ಜಿಣಿ, ಪಯ್ಣಾಂ ವರ್ಣಿಲ್ಯಾಂತ್. ಅಶೆಂ ಸೃಜನಾತ್ಮಕ್ ಸಾಹಿತ್ಯ್ ಉದೆಲಾಂ. ಗ್ಯಾನ್ ಬರವ್ನ್ ದವರ್ಲಾಂ. ಬರ್ಪಾಂ ಭರ್ಲ್ಯಾಂತ್ ಆನಿ ಭಾಶೆಚಿ ದಾಟಾಯ್ ಮೊಟಾಯ್ ಚಡ್ಲ್ಯಿ.

ಭಾಶೆಕ್ ಏಕೆ ಕುಡಿಕ್ ತಾಳ್ ಕರ್ಚೆಂ ತರ್: ಸಬ್ದ್ ಉತಾರ್–ಜೀವ್‌ಕಣ್. ಸಂಸ್ಕೃತಿ ಆನಿ ಪ್ರಾದೇಶಿಕತಾ – ಆಕಾರ್ ದಿಂವ್ಚಿಂ ಹಾಡಾಂ. ಸಾಹಿತ್ಯ್ – ಮಾಸ್ ಆನಿ ರಗಾತ್. ಅಲಂಕಾರ್–ನೆಟಯಿಲ್ಲೆಂ ಶೃಂಗಾರ್. ಉಲವ್ಪ್ಯಾನ್ ವ ವಾಚ್ಪ್ಯಾನ್ ಆಪ್ಲೊ ಶ್ವಾಸ್ ಭಾಶೆಚ್ಯೆ ಕುಡಿಕ್ ಮೆಳಯ್ಲ್ಯಾರ್ ಜೀವ್ ಭರುನ್ ಸಂತೊಸ್ ಜಾತಾ, ಭಾಸ್ ಸಕತ್ ಜಾತಾ.

ಭಾಶಾಂತರಾಚಿ ಗರ್ಜ್:

ವೆಪಾರ್–ವಹಿವಾಟ್, ಉದ್ಯೋಗ್, ಉದ್ಯಮಾಂ ಖಾತಿರ್ ಲೊಕಾನ್ ಎಕಾ ಜಾಗ್ಯಾ ಥಾವ್ನ್ ಆನ್ಯೇಕ್ ಕಡೆನ್ ವ್ಹಚಾಜಾಯ್ ಪಡ್ತಾ. ಹೆರ್ ಭಾಶೆಂಚಾ ಲೊಕಾ ಸಂಗಿಂ ಸಂವಾದ್ ಕರಿಜಾಯ್ ಪಡ್ತಾ. ತೆದ್ನಾ ತ್ಯಾ ಪ್ರದೇಶಾಚಿ ಭಾಸ್ ತಾಣಿಂ ಶಿಕಾಜಾಯ್ ವ ಕೊಣೆ ಪುಣೀ ಭಾಶಾಂತರ್ ಕರ್ನ್ ಸಾಂಗಾಜಾಯ್. ಎಕ್ಲ್ಯಾನ್ ಆಪ್ಲ್ಯೆ ಭಾಶೆಂತ್ ಸಾಂಗ್‌ಲ್ಲೆಂ ತೆಂ ಆನ್ಯೇಕ್ಲ್ಯಾಕ್ ವ ಜಮ್ಯಾಕ್ ತಾಂಚೆ ಭಾಶೆಂತ್ ಸಾಂಗ್ಚೆಂಚ್ ಭಾಶಾಂತರ್.

ಉಲಂವ್ಪ್ಯಾ ಆನಿ ಸಮ್ಜೊಂಚಾ ದೊಗಾಂ ವ್ಯಕ್ತಿ ಮಧೆಂ ತಿಸ್ರೊ ವೆಕ್ತಿ ಆಸ್ತಾ. ಹ್ಯಾ ತಿಸ್ರ್ಯೆ ವೆಕ್ತಿಕ್ ಮಾತ್ರ್ ದೊನೀ ಭಾಸೊ ಸಾರ್ಕ್ಯೊ ಕಳಿತ್ ಆಸಾಜಾಯ್. ತಾಕಾ ಭಾಶಾಂತರ್‌ಕರ್ತ್ ಮ್ಹಣ್ತಾಂವ್. ತುಳು ಭಾಶೆಂತ್ 'ಆಯೆ ಪದ್ರಾಡ್' ಮ್ಹಳ್ಳೆಂ ಭಾಶಾಂತರ್‌ಕರ್ತ್ಯಾನ್ 'ತೊ ಬಾರಾ' ಮ್ಹಣೊಂಕ್ ಜಾಯ್ನಾ 'He turned down the request' ಮ್ಹಳ್ಳೆಂ 'ತಾಣೆ ವಿನಂತಿ ಸಕಯ್ಲ್ ಘುಂವ್ಡಾಯ್ಲಿ' ಮ್ಹಣೊಂಕ್ ನಜೊ. ಪುಣ್ ಥೊಡೆ ಪಾವ್ಟಿಂ ಅಶೆಂಯ್ ಘಡ್ತಾ.

ಸಂಸಾರ್ ಆಜ್ ಎಕ್ವೀಸಾವ್ಯಾ ಶತಾಬ್ದೆಕ್ ಪಾವ್ಲಾ. ಜಾಗತಿಕ್ ಹಳ್ಳಿ ಜಾವ್ನ್ ವೆಗಾನ್ ಬದಲ್ತಾ. ಸಂಪರ್ಕ್, ಸಂವಹನ್ ಸಾಹೆತಿ ಉತ್ತೀಮ್ ಮಟ್ಟಾಕ್ ಪಾವ್ಲ್ಯಾತ್. ಮಾಹೆತಿ ಮಾಧ್ಯಮಾಂ ಬಳಾಧಿಕ್ ಜಾಲ್ಯಾಂತ್. ಹೆರ್ ಭಾಶೆಚಾ ಲೊಕಾ ಸಂಗಿಂ ಭರ್ಸುಂಚೆಂ, ಉಲಂವ್ಚೆಂ ಅನಿವಾರ್ಯ್ ಜಾಲಾಂ. ಹ್ಯೆ ಪರಿಗತೆಂತ್ ಭಾಶಾಂತರ್ ಬೋವ್ ಗರ್ಜೆಚೆಂ.

ಪರ್ಕಿ ಭಾಶೆಚಾ ಲೊಕಾಕ್ ಭಾಶಣ್ ದಿತಾನಾ, ತೆಂ ತರ್ಜಣ್ ಕರ್ನ್ ಪರಿಣಾಮ್‌ಕಾರಿ ರಿತಿನ್ ಸಾಂಗಾಜಾಯ್ ಪಡ್ತಾ. ವಿಶ್ವ ಸಂಸ್ಥ್ಯಾಚ್ಯೆ ಮಹಾಸಭೆಂತ್ ಭಾರತಾಚೊ ಪ್ರಧಾನಿ ಹಿಂದಿ ಭಾಶೆಂತ್ ಉಲಯ್ತಾನಾ ಸಭೆಚಾ ಸಾಂದ್ಯಾಂಕ್ ತಿಂ ಉತ್ರಾಂ ತಾಂಚೆ ತಾಂಚೆ ಭಾಶೆಂತ್ ಸಾರ್ಕಿ ತರ್ಜಣ್ ಕರ್ಚಿ ವ್ಯವಸ್ಥಾ ಕರ್ತಾತ್. ಭಾಶಾಂತರ್‌ಕರ್ತ್ಯಾಂಚೊ ಮಹತ್ವ್ ಹ್ಯಾ ದ್ವಾರಿಂ ಸ್ಪಷ್ಟ್ ಜಾತಾ.

ಖಬ್ರೆ ಪತ್ರಾಂಚಾ ದಫ್ತರಾಂತ್ ನಿರಂತರ್ ಭಾಶಾಂತರಾಚೊ ವಾವ್ರ್ ಜಾತಾ. UNI, PTI ತಸಲ್ಯಾ ಖಬ್ರೆ ಸಂಸ್ಥ್ಯಾಂನಿ ಇಂಗ್ಲಿಷ್ ಭಾಶೆನ್ ಧಾಡ್‌ಲ್ಲ್ಯೊ ಖಬ್ರೊ ವ ಬರ್ಪಾಂ ಪರ್ಗಟ್ಚ್ಯಾ ಪತ್ರಾಚ್ಯೆ ಭಾಶೆಕ್ ತರ್ಜಣ್ ಕರ್ತಾತ್. ಹ್ಯಾ ವರ್ವಿಂ ಸಂಸಾರಾಚಾ ಖಂಚಾಯ್ ಪೊಂತಾರ್ ಘಡ್‌ಲ್ಲಿ ಸಂಗತ್, ಖಂಚೆಯ್ ಹಳ್ಳೆಚಾ ಸಾಂದಿ ಮುಲ್ಯಾಂನಿ ಲೊಕಾಕ್ ತಾಂಚೆಚ್ಚ್ ಭಾಶೆಂತ್ ವಾಚುಂಕ್ ವ ಆಯ್ಕೊಂಕ್ ಮೆಳ್ತಾ. ಭಾಶಾಂತರಾ ವರ್ವಿಂ ಮನ್ಶ್ಯಾಕ್ ಮನಿಸ್ ಲಾಗಿಂ ಜಾತಾ, ಎಕ್ತಾರ್ ವಾಡ್ತಾ.

ಭಾಶಾಂತರ ವರ್ವಿಂ ವಿವಿಂಗಡ್ ಭಾಶಿಕ್ ಲೊಕಾ ಮಧೆಂ ಸಾಮಾಜಿಕ್ ಆನಿ ಸಾಂಸ್ಕೃತಿಕ್ ವಳಕ್ ಚಡ್ತಾ. ಜಣಾಂಚಾ ಎಕಾ ಸಮುದಾಯೆಚ್ಯೊ ರಿತಿ–ರಿವಾಜ್ಯೊ, ವರ್ತನಾಂ, ಪರಿಸರ್, ಚರಿತ್ರಾ ಆನಿ ತಾಚೊ ಪ್ರಭಾವ್, ಪಿಸಾಯೊ ಹೆರ್ ಸಮುದಾಯಾಚಾ ಜಣಾಂಕ್ ಕಳ್ತಾ. ನಾ. ಡಿಸೋಜಾನ್ ಕಾನಡಿ ಭಾಶೆಂತ್ ಬರಯಿಲ್ಲ್ಯೊ ಕಾಣಿಯೊ ಕೊಂಕ್ಣೆಂತ್ ವಾಚ್ತಾನಾ ಕೊಂಕ್ಣಿ ಲೊಕಾಕ್ ಸಾಗರ್, ಜೋಗ, ಭಟ್ಕಳ, ಹೊನ್ನಾವರ್ ಪರಿಸರಾಚಾ ಲೊಕಾಚಿ ವಳಕ್ ಜಾತಾ. ತ್ಯಾ ಪರಿಸರಾಂತ್ ನಂಯ್ಕ್ ಬಾಂಧ್ ಬಾಂಧ್‌ಲ್ಲ್ಯೆ ವೆಳಿಂ ಲೊಕಾನ್ ಭಗ್‌ಲ್ಲೆ ತಳ್ಮಳೆ, ಕೆಲ್ಲೊ ತ್ಯಾಗ್ ಕೊಂಕ್ಣ್ಯಾಂಕ್ ದೊಳ್ಯಾಂ ಮುಖಾರ್ ಯೆತಾ. ಭಾಶಾಂತರ್, ಸಂಸ್ಕೃತೆಚೊ ಆನಿ ಹ್ಯಾ ಮುಖಾಂತ್ರ್ ವೆವೆಗ್ಳ್ಯಾ ಸಮುದಾಯಾಂಚಾ ಲೊಕಾಚೊ ಮೆಳಾವ್ ಕರ್ತಾ. ಎಕಾಮೆಕಾ ಸಮ್ಜೊಂಚೆ ಅವ್ಕಾಸ್ ದಿತಾ.

ಭಾಶಾಂತರ್ ಜಣಾಂಚಿ ಚಿಂತ್ಪಾ ಮೇರ್ ವಿಸ್ತಾರಾಯ್ತಾ. ಜನೆಲಾಂ ಉಘಡ್ತಾನಾ ಭಾಯ್ಲಿಂ ವಾರೆಂ ಭಿತರ್ ಸರೊನ್ ಬದ್ಲಾವಣ್ ಘಡ್ತಾ. ಎಕಾ ಪ್ರದೇಶಾಂತ್ ವಾ ಭಾಶೆಂತ್ ಕುಡಾವ್ನ್ ಆಸ್‌ಲ್ಲ್ಯಾ ಲೊಕಾಕ್ ಪ್ರಗತಿಪರ್ ಬದ್ಲಾವಣೆಕ್ 'ಜನೆಲಾಂ ಉಘಡ್ನ್' ನವೆಂ ಚಿಂತಾಪ್ ವ್ಹಾಳೊಂಕ್ ಹೆರ್ ಭಾಶೆಚೆಂ ಬರಾಪ್ ಭಾಶಾಂತರ್ ಕೆಲ್ಲ್ಯೆ ವರ್ವಿಂ ಸಾಧ್ಯ್ ಜಾತಾ. ನವೆಂ ಚಿಂತಾಪ್ ನವಿ ದಿಶಾ ದಾಕಯ್ತಾ. ಪರ್ಕ್ಯೆ ಸಮಾಜಿಚೆಂ ಆಕ್ರಮಣ್‌ಯೀ ಜಾಯ್ತ್. ಭಾಶಾಂತರಾ ವರ್ವಿಂ ಕ್ರಾಂತಿಕಾರಿ ಪರಿಣಾಮ್ ಜಾತಿತ್.

ಗ್ಯಾನ್ ವಾಂಟ್ಚಿ, ದಿಂವ್ಚಿ ಆನಿ ಘೆಂವ್ಚಿ ಪ್ರಕ್ರಿಯಾ (Process) ತರ್ಜಣೆ ವರ್ವಿಂ ಜಾತಾ. ಥೊಡ್ಯಾಚ್ಚ್ ವೆಳಾನ್ ವ್ಹರ್ತೆಂ ಆನಿ ಜಾಯ್ತೆಂ (ವ್ಹಡ್ ಮಾಪಾನ್) ಗ್ಯಾನ್ ಪ್ರಸಾರುಂಚಾಕ್ 'ಗ್ಯಾನ್ ಸ್ಫೋಟ್' (Knowledge Explosion) ಮ್ಹಣ್ತಾಂವ್. ಆಜ್‌ಕಾಲ್ ಗ್ಯಾನ್ ಸ್ಫೋಟ್ ಅನಿವಾರ್ಯ್ ಜಾಲಾ. ಭಾಶಾಂತರಾ ಶಿವಾಯ್ ಹೆಂ ಸಾಧ್ಯ್ ನಾ, ಸರ್ವ್ ಬಗಾಂಚೆಂ ಗ್ಯಾನ್ ವೆವೆಗ್ಳ್ಯಾ ಭಾಸಾಂನಿ ಭಾಶಾಂತರ್ ಕೆಲ್ಲ್ಯಾ ವೆಳಾರ್ ವಾಂಟಾಪ್ ಜಾತಾ ಆನಿ ವಾಡಾವಳೆಕ್ ಕಾರಣ್ ಜಾತಾ.

ಕಾನಡೀ ಭಾಶೆಂತ್ ಬಿ. ಎಮ್. ಶ್ರೀನ್ 'ಇಂಗ್ಲಿಷ್ ಗೀತಗಳು' ಬೂಕ್ ಪರ್ಗಟ್ತಚ್ಚ್ ಕಾನಡೀ ಸಾಹಿತ್ಯಾಚ್ಯೊ ವಾಟೊ ಬದಲ್ಲ್ಯೊ. ನವ್ಯೊ 'ನವ್ಯ್' ಆನಿ ನವ್ಯೋತ್ತರ್ ಸಾಧ್ಯತಾ ದಿಸೊನ್ ಆಯ್ಲ್ಯೊ, ನವೊ ಶ್ವಾಸ್, ವೇಗ್ ಭರ್ಲೊ. ನವೆ ಚಿಂತಾಪ್ ರುತಾ ಜಾಲೆಂ. ಭಾಶಾಂತರಾ ದ್ವಾರಿಂ ನವ್ಯಾ ವರ್ಗಾಚೆಂ ಸಾಹಿತ್ಯ್ ಆಪ್ಲ್ಯೆ ಭಾಶೆಕ್ ಹಾಡುಂಕ್ ಜಾತಾ. ಸಾಹಿತ್ಯಾಚಿ ವಿವಿಧತಾ ಚಡ್ತಾ. ಬರ್ಪಾಂಚೊ ಪಾಂವ್ಡೊ ವಾಡ್ತಾ.

ಉತ್ತೀಮ್ ಬರಾಪ್ ಹೆರ್ ಭಾಶೆಂನಿ ಭಾಶಾಂತರ್ ಜಾತಾನಾ ಬರವ್ಪ್ಯಾಚೆಂ ಸ್ಥಾನ್‌ಮಾನ್‌ಯೀ ವಾಡ್ತಾ. ತಾಚಾ ದೆಣ್ಯಾಂಚೊ ಪ್ರಭಾವ್ ಆನಿ ಪರಿಣಾಮ್ ಚಡ್ ಆನಿ ಚಡ್ ವಾಚ್ಪ್ಯಾಂಕ್ ಪಾವ್ತಾ. ಠಾಗೋರಾಚಿಂ ಕವಿತಾಂ ಇಂಗ್ಲಿಷಾಕ್ ಭಾಶಾಂತರ್ ಜಾವ್ನಾತ್‌ಲ್ಲಿಂ ತರ್ ತಾಕಾ ನೊಬೆಲ್ ಪುರಸ್ಕಾರ್ ಲಾಬ್ತೊನಾ ಮ್ಹಣ್ ಎಕ್ಲೊ ಬರವ್ಪಿ ಲಿಖ್ತಾ. ಯೆಂಡಮೂರಿ ವೀರೇಂದ್ರನಾಥ್, ತೆಲುಗು ಭಾಶಿಕ್ ತರೀ ಕಾನಡಿ ಜಣಾಂಕ್ ತೊ ಖೂಬ್ ವಳ್ಕಿಚೊ. ಆಜ್‌ಕಾಲ್ ಕಾನಡಿ ಬರವ್ಪಿ ನಾ. ಡಿಸೋಜಾ, ಯಶವಂತ ಚಿತ್ತಾಲ, ನಾಗತಿಹಳ್ಳಿ ಚಂದ್ರಶೇಖರ್, ಪ್ರೇಮ್‌ಚಂದ್, ಜೇಮ್ಸ್ ಹ್ಯಾಡ್ಲಿ ಚೇಜ್, ಕೊಂಕ್ಣೆಚೆಚ್ಚ್ ಮ್ಹಣ್ ಭಗ್ತಾ! ತಾಂಚ್ಯೊ ಜಾಯ್ತ್ಯೊ ಕಾಣಿಯೊ ಕೊಂಕ್ಣೆಕ್ ಉತ್ರಾಯ್ಲ್ಯಾತ್.

ಹೆರ್ ಭಾಶೆಂಚೆಂ ಸಾಹಿತಿಕ್ ವಾರೆಂ ವ್ಹಾಳ್ತಾನಾ ಫಲಾಣ್ಯಾ ಭಾಶೆಚಾ ಬರವ್ಪ್ಯಾಚಿ ಜವಾಬ್ದಾರಿ ಚಡ್ತಾ. ತಾಚೆಂ ದೆಣೆ ಆನಿ ಕುಶಲತಾ ಮೆಚ್ವಣೆಚಾ ಆನಿ ಸ್ವೀಕಾರ್‌ಪಣಾಚ್ಯೆ ಪರೀಕ್ಷೆಕ್ ವಳಗ್ ಜಾತಾ. ಸ್ಪರ್ಧಾತ್ಮಕ್ ಮನೋಭಾವ್ ಚಡೊನ್ ಚಡೊನ್, ಶ್ರೇಷ್ಟತಾ

ಉಜಳ್ತಾ, ಕೋಯ್ರ್ ಉಸಾಳ್ತಾ. ಅಶೆಂ ಭಾಶಾಂತರ್, ಫಲಾಣ್ಯಾ ಭಾಶೆಚಾ ಸಾಹಿತ್ಯಾಚೆ ಉದರ್ಗತೆಕ್ ಕಾರಣ್ ಜಾತಾ.

ಕೊಂಕ್ಣಿ ಭಾಶಾಂತರಾಚಿ ರೀತ್, ನೀತ್ ಆನಿ ಮೀತ್

ಭಾಶಾಂತರ್ ಮ್ಹಳ್ಯಾರ್ ಕಿತೆಂ ಮ್ಹಣ್ ಸಂಪ್ಯಾ ದಾಖ್ಲ್ಯಾನ್ ಸಾಂಗ್ಚೆಂ ತರ್: ಸೆಜಾರ್ಲ್ಯಾ ಘರಾ ಕೆಲ್ಲೆಂ ವೋರ್ನ್ (ಪಾಯಸ್) ತಾಂಚಾ ಆಯ್ದಾನಾ ಥಾವ್ನ್ ಆಮ್ಚ್ಯಾ ಆಯ್ದಾನಾಂತ್ ಘೆಂವ್ಚೆಂ!! ಹ್ಯಾ ವೆಳಿಂ ವೋರ್ನ್ ತಾಂಚಾ ಆಯ್ದಾನಾ ಥಾವ್ನ್ ಆಮ್ಚ್ಯಾ ಆಯ್ದಾನಾಕ್ ಆಯ್ಲೆಂ, ಆಯ್ದಾನಾಂ ಬದಲ್ಲಿಂ ತರೀ ವೋರ್ನ್ ಮಾಪಾನ್ ಆನಿ ಗುಣಾನ್ ತಶೆಂಚ್ ಉರ್ಲೆಂ. ಎಕಾ ಆಯ್ದಾನಾ ಥಾವ್ನ್ ಆನ್ಯೇಕಾಕ್ ವೊತ್ತಾನಾ ಪುಸುನ್ ವೊತಿಜಾಯ್. ನಾ ತರ್ ರುಚಿಕ್ ವೋರ್ನ್ ಲುಕ್ಸಾಣ್ ಜಾತಾ.

ಕನ್ನಡ ವಿದ್ವಾಂಸ್ ಜಿ. ಎಸ್. ಶಿವರುದ್ರಪ್ಪ ಸಾಂಗ್ತಾಕೀ (ಸಮಗ್ರ ಗದ್ಯ, ಪಾನ್: 120) ಇಂಗ್ಲಿಷಾಚೊ Translation ಸಬ್ದ್ Trans-lates ಲ್ಯಾಟಿನ್ ಭಾಶೆ ಮುಳಾ ಥಾವ್ನ್ ಆಯ್ಲಾ. ತಾಚೊ ಅರ್ಥ್ Carry Across ಮ್ಹಣ್ ಜಾತಾ. ಭಾಸ್ ಎಕಾ ಪ್ರದೇಶಾಕ್ ಸೀಮಿತ್ ಜಾವ್ನಾಸ್ತೆತ್. ಹ್ಯಾ ವರ್ವಿಂ ಭಾಶೆಕ್ ಸಂಸ್ಕೃತಿ, ದೇಶ್, ಧರ್ಮ್ ಅಶೆಂ ಥೊಡ್ಯೊ ಮೆರೊ ಆಸ್ತಿತ್. ಸಾಹಿತ್ಯಾಕ್ ಮೇರ್ ನಾ. ತೆಂ ಕೊಣಾಯ್ಕೀ ಪಾವ್ತೆತ್; ಕೊಣೆಂಯ್ ಘೆವ್ಯೆತ್. ಪುಣ್ ತೆಂ ಸಾಹಿತ್ಯಾಚ್ಯೆ ಭಾಶೆಂತ್ ಉದೆತಾ ಜಾಲ್ಲ್ಯೆ ವರ್ವಿಂ ಥಂಯ್ಚ್ ಉರ್ತಾ. ಭಾಶಾಂತರ್, ಸಾಹಿತ್ಯಾಕ್ ಭಾಶೆಚ್ಯೆ ಮೆರೆ ಥಾವ್ನ್ ಉತ್ರಾಯ್ತಾ.

Translation – ಕೊಂಕ್ಣಿ ಉತ್ರಾಂವಳ್:
'ಇಂಗ್ಲಿಷ್, ಹ್ಯಾ Translation ಉತ್ರಾಕ್ ಕೊಂಕ್ಣೆಂತ್ ವಿವಿಧ್ ಉತ್ರಾಂ ವಾಪರ್ಲ್ಯಾಂತ್. ತರ್ಜುಮೊ, ತರ್ಜಣ್, ಅನುವಾದ್, ಅಣ್ಕಾರ್, ರುಪಾಂತರ್, ಭಾಶಾಂತರ್. ತರ್ಜುಮೊ ಆನಿ ತರ್ಜಣ್– ಹಿಂ ಉತ್ರಾಂ ಅರೇಬಿಕ್ ಭಾಶೆ ಥಾವ್ನ್ ಆಯ್ಲ್ಯಾಂತ್. ತರ್ಜುಮೊ=Summary, ತರ್ಜಣ್=Examine ಅನುವಾದ್ ಆನಿ ರುಪಾಂತರ್ – ಹಿಂ ಸಂಸ್ಕೃತ್ ಭಾಶೆಚಿ ಉತ್ರಾಂ. ಅನುವಾದ್=Repetition by way of explanataion or free translation, ರುಪಾಂತರ್ = Adaptation. ಗೊಯಾಂತ್ 'ಅಣ್ಕಾರ್' ಹೆಂ ಉತಾರ್ ಘೊಳ್ತಾ. ಹೆಂ ಉತಾರ್ ಮರಾಠಿ ಅನುಕಾರ್=Copying ಉತ್ರಾಂತ್ಲ್ಯಾನ್ ಆಯ್ಲಾಂ' – ಅಶೆಂ ವಿವರಾಯ್ತಾ ಪ್ರತಾಪ್ ನಾಯ್ಕ್ ಜೆ. ಸ., 'ಭಾಶಾಂತರಾಚಿಂ ತತ್ವಾಂ ಆನಿ ಕಲಾ' ಬರ್ಪಾಂತ್.

ಭಾಶಾಂತರಾಚ್ಯೆ ಪ್ರಕ್ರಿಯೆಂತ್ 3 ಘಟಕ್ ಆಸ್ತಾತ್.

1. ವಿಷಯ್ (ಸಾಹಿತ್ಯ್) 2. ಮೂಳ್‌ಭಾಸ್ 3. ಶೆವೊಟ್ ಭಾಸ್

ವಿಷಯ್ ಮೂಳ್‌ಭಾಶೆಂತ್ ಆಸ್ತಾ, ತೊ ಆಸಾ ತಸೊ ಶೆವೊಟ್ ಭಾಶೆಂತ್ ಘಾಲ್ಚಿ ಪ್ರಕ್ರಿಯಾ ಭಾಶಾಂತರ್. ಮೂಳ್ ಪ್ರಕ್ರಿಯೆಕ್ ಆನಿ ಭಾಶಾಂತರ್ ಕೃತಿಯೆಕ್ ಫರಕ್, ಭಾಸ್ ಮಾತ್ರ್.

ನಿಜಾಯ್ಕಿ ಅಶೆಂ ಭಾಶಾಂತರ್ ಕರ್ಚೆಂ ಸೈದ್ಧಾಂತಿಕ್ ಜಾವ್ನ್ ಅಸಾಧ್ಯ್ ಮ್ಹಣ್ತಾ ಪ್ರೊ. ಎನ್. ಬಾಲಸುಬ್ರಹ್ಮಣ್ಯ.

ತಾಚೆ ಪ್ರಕಾರ್ ಹರ್ಯೆಕೆ ಭಾಶೆಕ್ ತಾಚೆಂಚ್ ವ್ಯಕ್ತಿತ್ವ್ ಆಸಾ. 'ವಿಶ್ವನದರ್' ಆಸಾ. ಹೆಂ ವ್ಯಕ್ತಿತ್ವ್ ಆನಿ ವಿಶ್ವನದರ್ ತಿ ಭಾಸ್ ಉಲಂವ್ಚ್ಯಾ ಲೊಕಾಚಾ ಸಾಮಾಜಿಕ್ ಆನಿ ಐತಿಹಾಸಿಕ್

ಪರಿಸರಾಚೊ ಪರಿಣಾಮ್ ಜಾವ್ನಾಸ್ತಾ. ವೆವೆಗ್ಳ್ಯಾ ಭಾಶೆಂತ್ ವೆವೆಗ್ಳೆಂ ವ್ಯಕ್ತಿತ್ವ್ ಆಸ್ತಾ, ಎಕಾ ಸಬ್ದಾಚೊ ಅರ್ಥ್ ಆನ್ಯೇಕೆ ಭಾಶೆಂತ್ ಸಮಾಸಮ್ ಜಾಂವ್ಕ್ ಸಾಧ್ಯ್‌ಚ್ ನಾ. 'He ran away' ಮ್ಹಳ್ಳೆಂ 'ತೊ ಧಾಂವ್ಲೊ', 'ತಾಣೆ ಪೊಳಾಪಳ್ ಘೆತ್ಲಿ', 'ತಾಣೆ ಚುಕಾರಿ ಮಾರ್ಲಿ' ಮ್ಹಣ್ ಬರಂವ್ಕ್ ಸಾರ್ಕಿ ವಿಂಚವ್ಣ್ ಕರಿಜಾಯ್ ಪಡ್ತಾ. ವ್ಹರ್ತ್ಯಾ ಮ್ಹಿನತೆನ್, ಜಾಯ್ತ್ಯಾ ಚತ್ರಾಯೆನ್ ಬೈಬಲ್ ಭಾಶಾಂತರ್ ಕೆಲ್ಲೆ ಭಾಶಾಂತರ್‌ಕರ್ತ್ ಸೈತ್ ಆಪ್ಲ್ಯಾ ಸುರ್ವಿಲ್ಯಾ ಉತ್ರಾಂನಿ 'ಭಾಶಾಂತರಾಂತ್ ಚುಕಿ ಆಸ್ಯೆತ್' ಮ್ಹಣ್ ಮಾನುನ್ ಘೆತಾತ್. ಹೆಂ ಸಹಜ್. ಪ್ರೊ. ಎನ್. ಬಾಲಸುಬ್ರಹ್ಮಣ್ಯಾನ್ ಸಾಂಗ್ಚೆಪರಿಂ 'ಭಾಶಾಂತರ್' ತಾಚಾ ಸಾರ್ಕ್ಯಾ ಅರ್ಥಾನ್ ಅಸಾಧ್ಯ್.

ತಶೆಂ ಮ್ಹಣ್ ಸಗ್ಳಿ ಘೆಂವ್ಕ್ ಜಾಯ್ನಾ. ಭಾಶಾಂತರಿತ್ ಕೃತಿ, ಮೂಳ್ ಕೃತಿಯೆಕ್ ಬೋವ್ ಲಾಗಿಂ ಪಾವಯ್ಲ್ಯಾ ಶಿವಾಯ್ ಮೂಳ್ ಲೇಖಕಾಕ್ ಜಾಂವ್, ವಾಚ್ಪ್ಯಾಕ್ ಜಾಂವ್ ನ್ಯಾಯ್ ಕೆಲ್ಲ್ಯಾ ಪರಿಂ ಜಾಯ್ನಾ. ದೆಕುನ್ ಆದರ್ಶಾಚೊ 'ಭಾಶಾಂತರ್' ಸಬ್ದ್ ವಾಪರ್ತಾಂವ್.

ಭಾಶಾಂತರಾಚೆ ವರ್ಗ್:

i) ಅನುವಾದ್: ಮೂಳ್‌ಭಾಶೆ ಥಾವ್ನ್ ಶೆವೊಟ್ ಭಾಶೆಕ್ ವಿಷಯ್ ಉತ್ರಾಂವ್ಚೆಂ– ಅನುವಾದ್. ಯಶಪಾಲನ್ ಹಿಂದಿ ಭಾಶೆಂತ್ ಬರಯಿಲ್ಲಿ ಕಾಣಿ 'ಪರ್ದಾ' ಜೂಡಿ ಪಿಂಟೊನ್ 'ಪಡ್ದೊ' ನಾಂವಾನ್ ಅನುವಾದ್ ಕೆಲ್ಯಾ. ಹ್ಯೆ ಕಾಣಿಯೆಂತ್ಲೆಂ ಸಾಹಿತ್ಯ್–ವಿಷಯ್, ಹಿಂದಿ– ಮೂಳ್‌ಭಾಸ್, ಕೊಂಕ್ಣಿ–ಶೆವೊಟ್ ಭಾಸ್.

ಅನುವಾದ್ ಕರ್ತಾನಾ ಮೂಳ್‌ಕೃತಿಯೊ ಆಶಯ್ (Motif), ಸಬ್ದಾಂ ಆನಿ ಶೈಲೆ ದ್ವಾರಿಂ ಶೆವೊಟ್ ಭಾಶೆಕ್ ಜಾತಾ ತಿತ್ಲ್ಯಾ ಸಂಪೂರ್ಣ್‌ಕಾಯೆನ್ ಪಾವೊಂಕ್ ಪ್ರೆತನ್ ಕರ್ತಾತ್. ಅನುವಾದ್ ಕೆಲ್ಲಿ ಕೃತಿ ವಾಚ್ತಾನಾ ಚಡುಣೆ ಮೂಳ್‌ಕೃತಿ ವಾಚ್‌ಲ್ಲೊಚ್ಚ್ ಅನ್ಭೊಗ್ ಜಾಯ್ಜಾಯ್.

ಏಕ್ ಕೃತಿ ಹೆರ್ ಭಾಶೆಂಕ್ ಭಾಶಾಂತರ್ ಜಾಲ್ಲಿ ಯಾ ಹೆರ್ ಭಾಸಾಂನಿ ಆಸ್ಚಿ ಕೃತಿ ಶೆವೊಟ್ ಭಾಶೆಕ್ ಹಾಡ್ಯೆತಾ. ಬೈಬಲ್ ಭಾಶಾಂತರ್ ಕರ್ತಾನಾ ಹೆಬ್ರೆವ್, ಗ್ರೀಕ್, ಇಂಗ್ಲಿಷ್ ಹ್ಯೊ ಮೂಳ್‌ಭಾಸೊ ಜಾವ್ನ್ ಘೆತ್ಲ್ಯಾತ್. ಕೊಂಕ್ಣಿ ಶೆವೊಟ್ ಭಾಸ್.

ಚಡಾವತ್ ಆಮಿ ಭಾಶಾಂತರ್ ಮ್ಹಣ್ಚೆಂ ಅನುವಾದಾಕ್. 'ಅಣ್ಕಾರ್' ವ 'ತರ್ಜಣ್' ಸಬ್ದ್‌ಯೀ ವಾಪರ್ಯೆತ್. ಚಡ್ ಫರಕ್ ಪಡಾನಾ. ವಿಚಾರ್ ಸಾಹಿತ್ಯ್, ಸೃಜನಾತ್ಮಕ್ ಸಾಹಿತ್ಯ್ ಅನುವಾದ್‌ಚ್ ಕರಿಜಾಯ್ ಪಡ್ತಾ.

ii) ಭಾವಾನುವಾದ್: ಮೂಳ್‌ಭಾಶೆಚೊ ಸಬ್ದ್ ವ ವಾಕ್ಯ್ ತಶೆಂಚ್ ಶೆವೊಟ್ ಭಾಶೆಕ್ ಯೇನಾ. ಮೂಳ್‌ಭಾಶೆಚಾ ಎಕೆ ವಾಕ್ಯಾವಳಿಂತ್ (Paragraph) ಧಾ ವಾಕ್ಯಾಂ ಆಸಾತ್ ತರ್ ಶೆವೊಟ್ ಭಾಶೆಂತ್ ಸ ವ ಬಾರಾ (ಮ್ಹಳ್ಯಾರ್ ಚಡ್ ವ ಉಣೆ) ಆಸ್ತಿತ್. ಪುಣ್ ಶೆವೊಟ್ ಭಾಶೆಂತ್ಲ್ಯಾ ವಾಕ್ಯಾಂನಿ ಮೂಳ್‌ಭಾಸೆಚಾ ವಾಕ್ಯಾಂನಿ ದಿಂವ್ಚೊ ಅರ್ಥ್‌ಚ್ ದೀಜಾಯ್. ಶೈಲಿ ಆನಿ ರಚಪ್ ವೆಗ್ಳೆಂ ಅಸ್ಯೆತ್. ಹ್ಯೆ ರಿತಿಚಾ ಭಾವಾನುವಾದಾಕ್ ಸಂಗ್ರಹಾನುವಾದ್‌ಯೀ ಮ್ಹಣ್ತಾತ್. ಥೊಡಿಂ ಲಾಂಬ್, ಗಂಭೀರ್ ಲೇಖನಾಂ, ಪ್ರಬಂಧ್ ಸಂಗ್ರಹಾನುವಾದ್ ಕರ್ಯೆತ್. ಕಾಣಿಯೊ ವ ಕಾದಂಬರಿಯೊ ಅಶೆಂ ಕೆಲ್ಯಾರ್ ವೊರ್ನಾಕ್ ಉದಾಕ್ ಭರ್ಶಿಲ್ಲೆಪರಿಂ ರೂಚ್ ವ್ಹೆತಾ. ಪುಣ್ ಎ. ಎಕ್ಸ್. ಪತ್ರಾವೊನ್ ಆಪ್ಲೆಂ ಕೆದಾಳಾಗೀ ವಾಚುನ್, ಉಡಾಸ್ ದವರ್‌ಲ್ಲ್ಯೊ ಇಂಗ್ಲಿಷ್ ಕಾಣಿಯೊ ಭಾವಾನುವಾದ್ ಕರ್ನ್ ರುಚಿನ್ ಕೊಂಕ್ಣೆಂತ್ ಬರಯ್ಲ್ಯಾತ್. ಪತ್ರಾಂನಿ ಯೆಂವ್ಚ್ಯೊ ಖಬ್ರೊ, ಲೇಖನಾಂ ಅಶೆಂ ಕರಿಜಾಯ್ ಪಡ್ತಾತ್. 'ಆಧಾರಾನ್' ಬರಯಿಲ್ಲ್ಯೊ ಕಾದಂಬರಿ ಭಾವಾನುವಾದ್ ಜಾವ್ನಾಸ್ತಾತ್.

iii) ಸಾರಾಂಶ್: ಮೂಳ್‌ಭಾಶೆಂತ್ ಆಸ್ಚೊ ವಿಷಯ್ ಶೆವೊಟ್ ಭಾಶೆಂತ್ ಭೋವ್ ಮಟ್ವ್ಯಾನ್ ಸಾಂಗ್ಚೆಂ ವ ಬರಂವ್ಚೆಂ ಸಾರಾಂಶ್ ಜಾತಾ. ವಿಷಯಾಚಿ ಭಾಸ್ ಬದ್ಲ್ತಾತಾ ತರೀ ಖರ್ಯಾ ಅರ್ಥಾನ್ ಭಾಶಾಂತರ್ ಮ್ಹಣೊಂಕ್ ಜಾಯ್ನಾ. ಸಾಹಿತ್ಯ್ ಮ್ಹಳ್ಯಾರ್

ವಿಷಯ್ ಮಾತ್ರ್ ನ್ಹಯ್, ಸಬ್ದ್, ವಾಕ್ಯ್, ಅಲಂಕಾರ್, ವ್ಯಾಕರಣ್, ಶೈಲಿ, ಚಿಂತ್ಪಾ – ರಾಜಾಂವ್, ಪ್ರತಿಮಾಂ, ಸಬ್ದಾ–ಚಿತ್ರಣ್... ಸರ್ವ್ ಆಟಾಪುನ್ ಆಸ್ತಾ. ಸಾರಾಂಶಾಂತ್ ಹೆಂ ಸರ್ವ್ ಲಾಭಾನಾ.

iv) ರುಪಾಂತರ್ (**Adaptation**): ಮೂಳ್‌ಕೃತಿ ಶೆವೊಟ್ ಭಾಶೆಕ್ ಪಾವೊನ್, ತ್ಯೆ ಭಾಶೆಚೊ ಪ್ರಾದೇಶಿಕ್ ವ ಸಾಮಾಜಿಕ್ ವೇಸ್ ಪಾಂಗುರ್ನ್ರೆಂ ರುಪಾಂತರ್ ಜಾತಾ. ಹ್ಯೆ ವೆಳಿಂ ವಿಷಯ್ ಆಶಯ್ ತಸೊಚ್ಚ್ ಉರ್ತಾ. ಹಾಂಗಾಸರ್ ಭಾಶಾಂತರ್‌ಕಾರ್ ಚಡ್ ಸ್ವಾತಂತ್ರ್ಯ ವಾಪರ್ತಾ. ತಾಚಿ ಪ್ರತಿಭಾ ಗಳ್ಸಿತಾ. ಇಂಗ್ಲಿಷ್ ನಾಟಕ್ ಇಂಗ್ಲೆಂಡಾಂತ್ ರಚ್‌ಲ್ಲೊ ತೊ, ಕೊಂಕ್ಣೆಕ್ ಹಾಡ್ತಾನಾ ನಾಂವಾಂ, ಗಾಂವ್ ಆನಿ ಸಂಭಾಷಣಾಚಿ ರೀತ್ ಬದಲ್ನ್ ರಚ್ಲೊ ತರ್ ರುಪಾಂತರ್ ಜಾತಾ. ಸುಭದ್ರಕುಮಾರಿ ಚೌಹಾಣಾನ್ ಹಿಂದಿ ಭಾಶೆಂತ್ ಲಿಖ್‌ಲ್ಲಿ ಕಾಣಿ **'वे तीन बच्चे'** ಫ್ರಾನ್ಸಿಸ್ ಡಿಕುನ್ಹಾನ್ ಕೊಂಕ್ಣೆಂತ್ 'ತಿಂ ತೆಗಾಂ ಭುರ್ಗಿಂ' ನಾಂವಾನ್ ರುಪಾಂತರ್ ಕೆಲ್ಯಾ. ಘಡಿತಾಂ ಆನಿ ಕಥಾವಸ್ತು ತಶಿಂಚ್ ಉರ್ಲ್ಯಾಂತ್. ಪಾತ್ರಾಂಚಿಂ ನಾಂವಾಂ ಬದಲ್ಲ್ಯಾಂತ್.

ಅಲಹಾಬಾದ್‌ಚಾ ಪರಿಸರಾಂತ್ ಘಡ್ಚಿ ಮೂಳ್‌ಕಾಣಿ, ಶೆವೊಟ್ ಭಾಶೆಂತ್ ಮಂಗ್ಳುರ್, ಬಿದ್ರಾ್ಯಂ ಘಡ್ಚೆಪರಿಂ ಕೆಲ್ಯಾ. ಅಲಹಾಬಾದ್‌ಚೆಂ ಜೈಲ್, ಇಜಯ್ಚೆಂ ಜೈಲ್ ಜಾಲಾಂ. ಭುರ್ಗ್ಯಾಂನಿ ಗಾಂವ್ಚಿಂ ಹಿಂದಿ ಗಿತಾಂ, ಕೊಂಕ್ಣಿ ಕಂತಾರಾಂ ಜಾಲ್ಯಾಂತ್. ವಾಚ್ಪ್ಯಾಕ್ ತಿ ಕಾಣಿ ಆಪ್ಲ್ಯಾ ಪರಿಸರಾಂತ್‌ಚ್ಚ್ ಘಡ್ಚೊ ಅನುಭವ್ ಜಾವ್ನ್ ಮೂಳ್‌ಕಾಣ್ಯೆಗಾರ್ನಿಚಿಂ ಭಗ್ಣಾಂ ಆನಿ ಆಶಯ್ ಅರ್ಥ್ ಕರುಂಕ್ ಸಲೀಸ್ ಜಾಲ್ಯಾಂತ್. ಸಕ್ಕಡೀ ಸಾಹಿತ್ಯ್ ಅಶೆಂ ಕರುಂಕ್ ಜಾಯ್ನಾ. ಕಾನಡಿ ಭಾಶೆಂತ್ ಶೇಕ್ಸ್‌ಪಿಯರಾಚಿ ನಾಟಕ್ ರುಪಾಂತರ್ ಕೆಲ್ಲೆಂ ಆಸಾತ್. ಕೊಂಕ್ಣೆಂತೀ ಹೆರ್ ಭಾಶೆಂಚ್ಯೊ ಸಬಾರ್ ಕಾದಂಬರಿಯೊ ರುಪಾಂತರಿತ್ ಜಾವ್ನ್ ಉತ್ರಾಯ್ಲ್ಯಾತ್.

ರುಪಾಂತರಿತ್ ಕೃತಿ ಮೂಳ್‌ಕೃತಿಯೆ ಥಾವ್ನ್ ಚಿಕ್ಕೆ ಪಯ್ಸ್ ಪಾವ್ತಾ. ತರೀ ರುಚಿಚ್ಯೆ ಆನಿ ಉಪ್ಯೋಗಾಚ್ಯೆ ನದ್ರೆನ್ ಮಹತ್ವ್ ಆಸಾ.

v) ಸೃಷ್ಟ್ಯಾಂತರ್ (**Trans creation**): ಮೂಳ್ ಭಾಶೆಚಿ ಕೃತಿ ತಾಚಿ ಸೃಷ್ಟಿ ರೀತ್ ಬದಲ್ನ್ ಶೆವೊಟ್ ಭಾಶೆಕ್ ವ್ಹೆಲ್ಯಾರ್ ಸೃಷ್ಟ್ಯಾಂತರ್ ಜಾತಾ. ಹಿಂದಿ ಭಾಶೆಂತ್ ಆಸ್ಚಿ ಜಾನಪದ್ ಕಥಾ अंधेरी राजा चौपट शासन

ಕಾನಡಿ ಭಾಶೆಂತ್ ವೆವೆಗ್ಳ್ಯಾ ಬರವ್ಪ್ಯಾಂನಿ ನಾಟಕ್ ಜಾವ್ನ್ ಬದ್ಲಿಲ್ಯಾ. ಸಂಭಾಷಣಾಂ ಬರಯ್ಲ್ಯಾಂತ್. ಕಾನಡಿ ಪರಿಸರಾಂತ್ ನೆಟಯ್ಲ್ಯಾಂ. ಪುಣ್ ಮೂಳ್ ಆಶಯ್–ವಿಷಯಾಕ್ ಬಾಧಕ್ ಯೇಂವ್ಕ್ ನಾ. ಗೊಯಾಂತ್ 'ಸಂಸ್ಕಾರ' (ಯು.ಆರ್. ಅನಂತಮೂರ್ತಿ) ಕಾದಂಬರಿ ಕೊಂಕ್ಣೆಂತ್ ನಾಟಕ್ ಜಾವ್ನ್ (ದತ್ತಾರಾಮ್ ಕಾಮತಾನ್) ಸೃಷ್ಟ್ಯಾಂತರ್ ಕೆಲಾ. ಅಶೆಂ ಕರ್ತಾನಾ ಭಾಶಾಂತರ್‌ಕಾರ್, ಮೂಳ್ ಪಾತ್ ನವ್ಯೆಚ್ಚ್ ಸೃಷ್ಟೆಂತ್ ಭರ್ತಾ. ತಾಚಿ ಪ್ರತಿಭಾ ಆನಿ ಕುಶಲತಾ ವಾಪರ್ನ್ ಹಿ ಸೃಷ್ಟಿ ಕರ್ತಾ.

ಥೊಡ್ಯಾ ಜಾಗ್ಯಾಂನಿ ಸೃಷ್ಟ್ಯಾಂತರ್ ವರ್ ರುಪಾಂತರ್ ವರ್ಗಾ ಸಂಗಿಂ ಮೆಳವ್ನ್ ಘೆತ್ಲಾ. ಥೊಡೆ ಪಾವ್ಟಿಂ ಭಾಶಾಂತರ್, (Trans creation) ಜಾಯ್ಜಾಯ್ ಮ್ಹಳ್ಳೊ ಉಲೊ ದಿಲ್ಲೊ ಆಸಾ. ಹೆಂ ಕಿತ್ಲೆಂ ಸಾರ್ಕೆಂ ಮ್ಹಳ್ಳೆಂ ತರ್ಕಾಕ್ ಸೊಡಿಜಾಯ್ ಪಡ್ತಾ. (Trans creation) ವರ್ವಿಂ ಭಾಶಾಂತರಿತ್ ಕೃತಿ ರುಪಾನ್ ಆನಿ ಸೃಷ್ಟೆನ್ ಮೂಳ್ ಕೃತಿಯೆ ಥಾವ್ನ್ ಪಯ್ಸ್ ವ್ಹೆತಾ. ವಾಚ್ಪ್ಯಾಚಿ ಅಭಿರೂಚ್ ಭಾಶಾಂತರ್‌ಕರ್ತ್ಯಾಚಾ ದೆಣ್ಯಾಕ್ ಸರ್ಪಡ್ತಾ.

ಭಾಶಾಂತರಾಚಿ ಸಮಸ್ಯೆ:

ಭಾಶಾಂತರ್ ಕರ್ತಾನಾ ಉದೆಂವ್ಚೆ ಸಮಸ್ಯೆ 3 ವರ್ಗಾಂನಿ ಸಮ್ಜುವ್ಯೆತ್.

1. ಭಾಶೆಕ್ ಲಗ್ತಿ ಜಾಲ್ಲೆ ಸಮಸ್ಯೆ
2. ವಿಷಯಾಕ್ ಲಗ್ತಿ ಜಾಲ್ಲೆ ಸಮಸ್ಯೆ
3. ಭಾಶಾಂತರ್‌ಕಾರಾಕ್ ಲಗ್ತಿ ಜಾಲ್ಲೆ ಸಮಸ್ಯೆ

ಭಾಶೆಕ್ ಲಗ್ತಿ ಜಾಲ್ಲೆ ಸಮಸ್ಯೆ:

ಬ್ರಹ್ಮ ಪರಿಂ ಭಾಶೆಕ್‌ಯೀ ಚ್ಯಾರ್ ಮುಖಿಮಳಾಂ: ಆವಾಜ್, ಉತಾರ್, ಅರ್ಥ್ ಆನಿ ಭಾವನಾಂ.

ಆವಾಜಾಂಚಾ ರಾಜಾಂವಿಕ್ ಮೆಳಾವಾನ್ ಉತಾರ್ ಜಾತಾ. ಉತ್ರಾ ಥಾವ್ನ್ ಲಾಬ್ಚಿ ಸಮ್ಜಣಿ ಅರ್ಥ್. ಅರ್ಥಾ ದ್ವಾರಿಂ ಉಬ್ಜೊಂಚೊ ಪ್ರಭಾವ್ – ಭಾವನ್ (ಭಗಾಪ್) ಅರ್ಥ್ ಆನಿ ಭಗಾಪ್ ಸಾಂಗಾತಾ ಮೆಳ್ತಾನಾ ಭಾಶೆಚಾ ಉಪ್ಯೋಗಾಚೊ ಉದ್ಧೇಶ್ ಜ್ಯಾರಿ ಜಾತಾ. ಭಾಶಾಂತರ್ ಕರ್ತಾನಾ ಮೂಳ್‌ಭಾಸ್ ಆನಿ ಶೆವೊಟ್ ಭಾಶೆಚಾ ಹ್ಯಾ ಚಾರೀ ಸಂಗ್ತಿಂಚಿ ಸಮ್ಜಣಿ ಜೊಡ್ಚಿ ಗರ್ಜ್ ಆಸಾ.

ಇಂಗ್ಲಿಷಾಂತ್ಲೆಂ Hai, OK, Ya ಸಬ್ದ್ ಕೊಂಕ್ಣೆಕ್ ತಶೆಚ್ಚ್ ಹಾಡುಂಕ್ ಜಾಯ್ನಾಂತ್. ಕೊಂಕ್ಣೆಂತ್ 'ವ್ಹೆತಾಯ್‌ಗಿ ನಾ' ಹೆಂ ಇಂಗ್ಲಿಷಾಂತ್ ಭಾಶಾಂತರ್ ಕರ್ತಾನಾ ಭೋವ್ ಚತ್ರಾಯ್ ಜಾಯ್. 'His B.P. is normal' ಹೆಂ ಕೊಂಕ್ಣೆಕ್ ಭಾಶಾಂತರ್ ಕರ್ತಾನಾ Normal ಸಬ್ದ್ ಕಸಲೊ ಅರ್ಥ್ ದಿತಾ ಮ್ಹಣ್ ಆನಿ ತಾಚ್ ಪರಿಣಾಮ್ ವಾಚ್ಪ್ಯಾಕ್ ಕಸೊ ಜಾತಾ ಮ್ಹಣ್ ತಜ್ವೀಜ್ ಕರಿಜಾಯ್ ಪಡ್ತಾ.

ಭಾಶೆಂತ್ಲ್ಯಾ ಸಬ್ದಾಂಕ್ ಸಾಂದರ್ಬಿಕ್ ಅರ್ಥ್, ಉತ್ರಾಚೊ ಅರ್ಥ್ ಆನಿ ಪ್ರಾದೇಶಿಕ್ ಅರ್ಥ್ ಆಸ್ತಾ. Bill ಮ್ಹಳ್ಯಾರ್ ವೀಜ್‌ಸಕ್ತೆಚೆಂ ಬಿಲ್ಲ್ ಜಾವ್ಯೆತಾ. ವ ಪಾರ್ಲಿಮೆಂಟಾಂತ್ ಮಂಜೂರ್ ಕರ್ಚೆಂ ಬಿಲ್ಲ್ ಜಾವ್ಯೆತಾ.

'Tyagi tabled the bill'
'Member jumped into the well of the House'

ಹಾಂಗಾಸರ್ ಸಾಂದರ್ಬಿಕ್ ಅರ್ಥ್ ಘೆಜಾಯ್ ಪಡ್ತಾ. 'ಮ್ಹೊಸಿಕ್ ಬಾಂಧ್ಚೆಂ' ಆನಿ 'ಘರ್ ಬಾಂದ್ಚೆಂ' ಏಕ್ ನ್ಹಯ್. ಫಲಾಣ್ಯಾ ಪ್ರದೇಶಾ ವರ್ವಿಂ ವ ಐತಿಹಾಸಿಕ್ ಕಾರಣಾಂ ವರ್ವಿಂ 'ಬೊಲಿಯೊ' ರೂಪಿತ್ ಜಾತಾನಾ ಸಬ್ದಾಂಚೊ ಅರ್ಥ್‌ಯೀ ಬದ್ಲಾತಾ. 'ಪಾಯ್ ಭಾಯ್ರ್ ಪಡ್ಲಾ' ಮ್ಹಳ್ಳೆಂ 'ಬಾಪುಯ್ ದೆವಾದಿನ್ ಜಾಲಾ' ಮ್ಹಳ್ಳೊ ಅರ್ಥ್ ದಿತಾ.

'ಸಾಕರ್ ಸರ್ಲ್ಯಾ' ಮ್ಹಳ್ಳೆಂ ಕ್ರಿಸ್ತಾಂವ್ ಕೊಂಕ್ಣೆಂತ್ 'ಸಾಕರ್ ಮೆಲ್ಯಾ' ಮ್ಹಣೊಂಕ್ ಜಾಯ್ನಾ. ಕನ್ನಡಾಂತ್ 'ಕೂಗುತ್ತಾನೆ' ಮ್ಹಳ್ಯಾರ್ 'ಆಪಯ್ತಾ' ಮ್ಹಳ್ಳೊಯ್ ಅರ್ಥ್ ಜಾತಾ. ಮೂಳ್ ಸಾಹಿತ್ಯ ಖಂಚಾ ಪರಿಸರಾಂತ್ ಉದೆಲಾಂ, ತಾಂತುಂ ಆಸ್ಚಿ ಪಾತ್ರ್ ಕಸಲಿ 'ಬೊಲಿ' ವಾಪರ್ತಾತ್, ತ್ಯಾ ಉತ್ರಾಂಚೊ ಅರ್ಥ್, ತ್ಯಾ ಪರಿಸರಾಚಾ ವ ಸಂಭಾಷಣಾಚಾ ಸಂದರ್ಭಾರ್ ಕಸಲೊ ಮ್ಹಳ್ಳೆಂ ಭಾಶಾಂತರ್‌ಕರ್ತಾನ್ ಗುಮಾನ್ ಕರಿಜಾಯ್.

ಹ್ಯಾ ಖಾತಿರ್:

i) ಮೂಳ್ ಸಾಹಿತ್ಯಾಚೊ ಪರ್ಕಾರ್ (ಕಾಣಿ, ಕಾದಂಬರಿ ವ ಕವಿತಾ) ಘಡ್ಚ್ಯಾ ಪ್ರದೇಶಾಕ್ ಭೆಟ್ ದೀವ್ನ್, ಥಂಯ್ಚಿ ಸಂಸ್ಕೃತಿ, ಉತ್ರಾಂಚೊ ಖರೊ ಅರ್ಥ್, ಸಾರ್ಕೊ ಸಮ್ಜೊನ್ ಘೆಂವ್ಚಿ ಗರ್ಜ್ ಆಸಾ. ವ ತರ್ಜಣ್‌ದಾರಾಕ್ ತ್ಯಾ ಪ್ರದೇಶಾಚಿ ಸಾರ್ಕಿ ವಳಕ್ ಆಸಾಜಯ್ ಪಡ್ತಾ.

ii) ಮೂಳ್ ಭಾಸ್ ಆನಿ ಶೆವೊಟ್ ಭಾಶೆಚೆಂ ವ್ಯಾಕರಣ್, ಸಾಂಗ್ಣ್ಯಾಂಚೊ ಅರ್ಥ್, ಪ್ರಚಲಿತ್ ಗಾದಿಯೊ, ಬೊಲಿಯೊ ಭಾಶಾಂತರ್‌ಕರ್ತ್ಯಾಕ್ ಸಾರ್ಕೆಂ ಕಳಿತ್ ಆಸಾಜಯ್.

2. ವಿಷಯಾಕ್ ಲಗ್ತಿ ಜಾಲ್ಲೆ ಸಮಸ್ಯೆ:

ಬರಾಪ್, ವಿಷಯಾಕ್ ಲಗ್ತಿ ಜಾವ್ನ್ ರುಂದಾಯೆನ್ ದೋನ್ ಥರ್ ಕರ್ಯೆತ್. 1. ವಿಜ್ಞಾನ್ ಆನಿ ಶಾಸ್ತ್ರ್ 2. ಸಾಹಿತ್ಯ (ಸೃಜನಾತ್ಮಕ್) ವಿಜ್ಞಾನ್ ವ ಶಾಸ್ತ್ರ್, ಅರ್ಥ್‌ಪ್ರಧಾನ್ ಜಾವ್ನಾಸ್ತಾ. ಗಿನ್ಯಾನಾಕ್ ಚಡ್ ಲಗ್ತಿ ಜಾವ್ನಾಸ್ತಾ. ಪುಣ್ ಸಾಹಿತ್ಯ, ಭೆಗ್ಣಾಂನಿ ಆಟಾಪ್ತಾ. ರಸಾತ್ಮಕ್ ಜಾವ್ನ್ ಕಾಳ್ಜಾಕ್ ಲಾಗ್ತಿಲೆಂ ಜಾವ್ನ್, ಮತಿಕ್ ಸುಶೆಗ್ ದಿಂವ್ಚೆಂ ತಸಲೆಂ.

ವಿಜ್ಞಾನ್ ವ ಶಾಸ್ತ್ರಾಚಾ ಬರ್ಪಾಂತ್ ವರ್ಣನ್, ಅಲಂಕಾರ್ ವ ಭಗಾಪ್ ನಾ. ಆಸಾ ತಶೆಂ ಬರಂವ್ಚೆಂ. ವಸ್ತು ನಿಷ್ಟತಾ ಚಡ್. ಅಸಲೆಂ ಬರಾಪ್ ಭಾಶಾಂತರ್ ಕರ್ತಾನಾ ಬೋವ್ ಚತ್ರಾಯೆನ್ ಮೂಳ್ ಭಾಶೆಂತ್ ಜೊ ಅರ್ಥ್ ಆಸಾ, ತೊಚ್ಚ್ ಶೆವೊಟ್ ಭಾಶೆಕ್

ಅಚೂಕ್‌ಪಣಾನ್ ಯೇಜಾಯ್. ವಾಕ್ಯಾನ್ ವಾಕ್ಯ ಸಾರ್ಕೆಂ ಸಮ್ಜೊನ್ ಹೊ ವಾವ್ರ್ ಜಾಯ್ಜಾಯ್. ಶಾಸ್ತ್ರಾಚಾ ಫಲಾಣ್ಯಾ ವಿಭಾಗಾಂತ್ ಹೆಳ್‌ಲ್ಲ್ಯೆ ವ್ಯಕ್ತಿನ್ ಭಾಶಾಂತರ್ ಕೆಲ್ಯಾರ್ ಮಾತ್ರ್ ಸಾರ್ಕೆಂ ಜಾಯ್ತ್. ಜಾಯ್ತೆ ಪಾವ್ಟಿಂ ಮೂಳ್‌ಭಾಶೆಚಾ ಸಬ್ದಾಕ್ ಸಾರ್ಕೊ ಅರ್ಥ್‌ ದಿಂವ್ಚೊ ನವೊ ಸಬ್ದ್ ರಚಿಜಾಯ್ ಪಡ್ತಾ. ವ ಮೂಳ್‌ಭಾಶೆಂತ್ಲೆ ಸಬ್ದ್ ಶೆವೊಟ್ ಭಾಶೆಕ್ "ಸ್ವೀಕರಣ್' ಕರಿಜಾಯ್ ಪಡ್ತಾ.

ಸಾಹಿತ್ಯ ಚಾಕೊಂಕ್ (ರಸಾಗ್ರಹಣ್) ನೆಣಾ ಆಸ್ಚಾನ್ ಸಾಹಿತ್ಯಾಚೆಂ ಭಾಶಾಂತರ್ ಕರುಂಕ್ ಜಾಯ್ನಾ. ಆಪ್ಣೆ ಸಾಹಿತ್ಯ ವಾಚುನ್, ತಾಚಾ ಸರ್ವ್ ಅಂಶಾಚಿ ರೂಚ್ ಭಗುನ್, (ಬಾಪ್ ಪ್ರಶಾಂತ್ ಮಾಡ್ತಾನ್ ಸಾಂಗ್‌ಲ್ಲ್ಯೆ ಪರಿಂ: ಚೋದನಾಕ್ ಒಳಗ್ ಜಾವ್ನ್) ಹಿಚ್ಚ್ ರೂಚ್ ಶೆವೊಟ್ ಭಾಶೆಕ್ ಉತ್ರಾಂವ್ಚೆಂ ದೆಣೆ ಆಸ್‌ಲ್ಲೊ ಖರೊ ಭಾಶಾಂತರ್‌ಕರ್ತ್ ಜಾತಾ.

3. ಭಾಶಾಂತರ್‌ಕರ್ತಾಚಿ ಸಮಸ್ಯೆ:

ಭಾಶಾಂತರ್‌ಕರ್ತಾಕ್ ಪ್ರಮುಖ್ ಜಾವ್ನ್ ತೀನ್ ಸಕ್ತ್ಯೊ ಆಸೊಂಕ್ ಜಾಯ್. 1. ಸಬ್ದಾಂ ದಾಯ್ಜ್ 2. ವಿಷಯಾಚಿ ಪರಿಣತಾ 3. ಬರ್ಪಾ ಶೈಲಿ

ಬರ್ಯಾ ವಾಚ್ಪ್ಯಾ ವರ್ವಿಂ ಬರೊ ಬರವ್ಪಿ ಜಾಂವ್ಕ್ ಜಾತಾ. ಭಾಶಾಂತರ್‌ಕರ್ತಾನ್ ವಾಚುನ್, ಉಲವ್ನ್ ಚಡ್ ಆನಿ ಚಡ್ ಸಬ್ದ್ ಜಮೊ ಕರಿಜಾಯ್. ಜೊಕ್ತೊ ಸಬ್ದ್ ವಿಂಚುನ್, ಭಾಶಾಂತರ್ ಕರ್ಚಿ ಕುಶಲತಾ (Skill) ಹ್ಯಾ ವರ್ವಿಂ ರುತಾ ಜಾತಾ. ಜಾಯ್ತೆ ಪಾವ್ಟಿಂ ನವೆ ಸಬ್ದ್ ರಚಿಜಾಯ್ ಪಡ್ತಾತ್ ವ ಮೂಳ್ ಭಾಶೆಚೆ ಸಬ್ದ್ ಶೆವೊಟ್ ಭಾಶೆಂತ್ ರುಪಾಂತರ್ ಕರ್ನ್ ಘೆಜಾಯ್ ಪಡ್ತಾತ್. ಮರಾಠಿ, ಕನ್ನಡ, ಸಂಸ್ಕೃತ್, ಹಿಂದಿ ಭಾಸಾಂ ಥಾವ್ನ್ ರಚ್‌ಲ್ಲೆ ಸಬ್ದ್ ಸಲೀಸಾಯೆನ್ ಕೊಂಕ್ಣೆಕ್ ಮಿಸ್ಳಾತಾತ್. ಭಾಶಾಂತರ್‌ಕರ್ತಾಕ್ ಹ್ಯಾ ಭಾಸಾಂಚಾ ಸಬ್ದಾಂಚಿ ವಳಕ್ ಗರ್ಜ್ ಪಡ್ತಾ.

ಎದೊಳ್ಚ್ಚ್ ವಿವರಿಲ್ಲ್ಯಾ ಪರಿಂ ಶಾಸ್ತಿರಾಕ್ ಲಗ್ತಿ ಜಾಲ್ಲೆಂ ಬರಾಪ್, ಸಂಬಂಧಿತ್ ಶಾಸ್ತಿನ್ (ಪರಿಣತಾನ್) ಭಾಶಾಂತರ್ ಕರಿಜಯ್ ಪಡ್ತಾ. ಹೆರಾಂನಿ ಕರ್ಚೆಂ ತರ್ ತಾಣೆ ವಿಷೆಯ್ ಶಿಕಾಜಾಯ್. ಸಾಹಿತ್ಯಾಚಿ ವೋಡ್ ನಾತ್‌ಲ್ಲ್ಯೆ ವ್ಯಕ್ತಿನ್ ಸಾಹಿತ್ಯ ಭಾಶಾಂತರ್ ಕರುಂಕ್ ಜಾಯ್ನಾ.

ಭಾಶಾಂತರ್‌ಕರ್ತಾಚಿ ಶೈಲಿ ಸುಢಾಳ್ ಆನಿ ಸುಲಭ್ ಆಸಾಜಯ್. ಥೊಡಿಂ ವಾಕ್ಯಾಂ ಇತ್ಲಿಂ ಲಾಂಬ್ ಆಸ್ತಾತ್ ವ ಘುಸ್ಪಡಾಂವ್ಚಿಂ ಆಸ್ತಾತ್ ಕೀ, ತಿ ಶೆವೊಟ್ ಭಾಶೆಕ್ ತರ್ಜಣ್ ಕರ್ಚೆಂ ಭಾಶಾಂತರ್‌ಕರ್ತಾಕ್ ಏಕ್ ವ್ಹಡ್ ಸಾಹಸ್‌ಚ್ಚ್ ಜಾತಾ. ಹ್ಯಾ ವೆಳಿಂ ತಾಚೆಂ ದೆಣೆ ಪರೀಕ್ಷೆಕ್ ವಳಗ್ ಜಾತಾ. ಶೆವೊಟ್ ಭಾಶೆಂತ್ಲ್ಯಾ ವಾಚ್ಪ್ಯಾಕ್ ಸಾರ್ಕೆಂ ಸಮ್ಜೊಂಚಿಂ ವಾಕ್ಯಾಂ ರಚಿಜಾಯ್. ತಾಣೆಂ 'ಮೂಳ್ ಭಾಶೆಂತ್ ಕಶೆಂ ಆಸಾ ಪಳೆವ್ಯಾಂ' ಮ್ಹಣ್ ದುಬಾವ್ ಉಚಾರ್ಚೆಪರಿಂ ಜಾಂವ್ಕ್ ನಜೊ. ಸಾಹಿತ್ಯಾಂಕ್ ಮೂಳ್ ಬರ್ಪ್ಯಾಚಿಚ್ಚ್ ಶೈಲಿ ಅನುಕರಣ್ ಕರ್ಚೆಂ ಪ್ರೆತನ್ ಬರೆಂ ಲಾಗ್ತಾ. ಪುಣ್ ಶಾಸ್ತ್ರೀಯ್ ಭಾಶಾಂತರಾಂತ್ ಭಾಶಾಂತರ್‌ಕರ್ತಾಚಿ ಶೈಲಿ 'ವಾಚುನ್ ವ್ಹರ್ಚಾಕ್' ಪ್ರಚೋದಕ್ ಜಾವ್ನಾಸ್ತಾ.

ಧಾರ್ಮಿಕ್ ಬರ್ಪಾಂಚೆಂ ತರ್ಜಣ್

ಬರ್ಶ್ಪುರ್ ಧಾರ್ಮಿಕ್ ಜಾಗ್ವಣೆಚೊ ದೇಶ್ ಆಮ್ಚೊ. ಹ್ಯಾ ಧರ್ಮಾಂ ವರ್ವಿಂ ಸಾಹಿತಿಕ್ ಶ್ಥೆತ್ ಇಟಾಳ್ ಜಾಲಾಂ. ಪುರಾಣಾಂಚಾ ಆಧಾರಾಚೆರ್ ಭಾರತಾಚಾ ಸರ್ವ್ ಭಾಶೆಂನಿ, ವೆವೆಗ್ಳ್ಯಾ ಪರ್ಕಾರಾಂನಿ ಘಡ್ಲಲೆಂ ಸಾಹಿತ್ಯ ಸಂಸಾರಾಚಾ ಹೆರ್ ದೇಶಾಂನಿ ಆಸ್ಚೆಂನಾ. ಆಧ್ಯಾತ್ಮಿಕ್ ಭಗ್ಣಾಂ ಜಾಗಂವ್ಚೆಂ, ಥರಾವಳ್, ಉಂಚ್ಲೆಂ ಸಾಹಿತ್ಯ ಸರ್ವ್ ಭಾಶೆಂನಿ ನಿರ್ಮಿತ್ ಜಾಲಾಂ. ಭಜನಾಂ, ಗಿತಾಂ, ಮಾಗ್ಣಿಂ, ಕಾವ್ಯಾಂ, ಸಾಂತಾ ಭಕ್ತಾಂಚ್ಯೊ ಜಿಣ್ಯೆ ಕಥಾ, ಧಾರ್ಮಿಕ್ ಚಾಲಿಚಿಂ ಬರ್ಪಾಂ, ಧಾರ್ಮಿಕ್ ಗ್ರಂಥ್ ಜಾಯ್ತೆ ಉಜ್ವಾಡ್ಲ್ಯಾತ್. ಹಾಂತುಂ ಚಡಾವತ್ ಹೆರ್ ಭಾಶೆಂ ಥಾವ್ನ್ (ಸಂಸ್ಕೃತ್, ಇಂಗ್ಲಿಷ್, ಹಿಬ್ರು, ಲಾತೆಂ) ತರ್ಜಣ್ ಕೆಲ್ಲೆಚ್ಚ್ ಜಾವ್ನಾಸಾತ್.

ಕೊಂಕ್ಣಿ ಜಣಾಂನಿ ಆಪ್ಲ್ಯೆ ಮಾಯ್‌ಭಾಶೆಂತ್ ದೇವಾಕ್ ಒಳ್ಖುಂಕ್ ಆನಿ ಆರಾಧುಂಕ್ ಗ್ರಂಥ್ ಆನಿ ಪದಾಂ ಕೊಂಕ್ಣೆಕ್ ತರ್ಜಣ್ ಕೆಲಿಂ. ಕ್ರಿಸ್ತಾಂವ್ ಯಾಜಕಾಂನಿ ಮಿಸಾಂವಾಚಾ ಉದ್ಧೇಶಾಕ್ ಸರಿ ಜಾವ್ನ್ ಲಾತ್ಯಾಂತ್ ಆನಿ ಇಂಗ್ಲಿಷಾಂತ್ ಆಸ್‌ಲ್ಲೆಂ ಭಕ್ತಿಕ್ ಸಾಹಿತ್ಯ್ ಅಣ್ಕಾರ್ ಕರುನ್ ಕೊಂಕ್ಣೆಕ್ ಗ್ರೇಸ್ತ್ ಕೆಲಾಂ. ಸಂಸ್ಕೃತ್ ಥಾವ್ನ್ ಭಜನಾಂ, ಭಗವದ್ಗೀತಾ ಭಾಶಾಂತರ್ ಕರ್‌ನ್ ಕೊಂಕ್ಣಿ ಲೊಕಾನ್ ಧಾರ್ಮಿಕ್ ಗಿನ್ಯಾನ್ ಜೊಡುಂಕ್ ಅವ್ಕಾಸ್ ದಿಲಾ.

ಇಂಗ್ಲಿಷ್, ಕನ್ನಡ ಆನಿ ಮರಾಠಿ ಭಾಸಾಂಚಾ ಪ್ರಭಾವಾಂ ಮಧೆಂ ಕೊಂಕ್ಣೆಕ್ ಜೀವ್ ಧರುಂಕ್ ಆನಿ ಲ್ಹಾನ್ ಭುರ್ಗ್ಯಾಂ ಥಾವ್ನ್‌ಚ್ಚ್ ಕೊಂಕ್ಣಿ ವಾಚುಂಕ್, ಬರಂವ್ಕ್ ಶಿಕೊಂಕ್ ಕಾರಣ್ ಜಾಲ್ಲೆಂ ಧಾರ್ಮಿಕ್ ಸಾಹಿತ್ಯ್. ಹೆಂ ಅಣ್ಕಾರಾ ದ್ವಾರಿಂ ಕೊಂಕ್ಣೆನ್ ಜೋಡ್ನ್ ಘೆತ್ಲೆಲೆಂ, (ಕನ್ನಡ ವ ಇಂಗ್ಲಿಷ್ ಮಾಧ್ಯಮಾಂತ್ ಶಿಕ್ಚಿಂ ಭುರ್ಗಿಂ ಕ್ರಿಸ್ತಾಂವ್ ಶಿಕಾಪ್ ಕೊಂಕ್ಣೆಂತ್ ಶಿಕ್ತಾತ್ ಆನಿ ಕೊಂಕ್ಣೆಂತ್ ಬರಯ್ತಾತ್ ಕೊಂಕ್ಣೆಂತ್‌ಚ್ಚ್ ಮಾಗ್ತಾತ್.)

ಧಾರ್ಮಿಕ್ ಸಾಹಿತ್ಯಾಚಾ ಅಣ್ಕಾರಾ ದ್ವಾರಿಂ ಜಾಯ್ತೆ ಪೊರ್ತುಗೇಜ್ ಸಬ್ದ್ ರುಪಾಂ ಬದ್ಲುನ್ ಕೊಂಕ್ಣೆಕ್ ಸ್ವೀಕಾರ್ ಜಾಲ್ಯಾತ್.

ದಾಖ್ಲ್ಯಾಕ್: ತೇಂಪ್ಲ್, ಸ್ಪಿರಿತ್, ಸಾಕ್ರಾಮೆಂತ್, ಮಿಸಾಂವ್, ಆಲ್ತಾರ್, ಲಿತುರ್ಜಿ, ತಾಲೆಂತ್, ಆಪೊಸ್ತಲ್, ಮಾಡ್ತಿರ್, ಓಡ್ದ್, ಬಾಪ್ತಿಜ್ಮ್, ಸಾಕ್ರಿಫಿಸ್.

1918 ಇಸ್ವೆಂತ್ ಮುಲ್ಕಿ ನಾರಾಯಣ ಕಾಮತಾನ್ 'ಗೀತಾಮೃತ ಸಾಕಿ' ಮ್ಹಣ್ 'ಶ್ರೀಮದ್ ಭಗವದ್ಗೀತಾ' ಹಾಚೆಂ ಕೊಂಕ್ಣಿ ಭಾಶಾಂತರ್ ಕೆಲ್ಲೆಂ.

ಕಾರ್ಕಳ್ಚೊ ಪಂಡಿತ್ ಪಿ. ವಾಮನ ಪ್ರಭುನ್ 'ರಘುವಂಶ ಮಹಾಕಾವ್ಯ' ಚೆಂ ಅಣ್ಕಾರ್ ಕೆಲಾಂ.

ಬಿ.ವಿ. ಬಾಳಿಗಾ, ಪಿ. ಜಿ. ಕಾಮತ್ ಆನಿ ಮಟ್ಟಾರ್ ವಿಠಳ ಕಿಣಿ ಹಾಣಿಂ ಸಂಸ್ಕೃತ ಥಾವ್ನ್ 'ಭಗವದ್ಗೀತಾ' ಕೊಂಕ್ಣೆಕ್ ತರ್ಜಣ್ ಕೆಲ್ಯಾತ್.

ಕೆ. ಅನಂತ ಭಟ್ಟನ್ ಹಿಂದಿ ಭಾಶೆ ಥಾವ್ನ್ ಕವಿ ಕಾಳಿದಾಸ ಆನಿ ಕವಿ ಸೂರ್‌ದಾಸಾಚಿಂ ಕವಿತಾ (ದೋಹೆ) ಕೊಂಕ್ಣೆಕ್ ಅನುವಾದ್ ಕೆಲ್ಯಾತ್.

ಶರತ್‌ಚಂದ್ರ ಶೆಣ್ಯೆನ್ ಇಂಗ್ಲಿಷ್ ಮುಳಾ ಥಾವ್ನ್ 'ಶ್ರೀ ಕೃಷ್ಣ ಚರಿತಾಮೃತ' ಕೊಂಕ್ಣೆಕ್ ಅಣ್ಕಾರ್ ಕೆಲಾಂ.

ಕೆ. ಎನ್. ರಾವ್ ದಾಂಡೇಲಿ, ಹಾಣೆ ಮರಾಠಿ ಮುಳಾ ಥಾವ್ನ್ 'ತುಕರಾಮಾಲೆ 1000 ಭಜನೆ' ಆನಿ 'ಪುರಂದರದಾಸಾಚೆ ಭಜನೆ' ಕೊಂಕ್ಣೆಂತ್ ಭಾಶಾಂತರ್ ಕೆಲ್ಯಾತ್.

ದೇವ್‌ಸ್ತುತಿ ಕೊಂಕ್ಣೆಕ್:

ಕ್ರಿಸ್ತಾಂವಾಂಚೆ ದುಸ್ರೆ ವಾತಿಕನ್ ಮಹಾಸಭೆನ್ (1964) ಸ್ಥಳೀಯ್ ಭಾಶೆನ್ ದೇವ್‌ಸ್ತುತಿ ಕರುಂಕ್ ಉಲೊ ದಿಲ್ಯಾ ಉಪ್ರಾಂತ್, ಗೊಯಾಂ, ಕೆನರಾ ಆನಿ ಮಂಗ್ಳುರಿ ಪ್ರದೇಶಾಂತ್ ಭರಾನ್ ಬದ್ಲಾವಣ್ಯೊ ಜಾಲ್ಯೊ. ತೆದೊಳ್ ಪರ್ಯಾಂತ್ ಲಾತಿನ್ ಭಾಶೆಂತ್ ಆಸ್‌ಲ್ಲಿ ದೇವ್‌ಸ್ತುತಿ, ಮಾಗ್ಣಿಂ, ಗಿತಾಂ, ಧಾರ್ಮಿಕ್ ಶಿಕಾಪ್ ಕೊಂಕ್ಣೆಂತ್ ಅಣ್ಕಾರ್ ಕರುಂಕ್ ಸುರು ಕೆಲೆಂ. ಸಾಹಿತ್ಯ್ ರಚ್ಪಾಚೊ ವಾವ್ರ್ ಭರ್ಪೂರ್ ಜಾಲೊ. ಪತ್ರಾಂ ಆನಿ ಬೂಕ್ ಪರ್ಗಟ್ಲೆ.

"1964 ಇಸ್ವೆಂತ್, ಕೊಂಕ್ಣಿ ಉಲಂವ್ಚೊ ಲೋಕ್ ಆಸ್ಚಾ ಬೆಳ್ಗಾಂವ್, ಪೂನಾ, ಮುಂಬಯ್, ಚಿಕ್‌ಮಗ್ಳುರ್, ಗೊಂಯ್ ಆನಿ ಮಂಗ್ಳುರ್ ದಿಯೆಸೆಜಿಂಚಾ ಬಿಸ್ಪಾಂನಿ ಸಾಂಗಾತಾ ಮೆಳೊನ್ 'ಕೊಂಕ್ಣಿ ಭಾಸೆಚಿ ಪ್ರಾಂತೀಯ್ ಸೆವಾ ಧಾರ್ಮಿಕ್ ಸಮಿತಿ' ರಚ್ಲಿ.

"ಬೆಳ್ಗಾಂವ್ಚೊ ಬಿಸ್ಪ್ ಪೊರ್ತುನಾ ತೊ ದಾ ವಿಯೆಗಾ ಕುತಿನ್ಹಾ (1964-1967) ಹ್ಯೆ ಸಮಿತಿಚೊ ಅಧ್ಯಕ್ಷ್ ಜಾವ್ನಾಸ್‌ಲ್ಲೊ. ಲಾತಿನ್ ಆನಿ ಕೊಂಕ್ಣಿ ಭಾಸ್ ಸಾರ್ಕಿ ಜಾಣಾ ಆಸೊನ್ ಬರ್ಪಾಚೆಂ ದೆಣೆ ಆಸ್ಚಾ ಯಾಜಕಾಂಕ್ ಹ್ಯೆ ಸಮಿತಿಚೆ ಸಾಂದೆ ಜಾವ್ನ್ ನೆಮ್ಲೆ. ಮಾನಾದಿಕ್ ಬಾಪ್ ರೆನಾಟೊ ರೇಗೊ, ಕ್ರೆಸೆನ್ಸಿಯಾ ಮೊಂತೇರೊ, ಅಸುಸ್ಸಾಂವ್ ದೆಸಿಲ್ವಾ, ಕಾಜಿತಾನ್ ಕ್ರೂಜ್ ಫೆರ್ನಾಂಡಿಸ್, ಅಲೆಗ್ಸಾಂಡರ್ ಎಫ್. ಸೊಜ್, ಫಿಲಿಪ್ ನಜ್ರೆತ್, ಮಾರ್ಸೆಲಿನೊ ರೆಮೆದೆಯೊಸ್, ಮಾಸಿಲ್ಲಿಯೆನ್ ಫೆರ್ನಾಂಡಿಸ್ ಜೆ. ಸ., ವಾಸ್ಕೊ ದ ರೇಗೊ– ಹೆ ಸಾಂದೆ ಜಾವ್ನಾಸ್‌ಲ್ಲೆ.

1967 ವರ್ಸಾ ಉಪ್ರಾಂತ್ ಮಂಗ್ಳುರ್ಚ್ಯೊ ಬಿಸ್ಪ್ ಅ. ಮಾ. ದೊ. ಬಾಜಿಲ್ ಸಾಲ್ವದೊರ್ ಸೊಜಾನ್ ಸಮಿತಿಚೆಂ ಮುಖೇಲ್‌ಪಣ್ ಘೆವ್ನ್ ಉಮೆದಿನ್ ಭಾಶಾಂತರಾಚೊ ವಾವ್ರ್ ಮುಖಾರ್ಸಿಲೊ.

ಸಮಿತೆನ್ ಭಾಶಾಂತರ್ ಕರ್‌ನ್ ಪ್ರಗಟ್ ಕೆಲ್ಲೆ ಬೂಕ್:

1968 – ಯಾಜಕೀ ಸಂಸ್ಕರಣೆಚಿ ರೀತ್

1971 – ಲಗ್ನಾಚಿ ರೀತ್, ಭುರ್ಗ್ಯಾಂಕ್ ಪವಿತ್ರ್ ಸ್ನಾನ್ ದಿಂವ್ಚಿ ರೀತ್, ಮರ್ಣಾಚಿ ರೀತ್

1973 – ರೋಮಿ ವಾಚ್ಪಾ ಗ್ರಂಥ್

1974 – ಥಿರಾವ್ಣೆಚಿ ರೀತ್, ಪಿಡೆಸ್ತಾಂಚಾ ಮಾಖ್ಣೆಚಿ ರೀತ್

1975 – ಪ್ರಾಚಿತ್ ಸಂಸ್ಕಾರಾಚಿ ರೀತ್

1981 – ತೆಲಾಂ ಪವಿತ್ರ್ ಕರ್ಚಿ ರೀತ್, ರೋಮಿ ಮಿಸಾಗ್ರಂಥ್

1992 ಆನಿ 2004 – ಆಶೀರ್ವಾದ್

ದೇವ್‌ಸ್ತುತಿ, ಕೊಂಕ್ಣೆಕ್ ಭಾಶಾಂತರ್ ಕರ್ತಾನಾ, ಮೂಳ್ ಚಿಂತ್ಪಾಕ್ ಸಾರ್ಕ್ಯಾ ರಿತಿನ್ ತಾಳ್ ಪಡಾಜಯ್, ಹೊ ವಾವ್ರ್ ತಿತ್ಲೊ ಸಲೀಸ್ ನ್ಹಯ್. ಇಂಗ್ಲಿಷ್, ಹೆಬ್ರೆವ್, ಗ್ರೀಕ್, ಲಾತಿನ್ ಅಸಲ್ಯೊ ವಿದೇಶಿ ಭಾಸೊ ಶಿಕೊನ್ ತರ್ಜುಮ್ಯಾಕ್ ಹಾತ್ ಘಾಲಿಜಾಯ್ ಪಡ್ತಾ. ಭಾಶಾಂತರ್‌ಕರ್ತಾನ್ ಕೊಂಕ್ಣಿ ಭಾಶೆಚೆಂ ಗುಂಡಾಯೆಚೆಂ ಮಾತ್ರ್ ನ್ಹಯ್ ವಿಸ್ತಾರಾಯೆಚೆಂ ಅಧ್ಯಯನ್ ಕರಿಜಾಯ್. ನವೆ ಸಬ್ದ್ ಘಡುಂಕ್ ಗ್ಯಾನ್ ಜೊಡಿಜಾಯ್. ಬಾರಿಚ್ ಗಂಭೀರಾಯೆಚೊ ವಾವ್ರ್ ಹೊ. ಹ್ಯಾ ವೆಳಿಂ ಎದೊಳ್ ದಿಲ್ಲ್ಯಾ ದಾಖ್ಲ್ಯಾಂ ಪರ್ಮಾಣೆ ಥೊಡೆ ಸಬ್ದ್ ಕೊಂಕ್ಣೀಕರಣ್ ಕರ್‌ನ್ 'ಸ್ವೀಕಾರ್' ಕೆಲಾಂ ತರ್ ಹೆರ್ ಸಂಸ್ಕೃತ್ ವ ದ್ರಾವಿಡ್ ಕುಟ್ಮಾಂ–ಭಾಶೆಂ ಥಾವ್ನ್‌ಯೀ ರಚ್ಲ್ಯಾತ್.

ದಾಖ್ಲ್ಯಾಕ್: ಬಲಿದಾನ್, ದೇವ್‌ಸ್ತುತಿ, ಕ್ರಿಸ್ತ ಜಯಂತಿ, ಥಿರಾವ್ಣಿ, ಯಾಜಕೀ ದೀಕ್ಷಾ, ಮಂದಿರ್, ಕ್ರಿಸ್ತ್‌ಪ್ರಸಾದ್, ಪ್ರಾರ್ಥಯಾಂ, ವೆದಿ...

(ಉಲ್ಲೇಖ್: 'ರಾಕ್ಣೊ' ಅಕ್ತೋಬರ್ 30, 2003. ಲೇಖನ್: ಕೊಂಕ್ಣಿ ಭಾಶೆಚ್ಯೆ ವಾಡಾವಳೆಕ್ ಬುನ್ಯಾದ್ ಜಾಲ್ಲಿ ಕೊಂಕ್ಣೆಂತ್ಲಿ ದೇವ್‌ಸ್ತುತಿ. ಲೇಖಕ್: ಮಾ. ರೊನಾಲ್ಡ್ ಸೆರಾವೊ)

ದೇವ್‌ಸ್ತುತಿ ಕೊಂಕ್ಣೆಂತ್ ತರ್ಜಣ್ ಜಾಲ್ಲ್ಯಾ ವರ್ವಿಂ ಕೊಂಕ್ಣಿ ವಾಚಪ್ ಆನಿ ಬರಾಪ್ ಕ್ರಿಸ್ತಾಂವ್ ಲೊಕಾಕ್ ಅನಿವಾರ್ಯ್ ಜಾಲೆಂ. ಕೊಂಕ್ಣಿ ಸಬ್ದಾಂಚೆಂ ಘಡಾಪ್, ವ್ಯಾಕರಣಾಚೆಂ ಅಭ್ಯಾಸ್, ಭಾಶಾಂತರಾಚಿ ಕುಶಲತಾ – ಹ್ಯಾ ಸಂಗ್ತಿಂನಿ ಆಟವ್ ಗರ್ಜೆಚೊ ಜಾಲೊ. ಲೊಕಾಕ್ ಮಾಯ್‌ಭಾಶೆಚಿ ವೊಡ್ಣಿ ಆನಿ ಮೋಗ್ ಉಬ್ಜೊಂಕ್ ಬಳಾದಿಕ್ ಕಾರಣ್ ಜಾಲೆಂ.

ಮೊನ್ಸಿ. ಸಿಲಾ ಮಿನೆಜಾಚೆಂ ಸಾಧನ್:

ಎಕೆ ಕುಶಿನ್ ದೇವ್‌ಸ್ತುತಿ ತರ್ಜಣ್ ಜಾವ್ನಾಸ್ತಾಂ, ಸಾಂಗಾತಾಚ್ ಕೊಂಕ್ಣಿ ವಿದ್ವಾಂಸ್ ಮೊನ್ಸಿ, ಸಿಲ್ವೆಸ್ಟರ್ ಫ್ರಾನ್ಸಿಸ್ ಮಿನೇಜಾನ್ ಧಾರ್ಮಿಕ್ ಜಿಣ್ಯೆಕ್ ಲಗ್ತಿ ಜಾಲ್ಲೆ ವಿಷಯ್ ತರ್ಜಣ್ ಕರ್ಚೆಂ ಕಾಮ್ ಹಾತಿಂ ಧರ್ಲೆಂ. ಚಡಾವತ್ ಲಾತಿನ್ ತಶೆಂ ಹೆರ್ ಭಾಸಾಂ ಥಾವ್ನ್ ಹೆಂ ಸಾಹಿತ್ಯ್ ತಾಣೆಂ ಕೊಂಕ್ಣಿಕ್ ಹಾಡ್ಲೆಂ. ಭುರ್ಗ್ಯಾಂಕ್ ತಶೆಂ ವ್ಹಡಿಲಾಂಕ್ ಧಾರ್ಮಿಕ್ ವಾಚಪ್ ಕೊಂಕ್ಣೆಂತ್ ಮೆಳಾಜಾಯ್ ಮ್ಹಳ್ಳಿ ಉರ್ಬಾ ಮೊನ್ಸಿ. ಸಿಲಾ ಮಿನೆಜಾಚಾ ವಾವ್ರಾಕ್ ಪ್ರೇರಕ್ ಜಾವ್ನಾಸ್‌ಲ್ಲಿ. ತಾಣೆಂ ತರ್ಜಣ್ ಕೆಲ್ಲೆ ಚಡಾವತ್ ಬೂಕ್ ಲಿಯೊ ಡಿ'ಸೋಜಾನ್ (ಲಿಯಾಬ್) ಉಲ್ಲೇಖ್ ಕೆಲ್ಯಾತ್.

(ಕೊಂಕ್ಣಿ ಮಾನೆಸ್ತ್ ಲೇಖನ್‌ಮಾಲಾ –17, ಕರ್ನಾಟಕ್ ಕೊಂಕಣಿ ಸಾಹಿತ್ಯ್ ಅಕಾದಮಿ, ಎಪ್ರಿಲ್ 2003)

ತೆ ಬೂಕ್ ಹ್ಯೆ ಪರಿಂ ಆಸಾತ್:

ಕ್ರಿಸ್ತಾಚೊ ಪಾಟ್ಲಾವ್ (1962) ಲೂರ್ದ್ ಸಾಯ್ಬಿಣ್, ನಿಮಾಣೊ ಸುಕ್ರಾರ್, ಜೆಜು ಮೆಸ್ತ್ರಿ, ಮಹಿನ್ಯಾಚೆ ಪಯ್ಲೆ ಸುಕ್ರಾರ್, ಜೆಜುಚಿ ಕಥಾ, ನಿತ್ಯಾಧಾರ್ ಸಾಯ್ಬಿಣ್, ಜೆಜು ಜಿವೆಂತ್, ಫಾತಿಮಾ ಸಾಯ್ಬಿಣ್, ಆಗ್ಮೆಂತ್, ಚಾಲ್ತಿಂ ಮಾಗ್ಣಿಂ, ಅಬ್ರಾಂವ್, ಆಲ್ತಾರಿಚೊ ಪಾವ್ರೊ, ಇಜಾಕ್ ಆನಿ ಜಾಕೊಬ್, ಫಾತಿಮಾ ಸಂಸಾರಾಚೊ ಉಜ್ವಾಡ್, ಚರಯ್ ಮ್ಹಜಾ

ಶೆಳಿಯಾಂಕ್, ಕ್ರಿಸ್ತಾಂವ್ ಘರಾಣೆ, ಆಪಸ್ತಲಾಂಚಿಂ ಕೃತ್ಯಾಂ, ಆವಯಾಂಚೊ ಸಾಂಗಾತಿ, ಜೆಜು ಆನಿ ಹಾಂವ್, ಕ್ರಿಸ್ತಾಚೊ ಆರ್ರೊ, ದೆವಾಚಾ ರಾಜಾಚಿ ಕಥಾ, ಸಾಕ್ರಾಮೆಂತಾಚೊ ದಿವೊ, ಲೀಜನಾಚೆಂ ಹಾತ್ ಪುಸ್ತಕ್, ಜೆಜು ಸಂಸಾರಾಚೊ ಉಜ್ವಾಡ್ (1964), ತುಂ ಜಾವ್ನಾಸಾಯ್ ಖಡಾಪ್.

ಬೈಬಲ್ ಭಾಶಾಂತರ್:

ಹ್ಯಾ ಶಿವಾಯ್ ದೇವ್‌ಸ್ತುತೆಂತ್ ವ ಭಕ್ತಿಕ್ ವಾಚ್ಪಾಂಕ್ ವಾಪರ್ಚೆ ಜಾಯ್ತೆ ಬೂಕ್ ತರ್ಜಣ್ ಕರ್ಚ್ಯಾಂತ್ ಮೊನ್ಸಿ. ಸಿಲಾ ಮಿನೆಜಾನ್ ವ್ಹಡ್ ಜಯ್ತ್ ಸಾಧನ್ ಕೆಲಾಂ. ಹ್ಯಾ ಸಾಧನಾಂತ್ ಅಧಿಕ್ ಪರ್ಜಳ್ಚೆಂ ಥಿಕ್ ಜಾವ್ನಾಸಾ – ಜೆಜು ಕ್ರಿಸ್ತಾಚಾ ಪವಿತ್ರ್ ವಾಂಜೆಲಾಚೆಂ ಭಾಶಾಂತರ್ (1958). ಹ್ಯಾ ವಾವ್ರಾಕ್ ಪಂಚ್ವೀಸ್ ವರ್ಸಾಂಚೆಂ ಪ್ರೇತನ್ ಗರ್ಜ್ ಪಡ್ಲೆಂ ಮ್ಹಣ್ ಭಾಶಾಂತರ್‌ಕರ್ತ್ ಸಾಂಗ್ತಾ. 'ಕಿತ್ಲೆ ಪಾವ್ಟಿಂ ಮ್ಹಣ್ ನಾ ತೆ ತಿದ್ವಿಲಾಂ. ಆನಿ ಪರ್ತುನ್ ಪರ್ತುನ್ ಬರಯ್ಲಾಂ. ವಾಂಜೆಲಾಚಾ ಮೂಳ್ ಉತ್ರಾಂಕ್ ವಿಶ್ವಾಸ್ ಸಾಂಬಾಳ್ತಾನಾ, ಸಾಂಗಾತಾಚ್ಚ್ ಸಮ್ಜೊಂಕ್ ಸುಲಭ್ ಜಾಯ್ಜಾಯ್ ಆನಿ ವಾಚುಂಕ್ ಸುಢಾಳ್ ಜಾಯ್ಜಾಯ್ ಮ್ಹಳ್ಳೊ ಉದ್ದೇಶ್ ದೊಳ್ಯಾಂ ಮುಖಾರ್ ದವರ್‍ಲಾ. ಲಾತಿನ್ ಶಿವಾಯ್, ಗ್ರೀಕ್ ಆನಿ ಲಾತಿನ್ ಮೂಳ್ ವಾಂಜೆಲಾಂಚೊ ತರ್ಜುಮೊ ದಿಂವ್ಚಾ ಇಂಗ್ಲಿಷ್, ಮರಾಠಿ, ಕನ್ನಡ ಆನಿ ಹೆರ್ ಭಾಶಾಂತರಾಂಚೆಂ ವಾಕ್ಯಾನ್ ವಾಕ್ಯ್ ವಾಚುನ್ ತಜ್ವೀಜ್ ಕೆಲಾಂ. ತರೀಪುಣ್ ಹ್ಯಾ ಭಾಶಾಂತರಾಂತ್ ಜಾಯ್ತೆ ಊಣ್ ಆಸ್ತೆಲೆ ಮ್ಹಣ್ ಭಾಶಾಂತರ್‌ಕರ್ತ್ ಒಪ್ತಾ.

ಮಾ. ಬಾ. ವಿತೊರ್ ಎ. ಪೀಂತ್ ಹಾಣೆ 1979 ಇಸ್ವೆಂತ್ 'ನವೊ ಸೊಲ್ಲೊ' ಭಾಶಾಂತರ್ ಕೆಲ್ಲೊ ತೊ ಮಂಗ್ಳುರ್ ಧರ್ಮ್‌ಪ್ರಾಂತಾನ್ ಪರ್ಗಟ್ಲಾ.

ವಿಲ್ಯಮ್ ದ ಸಿಲ್ವಾನ್ 1977 ಇಸ್ವೆಂತ್ ಕ್ರಿಸ್ತಾಂವ್ ನೊವೊ ಸೊಲ್ಲೊ ಮ್ಹಣ್ತಾತ್ ತೊ ದುಸ್ರೊ ಖರಾರ್ ತರ್ಜಿಲೊ. ಆನಿ 'ಜೆಜು ಕ್ರಿಸ್ತಾಚೀ ಬರೀ ಖಬರ್' ನಾಂವಾನ್ ಪರ್ಗಟ್ಲೊ. 'ಫುಡ್ಲ್ಯಾ ವರ್ಸಾ ಭಾರತಾಚಾ ಭಾಸಾಂನಿ ಪರ್ಗಟ್ ಜಾಲ್ಲ್ಯಾ ಸಗ್ಳ್ಯಾ ತರ್ಜುಮ್ಯಾಂ ಪೈಕಿ ತೊಚ್ಚ್ ಚಡ್ ಬರೊ ತರ್ಜುಮೊ ಮ್ಹಣ್ ತ್ಯಾ ತರ್ಜುಮ್ಯಾಕ್ 'John Hand Memorial' ಇನಾಮ್ ಫಾವೊ ಜಾಲೆಂ. ಕೊಂಕಣಿಂತ್ ಹಾಚಾ ಪಯ್ಲೆಂ ಎಕುಣಿಸಾವ್ಯಾ ಶೆಕ್ಡ್ಯಾಂತ್ ಸೆರಾಮ್‌ಪುರಾಂತ್ ಕೆಲ್ಲೊ ನಾಗರಿ ಲಿಪಿಚೊ ತರ್ಜುಮೊ ಆಸ್ಲ್ಲೊ. ರಾಯ್ಮೊಂದ್ ಮಸ್ಕರೆಞಾನ್ ತರ್ಜಿಲ್ಲೊ ನೊವೊ ತೆಸ್ತಾಮೆಂತ್ ಆಸ್ಲ್ಲೊ. ಸಿಲಾ ಮಿನೇಜಾಚೆ ವಾಂಜೆಲ್ ಆಸ್‌ಲ್ಲೆ. ಆನಿ ಬರಾಬರ್ ತಾಣೆ ಕರುನ್ ದವರ್‌ಲ್ಲಿಂ ನವ್ಯಾ ಖರಾರಾಚಿಂ ಹೆರ್ ಪುಸ್ತಕಾಂ ಆಸ್‌ಲ್ಲಿಂ.'

1997 ಇಸ್ವೆಂತ್ ಪಯ್ಲೊ ಖರಾರ್ ಆನಿ ದುಸ್ರೊ ಖರಾರ್ ಸಾಂಗಾತಾ ಆಟಾಪ್ಚೊ 'ಬಾಇಬಲ್' ವಿಲ್ಯಮ್ ದ ಸಿಲ್ವಾನ್ ತರ್ಜಣ್ ಕೆಲ್ಲೊ ತೊ ಮಂಗ್ಳುರ್ಚಾ ಕೊಂಕಣಿ ಬಾಇಬಲ್ ಪಂಗ್ಡಾನ್ ಉಜ್ವಾಡಾಯ್ಲಾ. ಹ್ಯಾ ಗ್ರಂಥಾಂತ್ಲ್ಯಾ ಸುರ್ವಿಲ್ಯಾ ಉತ್ರಾಂನಿ ತರ್ಜಣ್‌ದಾರ್ ವಿಲ್ಯಮ್ ದ ಸಿಲ್ವಾನ್ ಆಪ್ಣೆ ಕಾಡ್‌ಲ್ಲ್ಯೆ ಮ್ಹಿನತೆ ವಿಶಿಂ ಆನಿ ವಾಪರ್‌ಲ್ಲ್ಯಾ ಉತ್ರಾಂ ತಶೆಂಚ್ ಬರ್ಪಾರಿತಿ ವಿಶಿಂ ವಾಚ್ಪ್ಯಾಂಕ್ ಸವಿಸ್ತಾರ್ ಸಮ್ಜಣಿ ದಿಲ್ಯಾ.

ಮಾ. ವಿಲ್ಯಮ್ ಬಿ. ಬಾರ್ಬೊಜಾನ್ ಪವಿತ್ರ್ ಬೈಬಲ್ (ಪರ್ನೊ ಆನಿ ನವೊ ಸೊಲ್ಲೊ) ಭಾಶಾಂತರ್ ಕೆಲ್ಲೊ ಮಂಗ್ಳುರ್ ಕಥೊಲಿಕ್ ಧರ್ಮ್‌ಪ್ರಾಂತ್ಯಾನ್ ಕ್ರಿಸ್ತ ಜಯಂತಿ –2000 ವೆಳಿಂ ಉಜ್ವಾಡಾಯ್ಲಾ.

ಹೆರ್ ಧಾರ್ಮಿಕ್ ಸಾಹಿತ್:

'ಜೆಜು ರಾಯ್' ಪತ್ರ್ ಫಾತಿಮಾ ರೆತಿರ್ ಮಂದಿರಾ ಥಾವ್ನ್ ಪರ್ಗಟ್ ಜಾತಾ. ಹಾಂತ್ಲೆಂ ಚಡಾವತ್ ಸಾಹಿತ್ಯ್ ಇಂಗ್ಲಿಷ್ ಆನಿ ಹೆರ್ ಭಾಶೆಂ ಥಾವ್ನ್ ಅಣ್ಕಾರ್ ಕರ್ನ್ ಪರ್ಗಟ್ತಾತ್. ಹಾಂತ್ಲ್ಯೊ ಲ್ಹಾನ್, ಲಿಸಾಂವಾಭರಿತ್ ಕಾಣಿಯೊ ಧಾರ್ಮಿಕ್ ಉದ್ದೇಶಾಂಚ್ಯೊ ತರೀ ಭುರ್ಗ್ಯಾಂಕ್ ಲ್ಹಾನ್ ಪ್ರಾಯೆರ್ ಕೊಂಕ್ಣಿ ವಾಚ್ಪಾಚಿ ರೂಚ್ ಲಾಗಂವ್ಕ್ ಸಕ್ಲ್ಯಾತ್. ಪಾಟ್ಲ್ಯಾ ಪನ್ನಾಸ್ ವರ್ಸಾಂ ಥಾವ್ನ್ ಮುಳಾವ್ಯಾ ಹಂತಾರ್ ಭುರ್ಗ್ಯಾಂಕ್ (ವಿಶೇಷ್ ಜಾವ್ನ್) ಮಾಯ್‌ಭಾಸೆಚಿ ವೊಡ್ ಲಾಗಯಿಲ್ಲೆಂ ಸಾಧನ್ ಉಲ್ಲೇಖ್ ಕರಿಜಾಯ್ ಜಾಲ್ಲೆಂ.

ಕೊಂಕ್ಣಿ ಭಾಶೆಕ್ ಲಾತೆಂ ಆನಿ ಇಂಗ್ಲಿಷ್ ಭಾಶೆಂ ಥಾವ್ನ್ ಜಾಯ್ತಿಂ ಭಕ್ತಿಕ್ ಗಿತಾಂ ಭಾಶಾಂತರ್ ಜಾಲ್ಯಾಂತ್. 'ನಾಂವಾಡ್ ಸಿಯೊನ್', 'ಎದ್ಯಾ ವೊಡಾ ಸಾಕ್ರಾಮೆಂತಾಕ್' ಅಸಲಿಂ ಗಿತಾಂ ಮೂಳ್ ತಾಳ್ಯಾಕ್ ಹೊಂದ್ವೊನ್ ಕ್ರಿಸ್ತಾಂವ್ ಯಾಜಕಾಂನಿ ತರ್ಜಣ್ ಕೆಲ್ಯಾಂತ್. ವೆಳಾ ಕಾಳಾಚೆ ಗರ್ಜೆ ತೆಕಿದ್ ಕೆಲ್ಲ್ಯೆ ಹೈ ತರ್ಜಣೆಚೆ ತರ್ಜಣ್‌ಕಾರ್ ಅನಾಮಿಕ್‌ಚ್ಚ್ ಉರ್ಲ್ಯಾತ್. ಮಾ. ಚಾರ್ಲ್ಸ್ ವಾಸ್ ಬಾಪಾನ್ ಆಪ್ಲಿಂಚ್ ಭಕ್ತಿಕ್ ಗಿತಾಂ ಕೊಂಕ್ಣೆಕ್ ತರ್ಜಣ್ ಕರ್ನ್ ಗಾಯ್ಲ್ಯಾಂತ್.

ಮಾ. ಟಿ. ಎ. ಲೋಬೊ ಎಸ್. ಜೆ., ಹಾಣೆ ಮಾ. ಪಾವ್ಲ್ ವೆನಿಶ್ ಎಸ್. ಜೆ.,ನ್ ಲಿಖ್‌ಲ್ಲ್ಯೊ The World on Fire ಬೂಕ್ 'ಮೊಗಾಕ್ ಮೋಗ್' ನಾಂವಾನ್ (1976) ಆನಿ ತ್ಯಾಚ್ಚ್ ಲೇಖಿಕಾಚೊ ಆನ್ಯೇಕ್ ಬೂಕ್ 'ಸ್ವಾಗತ್ ಜೆಜು ರಾಯಾಕ್ ಆಮ್ಚ್ಯಾ ಕುಟ್ಮಾಂತ್' (1980) ನಾಂವಾನ್ ಅಣ್ಕಾರ್ ಕೆಲಾ.

ವಿ.ಜೆ.ಪಿ. ಸಲ್ಡಾನ್ಹಾನ್ 'ಜಿವಿತ್ ಫುಲ್ಲೆಂ ದೆವಾಕ್' (1977) ಕೃತಿ ಅಣ್ಕಾರ್ ಕೆಲ್ಯಾ. 1974 ವ್ಯಾ ವರ್ಸಾಂತ್ 'ಭಾಗೆವಂತ್ ವರಸ್' (Mathias K. J.) ಕೊಂಕ್ಣೆಕ್ ತರ್ಜಣ್ ಕೆಲಾ.

ಮಾ. ಸಿಲ್ವೆಸ್ತರ್ ಮೊಂತೆರಾನ್ The bread that we break (ಲೇಖಿಕ್: Rev Erasto Fernand) ಬೂಕ್ 'ಆಮಿ ಮೊಡ್ಚ್ಯೊ ಉಂಡೊ' ನಾಂವಾನ್ ತರ್ಜಣ್ ಕೆಲಾ (1983).

ಜೆ. ಎಸ್. ಕ್ರಾಸ್ತಾನ್ 'ವೆಲಂಕಣಿ ಭಲಾಯ್ಕೆಚೆ ಮಾಯೆಕ್ ನೊವೆನಾಚೆಂ ಮಾಗ್ಣೆ' (1977) ಆನಿ 'ಪುಲ್ಗತ್ರೆಂತ್ಲೊ ತಾಳೊ' (ಮೂಳ್: Through Purgatory by Maric E. Kolz) ಭಾಶಾಂತ್ರ್ ಕೆಲ್ಯಾತ್.

ಲಿಯೊ ಡಿಸೋಜಾನ್ 'ಪ್ರಶ್ನೋತ್ತರ್ ರುಪಾರ್ ಮಾಗ್ಣ್ಯಾ ವಿಶ್ಯಾಂತ್ ಶಿಕ್ಷಣ್ (ಮೂಳ್: ಮಾ. ಬಾ. ಗಾಬ್ರಿಯೆಲ್) ಭಾಶಾಂತರ್ ಕೆಲಾಂ (1979).

ಸಿ. ಎಮ್. ರೊಸೆಟ್ಟಾ, ಎ. ಸಿ. ಹಿಣೆ 'ಯುವಜಣಾಂಕ್ ಏಕ್ ಸವಾಲ್' (1979) ಪುಸ್ತಕ್ ಭಾಶಾಂತರ್ ಕೆಲಾಂ. (ಮೂಳ್: Rev. Jerry Drinen s.j.) ಲೀನಾ ಮಾರ್ಟಿಸಾನ್ Christmas and the Saints (ಮೂಳ್: Hertha Pavli) ಕೃತಿ 'ಬೆತ್ಲೆಹೆಮಾಚೆ ವಾಟೆರ್' ನಾಂವಾನ್ ಅಣ್ಕಾರ್ ಕೆಲಾ (1960).

ರಿಚಾರ್ಡ್ ಆಲ್ವಾರಿಸಾನ್ 'ಫಾಲ್ಯಾಂ ಕಿತೆಂ?' ಪುಸ್ತಕ್ (1999) 'Serendipity New Testament for Groups' ಥಾವ್ನ್ ತರ್ಜಣ್ ಕೆಲಾಂ.

ಆಯ್ಲೆವಾರ್ ಶ್ರೀ ವೊಲ್ಟರ್ ಕುಲಾಸೊನ್ ಕ್ರಿಸ್ತಾಂವ್ ಕೊಂಕ್ಣಿ ಲೊಕಾನ್ ಅರ್ಗಾಂ ಜಾವ್ನ್ ಗಾಂವ್ಚೆಂ ಬೋವ್ ಲೊಕಾಮೊಗಾಳ್ ಲಾತೆಂ ಗೀತ್ 'ಲಾವ್ದಾತೆ ದೊಮಿನೊಮ್' ಕೊಂಕ್ಣೆಕ್ ತರ್ಜಣ್ ಕೆಲಾಂ. ತ್ಯಾ ಮೂಳ್ ಗಿತಾಚೊ ಫಾಮಾದ್ ತಾಳೊ ತರ್ಜಣ್ ಗಿತಾಕ್ ಮೆಳಾಸೊ ಕೆಲಾ. ಹ್ಯಾ ಗಿತಾಚಿ ಪಯ್ಲಿ ಪಂಗತ್ ಅಶಿ ಆಸಾ.

'ನಾಂವಾಡಾ ಆಮ್ಚ್ಯಾ ಸೊಮಿಯಾಕ್, ಸರ್ವ್ ಲೊಕಾಂನೊ,
ಸರ್ವ್ ಜನಾಂಗಾಂನೊ, ಹರ್ಸಿಯಾ ತಾಚಿ ವ್ಹಡ್ ದಯಾ'

ಹ್ಯಾ ಶಿವಾಯ್ ಜಾಯ್ತೆ ದೊತೊರ್ನೆಚೆಂ ಸಾಹಿತ್ಯ್, ಶೆರ್ಮಾಂವ್ 'ಮಂಗಳಜ್ಯೋತಿ' ಸಂಸ್ಥ್ಯಾನ್ ಕೊಂಕ್ಣೆಂತ್ ತರ್ಜಣ್ ಕೆಲಾಂ.

ಮಾ. ರೆಜಿನಾಲ್ಡ್ ಪಿಂಟೊನ್ 'Catechism of Catholic Church' ಗ್ರಂಥ್ 'ಕಥೊಲಿಕ್ ಪವಿತ್ರ್ ಸಭೆಚಿ ದೊತೊರ್ನ್' ನಾಂವಾನ್ ತರ್ಜಣ್ ಕೆಲಾ.

ಸೃಜನಾತ್ಮಕ್ ಗದ್ಯ್ ಸಾಹಿತ್ಯಾಚೊ ಅಣ್ಕಾರ್

ಭಾಶೆಚಾ ಆನಿ ಸಾಹಿತಾಚಾ ಅಣ್ಕಾರಾಚೊ ಫರಕ್:

ಮನ್ಶ್ಯಾಚಿಂ ಭಗ್ಣಾಂ ಉತ್ರಾಂನಿ ಉಚಾರ್ಚ್ಯಾಕ್ ಭಾಸ್ ಗರ್ಜ್ ಆಸಾ. ಎಕೆ ಭಾಶೆಂತ್ ಉಚಾರ್‌ಲ್ಲೆಂ ಭಗಾಪ್, ಆನ್ಯೇಕೆ ಭಾಶೆಂತ್ ತೊಚ್ಚ್ ಅರ್ಥ್ ದೀವ್ನ್ ಸಾಂಗ್ಲ್ಯಾರ್ (ಭಾಶೆಚೆಂ) ಭಾಶಾಂತರ್ ಜಾತಾ. ಹೆಂ ವಾಕ್ಯಾನ್ ವಾಕ್ಯ್ ಕರುಂಕ್ ಜಾತಾ. ಭಾಷಣ್ ಭಾಶಾಂತರ್ ಕರ್ತಾನಾ ಉಲಯ್ತೊಲೊ, ಮುಖಾರ್ ಕಿತೆಂ ಸಾಂಗ್ತಾ ತೆಂ ಪಯ್ಲೆಂ ಕಳಿತ್

ಆಸಾನಾ. ಜೆಂ ವಾಕ್ಯ್ ಉಚಾರ್ಲ್ಲಾಂ, ತೆಂ ಮಾತ್ರ್ ಭಾಶಾಂತರ್ ಕರ್ಯೆತ್. ಉಪ್ರಾಂತ್ ಉಲಯಿಲ್ಲ್ಯಾ ವಾಕ್ಯಾಂಚೊ ವಾಕ್ಯಾಂವಳ್ (ಪ್ಯಾರಾಗ್ರಾಫ್) ಜಾಯ್ನಾಸ್ತಾಂ ರಾವಾತ್, ವ ವಾಕ್ಯಾ-ವಾಕ್ಯಾ ಮಧೆಂ ವಿಷಯಾಂತರ್ ಜಾಯ್ತ್.

ಜಾಯ್ತೆ ಪಾವ್ಟಿಂ ಹೆರ್ ಭಾಶೆಂನಿ ಚಿಂತುನ್, ತೆಂ ಆಯ್ಕೊವ್ಪ್ಯಾಚ್ಯೆ ಭಾಶೆಂತ್ ಆಪ್ಲೆಸ್ಥಿಕಿಂ ಭಾಶಾಂತರ್ ಕರ್ನ್ ಉಚಾರ್ಚೆಂ ಆಸಾ. ಮರಾಠಿ ಪರಿಸರಾಂತ್ ಆಸ್ಚೊ ಕೊಂಕ್ಣಿ ಜಣ್, ಕೊಂಕ್ಣೆಂತ್ ಚಿಂತುನ್, ತಾಚೆಂ ಆಪ್ಲೆಸ್ಥಿಕಿಂ ಭಾಶಾಂತರ್ ಕರ್ನ್ ಕಷ್ಟಾಂನಿ ಮರಾಠಿ ಉಲಯ್ತಾ. ಇಂಗ್ಲಿಷ್ ದರಬಸ್ತ್ ಶಿಕ್‌ಲ್ಲಿಂ, ಆಜ್‌ಕಾಲ್ ಭಾಶಾಂತರಿಕ್ ಕೊಂಕ್ಣಿ ಉಲಯ್ತಾತ್. ಹ್ಯಾ ವೆಳಿಂ 'ಚಿಂತ್‌ಲ್ಲೆ' ಭಾಶೆಚೊ ಪ್ರಭಾವ್ 'ಉಲಂವ್ಚೆ' ಭಾಶೆಕ್ ಯೆತಾ. 'ಚಿಂತ್‌ಲ್ಲೆ' ಭಾಶೆಚಿಂ ಉತ್ರಾಂ, ವ್ಯಾಕರಣ್ 'ಉಲಯಿಲ್ಲೆಂ' ಭಾಶೆಕ್ ಯೆತಾ. ಆಯ್ಕಾತಾನಾ ಭಾಶೆಚಿ ದಗ್ದವ್ಣಿ ಜಾಲ್ಲೆ ಪರಿಂ ಭಗ್ತಾ.

ಅಶೆಂ ಸಾಹಿತ್ಯಾಚೊ ಅಣ್ಕಾರ್ ಕರುಂಕ್ ಜಾಯ್ನಾ. ಸಾಹಿತ್ಯಾಚೆಂ ರಚಾಪ್ ಏಕ್ ವಿಶೇಷ್ ದೆಣೆ. ಹ್ಯಾ ಬರ್ಪಾಂಕ್, ಬರ್ಪಾ-ಶೈಲಿ ಆಸ್ತಾ. ವಾಕ್ಯಾಂ ಆನಿ ವಾಕ್ಯಾವಳಿಂಚೆಂ ಘಡಾಪ್ ವಿಶೇಷ್ ಮಾಂಡಾವಳಿಚೆಂ ಆಸ್ತಾ. ವಾಚ್ಪ್ಯಾಕ್ ವಾಚವ್ನ್ ವ್ಹರ್ಚೆಂ ಆನಿ ಆನಂದ್ ದಿಂವ್ಚೆಂ ಹ್ಯಾ ವರ್ಪಿಂ ಸಾಧ್ಯ್ ಜಾತಾ. ಬರವ್ಪಿ, ಉತ್ರಾಂ ವಿಂಚುನ್, ಜೊಕುನ್, ಫಲಾಣ್ಯಾ ಅರ್ಥಾನ್ ಬರಪ್ ರಚ್ತಾ. ವಾಕ್ಯಾ ಆನಿ ವಾಕ್ಯಾವಳಿಂ ಮಧೆಂ ತಾರ್ಕಿಕ್ ಘಡಾಪ್ ಆಸ್ತಾ. ಹ್ಯೆ ವರ್ಪಿಂ, ಸಗ್ಳೆಂ ಲೇಖನ್, ಕಾಣಿ ವಾ ಕಾದಂಬರಿ ವಾಚುನ್ ಸಾಹಿತ್ಯ್ ರಚ್ಪಾಚ್ಯೆ ಘಡಾವಳಿಚ್ಯೆ ಸರ್ವ್ ಗೂಣ್, ಕಾಲೆತಿ ಪಾರ್ಕಿಲ್ಯಾ ಶಿವಾಯ್ ಅಣ್ಕಾರ್ ಕರುಂಕ್ ಜಾಯ್ನಾ. ಆಮ್ಸೊರಾನ್ ವ 'ಸಾರ್ಕೊ ವೇಳ್' ಯೇನಾಸ್ತಾಂ ಸೃಜನಾತ್ಮಕ್ ಸಾಹಿತ್ಯ್ ಜಶೆಂ ರಚುಂಕ್ ಜಾಯ್ನಾ ತಶೆಂ ಭಾಶಾಂತರ್ ಕೆಲ್ಯಾರ್ ತೆಂ ಸಾರ್ಕೆಂ ಜಾಯ್ನಾ. ಮೂಳ್ ಪಾಠಾಂತ್ಲಿ ಕಾಲೆತಿ ಭಾಶಾಂತರಾಚಾ ಪಾಠಾಂತ್ ಯೇಜಾಯ್. ಭಾಶೆಚಾ ಪ್ರಯೋಗಾ ವರ್ವಿಂ ಮೂಳ್ ಪಾಠಾಚೊ ಜೊ ಅನ್ಭೋಗ್ ವಾಚ್ಪ್ಯಾಕ್ ಮೆಳ್ತಾ ತೊಚ್ಚ್ ಅನ್ಭೋಗ್ ಭಾಶಾಂತರಿತ್ ಕೃತಿ ವಾಚ್ತಲ್ಯಾಂಕ್ ಲಾಭಾಜಾಯ್. ಸಾಹಿತ್ಯ್ ಸರ್ವಕಾಳಿಕ್, ಸಾಹಿತ್ಯಾಕ್ ಪ್ರಾದೇಶಿಕ್ ಮೇರ್ ನಾ. ಉಜ್ವಾಡ್‌ಲ್ಲೆಂ ಸಾಹಿತ್ಯ್ ಸರ್ವ್ ಲೊಕಾಚೆಂ. ತ್ಯಾ ದೆಕುನ್ ಭಾಶೆ ಥಾವ್ನ್ ಭಾಶೆಕ್ ಸಾಹಿತ್ಯಾಚೊ ಸಾರ್ ಮಾತ್ರ್ ಪಾವ್ಲ್ಯಾರ್ ಪಾವಾನಾ, ಸಾಹಿತ್ಯಾಚ್ಯೆ ಆಪ್ಲ್ಯೆ ಕಾಲೆತಿ ಸಂಗಿಂ ಪಾವಾಜಾಯ್ ಪಡ್ತಾ. ಹಾಂಗಾಸರ್ ಲೇಖನಾಂಕ್ ಥೊಡಿ ರಿಯಾಯ್ತಿ ದಿವ್ಯೆತ್. ಕಾಣಿಯೊ ವ ಕಾದಂಬರಿಯೆಂತ್ ಭಾಶಾಂತರ್ ಕೃತಿ ಮೂಳ್ ಕೃತಿಯೆಕ್ ಆರ್ಸೊ ಜಾಯ್ಜಾಯ್.

ಕಾನಡಿ ಲಿಪಿಂತ್ ಅಣ್ಕಾರಾಚೊ ವಾವ್ರ್ 85 ವರ್ಸಾಂ ಥಾವ್ನ್ ಚಾಲು ಆಸಾ. 1913 ವ್ಯಾ ವರ್ಸಾ ಮೆಸ್ತ್ರಿ ಪೆದ್ರು ಜುವಾಂವ್ ಸೊಜಾನ್ 'ಪಾರ್ಸ್ವೊ', 'ಆವ್ರ್', 'ಗುಲೊಬಾಂಚೆಂ ಝುಡ್' ಅಣ್ಕಾರ್ ಕೆಲ್ಯಾಂತ್. 1921 ವ್ಯಾ ವರ್ಸಾ ಫಾ. ಲುವಿಸ್ ಜುವಾಂವ್ ಸೊಜಾನ್ 'ಪೊಂಪೈ ಸಾಯ್ಬಿಣಿಚೆಂ ನೊವೆನ್' ಅಣ್ಕಾರ್ ಕೆಲಾಂ. (ಮೂಳ್: Bartolo Longo)

ಕೊಂಕ್ಣಿಂತ್ ಸಾಹಿತ್ಯಾಚೆಂ ಭಾಶಾಚಿತರ್

ಕೊಂಕ್ಣಿಂತ್ ಅಣ್ಕಾರ್ ಆನಿ ರುಪಾಂತರಾಚೊ ವಾವ್ರ್ 1818 -ಂತ್ ವಿಲ್ಲಿಯಮ್ ಕ್ಯಾರಿನ್ ಪರ್ನ್ಯಾ ಆನಿ ನವ್ಯಾ ಸೊಲ್ಲ್ಯಾ ಥಾವ್ನ್ ಸುರು ಕೆಲ್ಲೊ ತೊ ಶೆಣಯ್ ಗೊಂಯ್ ಬಾಬಾನ್ ಫುಡೆಂ ವ್ಹೆಲೊ. ತಾಣೆ ಅಣ್ಕಾರ್ ಕೆಲ್ಲಿಂ ಪುಸ್ತಕಾಂ: ಮೊಗಾಚೆಂ ಲಗ್ನ್ (1913), ಪೊವ್ಣ್ಯಾಚೆಂ ತಪಲೆಂ (1948), ಝಿಲ್ಬಾ ರಾಣೊ (1950), ಶ್ರೀ ಭಗವಂತಾಲೆಂ ಗೀತ್ (1959), ಜಾದೂಚೊ ಜುವೊಂ (1968).

ಅಣ್ಕಾರ್ ಸಾಹಿತ್ಯಾಚೆ ಹೆರ್ ಕರ್ತ್ (ನಾಗರಿ ಲಿಪಿಯೆಂತ್):

ರಾಮಚಂದ್ರ ನಾರಾಯಣ್ ನಾಯಕ್- ಸರ್ವೋದಯ್, ನಿತಿ ಧರ್ಮ್, ಸತ್ಯಚಿ ಸಾಧನಾಂ.

ರಾಮಚಂದ್ರ ಶಂಕರ್ ನಾಯಕ್– ಏಕ್ ಹಜಾರ್ ಆನಿ ತೆವೀಸ್, ಮ್ಹುಜೊ ಸರ್ಗ್ಗಾರ್ ಆಸ್ಲ್ಲೊ ಘರ್ಕ್ಕಾರ್.

ಬಾಕಿಬಾಬ್ ಬೋರ್ಕ್ಕರ್–ಗೀತಾ ಪ್ರವಚನ, ಪಯ್ಗಂಬರ್, ವಾಸವದತ್ತಾ, ಭಗವಾನ್ ಬುದ್ಧ್

ನಾಗೇಶ್ ಸೋಂದೆ– ವೈರಾಗ್ಯ್ ಶತ್ಯಾಮು, ಕತಾ ಸಂಗಮ್, ಉಪನಿಶದಾಚೆಂ ಅವಲೋಕನ್

ರವೀಂದ್ರ ಕೇಳೇಕರ್– ಸತ್ಯಾಗ್ರಹ ಆನಿ ತಾಂಕಾಂ ಮನ್ಶಾಂತ್ ಹಾಡ್ಲೆಂ, ದೊಗಿ ಭಯ್ಣಿ, ಸಗ್ಳೆ ಮನಿಸ್ ಭಾವ್ ಭಾವ್

ಫ್ರೆಂಚ್ ಪುಸ್ತಕ್ Petit Prince ಕೊಂಕ್ಣೆಂತ್ 'ಮಾಣ್ಕುಲೊ ರಾಯ್‌ಕುಂವರ್' ನಾಂವಾನ್ ಮಾಧವಿ ನಾಯ್ಕ್ (ಸರ್ದೇಸಾಯ್)ನ್ ಅಣ್ಕಾರ್ ಕೆಲಾ.

ತ್ಯಾ ಶಿವಾಯ್, ದೊ. ಮನೋಹರ್‌ರಾಯ್ ಸರ್ದೇಸಾಯ್, ದೊ. ಒಲಿವಿನೊ ಗೋಮ್ಸ್, ಪಾಂಡುರಂಗ ಭಾಂಗಿ, ಶ್ರೀಪಾದ್ ದೇಸಾಯಿ, ಶಾಂತಾರಾಮ್ ಹೆದೊ, ಲಕ್ಷ್ಮಣ್‌ರಾಯ್ ಸರ್ದೇಸಾಯಿ, ಯಶವಂತ್ ಪಾಲೇಕರ್, ಪುಂಡಲೀಕ ನಾರಾಯಣ್ ನಾಯಕ್, ರಾಮಕೃಷ್ಣ ಜುವಾರ್‌ಕರ್, ಅ. ನಾ. ಮಾಂಬ್ರೊ– ಹಾಣಿಂ ಆಪ್ಲ್ಯಾ ಅಣ್ಕಾರ್ ಸಾಹಿತ್ಯಾ ವರ್ವಿಂ ಕೊಂಕ್ಣೆಕ್ ಗ್ರೇಸ್ತ್ ಕೆಲಾಂ.

(ಉಲ್ಲೇಖ್ ಕುರ್ಪಾ: ಶ್ರೀ ಎಡ್ವಿನ್ ಜೆ. ಎಫ್. ಡಿಸೋಜ, ಹಾಣೆ ತಯಾರ್ ಕೆಲ್ಲೊ ಪಿ.ಜಿ. ಡಿಪ್ಲೊಮಾ ನೋಟ್ಸ್)

i) ವಿಚಾರ್ ಸಾಹಿತ್ಯ್:

ಕೊಂಕ್ಣೆಂತ್ (ಕಾನಡಿ ಲಿಪಿಯೆಂತ್) ವೈಜ್ಞಾನಿಕ್ ವ ಕಾಯ್ದ್ಯಾಂಚೆಂ ಭಾಶಾಂತರ್ ಸೊಧ್ಲ್ಯಾರೀ ಮೆಳಾನಾ. ಧಾರ್ಮಿಕ್ ಬರ್ಪಾಂ ಸೊಡ್ಲ್ಯಾರ್ ಹೆರ್ ಪ್ರಬಂಧ್ ಭಾಶಾಂತರ್ ಜಾಲ್ಲೆ ಬೋವ್‌ಚ್ ಉಣೆ. 1956–ವ್ಯಾ ವರ್ಸಾಂತ್ 'ರಗ್ತಾಚೊ ತಾಳೊ' ಮ್ಹಳ್ಳೊ ಅನುವಾದಿತ್ ಬೂಕ್ 'ಕೊಂಕಣಿ ಸಾಹಿತ್ಯ್ ಪ್ರಕಾಶನಾ' ನ್ ಪ್ರಕಟ್ಲಾ.

1968 ಇಸ್ವೆಂತ್ ವಿಲ್ಯಮ್ ದ ಸಿಲ್ವಾನ್ ABC of YCW ಮ್ಹಳ್ಳೊ ಬೂಕ್ 'ಯುವ ಕ್ರಿಸ್ತಾಂವ್ ವಾವ್ರಾಡಿ' ಮ್ಹಣ್ ಕೊಂಕ್ಣೆಕ್ ಭಾಶಾಂತರ್ ಕೆಲಾ.

ವಿ. ಜೆ. ಪಿ. ಸಲ್ಡಾಞಾನ್ 'ಆಪೊಕಾಲಿಪ್ಸಾಚೊ ಹೊ ಕಾಳ್' (This Apocalypstic Age, by Robert Bergin). 'ರಾಜಿ ಆನಿ ನವೆಂ ಜೀವನ್', 'ಭಾಗೆವಂತ್ ವರಸ್' ಭಾಶಾಂತರ್ ಕೆಲಾಂ.

ಜೆ. ಬಿ. ಮೊರಾಯಸಾನ್, ರಂ. ಶ್ರೀ ಮುಗಳಿಚೊ History of Kannada Literature ಕೊಂಕ್ಣೆಂತ್ 'ಕನ್ನಡ ಸಾಹಿತ್ಯಾಚೊ ಇತಿಹಾಸ್' ಅಣ್ಕಾರ್ ಕೆಲಾ.

ಪ್ರೊ. ಆರ್. ಕೆ. ರಾವಾನ್ ಮಲಯಾಳಮ್ ಸಾಹಿತ್ಯಾಚೊ ಇತಿಹಾಸ್ ಭಾಶಾಂತರ್ ಕೆಲಾ.

40 ವರ್ಸಾಂ ಆದಿಂ ಕಾರ್ಡಿನಲ್ ನ್ಯೂಮೆನಾಚೊ ಪ್ರಸಿದ್ಧ್ ಶೆರ್ಮಾಂವ್ ಕೊಂಕ್ಣೆಂತ್ ಅನುವಾದ್ ಕೆಲ್ಲೊ 'ಮಿತ್ರ್' ಹಫ್ತ್ಯಾಳ್ಯಾಚೆರ್ ಪರ್ಗಟ್ಲಾ.

ಎ. ಎಕ್ಸ್. ಪತ್ರಾವೊನ್ 'ರಾಕ್ಣೊ' ಪತ್ರಾ ಖಾತಿರ್ ಖಬ್ರೆ ಸಂಸ್ಥ್ಯಾ ಥಾವ್ನ್ ಯೆಂವ್ಚ್ಯಾ ಕಥೊಲಿಕ್ ಖಬ್ರೊ ಅಣ್ಕಾರ್ ಕೆಲ್ಯಾತ್. ಪಾಪಾಸಾಯ್ಬಾಚಿಂ 'ವಿಶ್ವ್ ಪತ್ರಾಂ' ಭಾಶಾಂತರ್ ಕೆಲ್ಯಾಂತ್.

ಮೆಲ್ವಿನ್ ರೊಡ್ರಿಗಸಾನ್ ಬೂಕರ್ ಪ್ರಶಸ್ತಿ ವಿಜೇತ್ ಆರುಂಧತಿ ರೊಯ್ ಹಿಣೆ ಮೇ 13, 2003–ವೆರ್ ನ್ಯೂಯೊರ್ಕಾಚಾ ದಿ ರಿವರ್‌ಸೈಡ್ ಚರ್ಚ್ ಹಾಂಗಾಸರ್ ಸಾದರ್ ಕೆಲ್ಲೆಂ ಭಾಷಣ್, 'ಜಟ್‌ಪಟ್ ಭರ್ಶಿಕ್ ರಾಯಾಳ್ ಪ್ರಜಾಪ್ರಭುತ್ವ್ ಜಾವ್ನ್ ತರ್ಜಣ್ ಕೆಲಾಂ. ('ಮಿತ್ರ್' ಜನೆರ್–ಫೆಬ್ರೆರ್ 2004) ಗಂಭೀರ್ ವಿಷಯ್ ಆಟಾಪುನ್, ಉಂಚ್ಲ್ಯಾ ಮಟ್ಟಾಚೆಂ ಇಂಗ್ಲಿಷ್ ಭಾಶೆಚೆಂ ಹೆಂ ಭಾಷಣ್ ಮೆಲ್ವಿನ್ ರೊಡ್ರಿಗಸಾಚಾ ಧಾರಾಳ್ 'ಸಬ್ದಾಜಮ್ಯಾ'ಚಾ ಬಳಾನ್ ಕೊಂಕ್ಣೆಕ್ ಉತರ್ಲ್ಲಾಂ.

ಮೆಲ್ವಿನ್ ಪಿಂಟೊ, ನೀರುಡೆ ಹಾಣೆ ಯು. ಆರ್. ಅನಂತಮೂರ್ತಿಚೆಂ ಲೇಖನ್ 'ಸಾವಿನ ಭಯವನ್ನು ಗೆದ್ದ ಗಾಂಧಿ' (ಪೂರ್ವಾಪರ' – ಅಕ್ಷರ ಪ್ರಕಾಶನ, ಹೆಗ್ಗೋಡು) 'ಮರ್ಣಾ ಭಿರಾಂತ್ ಜಿಕ್‌ಲ್ಲೊ ಗಾಂಧಿ' ನಾಂವಾನ್ ಅನುವಾದ್ ಕೆಲಾಂ. ('ರಾಕ್ಣೊ' ಅಕ್ಟೋಬರ್ 2, 2013) ಬರವ್ಪ್ಯಾಚ್ಯೆ ಮೂಳ್ ಆಶೆಕ್ ಬಾಧಕ್ ಹಾಡಿನಾಸ್ತಾಂ ಲಾಂಬ್ ಬರಪ್ ಮಟ್ವ್ಯಾನ್ ಕೊಂಕ್ಣೆಕ್ ಅನುವಾದ್ ಕೆಲ್ಲೊ ಹೊ ದಾಕ್ಲೊ (Example) ಜಾವ್ನ್ ಘೆವ್ಯೆತ್. ಹೆಂ ಭಾಶಾಂತರ್ ಜಾಯ್ನಾ. (ಮೂಳ್ ಪಾಠ್ ವಾಚ್‌ಲ್ಲ್ಯಾಂಕ್ ತೆಂ ಭಾಶಾಂತರ್ ಕೆಲ್ಯಾರ್ ಬರೆಂ ಜಾತೆಂ ಮ್ಹಣ್ ಭಗಾತ್. ಅನಂತಮೂರ್ತಿಚಾ ಬರ್ಪಾಚಿ ಆಶಾ ಕೊಂಕ್ಣಿ ವಾಚ್ಪ್ಯಾಂಕ್ ಪಾವೊಂಕ್ ಉಣ್ಯಾ ವಾಕ್ಯಾಚೆಂ ಅನುವಾದ್ ಪುರೊ ಮ್ಹಣ್ ಮೆಲ್ವಿನ್ ಪಿಂಟೊ, ನೀರುಡೆಕ್ ಭಗ್ಲಾಂ. ತೆಂ ತಾಣೆ ಬರ್‍ಯಾನ್ ಕೆಲಾಂ.)

ii) ಕಾಣಿಯೊ ಆನಿ ಕಾದಂಬರಿಯೊ:

ಆಪ್ಣಾಕ್ ಬರೀ ಮ್ಹಣ್ ದಿಸ್‌ಲ್ಲಿ ಹೆರ್ ಭಾಶೆಚಿ ಕಥಾ, ಕೊಂಕ್ಣಿ ವಾಚ್ಪ್ಯಾಂನಿ ವಾಚಿಜಯ್ ಮ್ಹಳ್ಳಿ ಉರ್ಬಾ.

ಆಪ್ಣಾಚ್ಯೆ ಚಿಂತ್ಪಾರಿತಿಕ್ ತಾಳ್ ಪಡ್ಚಿ ಹೆರ್ ಭಾಶೆಚಿ ಕಥಾ ಕೊಂಕ್ಣಿ ಲೊಕಾಕ್ ಪಾವಾಜಯ್ ಮ್ಹಳ್ಳಿ ಆಶಾ.

ಕೊಂಕ್ಣೆಂತ್ ಉಂಚ್ಲ್ಯಾ ಕಾಣಿಯಾಂಚೊ ಬರ್ಗಾಲ್ ಆಯ್ಲಾ, ವ ಕೊಂಕ್ಣಿ ಕಾಣಿಯಾಂಚೊ ಪಾಂವ್ಡೊ ಹೆರ್ ಭಾಸಾಂಚಾ ಕಾಣಿಯಾಂಚಾಕೀ ಉಣೊ ಆಸಾ ಮ್ಹಳ್ಳೆಂ ಭಗಾಪ್,

ಆಪ್ಣಾಕ್ ಕಾಣಿ ರಚ್ಚೆಂ ದೆಣೆ ನಾ, ಭಾಶಾಂತರಾಚಿ ಕುಶಲತಾ ಗಳ್ಸುನ್ ಕೊಂಕ್ಣಿ ಸಾಹಿತ್ಯ್ ಗ್ರೇಸ್ತ್ ಕರ್ತಾಂ ಮ್ಹಳ್ಳೆಂ ಚಿಂತಾಪ್,

ಫಲಾಣ್ಯಾ ಹೆರ್ ಭಾಶೆಚಾ ಸಾಹಿತಿಕ್ ಕೊಂಕ್ಣೆಂತ್ ವಳಕ್ ಕರ್ನ್ ದೀಜಾಯ್ ಮ್ಹಳ್ಳೊ ಅಭಿಮಾನ್.

ಪತ್ರಾಚ್ಯೆ ಮೆಚ್ವಣೆಕ್ ಜರೂರ್ ಬರೀ ಕಾಣಿ ಜಾಯ್ ಮ್ಹಳ್ಳೊ ಅನ್ಬೋಗ್ ಕಾಣಿಯೊ, ಕಾದಂಬರಿಯೊ ಕೊಂಕ್ಣೆಕ್ ಭಾಶಾಂತರ್ ಜಾಂವ್ಕ್ ಮೂಳ್ ಪ್ರೇರಣ್ ಜಾಲ್ಯಾತ್.

ವಿಲ್ಯಮ್ ದ ಸಿಲ್ವ, 'ಖೆಳ್ ಆನಿ ಹೆರ್ ಕಥಾ' ಹ್ಯಾ ಬುಕಾಂತ್ ವಾಚ್ಪ್ಯಾಂಲಾಗಿಂ ಸಂವಾದ್ ಚಲವ್ನ್ ಬರಯ್ತಾ. 'ಕೊಂಕ್ಣಿ ಭಾಸ್ ಆನಿ ತಿಚೆಂ ಸಾಹಿತ್ಯ್ – ಹಿಂ ದೋನ್‌ಯಿ ಫುಂಗ್‌ರ್ಗೆಲ್ಯಾಂತ್; ದುಧಾವೀಣ್ ಸುಕ್ಲ್ಯಾಂತ್; ತಿಂ ಆಂಕುಡ್ಚೆ ಪಯ್ಲೆಂ ಭಾಯ್ಲ್ಯಾ ಸಾಹಿತ್ಯಾಚಾ ವೀರ್‍ಯಾನ್ ಭರವ್ನ್ ತಿಂ ಪರತ್ ಫಳಾದಿಕ್ ಕರ್ಚಿ ಆಶಾ ಆಮ್ಕಾಂ ಆಸ್‌ಲ್ಲ್ಯಾನ್ ಆಮಿ ಭಾಯ್ಲ್ಯಾ ಭಾಸಾಂತ್ಲೆಂ ಉಂಚ್ಲೆಂ-ಲೊಕಾಮೊಗಾಳ್ ಜಾಲ್ಲೆಂ ತಶೆಂಚ್ ಪುರಸ್ಕಾರ್ ಮೆಳ್‌ಲ್ಲೆಂ ಸಾಹಿತ್ಯ್ ಕೊಂಕಣಿಂತ್ ತರ್ಜುಮೊ ಕರ್ಚ್ಯಾ ಕಾಮಾಕ್ ಹಾತ್ ಘಾಲಾ... ಭಿತರ್ಲೆ ಸಕ್ತೆನ್ ಆನಿ ಭಾಯ್ಲ್ಯಾ ವೀರ್‍ಯಾನ್ ಕೊಂಕಣಿ ಭಾಸ್ ಆನಿ ಸಾಹಿತ್ಯ್ ಪರತ್ ಜಿವಾಳುನ್ ಯೆಂವ್ಚೆಂ ಆಮ್ಕಾಂ ಜಾಯ್' (ದಶೆಂಬರ್ 19, 1986)

ರಾಕ್ಣೊ, ಪ್ರಗತೀ, ಪುನವ್ ಆನಿ ಸಾಳಕ್ ಪ್ರಕಾಶನಾಂನಿ ಕಾನಡಿ ಲಿಪಿಯೆಂತ್ ಆನಿ ಗೊಂಯ್ಚ್ಯಾ ಹೆರಾಂನಿ ದೇವ್‌ನಾಗರಿಂತ್ ತರ್ಜುಮೆ ಪರ್ಗಟ್ಲ್ಯಾಂತ್.

ಗೋಕುಲ್‌ದಾಸ್ ಪ್ರಭುನ್ ಎಮ್. ಟಿ. ವಾಸುದೇವನ್ ನಾಯರಾಚಿ ಜ್ಞಾನ್‌ಪೀಠ್ ಪುರಸ್ಕೃತ್ ಕಾದಂಬರಿ, 'ಚಕ್ಕಿ' ನಾಂವಾನ್ ಕೊಂಕ್ಣೆಂತ್ (ದೇವ್‌ನಾಗರಿ ಲಿಪಿಯೆಂತ್) ಅಣ್ಕಾರ್ ಕೆಲಾ. ಹ್ಯಾ ಅಣ್ಕಾರಾಕ್ ಕೇಂದ್ರ್ ಸಾಹಿತ್ಯ್ ಅಕಾದೆಮಿಚೊ ಪುರಸ್ಕಾರ್ ಲಾಭ್ಲಾ.

ವೊಲ್ಟರ್ ಲಸ್ರಾದೊನ್ ಜೇಮ್ಸ್ ಹ್ಯಾಡ್ಲಿ ಚೇಜ್, ಹಾಚ್ಯೊ 4 ಕಾದಂಬರಿಯೊ– ಜುದಾಸಾಚಿ ಜುಗಾರ್, ಚಲ್ಚೆಂ ಮೊಡೆಂ, ಆಕ್ರಮಿ ಜಾಳ್, ಮೊರ್ನಾಚೊ ತಾಳೊ ಭಾಶಾಂತರ್ ಕೆಲ್ಯಾತ್.

ಮೊನ್ಸಿ. ಸಿಲಾ ಮಿನೇಜಾನ್, ಕೆನನ್ ಶ್ಮಿಡಾಚ್ಯೊ ದೋನ್ ಕೃತಿಯೊ ಫುಲಾಂಚಿ ದಾಲಿ (1970), ಜೆನೆವಿವ್ (1961) ಇಸ್ವೆಂತ್ ಕೊಂಕ್ಣೆಕ್ ಹಾಡ್ಲ್ಯಾತ್. 'ಫಾಬಿಯೋಲ' ನಾಂವಾಚಿ ಕೃತಿ ಆಧುರಿ ಉರ್ಲಿ ಮ್ಹಣ್ ಲಿಯಾಬ್ ಸಾಂಗ್ತಾ.

ದುಸ್ರ್ಯಾ ಮಹಾಝುಜಾ ವೆಳಾರ್ ಆಸ್ಟ್ರೇಲಿಯಾಚಾ ಫೊನ್ ಟ್ರ್ಯಾಪ್ ಗಾವ್ಪಿ ಕುಟ್ಮಾಚೆರ್ ಆಯಿಲ್ಲ್ಯಾ ಕಷ್ಟಾಂಚೊ, ತಾಂಚಾ ದೇಶ್‌ಪ್ರೇಮಾಚೊ ದಾಖ್ಲೊ ಜಾವ್ನ್ ಮರೀಯಾ ಫೊನ್ ಟ್ರ್ಯಾಪ್ ಹಿಣೆ ಲಿಖ್‌ಲ್ಲ್ಯಾ ಆಪ್ಲ್ಯಾ ಕುಟ್ಮಾಚ್ಯೆ ಕತೆಚೊ ಭಾಶಾಂತ್ರ್ 'ಘರ್ ಭರ್‌ಲ್ಲೆಂ ಗೀತ್' ತಕ್ಲೆ ನಾಂವಾನ್ ದೊ. ವಿಲ್ಯಮ್ ದ ಸಿಲ್ವಾನ್ ತಯಾರ್ ಕೆಲ್ಲೆಂ ತೆಂ 'ರಾಕ್ಣೊ' ಪ್ರಕಾಶನಾನ್ (1967) ಪ್ರಗಟ್ ಕೆಲಾಂ.

ಮೆಲ್ವಿನ್ ರೊಡ್ರಿಗಸಾನ್ ಯಶವಂತ್ ಚಿತ್ತಾಲಾಚಿ 'ಕತೆಯಾದಳು ಹುಡುಗಿ' ಕಾದಂಬರಿ 'ಕಾಣಿ ಜಾಲ್ಲಿ ಚಲಿ' ಜಾವ್ನ್ ಕೊಂಕ್ಣಿ ದೇವ್‌ನಾಗರಿಂತ್ ಅಣ್ಕಾರ್ ಕೆಲ್ಯಾ. ತ್ಯಾಚ್ ಲೇಖಕಾಚಿ 'ಆಬೊಲಿನಾ' ಹ್ಯಾಚ್ಚ್ ನಾಂವಾನ್ ಕೊಂಕ್ಣೆಕ್ ಕಾನಡಿ ಲಿಪಿಯೆಂತ್ ಭಾಶಾಂತರ್ ಜಾಲಾ.

ಜೆ.ವಿ ಕಾರ್ಲೊನ್ ಇಂಗ್ಲಿಷ್ ಕಾದಂಬರಿ 'ಸೈತಾನಾಚೊ ವಕೀಲ್' ತರ್ಜಣ್ ಕೆಲ್ಲಿ 'ಮಿತ್ರ್' ಹಫ್ತ್ಯಾಳ್ಯಾಚೆರ್ ಪ್ರಗಟ್ ಜಾಲ್ಯಾ. ಚಂಬಲ್ ರಾಣಿ ಫೂಲನ್ ದೇವಿಚಿ ಜಿಣ್ಯೆ ಕಥಾ ಕಾನಡಿ ಥಾವ್ನ್ ಮೆಕ್ಷಿ ಪಿಂಟೊ ಕೆಲರಾಯ್ ಹಾಣೆ ಕೊಂಕ್ಣೆಕ್ ಅನುವಾದ್ ಕೆಲ್ಲಿ 'ಮಿತ್ರ್' ಹಫ್ತ್ಯಾಳ್ಯಾಚೆರ್ ಪ್ರಗಟ್ ಜಾಲ್ಯಾ.

ವಿಲ್ಯಮ್ ದ ಸಿಲ್ವಾನ್ ಮಲಯಾಳಮಾಂತ್ಲಿ ತಕಳಿ ಶಿವಶಂಕರ ಪಿಳ್ಳ್ಯೆಚಿ ಕಾದಂಬರಿ 'ಸುಂಗ್‌ಟಾಂ' ಮ್ಹಣ್ ಭಾಶಾಂತರ್ ಕೆಲ್ಯಾ. ಯಶವಂತ್ ಚಿತ್ತಾಲಾಚಿ 'ಆಟ ಮತ್ತು ಇತರ ಕತೆಗಳು' ಕೃತಿ 'ಖೆಳ್ ಆನಿ ಹೆರ್ ಕತಾ' ಜಾವ್ನ್, ನಾ. ಡಿಸೋಜಾಚಿ 'ಪ್ರೀತಿಯೊಂದೆ ಸಾಲದು' ಕೃತಿ 'ಮೋಗ್ ಮಾತ್ ಪಾವಾನಾ' ಜಾವ್ನ್, ಪೂರ್ಣಚಂದ್ರ ತೇಜಸ್ವಿಚಿ ಕಾಣಿ 'ಕುಬಿ ಮತ್ತು ಇಯಾಲ', ನಾ. ಡಿಸೋಜಾಚಿ 'ರುಜಾರಿ' ಕಾಣಿ, ಕೆನೆಡಿಯನ್ ಕಾಣಿ, 'ಲ್ಹಾನ್ ಚಲಿಯೆಚಿ ಕತಾ' ಕೊಂಕ್ಣೆಕ್ ಅಣ್ಕಾರ್ ಕರುನ್ ಕೊಂಕ್ಣಿ ಭಾಶೆಚಿ ಗ್ರೇಸ್ತ್‌ಕಾಯ್ ಚಡಯ್ಲ್ಯಾ. ಹ್ಯಾ ಅಣ್ಕಾರಾಂನಿ ವಿಲ್ಯಮ್ ದ ಸಿಲ್ವಾನ್ ವೆಗ್ಳಿಚ್ಚ್ ಅಧ್ಯಯನ್ ಯೋಗ್ಯ್ ಬರ್ಪಾರೀತ್ ವಾಪರ್ಲ್ಯಾ. ವಾಚ್ಪ್ಯಾಂಚಾ ಚಾಲ್ತ್ಯೆ ಉಲವ್ಣ್ಯೆ ಭಾಶೆಕ್ ಬರ್ಪಾ ಭಾಸ್ ಹಾಡ್ಚೆಂ ಪ್ರೇತನ್ ಭಾಶಾಂತರ್‌ಕರ್ತ್ಯಾನ್ ಕೆಲಾಂ.

ಎಡ್ವಿನ್ ಜೆ. ಎಫ್. ಡಿ'ಸೋಜಾನ್ 'ಕಮಲ್' ಲಿಖ್ಣೆ ನಾಂವಾನ್ 1969 ವ್ಯಾ ವರ್ಸಾಂತ್ 'ದೆವಾನ್ ವಿಂಚ್‌ಲ್ಲೆಂ ಫಳ್' (ಮೂಳ್: Heaven Knows Mr. Allison) ಅಣ್ಕಾರ್ ಕೆಲ್ಯಾ. 1971–ವ್ಯಾ ವರ್ಸಾಂತ್ 'ತುಂವೆ ಮ್ಹಾಕಾ ರಚ್ಲೊಯ್' ನಾಂವಾನ್ (ಮೂಳ್: ಡೊ. ಎ. ಜೆ. ಕ್ರೊನಿನ್ ಹಾಚಿ Shannon's Way) ರುಪಾಂತರ್ ಕೆಲ್ಯಾ.

ಫ್ರಾನ್ಸಿಸ್ ಡಿಕುನ್ಹಾನ್ ಹಿಂದಿ ಭಾಶೆಂತ್ಲಿ ಅಯೋಧ್ಯಾ ಪ್ರಸಾದ್ ಗೊಯಲಿಯ್ ಹಾಚಿ ಕಾಣಿ 'ಶಹೀದ್ ಬಕ್ರೆ', 'ಮಾಡ್ತಿರ್ ಶೆಳಿ' ನಾಂವಾನ್ ಅಣ್ಕಾರ್ ಕೆಲ್ಯಾ. ಶ್ರೀಮತಿ ಸುಭದ್ರ ಕುಮಾರಿ ಚೌಹಾನಾಚಿ 'ವೊ ತೀನ್ ಬಚ್ಚೆ' ಕಾಣಿ 'ತಿಂ ತೆಗಾಂ ಭುರ್ಗಿಂ' ನಾಂವಾನ್ ರುಪಾಂತರ್ ಕೆಲ್ಯಾ. ಗೊಂಯ್‌ಚ್ಯಾ ದಾಮೋದರ್ ಮೌಜೊ ಹಾಣೆ ಶಿವರಾಮ ಕಾರಂತಾಚಿ 'ಚೋಮನ ದುಡಿ' ಕಾದಂಬರಿ 'ಅಂತ್ ನಾತ್‌ಲ್ಲೆಂ ಸಪಾಣ್' ನಾಂವಾನ್ ಅಣ್ಕಾರ್ ಕೆಲ್ಯಾ.

ಕೇರಳಾಚಾ ಎಸ್. ಎನ್. ಆನಂದನ್ ಹಾಣೆ, ಗುಜ್ರಾಥಿ ಥಾವ್ನ್ 'ಸಾತ್ ಪಾವ್ಲಾಂ ಮೊಳ್ಬಾಂತ್', ಬಂಗಾಳಿ ಥಾವ್ನ್ ಠಾಗೋರಾಚಿ 'ದೊಳ್ಯಾಂತ್ಲೆಂ ಕಿಸರ್' ಆನಿ 'ಜೋಕರ್ ಬಾಳಿ' ನಾಂವಾನ್ ಬಂಗಾಳಿ ಕತಾ, 'ರಾಹುಲ ಸಾಂಕಯ್‌ತಾಯನ' ನಾಂವಾನ್ ಇಂಗ್ಲಿಷ್ ಕತಾ ಕೊಂಕ್ಣೆಕ್ ಹಾಡ್ಲ್ಯಾತ್.

ಶರತ್‌ಚಂದ್ರ ಶೆಣ್ಯೆನ್ 'ಅಗ್ನಿ ಸಾಕ್ಷಿ' ಕೃತಿಯೆಚೆಂ ಭಾಶಾಂತರ್ ಕೆಲಾಂ.

ರವೀಂದ್ರ ಕೇಳೇಕರಾನ್ ಬಂಗಾಳಿಂತ್ಲಿ ಠಾಗೋರಾಚಿ ಕಾಣಿ 'ದೊಗಿ ಭಯ್ಣಿ' ನಾಂವಾನ್ ಆನಿ ಇಂದಿರಾ ಗೋಸ್ವಾಮಿಚಿ ಗುಜ್ರಾಥಿ ಕೃತಿ 'ತಾಣಿಂ ತಾಂಕಾಂ ಮನ್ಶ್ಯಾಂತ್ ಹಾಡ್ಲೆಂ' ನಾಂವಾನ್ ಭಾಶಾಂತರ್ ಕೆಲ್ಯಾ.

ಮನೋಹರ್‌ರಾಯ್ ಸರ್‌ದೇಸಾಯ್‌ನ್ ಫ್ರೆಂಚ್ ಭಾಶೆಚಿ ಕೃತಿ 'ಉತ್ರಾಂ' ಜಾವ್ನ್ ಆನಿ ಬಂಗಾಳಿ ಭಾಶೆಚಿ 'ಆಯ್ಲೆಂ ಆಮ್ಚೆ ರಾಜ್' ಜಾವ್ನ್ ಅಣ್ಕಾರ್ ಕೆಲ್ಯಾ.

ಪ್ರೊ. ಆರ್. ಕೆ. ರಾವಾನ್ 'ದೋನ್ ದಂಗಳಿ ಭಾತ್', ಹರಿಶ್ಚಂದ್ರ ನಾಗ್ವೇಕರಾನ್ ಪಿ. ಕೇಶವದೇವಾಚಿ ಕೃತಿ 'ಶೆಜಾರಿ' ನಾಂವಾನ್ ತರ್ಜಣ್ ಕೆಲ್ಯಾ.

ಒಲಿವಿನೊ ಗೋಮ್ಸಾನ್ 'ಜಿವಿತ್ ಮ್ಹಳ್ಯಾರ್ ಸಪಾಣ್' ಆನಿ 'ಲಾಯೊ ಭಾತಾಂ' ಕೊಂಕ್ಣೆಕ್ ಫ್ರೆಂಚ್ ಭಾಶೆ ಥಾವ್ನ್ ಅಣ್ಕಾರ್ ಕೆಲ್ಯಾ.

ಪ್ರಕಾಶ್ ಥಳಿನ್ ಯು. ಆರ್. ಅನಂತಮೂರ್ತಿಚಿ ಕನ್ನಡ ಕಾದಂಬರಿ 'ಸಂಸ್ಕಾರ' ಕೊಂಕ್ಣೆಕ್ ಅಣ್ಕಾರ್ ಕೆಲ್ಯಾ.

ಯಶವಂತ ಪಾಲೇಕರಾನ್ ಶಿವರಾಮ ಕಾರಂತಾಚಿ ಕನ್ನಡ ಕಾದಂಬರಿ 'ಮರಳಿ ಮಣ್ಣಿಗೆ' ಕೊಂಕ್ಣೆಕ್ ಉತ್ರಾಯ್ಲ್ಯಾ.

ಲಿಲ್ಲಿ ಮಿರಾಂದ ಜೆಪ್ಪು ಹಿಣೆ ಕೆ.ಪಿ. ಪೂರ್ಣಚಂದ್ರ ತೇಜಸ್ವಿಚಿ ನಾಂವಾಡ್ದಿಕ್ ಕಾದಂಬರಿ 'ಕರ್ವಾಲೊ' ಕೊಂಕ್ಣಿ ವಾಚ್ಪ್ಯಾಂಕ್ ಅಣ್ಕಾರ್ ಕರುನ್ ದಿಲ್ಲಿ 'ಝೆಲೊ' ಪತ್ರಾರ್ ಪ್ರಗಟ್ ಜಾಲ್ಯಾ. 32 ಅಧ್ಯಾಯ್ ಮಹಿನ್ಯಾಕ್ ಎಕಾ ಲೆಕಾನ್ ಪರ್ಗಟ್ ಜಾಲ್ಯಾತ್.

ಕಾನಡಿ ವಾಕ್ಯಾಂ ಕೊಂಕ್ಣೆಂತ್ ಹಾಡ್ತಾಂತ್ ಹೆಳ್ಲ್ಲಿ ಲಿಖ್ಣಿ ಮೂಳ್‌ಕೃತಿ ವಾಚ್‌ಲೊಚ್ಚೆ ಅನ್ಭವ್ ದಿತಾ. ಭಾಶಾಂತರ್‌ಕರ್ ಬರವ್ಪಿಣ್, ಕಥಾ ಘಡ್ತಾ ಪರಿಸರಾಂತ್ ವಾಡ್‌ಲ್ಲಿ ದೆಕುನ್, ಮೂಳ್‌ಕೃತಿಯೆಕ್ ತಿಣೆ ನ್ಯಾಯ್ ದಿಲಾ ಮ್ಹಣ್ಯೆತ್. ಶಿವಾಯ್ 'ಪಾಕಿಸ್ತಾನಾಚಿ ಕತಾ' ತರ್ಜುಮೊ ಕೆಲ್ಯಾ. ಹಿ ನೀಳ್ ಕತಾ 'ಕುರೊವ್' ಪತ್ರಾನ್ ಫಾಯ್ಸ್ ಕೆಲ್ಯಾ. ಕೆ. ಪಿ. ಪೂರ್ಣಚಂದ್ರ ತೇಜಸ್ವಿಚಿ 'ಕಾಡಿನ ಕಥೆ'ಗಳು ಬುಕಾಂತ್ಲಿ ಕಾಣಿ 'ಬೆಳ್ಳಂದೂರ್ಚ್ಯೊ ನರಭಕ್ಷಕ್' ಮ್ಹಣ್ ಲಿಲ್ಲಿ ಮಿರಾಂದಾನ್ ಆಪ್ಲ್ಯಾ 'ಫುಲಾಂ ಫಳಾಂ' ಬುಕಾಂತ್ ಪರ್ಗಟ್ಲ್ಯಾ.

ಸಿರಿವಂತಾನ್ ಲಿಯೊ ಟಾಲ್ಸ್‌ಟಾಯ್‌ಚಿ ಕಾಣಿ 'ಚೆಲಿನ್ ಆನಿ ಡೀನಾ' ಜಾವ್ನ್ ಆನಿ ವಿಲಿಯಮ್ ಇ. ಬಾರೆಟ್ ಹಾಚಿ ಇಂಗ್ಲಿಷ್ ಕಾಣಿ Lillies of the Field, 'ಭುಂಯ್ ಕಮಳಾಂ' ಜಾವ್ನ್ (ಪ್ರದೀಪ್ ಆನಿ ಸಿರಿವಂತ್ ಹಾಣಿಂ ಸಾಂಗಾತಾ) ತರ್ಜುಮೊ ಕೆಲ್ಯಾ. ಹರ್ಮಿರಾಯ್ ಆನಿ ಪ್ರದೀಪ್ ಹಾಣಿಂ ಗ್ರೀಕ್ ಭಾಶೆ ಥಾವ್ನ್ 'ಕಿನ್ನರಿ ಕತಾ' ನಾಂವಾಚ್ಯೊ ಕಾಣಿಯೊ ಅಣ್ಕಾರ್ ಕೆಲ್ಯಾತ್.

ಎವ್ಲಾಲಿಯಾ ಆಲ್ವಾರಿಸಾನ್ ವಿಲಿಯಮ್ ಶೇಕ್ಸ್‌ಪಿಯರಾಚೊ 'ಒಥೆಲ್ಲೊ' ನಾಟಕ್ ಕೊಂಕ್ಣೆಕ್ ಹಾಡ್ಲಾ.

1958–ಂತ್ ಮಾರಿ ಕೊರೆಲ್ಲಿಚೆ ದೋನ್ ಮಹಾನ್ ಗ್ರಂಥ್ ರುಪಾಂತರ್ ಕರುನ್ 'ಪೊಕಿಚೆಂ ಕಾರ್ಬಾರ್ (ವೆಂಡೆಟ್ಟಾ) ಆನಿ 'ಫ್ಲೋರಾಚಿ ಕಥಾ (ತೆಲ್ಮಾ) ಹ್ಯಾ ಮಾತಾಳ್ಯಾಂನಿ ಪ್ರಗಟ್ಲೆ. 'ಪೆಟಾನಾತ್‌ಲ್ಲೆಂ ತಣ್', 'ದಿ ರೋಬ್' (ಲೋಯ್ಡ್ ಸಿ. ಡಗ್ಲಸ್) ಕೊಂಕ್ಣಿ ಭಾಶೆಕ್ ಅಣ್ಕಾರ್ ಕೆಲ್ಯಾಂತ್.

ಎಮ್. ಪ್ಯಾಟ್ರಿಕಾನ್ ಟಿ. ಸಿ. ಎನ್. ರಾಜ್‌ಚ್ಯೊ ಕನ್ನಡ ಕೃತಿಯೊ 'ಒಲಿವಿಯಾ' ಆನಿ 'ವಜ್ರಾಂಚೊ ಕುರೊವ್' ಅಣ್ಕಾರ್ ಕೆಲ್ಯಾತ್. (1986)

ರೈಮಂಡ್ ಮಿರಾಂದಾನ್ ಜೋನ್ ಕೊಸ್ಸ್‌ಗ್ರೊವಾಚೆ ಕಾದಂಬರಿಯಾಂಚೆ ದೊನೀ ಭಾಗ್ 'ಪಾತ್ಯೆಣೆಚೊ ಈಷ್ಟ್' ನಾಂವಾನ್ ಭಾಷಾಂತರ್ ಕೆಲ್ಯಾತ್. ಆನಿ ಮಿಸ್ಸ್ ಆ್ಯನ್ನ್ ಟ್ಯಾನ್ಸಿ ಹಿಣೆ ಇಂಗ್ಲಿಷಾಂತ್ ಲಿಖ್‌ಲ್ಲಿ Nephew of the Commissioner ಮ್ಹಳ್ಳಿ ಕಾಣಿ 'ಕೊಮಿಶ್ರಾಚೊ ಭಾಚೊ' ನಾಂವಾನ್ ಅನುವಾದ್ ಕೆಲ್ಯಾ.

ಎ. ಎಕ್ಸ್. ಪತ್ರಾವೊನ್ ಜರ್ಮನ್ ಥಾವ್ನ್ ಕೊಂಕ್ಣೆಕ್ Canon Schmidt ಹಾಚಿ ಕಾಣಿ 'ಲ್ಹಾನ್ ಗಾಯಕಿ' ನಾಂವಾನ್ ತರ್ಜಣ್ ಕೆಲ್ಯಾ.

ಮಾ। ಬಾ। ಧೀರಾತ್ಮ ಪ್ರಭುನ್ ಖ್ರಿಜ Scarlet Lilly (by Rev. Fr. Edward F. Murffi) ಕೃತಿ 'ಮೊಗಾಚಿ ರಾಣಿ' ನಾಂವಾನ್ ಅಣ್ಕಾರ್ ಕೆಲ್ಯಾ.

ಎಮ್. ಪಿ. ರೊಡ್ರಿಗ್ಸಾನ್ Joseph Spillman ಹಾಚಿ ಕಾದಂಬರಿ 'ಕಾಂಟ್ಯಾಂಚೊ ಖುರಿಸ್' ನಾಂವಾನ್ (1970) ಆನಿ Unto the last ಮ್ಹಳ್ಳಿ ಕಾದಂಬರಿ 'ನಿಮಾಣಿ ಆಶಾ', ತಶೆಂಚ್ ಆನ್ಯೇಕ್ ಇಂಗ್ಲಿಷ್ ಕಾದಂಬರಿ 'ಮೊಗಾಚಿ ಧಾಂವ್' ನಾಂವಾನ್ ಅಣ್ಕಾರ್ ಕೆಲ್ಯಾ.

ಲಿಯೊ ಡಿ'ಸೋಜಾನ್ (ಲಿಯಾಬ್) ವಾಶಿಂಗ್ಟನ್ ಇರ್ವಿಂಗ್ ಹಾಚಿ ಇಂಗ್ಲಿಷ್ ನವಾಲ್ ಕತಾ 'ವಿಂಕಲಾಚಿ ಕತಾ' ಜಾವ್ನ್, ಮಾರ್ಕ್ ಟ್ವೈನಾಚಿ ಇಂಗ್ಲಿಷ್ ನವಲ್ ಕತಾ 'ರಾಜು

ಆನಿ ರಾಯ್‌ಕುಂವರ್' ನಾಂವಾನ್ ಆನಿ ಮೇರಿ ಫೇಬಿಯನಾಚಿ ಲ್ಯಾಡ್ ಒಫ್ ಲೀಮಾ ಕೃತಿ 'ಲಿಮಾಚೊ ಭುರ್ಗೊ' ನಾಂವಾನ್ (1970) ಆನಿ 'ಮಾರ್ಸೆಲಿನೊ' (1970) ಕೃತಿಯೊ ಅಣ್ಕಾರ್ ಕೆಲಾ.

ಅನಿರುದ್ಧ್ ಕಾಮತಾನ್ Br. Ernest E.F.C. ಹಾಚಿ The man under the stairs ಲಾಂಬ್ ಕತಾ 'ವಿಚಿತ್ರ್ ಶಿಕಾರಿ' ನಾಂವಾನ್ ಆನಿ Anatol France ಹಾಣೆ ಲಿಖ್‌ಲ್ಲೊ ಮಟ್ವ್ಯೊ ಕಾಣಿಯೊ 'ಉದೆಂತಿಚೆಂ ನೆಕೆತ್ರ್' ನಾಂವಾನ್ ತರ್ಜಣ್ ಕೆಲ್ಯಾತ್.

ಮಾ। ಎಸ್. ಎಫ್. ಮಿನೇಜಾನ್ ಕಾನಡಿ ಭಾಶೆಚೊ ಕಾಣಿಯೊ 'ಹುಶಾರ್ ಭೊಟ್' ನಾಂವಾನ್ ಅಣ್ಕಾರ್ ಕೆಲ್ಯಾತ್.

ಜೊನ್ ಬಿ. ಟೆಲ್ಲಿಸಾನ್ 'ಆಚರ್ಯಾಂಚಿ ಕಾಳಿ' ಆನಿ 'ಸಾಂ. ಜೋನ್ ಒಫ್ ಆರ್ಕ್' ಪುಸ್ತಕಾಂ ಭಾಶಾಂತರ್ ಕೆಲ್ಯಾತ್.

ಸುನಂದಾನ್ ಜೇಮ್ಸ್ ಕ್ಲ್ಯಾಬೆಲ್ ಹಾಚಿ King Rat ಮ್ಹಳ್ಳಿ ಲಾಂಬ್ ಕತಾ 'ರಾಯ್ ಉಂದಿರ್' ನಾಂವಾನ್ ತರ್ಜಣ್ ಕೆಲ್ಯಾ. (1991)

ಸೋನಿಯಾ ದೆ' ಕೊಸ್ತಾನ್ 'ಝುಲೊ' ಪತ್ರಾರ್ ಠಾಗೋರಾಚ್ಯೊ ಮಟ್ವ್ಯೊ ಕಾಣ್ಯೊ ಭಾಶಾಂತರ್ ಕರ್ನ್ ಛಾಯ್ಸ್ ಕೆಲ್ಯಾತ್. ತ್ಯೊ ಹ್ಯೆ ಪರಿಂ ಆಸಾತ್: ಕಾಬೂಲಿವಾಲ, ಪೋಸ್ಟ್ ಮಾಸ್ಟರ್, ರುಕ್ಮಿಣಿಚೊ ಪೂತ್, ಪಾಟಿಂ ಘರಾ, ನಯಂಜೂರ್ಚೆ ಬಾಬು, ಸುಭಾ, ಥೊಡ್ಯೊ ಝುನ್ ಕತಾಯಿ ತರ್ಜುಮೊ ಕೆಲ್ಲ್ಯೊ ತ್ಯೊ ಝುಲೊ ಪತ್ರಾಚೆರ್ ಪರ್ಗಟ್ಲ್ಯಾತ್: ಸರ್ಗಾಚೆಂ ದಾರ್, ಶಿಮ್ಪಿ ಆನಿ ತಕ್ಲಿ, ಮಾಣ್ಕ್ಯಾಂಚೆಂ ಲಿಸಾಂವ್ ಆನಿ ರಡ್ಕುರಿ ಮಾತಾರಿ.

ಜೂಡಿ ಪಿಂಟೊನ್ ಹಿಂದಿ ಭಾಶೆಚಾ ಪ್ರಖ್ಯಾತ್ ಸಾಹಿತಿಂಚ್ಯೊ ಕಾಣಿಯೊ ಕೊಂಕ್ಣೆಕ್ ಭಾಶಾಂತರ್ ಕೆಲ್ಲ್ಯೊ 'ರಾಕ್ಣೊ' ಆನಿ 'ಆಮ್ಚೊ ಯುವಕ್' ಪತ್ರಾರ್ ಪರ್ಗಟ್ಲ್ಯಾತ್.

ತೊ ಪಾಟಿಂ ಗೆಲೊ – ಮೂಳ್ ಬರೊಪ್ಪಿ: ಉಷಾ ಪ್ರಿಯಂವದಾ

ವೇಳ್–ಯಶ್‌ಪಾಲ್

ಪಡ್ದೊ–ಯಶ್‌ಪಾಲ್

ಪಶ್ಚಾತ್ತಾಪ್–ಪ್ರೇಮ್‌ಚಂದ್

ಭೊಲಾರಾಮಾಚೊ ಪ್ರಾಣ್–ಹರಿಶಂಕರ್ ಪರ್ಸಾಯಿ

ಹಾಂವ್ ದೆವಾಚೊ ಪೆಟೊ–ಮೋಹನ್ ರಾಕೇಶ್

ಸಜಾ– ಮನ್ನು ಭಂಡಾರಿ

ಆಪ್ಲೊ ಪೆಲೊ–ಜೈನೇಂದ್ರ್ ಕುಮಾರ್

ವಿಲ್‌ಫ್ರೆಡ್ ಲೋಬೊ, ಪಡೀಲ್ ಹಾಣೆ ನಾಗತಿಹಳ್ಳಿ ಚಂದ್ರಶೇಖರಾಚಿ 'ಮಲೆನಾಡಿನ ಹುಡುಗಿ' ಕತಾ 'ಮೊಜಾ ಮೊಗಾಚೆಂ ಚೆಡುಂ' ನಾಂವಾನ್ ಅಣ್ಕಾರ್ ಕೆಲ್ಯಾ. ಅನುಜಯ ಕುಮಟೇಕರಾಚಿ ಕೃತಿ 'ವೋಂಯ್‌ಂತ್ಲೆಂ ಫುಲ್' ಜಾವ್ನ್ ಆನಿ ನಾ. ಡಿ'ಸೋಜಾಚಿ ನಾಂವಾಡ್ದಿಕ್ ಕಾದಂಬರಿ 'ಇಗರ್ಜಿಯ ಸುತ್ತಲಿನ ಹತ್ತು ಮನೆಗಳು' 'ಇಗರ್ಜೆಚಾ ಭೊಂವ್ತಿಂಚಿ ಧಾ ಘರಾಂ' ನಾಂವಾನ್ ಭಾಶಾಂತರ್ ಕೆಲ್ಯಾ (2004).

ಜೈಸನ್ ಸುವಾರೆಸ್ ತಾಕೊಡೆ ಹಾಣೆ ನಾಗತಿಹಳ್ಳಿ ಚಂದ್ರಶೇಖರಾಚ್ಯೊ ಮಟ್ವ್ಯೊ ಕಾಣಿಯೊ ಅಣ್ಕಾರ್ ಕರ್ನ್ 'ವಾದಾಳಾಂ' ನಾಂವಾಚೊ ಬೂಕ್ ಪರ್ಗಟ್ಲಾ. (2004) ಮೆಲ್‌ಕ ಮಿಯಾರ್ ಹಾಣೆ ಜಾನಕಿ ಬ್ರಹ್ಮಾವರ್ ಹಾಚಿ 'ಕುದುರುದ ಕೇದಗೆ' ಕಾಣಿ 'ಕುದ್ರ್ಯಾ ಭಿತರ್' ನಾಂವಾನ್ ಭಾಶಾಂತರ್ ಕೆಲ್ಯಾ. (2003)

ಶ್ರೀ ಜೆ. ಬಿ. ಮೊರಾಯಸ್ ನ್ಯಾಶನಲ್ ರೆಜಿಸ್ಟರ್ ಒಫ್ ಟ್ರಾನ್ಸ್‌ಲೇಟರ್ಸ್ ಹಾಂತುಂ ದಾಖಲ್ ಜಾಲ್ಲೊ ಅಣ್ಕಾರ್ ಸಾಹಿತಿ ಜಾವ್ನಾಸಾ. ಡೊ। ಶಿವರಾಮ ಕಾರಂತ ಹಾಚಿ 'ಚೋಮನ ದುಡಿ' ಕನ್ನಡ ಕಾದಂಬರಿ 'ಅಂತ್ಯ್ ನಾತ್‌ಲ್ಲೆಂ ಸಪಾಣ್' ನಾಂವಾನ್ 'ಪಯ್ಣಾರಿ' ಹಪ್ತ್ಯಾಳ್ಯಾರ್ ಛಾಯ್ಸ್ ಜಾಲ್ಲಿ. ಜೇಮ್ಸ್ ಹ್ಯಾಡ್ಲಿ, ಚೇಜಾಚ್ಯೊ ದೋನ್ ಇಂಗ್ಲಿಷ್ ಕಾದಂಬರಿಯೊ ಕೊಂಕ್ಣಿಂತ್ ರುಪಾಂತರ್ ಕೆಲ್ಯಾತ್. ಪಯ್ಲಿ 'ಪಯ್ಣಾರಿ' ಹಫ್ತ್ಯಾಳ್ಯಾಂತ್ 'ನಿಸ್ರಾಲ್ಲ್ಯಾಕ್ ಲೊಟುನ್ ಘಾಲೊ' ನಾಂವಾನ್ ಆನಿ ಉಪ್ರಾಂತ್ 1995 ವರ್ಸಾ 'ಚಿಂತ್ಲೆಂ

ಕಿತೆಂ ಜಾಲೆಂ ಕಿತೆಂ' ನಾಂವಾನ್ 'ದಿವೊ' ಹಫ್ತ್ಯಾಳ್ಯಾರ್ ಪರ್ಗಟ್ ಜಾಲ್ಲ್ಯೊ. ದುಸ್ರಿ ಕಾದಂಬರಿ 'ಬೊಲ್ಷ್ಯಾ ಮಧ್ಲಿ ಶೆಳಿ' ನಾಂವಾನ್ 'ಪಯ್ಣಾರಿ' ಹಫ್ತ್ಯಾಳ್ಯಾರ್ ಫಾಯ್ಸ್ ಜಾಲ್ಲಿ. ಅರ್ಥರ್ ಕೆನೊನ್ ಡೊಯ್ಲ್ ಹಾಚ್ಯೊ ಲೊಕಾಮೊಗಾಳ್ ಶೆರ್ಲೊಕ್ ಹೋಮ್ಸ್ ಕಾಣ್ಯೊ ಜರ್ಲೊ ಗೋಮ್ಸ್ ನಾಂವಾನ್ ರುಪಾಂತರ್ ಕರ್ನ್ 'ರಾಕ್ಣೊ' ಹಫ್ತ್ಯಾಳ್ಯಾರ್ ಫಾಯ್ಸ್ ಕೆಲ್ಲ್ಯೊ. ಹಿಂದಿ, ಕನ್ನಡಾಂತ್ಲ್ಯೊ ಮಟ್ವ್ಯೊ ಕಾಣಿಯೊ ಆನಿ ಓ. ಹೆನ್ರಿಚೊ ಇಂಗ್ಲಿಷ್ ಕಾಣಿಯೊ ಕೊಂಕ್ಣೆಕ್ ರುಪಾಂತರ್ ಕೆಲ್ಯಾತ್. 1954 –ಂತ್ ಶೇಕ್ಸ್‌ಪಿಯರಾಚಾ ರೋಮಿಯೊ ಜ್ಯೂಲಿಯೆಟ್ ನಾಟಕಾಚೊ ಮಟ್ವೊ ಅಣ್ಕಾರ್ ಪರ್ಗಟ್ ಕೆಲ್ಲೊ.

ಸಿರಿಲ್ ಜಿ. ಸಿಕ್ವೇರಾನ್ (ಸಿಜೈಸ್) ಕನ್ನಡ ಲೇಖಿಕಿ ತ್ರಿವೇಣಿಚಿ 'ಬೆಕ್ಕಿನ ಕಣ್ಣು' ಕೃತಿ 'ಜೀವನ್ ತುಫಾನ್' ನಾಂವಾನ್ ಅಣ್ಕಾರ್ ಕೆಲ್ಯಾ. DYSP ರಾಮಯ್ಯಾನ್ ಬರಯಿಲ್ಲಿ 'ತಲೆಬುರುಡೆ ಬಿಡಿಸಿದ ಕೊಲೆ ರಹಸ್ಯ' ಪತ್ತೇದಾರಿ ಕಾದಂಬರಿ 'ಪೆರಿಸ್' ನಾಂವಾನ್ ಕೊಂಕ್ಣೆಕ್ ಉತ್ರಾಯ್ಲ್ಯಾ. ಹೆರ್ ಮಟ್ವ್ಯೊ ಕಾಣಿಯೊ ಕನ್ನಡ ಆನಿ ಇಂಗ್ಲಿಷಾ ಥಾವ್ನ್ ಕೊಂಕ್ಣೆಕ್ ತರ್ಜುಮೊ ಕೆಲ್ಯಾತ್.

ಕವಿತಾ/ಕಾವ್ಯ್ ಭಾಶಾಂತರ್

ಅಲಂಕಾರ್, ಪ್ರತಿಮಾ, ವಾಚ್ಯಾರ್ತ್, ಧ್ವನ್ಯಾರ್ತ್ ಭಾವಾರ್ತ್ ಆನಿ ಛಂದ್ ಆಟಾಪುನ್ ಆಸ್ಚೆಂ ಕಾವ್ಯ್ ಆನಿ ಕವಿತಾ ಅನುವಾದ್ ಕರ್ಚೆಂ ಎಕಾ ಕವಿ ವರ್ವಿಂ ಮಾತ್ರ್ ಸಾಧ್ಯ್. ಹೊ ವಾವ್ರ್ Transcreation ಮ್ಹಣ್ಯೆತ್. ಕವಿತೆಂತ್ ಆಸ್ಚೆ ಸಬ್ದ್ 'ಜಿವಾಳ್' ಜಾವ್ನಾಸಾತ್. ವಾಕ್ಸರಿ (ಸಬ್ದ್‌ಕೋಶ್) ಪಳೆವ್ನ್ ಅರ್ಥ್ ಸಮ್ಜೊನ್ ಕವಿತಾ ಭಾಶಾಂತರ್ ಕರುಂಕ್ ಜಾಯ್ನಾ. ಮೂಳ್‌ಕವಿ ತ್ಯಾ ಕಾವ್ಯಾಂತ್ ಕಸಲಿಂ ಭೊಗ್ಣಾಂ ವೆಕ್ತ್ ಕರ್‍ತಾ, ತಿಂ ವೆಕ್ ಕರುಂಕ್ ಕಸಲಿಂ ಪ್ರತಿಮಾ ವಾಪರ್‍ತಾ ಆನಿ ಹ್ಯಾ ಪಾಸತ್ ತಾಣೆ ವಿಂಚ್ಲ್ಲೆ ಸಬ್ದ್ ಕಸಲೆ, ತೆ ಸಬ್ದ್ ತಾಣೆ ಕಸಲ್ಯಾ ಬಾಂಧಾವಳಿಂತ್ ಘುಂತ್ಲ್ಯಾಂತ್, ಹ್ಯಾ ವರ್ವಿಂ ಜಾಂವ್ಚೊ ಅನ್ಭೋಗ್ ಕಸಲೊ ಹೆಂ ಸರ್ವ್ ಜಿಕ್ಲ್ಯಾರ್ ಮಾತ್ರ್ ತೆಂ ಕಾವ್ಯ್ ಭಾಶಾಂತರ್ ಕರುಂಕ್ ಜಾತಾ. ಕವಿತಾ ಲ್ಹಾನ್ ವ ವ್ಹಡ್ ಜಾವ್ನಾಸ್ಯೆತ್. ತಾಚೆ ಪಾಟ್ಲ್ಯಾನ್ ಕವಿ ಪ್ರತಿಪಾದನ್ ಕರ್ಚೆಂ ಮಹತ್ವಾಚೆಂ ಸಿದ್ಧಾಂತ್ ವ ತತ್ವ್ ಆಟಾಪುನ್ ಆಸ್ಯೆತ್. ಅನುವಾದಕಾನ್ ಹೆಂ ಸರ್ವ್ ಪಾರ್ಖುಂಚೆಂ ಗರ್ಜೆಚೆಂ.

ಕವಿತಾ ಭಾಶಾಂತರ್ ಅಸಾಧ್ಯ್. ತ್ಯೊ ಅನುವಾದ್ ಮಾತ್ರ್ ಕರ್ಯೆತ್. ಆನಿ ಹೆಂ ಅನುವಾದ್ ನವಿ ಸೃಷ್ಟಿ ಜಾತಾ. ಮೂಳ್ ಕವಿಚಾ ಭೊಗ್ಣಾಂಕ್ ಆನಿ ಕವಿತ್ವಾಕ್ ನ್ಯಾಯ್ ದೀವ್ನ್ ಶೆವೊಟ್ ಭಾಶೆಂತ್ ಕರ್ಚಿ ಸೃಷ್ಟಿ ಹಿ. ಭೋವ್ ಸೂಕ್ಷಿಮಾಯೆಚೊ ವಾವ್ರ್ ಹೊ. ತರೀ ಮೂಳ್ ಕವಿತೆಕ್ ವ ಕಾವ್ಯಾಕ್ ಸಮಾಸಮ್ ಜಾಯ್ನಾ. ಸಂಪೂರ್ಣ್‌ಕಾಯೆಕ್ ಮಾಗಿರೀ ಅವ್ಕಾಸ್ ಉರ್‍ತಾತ್.

ಕನ್ನಡ ಸಾಹಿತ್ಯಾಂತ್ ಕವಿ ಬಿ. ಎಂ. ಶ್ರೀಕಂಠಯ್ಯಾನ್ 'ಇಂಗ್ಲಿಷ್ ಗೀತೆಗಳು' ಕವಿತಾ ಅಣ್ಕಾರ್ ಸಂಗ್ರಹ್ ಪರ್ಗಟುನ್ ನವಿ ದಿಶಾ ಆನಿ ಸಾಧ್ಯತಾ ದಾಖಯಿಲ್ಲಿ. ಕೊಂಕ್ಣೆಂತ್ ಭಜನಾಂ, ದೋಹೆ, ಪ್ರಾರ್ತನ್ ಗಿತಾಂ ಅನುವಾದ್ ಕೆಲ್ಯಾಂತ್. ಬೈಬಲಾಂತ್ಲಿಂ ಕೀರ್ತನಾಂ ಅನುವಾದ್ ಕೆಲ್ಯಾಂತ್ ವಿಲ್ಯಮ್ ದ ಸಿಲ್ವಾ ಆನಿ ವಿಲ್ಯಮ್ ಬಾರ್ಬೋಜ ಹಾಣಿಂ.

ಕನ್ನಡ ಕವಿ ಎಮ್. ಗೋವಿಂದ ಪೈನ್ ಕನ್ನಡ ಭಾಶೆಂತ್ ಲಿಖ್ಲ್ಲೆಂ ನೀಳ್ಗವನ್ 'ಗೊಲ್ಗೊಥಾ' ಎಡ್ವರ್ಡ್ ನೊರೊನ್ಹಾಚ್ಯೆ ಲಿಖ್ಣೆದ್ವಾರಿಂ 'ಜೆಜುಚೊ ನಿಮಾಣೊ ದೀಸ್' ನಾಂವಾರ್ ಅಣ್ಕಾರ್ ಕೆಲಾಂ (1983) ಹೆಂ ಮಹಾನ್ ಸಾಧನ್ ಜಾವ್ನಾಸಾ.

...ಸಿರಿಲ್ ಜಿ. ಸಿಕ್ವೇರಾನ್ ಇಂಗ್ಲಿಷ್ ಕವಿತಾ ಕೊಂಕ್ಣೆಂತ್ ಅನುವಾದ್ ಕೆಲ್ಯಾತ್. ಕವಿ ಮೌರಿಸ್ ಡೆಸಾನ್ ಸಬಾರ್ ಕವಿತಾ ಅಣ್ಕಾರ್ ಕರ್ನ್ ಪತ್ರಾಂನಿ ಫಾಯ್ಸ್ ಕೆಲ್ಯಾತ್.

ಫ್ರಾನ್ಸಿಸ್ ಡಿ'ಕುನ್ಹಾನ್ ಪಂಜೆ ಮಂಗೇಶ್‌ರಾವ್‌ಚಿ 'ತೆಂಕಣ ಗಾಳಿಯೂಟ' ಕವಿತಾ 'ತೆನ್ಕಾಚೆಂ ವಾದಾಳ್' ನಾಂವಾನ್ ಅನುವಾದ್ ಕೆಲ್ಯಾ. ವಾಚ್ಪ್ಯಾಂನಿ ಮೂಳ್ ಆನಿ ಅಣ್ಕಾರ್ ಭಾಗ್ ವಾಚ್ಲ್ಯಾರ್ ಅನುವಾದಾಚಿ ರೂಚ್ ಪಾರ್ಕಿಯೆತ್.

...ರವೀಂದ್ರನಾಥ ಠಾಗೊರಾಚೆಂ 'where the mind is' ಇಂಗ್ಲಿಷಾಂತ್, ಕನ್ನಡಾಂತ್ ಎಮ್. ಎನ್. ಕಾಮತಾನ್ ಅನುವಾದ್ ಕೆಲ್ಲೆಂ 'ಎಲ್ಲಿ ಮ ... ನಕಳುಕಿರದೊ...' ಗೀತ್ ಹೆಚ್. ರಾಘವೇಂದ್ರ ರಾವಾನ್ ಕೊಂಕ್ಣೆಕ್ ಅಣ್ಕಾರ್ ಕೆಲಾಂ.

PART FOUR

Selected Essays on the Cultural Politics of Transcription/Translation

This part comprises a selection of essays discussing different aspects of translation and transliteration in the context of Konkani. These have been divided into two sections, the first of which focuses on questions of script. The second section comprises essays that discuss cultural questions raised by translated texts, from manuals of confession, to the appearance of Konkani dialects in the earliest Marathi text printed in Goa, to questions of literary history. While some of these essays have been published before, others are original contributions to this volume.

S. M. Borges' article in Section I discusses two schemes for the transliteration of Marathi/Konkani and Portuguese religious terms in the Marathi *Kristapurana* of 1616. The text is significant in the light of later usages by indigenous Christians and the changing opinions regarding appropriate religious terms. Excerpts from Narayan B. Desai's PhD thesis, 'Politics of script: The Case Of Konkani (1961–1992)', illuminate contexts and phases of translation across Karnataka and Goa. Desai has a detailed account of the different caste interests, religious differences and questions of dialect that arose when particular sets of texts were translated. The excerpts from Jason Keith Fernandes' thesis, 'Citizenship Experiences of the Goan Catholics' complement Desai's work and draw attention to moments within the language movement and the nature of organisations and formations that emerged. The excerpts highlight the significance of linguistic geographies as they were imagined and used to harness support and carve out a community for the advocacy of the language.

Dr. Victor Ferrao's unpublished essay reads translation as a process in cultural politics through which subjectivities are formed and contested. His essay deploys theories that focus on the ambivalent nature of colonial power and subject formation under colonial rule. It suggests that Goan cultural politics is formed by a convergence of two processes of cultural translation, the Portuguese approach to colonial difference and the once remored but more influential epistemological constructions of the British colonial power. Dale Luis Menezes' essay 'Between Language and Scripts: The Controversies of Konkani Revisited' focuses significantly on recurring patterns in the manner in which different groups within Goa and Bombay articulated their positions in relation to language. This essay also suggests a shift in the manner in which contemporary linguistic politics is imagined and articulated.

In Section II, Teotonio de Souza's article, "*Confessionários*" or Manuals of Confession – missionary tools and their colonial uses: the case study of Goa', is an English adaptation of the original essay in Portuguese. De Souza provides a commentary on the creation of the *confessionário* in Konkani to facilitate a minimal conversation between priests new to the language and new converts. His essay examines the questionnaires that would guide conversation on principles of Christian doctrine. Vidya Pai's essay, 'Translation of Culture' is noteworthy for being a contribution by a translator. The essay discusses the decisions that have to be made when translating across cultures, where words and names that denote attitudes, practices and beliefs have to be conveyed at length in another cultural idiom, or have no equivalent that allows for meaning to travel. William Madtha's and Melvyn Rodrigues' essays assert the importance of translation for the growth of any literature, and the range of experiences and thoughts that are drawn into each language through translation. A second essay by S. M. Borges translated as *'Occurrence of Salcete Konkani Vocables and Dialectal Forms in the Kristapurana'* contends that although Thomas Stephens' *Kristapurana* is presented as a Marathi work, it abounds in Konkani words and phrases, which are currently in vogue in the Salcete taluka of Goa where Stephens spent much of his time. Lastly, Pratap Naik's *'Bhashantharachim Thathvamani Kala'* (Principles of Translation and Art) discusses translated literature as a third category of literature, with folklore being the first and creative literature being the second. He examines the different words used to designate 'translation' in Konkani and their connotations.

Section I

S. M. Borges translated R. N. Naik's biography, Shenoi Goembab *for the Sahitya Akademi in 2007. He published* The Triumph of Konkani – A Translation of Shenoy Goembab's Konkani Bhashechem Zoit *at New Age Printers, Goa in 2003. He was associated in an editorial capacity with the Konkani journals* Dalgadacho Sondex *and* Gulab *and contributed to the volume,* Dalgado on Konkani: A Translation of Msgr. S.R. Dalgado's Introductions to his Dictionaries *published in 2008. He also assisted in the preparation of English-Konkani vocabularies of administrative, legislative and scientific terms, initiated by the Department of Official Language, Govt. of Goa and the National Translation Mission, CIIL, Mysore.*

Evropev padrinim vaprillio lipyantarachio paddati

(Transliteration schemes devised by European missionaries)

This article discusses the schemes employed by European priests who worked in Goa during the sixteenth century to use the Roman alphabet for the transliteration of local languages. The Kristapurana*, published in 1616 in Marathi, has been the focus of linguistic study, transliteration and translation projects across the centuries. This article contends that it contains two distinct schemes, one for Marathi/Konkani words and another for (Portuguese) religious terms.*

एवरोपेव पाद्रींनी वापरिल्ल्यो लिप्यांतराच्यो पद्धती - प्रा. से. मा. बॉर्जिस

सोळाव्या शेंकड्यांत एवरोपेव पाद्री गोंयां आयले तेन्ना थळाव्यो भासो शिकचे खातीर तांकां त्या त्या भासांतलीं उतरां बरोवन घेवप अनिवार्य आसलें. पूण त्या काळावेल्या गोंयांत तीन, आपसांत सामक्यो वेगळ्यो, थळाव्यो लिपी चालंत आशिल्ल्यो.[1] सुरवेकच तीन वेगळ्यो लिपी शिकप म्हळ्यार कोणाकूय कटकटीचें दिसतलेंच. हाचे परस आपली संवकळीची रोमी लिपी वापरप अदीक सोयिस्कर थारलें, हातूंत दुभाव ना. पूण रोमी लिपीची एक मोटी अडचण म्हळ्यार तातूंतल्या लेत्रांक (वर्णांक) आपलो असो खास उच्चार ना; तो भाशेकणकणीं बदलता आनी कांय लेत्रांचे उच्चार तर एकेच भाशेंत लेगीत उतरांकणकणीं बदलतात.

रोमी लिपींत भासो बरयतात तांच्या उच्चारक्रमांची तुळना केली जाल्यार पुर्तुगेजीचो क्रम सगळ्यांत सोंपो थारता, आनी लातीं भाशेच्या क्रमाक तो बरोच लागीं आसा. शिवाय त्या सगळ्या पाद्रींक पुर्तुगेज आनी लातीं भासो येताल्यो. हें सगळें मतींत धरून तांणी पुर्तुगेज क्रम पत्करलो आनी ते भाशेंत वापरताले त्याच लेत्रांचो उपेग केलो : **a** [पुर्तुगेज नांव आ], **b** [बे], **c** [से], **d** [दे], **e** [ऍं], **f** [एफ्], **g** [जे], **h** [आगा], **i** [ई], **l** [एल्], **m** [एम्], **n** [एन्], **o** [ऑ], **p** [पे], **q** [के], **r** [एर्], **s** [एस्], **t** [ते], **u** [ऊ], **x** [शींज्], **y** [इग्रेग्], **z** [ज़े]. पुर्तुगेजींत वापरिनात त्या **k** [का] आनी **w** [दाब्लू] लेत्रांक सुवात दिली ना. हांचे शिवाय पुर्तुगेजींत कांय स्वरभार कुरवो [आसेंत], आनी स्वरभेदचिन्नां आसात. ख्रिस्तपुराणांत हांतली फकत ˜ [तील] आनी ç [सेसेदील] हींच वापरल्यांत. (हातबरपांनी तांणी ^ [आसँतु सिर्कुंफ्लॅक्सु] आनी ˘ [ब्रॅवि], ह्योय कुरवो वापरल्यात. घडये छापखान्यांत तांकां त्यो कुरवो मेळूंक नांत वा तांचो अभाव आशिल्लो जायत; ब्रॅवि तर आयजूय मेळना खंय. अशें आसुनय प्रियोळकर हांणी केल्ल्या 'दौत्रिन ख्रिस्तां'च्या देवनागरी लिप्यंतरांत, थंय e-चेर प्रत्यक्ष ब्रॅवि नासुनय, ती सारकी पारखिल्या. Raze, S*a*temanitam, divedan*a* हीं राज्य, सत्यमानितां, दिव्यदान अशीं लिप्यांतरीत केल्यांत.[2] ब्रागा ग्रंथालयांत मेळ्ळ्या ते बरपावळींत S*a*hinĕ (सहिन्य), R*â*zĕ (राज्य), M*a*chhĕg*a*nd*â* (मछ्यगंदा) अशीं उतरां

आडळटात.[3] 'ख्रिस्तपुराणां'त sixe (सिष्य) S*a*teu*a*ntu (सत्यवंतु) असलीं साबार उतरां e-चेर ब्रॅवि नासताना मेळटात. गोंयचे भाशेच्या मानान पुर्जुगेज भाशेंतले ध्वनी खुबच कमी आसात. देखून चडावत तरतुदी आनी तडजोडी करून ही समस्या तांणी सोडयली; कोंकणी खातीर एक नवो रोमी बरपाक्रम विकसीत केलो. फुडें वचून तांणी महाभारत आनी रामायणांतल्यो क था आनी मराठी कविता वाचून/ सांगून घेतल्यो आनी त्यो ह्या नव्या क्रमापरमाणें बरोवन काडल्यो. विसाव्या शेंकड्यांत हीं हातबरपां पुर्तुगालच्या ब्रागा ग्रंथालयांत मेळ्ळीं (ब्रागा बरपावळ) तांचो, आनी सतराव्या शेंकड्यांत छापिल्ल्या पुस्तकांचो, अभ्यास करून कांय विद्वानांनी त्या क्रमाची लिप्यांतर पद्दत सुटावी करपाचे यत्न केल्यात.[4]

पुर्तुगेजींत ˜ (तील) ही कुरू वापरून अनुस्वार व्यक्त करतात. ही कुरू एका स्वराचेर दवरल्यार तो नाकयो जाता, आनी ताचेर स्वरभारूय आपसूक येताः acensão (आसेंसांव), manhã (माय्न्यां). ही कुरू कोंकणी-मराठी उतरां खातीरय वापरल्या : *tãua* (तंव), dogã (दोगां). पुर्तुगेजींत m आनी n ह्या व्यंजनांचोय अनुस्वरा खातीर वापर जाता. b आनी p ह्या व्यंजनां आदीं अनुस्वार येता तेन्ना m जाल्यार हेर कडेन n : campo (कांपु), jantar (ज्यांतार). ही तराय कोंकणी-मराठी उतरां खातीर वापरल्या : S*a*mbh*a*v*a*la (संभवला), ch*a*ndru (चंद्रु).

आयज आमी देवनागरी लिपींत कोंकणी बरयतात तेन्ना विशेशनामां आनी तत्सम संस्कृत उतरां खातीर नेम शिथील करतात, तीं उतरां संस्कृतांतले वरीच बरयतात. होच तर्क त्या पाद्रींनीय वापरिल्लो दिश्टी पडटा. "ख्रिस्तपुराणां'त साबार पुर्तुगेज उतरां आनी विशेशनामां आयल्यांत; तीं पुर्तुगेजींतल्या वरीच बरयल्यांत, कोंकणी खातीर विकसीत केल्ल्या क्रमांत न्हय. देखून तीं वाचताना पुर्तुगेज क्रमूच वापरचो लागता आनी कोंकणी क्रम वापरल्यार घोळ जावंयेता. ह्या वावराखातीर तांणी पुर्तुगेज आनी कोंकणी भासांच्या ध्वनीविन्यासाचो विस्तृत अभ्यासूच न्हय तर कोंकणीच्या खाशेलपणांचेरय खोलायेन विचार केल्ल्याचो भास जाता. हाका लागून तांचे यत्न बरेच सुफळ जाले, कुरू आनी ध्वनी हांचो सुमेळ घालपांत तांकां बरेंच यश लाबलें. अग्रेसर यत्नांच्या ह्या तांच्या फळांत कांय त्रुटी उरल्यो, कांय उच्चार स्पश्टपणीं वेगळावंक जमलें ना, हें खरें आसल्यारय, कांय शेंकडे उपरांत, आनी साबार चडावत कुरवो वापरून, संस्कृत भाशेखातीर विकसीत केल्ल्या रोमी क्रमांचे तुळणेंत तो जबर सो फाटीं पडना. तशें पळेल्यार एक भास बरोवंचो खंयचेच लिपींतलो क्रम परिपूर्ण नासता. देवनागरी लिपींत कोंकणी बरोवंचो क्रम लेगीत हाका अपवाद ना. देखून शुद्धलेखन नेमांची दुरुस्ती परपरत करची पडटा, हें विसरचें न्हय.

पुर्तुगेज आनी कोंकणी बरपाक्रम – वेगळेपणां :

पुर्तुगेज बरपाक्रमाचो खोलायेन अभ्यास करूनच पाद्रींनी क्रम विकसीत केला, हातूंत मातूय दुभाव ना. दोनूय क्रम वापरताना कमींत कमी गोंदळ जावचो हेखातीर तांणी बरीच जतनाय घेतली.

एका बरपाक्रमांत प्रत्येक उच्चाराक एक बरपी कुरू आनी प्रत्येक कुरवेक एक उच्चार आसलो जाल्यार तो क्रम उत्तम आनी आदर्श थारता. पुर्तुगेज भाशेचें बरोवप आनी उच्चार तपासल्यार हो आदर्श बऱ्याच प्रमाणान साध्य जाला सो दिसता. तरूय क ांय कांय लेत्रां आसात जांचे उच्चार सान्निध्या प्रमाणें बदलतात, म्हणजे आजूबाजूचीं लेत्रां त्या लेत्राचो उच्चार थारायतात. हीं अथीर उच्चाराचीं लेत्रां म्हळ्यार a, e, o हे स्वर आनी c, g, s हीं व्यंजनां. हीं स वगळून उरिल्लीं 18 लेत्रां "एका वर्णाक एक उच्चार' हो नेम पाळटात. तांचे पुर्तुगेज उच्चार कोंकणी उतरां खातीरय कायम दवरल्यात. ते अशे : b = ब्, d = द्, f = फ् (फक्त पुर्तुगेज उतरां खातीर वापरलां), h = ह्, i = इ, j = ज्य् (फक्त पुर्तुगेज उतरां खातीर वापरलां), l = ल्, m = म्, n = न्, p = प्, qu = क्, r = र्, t = त्, u = उ, v = व्, x = ष्, y = य्, z = ज्. दोन लेत्रां स्वर आनी व्यंजन म्हणनूय घोळटात : u = उ/व् आनी y = ई/य्. दोन अनुनासीक व्यंजनां m आनी n अनुस्वाराचीय भुमिका करतात.

पुर्तुगेजींत h मोनें आसता, ताका उच्चार ना. पूण कोंकणी खातीर ताका इंग्लिशींतलो ह् उच्चार घेतला. पुर्तुगेजींत एकूय म्हाप्राण ना, पूण कोंकणींत खुबच आसात. ही अडचण निवारूंक त्या त्या व्यंजनाक h जोडला : bh = भ्, gh = घ्, ph = फ्, qh = ख्, th = थ्, zh = झ्. पुर्तुगेजींत ट्, ड्, ळ् आनी ण् हांचे पर्याय मेळनांत. ते दाखोवंक तीं तीं व्यंजन लेत्रां दोट्टी बरयल्यांत. tt = ट्, tth = ठ्, dd = ड्, ddh = ढ्, ll = ळ, nn = ण्. (जेन्ना उतर पुर्तुगेज आसता तेन्ना त्या उतरांत ह्या निमाण्याचो उच्चार न्न् जाता, देखीक Manna मान्ना, Anna आन्ना; पूण ann*a* हे कोंकणी/मराठी उतर आसता तेन्ना ताचो उच्चार आण असो जाता.)

आयज जितल्याय पुर्तुगेज उतरांनी फ् उच्चार जाता, थंय f-च वापरतात. पूण "ख्रिस्तपुराणां'त हें लेत्र कोंकणी-मराठी उतरां खातीर वापरूंक ना; फक्त तें वापरून त्या काळार जीं पुर्तुगेज उतरां बरयताले तितल्या पुरतेंच मर्यादीत दवरलां : confess*a*rī (काँफेसरीं), Luciferu (लुसिफेरु). कोंकणी-मराठी उतरां खातीर ph च वापरलां : ph*a*ll*a* (फळ), phouzancha (फौजांचा), phuddã (फुडां). कांय पुर्तुगेज उतरां खातीरय ph वापरलां. त्या काळार हीं उतरां ph वापरुनच बरयताले. मों. दालगादाच्या, 1905 वर्सा उजवाडायल्ल्या, पुर्तुगेज-कोंकणी कोशांतूय हीं उतरां ph वापरून बरयल्यांत.[5] पूण 1911 वर्सा सावन पुर्तुगेजींत ही चाल मोडली. "ख्रिस्तपुराणां'तलीं असलीं कांय उतरां म्हळ्यार prophet*a*

(प्रॉफेत), pharizeu*a* (फारिजेव), Capharnaũ (काफार्नाऊं) हीं आसात. इंग्लिश उतरांचे मदेकत स्वरा विरेत n येता तेन्ना ताचो उच्चार न् असो करतात. पूण पुर्तुगेजींत (आनी हांगा कोंकणी-मराठींतय) ताचो अनुस्वारूच जाता. देखून confessor हें कॉंफेसोर अशेंच वाचचें आसता, इंग्लिशींत उच्चारतात तशें कॉन्फॅसर न्हय.

सुरवेच्या काळांत (सत्राव्या शेंकड्याचे सुरवाते मेरेन तरी) रोमी लिपींत j (ज्यॉत) लेत्र नाशिल्लें; तें i लेत्राचीच एक तरा म्हणून विकसित जालें आनी ताचो उच्चारूय इ (स्वर) य् (व्यंजन) असोच जातालो. उपरांत ताका ज्य् उच्चार लाभलो. 1616 वर्सा उजवाडायल्ल्या "ख्रिस्तपुराणां'त ताचो वापर क्वचित जाला खरो, पूण 1611 सालांत जें इंग्लिश बायबल उजवाडा आयल्लें तातूंत Jesu हे नांव लेगीत Iesu अशेंच बरयल्लें मेळटा. त्या बायबलांत j वापरलेंच ना. "ख्रिस्तपुराणां'त Jesu (जेजू) आनी anj*a* (आंज्य) ही उतरां आयल्यांत. जाल्यार इग्रेज्य हें Igrei*a* आनी Igrej*a* अशेंय बरयलां. "दौत्रिन ख्रिस्तां" ह्या थॉमस स्टीफन्सच्या पुस्तकांत (1622), Jesu हें IESV अशेंच बरयल्लें मेळटा. इल्लें इल्लें करून व्यंजनी J-क ज्य-चो उच्चार कायम जालो. "ख्रिस्तपुराणां'त मेळटात तीं व्यंजनी I-न सुरू जावपी साबार विशेशनामां आयचे पुर्तुगेजींत J-न सुरू जातात : Ioaõ - João ज्युआंव), Iordaõ - Jordão (ज्यॉर्दांव).

त्या सुरवातेच्या काळांत u आनी v ही वेग्ळीं लेत्रां म्हूण घोळनाशिल्लीं; धाकट्या लेत्रा खातीर u जाल्यार कॅपिटल लेत्रा खातीर V वापरताले, आनी दोनांकय ऊ म्हणटाले. पोरण्या थडग्यांचेर नदर मारल्यारय हें स्पश्ट दिसून येता. थंय U चे बदला V-च दिश्टी पडटा, U मेळना. ब्रागा बरपावळींत v मेळच ना म्हणल्यार जाता; थंय उतराचे सुरवेक लेगीत u-च वापरलां. म्हणजे सोळाव्या शेंकड्यांत v विकसीत जावंक ना. सतराव्या शेंकड्यांत उजवाडायल्ल्या "ख्रिस्तपुराणांत' हीं दोनूय लेत्रां आयल्यांत खरीं पूण तांचे उच्चार मात् स्पश्टपणीं वेगळे जावंक नांत, "ख्रिस्तपुराणांत' जितलेय कडेन v आयलां थंय तें उतराचे सुरवेक आसा. ह्या लेत्राचो उच्चार उ जाल्लो खंयच मेळना. पूण "दौत्रिन ख्रिस्तां' पुस्तकांत vcharita (उचारिता) vp*a*dessu (उपदेसु) vp*a*rantem (उपरांतें) अशींय बरयल्लीं उतरां मेळटात. v-चो उच्चार व् जाता (इंग्लिशींतल्या वरी व्ह् न्हय), जाल्यार u-चो स्वर म्हणून उ आनी व्यंजन म्हणून (म्हणजे स्वरा आदीं) व्. तरूय वाचपांत व्हडलोसो गोंदळ जायना. v-चो उच्चार व्-च आणि व्ह् न्हय म्हणपाक "ख्रिस्तपुराणांत' पुरावो आसा: व्हाराडिया हें vharaddiya अशें बरयलां, varaddiya अशें न्हय.

आतां तीं सात लेत्रां पळेवंया. पुर्तुगेजीत a लेत्राचो उच्चार अ वा आ जाता. पूण कोंकणी-मराठी उतरां खातीर हे दोनूय उच्चार वेगळायल्यात. 'ख्रिस्तपुराणांत' आनी हेर छापील साहित्यांत *a* (म्हणजे तिरपो वा इटॅलीक a) = अ आनी a (ताठ वा रोमन a) = आ (हातबरपांनी *ă* = अ आनी *â* = आ)

पोर्तुगेज उतरांत जेन्ना सुरवातेक वा मदेकत e येता तेन्ना ताचो उच्चार ए असो जाता. पूण शेवटाक येता तेन्ना इ. देखीक pente (पँति). कोंकणी-मराठी उतरांनी e-चो उच्चार सादारणपणी ए असोच दरवला.

पुर्तुगेज उतराचे सुरवातेक वा मदेकत o येता तेन्ना ताचो उच्चार ओ असो जाता, पूण शेवटच्या o-चो उच्चार उ. देखीक porto (पोर्तु). कोंकणी-मराठी उतरां खातीर ही तर्तूद वापरूंक ना; सगले कडेन o-चो उच्चार सादारपणी ओ असोच दवरला. मात् कांय उतरां वु अशीं सोंपतात तेन्ना uo वापरलां: rauo (रावु) deuo (देवु). हाचें कारण म्हळ्यार u हें लेत्र उ ह्या स्वरा खातीरच न्हय तर व् ह्या व्यंजना खातीरय वापरलां. तेन्ना वु हें uu अशें बरोवप बरेंशें दिसलें ना जायत.

पुर्तुगेजींत c व्यंजना उपरांत a, o, u, हांतलो एक स्वर आयल्यार ताचो उच्चार क् जाता. देखून क, का, को, कु, हांचे खातीर c*a*, ca, co, cu वापरल्यांत जाल्यार के, कि, की, हांचे खातीर que, qui, quy हीं. हांगा u-चो उच्चार जायच ना; आनी हें पुर्तुगेज पद्दतीक धरून आसा. c व्यंजनाचे उपरांत e, i हे स्वर आयल्यार ताचो उच्चार स् जाता; पूण हो उच्चार फ कत पुर्तुगेज उतरांनी मेळटा: तरूय थंय लेगीत चडावत काळजी घेतल्या - ç (सेसेदील) वापरलां. पुर्तुगेज भाशेंत a, o, u ह्या स्वरां आदीं आशिल्या c-चो उच्चार स् करूंक जाय जाल्यार ताचे पोंदाक "सेदील' नांवाचो गरो जोडटात, म्हणजे सेसेदील ç. देखीक, praça (प्रास), açucar (आसूकर). आनी e, i हांचे आदीं c-चो उच्चार आपशींच स् जाता, सेदील जोडिनासतानाच. पूण "ख्रिस्तपुराणांत' असले सुवातेरूय सेदील वापरलां. पुर्तुगेजींत Sacerdote (सोसेर्दोति), sacrificio (साक्रिफीसियु) अशींच बरयतात. पूण "ख्रिस्त पुराणांत' तीं saçerdoti, sacrifiçiu अशीं बरयल्लीं मेळटात; म्हणजे दोट्टी काळजी घेतल्या. पुर्तुगेजींत ch हाचो उच्चार नेमकोच च् असो जायना; देखीक achar ह्या पुर्तुगेज उतराचो उच्चार आशार असो जाता, आचार असो न्हय. तर कोंकणी-मराठी खातीर ch हाका इंग्लिशींतलो च् घेतलो सो दिसता. मागीर आनीक एक h जोडून म्हाप्राण केलो: ch = च्, chh = छ्.

पुर्तुगेज उतरांनी g व्यंजन जेन्ना a, o, u हांचे आदीं येता तेन्ना ताचो उच्चार ग् जाता. हो उच्चार कोंकणी-मराठी उतरां खातीरय वापरला. हें व्यंजन e आनी i हांचे आदीं येता तेन्ना ताचो उच्चार ज्य् जाता. हो उच्चार फकत पुर्तुगेज उतरां पुरतोच

मर्यादीत दवरला: vangelu (वांजेलु), Egiptantu (एजिप्तांतु). पुर्तुगेजींत गे, गि, उच्चारा खातीर gue, gui हीं वापरतात. हांगाय मदल्या u-चो उच्चार जायना. कोंकणी-मराठी उतरां खातीरय हीच पद्धत वापरल्या. म्हणजे गे, गि, गी हांचे खातीर gue, gui आनी guy वापरल्यांत : guele (गेले), bhoguita (भोगिता) laguy (लागी).

पुर्तुगेज भाशेंत s व्यंजनाक तीन तरी उच्चार आसात; तें उतराचे सुरवेक येता तेन्ना स् आनी शेवटाक येता तेन्ना श्. देखीक salas (सालश्). दोन स्वरां मदीं s आयल्यार ताचो उच्चार ज़् जाता. देखीक usar (उजार) "ख्रिस्तपुराणां'त असलीं उतरां Jesu (जेजू), Moise (मोइज़े), Eliseu (एलिज़ेव) हीं आसात. दोन स्वरां मदल्या s व्यंजनाक स् उच्चार जायच जाल्यार तें s दोट्टी बरोवंक जाय. देखीक, passo (पासु). कोंकणी-मराठी उतरां खातीर s-चो उच्चार स् असो कायम दवरला जाल्यारय दोट्टी s-चो वापरूय केला. देखीक sassureacha सासुऱ्याचा). अनुस्वाराचो n आयल्यार ताचे उपरांतय ss वापरला, जी पद्धत पुर्तुगेजींत ना. देखीक, पुर्तुगेज उतर manso (मांसु). पूण सौंसारीं = *s*aunssarī, भरवंसा = bh*ara*u*a*nssa हीं अशींच बरयल्यांत.

पुर्तुगेज उतराचे मदेकत जेन्ना c, f, p, t, v हांचे आदीं s येता, तेन्ना ताचो उच्चार श् जाता. देखीक, gosto (गोश्तु), bispo (बीश्पु). ही तरतूद कोंकणी-मराठी उतरां खातीरय वापरिल्ली मेळटा: काश्टाचे casttache, पुश्कळ = pusc*a*ll*a*, परमेश्वरा = p*ara*mesu*a*ra, विश्वव्यापकु = visu*a*ueap*a*cu. ह्या निमाण्या उतरांत i आनी u स्वरां मदीं एकच s जें वापरलां ताचो अर्थ कितें काय म्हळ्यार हें उ स्वर नासून तें व्यंजन व् आसा.

पुर्तुगेज उतराचे मदेकत जेन्ना b, d, g, l, m, n, r हांचे आदीं s येता तेन्ना ताचो उच्चार ज/ज्य जाता. देखून, Israel = इज्राएल, Ismael = इज्माएल, bautismu = बाउतिज्मु. ही पद्दत कोंकणी-मराठी उतरां खातीर वापरूंक ना; वज्र हे v*a*zr*a* अशेंच बरयलां, v*a*sr*a* अशें न्हय. तरूय पुर्तुगेजीची संवकळ आशिल्ल्या वाचप्या कडल्यान चूक जावची न्हय म्हूण कांय कडेन चडावत काळजी घेतिल्ली दिश्टी पडटा. ब्रागा बरपावळींत सहस्र हें s*a*h*a*ssr*a* अशें बरयल्लें मेळटा. हांगा s हें दोट्टी करची गरज नासली. कारण तें दोन स्वरां मदीं ना. पूण ताचे उपरांत r येता देखून ताचो चुकून ज उच्चार जावंयेत; हो निवारुंकच तें s दुपेट केलां. "ख्रिस्तपुराणांत" तें s*a*h*a*sr*a* अशेंय बरयलां. घडये तेन्ना म्हळ्यार ताचो उच्चार सहज्र असो जावंक लागलो जायत, कारण आयज ताचें रुपांतर हजार अशें जालां. तशेंच उष्ण हे usttn*a* अशें बरयलां. हांगा tt हाची गरजच ना; खरें पळेल्यार ह्या उतरांत ताचो स्पश्ट उच्चारूय जायना, पूण s हें t चे आदीं आशिल्ल्यान त्या s-चो उच्चार ज नासून श् जाता, जसो तो जावंक जाय. हांगा n-चे आदल्या s-चो ज उच्चार निवारुंकच तांणी ही गरजेभायली दिसपी तरतूद केली, हें स्पश्ट दिसून येता. ब्रागा बरपावळींत तशेंच "ख्रिस्तपुराणा'त प्रष्णु हें prusttnu अशें जें बरयलां तें ह्याच कारणाक लागून म्हण दुभाव ना; पूण तांणी हांतलें पयलें अक्षर पृ अशें धरलां काय दिसता. ब्रागा बरपावळींत कृष्णु, विष्णु ही Crusttnnu, Uisttnnu अशीं, आलायतें tt घालून बरयल्लीं मेळटात; हाचेंय कारण तेंच.

पाद्रींनी कोंकणी भाशेचो खोलायेन अभ्यास केल्याचेंय जाणवता. कोंकणी उतरांनी से, सी, स्या हे उच्चार मेळनांत; ताचें आपसुकच शे, शी, श्या जाता. देखीक बरो आनी पिसो हीं विशेशणां घेवंया: बरो, बरी, बरें, बरे, बऱ्यो, बरीं, बऱ्याक अशें जें जाता तेच धरतेर पिसो, पिसी, पिसें, पिसे, पिस्यो, पिसीं, पिस्याक अशें सादाराणपणीं जावंक जाय आसलें, पूण प्रत्यक्षांत पिसो, पिशी, पिशें, पिशे, पिश्यो, पिशीं, पिश्याक अशेंच जाता. देखून जितल्याय देशी उतरांनी शे, शि, शी, श्या येता थंय तांणी se/sse, si/ssi, sy/ssy, sea/ssea वापरलें. पूण जंय शा वा षा येवंक जाय थंय मात xa वापरलें: seuity (शेविती); honssy (होंशी); assassi (आसाशि); xastr*a* शास्त्र; xaqha (शाखा); truxessi (तृषेशि). घडये हेंच मतींत दवरून पुर्तुगेज उतरांत जर से, सि असोच उच्चार आसा जाल्यार तांणी थंय ç वापरलां: circunçisaõ (सिर्कुंसिजांव), cruçī (क्रु सीं= कुरसार). हाका लागून, शुद्धलेखनांत विसंगती उप्रासची न्हय म्हणून कांय संलग्न मूळ उतरांच्या बरपांतूय फावो ते बदल करचे पडले: cruçu (क्रुसु) cruçachy (क्रुसाची); मूळ पुर्तुगेज उतराचो उच्चार क्रूस, जाचे वेल्यान कोंकणी उतर खुरीस आयलें. हें जर crussu अशें बरयलें जाल्यार मागीर crussī बरोवचें पडपाचें, जें उतर कृषी हाचे खातीर वापरलां.

अक्षरां घडोवपाचे बाबतींत देवनागरी आनी रोमी लिपींच्यो तरा सामक्यो वेगळ्यो: देवनागरी व्यंजनवर्णा उपरांत स्वरकुरू जोडटात जाल्यार रोमींत व्यंजनवर्णा उपरांत सरळ तो तो स्वरवर्ण जोडप आसता. हांगा वापरिल्ल्या रोमी स्वरवर्णांचे उच्चार अशे आसात: *a* = अ, a =आ, i = इ, y = ई, u = उ, û* = ऊ, e = ए, o = ओ. पुर्तुगेज भाशेंत ऋ स्वर ना; पूण हांगा ताचें ru अशें लिप्यांतर केलां. हे स्वरवर्ण b ह्या व्यंजनवर्णाक जोडल्यार जीं अक्षरां उपजतात तीं अशीं: b*a* = ब, ba = बा, bi = बि, by = बी, bu = बु, bû* = बू, be = बे, bo = बो, bru = बृ.

(* ही कुरू ख्रिस्तपुराणांत दिसना. हातबरपांनी मात मेळटा; छापखान्यांत ती नाशिल्ली जायत, कारण पुर्तुगेज वा हेर एवरोपी भासांनी तिचो उपेग जायना.)

स्वरां शिवाय पुर्तुगेजींत साबार संधीस्वरय आसात. तांचोय हांगा उपेग केला. ते संधीस्वर अशे :

*a*i = ऐ : dog*a*i (दोगै) ; c*a*issa (कैसा)

*a*u = औ : s*a*unssaru (सौंसारू) ; pass*a*uni (पासौनि)
ae = आए : hontae (होंताए) ; Ismaeli (एज्माएलि)
ai = आइ : Caifa (काइफा) ; Cain (काइन); tthaī (ठाईं)
ao = आओ : Abrahaonssi (आब्राहाओंशि) ; Salamaon*a* (सालामाओन)
aõ = आंव: हें फक्त पुर्तुगेज उतरां खातीर वापरलां. Adaõ (आदांव) ; vizaõ (विजांव)
au = आउ : daunu (दाउनु) ; bautismu (बाउतिज्मु)
ea = या : b*ara*uea (बरव्या) ; razeassi (राज्याशि)
ei = एइ : deī (देईं) ; yeī (येईं)
eo = यो : raqheõ (राख्यों)
eu = एउ : vic*a*leū (विकलेउं) ; gheuni (घेउनि)
ia = इय : s*a*iti*a* (सैतिय) ; Eli*a* (एलिय)
ia = इया : Elian*a* (एलियान) ; Ezeqhia (एजेखिया)
ie = इये : Ezeqhiel (एजेखियेल) ; Gabrielu (गाब्रियेलु)
io = यो : Iosen*a* (योज़ेन) ; Iossuue (योसुवे)
iu = यु : mrutiu (मृत्यु) ; aditiu(आदित्यु)
oa = ओआ : Ioaqhī(योआखीं)
oe = ओए : hoe (होए) ; Noessi (नोएशि)
oi = ओइ : Moise (मोइजे) ; hoil*a* (होइल)
ou = ओउ : houni (होउनि) ; dhulloura (धुळोउर)
ue = उए : Emanueli (एमानुएलि);

देवनागरी वर्णांचें रोमी लिप्यांतर :

अ = a: *a*neca (अनेक), *a*m*a*ru (अमरू), *Amolic*a* (अमोलिक)
आ = a: ar*ata* (आरत), suqhacha (सुखाचा), *Apule (आपुले), (* कॅपिटल A लेत्रांत अ/आ हो फरक करूंक ना; दोनुय उच्चारां खातीर ताठ A- च वापरलां.)
इ = i : it*ara* (इतर); nirbh*ara* निर्भर),
ई = y : ychhe (ईछे); sar*a*thy (सारथी), anny (आणी). ऱ्हस्व आनी दीर्घ इकार वेगळावंची तर्तूद केल्या खरी, पूण अनुस्वारा वांगडा इकार येतात तेन्ना ते वेगळावंक नात. (हातबरपांनी असली तर्तूद आसा, (ý) पूण छापखान्यांत ती कुरू उपलब्ध नासली दिसता.)
उ = u: ub*a*gu (उबगु), tuuã (तुवां).
ऊ = û : छापखान्याच्या अडचणींक लागून "ख्रिस्तपुराणां'त वापरूंक ना. हातबरपांनी मात्र मेळटा: matû (मातू). अनुस्वाराचो तील येता तेन्ना तो उकार दीर्घच धरपाचो.
ऋ = ru : crupanidhy (कृपानिधी); gruhī (गृहीं); srustti (सृश्टि).
ए = e : natodde (नातोडे); hella (हेळा). (कोंकणी-मराठी उतराचे सुरवेक हाचो वापर करूंक ना; थंय ए येता तेन्ना ye अशेंच बरयलां; एक हो आंकडो yecu असो बरयला. घडये हो थळावोच उच्चार आशिल्लो जायत. पुर्तुगेज उतराचे सुरवेक मात e वापरलां: Emanueli (एमानुएलि).
ऐ = *a*i: *a*isse (ऐशे); b*a*iss*a*ty (बैसती)
ओ = o : moho (मोहो); caroni (करोनि). (कोंकणी-मराठी उतराचे सुरवेक हाचो वापर करूंक ना; थंय ओ येता तेन्ना vo अशेंच बरयलां; ओगुले हें vogule केलां. घड्ये होवूय थळावोच उच्चार आशिल्लो जायत, कारण असले बदल आयजूय घडटात. देखीक, ओखद - वखद, ओडप - वोडप. पुर्तुगेज भाशेंतल्यान आयल्ल्या उतरांक लेगीत हो "नेम' लागू जाला: ओक्लां - वक्लां, ओरां - वरां. पाद्रींनी ही थळावी वृत्ती सारकी पारखिल्ली. पुर्तुगेज उतराचे सुरवेक मात् o वापरलां: Oliveti (ऑलिवेति)
औ = *a*u: c*a*unneque (कौणेके), s*a*mbh*a*unu (संभौनु).
अं : अनुस्वारा खातीर पुर्तुगेज भाशेंत ज्यो तीन तर्तुदी आसात त्यो जश्याक तश्यो वापरल्यात : ˜(तील), m आनी n: z*a*u*a*llī (जवळीं); zedh*a*uã (जेधवां); gh*a*rogh*a*rī (घरोघरीं); tū (तूं), dhumpacha (धुंपाचा); acantu (आक ांतु); simponiya (शिंपोनिया); gundde (गुंडे).

अः : पुर्तुगेजींत विसर्ग ना. आनी हांगाय ताचो वापर जाल्लो दिसना.

क् = c, qu: a, o, u हांचे आदीं c जाल्यार e, i, y हांचे आदीं qu: c*a*ri (करि); car*a*nne (कारणे); cotthã क ोठां); cuddi (कुडि); quele (केले); pataquy (पातकी).

ख् = qh : qu*a*ndd*a* (खंड); sariqhy (सारिखी).

ग् = g, gu : a, o, u हांचे आदीं g जाल्यार e, i, y हांचे आदी gu. gonny (गोणी); nigala (निगाला); n*a*l*a*gue (नलगे); guiu*a*ssuni (गिवसुनि).

घ् = gh : gh*a*tt*a* (घट); au*a*gh*a*ddu (अवघडु).

च् = ch : changu (चांगु); ch*a*ug*a*i (चौगे).

छ् = chh : chhedunu (छेदुनु); m*a*chheculle (मछ्यकुळे).

ज् = z, s, g, j : zannaua (जाणावा); uzuuaddu (उजुवाडु); tuzea (तुज्या). (कांय पुर्तुगेज उतरां खातीर s, g आनी j हींच वापरल्यांत: Jesu (जेजू); vangelist*a* (वांजेलिस्त); anj*a* (आंज्य).

झ् = zh: zhancuni (झांकुनि); zhigziguity (झिगझिगिती).

ट् = tt: pr*a*gh*a*tt*a* (प्रघट); bhatti (भाटि).

ठ् = tth : tthac*a*il*a* (ठाकैल); utthily (उठिली).

ड् = dd : ddollã (दोळां); b*a*ddiuar*a* (बडिवार).

ढ् = ddh : suddhall*a* (सुढाळ); ddhenc*a*r*a* (ढेंकर).

ण् = nn, n : prannu (प्राणु); r*a*ch*a*nnara (रचणारा). (साबार उतरांनी जंय र्ण येता थंय rn इतलेंच बरयलां, rnn न्हय. हो प्रकार ब्रागा बरपावळींतय मेळटा: v*a*rnacha (वर्णाचा), s*a*mpurnu (संपुर्णु), c*a*rni (कर्णी). मिरांद हांच्या मतान कोंकणीचे बाबतींत हें सभाविक आसा; रेफ कुरवे सकयल ण येता तेन्ना ताचें सहज नं त रुपांतर जाता. तांणी दिल्ल्यो देखी: भग्त+ इणि= भग्तिणि; पूण दुदकार+ इणि = दुदकार्नि - दुदकान्न, चामार+ इणि = चामार्नि - चामान्न.)

त् = t: tara (तारा); bhituri भितुरि).

थ् = th : path*a*r*a* (पाथर); thoru (थोरु).

द् = d : dataru (दातारु); z*a*dī (जर्दी).

ध् = dh: dhaculī (धाकुलीं); ridhy (रिधी).

न् = n : nary (नारी); mell*a*uni (मेळौनि).

प् = p : papy (पापी); pita पिता).

फ् = ph: ph*a*ll*a* (फळ); phuddã (फुडां); prophet*a* (प्रॉफेत). (कांय ठरावीक पुर्तुगेज उतरां खातीर f वापरला: confess*a*rī (काँफेसरीं)

ब् = b : bapuddi (बापुडी); ddimbiya (डिंबिया).

भ् = bh: bhoz*a*n*a* (भोजन); labhe (लाभे).

म् = m : mata (माता); cr*a*m*a*unu क्रमौनु; mh*a*nn*a*unu (म्हणौनु).

य् = ea, y, i, ĕ : bh*a*l*a*tea (भलत्या); d*a*yall*a* (दयाळ); yety (येती); chearyi (च्यारीय); s*a*tĕ (सत्य) (छापखान्याचे अडचणीक लागून छापील साहित्यांत s*a*tĕ हें s*a*te अशेंच आयलां).

र् = r : ranniye (राणिये); ch*a*r*a*nn*a* (चरण).

ल् l: l*a*u*a*l*a*uit*a* (लवलवित); m*a*dhilea (मधिल्या).

व् = v (उतराचे सुरवेक), u: vanchuni (वांचुनि), bh*a*r*a*u*a*nssa (भरवंसा).

श् = x, s. ss : xastr*a* (शास्त्र); seu*a*ttu (शेवटु); sidory (शिदोरी); ussiru (उशिरु).

ष् = x, s. ss: truxessi (तृषेशि); bhux*a*nn*a* (भुषण); crussy (कृषी). (पाद्रींनी श आनी ष ह्या वर्णा मर्दी फरक केल्लो दिसना; आनी तेन्ना तो नाशिल्लोय जायत. जनर्धन[8] हाच्या मतान, कोंकणींत ष सादारणपणीं मेळच ना. संस्कृतांतल्यान आयिल्ल्या उतरांनी तो आशिल्लो थंय एक तर तो गळून पडला, ना तर ताचें स, श, व, क हातूंत रुपांतर जालां (पान 376, 385 पळेयात). देखी खातीर, उष्ण - हून, उष्मा - हूम, वृषभ - बसव, भाषा-भास, कष्ट-कश्ट, कूष्मांड - कुवाळें, शुषति - सुकता हीं परिवर्तनां दिल्यांत. ही प्रक्रिया सोळाव्या शेंकड्यांत चालू आशिल्ली जायत.)

स् = s, ss, c: s*a*hit*a* (सहित); suass*a* (स्वास); sp*a*russ*a*nn*a* (स्परुसण); circunçisaõ (सिर्कुंसिजांव).

ह् = h : h*a*llu (हळू); vahila (वाहिला).

ळ् = ll: valluca (वाळुका); d*a*yalla (दयाळा).

क्ष् = qhe, qhi: Saqheat*a* (साक्षात); s*a*nqhepī (संक्षेपीं), qhiob*a*le (क्षोबले). (हें लिप्यांतर विचित्र दिसता. कारण खंय क्ष आनी खंय ख. शिवाय मिशनरी साहित्यांत क्ष हाचें kx अशें लिप्यांतर खंयच मेळना. हरशीं तांणी निश्ठेन लिप्यांतर केलां, हें मान्य करचेंच पडटा; आनी हांगा kx वापरप खुबच सोयस्कर आशिल्लें. तर हांगाच ते कशे चुकले जायत, हो प्रस्न पडटाच. पूण मातशे खोलायेन येवजिल्यार जापय सहज मेळटा. साबार संस्कृत उतरां कोंकणींत आयल्यांत जांतूंत हो वर्ण आसपावता. पूण असल्या खुबच उतरांनी क्ष चें खं त रुपांतर जाल्लें नदरेक पडटा: राक्षस-राखेस, नक्षत्र-नखेत्र. "ख्रिस्तपुराणां'त वृक्ष हे vruqhe (वृख्य) अशें बरयलां; पूण ताचें आयज रुख अशें रुपांतर जालां. ही प्रक्रिया तेन्नाय चालंत आशिल्ली अशें दिसता. कारण सोळाव्या शेंकड्यांत गोंय सोडून गेल्ले जे कोंकणे केरळांत स्थायीक जाल्ले तांचे भाशेंतूय हें जाणवता. हें विशीं जनर्धन[8] (पान 389) कांय उदाहरणां दितात: क्षमा - खेम, क्षीरकी - खीरि, क्षेत्र-खेति. पाद्रींनी हे परिवर्तन सर्रास वापरलां. वयर क्षोबले हाचे खातीर qhi जें वापरला तें क्षो हांतलो स्वर धांपतो म्हुण दाखोवंक.)

ज्ञ् = gne : gnean*a*m*a*ti (ज्ञानमति), agnea (आज्ञा). (ह्या जोडगिराचो उच्चार साबार भासांनी वेगवेगळो जाल्लो मेळटा: हिंदींत ग्य्, मराठींत द्न्य्, कानडींत ज्ञ्, गुजराठींत ग्न्य्. पोरणे मराठींतय तो ग्न्य् असोच जातालो म्हणपाचीं चिन्नां मेळटात. तर कोंकणींत तो असोच आशिल्लो म्हूण स्पश्ट दिसता. शिवाय, व्युत्पत्तीच्या नेमांक धरून (जनर्धन[8]), तेन्नाचें gnean*a* (ज्ञान) आयज गिन्यान जावन घोळटा. तेच खातीर पाद्रींनी gne वापरलें. आयज कोंकणींत जो द्न्य् असो उच्चार करतात तो आधुनीक मराठी शिक्षणाचो प्रभाव.

आधारावळ :

1. Dom Francisco Garcia - O Homem das trinta e duas Perfeições e Outras Histórias. (Ed. J. Wicki) Lisboa. 1958. pp. 323 -26.

2. दौत्रिन क्रिस्तां म्हणजे क्रिस्ती धर्मतत्त्व (अनुवादक: अनंत काकबा प्रियोळकर) पुणें विद्यापीठ. 1965.

3. कृष्णदास शामा आनी सांगाती हांची बरपावळ. हाची प्रत (तीन खंड) पणजेच्या कृष्णदास शामा केंद्रीय ग्रंथालयांत उपलब्ध आसा.

4. **लिप्यांतर पद्दतीचेर विस्कावन उजवाड घालपी विद्वान:**

(अ) वि. बा. प्रभु देसाई : (1) सतराव्या शतकांतील गोमंतकी बोली. मुंबई विश्वविद्यालय, मुंबय. 1963. पा. 109-121.

(2) तोच लेखक : गोमंतकाचा मराठी वारसा. गोमंतक मराठी अकादेमी, पणजी. 1997. पा. 195-199.

(आ) अनंत काकबा प्रियोळकर-वयलीच कृती. पा. 23-24.

(इ) Rocky V. Miranda - The Old Konkani Bharata. Vol. l. Central Institute of Indian Languages, Mysore. 2011. pp. xxvi - xxx.

5. Mons. S. R. Dalgado - Diccionário Portuguez - Komkani. Imprensa Nacional, Lisboa. 1905.

6. Doutrina Cristã em Lingua Concani - Tomas Estevão S.J. 1622 वर्सा उजवाडायल्ले मूळ आवृत्तीची १९४५ वर्सा केल्ली प्रतीप्रत आवृत्ती.

7. Rocky V. Miranda - वयलीच कृती. पा. 300.

8. A Higher Konkani Grammar - P. B. Janardhan. Madras 1991

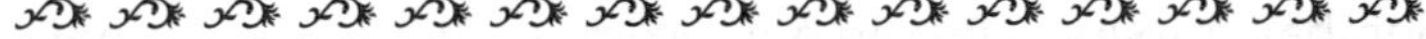

Narayan B. Desai is a regular contributor and columnist in Marathi and Konkani newspapers. His translated works include Rajwade Lekha Sangraha *published by the Sahitya Akademi, New Delhi, which received a translation prize in 2018, and a forthcoming Brazilian novel,* Dom Casmurro. *He is associated with Akashwani, the official public radio broadcaster of India as a translator, speaker, poet and theatre artist. He has worked on the editorial board for Konkani language textbooks of the Goa Board of Education.*

The following passages highlight various phases of translations from the time of a debate over a Bible translation in 1818, and their implication in different moments of linguistic and literary history. This thesis is particularly relevant for its ability to present the symbolic contexts and affiliations for language and script across the current states of Karnataka, Goa and Maharashtra. Relevant footnotes from the original text have been included below the main text. The excerpts are intended to provide thumbnail historical contexts for the occurrence of translations, and a fuller context for some of the emphatically expressed positions in this thesis, as they appeared in 2002 can be read online at http://library.unigoa.ac.in.8081/xmlui/handle/123456789/380

Excerpts from Narayan B. Desai's PhD thesis, 'Politics of Script: The Case Of Konkani (1961 – 1992)', 2002, Goa University.

KONKANI AND ITS SCRIPTS

The British ascendancy in India displaced the Peshwa rule that concluded the Maratha epoch. The issue of Konkani as a language figured in the early years of this transition in the beginning of the nineteenth century. Problems concerning its name and status cropped up in a dispute with regard to the translation of the New Testament called as the *Kunkuna Bible* Vol. V published in 1818 by the Serampore missionaries 'in another dialect of the Marathi language', in use 'in southern Konkan, in the vicinity of Goa' (Pinge, 1960: 61). The Bombay missionaries did not recognise this *kunkuna*, saying that:

> `We are prepared to state that from Goa northward through the whole of the Kunkun, the Mahratta language is universally spoken with only a slight provincial variation from the same language as spoken at Poona. From the name of the country this language has been called the Kunkunee language, but it differs in so slight a degree from the Mahratta, that in our judgment of able brahmuns whom we have consulted, a distinct version is neither at all desirable nor justifiable.'[1]

---

[1] Narayan B. Desai, "Politics of Script: The Case of Konkani (1961–1992)" (Goa University, 2002), 146, http://library.unigoa.ac.in:8081/xmlui/handle/123456789/380.

According to these missionaries, the name *Kunkunee* (Konkani) came `from the name of the country' and the language was not much different from the *Mahratta* (Marathi). Therefore, they opined, 'a distinct version (of the Bible) [sic] is neither at all desirable nor justifiable'. The version, printed in `the Balbodh character' i.e. Devanagari script, according to Rev. Bruce, is 'much more easily read than the Marathi version, but its idioms are less easily understood'. One can gather that the idioms were not as Marathi as the character in which the work was printed. Also it is easy to understand what makes the work 'undesirable' and 'unjustifiable', if one notes that the 'judgement' (sic) was the result of 'consultation' with 'able brahmuns', who, almost certainly, had to be the Marathi Brahmins, for whom Marathi was the language of the region. The dialect used in the translation was similar to the one current in Mangalore in the 20th century, which possibly occurred in Goa in the sixteenth and the seventeenth centuries. Court Pundits from south Konkan who were consulted, discounted the effort as 'no language at all' (Pinge, 1960: 62 quoting *The Oriental Christian Spectator*, July 1836). Serampore missionaries considered this criticism as unfounded and in their bid to counter the attack, solicited a recommendation on the usefulness of the specific version from an officer of the Madras Civil Service. But in this battle, the Konkani Bible was the victim. It failed to gain popularity while the other language editions, particularly Marathi ones, had widespread use in the region.[2]

...

In Kerala the literary history starts with certain *Puranas* in translation and *charitras* in original, manuscripts of which are said to be in the custody of the Konkani Brahmins at Ernakulam: and in secular sphere, the testimonial in Devanagari script by three Konkani Brahmins to *Hortus Indicus Malabaricus*, a botanical compendium of the 17 th century (Da Cunha, 1991 [1881]: 43–44).

John Leyden (1775–1811) in his visit to Malabar and Cochin at the turn of the eighteenth century met some Konkani Brahmins, who showed him `*Bhagavatam, Linga Purana, Ramayana and Bharata'* in their Konkani translations and also '*Virabhadra Charitra and Parasurama Charitra*' among original works (Mallaya, 1993:2).[3]

...

Goa Konkani Akademi came into being (1985) with its focus on Devanagari as the official representation of Konkani. Its activities, mainly the scheme *Pailo Chonvor* (literally meaning first flowering)

---

[2] ibid.

[3] ibid., 149. Footnote to p. 149.

of financial grants and subsidies to the first books of budding writers, projects such as *Sahitya Saptak* (Literary Week), workshops for young Konkani writers on different literary forms etc. helped in broadening the base of Devanagari. The Akademi also supported the publication of `transcreation' of the epic Mahabharata by Ravindra Kelekar soon after the language became the Official Language of Goa in 1987, and its release in New Delhi at the hands of the then Prime Minister Rajiv Gandhi was viewed as a great step forward in the direction of the constitutional recognition that was awaited. This or the earlier translations of '*Yakshaprashna*' and '*Raghuvansho*' of Kalidasa from Sanskrit to Konkani by Shripad Desai published in 1976, translations of the *Bhagavad Gita* both in prose and in verse were claimed as the proof of competency of the language to express the rich ancient Indian thought and ideas, in the line of Shenoi Goembab's *Gomantopanishat*. All this shaped the common standard of Konkani in Devanagari, for Goa, and also prepared a base for staking claims to the 'national' status.

The prose version '*Geeta Pravachanam* (1956) was the translation of Vinoba's discourses on *Geeta.* ('*Geeta Pravachane*') in Marathi and in many other Indian languages, and the verse form '*Gitay*' appeared in print in 1960. Shennai Goembab's translation in prose, '*Bhagavantalem Geet*' was completed in 1935 but published in 1959. At least ten other translations by individuals from North and South Kanara and also Kerala are mentioned in the latest translation (2002) by Suresh Amonkar.[4]

CAUSES OF MULTILITERALISM – POLITICAL FACTORS

The Roman script was made compulsory for use in local administration by the beginning of the 17th century as almost all the communidades in the Old Conquests were transferred to new converts. Many converts had to leave the territory to avoid persecution for continuing with their old practices. Bardeskars who shifted to the areas across the ghats in the Marathi-speaking areas such as Ajra, Gadhinglaj, Ichalkaranji, some villages in Belgaum district, and some others in Dharwar district were left to the care of irmaos without any religious authority for some years before they were organised by the priests (Fernandes 1996). In the coastal areas of Ratnagiri, Malvan, Vengurla in the present Sindhudurg (Maharashtra), the study and practice of Marathi and Devanagari became common. All these Catholics

[4] ibid., 158. Footnote to p. 158

living under local rulers adopted the local languages for social communication and education (even in schools run by Christian missionaries) but continued the use of Konkani in their houses and the Church. With Devanagari script many of their prayers are in Marathi; Church services and sermons are also in Marathi.

During the period starting from the Portuguese Republic (1910) many Goan writers — both Hindu and Catholic — started exploring the old documents of the early colonial period and as a part of nationalist campaign quoted liberally from them often in translation, to arouse anti-colonial sentiments. T.B.Cunha, Menezes Braganza, Dr. Govind Pundalik Hegdo Desai, Adv. Laxmikant Bhembre, and many others have done this. Dr. Panduronga Pissurlenkar was instrumental in making many of these available through his writings and also as the Chief of Goa Archives during Portuguese rule between 1931 and 1961.[5]

LINGUISTIC AND CULTURAL CONCERNS

Goan Catholics, who were the main among Roman script users for Konkani had intellectuals and scholars of renown whose contributions to literatures in different languages have been recognised. Their knowledge of linguistics too should be quite remarkable considering that many of these were priests or teachers of old and new languages. Hence it is unlikely that they were not aware of the need to regulate and modify syntax and orthography of Konkani in the Roman script. There should have been deliberations on these aspects through their journals and newspapers. But with growth in printing and publishing activity in Devanagari script, some among the Roman script users initiated some attempts at purification of their language and following the Vatican II there were translations of religious texts for regular use, which was somewhat resented by a section of Catholics (Gomes in Souvenir, 1967: n.p.). They favoured preserving their old words and expressions in liturgical translations.

Felicio Cardozo started replacing the syntax used in the Roman script writings through his periodicals in the mid-60s; The church authorities too, prepared liturgical translations for use in Bombay and Goa but some resented the Goa translation as they saw it as 'purism with a vengeance' due to Sanskritic words included therein.[6]

[5] ibid., 174–5.

[6] ibid., 201.

Recognition of the multi-literal reality in case of Konkani over the century is accompanied by the recent suggestions and experiments in transliteration. There are attempts in this direction mainly in Kerala and Karnataka. With the switch over to Devanagari from Malayalam as a policy in Kerala, transliterations of folk and religious literature have taken place. The transliterations from Devanagari to Malayalam script in Konkani are not many in creative literature as the large majority of Konkani speakers are still with the Malayalam language, and thus translations from Konkani to Malayalam are few.

In Karnataka on the other hand there have been consistent attempts to transliterate the works from Devanagari to Kannada and some works from Kannada to Devanagari. The two journals – *Amar Konkani* and *Panchakadayi* are printed in both the scripts – Kannada and Devanagari. There are few books printed in two scripts one of which was awarded the Sahitya Akademi award in 1985. In Goa publishers in Devanagari script are not so enthusiastic about this though there have been some pieces published in periodicals. The transliterations from Kannada script are restricted to the works of C.F. D'Costa (*Chafra*), one of which got him the Sahitya Akademi award.

SOUTH KANARA: THE REAL BATTLE GROUND

In Karnataka the organised Konkani language movement is seen mainly in Mangalore-Udupi area where the contesting groups within the movement are more defined and their respective activities more pronounced. The GSBs as a business community have limited practical utility for the language in terms of literature or culture. But their search for status is focused on 'language as an asset' to acquire certain political and administrative advantages. The GSBs in trade and business have supported the language activities mostly as their community work. Their contribution to academic or creative side of language is...limited as compared to that of the Catholics, who have worked both through the church and outside.

Organisations in the early part of the twentieth century were essentially community-based, giving a prominent role to the church and temples. The church service and liturgy were in Konkani. In this context creative writing in Konkani got a boost with the appearance of '*Konkani Dirvem*' but only among Catholics. The *Catholic Association of South Kanara* (CASK) and other organisations, guided by the missionaries, and the *Saraswat Associations*, connected to the GSB temples, worked for their respective communities making use of Konkani. In the year 1940 the second *Konkani Parishad* was held in Udupi (with the support of Dr. T. M. A. Pai) in which the participation of Catholics was ensured. Jerome Saldanha, the Member of Madras Legislature, who presided over the event, was not in favour of a single script as was resolved in the first conference. The first Parishad held in Karwar had included as one of its objectives – 'To use Devanagari, the original/ natural and national script for Konkani.

...

This emphasis on Devanagari has to be seen in the light of consolidation of Kannada forces through the *Samyukta Karnataka* movement of 1930s and ridicule suffered by the Konkani speaking children in Kannada schools, which they had to attend.[7]

...

The major formations in the region were three:

(i) The GSB community and its institutions led by the Pais of Manipal,

(ii) The Jesuits and their institutions,

(iiI) The Catholic writers with secular/leftist leanings.

As the GSBs had to counter the hostility of the regional Brahmin groups such as Shivallis and also to consolidate the forces scattered in different states they worked towards promotion of Konkani language as their symbol of identity and Devanagari script as the distinct Aryan heritage to which they had a claim. This would also help in developing the distinct identity of the community... Their views on script, however, were not clear, because, for them, Konkani as a language carried value, which was more symbolic than real.

The role of Jesuits in the work of Konkani has a history of over a century in Mangalore.[8] ... The use of Konkani in the church was popularised through the efforts of such priests. St. Aloysius College in Mangalore became a centre of activities for Konkani through the priests and teachers. The prime focus was, however, on religion and the idea of free thought and action outside the church domain was promptly curtailed.

Konknni Dirvem could not continue for long though it shifted to Canara Press for printing after the Jesuit Kodialbail Press refused to print it. The controversy between *Dirvem* and *Raknno* finds mention in the issue of *Dirvem* dtd. 2nd Dec. 1938. Another journal '*Samajicho Divo*' was banned by the church as it propagated the socialist

[7] ibid., 241–242.

[8] ibid., 245.

ideas. *Dirvem* issue dtd. 16th Dec. 1937 mentioned about Bishops proclamation proscribing the journal.[9]

...

The third group consists of writers, artists and activists whose commitment to language, literature and culture is based on their socialist ideas and concern for well-being of the masses. Their experience of cosmopolitan life and exposure to the industrial culture in Bombay led them to question the functioning and policies of the church. Late Charles Francis Da Costa (*Chafra* to the Konkani literary world), the first among Mangaloreans to receive the Sahitya Akademi literary award (1989) tops the list of this group.[10]

....

The associational scenario of Konkani in Karnataka is characterised by the contesting roles of the first two groups to control centres of power. *Konkani Bhasha Mandal Karnataka* (KBMK), *Akhil Karnataka Konkani Sahitya Parishad* (AKKSP) with its affiliates such as the *Uttara Kannada Zilla Konkani Sahitya Parishad* (UKZKSP), and *Karnataka Konkani Sahitya Akademi* (KKSA) are seen as the arenas of this contest. KBMK as the veteran body with secular standing was formed in 1974.[11]

Even though some GSB individuals were to take up the position of Secretary, the scope for Devanagari is not likely to be created because of the language environment surrounding the Konkani community in Karnataka. Tulu, which is the language of the region, has Kannada as its script and Konkani is no different in the eyes of the state. The language policy of the Karnataka state government makes Kannada language and script compulsory and knowledgeable people feel that getting state support is possible only with Kannada script. Devanagari has no practical, significant role in Karnataka, especially after the establishment of the *Karnataka Konkani Sahitya Academy* which has to use Kannada script as the government body.[12]

...

Dr. Willy D'Silva had problems with the church authorities in the matter of Konkani translation of Bible too. Fr. Willy completed it [the task of translating] on his own...He also achieved the goal of freeing the Mangalore Catholic Konkani from massive Kannadisation that was noted by many but not acted upon in the past (Interview-Fr.

---

9 ibid., 246.

10 ibid., 247.

11 ibid., 248.

12 ibid., 250.

Mark Valdar). But his translation was not allowed for circulation on technical/procedural grounds. The Bible translation was printed but copies could not be sold as officially approved as Willy D'Silva asked for 'imprimatur' after it was printed and it was refused by the Bishop. The official translation was not available till 2001. Willy's work had to be sold at a heavy discount unofficially. The concern for Konkani on the part of the church authorities has also seen ups and downs.[13]

[13] ibid., 251.

Jason Keith Fernandes' PhD on 'The Citizenship Experiences of Goan Catholics' was awarded by the Instituto Univeritário de Lisboa (ISCTE-IUL), Portugal in 2013. His other publications include, Invoking the Ghost of Mexia: Community and State in Post-colonial Goa: *in Dossier Goa: 1510–2010, Entre a história e a memória, Ler História, nº 59, 2010.*

The excerpts from the thesis detail the formation of organisations like the Saraswat Parishad and the Konkani Parishad, which consolidated community identities and support for Konkani outside of Goa. The thesis indicates the convergence between imagined geographies for a Konkani-speaking region and caste affiliations and complements the excerpts from Narayan B. Desai's thesis.

Excerpts from Jason Keith Fernandes' PhD thesis, 'Citizenship Experiences of the Goan Catholics' 2013, Instituto Universitário de Lisboa

FIXING KONKANI AS A BRAHMIN TONGUE[1]

A good part of Valaulikar's [Vaman Varde Valaulikar, or Shenoi Goembab as he was called] writings that are translated into English were delivered in the context of a specific associational setting. He was involved with the establishment of, and subsequently the running of the Goa Hindu Association, a cultural association for the Goan "Hindus" of Bombay akin to those available to the Goan Catholics (Budkuley 2003). The most substantial of his works, *Goenkaranchi Goianbhaili Vosnook* ("The Travels of Goans outside of Goa") was originally a lecture delivered to a "public" audience hosted by the Goa Hindu Association and the *Saraswat Brahman Samaj*. The aim of this lecture series was to boost *Saraswat* pride and to create a history for this group fighting for place in the public spaces of the Bombay Presidency.

...

Like other reformists, Varde Valaulikar extols the brahmin community when they shed traditional prejudices and taboos to participate in the opportunities being opened by colonial modernity (Varde Valaulikar 2008: 30). More specifically, it encourages the younger generation of the *Saraswat* to follow their noble learned ancestors and challenge the idea that the *Saraswat* was backward in education (Varde Valaulikar 2008: 16; 13–15; 23–33). The

---

[1] Jason Keith Fernandes, "Citizenship Experiences of the Goan Catholics" (ISCTE/Instituto Universitário de Lisboa, 2013), 108.

setting of modernity that Valaulikar established then involved the rejection of traditional interdictions of a provincial community, an encouragement of entering into "modern" professions, especially those within Government service, and a stressing of the Aryan heritage.

...

A SEPARATE HOMELAND AND CASTE UNIFICATION[2]

Given the nature of the debate that was concerned with marking out the difference of the Konkani speaker, it was not long before the idea of a separate homeland should also have emerged.[3] Though Varde Valaulikar may not have been the first person to articulate it, given his centrality in the imagination of Konkani language activists, he is regarded as having first come up with this idea. Subsequently, Pereira points out, the idea of a Konkan state, as a *Sagari Pranta* or "Maritime Province", was articulated by a prominent lawyer from Karwar, Madhav Manjunath Shanbhag. This concept was later elaborated by "Kakasaheb Kalelkar ..., but was first presented in cogent intellectual terms by George Mark Moraes ..., whose arguments were reinforced by the fervent rhetoric of Bhaskar Anand Saletore ..." (Pereira 1992: 20–21). Among these many activists, it is Madhav Shanbhag who is important to my narrative of the political history of Konkani for another significant reason.

Both Madhav Shanbhag and Bhaskar Anand Saletore, are as evidenced by their surnames, from the North Kanara region of the former Bombay Presidency. In his work, Desai suggests that in the case of the Mangalore GSBs like the Pais, the need to "counter the hostility of the regional brahmin groups such as the *Shivallis* and also to consolidate the forces scattered in different states" made them work toward "promotion of Konkani as a symbol of their identity, and Devanagari script as the distinct Aryan heritage to which they had claim" (Desai 2007: 245). It is in this context of inter-caste rivalries, that the support for the *Sagari Pranta* as a bastion of Konkani (read *Saraswat*) interests should be seen.[4]

---

[2] This title has been added to facilitate changes in themes and is not part of the original thesis.

[3] Jason Keith Fernandes, "Citizenship Experiences of the Goan Catholics," 109.

[4] ibid., 110 footnote 89.

KONKANI ORGANIZATIONS, CASTE AND THE APPEARANCE OF SECULARISM[5]

Shanbhag was another of the activists who had been involved in the caste unification process.[6] Impressed by Varde Valaulikar's efforts Shanbhag supported him, and together, worked to establish the Konkani Parishad (Konkani Conference). Founded in 1939, it held its first convention in the same year in Karwar, Karnataka. What should also be remembered is that this Konkani Parishad was held in the context not only of the recognition of the linguistic principle for organisation of the Indian National Congress, but also of the establishment of the Kannada Sahitya Parishad in 1915. This Parishad was committed to the idea of *karnataka ekikarana* (consolidation of Karnataka as the space of Kannada speakers). Conducting its first conference in Bangalore in 1915, the Parishad followed a pattern, latter taken up by the Konkani Parishad, of conducting its annual meetings at different locations in the Kannada speaking areas (Nair 2011: 61). Similarly the *Saraswat Parishad* also moved the location of its conferences, being one way to attract the interest of those who could not afford to travel to a single fixed location. What should be also stressed is that these strategies, as well as the forms that the conferences would take, were also drawn from the patterns of the early Indian National Congress, and other national public interest associations that formed civil society, both in the colonial period, and later the post-colonial period.

...

A number of these sentiments are also plainly visible in the Presidential address to the third Konkani convention, by Armando Menezes, a prominent Catholic man of letters.[7]

> I am afraid I was one of the most responsible for compromising on the Roman script for Konkani, in the hope of weaning my Christian countrymen back to their mother-tongue. But I was convinced even then that the chief stumbling-block to the unification and systematization of Konkani was the script; and that the Devanagari was, logically, the only script for Konkani; so I was glad to hear Mr. Shanbag, a Kanarite and therefore presumably more interested in the Kannada script, agree with Mr. Valaulicar on this vital question. (Menezes 1976: 86)

---

[5] Title not in original thesis

[6] Jason Keith Fernandes, "Citizenship Experiences of the Goan Catholics," 110.

[7] ibid., 114.

The establishment of the Konkani Parishad, that Menezes was addressing, ensured a number of gains for the Konkani activists.[8] It engendered the establishment of a number of Konkani language institutions, not least of which being the Konkani Bhasha Mandal. Other organisations were similarly established, with the Konkani Sahitya Samithi, founded in 1944, in Bombay; and the Konkani Cultural Association in 1965. Another Konkani Bhasha Mandal was founded in Mangalore in early 1974. With the integration of Goa into the Indian Union, in 1961, a Konkani Bhasha Mandal was founded first at Margão (Sar Dessai 2000: 11). Subsequent to Goa's integration into the Indian Union, these institutions, and especially the Konkani Bhasha Mandal in Goa, would play active roles in introducing the Konkani language into the governmental school system. The other significant factor was its ability, through using the logic of caste interests to attract members from the Catholic dominant castes and present the Konkani language movement and agenda as being secular.

FIXING GOA'S SECULAR CULTURE… THE BACKSTAGE FIXING OF KONKANI AS A LANGUAGE[9]

The Opinion Poll resolved the question of Goa's administrative status and provided a lull to linguistic politics for the next 20 years when the matter resurfaced in the form of the demand for the recognition of Konkani as the Sole Official Language of the state. In the meantime, the pro-Konkani forces had continued silently working to ensure that a framework for the construction of Goan identity within Konkani frames had been set in place. This was ensured by, among other things, introducing Konkani into the schooling system, an achievement managed through the networking of two pro-Konkani forces. The first was that of the Konkani Bhasha Mandal (KBM), based in Margão, and largely dominated by the GSB of that town, but also supported by nationalist minded dominant-caste Catholics. In particular was the support of the Correia Afonso family, through the person of Pedro Correia Afonso, who was the first President of the KBM, and the maternal uncle of one of the prime actors in the insertion of the teaching of the Konkani language into the school curriculum.

[8] ibid., 115.

[9] ibid., 128.

Before moving to this unfolding of history, there is a need to appreciate more fully the depth of the habitus of the Pedro-Correia household in matters of the thinking about Konkani, or vernacular culture, and the culture of the Goan Catholic elite. This thinking is captured perfectly in the words of Propercia Correia-Afonso, sister to Pedro Correia-Afonso. In the context of her colleague, the Hindu Professor Ramachandra Naique, she wrote:

> "A true Indian in heart and mind yet with no vestige of chauvinism; a teacher who is yet a true apostle, Ramachandra Naique possesses much that he can teach the Indo-Portuguese, who is immersed in a hybrid civilization which creates nothing. Vande Mataram, comrade and master."[10]

Through the goodwill generated by these Catholics, the KBM was able to introduce teaching of the Konkani language in four local schools; the Loyola High School run by the Jesuits, the Holy Spirit school attached to the parish of the Holy Spirit Church, and two other convent schools in the city of Margão. The KBM helped train the teachers as well as produced books that would accompany the students as they graduated from the lower to higher grades (Botelho 2002: 222). This Konkani was the kind of Konkani that Varde Valaulikar has in the early part of the century promoted, the language of the brahmin (or the Antruzi dialect) and scripted in Devanagari.

...

Before I convey the sense that this shift towards the Sanskritic was a unanimous project of the Goan Catholic elites, or upper-castes, I should point out that this project was, and continues to be, a highly contested one. Reflections of this contestation are more than evident in issues of *Renovação*, the magazine of the Archdiocese of Goa, through letters that are written to the editors, who at least in the person of Fr. Martinho Noronha, appear to be in favour of this shift. See for example, the letter titled "Krist Prosad" written by Fr. V. Azavedo in the *Renovação* dated 15 March, 1990. Or the letter titled "Translations" by Fr. Anastasio Gomes O.C.D dated 1 May, 1991.[11]

---

[10] ibid., 129 footnote 109. Translation from Couto (2004: 245)

[11] Footnote 115 ibid., 132.

Victor Ferrão is the author of The Horizons of Sangam: A Creative Dialogue between Science and Religion *and co-author (with Dr. James Ponniah) of* Identity Difference and Conflict: Postcolonial Critique, *Asian Trading Corporation & Association of Christian Philosophers of India, 2013, and* Being a Goan Christian: The Politics of Identity, Rift and Synthesis, *Boradway, 2011 among other books. His publications also include* Beyond the Beyond: Primordial Levels of the Symbiosis between Science and Religion, *in the Indian Journal of Science and Religion, Vol. 5, 2007.*

His essay, 'Translation between the Self and its colonial Other' reads translation as a process in cultural politics through which subjectivities are formed, selves are posited, and limits, boundaries and contours of political entities such as the post-colonial nation are formed. This engagement with a range of post-modernist thinkers also tries to suggest how Goa may provide a particular vortex of cultural relations from which to think about translation.

TRANSLATION BETWEEN THE SELF AND ITS COLONIAL OTHER

Translation has become a visible and vibrant field and translatology as an academic field has come into being and has acquired remarkable momentum in our days. Translation is not mere substitution of words within two languages but a search for convergence and overlaps in between two cultures. It is highly complex because a text often becomes cultural capital across cultural boundaries. Translation is a political process; a process of being in the world. However, translation often becomes the maid servant of imperialism as imperial culture often enters cloaked in the mode of translation. Hence, this essay attempts to study what came to be called cultural translation inspired by postmodern and post-colonial studies. It is non-textual and non-linguistic in its approach. Tejaswini Niranjana in her book, *Siting Translation: History, Post-Structuralism and the Colonial Context* uses the term translation to drive home the power-play between the British rulers and Indian Subjects.[1] Hence, like her, this study also uses the term translation under erasure.

Gayatri Spivak tells us that translation is the most intimate act of reading. Often, the colonized is involved in an act of translation wherein he/she attempts to hide the colonizer in him/her. It is an act of hybridization which brings an untranslatable dimension to the fore. Salman Rushdie said of himself and other diasporic people: 'We

[1] See Tejaswini Niranjana, *Siting Translation: History, Post-structuralism, and the Colonial Context* (Oxford: University of California Press, 1992).

are translated men'.[2] Translation in this sense becomes a strategy for survival (*sur-vivre*). It is an act of living on the borderlines. That is why non-European language, culture and values do not automatically construct a site of resistance to European languages, cultures and values. Hence, the colonizer is often translated by the colonized through his/her praxis. The native signifier thus binds to the colonizer's colonizing ways and reproduces the relations of coloniality in the post-colonial societies. Resistance to European culture, religion and languages in colonial societies is therefore complex and may clone the colonizer in different ways. This hides the loss of our nativeness by producing an illusion of unbrokeness with our tradition as the native begins to use cultural artifacts for domination and thus seeks a realm of mastery like the imperial masters. While approaching the complexities of our study, we wish not to get trapped into the standard binary of the colonizer and the colonized but focus our energy on the dynamic rhythm/play of unequal/ asymmetrical relations between the two.

The politics of translation takes on a life of its own if we see it in the context of meaning-construction of humans. Indeed, our quest for meaning has a political grammar of its own and can become an instrument of domestication as well as the eruption of the native in the context of domination. Humans can digest and uncritically assimilate the narratives of their oppressors as well as generate counter narratives that strive to dismantle the dominant narratives. The colonized internalized the hegemony of the colonizer by transforming the mode of being of the colonizer into their substance. Hence, this assimilation and translation of the mode of being of the colonizer re-invents domestic imperialism in post-colonial societies leading to a cultural metamorphism not less than a culturecide.

THE COLONIAL HABITUS OF HEGEMONY

The colonial habitus is uncritically internalized and unequal relations of power are normalized and naturalized by the colonized. This led to the acceptance and mimesis of the mode of existence of the colonizer. The colonizer's way of life became normative and the colonized steadily appropriated the disabling imperative to become the clone of the colonizer. It is in this context of cloning the mode of existence of the colonizer that translation becomes a

[2] http://iwp.uiowa.edu/91st/vol4-num1/translating-culture-vs-cultural-translation. Accessed February 21, 2014.

powerful tool. V.S Naipaul's *Mimick Men*, effectively brings home how colonial power became a site of subjectification. Ralph Singh, the hero of *Mimick Men* narrates an incident that on first impression might be counted as an act of mis-remembering: My first memory of the school is of taking an apple to the teacher. This puzzles me. We had no apples on Isabella. It must have been an orange: yet my memory insists on the apple. The editing is clearly at fault. But the edited version is all I have."[3] We can certainly trace in the quote above, a translation by way of substitution, of the apple for an orange based on the sense of empowerment that one derives in the interchanging of an asymmetrical power relation through the native orange for the metropolitan apple. Thus, we can trace that colonial habitus generates a symbolic structure that subjects the colonized to internalize both material and ideological asymmetries. This assimilation of the asymmetries is often believed to be civilizing and progressive. The sense of inferiority induced by the colonial culture produces an insatiable imperative to mimic the mode of existence of the colonizer. All this brings about dislocation, placelessness, fragmentation and loss of identity. They become mimic men who imitate and reflect the life style, values and views of their colonizers.

Indeed, this mimicking of the mode of existence of the colonizer is a sign of double articulation. Homi Bhabha hails it as a complex strategy of reform, regulation and discipline which appropriates the other as it visualizes power. Thus, we have those who mimic the colonizer readily while those who mock everything colonial are also not free from cloning the civilizing mission of the colonizer. Those who are driven by the need to civilize the colonized through what they consider as nationalism are also subject to the menace of practicing the civilizing mode of the colonizers. This means we cannot catch the shadow of the colonizer that is already living in us.

The end result of a process of translation is different from the original. This is specially the case in the context of translation of culture. Following Roman Jakobson, we can view translation as an inter-semiotic process. It involves the transmutation of one sign system into another another sign system.[4] Culture being a sign system, depends on translation in this sense for its dynamism, coherence, resistance and innovation. C. S. Pierce teaches that meaning in its primary sense is the translation of a sign into

---

[3] http://www.jstor.org/discover/10.2307/23112367? uid=3738256&uid=2&uid=4&sid=21103492595347. Accessed on Feb. 21, 2014.

[4] See Peeter Torop, " Translation as translating as Culture" , p. 557. http://www-1.ut.ee/SOSE/sss/pdf/torop302.pdf. Accessed March 21, 2014.

another sign system.[5] But meaning does not remain in a fixed sense but manifests the ability to dynamically spring forth within the boundaries of a framework of culture. This dynamism in the shifting meanings, codes, customs and practices with cross-cultural exchange due to colonization and globalization has led to the Creolization (hybridization) of cultural codes resulting in the emergence of some entirely new cultural forms. Thus, creolization is a process whereby cultures undergo change and continuity as a result of cross-fertilization and interaction among them. Globalization has effectively de-territorialized and dislodged cultures and revalorized 'traveling cultures'. This is what has brought about creolization of cultures, making cultural boundaries fuzzy, fluid and indeterminate. Though the term creole and creolization has a racist and colonial history, today it seems to have come to acquire subversive meaning asserting hybridization and syncretic and mixed heritage against racist, fundamentalist as well as ethnically oriented mono-cultural tendencies.

Humans as agents as well as products of cultural translation not only translate themselves but also their others. This process of translating the other opens up the space where we strive to articulate cultural differences and otherness. But we cannot digest and transmute the otherness into our sameness. We reach a point of untranslatability, an incommensurable moment that becomes a moment of enunciative disturbance. This enunciatory moment produces the anxiety of facing otherness or difference that leads to the reduction of the otherness into sameness. This means we seem to feel the void of otherness by avoiding it. But this translating of the other is also the translation of the self in as much the other is translated in reference to one's self.

CANNIBALISM IN TRANSLATION

Post-modern approaches to translation present it as an act of cannibalism assimilating the voices and discourses into hybrids that often set boundaries and hierarchies between the self and the other.[6] The social elite/power elite translate/re-translate cultural

[5] ibid., p 597.

[6] The master narratives of the colonizers attempted to assimilate the colonized people and their cultures into their universalizing liberal-humanistic rhetoric of progress. This means the origin of the colonized people had to be re-presented. Of course, this strategy of translation is based on the narrow, positivistic and essentialist paradigm that undergirds it.

productions to suit their ends. They often wage discursive battles to domesticate truth and power through which self and its other is continuously constructed. The politics of transmuting every shade of otherness into a totalized sameness that is at the service of the power elite is the egoistic dynamism of the self facing its other. But this egoistic dynamism is interrupted by a fugitive power as there is an irreducible dimension of the other which cannot be erased. Yet we cannot undermine how the power elites translate the self and its other by means of a fantasy and fiction and claim truth to all their stakes. Thus, the strategies of translation conceal their imperialist logic to maintain power and privilege. In this context self and its other and truth itself become fugitive.

The binding power of traditional structures is steadily collapsing in the context of the new hybridized cultures. This new scenario offers new space for the subaltern self to translate itself and its oppressors. We can trace an emergence of a new form of power that is increasingly mobile, slippery, shifting, evasive and fugitive. This has multiplied the points of resistance and their peripheral effects are already felt in different degrees in our society. This means the subalterns are discovering new forms of translation that has the power to dismantle the armour of their oppressors and bring about a re-distribution of the power regime. Power comes to be seen to reside in its very exercise rather than in some institution and position. This has created a new space that is greeted by Homi Bhabha as the third space, a space of heterogenesis. This new space provides opportunity to escape the politics of polarity. This new realization of a hybridized self interrupts and disrupts the politics of polarity that builds the self in a contrasting binary relation to its other and is the space of harmony and co-existence.

THE GAZE OF THE OTHER AND THE SELF

Gaze is often seen as having an interruptive, disruptive and dismantling power. It interrogates the position of comfort and privilege that one enjoys. It triggers anxiety and even a feeling of shame. It gives one a feeling of being externally scrutinized and being watched over by an external invisible anonymous other. This means a gaze is an anxiety provoking external point that assails a subject. It is point of failure of the visual field, a point where perception breaks down and triggers a disturbance in the self. The gaze is imagined by the self in the horizon of the other. The presence in the absence of the other triggers a horizonal and aural presence that interrupts and redirects the self to an inward look. This awareness leads the self to recognize that there is a hole or a lack in him. This relation of lack apprehended in the horizon of the other creates a desire to translate oneself as the other. Hence, Lacan says that Gaze is governed by the function of a stain.[7] A stain blocks vision rather than offering itself as a thing to be seen, it becomes a point of disruption where the subject fails to see. Having perceived oneself as a lacking self in the absent presence of the other/ translated other, the self is led on a journey of mimicking the other and thus emerge as a translated self.

Europe translated its Other by ascribing a subject position that is inferior and thus constructed locations that allowed a dominant translation of self.[8] Since the other of Europe did not remain a passive and silent interlocutor, we can trace a wide range of responses that exhibit mimesis as well as a violent rejection of the subject position offered by Europeans to their subordinated subjects. Indeed, Europe constituted itself by appropriating its other. This process brought about complex, dynamic, conflictual and shifting relationships between the colonizer and the colonized wherein each side required the other. This is based on the vulnerability of the dominant who feel it imperative that the subordinated other should authorize the dominant self and recognize its priority and superiority.

The colonizers employed technologies of Knowledge/power from multiple sites to construct the colonized subject. But the fact that this process occludes the violence that accompanies the construction of the colonial subject is adequately and effectively exposed by the postcolonial discourse. This process of representation/translation of the colonized has been viewed as a hegemonic construction of the colonized as objects without history by Edward Said.[9] Paradoxically, the conversion of the colonized as ahistoricals provides a place

---

[7] http://www.cultureunbound.ep.liu.se/v2/a06/cu10v2a6.pdf. Accessed on Feb. 26, 2014.

[8] James Mill's remark, 'India must discard her Indianness in order to become civilized', illustrates how Indians were given an inferior subject position which they had to abandon in order to become civilized. See Tejaswini Niranjana, *Siting Translation*, p. 58. The same can be traced in the project of 'anglicizing' Indians articulated by Macaulay. See 'Minute on Indian Education' in *Macaulay, Prose and Poetry*, selected by G.M. Young (Cambridge: Harvard University Press, 1967). William Jones' construction of the 'Hindus' as indolent, submissive and unable to appreciate freedom manifests how he translated the colonial rule of the British as benevolent and necessary for Indians. See Tejaswini Niranjana, *Siting Translation*, p. 14.

[9] See Tejaswini Niranjana, *Siting Translation*, p. 3.

for the colonized in history, particularly in the progressive march of the Spirit in the Hegelian sense while simultaneously endorsing the teleological and hierarchical model of civilization, wherein the colonizers enjoy the privileged location of being on a higher rung. This imperial locus informed and triggered the civilizing mission of the colonizers and is cloned and reproduced by the colonized in diverse ways in post-colonial societies leading to the formation of a native neo-colonization. This means the colonized subject continues to live in translation, imaged and reimaged by colonial ways of seeing though we might view it as strategies of resistance by mimesis.

CONSTRUCTION OF THE SELF OF THE COLONIZER

In the relation between the colonizer and the colonized the translative process mostly constructs, maintains, naturalizes and normalizes the asymmetrical colonial relations. But this does not mean it only results in a dynamic uncritical mimesis as exposed by Ashis Nandy in book, *The Intimate Enemy*.[10] Indeed, in the light of the work of Luce Irigaray as well, we can see how mimesis masquerades as a covert strategy of resistance from both sides of the line of divide.[11] Yet alongside this mimesis, we can trace direct and overt resistance that translates the self as an agitator against the perceived or real oppressor. This can be viewed as crypto-mimesis. This means that the colonized native learns to play by the rules of the hegemon's rule and emerges as the new avatara of the colonizer. We can trace how the colonial mantle is worn by the natives who in turn have turned out to be in some cases the worst oppressors of their own people. In fact post-colonial societies across the globe exhibit regimes that are willing to do what the colonizers did. Pointing to this fact, Malcom Muggeridge is reported to have said with reference to Indians 'Indians are the only surviving English in the world'.[12]

In fact the territorialisation of India was a dynamic process and reached its final completion with the integration of Goa into the Union of India.

---

[10] See Asish Nandy, *The Intimate Enemy: Loss and Recovery of Self Under Colonialism* (New Delhi: Oxford University Press, 1983).

[11] Luce Irigaray, *This Sex which is not One*, Trans. Catherine Porter and Carolyn Burke (New York: Cornel University Press, 1985), 133–134.

[12] http://radioopensource.org/real-india-ashis-nandys-post-colonial-intimate-enemies/. Accessed March 27, 2014.

BRITISH INDIA: COLONIZED MINDS LEADING TO TRANSLATED SELF

The geographical entity of Europe and Britain in particular is transformed into a psychological entity in the minds of Indians. Ashish Nandy suggests that under colonization, the Indian self became a passive, life-denying feminine subject, which attempts to recover its lost masculinity through the reinvention of Gods like Rama and Krishna. It is said that Michael Madhusudan Dutt's epic *Meghnadvadh Kavya* redefined (translated) popular Hindu Mythology to fit the shift in values of the period. It appears that he translated the sacred figures Ram and Lakshman as more feminine than masculine characters to bring into focus the passive feminine self acquired under colonial influence and in contrast created the masculine heroes of Ravan and his son Meghnadh so that the defeat of these demons inspired Indians to fight the proud and imperial masculine British Empire in India.[13] Nandy further shows how Bankimchandra Chattopadhyay wrote an essay on Krishna, the Hindu God, who has been traditionally characterized as child-like, innocent and playful God but is transformed (translated) into a respectable, righteous and hard God. His aim was to militate against the humiliation that we felt in the face of arrogant and aggressive colonizers.[14] The emergence of the metaphor of Mother India is attributed to Bankimchandra Chattopadahyay's *Anandamath* by postcolonial researchers.[15] Indeed, Bankimchandra's novel *Anandamath* has been credited with constructingthe first nationalist imagination of the nation as 'mother' in Indian fiction. From that time onwards, the hymn *Bande Mataram* (Hail mother) has become an unofficial national anthem. Thus, Bankim successfully translated our territorial geography into a divinized geo-body and created a patriotic cartography. This construction of nation as a mother has gained great prominence in the politics of the right wing Hindu nationalism in the 1980s. The Hindutva ideologues have appropriated this metaphor of Mother India and translated themselves as the bearers of the mantle of true Indian nationalism. As a result, we notice the resurgence of the Hindu right, both at the regional as well as the national level. Thus, we can see how resurgent nationalism recasts the white men's burden to use Rudyard Kipling's popular phrase as the brown men's burden

---

[13] See Asish Nandy, *The Intimate Enemy* , p. 19.

[14] ibid, p. 23.

[15] http://postcolonial.org/index.php/pct/article/viewArticle/446/841. Accessed March 12, 2014.

and translated the civilizing mission of the British into a recovery of a golden nation through the construction of a neo-Hinduism.

This means the hegemonic Hindu nationalism erases and undercuts other narratives that manifest the synchronic origins of India as a nation in the nineteenth century. Thus, we can trace how right wing nationalism relies on a selective, linear and religious narrative of the rise of a nation.

PORTUGUESE INDIA

The substantial role of the Portuguese in relation to translation of India from a European point of view cannot be dismissed. One can trace a play of epistemology of ignorance as well as the politics of territorialisation in the entire saga of the Portuguese engagement with India. The quest for a lost Christian empire in the East is very much central to the epistemology of Ignorance. The *Estado da India* that the Portuguese established included territories that are beyond the Indian Union of today and excluded the main land of what we know today as India. Since the chief motivation of the Portuguese expedition was to displace the power of the Muslims in Europe and the Middle East and monopolize the spice and other trades in Europe, they only occupied strategic locations that would give them power and domination over the sea routes in the Arabian Sea.[16] Within this scheme of things, Goa emerged as the capital of the Portuguese possessions in the East. That is why it has been argued that without the Portuguese in the Arabian Sea, the entire history of India would have been very different. The colonial agents translated the local ways of speaking into objects of study so that their speakers could be made subjects of colonial rule. It is a saga of the West's confrontation with the confusion of tongues, in the legacy of the tower of Babel. The biblical story of the tower of Babel informed the colonial matrix as it shaped their pre-suppositions about human conditions that they encountered. The imperative to render these languages into writing resulted in fixing the speakers in colonial hierarchies. The language of colonial command required the command of colonial languages.[17] Thus, the colonial attempts to conquer the local languages were aided by tools such as lists of

---

[16] See M.N. Pearson, *The Portuguese in India* (New York: Cambridge University Press, 2006)

[17] See Joseph Errington, *Linguistics in Colonial World: a Story of Language, Meaning and Power* (Oxford : Blackwell, 2008), pp. 2–3.

words, dictionaries and grammars. Besides this linguistic conquest, the translative process embraced the pluri-religious as well as the complex cultural milieu of the colonized people. Indeed, the translative process led to the translation of geographical habitat of the colonized people. Goa underwent all these processes and in fact is a product of these modes of domination.

Konkani, the mother-tongue of Goans became the object of the translative process at the hands of the Portuguese missionary. The first Provincial Council (1567) of the Christian religious orders in Goa made it mandatory for the religious to study Konkani in order to be effective in their preaching.[18] Following this, the Franciscan and Jesuit educational institutions were established.[19] The schools chiefly worked to mediate the plantation of the catholic faith among the Goans. Both schools produced the first lists of words in Konkani-Portuguese vocabularies. Fr. Thomas Stephens SJ, of the Jesuit School, produced the first Konkani grammar[20] in Konkani. The religious pioneers of Konkani translated Konkani as 'lingua Brahmanica', the language of the Brahmins. This translation seems to have been appropriated by Goans as the brethren from Bahujan Samaj still consider Konkani as marked by caste and prefer Marathi to Konkani. Moreover, the entire Konkani movement is construed as a caste-based movement and the recent script conflict among the Catholics and the Hindus largely brought these conflicts into the open. Besides these inter-lingual translations, Fr. Thomas Stephens translated the Christian message into a *Vaisnava* medium in his famous book; *Kristapurana*[21], thereby inaugurating a process of cultural translation. This process of cultural translation developed to appropriate civic dimensions of Goan society such as the *Gaunponn* (*Gaunkaria* system), the ancient Goan land and village administrative bodies, which were translated as *Communidades* (village communes).[22] The translative process led to the steady emergence of Goa as the political as well as ecclesiastical capital of the Portuguese possessions in the East.

---

[18] See Manohar Rai Sardessai, *A History of Konkani Literature: From 1500 to 1992* (New Delhi: Sahitya Akademi, 2000), p. 12.

[19] Antonio Pereira, *The Makers of Konkani Literature* (Pilar: Antonio Pereira SJ, 1982).

[20] See Thomas Estevao, *Arte da lingua Canarim* (Goa: 1640).

[21] See Thomas Stephens, *Kristpurana*, Sixth edition, Ed. Caridade Drago, (Mumbai: Popular Press, 1996).

[22] Rui Gomes Pereira, *Gaunkari: The Old Village Associations* (Panjim : A Gomes Pereira, 1981). Also see Olivinho J. F. Gomes, *The Goan Village Communes* (Panjim: Vasantrao Dempo and Research Foundation, 2006).

CONTRASTING TRANSLATIVE PROCESS IN GOA

The discourse of the de-nationalisation of Goans[23] under colonization, championed by Tristao de Braganca Cunha also views Goans as translated people. This perspectve flowed from a nationalist paradigm which itself was born in dialogue with British colonization in India. Cunha's idea of denationalisation may be viwed within the framework of nationalism that emerged in the nineteenth and twentieth centuries in our country. This framework can help us comprehend the vision of pre-Portuguese Goa as *Konkan Kashi* by some historians of the post-colonial era.[24] The fact that such a translation of Goa forgets and keeps under erasure the Islamic sway over Pre-Portuguese Goa is clearly evident even in our day. This version of Goan history has steadily emerged as legitimate, normal and in accordance to the order of things while simultaneously concealing its process of construction. The specters of this nationalist translation are divisive and remain communal. Besides this translation, Goa and Goans are rendered by the reigning tourism industry as an exotic tourism destination.

One might identify two kinds of translative processes in conflict in Goa. One initiated by the Portuguese while the other is that which emerged under the British colonization of India. The theoretical optic that has reinforced the translatative processes that were triggered by British colonization legitimizes itself by putting on a mask of crass nationalism. The collision of these translative processes in Goa opens a new window on India and shows how the translative processes originating under British colonization are blind to some of the pervasive ways they lend themselves to be exploited by vested interests to serve their communal agenda. In fact a dialogical encounter of these two processes can expose how one of them authorizes a narrow and bigoted translation of India and its people that remains tainted by its leanings towards a majoritarian religious nationalism. The fact that Goan society is experiencing this collision of these processes is quite evident from the identity politics that emerged in Post-colonial Goa.[25] It only made evident

---

[23] http://www.lusotopie.sciencespobordeaux.fr/desai.pdf. Accessed on March 30, 2014.

[24] See Arun Sinha, *Goa Indica: A Critical Potrait of Post-colonial Goa* (Panjim: Promilla /BSA, 2002).

[25] See Victor Ferrao, "Between Two Communities: Past Disruption and Present Inter-relation" in Savio Abreu and Rudolf C. Heredia, *Goa 2011: Reviewing and Recovering Fifty Years* (New Delhi: Concept Publishing Company, 2014).

that if we study the other orientalism of the Portuguese, we have a new window on India that might dismantle the communal narrow nationalist translations of our country by exposing their origin in time and space.

Goa is in a unique position from where a politics of Knowledge that reproduces diverse shades of the European translative process in India can be interrogated and even dismantled. Although Goa and its unique history enjoys a subaltern location in the scheme of epistemic orientations among the intelligentsia in our country, its experience of an alternate colonization that was temporally prior to British colonization and and out lived it for some time, as well as its insulation from mainstream India for four hundred and fifty years of colonization provide a different historical durée and perspective. This colonial difference can provide a new window from which to understand the afterlife of British colonization that afflicts India as well as Goa.

TOWARDS A COUNTER EPISTEMOLOGY FROM GOA

No counter epistemology can be simply reduced to an end result of a linear history of knowledge production. There is always a circular horizon that informs such epistemologies as they look back and look ahead simultaneously and are grounded firmly on the silence of History. The scrutiny from the perspective of a worldview that is free from the taint of progress and modernity of enlightenment can indeed be a great way at looking at pre-colonial India. The counter epistemology is not a celebration of the creolized lusitanized translation of India and Goa in particular but a sincere effort to bring it into dialogue with the hegemonic process set into motion by British colonization. In this project one might find that the sociology of absence championed by Boaventura de Sousa Santos[26] can be of great help as it manifests how absences, exclusions and silences are actively produced as non-existent and hidden as non-credible alternatives to what is granted existence.

The forgetting of the Portuguese contribution to the understanding of India, which I have translated as the other orientalism,[27] renders

---

[26] http://www.eurozine.com/articles/2003-02-10-santos-en.html. Accessed March 21, 2014.

[27] See Victor Ferrao, "The Other Orientalism and its Challenges and Opportunities to the Church in Goa", in Alexio Menezes (ed.) *Luceas*, Patriarchal Seminary of Rachol, 2013–2014, pp. 66–82.

invisible, trivial and hence of negligible importance, critical dimensions of the reigning production of knowledge that legitimizes and serve some powers that be in contemporary India.

The imperial, hegemonic and oppressive praxis of the colonizers have a second life in the elite among the colonized. The elite seem to have successfully cloned the mode of production of hegemony of the imperial colonizer. This cloning of the imperial praxis of the colonizers often hides under the cover of a nationalistic discourse and as a result becomes invisible. Yet a critical articulation of these translated versions of the praxis of power and hegemony can certainly help us demonstrate how they reproduce the coloniality of power[28] by inventing a colonial difference that masquerades as orthodox nationalism. Like *Mimic Men* of V.S Naipaul, the elite exchange the native oranges for colonial apples.

[28] The term coloniality of power was coined by Anibal Quijano. See http://www.unc.edu/~aescobar/wan/wanquijano.pdf. Accessed March 21, 2014.

Dale Luis Menezes is a regular contributor to Goan newspapers and his reviews of Konkani publications and cultural issues can be accessed at www. daleluismenezes.blogspot.com. His publications include 'Gossiping about the Goan Ayah: Migration, Diaspora, and Anxieties at Home in Karmelin', in the Interdisciplinary Journal of Portuguese Diaspora Studies, *and 'Christians and Spices: A Critical Reflection on Indian Nationalist Discourses in Portuguese India', in* Práticas da História: A Journal of Theory, Historiography, and Uses of the Past, *and* Renver Borovp: Nibond & Niyaji (Writings on Sand: Essays & Reflections), *writings by the late Fr. Martinho Noronha, published by Dalgado Konkani Akademi.*

The essay attempts to discuss the issue of the controversy of scripts within the politics of the Konkani language. It traces the roots of the conflict over script to the nineteenth-century political manoeuvres in Goa and Bombay. Chiefly focusing on recurring patterns in the manner in which different groups within Goa and Bombay articulated their positions, this essay also suggests a shift in the manner in which contemporary linguistic politics is imagined and articulated.

BETWEEN LANGUAGE AND SCRIPTS: THE CONTROVERSIES OF KONKANI REVISITED

I

The purpose of writing this essay is to give the reader a fair representation of the linguistic politics surrounding the 'script issue' of Konkani, a language spoken in areas on the west coast of India. The issue of script in Konkani is primarily fought by two opposing camps: nagri[1] on the one hand, and romi and Kannada[2] on the other. The issue of the script controversy needs to be understood in its proper context, as it is only post-1987 when the Official Language Bill was passed in the Goa Legislative Assembly, that the issue of which script is natural and legitimate (*nizachi*) to Konkani started gaining political importance and significance. The issue of script was never central to the Konkani-Marathi controversy, but one would always come across sporadic references to the issue of script. The Catholic

---

[1] Conventional wisdom dictates that this script be known as 'devanagari'. But using such a term unnecessarily gives it a sacral veneer, thus for all my purposes the term 'nagri' will be used. 'Devanagari' (and its spelling variants) will be retained in quotations as and when they appear.

[2] As far as Konkani written in the Kannada script in Mangalore, Karnataka and the surrounding areas is concerned, a petition is pending in the Bangalore High Court which seeks to gain the recognition of the Sahitya Akademi, New Delhi.

and Hindu upper-caste intellectuals who espoused the cause of Konkani, whether before or after 1961, were clear in their dubious understanding that a "true 'lipi'" could only be nagri as "it goes without saying that a language derived from Sanskrit should inherit not only word material and grammatical rules from its source but also the script. When other daughters of Sanskrit (*sic*) have adopted Nagari, or script slightly deviating from Nagri (e.g. Marathi, Hindi, Gujarati), Konkani should also use 'Nagari' as its true 'lipi'."[3] Despite the clear leaning towards the nagri script, one also comes across such statements that further testify to the fact that the issue of script was not central to the Konkani-Marathi controversy: "...something must be done to secure uniformity of script. We acknowledge this to be a difficult task, but it cannot be definitely solved by making Devanagari THE script for Konkani. If the reader expects to find our opinion in these pages, then we venture to say that after much thought and effort to understand the genius of our people, we find that the Roman script is the best..."[4]

The genealogy of the script controversy goes back to the Konkani-Marathi controversy, which was a conflict between two opposing camps in the nineteenth century: Marathi-sympathizers on the one hand who argued that Konkani is merely a dialect of Marathi and Konkani defenders on the other who were of the strong opinion that Konkani is an independent language with a long literary tradition to its credit. It is possible for us to trace the genealogy of the script controversy between nagri and romi to the politics of nineteenth century Goa (and also Bombay) which was played out chiefly by the Catholic and Hindu elites, who had access to print by way of pamphlets, newspapers, magazines, and books.[5] This enterprise is also aided by a theoretical position that I wish to subscribe to in this essay. This theoretical position was chiefly developed by Susan Gal and Judith T. Irvine, who argue that in languages, ideologies of difference are chiefly constructed through three processes: iconicity, fractal recursivity and erasure.[6] For our purposes fractal recursivity best illustrates the case of the controversies of Konkani. Fractal recursivity is defined as "the projection of an opposition, salient at some level of relationship, onto some other level." In this schema,

[3] Mallaya, "Place and Future of Konkani in Present-day India," 6.

[4] Lima, "Konkani as a Medium of Instruction," 51–2.

[5] See Pinto, *Between Empires: Print and Politics in Goa*, 2007.

[6] See Gal and Irvine, "The Boundaries of Languages and Disciplines: How Ideologies Construct Difference"; Gal, "Language Ideologies Compared: Metaphors of Public/Private"; Gal, "A Semiotics of the Public/Private Distinction."

conflicts within groups "might be projected outward onto intergroup relations, or vice versa."[7] The second theoretical position in this essay is borrowed from the work of Victor Ferrao who in analyzing the colonial encounter with Christianity in Goa talks about the loss of self of native Goans due to Portuguese colonial practices and its subsequent recovery (largely in post-decolonized Goa) wherein the Catholic as well as the markers of his/her self (such as romi script or the writings in it for instance) are seen as 'polluted' and the dominant discourse and community in Goa, which is Hindu, therefore, views the Catholic and the markers of his/her self and identity as foreign and polluted.[8]

Thus, the politics of print, fractal recursivity and the notions of purity and pollution along with the loss of self due to Portuguese colonialism will, I believe, give a much needed theoretical perspective on the whole issue of the script controversy that has raged for so many decades. These theoretical assumptions will illustrate the manner in which ideologies of difference and conflicts created or established in the nineteenth century around the Konkani-Marathi controversy, also emerged during the romi-nagri controversy in the late twentieth century. This paper would also like to demonstrate that fractally recursive processes are also found within the romi script movement.

II

Before the Official Language Act of 1987, which made Konkani in the nagri script the official language of the state of Goa, the most pressing task that the defenders of Konkani had was to offer counter-arguments to the claims of Marathi-loyalists. Even at the All India Konkani Sahitya Parishad held at Bombay in April 1980, the issue of script was not central as R. N. Nayak writing an article for the souvenir discussed the problem of the dispersal of Konkani speakers across the west coast by suggesting that nagri should be the unifying script.[9]

The controversy between the protagonists of Konkani and those of Marathi emerged in the nineteenth century. It is interesting to

[7] Gal and Irvine, "The Boundaries of Languages and Disciplines: How Ideologies Construct Difference," 974; See also Messing, "Fractal Recursivity in Ideologies of Language, Identity and Modernity in Tlaxcala, Mexico," 96.

[8] See Ferrao, *Being a Goan Christian: The Politics of Identity, Rift and Synthesis*.

[9] Nayak, "Konknnicheo Kaim Somosya."Nayak's essay was published in the souvenir brought out on the occasion of the 13th All India Konkani Sahitya Parishad, held at Bombay from 12–13 April, 1980.

note here, as Rochelle Pinto does, that the Inquisition as well as the Portuguese state directed prohibitions only against Konkani because "no language other than Konkani seemed to pose a threat to the desired lusophone identity" but nonetheless "it was Marathi and English that grew in dominance through the nineteenth century. In a situation in which the Portuguese state had a bare legislative infrastructure to influence linguistic policy, the place and form of print and language in Goa were substantially shaped by the linguistic formation of the Goan elite and by its interests."[10] The propagation of languages other than Konkani allowed those elite Goans to skillfully use such "cultural and linguistic power" for a variety of purposes such as access to jobs, which could be denied to speakers who spoke only in Konkani. As a result there was nobody to speak for the cause of Konkani (and by extension its speakers) and hence, "its speakers were excluded from those circuits of power to which Marathi, English, and Portuguese [were] granted access."[11] It is against such a background that a key figure emerges, a figure who is central to the historiography and literature of the Konkani-Marathi controversy (from the vantage point of Konkani protagonists) as many later writers in favour of Konkani took inspiration from his writings. Joaquim Heliodoro da Cunha Rivara, for the first time advocated the use of Konkani as well as suggested measures for its uplift. In 1858, Cunha Rivara linked linguistic history with cultural identity and language rights, but his essay had negligible influence on Portuguese legislation and policy, despite Cunha Rivara being part of the Portuguese state machinery.[12]

The reason why Cunha Rivara is such a key figure in this controversy is because being the first to speak for Konkani he provided a justification for the protagonists of Konkani when they started defending and counter-arguing the claims of the protagonists of Marathi almost a century later. In fact, if one closely observes the narratives of the Konkani-protagonists who wrote from Bombay, Dharwar and Goa (and I have chiefly José Pereira in mind), it follows a particular trajectory where the controversy emerges due to claims of British orientalists like John Leyden which led to the oppression of Konkani and the coming of Cunha Rivara marks the point from where Konkani starts to shake off the shackles that had until now kept *her* in bounds, in a sense it starts resurrecting itself, despite the fact that Cunha Rivara barely knew

[10] Pinto, *Between Empires: Print and Politics in Goa*, 87.

[11] ibid., 95–6.

[12] ibid., 101–2.

any Konkani.[13] Pereira further remarks that by 1855, "the Konkani language was not highly esteemed by its speakers when Cunha Rivara landed in India." The reason, Pereira believed, for Goa's Hindus to support Marathi was because of "past Inquisitional harassment and present Governmental discrimination..."[14] Although Pereira's assessment of the situation may seem correct or logical, he did not figure out the whole story as such resources like jobs and land were intimately linked up with the linguistic politics of Goa. Further, new research and perspectives in the history of the Inquisition in Goa do suggest that Konkani was used despite the harassment.

Writing in 1971, when a move to get the recognition of the Sahitya Akademi for Konkani was gaining momentum (which was eventually given in 1975), and the age old Konkani-Marathi controversy appears to have been raked up again, Pereira published *Konkani: A Language; A History of the Konkani Marathi Controversy*. Pereira's book gives us an introduction to the debates that took place over the nineteenth and the twentieth centuries in Bombay, in Goa, and to a certain extent in Dharwar as well. Pereira's aim was obviously to delegitimize the claims of the Marathi protagonists. Thus, he starts by demolishing the arguments of British linguists/orientalists like John Leyden, William Carey, John Wilson, Francis Hamilton Buchanan etc. whom he believes were responsible for the emergence of the Konkani-Marathi controversy by making baseless and irresponsible arguments and statements. The actual physical site of the controversy appears to be Bombay, from a reading of Pereira's work because he largely focuses on the writings of such persons like Gerson da Cunha, R. G. Bhandarkar, Varde Valaulikar, and Jerome Antony Saldanha, who were all based in Bombay and were vigorously debating amongst themselves.[15]

---

[13] For instance, Pereira says, "It is saddening to think that the present controversy [Konkani-Marathi] started with a brilliant man's [Leyden's] confessed ignorance [about Konkani]." Pereira, *Konkani: A Language; A History of Konkani Marathi Controversy*, 5 and also see the discussion on pp. 6–16; A much more recent work but drawing from the same paradigm as Pereira's is Gomes, *Konkani Literature in Roman Script – A Brief History*, 169–172.

[14] Pereira, *Konkani: A Language; A History of Konkani Marathi Controversy*, 21. For a brief discussion of the effects of Portuguese colonial policies on Goan Hindu intellectuals like A. K. Priolkar and Prabhakar Angle see Souza, "Some Contrasting Visions of Luso-Tropicalism in India."

[15] See Pereira, *Konkani: A Language; A History of Konkani Marathi Controversy*, chap. 7 and 8.

Cunha Rivara's pronouncements were vehemently opposed by one Suriyaji Anand Rau, who was a contemporary of Cunha Rivara and also the official translator of the Portuguese government and who realized the effects that Cunha Rivara's pronouncements could have if Konkani received the support of the state as it would threaten "to overturn what had already been achieved through their own efforts and through the official support of the Catholic elite."[16] What emerges from Pinto's reading of the politics of Konkani-Marathi controversy in the nineteenth century when Cunha Rivara was writing is that the access to Marathi, chiefly a Marathi education, enabled the Hindu elite to gain access to government jobs amongst other things through the use and patronage of Marathi, which scholars like José Pereira who operated in a British orientalist paradigm completely missed. Instead, we find explanations that tend to blame a faceless, nebulous, non-existent outsider[17] – "the Marathas". It is interesting to note the link that Pereira provides, in this context: "But what a Britisher [John Leyden] has done in ignorance, was put to deliberate political use, in the latter years of the same century, by Britain's conquered enemies, the Marathas. The latter, having lost India, made use of the dialect theory to seek to acquire Goa. Through these and other efforts, the Konkani way of life was relegated to the status of a sub-culture,with the Konkanis, like the Greeks under Turkish rule, becoming ashamed of their own speech and often affecting only that to which official prestige has been accorded."[18] For Pereira, the supporters of Marathi were outsiders or non-Goans, but as mentioned above this does not seem to be the case. The assertion of Prabhakar Angle that "[a]n attempt is made in some quarters to create the impression that Marathi is an alien language in Goa and that some outside elements with vested interests are sponsoring the Marathi agitation…[n]othingcould be further from the truth" makes us understand that it was the Hindu Goan elites that were the actual Marathi-protagonists. Angle further asserts that it is the Goan Hindu who has always backed Marathi

[16] Pinto, *Between Empires: Print and Politics in Goa*, 105.

[17] I refer to it as such because, in the writings that the controversy had spawned, one does not get to hear about non-Goan names who vehemently supported Marathi against Konkani. The Konkani-Marathi controversy was fought by upper-caste Goans in Bombay and Goa. Throughout the nineteenth and twentieth centuries it was the caste elites who spoke for and against Konkani and Marathi.

[18] Pereira, "The Struggle for Konkani Schools," 41.

because Goan Hindus during the Portuguese time had imparted primary education to their children in Marathi and subsequently sent them to Portuguese or English medium schools. This practice, he asserted, continues even today as "the number of pupils in Marathi schools" in post-decolonization Goa bears "eloquent testimony to the continuance of the old practice."[19]

Thus, having established the historical background in which the Konkani-Marathi controversy emerged, we can proceed to study and understand some key arguments in this debate that would help us in establishing the links with the romi-nagri controversy of recent times through our theoretical positions of the politics of print, fractal recursivity and the politics of purity and pollution along with loss of self due to Portuguese colonialism.

A crucial figure in our understanding of recursivity in the first half of the twentieth century is Vaman Verde Valaulikar (also known as Shennoy [or Shenoi] Goembab) whose work and life also reveal in a sense, the mimesis of arguments advanced by the Marathi protagonists against Konkani. Similar arguments and accusations were leveled against romi by the nagri protagonists, who see themselves as legitimate successors of the legacy of Valaulikar. José Pereira discusses the reasons that made Valaulikar turn to Konkani despite the fact that he started writing in Marathi first when he was in Bombay. Valaulikar, it seems was criticized for writing in "inauthentic" Marathi. Further, "When in Bombay the servility of the Goan Hindu to their Maratha opposite numbers and *their shame for Konkani (which they shared with the Goan Christians)* saddened and angered him." Such "pedagogical difficulties" that Valaulikar faced made him, argues Pereira, to turn "the Marathists' argument against themselves, alleging that, if Marathi was indeed the language of Goa, the Goans did not need men coming from above the Ghats to teach it to them."[20]

Pereira's analysis, we are afraid, tells a partial story. Reading one of Valaulikar's texts, produced in the 1930s, it becomes at once clear that persons supporting the cause of Marathi viewed Konkani (whether in nagri or romi) through the lenses of 'purity and pollution'. Valaulikar alludes to the fact that Marathi protagonists called Konkani as "impure Marathi" while also discussing the *shuddhikarann*(purification or purging) of names of places and persons by protagonists of Marathi,

---

[19] Angle, *Myth and Truth: Marathi in Goa*, 3.

[20] Pereira, *Konkani: A Language; A History of Konkani Marathi Controversy*, 66–7. Emphasis mine.

giving copious examples too. What Valaulikar is alluding to is the rendering of Konkani words in Marathi diction and intonation: "According to their own standards they [Marathi protagonists] are purifying these names," he said.[21] In the introduction of the same book, Valaulikar believed that many obstacles in the path of Konkani have been removed by him as he had systematically managed to demolish the arguments of the Marathi protagonists and thus, Konkani speakers should start working for the development of their language and give it world recognition. It should also be borne in mind, that by choosing the nagri script, Valaulikar was writing for a very small audience which automatically excluded the low-caste, working-class, romi-using Catholic population of Bombay.

At this point we need to focus on the arguments put forward by Marathi protagonists. It is a curious case of how politics is repeating itself as and when the issue of language becomes a site of contestation in the political sphere, which further lends credence to our theoretical position of fractal recursivity. I have selected here a set of articles originally written in 1939 in the Portuguese newspaper *O Ultramar* by Balkrishna Waman Sawardekar. These articles were collected and published in a book[22] in 1971 as well. What is interesting here is that Sawardekar wrote at a time when an All India Konkani conference was held in Karwar in 1939; a conference that laid the ground for the further consolidation of Konkani (in the nagri script) in Goa. In 1971 when these articles were published (posthumously), we need to remember that Konkani protagonists were vigorously making arguments for recognition from the Sahitya Akademi.What also needs to be borne in mind was that José Pereira was writing simultaneously. The choice of *O Ultramar* by Sawardekar to argue for the case of Marathi is curious if not clever as this paper largely stood for the interests of Catholic brahmins against the Catholic *chardos* (loosely Kshatriyas).[23] Getting a three-part article in a newspaper such as *O Ultramar* does tell us something about the alignment of various groups in the linguistic politics of Goa. Sawardekar being a brahmin himself, albeit a supporter of Marathi, had to seek the print space controlled by Catholic brahmins.

Sawardekar makes a distinction between Konkani spoken/written by a Catholic (i.e. the Portuguese inflected and written in romi script) and that spoken/written by a Hindu (obviously in the nagri script);

---

[21] Goembab, *Konknni Bhaxechem Zoit*, 47. This book was written in nagri and the translation is mine.

[22] See Sawardekar, *The Language of Goa*.

[23] Pinto, *Between Empires: Print and Politics in Goa*, 45.

the latter he considered as "less faulty". Therefore, Sawardekar says, "So the questions before us are: which Konkani should we accept? Should we accept that Konkani which contain sentences that begin with relative pronouns like 'jo', 'joslo' etc. and is filled with Portuguese words? Or should we accept that Konkani which flaunts the Arabic and Persian words like 'nyaya-kacheri'...? Or should we accept that John Bull type of Konkani...full of harsh words such as 'leader', 'worker', 'journalist', 'butler', etc.?"[24] Sawardekar tries to demonstrate that the Konkani that the Catholics and Hindus speak is impure and inadequate because Portuguese and Marathi words (in Roman script publications and in the writings and speeches of Hindu protagonists of Konkani, respectively) are found.[25] Sawardekar ends his essay by asserting that Konkani "...has neither body nor soul. Whatever exists is hotch-potch, *impure* and *contaminated*. We will have to purge it first if we are going to adopt it. *We will have to dress it properly before using it*."[26]

Sawardekar's views need to be understood in relation to Valaulikar's ideas for the simple reason that Sawardekar had managed to provide a trenchant critique of Valaulikar'sideological position. Sawardekar accuses Valaulikar of "cloth[ing] Konkani in sacred robes and as such it has assumed a very beautiful and chaste form. His is a completely Konkani diction no doubt but this is what has made it very *unintelligible*."[27] Sawardekar believed that the cause of the "rigidity" of Valaulikar's Konkani can be found in *Konknni Bhaxechem Zoit* written by Valaulikar himself. Sawardekar says, "[Valaulikar] maintains in this book that for hundreds of years this Konkani was spurned by all the people and using his pet weapon of the sad tale of the collection of Konkani books that the Portuguese had burnt down during their conquests in India sharply criticizes Hindus alone for their lack of love for their language and region and holds them responsible for this affront. The archaeologist (*sic*) Cunha Rivara is responsible for this fabrication of this tale...From what Shri Shanai Goebab [Shenoi Goembab] admits, it appears that the Konkani that he seeks to resuscitate is not the Konkani that Hindus or Christians in Goa or other people in the rest of India speak or write but the Konkani that was spoken hundreds of years ago and which is even now found at times being used in some out-of-the-way village by old or illiterate women."[28]

[24] Sawardekar, *The Language of Goa*, 11.
[25] ibid., 2–4.
[26] ibid., 71. Emphasis mine.
[27] ibid., 19. Emphasis mine.
[28] ibid., 22.

Sawardekar's main problem with Valaulikar was his pungent critique of the relationship that Goan Hindus had with Marathi. Valaulikar maintained that the Hindus of Goa mistakenly considered Marathi as the sacred language of Hinduism and he also maintained that during the religious sessions where the stories in the Puranas were read out in Marathi "most of the men doze [off] and women as a rule chat loudly about their everyday affairs." Valaulikar also believed that the Hindus took to Marathi because a "ready-made literary medium in Marathi" already existed and thus if Konkani was adopted by the Goan Hindu, it first needed development and this needed effort. Valaulikar also found the argument that Marathi was the business language of Goa baseless.[29]

At this point we also need to take into consideration another essay that was published in the pages of *O Ultramar* by Roque Correia Afonso in 1914. This essay was translated into English and published *circa* 1980s by a Vincent of Benaulim.[30] Afonso here tries to advocate primary education in Konkani using the Roman script for the illiterate Catholics of Goa, emphasizing also that this education should be largely "oral" in nature. But it is also interesting how he ends his essay saying that "[a]s for our vision, I do not hesitate, for the time being, in choosing Marathi and not a resuscitated Konkani as the point towards which we should direct our progress in regional language." Correia Afonso also ends up reiterating his original thesis that "spoken Konkani" is "the *actual* vehicle for public education."[31] Here, we need to ask why a paper such as *O Ultramar* with its sympathy for the Catholic brahmin, would espouse the cause of Konkani for illiterate Catholics? The answer may lie in the comments of Mariano Saldanha, who taught Sanskrit in Lisbon. For Saldanha, "An education in Konkani...would keep them [Goan peasants and migrants] in their place, and equip them with a vibrant organic culture."[32] Saldanha's concerns arose due to anxiety that if the Goan peasant was given an education in Portuguese, he would then aspire to a less laborious life thereby upsetting the existing power relations in the village.

If Pereira believed that discriminatory Portuguese colonial policies had made the Hindus take refuge in Marathi (as mentioned above), Angle, a protagonist of Marathi, was not far off from Pereira when he

---

[29] See Pereira, *Konkani: A Language; A History of Konkani Marathi Controversy*, 68.
[30] Unfortunately, very little bibliographical details are available for this publication, which is available in the Krishnadas Shama Library, Panjim, Goa.
[31] Correia Afonso, *Konkani for Christians*, 11. Emphasis in original.
[32] Pinto, *Between Empires: Print and Politics in Goa*, 62.

asserted that the 'assimilationist' policies adopted by the Portuguese had divided Goa's population into "Hindus and Christians" with "[t]he 'assimilated' section of the population gradually divorced from its original Indian culture. It was alienated from Marathi and instead, adopted Portuguese as its language of conversation and correspondence. The lower echelons of society started writing in Konkani in Roman characters. Such a situation gave rise to two categories of Konkani-speaking people: one speaking a *pure Konkani* by virtue of having studied Marathi and the other speaking Konkani influenced by Portuguese and deprived of a chance to learn Marathi."[33] Dubious as Angle's claims may sound, it is important for us to note how he structures his understanding of the politics and history of the Konkani-Marathi controversy, as well as the history of Konkani itself, through notions of purity and pollution.

Thus, to sum up this section, the Konkani-Marathi controversy saw the emergence of certain claims and arguments by the Marathi protagonists against Konkani. First, the Marathi protagonists viewed Konkani and its speakers as 'impure', secondly, it was alleged that Konkani had no classical literature. To counter such an orientalist preoccupation with origins, antiquity and sequential ordering, Konkani protagonists like José Pereira started emphasizing the "achievement" of Konkani vis-à-vis Marathi by stressing that prose in Konkani predated Marathi and as far as poetry was concerned "the versifiers of the Ghats continued to turn out their interminable doggerels..."

Further Pereira states that "[i]t was fortunate for Konkani that its sixteenth and seventeenth century scholars wrote their verses in Marathi[34] – which could not have been otherwise that what they are, "dreary and soporific."[35] To the Marathi protagonists' allegation that Konkani did not exist because this language was never known by the name of Konkani, Pereira gives a chronological list of references to the word *Konkani* in its various forms.[36] Lastly,

[33] Angle, *Myth and Truth: Marathi in Goa*, 4–5. Emphasis mine.

[34] Most likely Pereira is referring to such works of poetry like the *Kristapurana* of the Jesuit Thomas Stephens. For many years now, Stephens' composition was believed to be in Marathi. Vinay Dharwadker, writing about the history of English writing in India has this to say about the *Kristapurana*, "...Father Estavam [Thomas Stephens], lived in Salsette and Goa for over thirty-five years, studied Indian languages, and composed a mixed Marathi-Konkani version of the Gospel known as the *Christian Purana*, which was published posthumously in Goa in 1640." See Dharwadker, "English in India and Indian Literature in English: The Early History, 1579–1834," 97.

[35] Pereira, *Konkani: A Language; A History of Konkani Marathi Controversy*, 2.

[36] ibid., 82ff.

the shame that is very much part of the discourse of this controversy also needs to be factored in while understanding the Konkani-Marathi controversy.

III

The passing of the Official Language Act brought with it new problems for the people who used the Roman script. It appears that at the time of the passing of the Act, the major concern was with the loss of cultural identity. Later commentators have taken such arguments at face value and have not explained why the Hindu community was opposing the move to make Konkani the official language of Goa. Here is a comment by Alexandre Moniz Barbosa, a journalist who had witnessed closely these times, "It did appear absurd that the Marathi lobby feared that the majority community could stand to lose its cultural identity if Konkani and not Marathi was to be made the sole official language. Their mother tongue was after all Konkani and the supporters of Marathi were just a few among them. Marathi was used for cultural and religious purposes."[37] What Barbosa misses over here is that Marathi apart from being a cultural and religious language of the Hindus in Goa could also provide access to government jobs by sidetracking the Catholic, just like in the case of the nineteenth century when Cunha Rivara was writing in favour of Konkani.

So, the question of when the script becomes a contentious issue is still persisting. It is my claim here that the romi-nagri issue gained center-stage only post-1990 due to a crucial move by Shashikala Kakodkar, who at that time held the education portfolio.[38] Without naming Shashikala Kakodkar, Barbosa holds her responsible for "stok[ing] the embers of the Konkani-Marathi feud by refusing government grants to schools that did not switch to the *regional language* as a medium of instruction. Overnight hundreds of schools in the State rushed to make the change, a move in which Marathi gained tremendously...The duel did not end at that. Instead of laying to rest the language controversy in Goa, the Act led to further polemics of script..."[39] Although Barbosa is spot-on in reading the

---

[37] Barbosa, *Goa Rewound: A Land Liberated, A People Beleaguered*, 83.

[38] This despite the fact that the Dalgado Konknni Akademi was formed *circa* 1987. For reasons that I shall discuss below, it is my claim that the Dalgado Konknni Akademi could gain prominence only at the turn of this century.

[39] Barbosa, *Goa Rewound: A Land Liberated, A People Beleaguered*, 61. Emphasis mine.

problem of script in the Konkani-Marathi controversy, the actual moment of script being contentious only comes with the switch-over of the Diocesan schools, more than 120 in number, to Konkani in the nagri script. It is my claim over here, taking Barbosa's point forward, that the Catholics for the first time realized the nature and degree of their disenfranchisement because, as stated at the outset, the markers of their self were denied to them and an alien script (and a language as well, some might say) was heaped on them.

The Catholics that had fought for the recognition of Konkani in the 1980s, suddenly found themselves at a disadvantage because Konkani in the nagri *script* was made the official *language* of Goa. The Official Language Act provided Marathi for "all official purposes", thus, denying the Roman script user access to governmental jobs, as Olivinho Gomes rightly points out.[40] My point can also be understood in the context of the recent controversy over the Medium of Instruction that erupted somewhere around 2011, wherein Catholics were accused of supporting and demanding English at the primary level at the cost of *regional languages*. Thus, Ferrao clarifies and contextualizes the issue for us, "The Goan Christian feels the ambiguity, familiarity and foreignness, of the Konkani that is taught at the primary level. There is a familiarity as well as foreignness to it. From the Christian point of view the familiarity mostly comes from the meaning (semantic) while the phonetic as well as the script brings in a feeling of its alieness. Thus, for instance, the meaning of 'aslo'and'axil'lo' is same but certainly there is a phonetic gap as well as a void of the script. That is why Konkani as it is taught in our schools will always remain an acquired tongue for the Christians. This brings us to a real but disconcerting trauma felt by the Christians of Goa which seem to suggest that they are losing their grasp over their mother tongue."[41] Ferrao further asserts that since nagri is forced down the throat of Catholic children, such a move "calls for an effort to decipher this feeling that seems to lie behind the choice for English. Hence, in the choice for English lies the hidden choice for Konkani as spoken by the Christians in their homes. It is the breaking of the silence of the muted tongue in the Roman script. The choice of English demonstrates that cultural memory cannot be erased."[42] New research and views in the field of linguistics have argued very convincingly that "language shift must be viewed as

[40] See the brief discussion in Gomes, *Konkani Literature in Roman Script – A Brief History*, 177–8.
[41] Ferrao, "The Shadow of the Past."
[42] ibid.

a fundamentally social process in which individuals react to social changes that in turn affect their linguistic ideologies and social identities, and ultimately their language use."[43]

I wish to focus the attention of the reader, now, toward the formation of Dalgado Konknni Akademi and one of its founding members, Fr. Freddy J. da Costa. The story goes that after the Official Language Act was passed a meeting was convened by the Thomas Stephens Konknni Kendr under the aegis of Frs. Matthew Almeida and Pratap Naik. When Fr. Matthew Almeida asserted that all the people of Goa have accepted the Official Language Act, Fr. Freddy lodged his protest saying, "Who told you that the Bill (*sic*) has been accepted by everybody?"[44] The reason why Fr. Freddy pushed for the establishment of the Dalgado Konknni Akademi was because, "This [Dalgado Konknni Akademi] academy is not against Devnogri. The Goa Government's choice of Devnogri for Konkani is accepted by us with all our heart. But still we cannot count out the hundreds of writers who have produced *sahit'ya* using the Roman script. And because we cannot forget or exclude the writers and the romi script, it is necessary to form the Dalgado Konknni Akademi."[45]

The Dalgado Konknni Akademi could not pursue its goals vigorously after its establishment. Many would attribute this to the fact of the untimely demise of Fr. Freddy himself along with Felicio Cardozo in a car crash. That may very well be the case. But along with it we also need to factor in the aims of the Akademi and a closer reading of it reveals that it was primarily designed to protect the interest of the writers. In 1988, when the idea to establish the Dalgado Konknni Akademi was first mooted in a meeting, four motions were passed and one of them goes thus: "The Sahitya Akademi, New Delhi which gives awards to Konkani, should consider books written in Devnogri, Romi and Kannadda. Similarly, the Goa Konkani Akademi, Kala Akademi (Goa), Konkani Bhasha Mandal and other institutes and academies should take note of *sahit'ya* written in Devnogri as well as romi."[46] For me this is crucial to explain why the issue of script became so contentious for the Christians of Goa. It is only with the political move effected by Shashikala Kakodkar post-1990 that a space was created to take

---

[43] Messing, "Fractal Recursivity in Ideologies of Language, Identity and Modernity in Tlaxcala, Mexico," 95.

[44] Gomes, *Konknni Bagentlem Pormollit Ful – Padri Freddy*, 69–70.Fr. Freddy said, "Konnem sanglam tumkam hem Bill soglleamnim manun ghetlam mhonn…"

[45] ibid., 72. Translation mine.

[46] ibid., 77–8. Translation mine.

up the cause of the romi script in a wider political arena which the Dalgado Konknni Akademi filled. For how else would one explain the dormancy of the Dalgado Konknni Akademi till 2001 when a "revived" Akademi "went all out to secure justice to Konkani in the Roman script by virtually launching some sort of an agitation to press for its legitimate demands"?[47] The Akademi (especially) post-2006 has been very active in conducting various activities and also undertaking publication of romi books.

IV

Having analyzed the long and tortuous genealogy of the script controversy by way of the Konkani-Marathi controversy, it is time to engage more deeply with the arguments advanced by the nagri lobby or nagri protagonists against the Roman script through the theoretical positions adopted at the outset of this essay. But before we look at some of the arguments, it is appropriate here to introduce and define the theoretical positions that I had assumed at the start of this essay in the form of fractal recursivity and notions of purity and pollution along with the loss of self due to Portuguese colonialism. Doing so, I believe, will give the reader a better grasp on the operations of such processes in the linguistic politics of Konkani.

Since fractal recursivity involves the process of projecting difference at multiple levels, I will in this section demonstrate how the arguments and allegations that were advanced by the Marathi protagonists against the Konkani protagonists recur in the controversy between the nagri and romi scripts.

Victor Ferrao, a priest in the Archdiocese of Goa and Daman, in his *Being a Goan Christian* argues that the dominant discourse which is Hindu and upper-caste in Goa views "the colonial period as an era of pollution..." Thus, the principle of purity and pollution becomes the chief basis of 'othering' the Goan Christian.[48] Goan self and identity before the Portuguese, argues Ferrao, "was inseparable from the community owned land (*ganvkari* system) and Portuguese colonialism which resulted in a loss of the land also resulted in the 'loss of self'."[49] The problem that now faced the Hindu and the Catholic was the recovery or regaining of the 'self'; the upper-caste Hindus looked towards the Hindu culture of mainland India and

[47] Gomes, *Konkani Literature in Roman Script – A Brief History*, 180.
[48] Ferrao, *Being a Goan Christian: The Politics of Identity, Rift and Synthesis*, 22.
[49] ibid., 21.

the upper-caste Catholics identified themselves with the Portuguese Empire. Therefore, the question that needs to be asked of Ferrao's work is how the low-caste, working-class Catholic recovered their 'self'? The answer would definitely lie in the romi*lipi*.[50] Romi was a crucial marker of the Catholic self which was denied to the Catholic by the hegemonic imposition of nagri on them. The arguments of the nagri lobby – chiefly the Konkani litterateur Ravindra Kelekar – from the 1970s at least, reveal that the romi script was viewed as 'polluted' and thus not legitimate for carrying forward or progressing Goa's culture and identity.

Ferrao calls this as "[t]he politics of exclusion [which] in Goa is complex but one can somehow construct its trajectory, if one chiefly follows the politics of language as it unfolds in Goa. At the time of the Opinion Poll, the Christians who promoted the unique identity of Goa were seen as anti-national..."[51] Similarly, those demanding the official recognition of the Roman script in Goa are also seen as anti-nationals and agents of the Portuguese.

To understand the fractally recurring processes in the romi-nagri controversy, we can profitably refer to an essay that Ravindra Kelekar wrote for the romi weekly, *Vavraddeancho Ixtt* in 1980. He says that in 1962, when he was preparing a bibliography of Konkani works from the seventeenth century till present-times, he had browsed through all books published in the Roman script and except Joaquim Antonio Fernandes' *Amcho Soddvonddar* [Our Saviour] there is absolutely no "standard" book published in the Roman script.[52] What the late Kelekar, who was recently awarded the Dnyanpith award, is trying to do is deny the legitimacy of writings produced in the Roman script. The process of *erasure*, as explained by Gal and Irvine is also visible here.[53] In further denying the legitimacy of romi, Kelekar claims that the *sahitya* or literature in the Roman script is for the "neoliterates or illiterates" and that it cannot be included in the "classics."[54] It is

---

[50] *Tiatr* and *cantaram* are other markers that are chiefly carried through the vehicle of romi.

[51] Ferrao, *Being a Goan Christian: The Politics of Identity, Rift and Synthesis*, 28. The Opinion Poll decided that Goa would remain a separate state and not get integrated into the neighbouring Maharashtra.

[52] Kelekar, "Koddu Okhdacho Ghontt," September 6, 1980.

[53] Gal and Irvine, "The Boundaries of Languages and Disciplines: How Ideologies Construct Difference," 974. They say, "*Erasure* is the process in which ideology, in simplifying the field of linguistic practices, renders some persons or activities or sociolinguistic phenomena invisible. Facts that are inconsistent with the ideological scheme may go unnoticed or get explained away."

[54] Kelekar, "Koddu Okhdacho Ghontt," September 6, 1980.

my claim here that Kelekar was viewing and understanding the romi literature and culture through the lens of purity and pollution, as it is clear that Kelekar is directing his condescending remarks about "neo-literates or illiterates" to especially the low-caste Catholics. This is amply demonstrated by the following excerpt from Kelekar's essay: "The Gavddis, Kunbis, Velips and Dhangars [Scheduled Tribes and Castes] are the most backward people in Goa. How is it that a *lipi* that children of such backward people (*sic*) can learn with ease is found to be difficult by Catholic children? Are our Catholic children more backward than the Gavddis...Educated Christian feels ashamed to speak Konkani; he feels that he would be considered a simpleton if he does so. 20–25 years in the future when all the backward classes and castes of Catholics will get educated in Goa, there would be not even a single Catholic household that would speak in Konkani. Till their mothers are alive they will speak in Konkani and then give it up. In the next generation there will not be a single Catholic who will speak Konkani."[55] Kelekar, like Mariano Saldanha mentioned above, is reacting to an anxiety that he and persons like him felt at that time, for the mass of Catholics was very much important for the imposition of Konkani in the nagri script. If this did not happen and the Catholic gained in self-respect and self-esteem, it would automatically pose a challenge to the brahmanical power and hegemony in Goa, manifested through the politics and domination of the nagri script.

Further Kelekar says, "As a language Konkani is not inferior to Marathi and Hindi. But a person writing in the Roman script does not improve his literary standard; on the contrary he pulls down the literary standard to his level. Thus, such writings cannot be included in *classics*...There is only one reason why the writings in the Roman script appear to be anemic and it is due to the fact that romi writers do not know any *desi* (regional or Indian) language like Marathi, Hindi, Sanskrit etc. and hence a feeling of nationalism do not course through their veins (*sic*)."[56]

It is my claim here that just like the protagonists of Marathi were trying to deny Konkani any legitimacy by calling it a mere dialect of Konkani, the protagonists of nagri have done the same by making such arguments of which, I believe, Kelekar's essay provides a brilliant representation.

Secondly, focusing on the issue of standardizing the orthography of Konkani in the Roman script, the patterns recurring from

---

[55] Kelekar, "Koddu Okhdacho Ghontt," September 13, 1980. Translation mine.
[56] ibid., September 6, 1980. Translation mine.

the nineteenth century can also be observed. These patterns are embedded in the culture of print politics of that century as well as the succeeding one. In the beginning of the twentieth century when the subaltern, working-class, low-caste Catholic gained access to print, the elite Catholics would often criticize such people about the way they wrote Konkani. This was "volubly" protested and rejected.[57] The reader will also remember how Valaulikar had criticized the practice of Marathi protagonists to Marathicize or in a sense *standardize* Konkani words in a Marathi diction and intonation.

Such processes of standardizing orthography do fractally recur as even within the romi groups there is no consensus regarding the standardization and repeated attempts have met with frustration. The Dalgado Konknni Akademi had published an orthography[58] aimed at standardization, but differences of opinions do persist. Let us take here the case of a recent cover story in a romi magazine. This story was written by its own editor, Fausto V. da Costa. Da Costa begins by observing the process of fractal recursivity (without realizing it). He says, "We Goans are a curious (*vichitr*) case. First we fought for our language together and later because of the script issue. Further, the issue of how to write Konkani in a standardized form has divided the writers of this [Roman] script into various groups."[59] The issue of standardization within romi is also intimately linked to a certain notion of 'purity' whereby, if this is not achieved one is considered to have erred and in a sense one is considered not to have lived-up to a certain high, pure ideal of language and also culture. Da Costa's quote will illustrate this: "I remember the time when I would write for such weeklies like *Goencho Mog* and *The Goa Times*. Both these weeklies had their own way of writing and I had to adjust according to their respective orthographies. The editor of *The Goa Times* would not accept my articles if I had used the language (*bhas*) that was demanded in *Goencho Mog*. When Dr. Simon C. Fernandes, the then editor of *The Goa Times* expired, I took over the reins from him. I had to stick to the style and orthography that was used before me. My point here is this: despite knowing proper grammar and orthography I had to write in wrong (*chukichi*) Konkani."[60]

---

[57] See Pinto, *Between Empires: Print and Politics in Goa*, 114–6.

[58] Naik, *Romi Lipient Konknni Brounchi Promann Rit (The Standard Orthography of Konknni in Roman Script)*; In this context see also Halarnakar et al., *Romi Lipint Konknni Borounchi Nemavoll* which was published by the Goa Konkani Akademi three years before the Dalgado Konknni Akademi's standardized orthography.

[59] Costa, "Konknniche Bara Brestar, Tera Sukrar," 31. Translation mine.

[60] ibid. Translation mine.

If Valaulikar and José Pereira did allude to the shame that speakers of Konkani felt during the period of the Konkani-Marathi controversy, Ravindra Kelekar also mentions the shame that the Catholic felt in speaking Konkani in the context of the romi-nagri controversy. While the issue of shame needs a greater study through a sympathetic approach to the situation, it will suffice here to say that 'shame' has been very much a part of the discourse of the controversies of Konkani and it is a process that has recurred fractally as well. This shame can also be linked to Ferrao's argument of the loss of self which curiously provides a unique window for understanding 'shame' in the context of Konkani but,in the bargain, also creates a problem as well. For the recovery of the self, Sawardekar looked towards mainland India, and particularly Maharashtra and Marathi culture whereas Valaulikar wanted to search within his own culture which though ostensibly Konkani and Goan was also Hindu. The problem emerges because Valaulikar was the only person to suggest such a method (for which he was often ridiculed) as opposed to Sawardekar, who, it can be safely presumed, belonged to a group of like-minded, sympathetic-to-Marathi, individuals. But still a case can be made that Valaulikar was engaged in an enterprise for the recovery of his self as well as the markers of his self such as Konkani which was denied to him by the Marathi protagonists because more than fifty years later when José Pereira was writing in defense of Konkani, he too tried to look inside his own culture rather than identifying with the mainland Indian culture or with the Portuguese Empire (or Portuguese-ness), for the claim that he makes is very interesting in this context of recovering the self due to colonialism.

He says, "*Konkani is incontrovertibly a distinct language. Its greater antiquity, more integral Indianess and the profounder originality of its grammar further establish it in place of Marathi as the standard of comparison among the two tongues.* It is therefore less absurd to inquire whether Marathi is a dialect of Konkani than Konkani of Marathi."[61]

While defining *fractal recursivity*, Gal and Irvine further say that these "myriad opposition" that are projected at multiple levels "can create identity [and] may be reproduced repeatedly, either within each side of a dichotomy or outside it." They further clarify that "[i]n any case, the oppositions do not define fixed or stable social groups. Nor can the mimesis they suggest be more than partial. Rather, they provide actors with the discursive or cultural resources to claim and thus attempt to create shifting 'communities,' identities,

[61] Pereira, *Konkani: A Language; A History of Konkani Marathi Controversy*, 107. Emphasis in original.

and selves, at different levels of contrast, within a cultural field."[62] What ultimately Gal and Irvine's thinking invites us to do is to place language and linguistic politics within a socio-cultural realm and not to treat linguistic politics as divorced from the larger society. Because ideologies of difference are constructed through fractally recurring processes that empower groups to form new identities, the processes whereby identity of Konkani (in opposition to Marathi) giving way to Konkani in the Roman script (in opposition to nagri) which is now creating fractally recursive groups within romi as well, fall into a better perspective. Thus, what needs to be recognized and celebrated is the fact that the romi movement is not a monolithic one. It has its own internal diversity which gets suppressed if and when arguments in favour of 'standardization' are made.

For well over two centuries, the linguistic politics of Goa – through Portuguese, Marathi, Konkani and nagri Konkani – was mediated and led by the elites of Goa. Only post-1990, in the realm of language politics, a truly democratic move emerged where the control of language was attempted to be freed from the shackles of the caste elites. The demand for romi (and more recently the demand for English as a medium of instruction in primary schools, which includes both Catholics and Hindus) is truly a democratic turn in the realms of politics and culture in Goa.

ACKNOWLEDGEMENTS

Thanks to Alito Siqueira, from the Goa University for introducing me to the concept of *fractal recursivity* and for having lengthy discussions on many topics and themes that are linked to the script and language issues in Goa. For reading through the draft of this paper and making helpful suggestions, I would like to acknowledge the help rendered by Jason Keith Fernandes. Finally, I thank my parents for all their support.

REFERENCES

Angle, Prabhakar. Myth and Truth: Marathi in Goa. Margao: Gomant Vidya Niketan, ND.

Barbosa, Alexandre Moniz. Goa Rewound: A Land Liberated, A People Beleaguered. Panjim: Broadway Publishing House, 2012.

---

[62] Gal and Irvine, "The Boundaries of Languages and Disciplines: How Ideologies Construct Difference," 974.

Correia Afonso, Roque. Konkani for Christians. Translated by Vincent of Benaulim. No Place: Vincent of Benaulim, 1914.

Costa, Fausto V. da. "Konknniche Bara Brestar, Tera Sukrar." Gulab 31, no. 6 (2013): 31–37.

Dharwadker, Vinay. "English in India and Indian Literature in English: The Early History, 1579–1834." Comparative Literature Studies 39, no. 2 (2002): 93–119.

Ferrao, Victor. Being a Goan Christian: The Politics of Identity, Rift and Synthesis. Panjim: Broadway Publishing House, 2011.

———. "The Shadow of the Past." Navhind Times, July 16, 2011, sec. Panorama.

Gal, Susan. "A Semiotics of the Public/Private Distinction." Differences: A Journal of Feminist Cultural Studies 13, no. 1 (2002): 77–95.

———. "Language Ideologies Compared: Metaphors of Public/Private." Journal of Linguistic Anthropology 15, no. 1 (2005): 23–37.

Gal, Susan, and Judith T. Irvine. "The Boundaries of Languages and Disciplines: How Ideologies Construct Difference." Social Research 62, no. 4 (1995): 967–1001.

Goembab, Shennoi. Konknni Bhaxechem Zoit. Edited by K. S. Nayak. Bombay: Gomantak Press, 1930.

Gomes, Fr. Manuel. Konknni Bagentlem Pormollit Ful – Padri Freddy. Panaji: Dalgado Konknni Akademi, 2012.

Gomes, Olivinho. Konkani Literature in Roman Script – A Brief History. Panaji: Dalgado Konknni Akademi, 2010.

Halarnakar, Tanaji, Tomazinho Cardozo, S. M. Borges, Nagesh Karmali, Jose Salvador Fernandes, and Jayanti Naik. Romi Lipint Konknni Borounchi Nemavoll. Panaji: Goa Konkani Akademi, 2007.

Kelekar, Ravindra. "Koddu Okhdacho Ghontt." Vavraddeancho Ixtt. September 6, 1980.

———. "Koddu Okhdacho Ghontt." Vavraddeancho Ixtt. September 13, 1980.

Lima, Fr. Antonio F. X. de. "Konkani as a Medium of Instruction." In Essays on Konkani Language and Literature [Professor Armando Menezes Felicitation Volume], edited by D. N. Shanbhag, 45–52. Dharwar: Konkani Sahitya Prakashan, 1970.

Mallaya, N. Purushothama. "Place and Future of Konkani in Present-day India." In Essays on Konkani Language and Literature [Professor Armando Menezes Felicitation Volume], edited by D. N. Shanbhag, 1–15. Dharwar: Konkani Sahitya Prakashan, 1970.

Messing, Jacqueline. "Fractal Recursivity in Ideologies of Language, Identity and Modernity in Tlaxcala, Mexico." Texas Linguistic Forum 45 (2002): 95–105.

Naik, Pratap. Romi Lipient Konknni Brounchi Promann Rit (The Standard Orthography of Konknni in Roman Script). Ponnji [Panjim]: Dalgado Konknni Akademi, 2010.

Nayak, R. N. "Konknnicheo Kaim Somosya." In Proceedings of the 13th All India Konkani Sahitya Parishad, Bombay, 12–13 April 1980. Bombay: All India Konkani Sahitya Parishad, 1980.

Pereira, José. Konkani: A Language; A History of Konkani Marathi Controversy. Dharwar: Karnatak University, 1971.

———. "The Struggle for Konkani Schools." In Essays on Konkani Language and Literature [Professor Armando Menezes Felicitation Volume], edited by D. N. Shanbhag, 41–44. Dharwar: Konkani Sahitya Prakashan, 1970.

Pinto, Rochelle. Between Empires: Print and Politics in Goa. SOAS Studies on South Asia. New Delhi: Oxford University Press, 2007.

Sawardekar, Balkrishna Waman. The Language of Goa. Panaji: Prof. B. V. Sawardekar Memorial Committee, 1971.

Souza, Teotonio R. de. "Some Contrasting Visions of Luso-Tropicalism in India." Lusotopie (1997): 377–387.

Section II

Teotónio de Souza (1947–2019) was a prolific historian whose work brought various sources and fields of Goan history to the public eye. He was associated with the formation of the historical collections at the Xavier Centre for Historical Research. Among his publications are Medieval Goa: a Socio-Economic History *which was republished in 2009,* Goa to Me *in 1994 and most recently,* Goa outgrowing Postcolonialism: Historical Explorations *in 2014. He also edited* Indo-Portuguese History – Old Issues, New Questions, *and* Discoveries, Missionary Expansion *and* Asian Cultures. *De Souza has a range of articles in various journals as well as popular publications on various aspects of the history of Goa.*

The article, '"Confessionários" or Manuals of Confession – missionary tools and their colonial uses: the case study of Goa', appeared in Sod, *Matthew Almeida S. J. felicitation volume, Thomas Stephens' Konkani Kendra, No. 9, 2005. This is an English adaptation of an earlier paper published in Portuguese in* Amar, Sentir e Viver a História, *a two-volume work dedicated to the Portuguese historian Joaquim Veríssimo Serrão in 1995. In the following excerpt from the article De Souza provides a commentary on the creation of the confessionário in Konkani to facilitate a minimal conversation between priests new to the language and new converts. His study of the questionnaires that are part of the* confessionários *details the questions that range from a regular catechism about basic Christian doctrine, to questions about possible infringements of the commandments, including queries about worship, illicit sexual practices, etc.*

SYNOPSIS

The pioneering role of the Portuguese Discoveries in extending the impact of "modernity" was far from a secular exercise. The age of "Lights" was yet to dawn. The Portuguese "Padroado" system was a wedding of the State and Church interests on a world scale. The Society of Jesus played a pivotal role in the practical functioning of this joint venture, saving the State much cost in violent domination of the Eastern cultures.

The missionary activity of the Jesuits, and particularly their pedagogy of catching the youth to mould them more effectively, showed itself in the importance they gave to the sacrament of "Confession". Through this pastoral activity they tendered "delicate" consciences that would be submissive to colonial authorities and denounce any behaviour that could defraud or de-stabilize the State authority. The Jesuits produced "manuals" in vernacular languages to help the natives to make "good" confessions. This essay seeks to contextualize this type of religious literature and to examine the contents of some of them now preserved in the British Library (London) for the mid 17th century Goa (Portuguese India).

"CONFESSIONÁRIOS" OR MANUALS OF CONFESSION

Missionary tools and their Colonial uses: The Case Study of Goa

– *Teotonio R. de Souza**

Joaquim Heliodoro da Cunha Rivara spent nearly two decades in Goa as Secretary-General of the Government of Portuguese India 1855–1877). In addition to his administrative duties, he found time to promote valuable publications on the History of Portuguese India, as well as on the local society. His multi-volume Archivo Portuguez-Oriental, recently reprinted by AES, New Delhi, will remain a classic source of primary documentation for the history of the Portuguese in India during 16th to 18th centuries.

Cunha Rivara was convinced that Portuguese language could be better promoted through the native languages. As a result of this conviction, he published *Ensaio Histórico da Lingua Concani*,[1] wherein he traced the difficult evolution of Konkani language. The missionaries called it Língua Canarina, and at times Brachmana, because they believed that the early inhabitants of Goa had come from Canara region[2] or because the language was written and cultivated by the Brahmins. Konkani continues to be spoken by the inhabitants of Konkan, widely dispersed among other regions where Marathi, Kannada, Tulu and Malayalam are spoken by the local populations. The influence of these languages upon Konkani are obvious. The same had happened to Konkani under the Portuguese political rule, particularly to Konkani spoken by the Goan Christians who had been closer to the Portuguese missionaries. It had become so corrupt that language researchers were generally convinced that it was a dialect of Marathi. Lack of rigour in the use of Roman script in Konkani written by Goan

---

* Former Director of the Xavier Centre of Historical Research (19791994). Presently in Lisbon. Head of the Department of History, Universidade Lus6fona de Humanidades e Tecnologias, Member of the Portuguese Academy of History, Editor of Campus Social. Journal of Social Sciences. For updated bibliography consult: http://www.geocities.com/Athens/Forum/ 1503/teo_publ.html

[1] Nova Goa, Imprensa Nacional, 1858, pp. XLIlI+(l]+ 496.

[2] Joao de Barros, Da Asia, Dec. II, P. I, Lisboa, Livraria Sam Carlos, 1973, p. 440.

Christians further strengthened this opinion. However, Cunha Rivara, who knew about the similarity and difference between the Castillian and the Portuguese languages, was able to apply the same to the case of Konkani and Marathi.[3] He pointed out that the contribution of the missionaries of the XVII century was unknown to the orientalists, and tried to make it known through his Ensaio, and other publications of that kind, in order to minimise the harm already caused to the language by the Portuguese colonial presence. It is worth quoting a passage in which he distinguishes Portuguese India from America "discovered" by the Iberians: "India was not America. In this latter region the European conquerors could exterminate the simple and almost Primitive races, and populate it with imported European settlers; the great distance which separated the Indian conquest from the home country. and above all, the unbeatable resistance offered by a numerous population, whose leaders possessed a high level of civilization, forced the conquerors to avoid open violence, and to choose subtle means, though not always mild. to attain the same goals".[4]

From what we know of the written history, open violence was not always eschewed. The same author confirms it also: "In the early fervor of conquest, Temples were demolished, the symbols of the pagan cult were pulverized, and the books written in vernacular languages were burnt, for being judged or suspected of containing precepts and doctrine of idolatry. The wish to exterminate all those who did not convert was not entirely absent. This was not just the case at that time, but even two centuries later there were some wise counselors who recommended such measures to the State authorities."[5]

One could conclude that the times were far from "ecumenism", as the Portuguese scholars seem to suggest at times, referring to the policy of mix-marriages adopted by the Portuguese conqueror of Goa.[6] The fury of Reformation and Counter-Reformation tended to

---

[3] J. H. Cunha Rivara, *Ensaio Historico da Língua Concani,* p. XLlII.

[4] Ensaio. p. XLXL.

[5] Loc. Cit.; *Documenta Indica,* VI, ed. J. Wicki, Roma, 1969, pp. 387–96. The Jesuit Gomes Vaz gives us a contemporary picture of the happenings. "E porque deslruiremse todos juntos nao deixaria de causar algum escandalo nos gentios moradores e alteraçao da terra, buscou-se modo de pouco e pouco se fossem destruindo". The Jesuits soon lost patience with the slow pace of demolitions and adopted a more aggressive posture which cost them lives of the so-called "martyrs of Cuncolim", in 1583.

[6] J. Verissimo Serrao, Portugal e o Mundo nos séculos XII a XVI, Lisboa, Verbo, 1992, p. 244, operated in the Portuguese empire.

prevail, and the Inquisition in Goa proved to be the harshest among all that operated in the Portuguese empire.[7] ...

THE MISSIONARIES AND THE MANUALS FOR CONFESSING

Even though it is not uncommon nowadays to read derogatory comments about the missionaries as accomplices of the Western colonial expansion, we need to admit that colonialism could have been a much more brutal reality without such a missionary accompaniment. The Church took upon itself the task of checking the colonial abuses, reducing thereby more situations of injustice and violence that could occur. In a report sent by the Vicar General Miguel Vaz to king John III in 1545, we read that "the Portuguese are accustomed to beach their fleet and take it to the sea with the assistance of the poor natives. These inhabitants are thereby prevented from working for themselves, cultivating their fields or in something else to earn their livelihood. I believe that none should be deprived from his gainful occupation, and certainly not for free services. These natives are very poor and pay rent for the fields they cultivate. I consider their plight a grave case of oppression. I know this situation well, and cannot bear to describe it in more detail to Your Highness." The oppression was not always from the colonial agents, as we can read in the same report. There were also natives oppressing natives. The Vicar General defended the need of converting all the natives of Bardez and Salcete as a way of freeing them from the clutches of the all powerful Krishna and Gopu, the Brahmins and "great tyrants" known to me.

Francis Xavier, who started the activities of the Jesuits in the East after his arrival in Goa in May 1542, was writing the following to a colleague and superior in Portugal: "Please do not permit any of your friends to come to India as state official, because to them could be applied the biblical sentence: *Deleantur de libro viventium et cum iustis non scribantur* [may their names be deleted from the book of life and not be counted among the just men). The Saint also expressed his sadness and frustration with the behaviour of the Portuguese. He wrote to the king of Portugal that as soon as these set foot in India they learn to conjugate the verb "to rob" (*rapio*) in all its moods, tenses and participles".[8]

---

[7] A. Baiao, *A Inquisiçao de Goa*, 2 vols., Coimbra, 1930–45; A. K. Priolkar, *The Goa Inquisition*, Bombay, 1961; Francisco Belhencourt, *História das Inquisiçoes: Portugal, Espanha e Itália, Lisboa, Circulo de Leitores*, 1994, p. 273, passim.

[8] *Epistolae S. Francisci Xaverii aliaque eius scripta*, I, ed. G. Schurhammer & J. Wicki, Roma, 1944, pp. 281–2.

The lack of exemplary behaviour of the Portuguese in India was seen by Francis Xavier as a serious obstacle to the success of the missionary efforts of the Society of Jesus. It was through confessions and preaching that the Fathers of the Society of Jesus sought to combat the vices and other customs that they saw as contrary to the teachings of the Church. Together with catechizing and baptizing (general baptisms were a common practice) the natives, hearing confessions of the whites and the natives was an important pastoral activity of the missionaries. Fr. A. Quadros, Provincial of the Goa Jesuits, was writing in his annual letter of 1555: "General confessions have begun. Many come with questions and to manifest their scruples. Praised be God for these blessings. So many come to our college for confession that it is hard for us to attend to all of them."[9]

The Jesuits did not treat the whites and the natives with the same degree of rigour in their spiritual treatment. They were convinced that the natives could be helped more with confessions than with the punishments of the Inquisition (which Francis Xavier had asked the king to set up in Goa to check the crypto-Jews and to protect the native converts).[10]

While still in India, and before leaving for Japan, Fr. Melchior Carneiro wrote to the General Borgia of the Society of Jesus in 1555: "This Christianity is still a weakling and His Highness had decided to send the Inquisition. It will be the end of this Christianity. For God's sake, please write to the king that at least for another 20 years these natives should not be submitted to harsh procedures of the Inquisition. They should be handled with tenderness. and Our Lord would certainly not demand more from them than what is compatible with the capacity and nature He has given them."[11]

That same year the Jesuit Aires Brandão was writing to his colleagues in Portugal: "We see growing number of confessions in this college [St. Paul's] to the honour and glory of God our Lord. This is the main fruit of this land, where the people were not used to this practice and would rarely come for confession in the early days. Many even considered the practice repugnant. But now there are many who love confessing, and there is not a single day when our Church is not filled with persons who come every Saturday for confession and every Sunday for connnunion".[12]

---

[9] *Documenta Indica,* III, pp. 351–2.

[10] *The Letters and Instructions of Francis Xavier.* trans. M. Joseph Costelloe, Anand Press, 1992, p. 149; *Epistolae,* I, pp. 346–7: Francis Xavier had written to the king John III about it in 1546.

[11] *Documenta Indica,* III, p. 357.

[12] *Documenta Indica,* III, p. 369.

The correspondence of the Jesuits from India is replete with references to confessions. It permits us to gauge the importance they placed on this pastoral activity for the reform of life or to end well the Christian life. Fr. Sebastiao Fernandes wrote to Fr. General in 1569: "Ours are also called to hear confessions of the sick and to assist them to die well. Such calls come from all over the city because Ours are known to be always ready to respond at any time. We visit the prisons and hear confessions of those who are condemned by justice... Those of Ours who understand native tongue do better in accompanying those condemned by the Inquisition, from the day they hear the sentence till the day of punishment. Also the other prisoners in the *Sala*[13] and the galleys are visited by Ours on Sundays and days of obligation to teach them doctrine, to hear their confessions and to help them with any material means at their disposal..."[14] The missionaries faced the language problem when administering the sacraments to the natives. Not all were competent to provide spiritual assistance to the natives: "Ours who know the language move around the villages and parishes confessing the Christians and helping them in their spiritual needs. Since they are few and the needy are many, it means extra trouble. During the season of Lent they hear confessions in the city churches, and during the rest of the year in the churches outside, both those belonging to us and as well as to others."[15]

The Jesuits' pedagogy was based on the principle of catching the people young. The same pedagogy was applied in the spiritual care. Fr. Sebastiao Fernandes describes how they started in the village of Cortalim: "Wishing to confess the parishioners, he started with the young boys and moved them to such a sense of devotion and repentance of sins, which they lacked until then, that one lad of barely 10 years of age, had found a piece of cloth of no great value some six months earlier brought it to the priest to return it to its rightful owner. The same boy had some days earlier robbed a needle and wanted now to return it."[16]

Francis Xavier had foreseen the need of learning native languages in order to enable the Jesuits to peform with greater efficacy their activities in the East. He had initiated a school for the boys,

---

[13] *Viagem de Frallcisco Pyrard de Laval,* II, ed. J. H. Cunha Rivara, Porto, Liv. civilização, 1944, p. 21: Describes *Sala* as one of the four prisons in the city of Goa. It was a complement to the major State prison or *Tronco.* Pyrard de Laval had a taste of *Sala,* which he describes as the "dirtiest place on earth".

[14] *Documenta Indica,* VIII, pp. 48–52.

[15] ibid., p. 65.

[16] ibid., p. 81.

attached to the College of St. Paul in Goa. Boys from all over the East were brought there for education, and some of them became interpreters for Francis Xavier himself in the Fishery coast and in Japan. It was known as the "colégio dos moços da terra" (school for the native boys). It had 645 boys in 1563. Some years later the number had reached 800, including many ethnic groups.[17] Fr. Lourenlço Pires was writing to Portugal in 1563, describing the services rendered by these boys: "One is a Goan *canarim,*[18] and is already able to preach to the natives in various parishes in their own language. He also teaches the language to some of our Brothers with the help of a grammar he has composed. Some of these Brothers are already showing progress and could very soon converse with the natives in their language."[19] In this manner a native boy helped the Jesuits to prepare the first grammar of Konkani and assisted to teach the language to some Jesuits. The Jesuits had been working hard at learning the language, and the younger ones were chosen and given time to devote themselves to that study in a residence at Chorao, where the Jesuits owned a parish, and later a Novitiate. Fr. Gomes Vaz was writing to the Provincial in Portugal about this place in 1556: "Five are presently learning Konkani language (lingua canarim). They are considerably good in writing and their ability to speak it will soon allow them to preach and hear confessions. Two among them are doing so well that they can preach the Gospel and teach catechism during Mass. Fr, Pero d'Almeida does it also when he gets an opportunity. Three other Brothers have been residing there and doing the same, As they need more practice than just learning the grammar, those who have made more progress are advised to go to our parishes and get into direct contact with the Christians and gentiles."[20]

In order to facilitate the use of vernacular languages in their pastoral activities, the Jesuits composed vocabularies, grammars and manuals for confessing ("confessionários") in those languages. Fr. Henrique Henriques was a pioneer in this sense. Fr. Joao de Mesquita was writing about his work to the Jesuits in Portugal in 1558: "Fr. Henrique Henriques had composed a grammar *(arte)* in Malabar language [read TamilJ which is a great help for those who wish to leam that language. He speaks better than the natives, and

[17] *Documenta Indica,* VII, p. 49.

[18] Designation for native Goan Christians. It acquired later a pejorative sense, especially due to frictions with the *descendentes* and *mestiços,* It was equivalent to *canecos* in Mozambique.

[19] *Documenta Indica,* VI., p. 111.

[20] *Documenta Indica,* VII., p. 58.

has no need of interpreters [*topazes*]".[21] Henrique Henriques also wrote about his own activities: "Some years back I sent a copy of the same grammar. I have improved on it by now, but could not finish it due to my many occupations. I have also prepared some catechisms in Tamil. Since we have no preachers, they are read in churches on Sundays. I wish I could do more in this line, but I have no time for it. I want to finish a vocabulary on which I am working, and also a "conficioneyro" to help in confessions, a *Flos Sanctorum*,[22] and a few other such things."[23]

CONFESSIONÁRIOS IN THE BRITISH LIBRARY

I chanced to find a small sized, leather-bound codex (4.5" x 7") in the *Additional Manuscripts* collection of the British Library some years ago. It begins with "*Arte do Canarym, composta pelos nossos padres, e tresladada pela mão do clérigo António da Silva Brâmane de Margão*". The title page mentions that this cleric copied it with much care and without any mistakes, to send it with Fr. Antonio Magalhães to Rome, when he went there as Procurator. It was brought back by Fr. Francisco Carvalho, when he went as Procurator.[24] Since both left Portugal for India in 1630, we could date this manuscript as belonging to mid XVll century, It has 164 written folios. The "confessionários" are found in fls 67–121. The codex also includes: "A doutrina Christã abreviada com todo o essencial q hu xpão deve saber. A cartilha é Doutrina toda intr[a] tresladada da impressa, composta pello Padre Thomas Estêvao" (fls.109–121v). Follows "Doutrina Christam em língoa Bramana Canarim ordenada a manr[a] de dialog[o] pêra ensinar os mininos" (fis.122–163). The ending text on pp. 164–164v is the "benção das redes dos pescadores" [blessing of the fishing nets] in Latin.[25] The codex is invaluable as a contemporary copy of Arte and Doutrina of Fr. Thomas Stephens.[26] Even though the confessionários

[21] *Documenta Indica,* IV., p. 127.

[22] Was published in Tanlil in the Fishery Cosat in 1587 and a copy is preserved the Vatican Library.

[23] *Documenta Indica,* IV., p. 159.

[24] J. Wicki, *Liste der Jesuiten-Indienfaher* 1541–1758, 1967. p. 293.

[25] British Library, Add. Mss, 10359.

[26] See the *Doutrina Cristã* edited by Prof. Mariano Saldanha. Lisboa. Agência Geral das Colónias, 1945. It says that the Confessionários mentioned by L. Frósi could not be more than one, and adds that the use of plural was stylistic. Contrarily, we see in the codex of the British Library that there were in fact various manuals of confession with different formulae, some meant for general confessions and

printed in 1557 may have been distributed quite generously, and without knowing if there were any in Konkani,[27] the absence of any earlier known confessionários makes us consider the copies in this codex as unpublished. It is very likely that the style of composing the confessionários would have remained substantially the same during long period of time.

Cunha Rivara refers to a confessionário belonging to the end of the XVII century and composed by father and son, both natives of Chorão.[28] I tend to agree with Mariano Saldanha, and to believe that existing confessionários are translations or improvements in Konkani and composed by the major Jesuit Konkani experts of the first half of the XVII century, such as Tomas Stephen, Miguel D'Almeida, Diogo Ribeiro, Antonio Saldanha, João de Pedrosa and Etienne de la Croix.[29] They worked in parishes of Salcete during long periods of time and knew well the routine lifestyle of their native parishioners. That is the reason why these manuals can be considered also as very useful source for the socio-economic history of Goa. The questionnaire of the manuals for confessions makes sense only in the context of the daily lives of the people, with reference to the localities, to relationships. to certain practices that were deemed pagan, violation of certain fiscal rules, etc. Let us start reading parts of the text entitled O Confessionario em Canarim, The sub-title reads: Algumas perguntas que se fazem no princípio [Some initial questions]. The rest is in Konkani and extends from fl. 67 to fl. 78v. Here begins the next "Confessionário, ou interrogatório p[a] confissõis ordinárias" in Portuguese language. From fl. 83 to fl. 88v we have "Interrogatório pera confissoens ordinárias em Canarim", and from fl. 89 to 92v: Outra versão deste interrogatório" also in Konkani. Hence, we have three questionnaires in Konkani. We shall concentrate here largely upon the first one and comment upon the peculiarities and implications of its contents, noting the use of the Portuguese terms to denote

---

others for ordinary confessions. In this codex we can find three in Konkani and two in Portuguese.

[27] ibid., p.5. Mariano Saldanha is of the view that they were only in Portuguese, because there were no Jesuit experts in Konkani yet.

[28] Ensaio, p. CCXXX–CCXXXI. This too contained 3 questioning models. Cunha Rivara found them all in a single manuscript book of the XVIII century. The 2nd was entitled "breve confissionário na lingua vulgar" he starts with the same question" as the main manual of this codex. The question is: Confessar zatalossi? Probably it was already a standard formula.

[29] Bibl Nac. Vittorio Emanuele: Ms Gesuitici 1153 – De Sasatana Península by Ignacio Archamone, fls. 81v–84v.

certain objects and practices of the new religion, and pointing to some elements which could be considered as characteristic of the daily life of village folks. From the nature of the questions one could conclude that they are addressed to newly converted, and as such they seem to belong to the period when the conversion drive was still on, that is, from second half of the XVI century till mid XVII century. This is suggested by the following questions:

Christão keleari tuka kitule kalla zale? Konny Igrezē kelelo? Kossiena Christão zālolo mā? [Since when are you Christian? In which Church did you become Christian? Did you become Christian willingly?]

Following some initial questions there is a brief instruction about the sacrament of Penance. The penitent is told that the sacrament was instituted by Jesus Christ to cure the diseases of the soul just the same way as the doctors (vaida) cure the physical ills (āngāchi ballalika). The penitent is also told that Jesus Christ appointed the priests to be doctors of the souls and to forgive sins (tankā Paramesparana hukuma dilla patakā bhagasunchī). And goes on: Zaisso yecu mannussu vaidā laguy vetāchi, āpanna zari anlmāna zātalo, taka kāi lipainā, sāmesti āpuki ballalika sāngatā ... tāissechi confessor zāu'k gueleāri samestā patakā Padrika sānguchl'. Tākā kāi lipauche' nhoe. Anny confessar karitatl Padry mannussa zālei tari, lazena, ou behāna kāi' tāka lipauche' nhoe, Quitea confessar karite velie Parameshparāchie suateri, zituqui' patakā' tākā sa'nguilī, tituli tāncheāna ziteā zivāka sāngavanāti. [Just like a person that goes to the doctor wishing to be cured and tells him all his sickness without hiding anything ... so also he who goes to confession tells all his sins to the priest without hiding any thing. Even though the priest confessor is human, nothing should be hidden from him with shame or fear, because at the time of hearing the confession he is in the place of God, and all the sins told to him he cannot tell to any living being.]

The section that follows about introductory instructions seem to indicate that both the penitent and the confessor need this manual for confession: the penitent for being new to the new doctrine and in need of knowing where he failed; and the priest confessor who has difficulties with language and needs to understand what the penitent wants to say, even when he responds with just Yes or No to the questionnaire. One could conclude that not all Jesuits were yet very familiar with Konkani and would not easily follow a normal response of the penitent. It was therefore important that the questions were brief, precise and direct. The manual begins with questions about the first commandment, defining it as: Yeca satevantā Paramesparakā manu diu'cho [Honour the only and holy Lord]. Follow 21 questions about this commandment and the most curious questions proposed for an examination .of conscience are: Did you oppose the conversion of others? Did you wish to retum to your caste or suggested to a convert to do so? Did you advise a convert to prostitute with Hindu females [rom across the border? [Bhallateāka zāti gheu'ku, ou pellatāddy konkannea' laguy zāu'ka vachu' sānguilalem?] Did you think that a Hindu or a Muslim who did good works could go to Heaven? [Conkanne mussalmāna pune' keleāri, dana-dharma kelefui vaincuttā vety se tukā distāti?] Did you go across the border for any Hindu festival? Did you deny when asked if you were Christian? Or had the intention of denying? Did you mix water with sura or milk, believing that the pahn-tree.or the cow would not be productive. otherwise? Did you resort to any. diviner (ghāddy, zhoyssy) or to witchcraft to seek any cure or to fix auspicious day for a feast or a wedding? [tāche lāguy kāi paraba assamy ou vhaârâddika sobana kamnka murtu nīmiguilálo?][30] Did you make use of salt to ward off the evil eye when you thought your daughter was affected by it? [Tugelea cheddvāka distti zālia mhonnu kāi mittha bittha vuāllnu ghâlāle'?][31]

Questions relating to the second commandment want to find out if the penitent swore falsely invoking God, land, parents, children, eyes, or life. It was common practice among Hindus to use such invocations and expect harm to result to the invoked subjects in case of perjury.[32]

As regards the third commandment it was asked if the penitent attended the Mass and did not work without need or made others work on a Sunday or day of obligation. Another question points to the practice of frequent abstinence in those times: Sucrarā, Sanivâra, ou yekā bhagtacheâ dissa, ou kâresmaantu massa khelāle'? [Did you eat meat on a Friday, Saturday or a day of penance during the Lent?] In the same context could be read another question:

---

[30] Bibl Nac. Vittorio Emanuele: Ms Gesuitici 1153 – De Sasatana PenInsula by Ignacio Archamone, fls. 81v–84v. The term Konkanno appears already to designate a Hindu. Pelatâdi meant literally across the river (Zuari), but implied border separating the non-Portuguese jurisdiction. The terms ghāddy and zhoyssy referred to the temple servants practicing astrology and divination.

[31] Add: Mss. 10359. fl. 70, question n. 15

[32] Felippe Nery Xavier, Repertório Geral ou Indice Alfabético das differentes providencias, resoluçoes, usos e costumes... das Novas Conquistas, vols. III, Nova Goa, 1851, p. 65. Faz parte da Colleçao de Bandos.

Did you drink wine or toddy [sura] till losing senses or causing unpleasant situations?

Concerning the fourth commandment the penitent was asked if he respected the parents and cared for them. The married penitent was asked if he cared for his spouse and childreh. He/she was also asked if there was any family member who was not yet baptized.

Regarding the fifth commandment the penitent was asked if he/she had desired to kill or actually killed anyone, or had tried to poison anyone, or had taken any poison with the intention of committing suicide. Did he/she commit or helped committing abortion? [Bhaltate' bāllasse' māecheā pottantū' marasī quelem? Ou hollunu bhāira paddu'cheāka okhada ghetalâle'?][33]

When it comes to questions about the sixth commandment entitled Paraduara caru' naye, it distinguishes illicit sexual relations with four types of women: kazary, solten, ankvâri and cheddy, Tries to define solteri: "mhannazi dáduleachy nhoe, anny āncuâri nhoe."[34] Asks if the penitent desired to have sexual relations with other women, with or without their wish. Another questionnaire on the same commandment on fl. 91 asks if he' had winked to a woman on the road (Vattê vetanâ conny báileka dekhleári tiká ddollo moddilo?)[35] This questionnaire goes even deeper into details of homosexual relations. asking if he had genital contact in front or from behind: Bhallateâ cheddeâ lâguy guelālossii, mukhā veleanā, ou māguileâna? There is also a question about masturbation: Apuleâ hátana modu poro ghâlálo? Dussrea lâguy tennepramânny kele'?[36] Apnnapeâthát kai áphaddásáphaddy quelály? Mhannaze tuve'chi tuzea ângâca átu bottu láunu cái paâtaca quelâle'? Tāvalli polluçā zâlâle' mhannaze vrahe madhu paddalálo?[37]

The seventh commandment which prohibits coveting goods of others, is covered by the confessionário with the greatest number of questions, including some about cheating the State treasury, when the areca-groves (kullagar) were rented out, or by influencing the decisions of the village councils [Gavayântu bhalla-teâgule'

[33] Add. Mss. 10359, fl. 73, question n. 4.

[34] ibid., n. 86. question n. 3.

[35] ibid., fl. 91. question n. 4

[36] Loc. Cit.

[37] Add, Mss. 10359, fl. 86. questions n. 10–11. The proceedings of the Pastoral Visits provide many details about prostitution in Goa. Cf. Teotonio R. de Souza, "The Voiceless in Goan Historiography: A Case for the Source Value of Church Records in Goa", *Indo-Portuguese History: Sources & Problems*, ed. John Correia-Afonso, Bombay, Oxford University Press, 1981, pp. 114–131.

kullâgra sidāyka pāvāta tâvalli zâvo karu' naká mhonnu' bhalteâka sánguilálale' toddeâchi mola dharnu tuzielaguy paucheaka? Kāi lanchu kanchu guetalâlo bhallatca lâguy ápanna gâvancho nemu gheunu dina au ânnyeki kāi mazati karina mhonnu'?].[38] Some of the other questions are: Were you responsible for cheating in the construction of bunds and sluicegates, causing flooding of paddy fields? [Tuve' kāi bându kelālo? Bându baro kornu nâbfândilea pâssâvata bhateāle' setakamatu nāsslale'?][39] Did you manipulate any accounts or tear any page of the village account-book? (kai'vāyeche' tallata chirtlale'? pinzunu kāddunu annyeka ghālele'? bhalateaka kāi nasta yeu'cheaka ou vaitta zau'cheaka?)[40] When the village ganvkars take some administrative decision (nemu) in the village council, was it recorded fully in the proceedings, or was it modified while recording? [Gau'karâcho nemu gāvatu ditāti to taissochi vayert baraitâssi, ki na? Hou kâi adika unne' karttassi?][41] This question implies the collective responsibility of the village elders, each one being held responsible for the collective action. Hence, the implication of individual responsibility to denounce any collective misbehaviour, Those responsible for collecting village dues are asked if they collected anything more in silver or by cheating in exchange rate. [Gāviche' pota queleari lokāri kâi' adika ukhalilale ou rupeache nânne' ghetalalea pâssavata annyeku vâttau ghetakālo? Tu' anny kullakaranny' mellunu lokāri adiku phallo quelālo? Ou kāi adika prazeri ukhallilâlo? Maguiri dogāny vântuonu vharu'cheâka?][42] The Province captain and the clerk treasurer are asked if they forced a debtor to pay in kind by surrendering more cattle or chicken than their dues, or if received any bribes for not doing so. [Capitana, au escrivãona, ou konneitari gāi dharu'ka dhaddileari, au kombiyo dharu'ka dhaddileari lhâite mola naditanā haddillio? ou na haddu'cheaka kāi lanchu kanchu ghetalâlo?][43]

The questions about the eighth commandment relate to respecting the rights of others. The penitent is asked if he tried to hann the reputation and interests of others or had intention of doing so.

---

[38] Add. Mss. 10359. fl. 75, question n. 8.

[39] ibid., fl. 75v, question n. 11.

[40] ibid., fl. 76, question n. 17.

[41] ibid., fl. 76, question n. 18.

[42] ibid., fl. 76, question n. 20–21.

[43] Add. Mss. 10359, fl. 76, question n. 22. Many of these details tend to confirm the kind of abuses that prevailed in the villages as studied by Teotonio R. de Souza. Medieval Goa, New Delhi, Concept Publ. Co., 1979 with the help of the 17th century village community books in the Goa Historical Archives.

Questions about this and the last two commandments do not provide any specific insights about the daily life of Goan people.

Another interesting feature in the confessionário consists of two lists: one of numbers till 100, and the other with degrees of family relationships (by affinity and by consanguinity), The numbers were required to let the confessor know how many times a sin was committed or the amount involved in cases of robbery or cheating. The knowledge of the degree of relationship was also important to decide about the gravity of some sins. I have organized the second list into an Appendix for easier reference. [The Appendix has not been included in this excerpt.] I have opted for keeping the Portuguese terminology as it occurs in the confessionários.

By way of Conclusion, we hope that this brief presentation will rouse the interest of Konkani linguists and social scientists interested in Goa to pursue further their research by exploring this type of religious source material. We know for instance that "direct contact with God" was frowned upon by the spirit of Counter-Reformation which prized "mediation". The sacrament of Penance, that was belittled by the Reformed Church was thus reinforced by the Catholic Counter-Reformation. One could also study the use of Prayer Manuals over centuries among the Catholics, till at least the Vatican II made them largely obsolete. While the common folks said their beads, it was a common sight to see the educated faithful reading their Manuals during the Masses and Liturgy in Latin. The predominant themes of those Prayer Manuals at various times could be analysed to check what were the chief worries of the faithful as individuals and communities at the corresponding times.

Vidya Pai is a translator from Konkani to English. She has translated various Konkani novels: Mahabaleshwar Sail's Age of Frenzy, *Harper Perennial 2017, Pundalik Naik's* Acchev *(The Upheaval), OUP, 2002,* Havthan *('The Kiln'), Konkani Language and Cultural Foundation, Mangalore 2011,* 'Kali Ganga', *NBT, 2003, and Damodar Mauzo's novel* Karmelin, *Sahitya Akademi, 2004 among others. Her translation of Jayanti Naik's short story* 'Basavo' *is part of a British Council Project at www.womenswriting.com, and other stories have appeared in various publications such as* Visions Revisions *1, 1995,* Yuvkatha, *1996,* Katha Prize Stories *(vols. 12, 2002 and 13, 2004);* Ferry Crossing – *Short Stories from Goa, 1998, and in the Sahitya Akademi's journal,* Indian Literature, *2005.*

Vidya Pai's essay, 'Translation of Culture', discusses the decisions that translators have to make when words and names that denote attitudes, practices and beliefs have to be conveyed in another cultural idiom. In this regard, she suggests that, translations between some languages are more viable than between others where cultural difference seems greater.

'TRANSLATION OF CULTURE'

Culture has been defined as 'the way of life and its manifestations that are particular to a community that uses a particular language as its means of communication' (Peter Newmark, 1998). These cultural terms could be specific words related to flora and fauna, clothes, food, occupations or articles of daily use. They could also be abstract concepts based on religious belief or social practice or traditional customs followed by members of a community.

Cultural concepts are deeply embedded in the structure of a language, so a literary translator who seeks to 'carry across' a text from one language to another has to grapple with the process of transferring these concepts as well. The translation process is easier when one deals with languages that stem from the same roots or are spoken in contiguous regions, as is the case when one translates from one Indian language to another. Even in the case of dissimilar Indian languages like Konkani and Malayalam or Punjabi and Konkani, the chance of finding equivalence while translating cultural concepts is greater because the basic climate and lifestyle and myths and beliefs that shape the consciousness of people in different parts of the Indian subcontinent are largely the same.

The process becomes more complicated when one works with languages from disparate groups, like Konkani and English for instance. Konkani is an off-shoot of Maharashtri Prakrit and belongs to the Indo-Aryan group of languages. The 450 years of Portuguese rule in Goa ensured that Portuguese words and phrases entered the Konkani language, though this influence is more pronounced in Goan Christian dialects. Words and cultural terms that date back to the indigenous tribes who lived in this region also find a place in this linguistic melting pot.

The English language, though laden with a robust vocabulary culled from Greek and Roman and Teutonic roots is often ill-equipped to express Konkani cultural concepts and the translator who seeks to bring a Konkani literary work into English is often forced to make a choice. Should a word with cultural connotations be replaced by a descriptive group of words or an explanatory phrase which does not figure in the original text? Should the Konkani term be retained so that it adds some local colour to the translated text, should it be italicized? Should the word be glossed? Will too many footnotes distract the reader and mar the reading experience?

As one who has been translating Konkani writing into English for over a decade, let me touch on some of the problems I faced while translating cultural terms and concepts in Pundalik Naik's *Acchev* (The Upheaval, OUP, 2002), Mahabaleshwar Sail's *Kali Ganga* (Kali Ganga, NBT, 2003) and Mahabaleshwar Sail's *Havthan* (The Kiln, Konkani Language and Cultural Foundation, Mangalore, 2011).

Acchev is a novel about a traditional Goan village that is transformed when it comes into contact with modern mechanized ways of life. *Kali Ganga* depicts life in a village on the bank of the river Kali near the Goa-Karnataka border. Both novels paint pictures of an agricultural tradition with its shared belief in legends, fables and myths. Since Pundalik Naik and Mahabaleshwar Sail hail from traditional agrarian families, they bring the authenticity of experience and a wealth of detail into their depiction of peasants sowing and reaping and gathering the grain. I realized, much to my dismay, that English has a limited vocabulary for depicting these typically Indian agricultural terms and processes and was forced to fall back on words like 'plough' and 'reap' and 'harvest' despite the association with mechanized agriculture that these words would conjure up in the reader's mind.

Acchev opens with a vivid description of Pandhari working in his field. *Sarki chaar taasam ghalun kamashi kelli*, Naik claims. Pandhari has guided the oxen drawing the plough during the *aadas* and the *atras* and the *optasai* --- words that depict the process of guiding the plough in different directions following a traditional agricultural plan. These three words conjure up a vivid picture of the oxen drawing the plough across the field so that every bit of soil is tilled and the land is ready to be sowed. What the author conveyed with such economy of words in the Konkani text had to be explained and expanded in the translation. It became necessary to point out that '... once the entire length had been ploughed ....he moved cross-wise to cover the breadth .... covering the length and breadth of the field yet again .... he'd worked it four times in all and the field was now well prepared'.

Konkani has a vast store house of words for implements and tools and activities that form part of the agricultural process. In *Kali Ganga* Sail refers to fields that are *dhulavpek* (on low flat land that can be easily ploughed) and *makki-barad* (upland stretches that require furrows to be cut on the slopes and holes to be dug in the ground before the seeds are sown). He lists agricultural tools like *khorem-kuddal, nangar-junv, aalai-datem, dori-dayem, kanvkal-markal, manch-taat, hattar-hattri* with practiced ease. Describing each tool and explaining its significance proved too cumbersome in the English text, so I settled for pickaxe and spade, halter rope and reed matting and dubbed everything else as 'other implements that are used in the fields'.

Kali Ganga has a segment where Sail describes Suman's frustration when she is unable to assemble the different sections of the plough. She strings the parts together in a hap-hazard fashion and the unwieldy contraption wobbles crookedly over the ground. The Konkani text refers to the *junv* and the *kaani,* the *nangartya dori,* the *reesh* and the *nirmane* (all of which are parts of the plough); it describes the sequence of actions involved in the ploughing process and the manner in which the plough stops short because it is incorrectly assembled. *Bail vachunk lagley poon nangar bhuyant ubbo khonchtalo... taasai bhuyant sarko padnaslo ... bail kashakashi vankde tikde vachunk lagley, nangar tanchya payank ghuspunk laglo.* The translation into English can convey the general sense of what has been described but much of the detail is inevitably lost.

Pundalik Naik is a poet and dramatist who draws deeply from the folk tradition of the indigenous tribes who were the original inhabitants of the Goan region. The atmosphere in Mahabaleshwar Sail's novels is charged with the customs and beliefs that shape the lives of the rustic farming communities by the river Kali and the settlements of potters struggling to stay alive in the area around Karwar. It is this folk element that gives their writing a distinctive edge, but the translator into English is caught in a bind. Will this folk idiom survive the transfer to an alien language? Can it retain the interest of a new readership unfamiliar with the lifestyle and religious and social practices of the people depicted in the source text?

The *Dhalo*, a festival of traditional songs and ritualistic dances performed by village women finds a place in *Kali Ganga* and *Acchev*. Sail dwells at length on the myths and traditions associated with this festival. He describes how some women go into a trance and sway and leap about as the spirits of the *Rambhas*, (celestial dancers in Lord Indra's court) allegedly take possession of their bodies. This section of *Kali Ganga* has traditional songs invoking the various deities and lesser spirits that guard the village. Though these contribute to the folksy feel of the Konkani text they read like mere lists of unfamiliar names repeated at frequent intervals, when transcribed into English. I chose to condense and curtail these lengthy invocations, replacing snatches of repetitive verse with a few lines describing the action, in the translated text.

Naik's skill as poet and dramatist can be seen in his depiction of the *Dhalo* in *Acchev*. He uses more than a dozen snatches of religious and secular songs interspersed with lively banter where characters use these traditional songs to comment on happenings in the novel and to nudge the action along. As a translator, how was I to explain the various references in these songs, which ranged from religious ones dealing with infant Krishna's exploits and Sita's woes to popular ditties about a Shet visiting prostitutes in Mhardol? Since it wasn't possible to provide footnotes for all these references I chose to ignore the cultural undertones and retain only the literal meaning of the lyrics in this section of the translated text.

A concept that recurs in Sail's work is that of the *suvashin* or 'woman whose husband is alive' and the constraints faced by widows in traditional Indian society. *Kali Ganga* ends with Suman drawing off her bangles and wiping the spot of kumkum on her forehead when she hears of Govind's death. 'I wanted to die before you, a married woman with all the emblems of my marital status intact! But look at my fate! I'm a widow even before I am wed!' she wails.

Havthan, Sail's requiem for a community of potters faced with extinction, also deals with this concept. A widow may shape clay lamps and rimless saucers and lids which she must stack in the crevices between pots when a neighbour fires his kiln. She may not sit at the wheel and mould clay pots because this is an act of creation and signifies a new birth. The auspicious aura that surrounds the *suvashin* and the negative light in which widows are viewed can only be inferred from the translated text. They resist translation into English since neither concept has a place in western culture.

Cross-cousin marriages (where a man marries the daughter of his maternal uncle) are accepted amongst Konkani people, but marriages between parallel cousins (the children of two sisters or two brothers) are taboo. One of the important strands in the plot of *Kali Ganga* is the relationship between Suman and Govind, who belong to different clans. If Govind's uncle Bhaskar adopts the youth he will have to take his uncle's surname, he will be like a 'son' to everyone in the village and like a 'brother' to Suman, making it impossible for him to marry her. It is this that leads to Govind's suicide and the book ends on a tragic note. It was important that this concept be explained to the reader since a relationship between cousins is generally viewed as incest. The only way this could be done was through a lengthy footnote.

In his introduction to the English translation of *Kali Ganga*, noted Konkani writer Damodar Mauzo touches on the cultural baggage that is an intrinsic part of any language when he says that 'the title of the book is pregnant with allusions and draws deeply from tradition. On one plane Sail refers to the Kali river as the "Ganga" of that region, hence the name "Kali Ganga". On the other hand he puns on the word "Kali", which means "dark". This river, which is as [sacred as] the Ganga to those who live on its banks, is dark and foreboding and capable of spreading sorrow.'

Each translator has to decide how the rhythms of colloquial speech and interplay of rural dialects in the source text should be carried into an alien language. In *Acchev* the Goan Christian dialect of Konkani used by truck driver Manuel is easily identifiable and sets him apart from Nanu and the other Hindu drivers at the mine. The ritualistic framework of the incantations with which the Ghadi exhorts the local spirits and guardian deities makes his language different from that of the common villagers. I feel that the awkward construction and ungrammatical language that is produced when one tries to render diverse voices into another language often has a jarring effect. It might not be acceptable to the culture of readership in English. So, except for infusing a degree of informality into Manuel's speech and rendering the Ghadi's exhortations in a more ornate tongue, I chose to translate the diverse Konkani voices into a uniform English one.

A translator can render a text into an alien language as honestly as possible, but a range of associative cultural meanings are often lost in this process. The translated text, therefore, should not be viewed as a carbon copy of the original. Its merits should be judged on its ability to introduce a new set of readers to a writer and a text in an unfamiliar language that would have been out of bounds for them *but* for the translator's efforts.

William Madtha's essay 'Bhashanthar: Bhashevyjnanik Siddhanth' (Translation: Linguistic Theory) was published in Amar Konkani, *issue 43, 2005. The essay is divided into five subheadings: definition of translation, form of written language, similarity in translation, language types and abhhashantharikarann.*

Madtha asserts the importance of translation for the growth of any literature. Without the thoughts, feelings, and experiences of other languages being made available in Konkani, Konkani literature would remain poor according to him. Aside from emphasizing how the translated work is a new creation as the target language is different from the original language in form, Madtha points out the syntactical changes in translations from English to Konkani and Kannada.

As he explains language components such as idiolect, dialect, register, style and mode he emphasises the need for language variation/dialect to be kept in mind. The geographical, temporal and social differences within languages need to be considered. If Mangalorean, Goan, and Kerala Konkani are language dialects, ancient, middle and contemporary Konkani variations are temporal. In the same way Kudmi, Saraswat, Christian and Navayat Konkani are social variations. While producing literature, these language variations should have a distinct place.

When there is a wide gap between the culture and language formation of the original and the target language, abhhashantharikarann occurs as cultural words are difficult to translate. One must retain the original words in order to convey a sense of those aspects of the culture of the original language.

ಭಾಶಾಂತರ್: ಭಾಶೆವೈಜ್ಞಾನಿಕ್ ಸಿದ್ಧಾಂತ್

ದೆ। ದೊ। ವಿಲ್ಯಂ ಮಾಡ್ತಾ

ಸುರ್ವೆಚಿಂ ಉತ್ರಾಂ:

'ಭಾಶಾಂತರ್' ಮ್ಹಳ್ಳ್ಯಾ ಸಬ್ದಾಕ್ 'ತರ್ಜುಮೊ', 'ಅನುವಾದ್', 'ಅಣ್ಕಾರ್', ಮ್ಹಳ್ಳೆ ಸಬ್ದ್‌ಯಿೀ ಆಮ್ಚೆ ಮಧೆಂ ಪರ್ಯಾಯ್ ಜಾವ್ನ್ ಆಸಾತ್. ಮೂಳ್ ಭಾಶೆ (SL) ಥಾವ್ನ್ ಉದ್ದಿಶ್ಟ್ ಭಾಶೆ (TL)ಕ್ ಎಕಾ ಪಠ್ಯಾಕ್ ವ್ಹರ್ಚ್ಯಾ ಪ್ರಕ್ರಿಯೆಕ್ 'ಭಾಶಾಂತರ್' ಮ್ಹಣ್ತಾಂವ್. ಅಶೆಂ ಮುಳಾವಿ ಕೃತಿ 'ಬಿಂಬ್' ಜಾಲ್ಯಾರ್ ಭಾಶಾಂತರ್, 'ಪ್ರತಿಬಿಂಬ್' ಜಾವ್ನಾಸಾ. The Imitation of Christ ಮ್ಹಳ್ಳಿ ಕೃತಿ ಜೆಜ್ವಿತ್ ಪ್ರಶಾಂತ್ ಮಾಡ್ತಾನ್ ಕ್ರಿಸ್ತನ ಅನುಕರಣೆ ಮ್ಹಳ್ಳ್ಯಾ ತಕ್ಲೆ ನಾಂವಾಖಾಲ್ ಕೊಂಕ್ಣೆಕ್ ಹಾಡ್ಲ್ಯಾ. ತಿ ಮುಳಾವಿ ಕೃತಿ 'ಬಿಂಬ್' ಜಾಲ್ಯಾರ್, ಪ್ರಶಾಂತಾಚಿ ಕೃತಿ ಪ್ರತಿಬಿಂಬ್ ಯಾ ಭಾಶಾಂತರ್/ಅನುವಾದಿತ್ ಕೃತಿ.

ಖಂಚೆಂಯಿ ಸಾಹಿತ್ ವಾಡಾಜಯ್ ಜಾಲ್ಯಾರ್ ಭಾಶಾಂತರ್ ಸಾಹಿತ್ ಗರ್ಜೆಚೆಂ. ಎಕ್ಸುರಾಯೆಂತ್ ವಾಡಾವಳ್ ಜಾಯ್ನಾ. ವಾಡಾವಳಿಕ್ ಹೆರಾಂ ಥಾವ್ನ್ ಪೋಸ್ ಗರ್ಜೆಚೊ. ಅಶೆಂ ಸಂಸ್ಕೃತ್, ಪ್ರಕೃತ್ ಥಾವ್ನ್ ಆನಿ ಆಯ್ಲೆವಾರ್ ಇಂಗ್ಲಿಷ್ ಆನಿ ಹೆರಾಂ ಆಧುನಿಕ್ ಭಾಶೆಂ ಥಾವ್ನ್ ಭಾಶಾಂತರ್ ಸಹಿತ್ ಕನ್ನಡ್ ಆನಿ ಇತರ್ ಭಾಸಾಂನಿ ವ್ಹಾಳ್ಳಾಂ. ಕೊಂಕ್ಣೆಕ್‌ಯಿೀ ಭಾಶಾಂತರ್ ಸಾಹಿತ್ ಗರ್ಜೆಚೆಂ ಮ್ಹಳ್ಳೆಂ ಮಾಂದುನ್ ಘೆಜಯ್. ಭಾಶಾಂತರಾ ವರ್ವಿಂ ಹೆರಾಂ ಸಾಹಿತಾಂತ್ಲಿಂ ಮೊಲಾಂ, ಚಿಂತ್ನಾಂ, ಭಾವನಾಂ, ಅನ್ಭೋಗ್ ಇತ್ಯಾದಿ ಕೊಂಕ್ಣೆಕ್ ಮೆಳ್ತಾತ್. ಹೆಂ ಸರ್ವ್ ನಾಸ್ತಾನಾಂ ಕೊಂಕ್ಣಿ

ದುರ್ಬಳಿ ಜಾವ್ನ್ ಉರ್ತಾ. ಹೆ ಊಣ್ ನಿವಾರ್ಚ್ಯಾ ಖಾತಿರ್ ಭಾಶಾಂತರ್ ತರ್ಭೆತಿ ಆಮ್ಚ್ಯಾ ಸಾಹಿತಿಂಕ್ ಗರ್ಜೆಚಿ. ಅಶೆಂ ಭಾಶಾಂತರ್ ಮರ್ಜೆಚೆಂ ಜಾವ್ನ್ ಉರಾನಾಸ್ತಾಂ ಭೋವ್ ಗರ್ಜೆಚಿ ವಿದ್ಯಾ ಜಾಲ್ಯಾ.

ಭಾಶಾಂತರ್ ಆಮ್ಚ್ಯಾ ಭಾರತಾಂತ್ ಸುರ್ವಿಲ್ಯಾ ಕಾಳಾರ್ ಥಾವ್ನ್ ಆಸ್ಲ್ಯಾರ್‌ಯೀ ತೆಂ ಏಕ್ ವಿಜ್ಞಾನ್ ಜಾವ್ನ್ ಆಯ್ಲೆವಾರ್ ಭಾಶೆವಿಜ್ಞಾನಾಚೆಂ ಆನ್ವಯಿಕ್ ಶಿಸ್ತ್ ಜಾವ್ನ್ ಶಿವಾಯ್ ತಾಚಾ'ದಿಂ ನಹಿಂ. ಗಜಾಲ್ ಅಶಿ ಆಸ್ತಾಂ ಭಾಶಾಂತರಾಂತ್ ಭಾಶೆವಿಜ್ಞಾನಾಚೊ ಪಾತ್ರ್ ಮಹತ್ವಾಚೊ ಜಾವ್ನಾಸಾ. ಭಾರತೀಯ್ ಕಾವ್ಯ್ ಮಿಮಾಂಸೆಂತ್ ಸಬ್ದಾಂ–ಪ್ರಯೋಗಾಚೆ ಗೂಣ್ ಆವ್ಗುಣ್ ಇತ್ಯಾದಿಂಚೆ ವಿಶ್ಲೇಷಣ್ ಆಸ್ಲ್ಯಾರ್‌ಯೀ ಭಾಶಾಂತರ್ ಏಕ್ ವಿಜ್ಞಾನ್ ಯಾ ಶಿಸ್ತ್ ಮ್ಹಣ್ ಲೆಕ್‌ಲ್ಲೆಂ ನಾಂ.

ಭಾಶಾಂತರಾಚೆಂ ವ್ಯಾಖ್ಯೆ

ಮೂಳ್ ಭಾಶೆಚ್ಯೆ ಕೃತಿಯೆಚೆಂ ಅರ್ಥ್ ವ್ಯತ್ಯಾಸ್ ನಾಸ್ತಾನಾ ಉದ್ದಿಶ್ಟ್ ಭಾಶೆಂತ್ ಹಾಡ್ಚಿ ಪ್ರಕ್ರಿಯಾಚ್ ಭಾಶಾಂತರ್. ಅಶೆಂ ಉದ್ದಿಶ್ಟ್ ಭಾಶೆಂತ್ ಮೂಳ್ ಕೃತಿಯೆಚಿ ಅಭಿವ್ಯಕ್ತಿ ಕರ್ಚೆಂಚ್ ಭಾಶಾಂತರ್ ಜಾವ್ನಾಸಾ. ಹ್ಯಾ ಪ್ರಕ್ರಿಯೆಂತ್ ರೂಪ್ ವ್ಯತ್ಯಾಸ್ ಜಾಲಾಂ ಶಿವಾಯ್ ಅರ್ಥ್ ವ್ಯತ್ಯಾಸ್ ನ್ಹಯ್. ಹ್ಯಾ ಪ್ರಕ್ರಿಯೆಂತ್ ಅರ್ಥ್ ವ್ಯತ್ಯಾಸಾಕ್ ಕಸಲೊಚ್ ಬಾದಕ್ ಜಾಯ್ನಾ ಮ್ಹಣ್ ಸಾಂಗೊಂಕ್ ಅಸಾಧ್ಯ್ ಜಾಲ್ಯಾರ್‌ಯೀ, ಅರ್ಥ್ ವ್ಯತ್ಯಾಸ್ ಜಾಯ್ನಾಶೆಂ ಗಮನ್ ಆಸ್ತಾ. ಕಿತ್ಯಾಕ್ ಮ್ಹಳ್ಯಾರ್ ಸಬ್ದಾಂಕ್ ಅರ್ಥ್ ಯೆಂವ್ಚೊ ಸಂಸ್ಕೃತೆ ಥಾವ್ನ್ ಆಸ್ತಾಂ, ಸಂಸ್ಕೃತಿ ಯಾ ತಾಚಿ ಅಭಿವ್ಯಕ್ತಿ ಜಾವ್ನಾಸ್ಚಿ ಭಾಸ್ ಬರಯ್ತಾನಾಂ ಅರ್ಥ್ ಆಸಾ ತಶೆಂ ಉರ್ಚೆಂ ಕಷ್ಟಾಂಚೆಂ. ಕಿತ್ಲೊ ಮೂಳ್ ಅರ್ಥ್ ಆಸ್ತಾ, ತಿತ್ಲೆಂ ಬರೆಂ ಭಾಶಾಂತರ್ ಮ್ಹಣ್ ಲೆಕ್ಚೆಂ.

ಭಾಶಾಂತರ್, ಏಕ್ ಪುನರ್‌ಸೃಷ್ಟಿ ಕಾರ್ಯೆಂ ಜಾವ್ನಾಸಾ. ಉದ್ದಿಶ್ಟ್ ಭಾಸ್, ಮೂಳ್ ಭಾಶೆ ವರ್ನಿಂ ವಿಂಗಡ್ ಸುರ್ಪಾಯೆಚಿ ಜಾವ್ನಾಸ್ತಾನಾ ಪುನಸ್ಸೃಷ್ಟೆ ಶಿವಾಯ್ ಹೆರ್ ವಾಟ್ ನಾಂ. ಹ್ಯಾ ವರ್ವಿಂ ಭಾಶಾಂತರ್‌ಕಾರಾಚಿ ಜವಾಬ್ದಾರಿ ಆನಿ ಜಾಗ್ರುತ್ಕಾಯ್ ಭೋವ್ ವರ್ತಿ. ಏಕಾ ಭಾಶೆಂತ್ ಉದೆವ್ನ್ ಆಯಿಲ್ಲಿಂ ಭಾವನಾಂ ಆನ್ಯೆಕಾ ಭಾಶೆಕ್ ವರ್ಗಾವಣ್ ಕರ್ಚೆಂ ಏಕ್ ಉತ್ತೀಮ್ ಕಲಾಚ್ ಸೈ. ಅನುವಾದಿತ್ ಕೃತಿ ವಾಚ್ತಾನಾ ಮೂಳ್ ಕೃತಿ ವಾಚ್ಚೊ ಅನ್ಭೋಗ್‌ಚ್ ಯೇಂವ್ಕ್ ಜಾಯ್; ಭೊಗ್ಣಾಂನಿ ಚಡುಣೆಂ ಜಾಯ್ನಾಯೆ. ಜೆ. ಸಿ. ಕ್ಯಾಟ್‌ಫರ್ಡ್ (J. C. Catford) ಹಾಣೆಂ ಸಾಂಗ್ಚ್ಯಾ ಪರ್ಮಾಣೆ "ಏಕಾ ಭಾಶೆಂತ್ಲ್ಯಾ ಪಠ್ಯವಸ್ತ್ ಬದ್ಲಾ ಆನ್ಯೆಕಾ ಭಾಶೆಂತ್ ಸಮಾನ್ ಪಠ್ಯವಸ್ತ್ ದಿಂವ್ಚಿ ಪ್ರಕ್ರಿಯಾ ಜಾವ್ನಾಸಾ ಭಾಶಾಂತರ್". ಹಾಂಗಾಸರ್ 'ಪಠ್ಯವಸ್ತ್' ಮ್ಹಣ್ತಾನಾ ಅರ್ಥ್, ಶೈಲಿ/ರೀತ್ ಆಟಾಪ್ತಾ. ತಶೆಂಚ್ 'ಸಮಾನ್' ಮ್ಹಳ್ಯಾ ಸಬ್ದಾಂತ್ ಸರ್ವ್ ಸಾಹಿತಿಕ್ ಗೂಣ್ (Values) ಆಟಾಪ್ತಾತ್. ಭಾಶಾಂತರ್ ಕರ್ತೆಲ್ಯಾನ್ ಮೂಳ್ ಪಠ್ಯಂತ್ಲಿಂ ಭೊಗ್ಣಾಂ, ಅರ್ಥ್ ಇತ್ಯಾದಿ ಸಮ್ಜೊನ್ ಘೆಜಯ್. ಉದ್ದಿಶ್ಟ್ ಭಾಶೆಚ್ಯಾ ಸಮಾನಾರ್ಥಕ್ ಸಬ್ದಾಂಚಿ ವಳಕ್ ಆಸಾಜಯ್. ಆನಿ ಹೆ ಸಬ್ದ್, ಮೂಳ್‌ಪಠ್ಯಚ್ಯಾ ಸೊಭ್ಚ್ಯಾ ವಿನ್ಯಾಸಾಕ್ ಆನಿ ಶೈಲಿ ಸೊಭಾಯೆಕ್ ಅನುಗೂಣ್ ಜಾವ್ನ್ ಗಳ್ಸಿಜಯ್. ತೆದಾಳಾ ಮಾತ್ರ್ ಭಾಶಾಂತರ್, ಮೂಳ್ ಕೃತಿಯೆಚೆಂ ಪ್ರತಿರೂಪ್ ಜಾಂವ್ಕ್ ಪಾವ್ತಾ. ಅಶೆಂ ದೋನ್‌ಯಿ ಕೃತಿಯಾಂನಿ ಭೊಗ್ಣಾಂತರ್ ಜಾವ್ನೊಚೊ. ಥಂಯ್ಸರ್ ಜಾಂವ್ಚೆಂ 'ಭವಾಂತರ್' ಮಾತ್ರ್. ಅಶೆಂ ಮಟ್ವ್ಯಾನ್ ಸಾಂಗ್ಚೆಂ ಜಾಲ್ಯಾರ್, ಭಾಶಾಂತರ್ ಏಕ್ ರೂಪಾಂತರ್ ಶಿವಾಯ್ ಭೊಗ್ಣಾಂತರ್ ನ್ಹಯ್. ಹೆಂ ಕಾರ್ಯೆಂ ಕಿತ್ಲೆಂ ವೈಜ್ಞಾನಿಕ್‌ಗೀ ತಿತ್ಲೆಂಚ್ ಕಲಾತ್ಮಕ್/ಸೌಂದರ್ಯಾತ್ಮಕ್‌ಯೀ ವ್ಹಯ್.

2.0 ಬರ್ಪಿ ಭಾಶೆಚಿ ಸುರ್ಪಾಯಿ

ಬರ್ಪಿ ಭಾಸ್ ಮ್ಹಳ್ಯಾರ್ ಸಬಾರ್ ಮೂಳ್ ದ್ರವ್ಯಾಂಚೆಂ ಏಕ್ ವ್ಯವಸ್ಥಿತ್ ರೂಪ್. ಭಾಶೆಧ್ವನಿ, ಲಿಪಿ, ಅರ್ಥ್, ವ್ಯಾಕರಣ್, ಸಬ್ದಾಂವಳ್, ಸನ್ನಿವೇಶ್ – ಹಿಂ ಸರ್ವ್ ಬರ್ಪಿಭಾಶೆಚೆಂ

ಮೂಳ್ ದ್ರವ್ಯಾಂ ಜಾವ್ನಾಸಾತ್. ಹಿಂ ದ್ರವ್ಯಂ ಏಕ್ ಭಾಶೆಘಟಕ್ ಜಾವ್ನ್, ತ್ಯಾ ಘಟಕಾಂ ಮಾರಿಫಾತ್, ವಾಕ್ಯ್ ಸಂಘಟನ್ ಜಾವ್ನ್ ಹ್ಯಾ ವಾಕ್ಯಾಂದ್ವಾರಿಂ ಏಕ್ ಸಾಹಿತ್‌ಪತ್ಯ್ ನಿರ್ಮಾಣ್ ಜಾತಾ. ಅಶೆಂ ಸಾಹಿತ್‌ಪತ್ಯ್ ಏಕ್ ಭಾಶೆವಿನ್ಯಾಸ್ ಜಾವ್ನಾಸಾ. ಹ್ಯಾ ವಿನ್ಯಾಸಾಂತ್ ಘಟಕಾಂಚಿ ಶ್ರೇಣೀಕೃತ್ ಮಾಂಡಾವಳ್ ಆಸಾ.

'ಜೊನಿ ಆಂಬೊ ಖಾತಾ' ಮ್ಹಳ್ಳ್ಯಾ ವಾಕ್ಯಾಂತ್ 'ಜೊನಿ' ನಾಮ್ ಪುಂಜೊ ಜಾಲ್ಯಾರ್, 'ಆಂಬೊ ಖಾತಾ' ಕ್ರಿಯಾ ಪುಂಜೊ ಜಾವ್ನಾಸಾ. ಹಾಂತುಂ 'ಖಾತಾ' ಕ್ರಿಯಾಪದ್ ಜಾಲ್ಯಾರ್ 'ಆಂಬೊ' ಕರ್ಮ್‌ಪದ್ ಜಾವ್ನಾಸಾ. ಹ್ಯಾ ಘಟಕಾಂಕ್ ಉದ್ದಿಶ್ಟ್ ಭಾಶೆಂತ್ ಸಮಾನಾರ್ಥಕ್

ನಾಮ್ ಪುಂಜೊ : ಜೊನಿ
ಕರ್ಮ್‌ಪದ್ : ಮಾವಿನ ಹಣ್ಣನ್ನು
ಕ್ರಿಯಾಪದ್ : ತಿನ್ನುತ್ತಾನೆ.

ಅಶೆಂ ವಾಕ್ಯ್ # ಜೊನಿ ಮಾವಿನ ಹಣ್ಣನ್ನು ತಿನ್ನುತ್ತಾನೆ # ಉತ್ಪಾದನ್ ಜಾತಾ.

ವಯ್ಲ್ಯಾ ವಾಕ್ಯಾಂತ್ ನಾಮ್ ಪುಂಜೊ + ಕರ್ಮ್‌ಪದ್ + ಕ್ರಿಯಾಪದ್ ಮ್ಹಳ್ಳಿ ವ್ಯವಸ್ಥಾ ತ್ಯಾ ವಾಕ್ಯಾಚೆಂ ವ್ಯಾಕರಣಾರ್ಥ್ ಜಾವ್ನಾಸಾ. ಹೆಂ ಎಕಾ ಭಾಶೆ ಥಾವ್ನ್ ಆನ್ಯೆಕಾ ಭಾಶೆಂತ್ ವೆಗ್ಳೆಂ ಆಸ್ಯೆತಾ. ಧಾಕ್ಲ್ಯಾ ಕ್ ತೆಂ ನಾಮ್ ಪುಂಜೊ + ಕ್ರಿಯಾಪದ್ + ಕರ್ಮ್‌ಪದ್ ಅಶೆಂ ಜಾತಾ. # Johnny eats mango #. ಅಶೆಂ ಕೊಂಕ್ಣಿ, ಕನ್ನಡ್, ಇಂಗ್ಲಿಶ್ ಭಾಶೆಂನಿ ವಾಕ್ಯಾರ್ಥ್ ಎಕ್‌ಚ್ಚ್ ಜಾಲ್ಯಾರ್‌ಯೀ ವ್ಯಾಕರಣಾರ್ಥ್ ವಿಂಗಡ್ ಜಾವ್ನಾಸಾತ್.

ಆತಾಂ ಆನ್ಯೆಕ್ ಧಾಕ್ಲೊ ಘೆಂವ್ಯಾಂ:

uncle ಕೊಂಕ್ಣೆಂತ್ ಮಾಮ್ ಜಾವ್ಯೆತ್ ಯಾ ಬಪ್ಪು ಜಾವ್ಯೆತ್.

ಅಸಲ್ಯಾ ವೆಳಾರ್ ಸಬ್ದಾಚೆಂ ಸಂದರ್ಭ್ ಅರ್ಥ್ ಸಮ್ಜೊನ್ ಘೆಜಯ್. ಹೊ ಅಸೊ ಆಸ್ತಾ:

Uncle (C) ಪುಲ್ಲಿಂಗ್, ಬಾಪಾಯ್ಚೊ ಭಾವ್: 'ಬಪ್ಲೊ'
(D) ಪುಲ್ಲಿಂಗ್, ಆವಯ್ಚೊ ಭಾವ್: 'ಮಾವ್ಲೊ'
(E) ಪುಲ್ಲಿಂಗ್, ಬಾಪಾಯ್ಚ್ಯಾ ಭಯ್ಣಿಚೊ ಘೊವ್: ಆಕಯ್ಚೊ ಘೊವ್/'ಮಾವೊ'.

3.0 ಭಾಶಾಂತರ್ ಸಮಾನಾರ್ಥಕ್

ಮೂಳ್ ಭಾಶೆಚ್ಯಾ ಪತ್ಯಬದ್ಲಾಕ್ ಉದ್ದಿಶ್ಟ್ ಭಾಶೆಂತ್ ದಿಂವ್ಚೊ ಪತ್ಯ್‌ಚ್ಚ್ ಭಾಶಾಂತರ್ ಸಮಾನಾರ್ಥಕ್ ಜಾವ್ನಾಸಾ. ಅಶೆಂ ಸಮಾನಾರ್ಥಕ್ ದಿತಾನಾ ಮೂಳ್ ಭಾಶೆಚ್ಯಾ ಸಬ್ದಾರ್ಥ್, ಉದ್ದಿಶ್ಟ್ ಭಾಶೆಚ್ಯಾ ವ್ಯಾಕರಣಾರ್ಥಕ್ ಆನಿ ಸಂದರ್ಭಾರ್ಥಕ್ ಹೊಂದೊನ್ ಆಸಾಜಯ್. ಅಶೆಂ ಕೊಂಕ್ಣೆಂತ್ಲ್ಯಾ 'ಮಾಮ್' ಯಾ 'ಬಪ್ಪು' ಮ್ಹಳ್ಳ್ಯಾ ಸಬ್ದಾಂಕ್ ಇಂಗ್ಲಿಷಾಂತ್ Uncle ಮ್ಹಳ್ಳೆ ಸಬ್ದ್‌ಚ್ಚ್ ಸಮಾನಾರ್ಥಕ್ ಶಿವಾಯ್ ಹೆರ್ ನ್ಹಯ್. ಅಸಲೆ ಸಮರ್ಪಕ್ ಸಮಾನಾರ್ಥಕ್ ಉದ್ದಿಶ್ಟ್ ಭಾಶೆಂತ್ ಒದಗ್ಸಿತಾನಾ ಸಾರ್ಕೆಂ ಭಾಶಾಂತರ್ ಆಸಾ ಜಾತಾ ಹೆ ಸಮಾನಾರ್ಥಕ್ ಸಬ್ದ್ ಉದ್ದಿಶ್ಟ್ ಭಾಶೆಚ್ಯಾ ವ್ಯಾಕರಣಾ ಪರ್ಮಾಣೆ ಮಾಂಡಿಜಯ್. ಅಶೆಂ ಭಾಶಾಂತರಾಂತ್ ಸಮಾನಾರ್ಥಕ್ ಸಬ್ದ್, ಸಂದರ್ಭಾರ್ಥ್, ವ್ಯಾಕರಣ್ ಪರ್ಮಾಣೆ ಸಬ್ದಾಂಚಿ ಮಾಂಡಾವಳ್, ಶೈಲಿಯಾತ್ಮಕ್ ಗುಂತಾವಣ್ ಮ್ಹಳ್ಳಿಂ ಆಯಾಮಾಂ (Dimensions) ಆಸಾತ್. ಹೆಂ ಸರ್ವ್ ಲೆಕ್ತಾನಾ ಸಮರ್ಪಕ್ ಭಾಶಾಂತರ್ ಉಬ್ಜಾತಾ. ಹ್ಯಾ ಸರ್ವ್ ಸಂಗ್ತಿ ವಿಶಿಂ ಭಾಶೆ ವೈಜ್ಞಾನಿಕ್ ಸಾಮರ್ಥ್ಯ್ ಭಾಶಾಂತರ್ ಕರ್ತೆಲ್ಯಾ ಥಂಯ್ ಆಸಾಜಯ್. ಹೊ ವಿಶಯ್ ವೈಜ್ಞಾನಿಕ್ ಜಾಲ್ಯಾರ್, ಸರ್ವಾಂಚಿ ವ್ಯವಸ್ಥಾ ಕಲಾತ್ಮಕ್ ಜಾವ್ನಾಸಾ.

ಮುಳಾವ್ಯಾ ಭಾಶೆಂತ್ಲ್ಯಾ ಹರ್ಯೆಕಾ ಸಬ್ದಾಕ್ ಉದ್ದಿಶ್ಟ್ ಭಾಶೆಂತ್ ಸರಿಸಮಾನ್ ಸಬ್ದ್ ಆಸಾಜಯ್ ಮ್ಹಣ್ ನಾ ಯಾ ವ್ಯಾಕರಣಾತ್ಮಕ್ ಸರಿಸಮಾನ್ ಘಡಾನಾವಳ್ (Formal correspondence) ಆಸಾಜಯ್ ಮ್ಹಣ್ ನಾ. ಇಂಗ್ಲಿಷಾಂತ್ಲ್ಯಾ The ಮ್ಹಳ್ಳ್ಯಾ ರೂಪಾಕ್ ಕೊಂಕ್ಣೆಂತ್ ಸರಿಸಮಾನ್ ರೂಪ್ ನಾಂ. The book to be translated ಮ್ಹಳ್ಳೆಂ ಅಧೀನ್ ವಾಕ್ಯ್ 'ಭಾಶಾಂತರ್ ಕರಿಜಯ್ ಜಾಲ್ಲೊ ಬೂಕ್' ಮ್ಹಣ್ತಾನಾ ಞುಜ ಮ್ಹಳ್ಳ್ಯಾ ರೂಪಾಕ್ ಸರಿಸಮಾನ್ ರೂಪ್ ಕೊಂಕ್ಣೆಂತ್ ಯೆಂವ್ಕ್ ನಾ ಜಾಲ್ಯಾರ್‌ಯೀ, ಕೆಲ್ಲೆಂ ಭಾಶಾಂತರ್ ಸಮಾನಾರ್ಥಕ್ ಜಾವ್ನಾಸಾ. ಅಸಲಿ ಬದ್ಲಾವಣ್ (Shift) ಭಾಶಾಂತರಾಂತ್ ಸಾಮಾನ್ಯ್ ಜಾವ್ನಾಸಾ. ಅಸಲ್ಯೊ ಬದ್ಲಾವಣ್ಯೊ ವ್ಯಾಕರಣಾಚ್ಯಾ ಮಟ್ಟಾಚಿ ಜಾವ್ಯೆತ್:

2. Deepak loves Deepti: ಕತೃ + ಕ್ರಿಯಾಪದ್ + ಕರ್ಮಪದ್

2 (a) ದೀಪಕ್ ದೀಪ್ತಿಚೊ ಮೋಗ್ ಕರ್ತಾ: ಕತೃ + ಕರ್ಮಪದ್ + ಕ್ರಿಯಾಪದ್
ಕೊಂಕ್ಣೆಂತ್, ಇಂಗ್ಲಿಶ್ ವ್ಯಾಕರಣ್ ವ್ಯವಸ್ಥೆಚಿ ಬದ್ಲಾವಣ್ ಜಾಲ್ಯಾ.

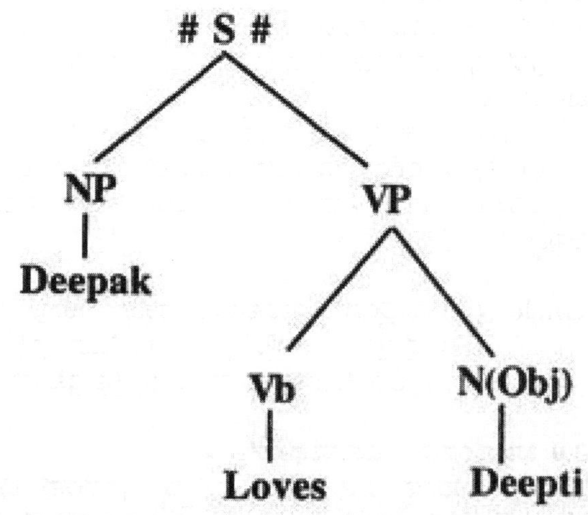

# S #	→	**NP + VP**
Vp	→	**Vb + N (obj)**
NP	→	**Deepak**
V	→	**loves**
N (obj)	→	**Deepthi**

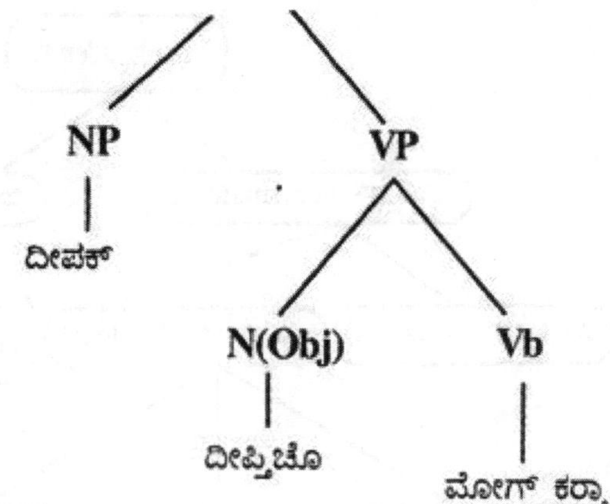

# S #	→	NP + VP
Vp	→	N (Obj) + Vb
NP	→	ದೀಪಕ್
N (obj)	→	ದೀಪ್ತಿಚೊ
Vb	→	ಮೋಗ್ ಕರ್ತಾ

Deepak loves Deepti (SL) : ಮೂಳ್ ಪತ್ಯ್
ದೀಪಕ್ ದೀಪ್ತಿಚೊ ಮೋಗ್ ಕರ್ತಾ (TL) : ಉದ್ದಿಷ್ಟ್ ಪತ್ಯ್

ಸಬ್ದ್ ಘಟನಾವಳಿಂತ್ ಬದ್ಲಾವಣ್
ಇಂಗ್ಲಿಷಾಂತ್: Trousers (pl)
ಕೊಂಕ್ಣೆಂತ್: Trousers (Sg) EAVè±ï {s}--->Æ //
ತಶೆಂಚ್ Pants > Pant: {s}--->Æ // ರೂಪ್ ಕೊಂಕ್ಣೆಂತ್ ಶೂನ್ಯ್/ಲೋಪ್ ಜಾತಾ.

4.0 ಭಾಶೆ ಪ್ರಭೇದ್:
ಭಾಶಾಂತರ್ ಕರ್ತಾನಾ ಭಾಶೆ ಪ್ರಭೇದ್ ವಳ್ಖೊನ್ ಭಾಶಾಂತರ್ ಕರಿಜಯ್.

ಭಾಸ್ ಏಕ್ ಅಪೂರ್ವ್ ಸುರ್ಪಾಯೆಚಿ. ತಾಂಚಿಂ ಮೂರ್ತ್ ಸುರ್ಪಾಂ ಭಾಶೆ ಪ್ರಭೇದ್ ಜಾವ್ನಾಸಾತ್. ತ್ಯೆ ಹ್ಯಾ ಪರಿಂ ಆಸಾತ್.

ಶಾಶ್ವಿತ್ ಆನಿ ಅಶಾಶ್ವಿತ್ ಸಂದರ್ಭಾಂ ಪರ್ಮಾಣೆ ಭಾಶೆಪ್ರಭೇದ್ ಉಬ್ಜಾತಾತ್. ಶಾಶ್ವಿತ್ ಭಾಶೆ ಪ್ರಭೇದಾಂನಿ ಬದ್ಲಾವಣ್ ಉಣೆ; ಅಶಾಶ್ವಿತ್ ಪ್ರಭೇದಾಂನಿ ಬದ್ಲಾವಣ್ ಚಡ್. ಹರ್ಯೆಕಾ ವ್ಯಕ್ತಿನ್ ಗಳ್ಸೊಂಚೆ ಸಬ್ದ್, ವಾಪರ್ಚಿ ರೀತ್, ಉಚ್ಚಾರಣ್ ಕರ್ಚೆಂ ಇತ್ಯಾದಿ ಆಪ್ಣಾಚೆಚ್ಚ್ ರಿತಿನ್ ಆಸ್ತಾ. ಅಸಲ್ಯಾ ವ್ಯವಸ್ಥೆಕ್ ವ್ಯಕ್ತಿ ಭಾಸ್ ಮ್ಹಣ್ತಾಂವ್.

ಎಕಾ ಪ್ರದೇಶಾಕ್, ಕಾಲಾಕ್ ಆನಿ ಸಮಾಜೆಕ್ ಲಾಗೊನ್ ಭಾಸ್ ಬದಲ್ತಾ. ಅಶೆಂ ಮಂಗ್ಳುರಿ, ಗೊಂಯ್ಚಿ, ಕೇರಳಿ ಕೊಂಕ್ಣಿ ಪ್ರಾದೇಶಿಕ್ ಕೊಂಕ್ಣಿ ಜಾಲ್ಯಾರ್, ಆದ್ಲಿ, ಮದ್ಲಿ ಆನಿ ಆತಾಂಚಿ ಕೊಂಕ್ಣಿ ಕಾಲಿಕ್ ಪ್ರಭೇದ್ ಜಾವ್ನಾಸಾತ್. ತಶೆಂಚ್ ಕುಡ್ಮಿ, ಸಾರಸ್ವತ್, ಕ್ರಿಸ್ತಾಂವ್ ಆನಿ ನವಾಯತ್ ಕೊಂಕ್ಣಿ ಸಾಮಾಜಿಕ್ ಪ್ರಭೇದ್ ಜಾವ್ನಾಸಾತ್. ಹ್ಯಾ ಪ್ರಭೇದಾಂತ್ ಸ್ಥಾನ್‌ಮಾನ್ ಆಸ್ತಾನಾ ಭಾಶಾಂತರಾಂತ್‌ಯೀ ಫಾವೊತೊ ಸ್ಥಾನ್‌ಮಾನ್ ದೀಜಯ್. ಅಶೆಂಚ್ ವೈಜ್ಞಾನಿಕ್ ಯಾ ಧಾರ್ಮಿಕ್, ಔದ್ಯೋಗಿಕ್ ಇತ್ಯಾದಿ ವಿಶಿಷ್ಟ್ ಸಂದರ್ಭಾಂಕ್

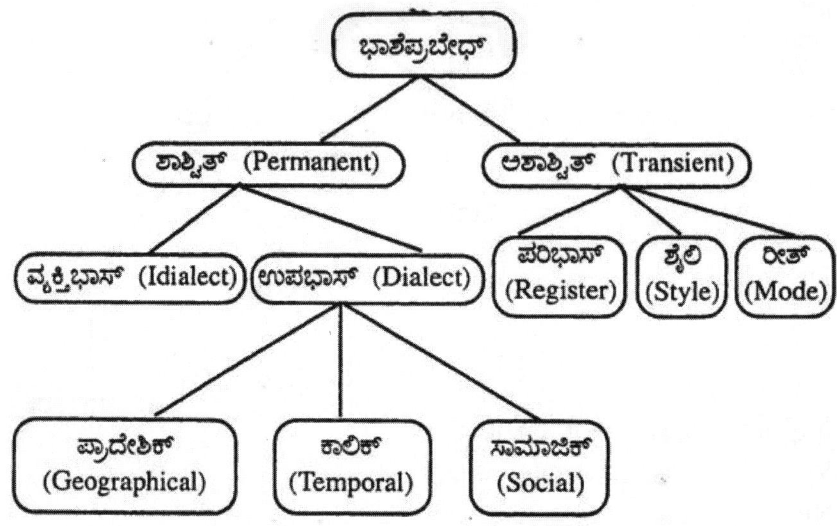

ಲಾಗೊನ್ ಪರಿಭಾಸ್ ಉದ್ಭವ್ ಜಾತಾ. ಅಶೆಂಚ್ ಸಾಮಾನ್ಯ್, ಶಿಶ್ಟ್, ಭಾವನಾತ್ಮಕ್ ಶೈಲಿವರ್ವಿಂ ಭಾಶೆರೂಪ್ ಬದಲ್ತಾ. ಉಲವ್ಣ್ಯಾಕ್, ಬರ್ಪಾಕ್, ಸಾಹಿತಾಕ್ ಹೊಂದೊನ್ ಭಾಶೆ ರೀತ್ ಬದಲ್ತಾ. ಅಸಲಿ ಅಶಾಶ್ವಿತ್ ಭಾಶೆಪ್ರಭೇದ್ ಭಾಶಾಂತರ್‌ಕಾರಾನ್ ಸಮ್ಜೊನ್ ಘೆಜಯ್. ತಶೆಂಚ್ ಪ್ರಾದೇಶಿಕ್ ಕಾಲಿಕ್ ಆನಿ ಸಾಮಾಜಿಕ್ ಉಪಭಾಶೆ ವಿಶ್ಯಾಂತ್‌ಯಿ ಗರ್ಜೆಚಿ ಸಮ್ಜೊಣಿ ಜಾಯ್.

ಅಶೆಂ ನಾನಾ ಭಾಶೆಪ್ರಭೇದಾಂನಿ ಗಳ್ಸುಂಚೆ ಸಬ್ದ್, ಸಬ್ದಾ ಸಂಘಟನ್ ಜಾಣಾ ಆಸ್ಲ್ಯಾರ್ ತಿ ಸಂದರ್ಬಾನುಸಾರ್ ಉಪಯೋಗ್ಸುಂಕ್ ಅನ್ಕೂಲ್ ಜಾತಾ. ತಶೆಂಚ್ ಸಬ್ದೋಚ್ಚಾರ್. ಹೆಂ ಸರ್ವ್ ಭಾಶಾದ್ರವ್ಯ್ ಔಚಿತ್ಯ್ ಸರ್ವ್ ಜಾವ್ನ್ ವಾಪರಿಜಯ್ ಶಿವಾಯ್ ನವೆಸಾಂವಾ ಖಾತಿರ್ ನ್ಹಯ್, ದೆವಾಸಾಂವಾ ಖಾತಿರ್‌ಯೀ ನ್ಹಯ್. ಅಶೆಂಚ್ ಭಾಸ್ ಸಂಸ್ಕೃತೆ ಥಾವ್ನ್ ಉಬ್ಜಾತಾ ಜಾಲ್ಲ್ಯಾನ್ ಭಾಶಾಂತರಾಂತ್ ಉದ್ದಿಶ್ಟ್ ಭಾಶೆಚ್ಯಾ ಸಂಸ್ಕೃತೆಕ್‌ಯೀ ಸ್ಥಾನ್‌ಮಾನ್ ಆಸಾಜಾಯ್. ಅಶೆಂ 'ರಾಂಡ್', 'ಮೆಂಡ್ರೊ' ಕೊಂಕ್ಣಿ ಸಬ್ದ್ ಜಾಲ್ಯಾರ್‌ಯೀ ಮಂಗ್ಳುರಿ ಸಂಸ್ಕೃತೆಕ್ ತೆ ಸರಿ ಜಾತಾತ್‌ಗಿ ಪಳಯ್ಜಯ್. ತಶೆಂಚ್ ಸಬಾರ್ ಪಾರಿಭಾಶಿಕ್ ಸಬ್ದಾ ವಿಶಿಂಯೀ ಜಾಗ್ರುತ್ಕಾಯ್ ಸಾಂಬಾಳಿಜಯ್. ಸಾಂಸಕೃತಿಕ್ ಗುರ್ತ್ (Cultural Marker) ಸಾಂಡುಂಕ್ ಸಾಧ್ಯ್ ನಾಂ. ಶೆತ್, ಬಾಟ್, ಪಾವ್ಲಾಂ, ಪಾಂಯ್ ಇತ್ಯಾದಿ ಸಬ್ದ್ ಪ್ರಾದೇಶಿಕ್/ಸಾಂಸ್ಕೃತಿಕ್ ಗುರ್ತ್ ಜಾವ್ನಾಸ್ಲ್ಯಾರ್ ತೆ ಹೆರಾ ಜಾಗ್ಯಾಂನಿ ಅರ್ಥಾಭರಿತ್ ಜಾಯ್ನಾಂತ್ ಆನಿ ವಾಚ್ಪ್ಯಾಂ ಥೈಂ ಗೊಂದೊಳಾಕ್ ಕಾರಣ್ ಜಾತಾತ್. ಹಾಚೊ ಅರ್ಥ್, ಸ್ವೀಕರಣ್ ನೆಗಾರ್ ಕರಿಜಾಯ್ ಮ್ಹಣ್ ನ್ಹಂಯ್. ಬಗಾರ್ ಜಾಗ್ರುತ್ಕಾಯೆಚಿ ಗರ್ಜ್ ಆಸಾ ಮ್ಹಣ್, ತಿತ್ಲೆಂಚ್. ಪ್ರಾದೇಶಿಕ್/ಸಾಂಸ್ಕೃತಿಕ್ 'ಭಾಶೆಗುರ್ತ್' ಇತ್ಯಾದಿ ಕರ್ಚೆಂ ಕಾಮ್ ಭಾಶಾಂತರ್‌ಕಾರಾಚೆಂ ನ್ಹಯ್ ಮ್ಹಳ್ಳೆಂ ಸಮ್ಜೊನ್ ಘೆಜಯ್.

5.0 ಅಭಾಶಾಂತರೀಕರಣ್: ಮೂಳ್ ಆನಿ ಉದ್ದಿಶ್ಟ್ ಭಾಶೆ ಸಂಸ್ಕೃತಿ ಮಧೆಂ ಆನಿ ಭಾಶೆ ಘಟನಾವಳಿಂ ಮಧೆಂ ಚಡ್ ವ್ಯತ್ಯಾಸ್ ಆಸ್ತಾಸ್ತಾನಾ ಅಭಾಶಾಂತರೀಕರಣ್ ಉಬ್ಜಾತಾ.

5.1 ಸಾಂಸ್ಕೃತಿಕ್: ಸಾಂಸ್ಕೃತಿಕ್ ಸಬ್ದಾಂಚೆಂ ಭಾಶಾಂತರ್ ಭೋವ್ ಕಷ್ಟಾಂಚೆಂ. ಇಂಗ್ಲಿಶಾಂತ್ಲಿ cake, Christmas-tree, snow ಇತ್ಯಾದಿಂಕ್ ಕೊಂಕ್ಣೆಂತ್ ಸಮಾನ್

ಸಬ್ದ್ ದಿಂವ್ಚೆಂ ಕಷ್ಟ್. ತಶೆಂಚ್ ಕೊಂಕ್ಣೆಂತ್ಲಿ ಪಾತೊಳಿ, ಮುಟ್ಲಿಂ, ಪೊಳೆ, ಸನ್ನಾಂ, ಪಿಡ್ಡುಕ್ ಇತ್ಯಾದಿ ಸಾಂಸ್ಕೃತಿಕ್ ಸಬ್ದ್, ಇಂಗ್ಲಿಶಾಂತ್ ಭಾಶಾಂತರ್ ಕರ್ಚೆಂ ಸುಲಭಾಯೆಚೆಂ ನ್ಹಯ್. ಅಸಲ್ಯಾ ಸಂದರ್ಭಾಂನಿ ತ್ಯೊ ವಸ್ತುಂಚಿ ಕಲ್ಪನಾ ಯೆಂವ್ಚೆ ಬರಿಂ ವಿವರ್ ದಿಜಾಯ್ ಪಡ್ತಾ ಯಾ ಸಬ್ದ್‌ಚ್ಚ್ ಗಳ್ಸಿಜಾಯ್ (Transference of the original) ಪಡ್ತಾ.

5.2 ಭಾಶಾತ್ಮಕ್:

5.2.1 ಭಾಶೆ ಘಟನಾವಳ್ ಲೆಕುನ್ ಭಾಶೆಂನಿ ನಾನಾ ಥರ್ ಆಸಾತ್:

(C) ವಿವಿಕ್ತ್ ವರ್ಗ್ (Isolating type)

(D) ಪ್ರಾತ್ಯಾಯಿಕ್ ವರ್ಗ್ (Agglutinative/affixation type)

(E) ಅಂತರ್ಗತ್ ವರ್ಗ್ (Inflective type)

EAVèμï <u>ಅಂತರ್ಗತ್</u> ವರ್ಗಾಚಿ ಭಾಸ್. ಹಾಂಗಾಸರ್ ಪ್ರಕೃತಿ ಆನಿ ಪ್ರತ್ಯಯ್ ಸುಟಂವ್ಕ್ ಕಷ್ಟ್.

Think + past > thought
Do + past > did
Feel + past > felt

ಭೂತ್ಕಾಲ್ ರೂಪಾಂನಿ ಪ್ರಕೃತಿ ಆನಿ ಪ್ರತ್ಯಯ್ ರೂಪಾಂ ಸುಟಂವ್ಚೆಂ ಕಶ್ಟಾಂಚೆಂ ಜಾವ್ನಾಸಾ.

ಹಾಂಚೊ ಬಾಂದ್ ವೆಗ್ಳೊ ಕರ್ಚೆಂ ಸುಲಭಾಯೆಚೆಂ ಕಾಮ್.

ಕನ್ನಡ್: ಮಾಡ್ + ಇದ್ + ಅನು > ಮಾಡಿದನು
ತಿಳಿ + ದ್ + ಅನು > ತಿಳಿದನು
ಕೊಲ್ + ನ್ದ್ + ಅನು > ಕೊನ್ದನು

ಕೊಂಕ್ಣಿ: ಜೇವ್ + ಲ್ + ಒ > ಜೆವ್ಲೊ
ವಾಚ್ + ಲ್ + ಒ > ವಾಚ್ಲೊ
ಕರ್ + ತ್ + ಆ > ಕರ್ತಾ

ವಿವಿಕ್ತ್ ವರ್ಗಾಚಾ ಭಾಶೆಂನಿ ಪ್ರತ್ಯಯೀಕರಣ್ ನಾಂ. ತಾಚ್ಯಾ ಬದ್ಲಾಕ್ ವಾಕ್ಯಾಂನಿ ಸಬ್ದಾಂಸ್ಥಾನ್, ವ್ಯಾಕರಣಾ ಬಾಂದ್ ತಿಳ್ಶಿತಾತ್:

ಚೀನಿ ಭಾಸ್: 1. /ta kuok / ವ್ಹಡ್ಲೆಂ ರಾಜ್ಯ್
2. /kuok ta / 'ರಾಜ್ಯ್ ವ್ಹಡ್ಲೆಂ ಜಾವ್ನಾಸಾ'
3. /wang pao ci min / 'ರಾಯಾ ಥಾವ್ನ್ ರಕ್ಷಿತ್ ಜಾಲ್ಲಿ ಪರ್ಜಾ'
4. /pao min ci wang/ 'ಪರ್ಜೆಕ್ ರಾಕ್ಚೊ ರಾಯ್'

ಅಶೆಂ ವಿವಿಧ್ ವರ್ಗಾಚ್ಯಾ ಭಾಶೆಂ ಮಧೆಂ ವ್ಯಾಕರಣ್ ವ್ಯತ್ಯಾಸ್ ಆಸ್ತಾ ಧಾಖ್ಲ್ಯಾಕ್:

ಕೊಂಕ್ಣಿ : ಹಾಂವ್ ದೂದ್ ಪಿಯೆತಾಂ : ಖ–ಔ–ಗಿ
I drink milk : ಖ–ಗಿ–ಔ

5.2.2 ಅರ್ಥ್ ವ್ಯಾಪ್ತಿ ಭಾಸ್ ಭಾಸಾಂನಿ ವಿಂಗಡ್ ಆಸಾ.

ಕೊಂಕ್ಣಿ : 1. ಮಾಸ್ : 'Flesh/meat'
2. ಸಕತ್ : 'capacity, power, efficiency etc.'

5.2.3 ಸಬ್ದ್ – ಮೆಳಾವ್ಣಿ (ಛಿಂಟಟಠಛಿಚಿಣುಠಟಿ) ಭಾಸ್ ಭಾಸಾಂನಿ ಬದ್ಲೊನ್ ವೆತಾ

1. Eng . : Leg is injured

ಕೊಂಕ್ಣಿ : ಪಾಯಾಕ್ ಮಾರ್ ಜಾಲೊ.

2. ಕೊಂಕ್ಣಿ : ಕಾರಾಕ್ ಮಾರ್ ಜಾಲೊ
Eng: *Car is injured
(+ living collocated with injury)
3. Eng. White Paper
Kon: ಧವೆಂ ಕಾಗದ್
4. Kannada : ©½ ºÉArÛ
Eng: * White wife

ಇಂಗ್ಲಿಷ್: 1 (a) I Go/I am going (present and Present continuous tense) ಕನ್ನಡ ನಾಮ್‌ಪದ್, ಇಂಗ್ಲಿಷಾಂತ್ ನಾಮ್ ವಿಶೇಷಣ್ + ನಾಮ್‌ಪದ್
ಅಣುಬಾಂಬು (ನಾ. ಪ) > Atom Bomb (satellite + Nucleus)
ಕೆಂದುಟಿ > Red lips

5.2.5. ವಾಕ್ಯ ರಚನ್ ವ್ಯತ್ಯಾಸ್

Eg: Gopal loves Gopi

#S# → NP_1 + VP
VP → Vb + NP_2
NP_1 → Gopal
Vp → loves
NP_2 → Gopi

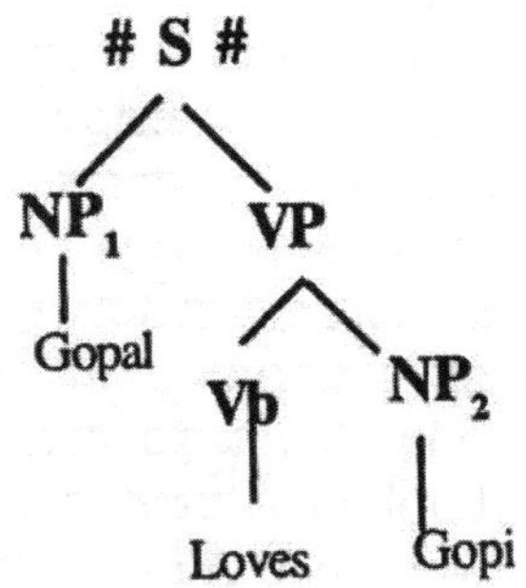

ಕೊಂಕ್ಣೆಂತ್: ಗೋಪಾಲ್ ಗೊಪಿಚೊ ಮೋಗ್ ಕರ್ತಾ.

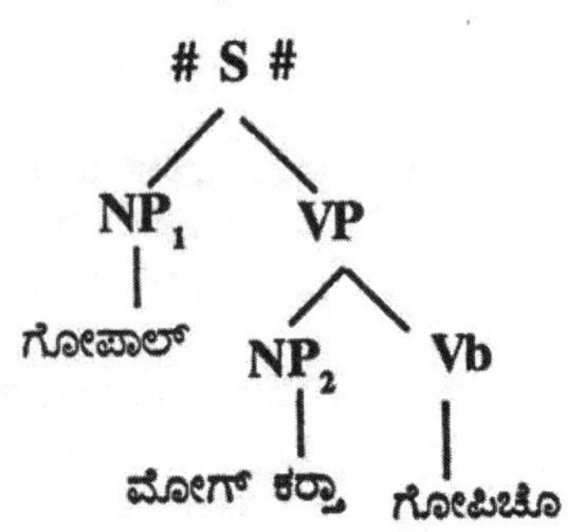

ಮೂಳ್ ಭಾಶೆಂತ್ ದ್ವಂದ್ವಾರ್ಥ್ ಆಸ್ತಾನಾ ಉದ್ದಿಶ್ಟ್ ಭಾಶೆಂತ್ ತೆಚ್ಚ್ ದ್ವಂದ್ವಾರ್ಥ್ ಆಸಾನಾಂತ್. ತೆದಾಳಾ ಖಂಚೊ ಅರ್ಥ್ ಸಾಂದರ್ಭಿಕ್ ಮ್ಹಳ್ಳೆಂ ಸಮ್ಜೊನ್ ಘೆಜಯ್.

eg. 1. Flying kite is dangerous

1a. Somebody flies a kite
1b. that kite is dangerous } → **Flying kite is dangerous**

1A somebody flies a kite
1B that activity is dangerous } → **Flying kite is dangerous**

ಸಾರ್ಕೆ ಅರ್ಥ್ ಸಮ್ಜೊನ್ ಉಪ್ರಾಂತ್ ಭಾಶಾಂತರ್ ಕೆಲ್ಯಾರ್ ಉದ್ದಿಶ್ಟ್ ಭಾಶೆಂತ್ ಅರ್ಥ್ ಸಾರ್ಕೆ ಸಮ್ಜಾತಾತ್.

1.0 ನಿಮಾಣೆಂ ಉತ್ರಾಂ:

ಭಾಶಾಂತರ್ ಮ್ಹಳ್ಯಾರ್ ಮೂಳ್ ಭಾಶೆಂತ್ ಆಸ್ಚ್ಯಾ ಪತ್ಯಸಂಗ್ತಿಂಕ್ ಉದ್ದಿಶ್ಟ್ ಭಾಶೆಂತ್ ಪತ್ಯ್ ಸಂಗ್ತಿ ಒದಗ್ಸುನ್ ದಿಂವ್ಚ್ಯೊ. ಅಶೆಂ ಮುಳಾವ್ಯಾ ಸಬ್ದ್, ಅರ್ಥ್, ವ್ಯಾಕರಣ್, ಧ್ವನಿ, ಲಿಪಿ ಇತ್ಯಾದಿಂಕ್ ಸಮಾನಾರ್ಥಕ್ ಉದ್ದಿಶ್ಟ್ ಭಾಶೆಂತ್ ದಿತಾನಾ ಭಾಶಾಂತರ್ ಪ್ರಕ್ರಿಯಾ ಜಾತಾ. ಹ್ಯಾ ಪ್ರಕ್ರಿಯಾ ಭಾಶೆಕ್ ಸಂಬಂಧ್, ಜಾಲ್ಲಿ ಆಸ್ತಾಂ, ಭಾಶೆ ವಿಜ್ಞಾನ್ ಹ್ಯಾ ಪ್ರಕ್ರಿಯೆಚ್ಯೆ ವಿವರ್, ಸಿದ್ಧಾಂತಾದ್ವಾರಿಂ ದಿತಾ. ಹಾಕಾ ಆಮಿ ಭಾಶಾಂತರ್: ಭಾಷಾ ವೈಜ್ಞಾನಿಕ್ ಸಿದ್ಧಾಂತ್ ಮ್ಹಣ್ ವೊಲಾಯ್ತಾಂವ್/ನಾಮಕರಣ್ ಕರ್ತಾಂವ್.

7.0 ಪರಾಮರ್ಶನ್ ಸಾಹಿತ್:

7.1 **ಪರಮಶಿವಯ್ಯ, ಜೇ. ಸಂ.**
1979 ನಾಗವಲ್ಲಿ: ಶ್ರೀ ನಾಗೇಗೌಡ್ ಗೌರವ ಗ್ರಂಥ. ಚಾಮರಾಜ ಪೇಟೆ, ಬೆಂಗಳೂರು: ಶ್ರೀ ಎಚ್. ಎಲ್. ನಾಗೇಗೌಡ್ ಸನ್ಮಾನ್ ಸಮಿತಿ

7.2 BROWER, R.A. (ed)
1959 On Translation. Cambridge Massachusetts: Harward University Press

7.3 CATFORD, J.C
1965 A Linguistic Theory of Translation London: Oxford University Press

7.4 CITROEN, I. J. (ed.)
1967 Ten Years of Translation

7.5 DIL, A.S. (ed.)
1975 Language Structure and Translation: Essays by Eugene A. Nida. Stanfording

7.6 SAVORY, T.H California: Standard University Press.
1957 The Art of Translation, London: Cape

Melvyn Rodrigues received a Sahitya Akademi award in 2011 for his collection of poems, Prakriticho Paas. *He has at least six other published books, among which are a novel, a collection of essays and collections of poetry. He is associated with various Konkani associations and is the founder of* 'Zage Kavi' *and* 'Kavita Trust'; *co-founder of* Mandd Sobhann, *founder member of* Daiji Dubai *and the editor of www.konkanipoetry.com.*

The following essay discusses aspects of translation as encountered by Rodrigues in the course of his work. Rodrigues has translated Yashwanta Chittal's short stories 'Kanni Zali Choli' *into Konkani in the Devanagari script in 1995 for the Sahitya Akademi. He also published serialised translations of autobiographies of Tenzing Norgay,* 'Evarestacho Monis' *for the Konkani publication,* Raknno *and of Florence Nightingale for the Konkani weekly,* Divo.

ಎಕಾ ಅರ್ಥಾಚೆ ಪಾಟಿಕ್ ಪಡುನ್.

ಅನುವಾದಾ ತಸಲೆಂ ಕಷ್ಟಾಂಚೆಂ ಕಾಮ್ ದುಸ್ರೆಂ ನಾ. ಅನುವಾದ್ ಮ್ಹಳ್ಯಾರ್ ಫೊಟೊಗ್ರಾಫಿ ಕಾಡಲ್ಲ್ಯಾ ತಿತ್ಲೆಂ ಸಲೀಸ್ ಕಾಮ್ ನ್ಹಯ್. ಎಕಾ ಚಿತ್ರಕಾರಾನ್, ಏಕ್ ಪಿಂತುರ್ ಪಳೆವ್ನ್ ತಸಲೆಂಚ್ ಆನ್ಯೇಕ್ ಪಿಂತುರ್ ಚಿತ್ರಾಯಿಲ್ಲ್ಯಾ ಬರೀಯ್ ನ್ಹಯ್. ಅನುವಾದ್, ಸರ್ಜನ್‌ಶೀಲ್ ಕೃತಿ ರಚ್ಚ್ಯಾ ಕಯ್ ಕಠಿಣ್ ಕಾಮ್.

ಎಮಿರೆತಾಂತ್ ಎಕ್ಲೊ ಕೇರಳಾಚೊ ಮನೀಸ್ ಕೃಷಿದ್ವಾರಿಂ ತಾಂದೂಳ್ ಕರ್‌ತಾ ಮ್ಹಣೊನ್ ಜ್ಯೂನ್ ಮ್ಹಯ್ನ್ಯಾಂತ್ ಪತ್ರಾಂನಿ ವಾಚುಂಕ್ ಮೆಳ್ಳೆಂ. ಭಾರತಾಂತ್ ಭಾತಾಚಿ ಕೃಷಿ, ವ್ಹಡ್ ಕಾಮ್ ನ್ಹಯ್. ಪುಣ್ ಹಿಚ್ ಕೃಷಿ ಎಮಿರೆತಾ ತಸಲ್ಯಾ ವೆಗ್ಳ್ಯಾಚ್ ಎಕಾ ವಾತಾವರಣಾಂತ್, ಮಾತಿಯೆಂತ್, ಉದ್ಕಾಂತ್, ಹವ್ಯಾಂತ್ ತುಂವೆಂ ಕರ್‌ಚಿ ಸಲಿಸಾಯೆಚೆಂ ಕಾಮ್ ನ್ಹಯ್. ಹಾಕಾ ಜಾಯ್ತಿಂ ಸವಾಲಾಂ ತುಂವೆಂ ಫುಡ್ ಕರಿಜಾಯ್ ಪಡ್ತಾ. ಎಮಿರೆತಾಂತ್ ತಾಂದ್ಯಾಚಿ ಕೃಷಿ ಕರ್‌ತಲ್ಯಾನ್, ಮಾತಿಯ್ ಪೊಂದಾ ಉದಕ್ ಜಿರನಾತಲ್ಲೆಬರಿ ಕೊಂಕ್ರಿಟಿಚಿ ವೋಲ್ ಹಾಂತುಳ್ಳಲಿ. ಎಮಿರೆತಾಂತ್ ತಾಂದೂಳ್ ಕಾಡ್ತಲ್ಯಾನ್, ಭಾರತಾಂತ್ ತಾಂದೂಳ್ ಕಾಡ್ಚ್ಯಾ ಕಯ್ ಚಡಿತ್ ಶ್ರಮ್ ಕರಿಜಾಯ್ ಪಡ್ತಾ ಆನಿ ತಿತ್ಲೇಂಯ್ ಕರುನ್ ತೊ ತ್ಯಾಚ್ ಮಾಪಾನ್ ಆನಿ ತ್ಯಾಚ್ ಗುಣಾಮೊಲಾಚೊ ತಾಂದೂಳ್ ಜೊಡುಂಕ್ ಪಾವ್ತಾ ಮ್ಹಣೊನ್ ಸಾಂಗೊಂಕ್ ಪಾವನಾ.

ಹಿಚ್ ಗತ್ ಅನುವಾದಾಚಿ ಆನಿ ಅನುವಾದ್‌ಕಾರಾಚಿ!

ಇತ್ಲೇಂಯ್ ಪೂರಾ ಬರೊಂವ್ಕ್ ಕಾರಣ್ ಆಯ್ಲೆವಾರ್ ಹಾಂವೆಂ ಅನುವಾದ್ ಕೆಲ್ಲೆಂ ಪುಸ್ತಕ್. ಕನ್ನಡಾಚ್ಯಾ ಕೆ.ಎಸ್.ನರಸಿಂಹಸ್ವಾಮಿಚ್ಯಾ ಕವಿತಾಂಚೆಂ ಪುಸ್ತಕ್ ';ತೆರೆದ ಬಾಗಿಲು'; - ಮ್ಹಳ್ಯಾರ್ ';ಉಗ್ತೆಂ ದಾರ್';.

ಕೆ.ಎಸ್.ನ. ';ಮೈಸೂರು ಮಲ್ಲಿಗೆ';ದ್ವಾರಿಂ ನಾಂವ್ ವೆಲ್ಲೊ ಕವಿ. ತಾಚ್ಯಾ ';ತೆರೆದೆ ಬಾಗಿಲು'; ಪುಸ್ತಕಾಕ್ ಸಾಹಿತ್ಯ ಆಕಾಡೆಮಿ, ನವಿ ಡೆಲ್ಲಿಚಿ ಪ್ರಶಸ್ತಿ ಲಾಭಲ್ಲಿ. ಹೆಂ ಪುಸ್ತಕ್ ಕೊಂಕಣಿಕ್ ಅನುವಾದ್ ಕರುಂಕ್‌ಜಾಯ್ ಮ್ಹಣೊನ್ ಅಕಾಡೆಮಿನ್ ಮ್ಹಜೆಲಾಗಿಂ ವಿಚಾರಲ್ಲೆಂ.

ಸುರ್‌ವೆರ್ ಮ್ಹಾಕಾ ಕಳ್ಚೆಬರಿ ಸಗ್ಳೆಂ ಪುಸ್ತಕ್ ಹಾಂವೆಂ ಅನುವಾದ್ ಕೆಲೆಂ. ಕಳನಾತಲ್ಲೆ ಕನ್ನಡ ಸಬ್ದ್, ಕನ್ನಡಾಚೆಂ ಮುಕಾವರಾಂ ಆಸಾ ತಶಿಂ ಸೊಡ್ಲಿಂ. ಚಡಿತ್ ವೇಳ್ ಖರ್ಚುಂಕ್ ಗೆಲೊಂನಾ. ಉಪ್ರಾಂತ್ ಅರ್ಥಕೋಶ್ ಭಾಯ್ರ್ ಆಯ್ಲೆ. ಮನೋಹರ್ ಸರ್ದೆಸಾಯಿ, ಸ್ಟೀವನ್ ಕ್ವಾಡ್ರಸಾಚೆ ಅರ್ಥಕೋಶ್ ಆಸ್ಲೆಚ್ ಮ್ಹಣ್ಯಾಂ, ಪುಣ್ ಚಡಿತ್ ಚಾಳಲ್ಲೊ

ಅರ್ಥಕೋಶ್ ಮ್ಹಳ್ಯಾರ್ ರಾಜ್‌ಹಂಸ್ ವಿತರಣಾನ್ ಪರ್ಗಟ್ ಕೆಲ್ಲೊ ';ಕೊಂಕಣಿ ಸಚಿತ್ರ್ ಅಷ್ಟಾಂಗಿ ಅಭ್ಯಾಸ್‌ಕೋಶ್';. ಹೆಂ ಪುಸ್ತಕ್ ಹಾತಾಂತ್ ಧರ್‌ಚೆಂಚ್ ಏಕ್ ಸಾಹಸ್. ತಿತ್ಲೆಂ ದಾಟ್ ಆನಿ ವಜನಾಚೆಂ. ಹಾಂತ್ಲಿಂ ಪಾನಾಂ ಚಾಳ್ಟೆಂಚ್ ಏಕ್ ನವ್ಯಾ ಅನ್ಭೋಗಾಕ್ ಕಾರಣ್ ಜಾಲೆಂ. ಕೆ.ಎಸ್.ನ.ಚೆಂ ';ತೆರೆದ ಬಾಗಿಲು'; ಕನ್ನಡಾಚೆಂ ಪುಸ್ತಕ್ ಜಾಲ್ಲ್ಯಾನ್ ಎಂ. ಮಾಧವ ಪೈಚೆಂ ';ಕನ್ನಡ-ಕೊಂಕಣಿ ರತ್ನಕೋಶ'; ಚಡಿತ್ ಉಪೆಗಾಕ್ ಆಯ್ಲೆಂ. ಚಡೀತ್ ದೀಸ್ ಹ್ಯಾ ಅರ್ಥಕೋಶಾಂ ಸಾಂಗಾತಾ ಆನಿ ಇಂಟರ್ನೆಟಾಂ ವಯ್ಲ್ಯಾ ಕನ್ನಡ-ಇಂಗ್ಲಿಷ್-ಕನ್ನಡ ಅರ್ಥಕೋಶಾಂಚೊ ಸಾಂಗಾತ್ ಜೊಡ್ಲ್ಯಾ ಉಪ್ರಾಂತ್ ಮ್ಹಜ್ಯಾ ಅನುವಾದಾಚಿ ದುಸ್ರಿ ಕರಡ್ ಪ್ರತಿ ತಯಾರ್ ಜಾಲಿ.

ಇತ್ಲೆಂ ಆಸುನಯ್ ಕನ್ನಡಾಚ್ಯಾ ಜಾಯ್ತ್ಯಾ ಸಬ್ದಾಂ-ಕಾಟಾಚಿ (ಫ್ರಸೆಸ್), ಮುಕಾವರಾಂಚೆ ಅರ್ಥ್ ಸಮ್ಜೊಂಕ್ ಹಾಂವ್ ಪಾವ್ಲೊನಾ. ಕೆ. ಎಸ್. ನ. ಚಿ ಪಯ್ಲಿ ಕವಿತಾ ';ಕುಂಕುಮ್ ಭುಂಯ್'; ಹಾಂತುಂ ';ನೀರೊಡಲ ಹಾವಿನ ಹೊಲಿಗೆ'; (ಆಸಾ ತಶ್ಯಾ ಅನುವಾದಾಂತ್ - ಉದ್ಕಾವೊಂಟ್ಯೆಂತ್ಲಿ ದಿವ್ಡಾ ಶಿಂವಣ್) ಮ್ಹಳ್ಳೊ ಸಬ್ದಾಂಕಾಟ್ ಯೆತಾ. ಕಶೆಂ ಕೆಲ್ಯಾರಿ ಮ್ಹಾಕಾ ಹಾಚೊ ಅರ್ಥ್ ಸಮ್ಜಲೊನಾ. ಹ್ಯಾಚ್ ಸಂದರ್ಭಾರ್ ಮ್ಹಾಕಾ ಕನ್ನಡಾಚೊ ವಿಮರ್ಶಕ್ ರಹಮತ್ ತರೀಕೆರೆಚೊ ಉಡಾಸ್ ಆಯ್ಲೊ. ತಾಕಾ ಫೊನ್ ಕರುನ್ ಸಮ್ಜೊಂಚೆಂ ಪ್ರೇತನ್ ಕೆಲೆಂ. ತಾಕಾಯ್ ಕಳ್ಳೆಂನಾ. ಜಾಯ್ತ್ಯಾ ಅರ್ಥಾಂ ಭೊಂವಾರಿಂ ಭೊಂವಾಡೆ ಕಾಡ್ಲೆ ತರೀ ಕವಿತೆಚ್ಯಾ ಸಂದರ್ಭಾಂತ್ ಅರ್ಥ್ ಝುಳ್ಕಲೊನಾ. ನಿಮಾಣೆ ತರಿಕೆರೆ ಮ್ಹಣಾಲೊ: "ಕೆ.ಎಸ್.ನ.ಕ್ ಆಪ್ಣಾಕ್ ಮಾತ್ರ್ ಸಮ್ಜೊಂಚ್ಯಾ ಅರ್ಥಾಂಚೆ ಸಬ್ದಾಂಕಾಟ್ ಆಪ್ಲ್ಯಾ ಕವಿತಾಂನಿ ಘಾಲ್ಚಿ ಮಸ್ತು ಸವಯ್ ಆಸಲ್ಲಿ. ಥೊಡೆಪಾವ್ಟಿಂ ವ್ಹಡ್ ಕವಿ ಜಾಲ್ಯಾರಿ, ತಾಂಣಿ ಬರಯಿಲ್ಲೆಂ ಸಗ್ಳೆಂ ಸಾರ್ಕೆಂ ಆಸ್ತಾ ಮ್ಹಣೊಂಕ್ ಜಾಯ್ನಾ. ತಾಚ್ಯಾ ಕವಿತಾಂಚೆರ್ ಡೊ. ನರಹಳ್ಳಿ ಬಾಲಸುಬ್ರಹ್ಮಣ್ಯಮಾನ್ ಪಿಎಚ್‌ಡಿ ಕೆಲ್ಯಾ. ತಾಚೆಂ ಡೊಕ್ಟರೇಟ್ ಜೊಡಲ್ಲೆಂ ಪುಸ್ತಕ್ ';ಇಹದ ಪರಿಮಳದ ಹಾದಿ'; ಮ್ಹಜೆಲಾಗಿಂ ಆಸಾ. ಮಂಗ್ಳುರಾಕ್ ಯೆಂವ್ಚೊ ಆಸಾಂ. ತುಕಾ ದಿತಾಂ" ಮ್ಹಣ್ತಾನಾ ಖುಶಿ ಜಾಲಿ. ಪುಣ್ ದುಸ್ರ್ಯಾ ದಿಸಾ ತಾಣೆಂಚ್ ಫೊನ್ ಕರುನ್ ಪುಸ್ತಕ್ ಕಿತ್ಲೆಂ ಸೊದ್ಲ್ಯಾರಿ ಮೆಳ್ಳೆಂನಾ ಮ್ಹಣ್ತಾನಾ ನಿರಾಶಾ ಜಾಲಿ. ಉಪ್ರಾಂತ್ ಸಪ್ನ ಬುಕ್ ಹೌಸಾಚ್ಯಾ ಜಾಳಿಜಾಗ್ಯಾಂನಿ ಸೊಧ್ನಾಂ ಕರ್‌ತಾನಾ, ಆಖ್ಯಾ ಕರ್ನಾಟಕಾಂತ್ ಮೈಸೂರಾಂತ್ ಮಾತ್ರ್ ಏಕ್ ಪ್ರತಿ ಆಸಾ ಮ್ಹಳ್ಳಿ ಮ್ಹಾಯಿತ್ ಲಾಬ್ಲಿ. ತಾಂಚೆಕಡೆ ಉಪ್ಕಾರ್ ಮಾಗಲ್ಲ್ಯಾನ್, ಹಿ ಪ್ರತಿ ತಾಂಣಿ ಬೆಂಗ್ಳುರಾಕ್ ಧಾಡ್ಲಿ ಆನಿ ಥಂಯ್ ಥಾವ್ನ್ ಮಂಗ್ಳುರ್ ಪಾವ್ತಚ್ ಮ್ಹಾಕಾ ಫೊನ್ ಆಯ್ಲೆಂ ಆನಿ ಹಾಂವೆಂ ತೆಂ ಪುಸ್ತಕ್ ವಿಕ್ತೆಂ ಘೆತ್ಲೆಂ.

ಪುಸ್ತಕಾಂತ್ ಹಿ ಕವಿತಾ ದಿಲ್ಯಾ ಜಾಲ್ಯಾರಿ ಖಂಯ್ಸರಯ್ ಹ್ಯಾ ಸಬ್ದಾಂಕಾಟಾಚೊ ಅರ್ಥ್ ನಾ. ಪುಣ್ ಹ್ಯಾ ಪುಸ್ತಕಾಂತ್ ಏಕ್ ಗಜಾಲ್ ಸಾಂಗ್ಲ್ಯಾ : "ಕೆ.ಎಸ್.ನ.ನ್ ಸಬ್ದಾಂಚೆಂ ಚಿತ್ರಾಂ ರಚ್ಚ್ಯಾಂತ್ ವಿಶೇಸ್ ಪ್ರತಿಭಾ ದಾಕಯಿಲ್ಲೆಂ ವಿಮರ್ಶಕಾಂನಿ ಪಾರ್ಕಿಲಾಂ. ಡಿ.ಎಲ್. ನರಸಿಂಹಾಚಾರ್ ಹಾಂಣಿ ಹಾಂಕಾಂ ';ಸವಿನುಡಿ ಚಿತ್ತಾರಗಳು'; ಮ್ಹಣ್ ಸಾಂಗುನ್ ಪ್ರಶಂಸಾ ಕೆಲ್ಯಾ. ತಾಂಚ್ಯೊ ಜಾಯ್ತ್ಯೊ ಕವಿತಾ ಅಸಲ್ಯಾ ಪಿಂತುರಾಂಚೆ ಸರ್. ಸುರ್‌ವೆಚ್ಯಾ ಕವಿತಾಂನಿ ಅಸಲಿಂ ಚಿತ್ರಾಂ ಸುಟಿಂ ಸುಟಿಂ ಜಾವ್ನ್ ಆಪ್ಣಾಯಿತ್ಲ್ಯಾಕ್ ಸೊಭಿತ್ ದಿಸ್ತಾಲಿಂ. ಉಪ್ರಾಂತ್ಲ್ಯಾ ಕವಿತಾಂನಿ, ಕವನಾಂಚೊ ಅರ್ಥ್ ಚಿತ್ರಾಂದ್ವಾರಿಂ ವಾಡೊವ್ನ್ ವೆಚಿ ರೀತ್ ಕೆ.ಎಸ್. ನ. ನ್ ಆಪ್ಣಾಚಿ ಕರ್ನ್ ಘೆತ್ಲಿ. ಪುಣ್ ಕಾವ್ಯವಸ್ತುಸಾಂಗಾತಾ ಹಿಂ ಚಿತ್ರಾಂ ಕಸಲೋಯ್ ಸಂಬಂಧ್ ಜೊಡುಂಕ್ ಸಕನಾಂತ್ ಮ್ಹಳ್ಳೆಂ ದುರ್‌ಸಣೇಂಯ್ ಕೆ.ಎಸ್.ನ.ಚೆರ್ ಆಸಾ."

ಹೆಂ ವಾಚ್ತಾನಾ ತರಿಕೆರೆಚೆಂ ಚಿಂತಪ್ ಸಾರ್ಕೆಂ ದಿಸ್ಲೆಂ ತರೀ ವಿವೇಕ ಶಾನಭಾಗಾಕ್ ಫೊನ್ ಕೆಲೆಂ. ತಾಣೇಂಯ್ ಮಾತೆಂ ಖೊರ್ಪಿಲೆಂ. ಈಮೇಯ್ಲಾಂ ಆಶಾರ್ ಪಾಶಾರ್ ಜಾಲಿಂ. ಹ್ಯಾಮಧೆಂ ನರಹಳ್ಳಿಕ್ ದೋನ್ ಪಾವ್ಟಿಂ ಫೊನ್ ಕೆಲೆಂ ತರೀ ತಾಚೆಥಾವ್ನ್ ಕಸಲಿಚ್ ಜಾಪ್ ಮೆಳ್ಳಿನಾ. ಮಾಗೀರ್ ವಿವೇಕಾನ್ ಎಚ್. ಎಸ್. ವೆಂಕಟೇಶಮೂರ್ತಿಕ್ ಬರಯ್ಲೆಂ. "ಮ್ಹಜೊ ಈಷ್ ಮೆಲ್ವಿನ್ ಕೆ.ಎಸ್.ನ. ಹಾಂಚೆಂ ';ತೆರೆದ ಬಾಗಿಲು'; ಪುಸ್ತಕ್ ಕೊಂಕಣಿಕ್ ಅನುವಾದ್ ಕರೀತ್ ಆಸಾ. ತಾಕಾ ';ಕುಂಕುಮ ಭೂಮಿ'; ಕವಿತೆಂತ್ಲಿ ';ನೀರೊಡಲ ಹಾವಿನ ಹೊಲಿಗೆ'; ವೋಳ್ ಅರ್ಥ್ ಜಾಂವ್ಕ್ ನಾ. ಮ್ಹಾಕಾಯ್ ಜಾಂವ್ಕ್ ನಾ. ತುಮ್ಕಾಂ ಕಳಿತ್ ಆಸ್ಲ್ಯಾರ್ ದಯಾ ದವ್ರುನ್ ಸಾಂಗ್ಯಾತ್?"

ಎಚ್ಚೆಸ್ವಿಚಿ ಜಾಪ್ ಆಯ್ಲಿ. "ನೀರೊಡಲ ಹಾವಿನ ಹೊಲಿಗೆ - ಹೆಂ ಕೆ.ಎಸ್.ನ. ಚ್ಯಾ ಪಸಂದೆಚೆಂ ರೂಪಕ್. ಸುತ್ ನಾತಲ್ಲಿ ಸುವಿ ನಿಳ್ಯಾ ವಸ್ತುರಾಚೆರ್ - ಅಶೆಂ ಏಕೆ ಕವಿತೆಂತ್ ವಿಮಾನಾಚಿ ಉಬ್ಣಿ ತಾಣೆ ವರ್ಣಿಲ್ಯಾ. ತ್ಯಾ ಅರ್ಥಾಕ್ ಸಮಾನ್ ಜಾಲ್ಲೆಂ - ಹೆಂ ನೀರೊಡಲ ಹಾವಿನ ಹೊಲಿಗೆ.

ಉದ್ಕಾಂತ್ ಆಡ್ವೆ ತಿಡ್ವೆಂ ಉಪ್ಯೆಂವ್ಚ್ಯಾ ಯೆವಾಳ್ಯಾಕ್ ಚೆಂತ್ಯಾಂ. ತೆಂ ಉದ್ಕಾವೊಂಟ್ಯೆಂತ್ಲೆ ಶಿಂವ್ಣೆಭಾಶೆನ್ ತುಕಾ ದಿಸ್ತಾ. ಝುಳ್ಕಲ್ಲೆಂಚ್ ನಪಯಿಂಚ್ ಜಾಂವ್ಚೆಂ ಹೆಂ ಶಿಂವ್ಣೆಚೆಂ ಚಿತ್ರ್ ಆಪ್ಣಾಯಿತ್ಲ್ಯಾಕ್ ನಿರರ್ಥಕ್. ಥಂಯ್ಸರ್ ಶಿಂವ್ಣೆಚೊ ಸಮಾನ್ ಧರ್ಮ್ ಆಸಾ. ಪುಣ್ ನಿಜಾಯೆಂತ್ ಕಸಲೀಯ್ ಶಿಂವಣ್ ನಾ. ಘಡನಾತಲ್ಲಿ ಏಕ್ ಕರ್ನಿ, ಹ್ಯೊ ವೊಳಿ ವರ್ಣಿತಾತ್. ಸುತ್ ನಾತಲ್ಲಿ ಸುವಿ ನಿಳ್ಯಾ ವಸ್ತುರಾಚೆರ್ - ತಸಲೆಂಚ್ ರೂಪಕ್. ವಿಮಾನ್ ಮ್ಹಳ್ಯಾರ್ ಸುವಿ. ಪುಣ್ ಸುತ್ ನಾತಲ್ಲಿ ಸುವಿ. ಸುತ್ ನಾತಲ್ಲಿ ಸುವಿ ಆಪ್ಲ್ಯಾ ಧರ್ಮಾಂತ್ ಆಸುನಯ್ ಕಸಲ್ಯಾಯ್ ಉಪ್ಕಾರಾಕ್ ಪಡನಾತಲ್ಲಿ. ಫಳಾವೀಣ್ ಕರ್ಮಾಚೆಂ ಚಿತ್ರ್ ಹೆಂ. ಅಸಲಿಂ ಚಿತ್ರಾಂ ';ಸವಿನುಡಿ ಚಿತ್ತಾರ'; ಮ್ಹಣೊನ್ ಕನ್ನಡ ವಿಮರ್ಶಕಾಂನಿ ಪಾರ್ಕಿಲ್ಯಾಂತ್. ತಿಂ ಎಕಾ ಸಂವೇದನಾಚ್ಯಾ ಥಳಾರ್ ಮಾತ್ರ್ ಸ್ವೀಕಾರ್ ಕರಿಜಾಯ್ ಪಡ್ತಾತ್. ಅನುವಾದ್ ಕರ್ತಾನಾ ಜಾಲ್ಯಾರೀ, ತೆಂ ಚಿತ್ರ್ ತಶೆಂಚ್ ಸಾಂಬಾಳ್ಳ್ಯಾರ್ ಪುರೊ ದಿಸ್ತಾ.

ಇತ್ಲೆಂ ವಾಚ್ಲ್ಯಾ ಉಪ್ರಾಂತ್ ';ಉದ್ಕಾವೊಂಟ್ಯೆಂತ್ಲಿ ದಿವ್ಳಾಶಿಂವಣ್'; ಹಾಂವೆಂ ತಶೀಚ್ ಸಾಂಬಾಳ್ಳಿ.

ಉಪ್ರಾಂತಯ್ ಜಾಯ್ತೊ ಗುಸ್ಪಡ್ ಗೊಂದೊಳ್ ಆಸಲ್ಲೊ. ಅನಂತಮೂರ್ತಿಕ್ ಬರಯ್ಲೆಂ. ಕಾಯ್ಕಿಣಿಕ್ ಬರಯ್ಲೆಂ. ಪ್ರಭಾಕರ ಜೋಶಿ ಸಾಂಗಾತಾ ಬಸ್ಲೊಂ. ಗುರು ಬಾಳಿಗಾನ್ ಥೊಡಿ ಜಾಣ್ವಾಯ್ ದಿಲಿ. ವಿತೊರಿ ಕಾರ್ಕಳಾನ್, ಎಚ್ಚೆಮ್ ಪೆರ್ನಾಳಾನ್ ಥೊಡಿ ಮಜತ್ ಕೆಲಿ. ಮಧೆಂ ಏಕ್ ಪಾವ್ಟಿಂ ಸಂಸ್ಕೃತಿಕ್ ಸಂಬಂಧ್ ಜಾಲ್ಲ್ಯಾ ಸಬ್ದಾಂಚೆರ್ ಶಿರ್‌ಕಲೊಂ ಜಾಲ್ಲ್ಯಾನ್ ಗೋಪಾಲ್ ಗೌಡಾಕ್ ಫೊನ್ ಕೆಲೆಂ. ಅಶೆಂ ತಿಸ್ರಿ ಕರಡ್ ಪ್ರತಿ ತಯಾರ್ ಜಾಲಿ.

ಆತಾಂ ಹೊ ಅನುವಾದ್ ದೇವನಾಗರಿಂತ್ ಪರ್ಗಟ್ ಜಾತಲೊ ಜಾಲ್ಲ್ಯಾನ್, ಆನಿ ಚಡಿತ್ ವಾಚ್ಪಿ ಗೊಂಯ್ಕಾರ್ ಆಸ್ತಲೆ ಜಾಲ್ಲ್ಯಾನ್, ಅನುವಾದಾಚಿ ಬೋಲಿ ಬದ್ಲುಂಚೊ ನಿಚೆವ್ ಕೆಲೊ. ಹ್ಯಾ ಸಂದರ್ಭಾರ್ ಕವಯಿತ್ರಿ ನೂತನ್ ಸಾಖರ್ ದಾಂಡೆನ್ ಮ್ಹಜಿ ಮಜತ್ ಕೆಲಿ. ಏಕ್ ಪಾವ್ಟಿಂ ಆಮಿ ದೊಗಾಂಯ್ನಿ ಸಾಂಗಾತಾ ಬಸುನ್, ಉಪ್ರಾಂತ್ ಥೊಡೆಂ ಫೊನಾಚೆರ್ ವೊರಾಂಗಟ್ಲ್ಯಾನ್ ಉಲೊವ್ನ್, ಹೊ ವಾವ್ರ್ ಸಂಪಯ್ಲೊ.

ಚವ್ತಿ ಪ್ರತಿ ಹಾಂವೆಂ ಅಕಾಡೆಮಿಕ್ ಧಾಡುನ್ ದಿಲ್ಯಾ ಆನಿ ಪರ್ಗಟ್ ಜಾಂವ್ಕ್ ವಾಟ್ ಪಳೆತೇ ಆಸಾ.

ಅಸಲೆ ಅನುವಾದ್ ಕೊಣಾಖಾತೀರ್? ಮೆಲ್ವಿನ್ ಇತ್ಲೆ ಕಷ್ಟ್ ಕಾಡುನ್ ಆಪ್ಲೊ ವೇಳ್ ಕಿತ್ಯಾಕ್ ವಿಭಾಡ್ತಾ? ಆಕ್ರೇಕ್ ಕೊಣ್ ಕಿತೆಂ ಜೊಡುಂಕ್ ಪಾವ್ತಾ ಮ್ಹಳ್ಳೆಂ ಸವಾಲಾಂ ಉದೆತಲಿಂ. ಏಕ್ ಅನುವಾದಾವರ್ವಿಂ ಆನ್ಯೇಕೆ ಭಾಶೆಚಿ ಗ್ರೇಸ್ತ್‌ಕಾಯ್ ಕಿತೆಂ, ಆನ್ಯೇಕಾ ಸಮುದಾಯಾಚಿ ಸಂಸ್ಕೃತಿ ಕಸಲಿ ಮ್ಹಳ್ಳೆಂ ಸಮ್ಜೊಂಕ್ ಸಾಧ್ಯ್ ಜಾತಾ. ಹ್ಯಾವರ್ವಿಂ ಭಾಸೊ ನೆಣಾಸಲ್ಲ್ಯಾಂಕ್ ಆಪ್ಲಿ ಜಾಣ್ವಿಕಾಯ್ ವಾಡೊಂವ್ಕ್ ಸಲೀಸ್ ಜಾತಾ ಮ್ಹಣ್ತಲೇಯ್ ಆಸ್ತಲೆ.

-ಮೆಲ್ವಿನ್ ರೊಡ್ರಿಗಸ್

S. M. Borges translated R. N. Naik's biography, Shenoi Goembab *for the Sahitya Akademi in 2007. He published* The Triumph of Konkani – *A translation of Shenoy Goembab's* Konkani Bhashechem Zoit *from Verna at New Age Printers, Goa in 2003. He was associated in an editorial capacity with the Konkani journals* Dalgadacho Sondex *and* Gulab. *He contributed to the volume,* Dalgado on Konkani: A Translation of Msgr. S.R. Dalgado's Introductions to his Dictionaries *published in 2008. He also assisted in the preparation of English-Konkani vocabularies of administrative, legislative and scientific terms, initiated by the Department of Official Language, Govt. of Goa and the National Translation Mission, CIIL, Mysore.*

Christpuranant Sashtintli Konkani utravol ani boli

(Occurrence of Salcete Konkani vocables and dialectal forms in the Christapurana)

S. M. Borges contends that although Thomas Stephens' Kristapurana is presented as a Marathi work, it abounds in Konkani words and phrases, which are currently in vogue in the Salcete taluka of Goa where Stephens spent almost the entire time that he stayed in India. The book also contains words/phrases presently out of circulation, even in Salcete, but which were in use in the sixteenth century as evidenced by the Braga codices and the dictionaries produced by the missionaries.

The Kristapurana and the evidence it does or does not offer for the genealogy of the Konkani language has been the focus of many linguistic studies. Aside from the mid-twentieth century assertions of the linguist and historian A. K. Priolkar who opposed the recognition of Konkani as a distinct language, the Kristapurana has seen Devanagari, and Roman transliterations and editions that seek to reinterpret it in keeping with contemporary theological beliefs, or seek to restore, revive, or correct its script/idiom.

खिस्तपुराणांत साश्टींतली कोंकणी उतरावळ आनी बोली

–प्रा. से. मा. बॉर्जिस

''हें सर्व मराठी भाशेंत बरयलां'' अशें ह्या ग्रंथा खातीर बरयल्ले गद्य प्रस्तावनेंतूच न्हय तर पयल्या आनी निमाण्या अवेस्वरांतूय स्टीफन्सान स्पश्टपणीं सांगलां. पूण ताणें आनीक्य सांगून दवरलां, ''हो ग्रंथ सामान्य (मधिमा) लोकांक समजुंचो ह्या हेतून, आपणें आदल्या कवींचीं कठीण उतरां वगळून ''ब्राह्मणांचे भाशेंतलीं'' साबार सोंपीं उतरां गरज थंय भरशिल्यांत. ही ''ब्राह्मणाची भास'' म्हळ्यारीच साश्टींतली कोंकणी जिका ते मिशोनार पाद्री ''लिंग्व ब्रामान कानारीं'' म्हणून पाचारताले. ती भास आयज आमकां ब्राग संहितेंत[1] सांभाळून दवरलली मेळटा. हे संहितेचोच अभ्यास करून मिशोनारींनी विस्तृत उतरावळी (कोंकणी-पुर्तुगेज, पुर्तुगेज-कोंकणी)[2] आनी व्याकरणां बरयल्लीं. हे संहितेंतल्या एका भागाचो - म्हाभारत हांतल्या कथांचो - सखोल अभ्यास प्रोफसर रॉकी मिरांद हांणी केला; ह्या वावराचो पयलो भाग ''प्राचीन कोंकणी भारत'' उजवाडा आयला.[3] आनी फुडलो वावर प्रकाशनाचे वाटेर आसा. हें प्रकरण बरयताना तांच्या अप्रकाशीत वावराचोय उदंड लाव हांवें धिनवाशी मनान घेतला.

कोंकणी आनी मराठी ह्यो दोनूय भासो आर्यभारती वंशांतल्यो आसून तांचे उतरावळींतूच न्हय तर व्याकरणांतूय बरेंच साम्य जाणवता. हें साम्य इतलें खोल आसा की हालींसरा मेरेन कांय विद्वान भासशास्त्री कोंकणी भाशेक मराठीची बोली मानताले. स्टीफन्सान आनी हेर मिशोनारींनी ब्राग संहितेचो खोलायेन अभ्यास केल्लो हातूंत मातूय दुभाव ना; ते संहितेंत जीं समासटिपां आदळटात तीं हाची गवाय दितात. ते संहितेचो कांय वांटो स्टीफन्साच्याच हातान बरयल्लो आसा. शिवाय, एक

व्याकरणकार आशिल्ल्यान (ताणें कोंकणी भाशेचें व्याकरण बरयलां.) ताका दोनूय भासां मदलें हें साम्य होल्मलां आसतलेंच. दोनूय भासांनी असंख्य उतरां समसमान आसात. हांचे कांय व्याकरणी बदल दोनूय भासांनी इतले जुळटात की परिणामी उतर मराठी काय कोंकणी म्हूण सांगप अशक्य थारता. तर कांय बदल भाशे प्रमाणें वेगळे आसून विंगड उतरां तयार जातात. हे बदल उतरांच्या अंत्यस्वरांचेर अवलंबून आसतात. देखून कोंकणी उतराचो अंत्यस्वर वळखून आनी मराठी नेमाक धरून ताचे व्याकरणी बदल केले जाल्यार तें परिणामी उतर मराठीच कशें दिसता. ख्रिस्तपुराण बरयतना, स्टीफन्सान हे जाणविक ायेचो उदंड वापर केलो - असंख्य कोंकणी उतरां, वाकप्रचार आनी वाक्यां लेगीत मराठी भेस चडोवन उपेगायलीं. इतलेंच न्हय तर, यमका खातीर बी, गरज पडली तेन्ना कोंकणी उतर तशेंच दवरलें.

लोकांचे जिबेर खेळटली भास जिवंत आसता, आनी थळाकणकर्णी (आनी उलयतल्याचे जाती तशेंच वेवसायाप्रमाणें लेगीत) तिच्यांत विविधताय दिश्टी पडटा. कोंकणीचेंय तशेंच. काळगती प्रमाणेंय एकाच थळांतली भास बदलत आसता; खंयचीच भास सोळाव्या शेंकड्यांत चालंत आशिल्ली त्याच रुपान आयज घोळना. साश्टींतली कोंकणीय बदल्ल्या हातूंत दुभाव ना. पूण साश्टींतल्या क्रिस्तांव लोकां मदीं आयज जी कोंकणी घोळटा ती ब्राग संहिते कडेन सर केल्यार तांच्यांत जायतें साम्य जाणवता. त्या काळार गोंय सोडून वचून जे लोक केरळांत/कर्नाटकांत स्थायीक जाल्ले तांच्यो बोलयोय ते संहिते कडेन बऱ्योच जुळटात. केरळांतले बोलयेचें एक विस्तृत व्याकरण उजवाडायल्लें आसा.[4]

साश्टींतली आयची भास गोंयांतल्या हेर वाठारांनी घोळटल्या बोलयां परस चिके वेगळी आसा, जाल्यार तींच वेगळेपणां ब्राग संहितेंत आदळटात; म्हणजे, साश्टींत तीं आजून कायम उरल्यांत, पुर्तुगेज भाशेच्या वा रोमी लिपीच्या प्रभावान तीं नव्यान उपजोंक नांत, हें सिद्ध जाता.

ख्रिस्तपुराणाचें साश्टींतले कोंकणी कडलें नातें तीन तरांनी जाणवता:

(1) कोंकणी उतरां जीं मराठींत घोळनांत,

(2) कांय उतरां जीं ''प्रमाण'' कोंकणींत मेळनांत पूण आयज साश्टींतूच घोळटात,

(3) उतरांचे व्याकरणी बदल जे मराठींत जांव ''प्रमाण'' कोंकणींत मेळनांत पूण साश्टींत आनी ब्राग संहितेंत आसात.

ऱ्हस्व मध्यस्वर :

साश्टींतले मोडीचीं जीं खाशेलपणां आसात, तांतलीं दोन हांगा नोंद करिसारकीं थारतात.

(1) तीन-अक्षरी उतरां, (2) ऱ्हस्व मध्यस्वर.

पयलें आसा तें कोंकणी भाशेचें मुलभूत खाशेलपण (पळेयात जनार्धन[4] अध्याय 9) : हेर खंयचेय भाशे कडल्यान उशिणें घेतिल्लें लांब उतर कोंकणी जिबेर मोटवें जाता आनी तें तीन अक्षरां परस लांब उरना. तांणी साबार संस्कृतजन्य उतरांच्यो देखी दिल्यात : नारिकेळ - नारलु, चन्द्रनीक - चांदिणें. साश्टींतले कोंकणींत जायतीं तीन-अक्षरी उतरां आसात तांचो उच्चार तीन-अक्षरीच जाता. ख्रिस्तपुराणांत तो तस्सो आयला. देखीक बैसता हें हेर कडेन बसता (उच्चार बस्ता) जालां पूण ख्रिस्तपुराणांत तें बैसता अशेंच आयलां. तीन-अक्षरी उतरांतलें मदलें अक्षर अ-कारी आसल्यार, हेर बोलयांनी तो अ-क ार गळून पडटा आनी व्यंजन शिल्लक उरता, जाल्यार साश्टींत तो अ-कार तिगून उरला. देखीक, सांगता हाचो उच्चार हेर कडेन सांग्ता असो जाता जाल्यार साश्टींत सां-ग-ता असो जाता.

तीनांतलें मदलें अक्षर ऱ्हस्व स्वरी आसता तेन्ना साश्टींत तो मध्यस्वर स्पश्ट आयकूंक मेळटा. देखीक, पांगुळो, वांकुडो, वाणियो, चांदिणें, डिंबियो, पाटियो पूण उत्तर गोंयांत (आनी मराठींत) तींच उतरां (मंदलो उ-कार/ इ-कार गळून) दोन-अक्षरी जातात. म्हणजे पांगळो (उ. पांग्ळो). चांदने (उ. चान्नें) बी. ख्रिस्तपुराणांत हीं उतरां तीन-अक्षरी रुपांतूच मेळटात. देखीक, (अ) तुवां आंकुवारपणाचा नेमु (निर्धार) केला. [II.3.110]; (आ) पाटिया (तुळई) जोडोनि थोरी [I.7-28]; (इ) येक (=कांय) पांगुळे उचलोनि आणिले. [II.25.76]; (इ) चालती डिंबिया वोडोनि [II.25.75].

तेन्नाची गोंयांतली मराठी :

त्या काळार गोंयांत बरयताले ती मराठी कशीकात आशिल्ली हाची झळक आमकां गांवकारींच्या बसकांचीं इतिवृत्तां दितात[5]. हीं इतिवृत्तां ख्रिस्तपुराणाक समकालीन आसात आनी तांच्यांतली मराठी ख्रिस्तपुराणांतले मराठी कडेन बरीच जुळटा; थंयसरूय जायती कोंकणी भरसल्ली दिश्टी पडटा. हाचे वेल्यान स्टीफन्सान, कोंकणी उतरांचें मराठीकरण करून, गोंयक ारांचीच मराठी बरोवंची पद्दत फुडें व्हेली काय, असो दुभाव तरी येता. आयचे सास्टींतले कोंकणीच्यो ज्यो पती ख्रिस्तपुराणांत आदळटात त्योच वा तसल्योच गांवकारी इतिवृत्तांनी मेळटात. साश्टींतल्या कुठ्ठाळ गांवच्या इतिवृत्तांनी अशें घडलां जाल्यार व्हडलेंशें अजाप न्हय, पूण हेंच बारदेसांतलो हळदोणें, तिसवाडींतलो करंबळी हागांसरल्या इतिवृत्तांनी लेगीत घडटाना दिश्टी पडटा. म्हणजे, तेन्नाच्या बोलयां मदीं बरेंच सारकेपण वसतालें, आनी त्यो आतांचे साश्टी बोलयेक लागीं आशिल्ल्यो. हेच खातीर जायत, ते बोलयेक डॉ. जुजे पेरेइर ''पोरणी प्रमाण'' म्हणटा. देखी खातीर, त्या इतिवृत्तांतले कांय नमुने: (क) कुळांचीं गोरुवां वेगळीं करुनु (पा. 67); (ख) तुमचे संचतीन (78); (ग) बारावेया दिवसा लेख सारावे। न सरि

होयील तरि (96); (घ) केळामुळा बयिसुनु (108); (ङ) म्हयिन्याच्या तरिके भितरि आणावे। न्हडी होयील तरि (141); (च) मडतीनान नेल्योति (169); (छ) घरा भितरलो वा (=आणी) येथे करबेळीय तथा घरवडीचो मालवंजु (188); (ज) मना आणुनु कुळकरणिया फर्मावि़लें (200); (झ) बरवी करुनु सरी करावी (227); (ञ) तो उभो रूखु (240); (ट) तरवळानीं धरुनु बादुनु दिवाणा न्यावे (242).

कोंकणी–मराठी समसमान उतरावळ :

ख्रिस्तपुराणांतले उतरावळीचें कोंकणी भाशेकडलें नातें वळखून तिचे अशे वर्ग घालुंयेत : (1) जीं उतरां दोनूय भासांनी कसलोच बदल नासताना एकसारकींच घोळटात; (2) हरशीं समसमान उतरां जांचो अंत्यस्वरूच तीं कोंकणी काय मराठी हें थारायता; (3) जीं सध्याचे मराठींत घोळनांत पूण कोंकणींतूच होल्मतात; (4) जीं आयज सास्टींतूच चालंत आसात; (5) जीं आयज मराठींतूय घोळनांत आनी कोंकणींतूय, पूण ब्राग संहितेंतल्या प्राचीन कोंकणी भारतांत मेळटात. हें ''कोंकणी भारत'' तेन्नाचे साश्टी बोलयेंतूच बरयलां म्हूण वेगळें सांगची गरज ना. उतरांचे व्याकरणी बदलूय दोनूय भासांनी सादारणपणीं एकसारकेच जातात. हे वर्ग सामकेच परस्पर विंगड नांत; मूळ उतर एका वर्गांत जाल्यार ताचेंच व्याकरणी रूप वेगळ्या वर्गांत आसुंये. देखीक, ''माता'' हें पयल्या वर्गांत जाल्यार ''मातेचो''/ ''मातेचा'' दुसऱ्या वर्गांत आनी ''तिसरो''/ ''तिसरा'' हें दुसऱ्या वर्गांत जाल्यार ''तिसऱ्या'' हें पयल्या वर्गांत.

पयल्या वर्गांतल्या उतरांच्यो कांय देखी. अंतराळ, मस्तक, राजा, राणी, लेंकरूं असलीं नामां; तूं, आमीं, तुमीं, एकमेक असलीं सर्वनामां; जिवंत, पवित्र, निट, असलीं विशेशणां; कर, मर, घे असलीं क्रियापदां; आतां, सदां असलीं क्रियाविशेशणां; जरि, तरि असलीं अव्ययां. अशें आसून साबार चरणांच न्हय तर अख्ख्यो ओवयो, कसलोच बदल करिनासताना, एका कोंकणी मनशाक, खास करून साश्टींतल्या क्रिस्तांवाक, सहज समजुंये अश्यो आसात. देखीक, (अ) जेतुकें पातक वर्तलें। तें देवचारा पासोनि निपजलें। नाना परिचे अवगुण प्रवर्तले। सौंसारा आंतु॥ [I.2.127]; (आ) ऐशी अजगाराची बोली। आइकोनि येरि चेतावली। मग तेया फळा दृश्टि लाविली। इछे करोनि॥ [I.4.123] (इ) देवा इज्राएलिच्या समरथा। पावईं आमंच्या आकांता। कवणु नाहीं सोडविता। तुजे विण॥ [I.15.74]; (ई) आरे मुर्खा हेरोदी राया। ऐशी कल्पना धरिशी वायां। कां भितोशि रे पापिया। आपुलिये साउळिये ॥ [II.13.51]; (उ) या परी समग्र तेंप्ल (देवालय) जळलें। खिणा येका भस्म जाहालें। वणतिंचे (भिंतीचे) पासाण करपले। उरले भिन होउनि॥ [II.42.129]

विभक्तीकुसांची अंतर :

बरींचशीं विभक्तीकुसां दोनूय भासांनी एक सारकींच आसात; तशेंच काळप्रत्ययूय बी. पूण मेजकेच जे फरक आसात ते अशे :-

1) कोंकणी उतराक जंय -क प्रत्यय लागता थंय मराठींत -थें वा -सि येता. स्टीफन्सान हेंच केलें. देखीक. (अ) ति दिधली आदांवाथें (आदांवाक) [I.3.55]; (आ) सातवें वरुदान तेयां दोगांथें (दोगांक) [I.4.15]; (इ) आतां हे निगतिल वैंकुंठासि (वैंकुंठाक) [I.4.63]; (ई) करु (हात) पण नलवावेया (= लावचो न्हय) तेया फळासि (फळाक) [I.4.118]; (उ) दिवसु नांव ठेविलें उजुवाडासि (उजवाडाक) [I.3.15]; (ऊ) म्हणौनि तेयां आदिपुरुसांसि (आदिपुरुसांक) [I.4.21]; (ए) आणी नैवेद्यु भेटावेयासि (भेटोवच्याक) [I.6.29]; (ऐ) एतुकें सांगा माथें (म्हाका) [II.16.96]; (ओ) मृत्यु नाहीं होयिल तुमांसि (तुमकां) [I.4.120]; (औ) तुमीं आपुल्यां बंदुंथें (बंदूक) [II.35.59]; (अं) माजेनि बापें तुथें (तुका) [II.33.78]. (अः) आपुल्या गुरूथें
(गुरूक) [II.29.53].

आयज साश्टींत विभक्ती-प्रत्यय वगळपाची चाल जी आसा ती तेन्नाय चालंत आशिल्ली जायत; स्टीफन्सान ती हांगा थंय वापरल्या. देखीक, (अ) दुजें स्वप्न जाहालें त्या भुपती (भुपतीथें) [I.12.97]; (आ) जे भुतां (भुतांसि) प्रेतां (प्रेतांसि) भजती [I.8.138]; (इ) मग पाठविलेया पडचारिकां (पडचारिकांथें) बोलाविलेया नणंदां (नणंदांथें) होनिकां (होनिकांथें) [I.12.28]; (ई) मेसोपोतामी देसा (देसासि) चालिला [I.10.12]; (उ) मज अपराधिया (अपराध्यासि) लाविली शिखा (=शिक्षा) [I.16.108] (ऊ) गोपिणी (गोपिणिचे) गुंडे
मारिती [I.23.5] ; (ए) तेंप्ला (तेंप्लाचां) आंगणीं देखता जाहाला [II.23.24]; (ऐ) दोरिये (दोरियेसि) बांदोनि गाघरी [II.24.21].

2) कोंकणी उतराक (करणाचें) -न लागता थंय मराठींत -एं येता. स्टीफन्सान होय बदल पतकरला. देखीक, (अ) देवें (देवान) रचिला मनुषु [I.3.71]; (आ) तंव स्वामियें (स्वाम्यान) परमेश्वरें (परमेश्वरान) उजुवाडु (= उजेड) केला [I. 3.13]; (इ) भारें (भारान) चोउं (= चारूय) कडां (कडेन) वोडवती (= झुकती) [I.4.80].

गरज भासली तेन्ना कोंकणी रूप तशेंच दवरलां. देखीक (अ) योज़ेन केणें दिधलें भरोनि [I.14.84]; (आ) तंव मोइज़ेन विनविला देवु [I.16.74]; (इ) ते तियेन (तिणें) लपौनि ठेविले [I.22.122]; (ई) तें वर्तमान मरियेन आइकिलें [II. 3.43]; (उ) तरुंवरांचिया (वृक्षांच्या) शाखा वाऱ्यान हालती लकलकां [I.5.21]; (ऊ) पुणती कोंब्यान केली बोबाटि [II. 46.130]. ही पद्धत इतिवृत्तांनीय मेळटा. देखीक (अ) कोंतादोरान आपविले तेधवा (पा.170); (आ) आपापुल्या कुळाग्रक ारान आपुल्या कुळाग्रातु उदक घ्यावे (227); (इ) नाडकरणियान कोकणा बरपान वा (= आनी) रकरसावाचा यिस्क्रिवाउनु फिरिग्या बरपान लिहावें (287);

3) मराठींत तशें कोंकणींत सातवे विभक्ती खातीर -अंत कूस लायतात. ताचे बदला हांगा, पोरणे कोंकणीं आनी साश्टीतले आयचे संवये प्रमाणें,-आंतु वापरलां. देखीक, (अ) स्वामियाच्या तेंप्लांतु तो बाळकु देखिला [II.16.91]; (आ) या येरू जाल्या राज्यांतु [II.16.77]. पोरणे कोंकणींतली देख : तोवोय घेउनु। उदकांतु घालुंक वेताली (आप. कथा 1).

कांय कडेन हें आंतु मेकळें दवरलां. देखीक, नाना परिचे अवगुण प्रवर्तले सौंसारा आंतु [I.2.127].

पूण पोरणे कोंकणींत आनी मराठींत (तशेंच कांय प्रमाणांत आयचे साश्टींतूय) -अंत हाचे सुवातेर -ईं लावपाची चाल मेळटा. ही चाल ख्रिस्तपुराणांत सर्रास वापरल्या. देखीक, (अ) वैंकुंठीं फांकली (पसरली) मातु [I.2.86]; (आ) इसाइ घातला खरवर्ती [I.29.71]; (इ) जळीं (जलांत) स्थळीं (थळांत) चराचरीं (चराचरांत) जरि देवु वर्ते सर्व सौंसारीं (सौंसारांत) [I. 2.65]. पोरणे कोंकणींतल्यो देखी: (अ) माजे मनीं ऐशें आस (आप. क.12); (आ) माजे मायेचे उधरीं पासणाचो फातरु जल्मलो ऐशें जाण (गप. क.3).

-अंतलो हो प्रत्यय, साश्टींतलें वरीच -आंतुलो करून वापरला. देखीक, तें गुप्तीं राखाव्या तेंप्लांतुलें घेउनि गेला [I. 29.118]. पोरणे कोंकणींत आनी मराठींत, तशेंच कांय प्रमाणांत आयचे साश्टींतुय -अंतलो हाचे सुवातेर -इंचो/-इचो वापरललें मेळटा. हीय पद्धत स्टीफन्सान वापरल्या. देखीक, तरि येमकोंडिचे (येमकोंडांतले) कश्ट अद्‌भुत [I.4.31]; (आ) पांचवी शिबिळ योनिये देशिंची (देसांतली) [I.36.20]; (इ) लिंबलोकिंचे (लिंबलोकांतले) समस्त विनंति करिती [II. 2.40]; (ई) नेलीं घोंटेरिचीं (घोटेरांतलीं) पिलें चोरूनु [I.14.2]; (उ) मार्था पाहे घरिंची (घरांतली) राटावळि [II. 36.16]. इतिवृत्तांतली देख: आमचे गांविचे लावणे निमितिं फायिआ (फाल्या) बउळ 8मी दिवसी [पा. 30]; प्राचीन कोंक णी भारतांतल्यो देखी: (अ) पाताळिंचो सर्व वृतावंतु सांगिलो (कप. क.2); (आ) हाची माय जी आस ती राखेस (= राक्षस) वंशिची (अश्वप. क.1).

अ-कारान्त उतरां :

कोंकणींत जायतीं अ-कारान्त अलिंगी नामां आसात जीं मराठींतूय त्याच रुपान घोळटात. देखीक चरण, ज्ञान, रुधन बी. हांच्या व्याकरणी बदलांची देख: चरण-चरणां (म.चरणें)- चरणाचें - चरणांचें. ह्या गटांत स्टीफन्सान साबार कोंकणी (आनी कांय पुर्तुगेजय) उतरां मराठी रूप दिवन वापरल्यांत. देखीक कूप (म. ढग), कोंड (खड्डा), खळ (खळें), खाड (दाढी), क डवळ (बरगडी), काराफूल (लवंग), खोर्न (भट्टी), सांसव (मोहरी), उचित (बक्षीस), घरवत (घरसंसार), नालकुत (जलोदर), निडळ (कपाळ), आइंस (आमिष), मोड (तुफान), वाजांत्र (वाद्य), नखेत्र (तारा), वरूस (वर्ष), उपपातक (गौण पाप,) जुझ (युद्ध), गायेन (गाणें), मुखकमळ (मुखडा), खत (कलंक), गंगाळ (आंगोळचे पाणी वेगळे काडायचे भांडे), कळिवर (प्रेत), चिबड (खरबूज), भाणसाघर (पाकशाला), कवड (दार), रिणस्व (कर्ज), कुड (खोली), आश्रवचन (आशीर्वाद); पुर्तुगेज उतरां (जीं आयजूय कोंकणींत घोळटात): आर्क, आल्तार, रेताब्ल, तेंप्ल. देखी:- (अ) सात कणसें मोटीं देखिलिंति [I.12.97]; कुपांतुनु थेंबे गळतां [I.4.106] (इ) मग आर्कांतु निगाला कुटंब सहित [I. 7.45] (ई) ऐशें स्वामियाचें शास्त्र निर्मळ। खत नाहीं अती नितळ [I.2.16]; यमकाची बी गरज म्हणून कांय कडेन कोंकणी भोववचनाचो आं-कार तसोच दवरला; देखीक फळां, कृपादानां बी.

कोंकणींत आनी मराठींत जायतीं अ-कारान्त स्त्रीलिंगी उतरां आसात; तीं दोनूय भासांनी एकसारकींच घोळटात. देखीक बाग - बागो (म. बागा) - बागेचें - बागांचें. हांच्यांत स्टीफन्सान कांय अमराठी कोंकणी उतरां भरशिल्यांत. देखीक, आंगवण (म. नवस), आस (आशा), माव (मोहिनी, व्रण), भेट (भेटवस्तू), प्राय (वय), भास (आज्ञा, वचन), बुजवण (सांत्वन), नाडवण (फसवणूक), येळ (वेलदोडा), दुर्बळिक (गरिबी), गंवळीक (पशूपालन), रेंव (वाळू). कांय पुर्तुगेज उतरांय आयल्यांत: एव, इग्रज. कांय देखी: (अ) आतां खैंची पुत्र आस [I.9.32], (आ) आणी त्र्याशि वरुसें आराओंसि प्राय होंती [I.15.123], (इ) मग हरिपलेया तेयाचें धन। पडे दुर्बळिकेचें दैन [I.5.13], (ई) अजगरा वरि एवेन परिहरु (निमित्त) द्यावेया लागोनु ठेविला बोलु [I.5.42].

उ-कारान्त विशेशणां अलिंगांत अ-कारान्त जातात. देखिक. देखोनि रायाचें मन निश्टुर [I.16.71].

ई–कारान्त उतरां :

हीं पुल्लिंगी वा स्त्रीलिंगी नामां, विशेशणां, क्रियारुपां आसुंये. पुल्लिंगी नामाचे बदल गवळी - गवळिये -गवळियाचें - गवळियांचें हे धरतेर जातात. स्त्रीलिंगी नामाचे बदल राणी - राणियो (म.राणिया) - राणियेचें -राणियांचें हे धरतेर जातात. ह्या गटांत कोंकणी उतरां आयल्यांत तीं अशीं :

पुल्लिंग : उदेमी (म. व्यापारी), विनाणी (सुतार), दाणी (कर वसुलदार), भावार्थी (भाविक), चक्रवती (सम्राट), मार्गी (यात्री), घाडी (मांत्रिक).

स्त्रीलिंग : मासळी (मासा), बोकडी (शेळी), आंतौरी (बायको), गोणी (पोतें), आइती (तयारी), विणी (वेणी), उडकी (उडी), हांडी (भांडी), चावी (किल्ली), किडविडी (''कों.''+ म. तिरडी).

ओ-कारान्त विशेशणाचें आनी क्रियारुपाचें स्त्रीलिंग ई-कारान्त जाता; आनी हाचें भोववचन -इया. देखी : (अ) तुमीं गुप्तिये जाणवे [I.13.57]; (आ) जेतुक्या मोनजाती होंतिया। येतुक्या जिंत उरलिया। [I.16.84]; (इ) तैसी त्यां उदेमियांची सांत। मोडोनि गेली अवचीत। पळतां विसरले समस्त। आपुली वाट॥ [II.23.33]; (ई) तें दाणियां पासीं द्यावें [II.35.10]; (उ) तें तैल तेयां हांडियांतु भरावें [I.28.87]

ऊ–कारान्त उतरां :

हीं पुल्लिंगी वा स्त्रीलिंगी नामां आसुंये. पुल्लिंगी नामाचे बदल लाडू - लाडू- लाडुवाचें - लाडुवांचें हे धरतेर जातात. स्त्रीलिंगी नामाचे बदल ताळू - ताळुवो (म. ताळुवा) - ताळुवेचें - ताळुवांचें हे धरतेर जातात. ह्या वर्गांतलीं पुल्लिंगी कोंकणी उतरां: मारू, हिंदू, चाटू . देखी :- (अ) आणी जो मारुवाचें कपाळ फोडितु। ता आमंचा स्वामी जेजू ख्रिस्तु [I.5.133]; (आ) चाटुवांतु कणिक जी ठेविली [I.27.102] . प्राचीन भारतांतली देख : ताच्या तोंडारि हो चाटू घश्टितलों. (वैप. क.3).

एं–कारान्त उतरां :

कोंकणींत आनी मराठींत एं-कारान्त अलिंगी उतरां आसात जीं दोनूय भासांनी एकसारकींच वागतात. (हालींच्या काळांत मात मराठी एं-तलो अनुस्वार गळून पडला.) तांचे व्याकरणी बदल गाराणें - गाराणीं - गाराण्याचें -गाराण्यांचें हे धरतेर जातात. ह्या गटांतूय कांय कोंकणी उतरां आयल्यांत : जोडें (जोडी), उशिणें(बदला), फळें (फळी), बाउलें (बाहुली), आटाळें (सज्जा), खाजें (खाण्याचा पदार्थ), केणें (माल, पुरवठा), मुलें (गाठोडें), पेणें (मुक्काम), रुपडें (मुखवटा), सवणें (पक्षी, ''कों.'' शेवणें), करें (उंट), चांदिणें (चंद्रप्रकाश), मडें (प्रेत), शेंवतें (पांढरे लिलीचे फुल), वोजें (ओझे), पिशें (वेड), तौशें (काकडी).

कोंकणी विशेशणां आनी क्रियारुपां जीं पुल्लिंगात ओ-कारान्त आसतात तीं अलिंगांत एं-कारान्त जातात; हांचें भोववचन ईं-कारान्त जाता. देखी : (अ) केणें विकोनि द्रव्य घेतलें। तें रायाचां भांडारीं निरोपिलें। तेणें करोनि निवारिलें। दुर्विख लोकाचें॥ [I.13.39]. (आ) मग खर्ग काडिलें तेयाचें। शिर छेदिलें गोलियाचें। मन उलासलें साउलाचें। थोरु आनंदु लोकासि॥ [I. 24.94]; (इ) जैशीं बाळकें धाकुलीं। काहीं वोखटें मनीं नाथिलीं। तैशीं तीं होंतीं वर्तलीं। लाजे विण॥ [I.4.132]; (ई) घरों घरीं रिघलीं। कुडीं वोव्हारियां भरलीं। येकें जाउनियां पड्लीं। रांधणी माजी ॥ [I.16.51].

अंत्यस्वर बदलपी उतरां :

ह्या वर्गांत चडांत चड उतरां येतात तीं म्हळ्यार कोंकणींत ओ-कारान्त. हो ओ-कार मराठींत वतना आ-कारांत बदलता. तीं नामां, सर्वनामां, विशेशणां वा क्रियारुपां आसुंयेत. एकवचनांत आसल्यार तीं पुल्लिंगी आनी भोववचन आसल्यार स्त्रीलिंगी. देखीक, कों. घोडो = म. घोडा; कों. जैसो = म. जैसा; कों. काळो = म. काळा; कों. लागलो = म. लागला. कांय कडेन सर्वनाम 'तो' हाचें मराठींत 'ता' अशेंय जाता. कों. शेळियो = म. शेळिया; कों. त्यो = म. त्या; कों. केलियो = म. केलिया.

हे गजालीचो उपेग करून स्टीफन्सान कांय कोंकणी ओ-कारान्त उतरां आ-कारान्त करून वापरल्यांत : नामां- एकवचन: भरवंसो (म. विश्वास), खोडो (बेडी), कडो (कोठार), करो (गार), गिमाळो (उन्हाळा), गरो (गळ), कोंबो (कोंबडा), दाटो (गुप्तहेर), चिरो (दगड), झेलो (तुरा), तुतियो (हातोडा), सरो (दारू), पोलो (''कों.'' = म. गाल), भरो (भारा), पारुवो (कबुतर), उमो (चुंबन), वळंबो (वारूळ), वळसो (लाट), होवळो (पाहुणा). शिर्को (आंब) हें कोंकणी उतर पयल्या पुराणांत शिर्को अशेंच वापरलां जाल्यार दुसऱ्यांत शिर्का ह्या मराठी रुपान. असले प्रकार इतिवृत्तांनीय मेळटात.

स्त्रीलिंगी (ई-कारान्त उतरांचें भोववचन): बोकडियो, काठियो, पाटियो, मासळियो बी.

सर्वनामां :

माजो, आमंचो, तुमंचो, आपुलो, पेलो (परका).

विशेशणां:

निको (नीट), उपराठो (उलट, ''कों.'' उरफाटो), धाकुलो/धाकुटो (लाहान), वेलो (वरचा), शिमरो (बसक्या नाकाचा), रुंवाळो (क्षतग्रस्त), कुडो (खोटा), दुर्बळो (गरीब), खैंचो (कुठला), पोलो (पोकळ), सटवो (सहावा), वेवेगळियो (वेगवेगळ्या).

क्रियारुपां : संतोसलो, जल्मलो, निखेपिलो (गाडला), जियेलो (जगला).

ओ-कारान्त विशेशणाचें/क्रियारुपाचें स्त्रीलिंग ई-कारान्त जाता जाल्यार अलिंग एं-कारान्त. हें मतीत धरल्यार फुडच्या ओवयांचें कोंकणी कडलें नातें सुस्पश्ट दिसून येता. (अ) आणी मनुषु ता कैसा। मातेच्या तत्वाचा। वेळा काळा माजी तेयाचा। जल्मु जाहाला देखोनि॥ [I.1.25]; (आ) माथां मकुटु रत्नांचा। करीं झेला पुश्पांचा। वासु फांकला (पसरला) तेयाचा। अवघे मंधिरीं॥ [II.5.35]; (इ) गोंवाचा उंडा (भाकरी) घेउनु करीं [II.45.108]; (ई) पाटिया जोडोनि थोरी [I.7.28]; (उ) काडोनि मृतिका वसुंधरिची। कुडि (देह) घडिली मनुषाची। सर्व संपुर्नि स्वरुपाची। केली देवें॥ [I.3.33]; (ऊ) मनीं कोपु (क्रोध) संचरला। तेणें कामबाणु विगडला (मोडला)। जैसा येम्नु (अग्नी) विजवला (विरजला)। उदकें क रोनि॥ [I.12.26];

न्हस्व अंत्यस्वर :

गोंयांत आयज ''प्रमाण'' म्हणून घोळटले कोंकणींत (''कों.'') न्हस्व स्वरान सोंपपी एकय उतर मेळना म्हणल्यार जाता. पूण सोळाव्या शेंकडयांत जी कोंकणी गोंयांत घोळटाली तातूंत न्हस्व स्वरान सोंपपी उतरां चांटेपावलाक गावतात. त्या अंत्यस्वराक लागुन, कोंकणी ध्वनिशास्त्राच्या नेमा प्रमाणें, ताचे आदल्या अक्षरांतलो अ/ए/ ओ धांपतो जाता. ख्रिस्तपुराणांत जीं उ-कारान्त आनी इ-कारान्त उतरां होल्मतात तांतलीं भोवतेक आजून साश्टींत जश्याक तशीं घोळटात. तीं उ-कारान्त उतरां आयचे ''प्रमाण'' कोंकणींत (आनी मराठींतूय) अ-कारान्त जाल्यांत. असल्या उतरांतलो उ-कार अडेचो आसा, देखून जनर्धन[4] तांकां ''उ-छन्न अ-कारान्त'' म्हणटा. अंत्यक्षरांतलो हो उ-कार/ इ-कार कांय बोलयांनी बदलून आयज अ-कार जाला जाल्यारूय अंत्यस्वरपूर्व अक्षरांतलो अ/ ए/ ओ-कार धांपतोच उरला. देखीक, जपु, मेळु, मोरु, झरि, केळि, घोणि. हीं उतरां आयज अनुक्रमान जप, मेळ, मोर, झर, केळ, घोण अशीं बरयतात. जाल्यारूय तांचे व्याकरणी बदल आदले वरीच उरल्यात; म्हणजे भोववचन अनुक्रमान जप, मेळ, मोर (उक्तो उच्चार), झरी, केळी, घोणी अशें जाता. सामान्यरुपांतूय बदल जावंक ना.

अशें आसून उ-कारान सोंपिल्लीं पुल्लिंगी नामां (आनी विशेशणां, क्रियारुपां) ख्रिस्तपुराणांत मेळटात. देखी खातीर एक ओवी: तैसा आमंचा येकुचि प्राणु। अघवा आहे सर्वांगीं परिपुर्नु। आणी गात्रां येकेका माजि वसुनु। अघवा असे॥ [I.3.77]; असलीं आनीक कांय कोंकणी उतरां अशीं आसात :

नामां :

(हांचे व्याकरणी बदल पुत्रु - पुत्र - पुत्राचें - पुत्रांचें हे धरतेर जातात.) चिकोलु (चिखल), दवु (दंव), घोंटेरु (म. घरटें), आंचोळु (ओंजळ, पदर), फारु (फटका), तगरु (एडका), कुल्हाळु (कोलाहल), ग्रासु (जेवण), पाडु (पर्वा), सांगणेकारु (निरोप्या), शिणु (तक्रार), रुपकारु (प्रतीक), दुकळु (दुष्काळ), वृतावंतु (वृत्तांत), धुंपु (''कों.''+ म. धूप), बुरिंजु (बुरू ज), धगु (उन्ह), उजुवाडु (उजेड, प्रकाश), जल्मु (जल्म), परिमळु (सुगंध), नेमु (निर्धार), फुडारु (भविष्य), बुधवंतु (फुडारी), पिडेवंतु (''कों.'' वायटकार, म. आजारी), चुळु (घोंट). ह्या गटांत कांय पुर्तुगेज उतरांय आसपायल्यांत जीं चडशीं पुर्तुगेजींत ०-न सोंपतात. (ह्या ०-चो उच्चार उ असो जाता.) देखीक मांदामेंतु, आपोश्तोलु, साक्रामेंतु, स्पिरितु सांतु, जेंतियु, नजरेनु, बाउतिज्मु, आउगुश्तु. कांय ०-न सोंपनाशिल्लीं उतरांय ह्या गटांत मेळटात: लुसिफेरु, साल्वादोरु, इंपेरादोरु, पात्रिआर्कु, आबेलु, फिलिपु बी. हीं सगळीं आयज कोंकणींत ह्याच रुपान घोळटात.

कांय देखी: (अ) मग पातला भाखेचा फुडारु। पवित्रु दिनु आदित्यवारु। तंव ते ब्रम्हपुरिचा भारु। मेळावा आला॥ [I. 1.171]; (आ) ऐसा विनविला काकुळतिचा बापु। तंव स्वामियाचा उतरला कोपु। प्रसण होउनि दिधला निरोपु। मोइज़ेसि देवें॥ [I.19.67].

वेगळे तरेचीं पुल्लिंगी उ-कारान्त नामां कोंकणींत आसात. हीं खरेलीं उ-कारान्त नामां. देखीक गुरु. हांचे व्याकरणी बदल गुरु - गुरू - गुरुचें - गुरुंचें हे धरतेर जातात. हांचे मदींय कांय पुर्तुगेच नांवां येतात. पेद्रु, लाजरु बी. देखीक, तेथें पेद्रुची सासुरी। ज्वरु संचरला तिये (तिच्या) शेरिरीं [II.25.54];

कांय उ-कारान्त स्त्रीलिंगी नामांय ख्रिस्तपुराणांत आसात जीं साश्टींत आयजूय तशींच घोळटात. तांचे व्याकरणी बदल पुल्लिंगी नामां वरीच जातात: मातु (खबर, बोलणें), पांगु (बंधन, ऋण), निथु (थुकी), वस्तु (वस्तू). देख: सकळां रचिलेयां वस्तूं होउनि [I.1.43]. ख्रिस्तपुराणांत ''रीति'' हें ''रितु'' अशें वापरलां, पूण तें आयज ''रीति'' अशेंच घोळटा. ख्रिस्तपुराणाच्या काळार मात ते ''रितु'' अशेंच घोळटालें म्हूण पुरावो मेळटा (घांटकार[5] पा. 49)

सर्वनामां:

कवणु, हाचें भोववचन कवण. देखीक (अ) म्हणे तुमीं कवणाचे कवण [I.13.48] ; (आ) ऐसा कवणु पां बुधियुक्तु। पाहांतां नदिसे एजिप्तांतु [I.13.1] ; (इ) ऐशें वोसद विसनिवारण (विषघ्न औषद)। नाहीं देखिलें कवणें [I.21.135].

विशेशणां :

ख्रिस्तपुराणांत, आनी साश्टींतले कोंकणींत, उ-कारान्त विशेशणां आसात; आनी तीं लिंग-वचना प्रमाणें बदलतात. (''कोंक णींत'' तीं अ-कारान्त जाल्यांत आनी लिंग-वचना प्रमाणें बदलनांत.) विचित्रु ह्या विशेशणाचे बदल अशे जातात. पु: विचित्रु; स्त्री. विचित्रि; अ. विचित्र; भोववचन अनुक्रमान विचित्र, विचित्री, विचित्रां (म. विचित्रें). ह्या वर्गांतलीं कांय विशेशणां : थोरु (मोठा), लानु/सानु (लाहान), लवलवितु (भुसभुशीत), अजाणु (अज्ञानी), परिकरु (सुंदर), ग्रेस्तु (श्रीमंत), चांगु (चांगला), उन्हु (गरम), तिखु (तिखट). असल्या विशेशणांच्या व्याकरणी बदलांच्यो देखी: उतमु प्रेत्नु, उतमि सुमुर्ति, उतम फळ, परिकरि कथा, अमोलिक रक्त, मोगाळि जननी, गर्विक भोडुवे, गुप्ती वस्तू (भोववचन), चांगें कृपादानें (भोववचन). एक ह्या आंकड्याचेय अशेच बदल जातात : येकु संधेवु, येकि स्त्री, येक हित, येके पंकती, येका परमेस्वराथें. येक हें ''क ांय'' ह्या अर्थान भोववचनांत वापरलां. देखीक, येक प्राणु राखावेया। जांती वैद्यां गिवसावेया। [I.25.52] ; दोग, तेग हीं ह्याच वर्गांतलीं भोववचन विशेशणां. देखून स्त्रीलिंगांत तीं दोगी, तेगी आनी अलिंगांत दोगां, तेगां (म. दोगें, तेगें) अशीं जातात. देखीक, मग येके दिवसीं दोगी जणी। वेशा आलिया संवादिणी [I.26.11].

अव्ययां :

पासौनु, वरौनु, तेथौनु. देख : मोइज़े निगाला तेथौनु। एजिप्ताचां मार्गीं [I.15.121].

क्रियारुपां :

करूनु, वर्जुनु, अनुसरूनु, देउनु. असलीं क्रियारुपां कोचींत आजून कायम आसात. जनर्धन[4] हांणी दिल्ली एक देख : हे चेल्ले चलचित्र चोवनु आयले. (पा.165). आनीक देखी (1) सुण्यान दिवडाक सुस्तवूनु सोडलो. (2) दकोवूनु दी (3) आपोवूनु हाडि (4) नांचूनु दाकेय (पा. 298). ख्रिस्तपुराणांतल्यो देखी: (अ) उतमी मोनजाती निवडूनु। प्रतियातिचीं तिनि जोडीं वेंचूनु। [I.7.40]; (आ) येतुकें अब्राहाउं बोलूनु। इसा हृदईं आळंगूनु। मोहें धरिला चुंबूनु। हृदया सरी [I.9.62].

इ-कारान्त उतरां :

साश्टींतलीं इ-कारान्त उतरां सोळाव्या-सतराव्या शेंकड्यांत बारदेसांत आनी तीसवाडींतूय तशींच घोळटालीं; गांवकारी बसकांच्या इतिवृत्तांनी हें स्पश्ट कळटा. हालींसरा मेरेन (म्हणजे पन्नास-साठ वर्सां फाटीं पर्यान) तीं मराठींतूय इ-कारान्त आशिल्लीं; आनी आयज ई-कारान्त जाल्यांत. ''प्रमाण'' कोंकणींत तांचे मदलीं कांय ई-कारान्त जाल्यार हेर अ-कारान्त जाल्यांत. अशें आसुनूय व्याकरणी बदल आदले वरीच जातात.

ख्रिस्तपुराणांतलीं साबार कोंकणी स्त्रीलिंगी उतरां ह्या वर्गांत आसपावतात. तांचे व्याकरणी बदल झरि - झरी - झरीचें - झरींचें हे धरतेर जातात. असल्या उतरांच्यो कांय देखी : कुडि (म. देह), झरि (झरा), काकुळति (दया), कुमरि (मुलगी), फातरि (शिळा), धरणि (जमीन), गोपिणि (गोफण), भाटि (भाटी), पडि (माप), बांदावळि (बांधणी), बिदि (रस्ता), बरि (बरगडी), संचति (संतती), कळंबि (म. जंग, ''कों.'' कळम), चाळणि (चाळण), पंकति (पंगत), उरि (उत्कंठा), रांधणि (चूल), निसणि, (शिडी). घाशि (कष्ट), गर्भेस्ति (गर्भवती), वैजि (म. सुईण, ''कों.'' वैजीण), कुंटि (लंगडेपणा), कुमरु (मुलगा, हाचें स्त्रीलिंगी रूप कुमरि). हेच धरतेर स्टीफन्सान पुर्तुगेज ''सांतु'' हाचें स्त्रीलिंग ''सांति'' अशें केलें आनी हाचें भोववचन, नेमाक धरून ''सांति'' अशें. तेच परीं ''प्रोफेतु'' हाचें स्त्रीलिंग ''प्रोफेतिणि.''

कांय देखी : (अ) दोगी वैजी होंतिया देसांतु [I.15.12]; (आ) आपुली गोपिणि घेतली करीं [I.24.55]; (इ) अदिक होउं नेदावी संचति तेयांची [I.15.6]; (ई) येकी (कांय) नारी प्रोफेतिणी दिधल्या जेंतियां
कारणें [I.35.89].

कोंकणींत/मराठींत इ-कारान्त पुल्लिंगी नामां आसात. देखीक कवि, प्राणि, अग्नि. स्टीफन्सान कांय पुर्तुगेज नांवां ह्या गटांत आसपायल्यांत, कारण पुर्तुगेजींत तीं तशींच सोंपतात. देखीक पाद्रि, सासॅर्दोति. पूण मिगेल, सामुवेल असलीं नावांय इ-क ारान्त केल्यांत आनी आयजूय तीं कोंकणींत अशींच घोळटात. हाचे फाटलें कारण म्हळ्यार लातीं भाशेंत ही नांवा मिखाएलिस (Michaelis), सामुएलिस (Samuelis) अशीं बरयतात. गांवकारी इतिवृत्तांनीय हीच पद्दत पळेवंक मेळटा : मनुवेलि, अंतोनि. देख: मिगेलिन अग्निची शृंखळा केली. [I.2.110].

कांय क्रियापदांचे, खास करून सकर्मक क्रियापदांचे, आज्ञार्थ इ-कारान्त आसतात. देखीक करि, काडि, मारि देख: वेगां भाजि म्हणत गोंवाच्या रोंटिया [I.9.27].

साश्टींतलीं खाशेलीं उतरां :

वयर सांगल्यात त्या अंत्यस्वरां शिवाय साबार कोंकणी उतरां ख्रिस्तपुराणांत आयल्यांत जीं आयज
साश्टींतूच घोळटात.

सर्वनामां :

तेणें (ताणें), तियेन (तिणें), तियेचें (तिचें); आमां (आम्हाला); तुमां (तुम्हाला), आपुलो (आपला).

देखी : (अ) येतुकें बोलिलें तेणें [I.28.99]; (आ) देखोनि तियेच्या उपकरासि [I.28.95]; (इ) ते आपुल्या रचणारा नेणती (ओळखत नाही) [I.2.3].

क्रियाविशेशणां :

आजि (आयज), पैरि (परवां), संवळीं (पाहाटे), शेवटीं (अखेर), जायेपणीं (म. जन्मतः, ''कों.'' जल्मजात), फायचां दिवशीं (उद्या). देख : हें अपुर्व मज निरोपावें आजि तुवां [I.4.115]:

आंकडे :

जितलेय आंकडे ख्रिस्तपुराणांत आयल्यात ते सगळे (एक ''शेतें'' वगळून) साश्टींत आयज उच्चारतात तशेच बरयल्यात : येकु, दोनि, तिनि, च्यारि, नव, बास्तरि, सतास्तरि, त्र्याशीं, इकुणणोवि. शिवाय दों, तीं, चोउं. देखीक, दोहीं कडां दों पर्वतां वरि [I.24.6]; इतिवृत्तांतली देख : दोयि वर्गानी जाउनुं दिलजेस

करावे [पा. 241].

संबोधन उद्गार:

रे, आरे, गे, आगे, गा, आगा. देखी : (अ) मागोनि आणि गे उसणिया [I.28.86]; (आ) म्हणे आगा ये सत्यार्थिया गुरू [I. 9.89].

खात्रेचो प्रत्यय :

''प्रमाण'' कोंकणींत आनी मराठींत हो -च असोच घोळटा. पूण साश्टींत तो, ख्रिस्तपुराणांत मेळटा तसोच, -चि असो चालंत आसा. देखीक, तुं येकिचि माता आंकुवारि [I.1.50]; (आ) लिहित लेखितार्थु थैंचि सांडिला [II.26.103]; (इ) तुमीं नेठवावी कदिंचि। मना माजि॥ [I.5.150]; (ई) तेयाचें काहींचि नाहीं नासलें (नष्ट जाहालें) [I.15.78].

क्रियापदां :

सगळ्या शब्दजातीं मदीं क्रियापद हेंच एके भाशेचो प्राण वा आत्मो आसता. साबार वेगळ्या भासांनी कांय नामां, विशेशणां बी एकसारकींच आसतात. तीं एके भाशे कडल्यान दुसरे भाशेन वा भासांनी उशणीं घेतिल्लीं आसतात. पूण दुसरे भाशेंतल्यान उशणें घेतिल्लें क्रियापद फावो तो बदल करुनूच वापरतात. समगोत्री भासांतल्या क्रियापदांच्या धातूंत जायतें साम्य जाणवता जाल्यार काळप्रत्यय वेगळे आसतात. कोंकणी, मराठी, हिंदीं, गुजराती ह्या भासांतलीं समानार्थी क्रियापदां तपासल्यार आमक ां हें सहज कळटा. देखीक कर, मर, खा, चल हीं क्रियापदां. पूण वेगळ्या गोत्रांतल्या भासांतलीं क्रियापदां सामकींच वेगळीं आसतात; देखीक, कोंकणी आनी कन्नड ह्यो शेजारी भासो. वयर दिल्ल्या क्रियापदांचे कन्नड पर्याय अनुक्रमान माडु, सायु, तिन्नु, नडे अशे आसात. समगोत्री क्रियापदांचे धातू सम आसल्यारीय, तांकां लागिल्लो काळप्रत्यय मात त्या त्या क्रियापदाची भास थारायता. अशें आसुनूय, कोंकणी आनी मराठी भासांतले कांय काळप्रत्यय, बरपांत तरी, एकसारकेच दिसतात; आनी हाका लागून मराठी वर्तमान पत्रांतले कांय माथाळे कोंकणीच कशे दिसतात आनी कोंकणी पत्रांतले मराठी.

ख्रिस्तपुराणांत साबार काळप्रत्यय आदळटात जे कोंकणीच आसात म्हणूंक कोणूच अनमनचो ना. देखीक, पडलेउं मुर्ख होउनि; तरि जेथें चुकतेउं देवाचें मुख; उदंड केलेति आचारी; सात कणसें देखिलिंति; मुर्ख जाहालाशि शेवटीं; जाणशि तेंचि नेणशि; कपट केलेंशि; स्वान काय देखिलाशि; तेया पळाविशि; मृत्यु जिणविशि; हे तरेचे काळप्रत्यय कोंकणी भारतात सर्रास मेळटात. देखीक, (अ) हात जोडुनु पायां जरि पडलेउं [सप. क.1]; (आ) आमी तुमंचे लागी मागतेउं [अरप. क.2] ; (इ) तैशेंचि करूंक पळेताशि [आप क.8]. (ई) दृपदियेचीं उतरां तुमीं आइकिल्यांति [सप. क. 4]. वयर दाखयलां तशें, इतिव ृत्तांनीय अशे तरेचीं क्रियारुपां आसात.

''प्रमाण'' कोंकणींत सगळ्याच क्रियापदांचीं कृदतां -ऊं, -ऊन अशीं सोंपतात. पूण साश्टींत आयज लेगीत साबार क्रियापदांचीं कृदंतां -ओंक, -ओन अशीं सोंपतात; तीं चडशीं अकर्मक आसतात. ख्रिस्तपुराणांत ह्या दोनीय तरांचीं क्रियारुपां मेळटात. तांचें अपूर्ण धातूविशेशणीय मुळावन अनुक्रमान -अत आनी -इत अशें सोंपता. देखीक करपता, खरपिता. तशेंच पूर्ण धांतूविशेशणीय मुळावन -अल आनी -इल अशें सोंपता. देखीक करपलें, खरपिलें. तरूय साश्टींत कांय क्रियापदां अशीं आसात जांचें अपूर्ण मुळावन -अत जाल्यार पूर्ण मुळावन -इल अशें सोंपता. देखीक राखता, राखिलें. ख्रिस्तपुराणांत ह्या सगळ्या तरांचीं क्रियारुपां मेळटात - आयज साश्टींत घोळटात तशींच आनी तींच. देखी: (क) चिंतूं लागला; (ख) देऊं सांगे; (ग) नसके करूं, (घ) दिसों लागले; (ङ) हिंडों गेला; (च) सांगों आधारिली; (छ) तळवटीं घालूनु; (ज) निगती धांवोनु; (झ) घेतीं मागोनु; (त्र) प्राणु वेचूनि; (ट) देव मानूनि; (ठ) मेले बुडोनि; (ड) मोडोनि वृख्याचा टाळा; (ढ) ऐशें चिंतिती; (ण) अस्ति काडिता जाहाला; (त) कदळी पत्रें काडिलीं; (थ) आर्क घडितां; (द) (देवें) मनुषु घडिला; (ध)

देवदुतां दोसु घडला; (न) मेंढिया गोधनें राखती; (प) लोकाचे प्राण राखिले; (फ) जें जागृतीं चिंतिलें देखिलें आइकिलें; (ब) सांडि मनिची दुखभ्रांति. साश्टींतली ही आयची चाल कोंकणी भारतांतूच न्हय तर इतिवृत्तांनीय मेळटा. देखीक, (अ) अस्नपया २८ वर्णिल्योति (पा. 103); (आ) पेगाउं मांडिताति घडिताति (111); (इ) निसाणिया केल्योति (112); (ई) वेदोरु फजेदान खबर आयिकिलें (286). कोंकेणी भारतांतल्यो देखी : (अ) अनुसाल्या तूं भोउ तृशेन सोखलाशि (अश्वप. क.2). (आ) अवकाळीं तांच्या राज्यांतु व्रख्य फळताति (सप. क.2) (इ) तुमच्या निरोपा प्रमाणी पौळिचे गणिकें राखेनैत राखूंक ठेइल्याति (अश्वप. क.1); (उ) हात जोडुनु पायां जरि पडलेउं (सप. क.1). (उ) ताका देखुनु भिमशेनु हांशिलो [गप. क. 1]; (ऊ) ऐशें त्या धनुजयाचें उतर आइकिलें
[गप. क. 1]; (ए) ते आमकां देखतले [गप. क. 1]; (ऐ) श्यामकोर्नु घोडो देखिलो [अश्वप. क. 1].

कोंकणी क्रियापद जेन्ना -अयता/ -आयता अशें सोंपता तेन्ना ताचें पर्याय मराठी क्रियापद -अविता/-आविता अशें सोंपता. देखीक, कों. सोडैता = म. सोडविता; कों फर्मायता= म. फर्माविता. अशे तरेन कोंकणी क्रियापदांचें मराठीकरण स्टीफन्सान केलां. (अ) तुजे प्रजेसि उपद्रविले (उपद्रव दिले) [I.16.23]; (आ) बुजाविली (सांत्वन केले) तिये स्त्रिये [II.23.101]; (इ) म्हणौनि तो दिनु सांतविला (आशीर्वाद दिला) [I.3.85]; हें निमाणें क्रियापद पुर्तुगेज सांतिफिकोव (Santificou) वा लातीं सांक्तिफिकावित (Sanctificavit) ह्या क्रियापदां वेल्यान घडयलां काय दिसलें. पूण ना. हें उतर कोंकणी भारतांत आसा: अर्जुनाक बरें जाऊं म्होणु सांतविताति (अश्वप. क.7)

असंख्य क्रियापदां ह्या दोनूय समगोत्री भासांनी घोळटात. पूण कोंकणींत आनीकय क्रियापदां आसात जीं मराठींत मेळनांत. स्टीफन्सान असल्या क्रियापदांचो सर्रास वापर केला, आनी तीं साश्टींत घोळटात तशींच उच्चारल्यांत. देखीक, कडकडले (काकडले), कुसला (सडला), गमली (समजली), चिंतिती (विचार करते), जल्मला (जन्माला आला), जियेला (जगला), निपजले (उत्पन्न झाले), नेणती (ओळखत नाही). पोंवती (पोहते), येकवटले (एकत्र गोळा झाले), वेचिला (खर्च केला), वेंचिली (निवड केली), वोडवती (झुकते), सांडिला (सोडला), सुस्कारिला (उच्छ्वास टाकला), हांतुरिलें (जमिनीवर पसरविले). कांय ओवयांच्यो देखी: (अ) ऐशें मरण तुज निर्मिलें (नशीबात आसलें) जरि [I.15.33], (आ) आणी बेडुकें निपजाविलीं (उत्पन्न केली) तेथ [I.16.66], (इ) कुपांचा शामवर्नु फांकला (पसरला) [I.18.33].

कांय क्रियापदांचे मदीं साश्टींतूच अनुस्वार येता. ख्रिस्तपुराणांत हीं अनुस्वारा सयत वापरल्यांत. कांय देखी: (अ) तंव फ राव्या मनीं भेवु (भय) सुंटला (उद्भवला) [I.16.103]; (आ) आंतुनि जळ झरि फुंटली (उत्पन्न झाली) [I. 17.107]. ''भंय सुंटप'' आनी ''झरि फुंटप'' हे साश्टींतले वाकप्रचार.

न्हयकारी क्रियापदां :

मराठींत क्रियापदाक नाहीं लावन ताचो न्हयकार व्यक्त करतात. देखीक, (अ) जेहीं देववचन नाहीं मानिले। म्हणोनि त्यांचें नाहीं आइकिलें [I.7.99]; (आ) येकाद्या थोरां कुळवंतां । निवडिले नाहीं सर्वथा। स्वामियें देवें ॥ [II.28.27]. पूण सोळाव्या शेंकड्यांतले कोंकणींत (आनी गोंयचे मराठींतूय) एके वेगळेच तरेचीं न्हयकारी क्रियापदां घोळटालीं म्हूण ब्राग संहितें त तशेंच इतिवृत्तांनी पुरावो मेळटा. तींच आनी तसलींच साबार हेर क्रियापदां ख्रिस्तपुराणांत सर्रास मेळटात. हीं क्रियापदां घडटाना, मूळ (हयकारी) क्रियापदाचे सुरवेक न लागता. देखीक, (अ) प्रजेथें नसोडित फरावा निश्टुरु [I.16.40]; (आ) हें कां नविचारिशी [I.2.99]. पूण वांगडाच आनीकय कांय बदल दिश्टी पडटात, कांय ''नेम'' पाळ्ळ्यात शें दिसता, पूण अपवादय आसात.

(1) मूळ क्रियापद इ वगळून हेर खंयच्याय स्वरान सुरू जाता जाल्यार तो स्वर न हातूंत विलीन जाता, म्हणजे न+उलैता = नुलैता. देखी: (अ) पण जे देवाथें नोळखती [I.2.1]; (आ) नांव मुखे नुचारी [I.8.69]; (इ) येर शिकविलेया नाइकती [I.7.35]; (क) मनुषांचें रक्त नइछ्तिु [I.9.94].

(2) मूळ क्रियापद अ-कारान सुरू जाता तेन्ना न लायतकच आनीक बदल जायना. देखी. (अ) यें येतुकें नघडे तरि [I. 1.137]; (आ) तरि नपडते अवगती [I.2.117]; (इ) हा नम्हणावा सोहधरु [I.11.17]; (ई) कश्टांचा पाडु नकरितां । भयेभ्रांति नधरितां [I.1.104].

(3) मूळ क्रियापद आ-कारान सुरू जाता तेन्ना तो आ-कार अ-कारांत बदलता. मात सुरवातेचें अक्षर पा/ बा/ मा आसल्यार तें तशेंच उरता; म्हणजे न+लायता = नलयता: पूण न+ मागता= नमागता. देखी: (अ) तेयासि पाहिजे नलगे क रहीं [I.2.29]; (आ) वोखटें बरवें तें नसंडिती कोणी वेळां [I.2.119]; (इ) आणी जरि तेयांथें नसंभाळित [I.15.146]; (क) लेंकुरुवां सवें माता त्यांचिया कां नमारिशी [I.15.35]; (ख) तंव कवण कवणा नमानिती [I.6.78]; (ग) तरि तीं म त्यु नपावती [I.4.14]; (घ) म्हणौनि तुजेन नबांदवत मंधिर माजें [I.25.18]; अपवाद: आमीं नपवतां लपौनि ठेविती बाळकें [I.15.18]. इतिवृत्तांतल्यो देखी: (आ) पाउणिकारु अतोनि परेरान सोमवारीं बादावे नबंदी होयील तरि (220);

(आ) दोग देसायी सागातीं वचुनु दिवाण सुरू करूनु यावें। देसायी न वचे होंती तरि (274). प्राचीन कोंकणी भारतांतल्यो देखी: (अ) ते तुमकां सर्वथा वाइट नकरिती (कप. क. 2); (आ) हो लाहाना-व्हडाक नपळे (कप. क. 2); (इ) येकमेकांचो घाउ आंगाक **नबै**सतनां दोगय आपापुल्या दळभारांतु गेले (अश्वप क. 6). (ई) आतां तरिय माज्यान नसंगतां विंदव नां (अश्वप. क. 6). विचित्र म्हळ्यार असलीं क्रियापदां आयज कोंकणीचे खंयचेच बोलयेंत मेळनांत.

साश्टींतली वापरचाल आनी वाकप्रचार :

ख्रिस्तपुराणांत अमराठी कोंकणी उतरां सर्रास मेळटात, तें जालेंच; पूण वयर पळेलां तशें, जेन्ना साश्टींतलें उतर ''प्रमाण'' कोंकणींत घोळटल्या पर्याय उतरा परस वेगळें आसता, तेन्ना साश्टींतलेंच उतर स्टीफन्सान वापरलां : अशीर (''कों.'' अरूं द), उपराटें (उरफाटें), कळंबि (कळम), गोपिणि (गोफण); घाशि (त्रास), पिडेवंत (वायटकार), पोलो (गाल), राखेशि (राक्षीण), रांधणि (रान्न), वैजि (वयजीण), सटवो (सवो), सवणें (शेवणें).

''प्रमाण'' कोंकणींत कूड ह्या उतराक दोन वेगळे अर्थ आसात. घराची खोली आनी मनशाचो देह; आनी दोनूय अर्थांनी तें स्त्रीलिंगी आसा : पूण साश्टींत हीं दोन वेगळीं उतरां आसात: अलिंगी कूड (खोली) आनी स्त्रीलिंगी कूडि (देह). हो फरक स्टीफन्सान ख्रिस्तपुराणांत केला: (अ) कवड घातलें कुडाशि [I.28.108]; (आ) कुडि घडिली मनुषाची [I.3.33]. शिवाय कवड घालप (दार धांपप) हो साश्टींतलो एक वाकप्रचार.

आनीक वाकप्रचारांच्यो देखी :

(अ) चोउं फेरीं मळेयानिळु खेळवी तेयाथें [I.1.176]. मळेयानिळु (सुगंधी वारो) हें उतर प्राचीन कोंकणी भारतांत मेळटां: तो बैसलो अशें कृष्णान देखून मळायानिळु सोडिलो (दृप. क.5). खेळोवप हाका भोंवडावप असो अर्थ कोंकणींतूच आसा.

(आ) डिंबिया घातलिया धरणी [I.1.177]; हें कोंकणी ''धरणीर (जमनीर) दिंबियो घाल्यो'' हाचें सरळ मराठीकरण. हाचें मराठींत ''गुडघे खाली टेकले'' अशें जाता.

(इ) येतुकेईं बाहिरि सरलिंति आर्कांतुलीं [I.8.1]; आनी गर्धवासी घालोनि पाखारी। बाहिरि सरला [I.9.42]. कोंकणींतलें ''भायर सरलो'' हें मराठींत ''बाहेर पडला/गेला/आला'' अशें जाता.

(ई) मारू भुतें बाहिर घाला तुमीं [II.30.121]. कोंकणींतलें ''भायर घालप'' हें मराठींत ''बाहेर टाकणे/हाकलणे'' अशें जातां.

(उ) घडिये घडिये रुधन करी [I.12.1]. घडिये घडिये ह्या साश्टींतल्या वाकप्रचाराचो मराठी पर्याय ''क्षणोक्षणी'' आनी ''प्रमाण'' कोंकणींतलो ''भोवन भोवन''.

ब्राग संहितेचें पडबिंब :

ख्रिस्तपुराणांत आस्पाविल्ल्या हिसपाभायर चालंत कोंकणी आनी प्राचीन कोंकणी उतरांची प्रचिती ह्या प्रकरणांत थोडे भितर दिल्लीच आसा. पुस्कळ कोंकणी उतरांक मराठी रूप (अंत्याक्षर, विभक्तिकूस बी) दिलां, जाल्यार साबार उतरां कोंकणी रुपांतूच आसात. हीं मूळ मराठी उतरांवेल्यान, कवित्व सोंपें करचे खातीर, कोंकणी केल्यांत अशें मानूंक कठीण लागता. थळाव्या गजालींचीं नांवां कोंकणीच आसात; हांचे मदीं फुलांचीं, फळांचीं, झाडांचीं, मसाल्यांचीं, सवण्यांचीं, शस्त्रांचीं, वाजंत्रांचीं, खड्यांचीं, सोरपांचीं इत्यादी नांवां आसपावतात. घडये तांचीं मराठी नांवां सोदून काडप स्टीफन्साक जमलें ना जायत, कारण आयजूय अशें करप सोंपें जायना. कांय देखी:-

फुलांचीं नांवां :- चांपीं, मोगरीं, शेंवतीं.

फळांची नांवां :- आंबे, पणस, केळीं, चिबडां, तौशीं.

झाडांचीं नांवां :- ताडमाड, कल्पतरू, फोफळी, येरंड, धुतरो, चांपो.

मसाल्यांचीं नांवां :- मिरीं, तिखी, येळ, काराफूल, सांसव, उलिचे कांदे.

सवण्यांचीं नांवां :- घार, गीद, घुमड, साळुवो, कावळो.

शस्त्रांचीं नांवां :- भाले, साभळ, कोंते, खर्ग, गोपिणि, वोडण.

वाजंत्रांचीं नांवां :- काळो, दमामे, भेरी, निसाण, निसणभेरी.

खड्यांचीं नांवां:- हिरो, नीळ, केंपु.

सोरपांचीं नांवां :- अजगरु, हारु, संकपाळु, माहुंडळु. ह्या निमाण्या दोन सोरपांक मराठींत नेमकेंच किर्तें म्हणटात तें आयजूय कळना. मराठींत मंडळ नांवाचो एक सोरोप आसा, पूण तो विखारी न्हय; ताका साश्टींत माळूंड म्हणटात. म्हांडळ तर अतिविखारी. ''घोणस'' हाचे अर्थ (कोंकणी कोशांत) भलतेच मेळटात. आनीकय नोंद करपासारकी गजाल म्हळ्यार, वयर उल्लेखिल्लीं सगळींच नांवां ब्राग संहितेंतल्या कोंकणी बाडांनी उपलब्ध आसात.

आदीं सांगलां आनी दाखयलां तशें ख्रिस्तपुराणांत साबार उतरां मेळटात जीं आयज मराठींतूच न्हय तर साश्टींतले कोंकणींत लेगीत मेळनांत. पूण ह्या ग्रंथांतलीं 90-95 टक्के तरी उतरां मिशोनारींच्या कोंकणी-पुर्तुगेज उतरावळींनी गावतात. आनी जीं

थंय झळकनांत तीं ब्राग संहितेंत सोदल्यार मेळटलीं. देखीक : (अ) घोडेयां राउतांची फळी। बुडौनि मारिली समुद्र जळीं। ऐसा देवु माहा बळी। भक्तांचा कोवासा ॥ [I.17.51]. कोवासा/कोवासो हें उतर आयचे मराठींतूय मेळना आनी कोंकणींतूय. कोंकणींत कवासो अशें उतर आसा. साश्टींत तें केतकीच्या (केवड्याच्या) घमघमीत फुला खातीर वापरतात. पूण हो अर्थ हांगा बसना. मिशोनरी उतरावळींनीय तें मेळना; पूण कोंकणी भारतांत मात मेळटा. दृणपर्वाचे पांचवे कथेंत हनुमंत श्रीकृष्णाक उलो करून म्हणटा : ''आतां कोणी एकी प्रकारीं ह्या अर्जुनाचो कोवासो जाउनु राख.'' दृणाचे बाण अर्जुनाचें वज्रकवच भेदून ताच्या आंगाक तोंपले आनी तो निचैतन्य जातो. आनीक बाण लागिल्ले जाल्यार अर्जून नक्की मरतलो आसलो. तेन्ना श्रीकृष्णान, सुदर्शन चक्र वापरून, दृणाचे फुडले बाण मोडले आनी अर्जून वांचलो.

(आ) रक्तमंष्य घेउनि मनुष्य शरिरीं, विस्वजनांचा कैवारी, सखावु होईल [I.33.62]; नभी नभी म्हणे देवु, मीं जाहालां तुजा सखावु [I.8.208]; ''सखावु'' हें उतर आधुनीक कोंकणी जावं मराठी कोशांत मेळना. पूण कोंकणी 'भारतांत' तें साबार कडेन आसा. थंय ताचो अर्थ ''संरक्षण दिवपी बळिश्ट सांगाती'' असो जाता. देखी: (1) राया द्रुणा सारिखो सखावु आसतनां कोण आमकां कितें करूं सख [भिप. क. 10]; (2) ह्या आकांताक तूं माका पाउनु सोडै. तुजे वेगळें माका, स्वामिया, कोण नां. माय-बापान सांडिलो. आतां तूंचि माजो सारथी, सखावु [अश्वप. क. 4].

कांय उतरां एकापरस चड अर्थांनी वापरिल्लीं मेळटात. ते सगळे अर्थ ब्राग संहितेंत गावतात. देखीक,

(अ) होउनु हें तीन अर्थांनी वापरलां : जावन, सावन आनी परस. (1) माहा मापी देवद्रुही होउनु (जावन) [I.29.25]; (2) देवें एजिप्ता होउनु (सावन) आणिला असे बोलाउनु. [II.12.19]; (3) अघवेयां आंकुवारीं होउनु (परस) बरवें पुण्य आचारूनु [II.3.21]. प्राचीन कोंकणी भारतांतल्यो देखी : (1) समेस्तां मधें लिण होउनु चमकताति [सप. क. 1]; (2) वरणावताक होउनु धर्मचें कागत आइलां [सप. क. 2]; (3) समस्ति ही माजी प्रजा माज्यां बाळकां होउनु बरें देखन [गप. क. 2].

(आ) 'क्रमऊंक'' हें क्रियापद दोन अर्थांनी वापरिल्लें मेळटा : वेळ सारूंक आनी वाट चमकूंक. देखी : गेली आनंदस्थाना भितुरि, क्रमावेया वेळु [I.4.78]; मनुष्यकुमरु पंथु क्रमउनि जांत असे तेथौनि [II.45.128]. हेच अर्थ प्राचीन कोंकणी ''भारत'' हातूंत मेळटात : च्यारि पार रात्रि आपुल्या घारा मधें क्रमविली [सप. क. 7]; कित्येक दिसानीं मार्गु क्रमउनु द्वारके पावलो [अश्वप. क. 2].

(इ) ''खेम'' हें उतर प्राचीन कोंकणींत दोन वेगळ्या अर्थांनी मेळटा : गळोवेंग आनी क्षमा. देखी : तिणें आपुल्या पुत्राक खेम दिली [अरप. क. 7]; जें हांवें नेणतां उलैलां ताचो अपराधु तूं खेम करि [अश्वप. क. 1]. पूण ख्रिस्त पुराणांत हीं दोन उतरां, खेम (गळोवेंग) आनी खेमा (क्षमा) अशीं वेगळायल्यांत : येरें धरिला खेम देउनि, हृदया सरी [II.19.51]; स्वामी खेमा किजे म्हणतु अपराधु माजा [I.25.28]. हे वेगळावणेची प्रेरणाय स्टीफन्साक कोंकणी ''भारतातूंच'' मेळ्ळी जायत: स्वामिया, सहस्र अपराध आमीं जरि केले तरि तूं हे वेळे आमकां खेमा करि [अश्वप. क. 9].

(उ) ''प्रति'' हें क्रियाविशेशण समोर ह्या अर्थान वापरलां. देखीक, सत्य मीं सांगतों तुमां प्रति [II.58.16]; स्वामी म्हणे शिष्यां प्रति [II.40.87]. शिवाय स्नेह ह्या अर्थान, प्रीति हाचें तद्भव म्हणून, नाम कशेंय वापरलां. देखीक, प्रति करा एकमेकाची जैशी म्यां केली तुमंची [II.58.39]; देवपुत्राची प्रति सेवा किजे अखंड तुमीं [I.5.155]. ह्या अर्थान केल्लो वापर कोंकणी ''भारतांतूय'' मेळटा: त्या पुत्राइ परस हिचेरि माजी प्रति थोरि [अश्वप. क. 10]; पातका ठाइं भोउ प्रति [अरप. क. 1].

विंगड अर्थान चालंत उतरां : ख्रिस्तपुराणांत साबार उतरां आसात जीं चालंत भाशेंत घोळटात पूण विंगड अर्थान. कांय देखी:-

(अ) ''नासता'' हें क्रियापद आयज ''आसना'' हाचो पर्याय जावनूच घोळटा. पूण प्राचीन कोंकणींत ताचो उच्चार ''ना-स-ता'' असो जातालो आनी अर्थ ''पाड पडटा, नश्ट जाता, काबार जाता'' असो. ख्रिस्तपुराणांत तें ह्याच अर्थान वारपलां. ब्राग संहितेंतल्यो देखीः हीं आपुल्ये माये लागी उदक जरि मागती, त्यो नेणतपणींचि तांकां पियेउंक जरि दिती तरि तीं नासती [अरप. क. 3]; आरे दुर्योधना, तुजी बुधि आतां लेगित नासली? आपुल्या बापलभावांक वाइट करिताशि, हें तुका बरें न्होय. [आप. क. 6]. ख्रिस्तपुराणांतल्यो देखी : बाईं पोखरणिचें जळ, सिहाळें नासलें सकळ [I.33.11]; पण तें झाड नाहीं जळलें, तेयाचें काहींचि नाहीं नासलें [I.15.78].

(आ) ''उचित'' हें उतर सध्याक मराठी आनी कोंकणी ह्या दोनूय भासांनी ''योग्य'' ह्या अर्थाचें विशेशण म्हूण घोळटा. पूण ब्राग संहितेंत तें ह्या अर्थान वापरिल्लें खंयच मेळना. थंय तें नाम म्हणुनूच घोळटा आनी ताचो अर्थ बक्षीस, मोबदलो बी. ख्रिस्तपुराणांत तें चडशें ह्याच अर्थान येता; इतलेंच न्हय तर ''उचितवंतु'' अशेंय एक उतर आयलां [II.42.170]. ब्राग

संहितेंतल्यो देखी : धर्मु संतोसुनु ताका उचिताक येकु लख्य द्रव्य दिलें [सप. क. 3]; आणी माका जरि सांगशात तरि तुमक ां उचित आसा [कप. क. 1]. ख्रिस्तपुराणांतल्यो देखी : कौण उचित दिधलें तेयां प्रति, तें देखिलें तुमीं [II.42.168]; देवा काय उचित देंसी मज लागोनि [I.8.209].

(इ) ''कदळी'' हें उतर मराठींत आनी संस्कृत भाशेंत केळ ह्या अर्थान आसा. पूण जितलेय कडेन हें उतर ख्रिस्तपुराणांत आयलां, तितलेय कडेन हो अर्थ, एके बायबलाचें ज्ञान आशिल्ले व्यक्तीच्या मनाक, पटपासारको ना. ''पवित्र पुस्तकांत'' साबार कडेन अंजिरेचो उल्लेख मेळटा; हांचे मदले तीन उल्लेख ख्रिस्तपुराणांत आयल्यात : (1) आदांव आनी एव पातकांत पडले उपरांत तांकां आपणालें विंगळेपण जाणवता तेन्ना तीं अंजिरेचीं पानां शिंवून आपणा खातीर पैरण तयार करतात [I. 5.5; उत्प. 3:7]; (2) नाथानियेलाक जेजु ख्रिस्त अंजिरेच्या मुळांत उभो आसतना चोयता [II.21.46; जुआंव 1:48]; (3) कांटयेच्या झाडाक अंजिरां जायनांत अशी ओपार जेजु ख्रिस्त आपल्या शिश्यांक सांगता [II.28.112; लुका 7:44].

वयल्या तिनूय प्रसंगांनी स्टीफन्स ''कदळी'' हें उतर वापरता. पूण ''केळ'' हो अर्थ एकाय संदर्भात बसना. आदिपुरुसांनी जर केळीचीं पानां वापरिल्लीं जाल्यार तांकां तीं शिंवचीं पडचीं नासलीं; हरशींय जाल्यार केळीचीं पानां शिंवूंक जायना. आनी केळीच्या मुळांत कोण उभो रावतलो? तिसऱ्या उल्लेखांत स्टीफन्साक जर ''केळीं'' म्हणपाचें आशिल्लें जाल्यार तो हेंच उतर वापरतलो आसलो, जशें ताणें II.22.33 हातूंत केलां.

अंजिरेच्याच Ficus ह्या वनस्पत कुळांतलो, ''केळ'' नांवाचो रूख गोंयात आसा; करंबली गांवकारीच्यो बसका चडश्यो ह्याच रुखामुळांत भरताल्यो.[5] स्टीफन्स ह्याच केळाची खबर करता काय? पूण लिंग बसना, आनी ह्या रुखाचीं फळां मनीस खायना. ''रुंबड'' हो त्याच कुळांतलो आनीक एक रूख आसून ताचीं फळां अंजिरा सारकींच आसात आनी तीं खातात. तरू य स्टीफन्सान ताचो वापर करूंक ना, जरूय हें उतर कोंकणी ''भारतांत'' आसा : पांडव वनवासांत आसले तेन्ना कं दमुळां आनी रुंबडां पुंजावन खाताले.

जाल्यार ''कदळी'' हाचो अर्थ हांगा नेमकोच कितें? हें उतर कोंकणी ''भारतांत'' एकेकडेन आदळटा खरें, पूण ताचो अर्थ स्पश्ट जायना. सभापर्वाचे सातवे कथेंत जगनाथ (श्रीकृष्ण) रुकमिणीचें ''कदळी व्रत'' मागून घेता आनी ताच्या आधारान द्रौपदीचें वस्त्रहरण भंग करता. परंत, हे कदळीचो अंजिरे कडेन कसलो संबंध?

अनुस्वार : हें कोंकणी भाशेचें खाशेलपण म्हूण मानतात. साबार उतरां अशीं आसात जांच्या कोंकणी रुपांत अनुस्वार आसा जाल्यार तांच्या मराठी पर्यायांत तो मेळना. देखीक, धोंतर - धोतर; पाणीं - पाणी; कोंपर - कोपर. हो एक ''नेम'' म्हणल्यार जाता, आनी फाटल्या पन्नास वर्सांच्या काळांत हो फरक आनीक तिव्र जाला; दांत, गांव, नांव असल्या उतरांतलो अनुस्वार मराठींत काडून उडयला.

अशें आसुनय कांय उतरां ह्या नेमाचे विरूध वागतात; म्हणजे मराठी उतरांत अनुस्वार आसा जाल्यार ताच्याच कोंकणी पड उतरांत अनुस्वार मेळना. देखीक, दव (म. दंव), विद्वास (म. विध्वंस), माजर (म. मांजर). असलीं कोंकणी उतरां ख्रिस्तपुराणांत आयल्यांत. देखीकः मग जें उरलें धरणी । तें सुर्ये उदेईं किरणीं । होय तेयासि विगरणी । दवाचे परी ॥ [I. 17.86]

''मांजर'' हें मराठींत अलिंगी, पूण कोंकणींत ''माजर'' हें तिनूय लिंगांनी घोळटा. ख्रिस्तपुराणांत तें पुल्लिंगी आनी अलिंग अशें वापरलां. देखी :

(अ) माजरु करी पिलेयांचा हारु [II.13.69]; (आ) येर कोश्टी जैशीं माजरें (कों. माजरां) [II.25.72]

आम्ही, तुम्ही, आमची, तुमची ह्या मराठी उतरांनी अनुस्वार ना; चालंत कोंकणींतय तो मेळना. पूण प्राचीन कोंकणींत हीं उतरां आमीं, तुमीं, आमंची, तुमंची अशींच वापरललीं मेळटात. हींच रुपां ख्रिस्तपुराणांत आसात, आनी तीं अनुस्वारा विरेत मेळच नांत. देखी: (अ) आमीं येका बापाचे पुत्र बारा [I.13.56]; (आ) जरि तुमीं भले म्हणती, तरि आणा बंदुथें [I. 13.62]; (इ) जि जि स्वामी अवधारा म्हणती, विनंति आमंची [I.13.45] (ई) तुमंचें नाणें आणिलें म्हणती, [I.14.15]. क ोंकणी ''भारतांतल्यो'' देखी : (अ) तैशेंचि आमीं करूं [गप. क. 1] (आ) तुमीं उभेचि राउनु पळ्या [गप. क. 1]; (इ) तूं आमंचो कैवारी [भिप. क. 4]; (ई) माज्या हातान तुमंचो शिरशेदु करीन [अश्वप. क. 2]

नाम विशेशण अन्वय : सध्याचे कोंकणींत आनी मराठींत अन्वया बाबतींत कसलोच फरक जाणवना. नाम विभक्तींत आसता तेन्ना ताका लागू आशिल्लें विशेशण सामान्यरुपांत आसता : काळो घोडो > काळ्या घोड्याक. आयज घोळटलीं अ-कारान्त विशेशणां जीं बदलनांत तीं प्राचीन कोंकणींत उ-कारान्त आशिल्लीं आनी वयर (उ-कारान्त उतरां संबंधीं) सांगलां तशीं, नामाच्या लिंग-वचना प्रमाणें बदलतालीं. हीच पद्दत ख्रिस्तपुराणांत पळेवंक मेळटा. देखी : स्रस्टा मनुष्याच्या कुमरासि आरोग्य दिधलें [II.24 माथाळो]; येकाद्या व्यादिस्टा प्राणिया वैद्यु वोसद दावितो [II.24.55]; ते पवित्री कथेची विवचना [II.28.122]; तूं जिवंता देवाचा कुमरु [II.46.151]; येणें साच जाहाली बोली प्रोफेता इसायाची [II.49.80]

नाम भोववचनांत आसल्यार लेगीत, चालंत कोंकणींत तशें मराठींत, विशेशणाचें सामान्यरूप एकवचनांतूच उरता : काळे घोडे > काळ्या घोड्यांक. पूण कांय क्रिस्तांव बोलयांनी (आनी ''पवित्र पुस्तकांतूय'') नाम भोववचनांत आसल्यार ताचें विशेशणय भोवचन सामान्यरुपांत आसता; म्हणजे, ''काळ्यां घोड्यांक'' देखीक, हालींच्या एका नेमाळ्यांतलें हें वाक्य पळेवंचें: ''संवसारांतल्यां असल्यां अप्रमाणीक मुकदमांच्यां कर्तुबांक लागून तांच्यां कुटुंबांक फावो जाल्ल्या वायटा विशीं पापा फ्रांसिस्क उलयतालो.'' हीच पद्दत प्राचीन कोंकणींत सगळे कडेन आदळटा. देखी : (अ) ऐसो निरोपु जाइत खेवीं परमेश्वराचे कृपेस्तंव सातां खणांचीं, आटां खणांचीं उतमां दामोधरां ततुखेणा भितरि बांदिलीं [वैप. क. 5]; (आ) फुडां पांचइ पांडव त्यां रथांरि आरुडले [भिप. क. 5]; (इ) आठांइ दिसां ठाउनु बाण येऊं लागले [द्रूप. क. 2]. ख्रिस्तपुराणांत ही पद्दत सर्रास मेळटा. कांय उदाहरणांः (अ) पैल्यां सातां वरुसां भितुरि [I.12.114]; (आ) पापियां मनुष्यांथें पाहुनि [II. 44.134] ह्यां माज्यां बंदू मधिल्या येकासि [II.44.133].

प्राचीन कोंकणींत आनीक एक विचित्र शी पद्दत पळेवंक मेळटा. नाम एकवचनी पांचवे विभक्तींत आसता तेन्ना ताचें विशेशण भोववचनी सामान्यरुपांत हाजीर रावता : (अ) ह्या वृख्याच्यां मुळांतु येकु माहा रुशेस्परु बैसला [अश्वप. क. 3] (आ) त्या अस्तनापुरिचां नगरांतु पावतचि रात्रिचोचि डांगिरो फिराइ [गप. क. 2]. हीच पद्दत ख्रिस्तपुराणांत वापरल्याः (अ) पाहुनि तुज्यां एजिप्तांतु, कार्य द्यावें तेया हातीं [I.12.113]; (आ) तुजे स्त्रियेचां उधरीं, पुत्रु होइल तुजां घरीं [II.4.32]; (इ) धन्य चरण माजां मंधिरीं लागले तुजे [II.6.19]; (ई) मध्यान रात्रिचां वेळीं, घनु वरुषणाचां प्रभळीं [II.7.78]; (उ) तदीं लागोनि माजा स्नेहु तुजां चितीं, लागला देवा [II.3.45].

ह्या सामान्यरुपां फाटलें कारण जाणकारांक सतायता.

पूण अन्वयाचे बाबतींत जनर्धन[4] जी फोडणिशी दिता, तातूंत हाची जाप सरळ मेळटा : काळो घोडो > काळ्या(क) घोड्याक; वापरांत विशेशण विभक्तीरुपांतलें (हांगा कंसांत दाखयलां तें) निमाणें अक्षर गळून पडटा आनी ''काळ्या घोड्याक'' अशें जाता. नाम भोववचनांत आसता तेन्ना, काळे घोडे > काळ्यां(क) घोड्यांक जाता, आनी विशेशणांतलें निमाणें अक्षर गळटा तेन्ना अनुस्वार गळना, तो निमाणचे आदल्या आक्षरांत आसून कायम रावता. देखून, ''काळ्यां घोड्यांक''. तेच परीं पांचवे विभक्तींत काळो घोडो > काळ्यां(त) घोड्यांत अशें जाता, आनी निमाणें अक्षर गळ्ळे उपरांत, अनुस्वार आदल्या अक्षराचेर कायम उरता, ''काळ्यां घोड्यांक'' हातूंत उरता तसोच. म्हणजे, हें सामान्यरूप भोवचनी कशें दिसता जायत, पूण तें एक वचनीच.

स्टीफन्साक ह्या तंत्राची जाणीव आशील्ली म्हणपाक वाव आसा; जंय ''आंतु'' हें नामाच्या सामान्यरुपा पासून वेगळें बरयलां, थंय विशेशणाच्या सामान्यरुपांत अनुस्वार फकत भोववचनांत येता. देखीकः कुडि नेली पैल्या कुडा आंतु [II. 50.177]; की उतमा कळपा आंतु [II.44.223]; तेयां दिवसांच्यां कश्टां आंतु [II.43.134].

ख्रिस्तपुराण मुळांत कोंकणी?

हें सबंद प्रकरण नियाळ्ळे अंतीं एक अनिवार्य निश्कर्श फाट सोडिना : उतरावळीचे तशेंच व्याकरणाचे बाबतींत, ख्रिस्तपुराणांत कोंकणीचो बरोच मोठो वांटो आसा. आनी थंयसून एक शंका - न्हय खात्रीच - मनांत प्रकर्शान उभी जाले बगर रावना :- स्टीफन्सान हें पुराण आदीं प्राचीन कोंकणी गद्यांत बरयलें आनी मागीर ताचें मराठी पद्यांत रुपांतर केलें कय? हय जाल्यार, ताणें अशें कित्याक केलें?

थळावे भाशेंत आनी लिपींतल्यान पुस्तकां छापून उजवाडावपाची आपणाली इत्सा 5 डिसेंबर 1608 दिसा पाद्रि क्लावदियुस आक्वावीव ह्या जेजुइत संघाच्या व्हडिलाक बरयल्ले चिटींत, स्टीफन्सान उक्तायल्ली आनी ते विशीं आदार-आशिर्वाद मागिल्लो.

थळावी भास म्हळ्यार कोंकणी हीच, हे विशीं दुमत ना. त्या काळार गोंयकानडी लिपीच तेन्नाच्या गोंयची ''देशी लिपी'' आशिल्ली आनी सरकारी दस्तावेजांनी हेच लिपीचो उल्लेख "Letra da terra" असो जाला.[5] गांवकारींच्या बसकांचीं इतिवृत्तांच न्हय तर थंय हाजीर आशिल्ल्या गांवकारांच्यो निशाण्यो लागीत हेच लिपींत आसताल्यो. मिशोनारींनी थळावे लिपींत बरयललें एकच कोंकणी पुस्तक आसा - फ्रेय आमादोर द सांक्ता आना हांचें "Flos sanctorum" वो ''सांतांच्यो जिणो''- आनी तें गोंयकानडी लिपींत आसा. तें 1607 वर्सा बरोवन जाल्लें. तर स्टीफन्सचें पुराणय तेच गोंयकानडींत बरयलले कोंकणींत आसप सभावीक जावपाचें. पूण तें आयलें मराठींत आनी रोमी लिपींत. अशें कशें? स वर्सांच्या काळांत स्टीफन्सचें धोरण इतलें कशें बदल्लें?

लिपीफाटलें एक कारण ते चिटींतय आयलां; थळावे लिपीचे खिळे तयार करपांत तांकां अपेस आयलें. शिवाय, हें पुस्तक बरोवन तयार जाल्लें त्याच वर्सांत पुर्तुगेजांनी थळावे लिपीचो उपेग हळू हळू काबार करपाचें पयलें पावल मारिल्लें; गांवकारींचीं इतिवृत्तां पुर्तुगेजींत बरोवचीं म्हूण ताकीद दिल्ली.[5] आनीक म्हळ्यार तेन्ना स्टीफन्सची पिराय 65 चेर पाविल्ल्यान खिळ्यांची वाट पळेत बसप शाणपणाचें जावचें नाशिल्लें. देखून ताणें, ना इलाजान, रोमी लिपी आपणायली.

आपल्या पुराणाचो हेतू ताणेंच पयल्या अवेस्वरांत (ओवी 154 -165) स्पश्ट केलाः जेजु ख्रिस्ताची जीण आनी कार्य, ताच्या येण्याची फाटभूंय तशेंच क्रिस्तांव धर्माचीं आदिमुल्यां नव्या क्रिस्तांवां मेरेन थोडक्यांत पावोवप. ही मोख कोंक णींतल्यानूच साध्य जावंयेताली देखून तशेंच ताणें केलें आसतलें, म्हणजे कोंकणी गद्यांत बरयलें आसतलें; कारण ताका क ोंकणी पद्याचो एकूय नमुनो मेळूंक नाशिल्लो. मराठींत तर पद्याचेच नमुने मेळिल्ले. पूण ताचे द्रश्टे बुधीन आनीक एक तथ्य पारखिलें.

आपणाले भाशेंत वाचिल्ली वो वाचून दाखयलली गजाल श्रोत्याक बरी समजता हातूंत दुभाव ना. पूण ती ताच्या ध्यानांत कि तलो वेळ तिगून उरता? तीच गजाल गावून दाखयली जाल्यार श्रोत्याच्या ध्यानांत चड वेळ उरता तें जालेंच; तो ती आपणाल्या मनांत आडवर गुणगुणायत रावलो जाल्यार ती गजाल ताच्या मनांत घर करून रावता. देखून तें पुराण पद्यांत, गायनाच्या स्वरुपांत, सादर करपाचें ताणें थारायलें जायत. त्या काळार, पुराय अस्तंत भारतांत एक धर्मीक प्रथा वसताली; लोक देवळांनी, घुमट्यां लागीं जावं मांडार एकठांय येवन भजनां करताले. हातूंत मराठी संत कवींचीं अभंगां आनी ओवयो गावप जाताले. (हांवें ही प्रथा गुजरातांतल्या एका पयसुल्या खेड्यांत प्रत्यक्ष पळेल्या. निराक्षर आदिवासी तीं भजनां गायतात.) गोंयांतूय ही प्रथा चालंत आशिल्ली म्हणपाक कसलीच अडचण ना. क्रिस्तांव जाल्ल्या गोंयकारांक त्या गायनांची चाल संवकळीची आशिल्लीच. तर त्याच छंदांत आनी तेच भाशेंत आपलें पुराण बरयलें जाल्यार आपणाली मोख वेगीं साक ार जायत म्हणपाचें ताका कळून आयलें आसतलें. शिवाय, गद्यांत बरयललें फकत शिक्षितां मेरेन पावता जाल्यार गायन अशिक्षीत मधिमा लोकां मेरेनय पावता. तेच खातीर ताणें तें मराठी पद्यांत, ओवी छंदांत रुपांतरीत केलें; पूण चडांत चड भाविकांक समजुंचें म्हणून चडसो भाग कोंकणीच दवरलो, अशें दिसता. ह्या अनुमानाक गवाय म्हूण साबार ओवयो दाखोवंयेत - वळेरी बरीच लांब जातली! पूण पयल्या पुराणांतलो सातवो अवेस्वर - प्रळयाची कथा - चिकित्सायेन वाचून पळेवंचो; पुराय कोंकणी आसा, कांय उतरांचें मराठीकरण मात्र जालां.

हें अनुमान जर खरें थारलें जाल्यार स्टीफन्सचें विधान लटकें थारचें ना? ना, ताच्या हिसपांत तरी ना! कोंकणी उतरांचेर मराठी भेस चडयतकच तीं कोंकणी उरनांत, मराठी किंवा ''मराठीछन्न'' जातात. तशें आसल्यार आपणें ठांय ठांय कोंकणी उतरां भरसून कवित्व सोंपें केलें, अशें कित्याक म्हणलें? तर हांगा तो बदलिनासताना कोंकणीच दवरिल्ल्या उतरांची खबर करता, जीं हांगा थंय, ठांय ठांय, आडळटात. पूण मराठीछन्न कोंकणी उतरां ठांय ठांय न्हय तर चांटे पावलाक गावतात. इतलेंच न्हय तर कांय उतरां पयल्या पुराणांत कोंकणी रुपांत आसात जाल्यार दुसऱ्यांत मराठीछन्न. देखीक, (1) जाइ जूइ [I.30.39], जाती जुती [II.40.184] ; (2) शिर्को [I.35.63], सिर्का [II.49.164].

स्टीफन्सची मोख साकार जाल्ली :

वयर वर्णिल्यात त्या कारणांक लागून मराठी शिकूंक नाशिल्ल्या साश्टींतल्या साद्या क्रिस्तांवाक ख्रिस्तपुराणाचो चडावत भाग सहज समजुंये असो आसा म्हणलें जाल्यार अतिताय थारची ना. फाटल्या चार शेंकड्यांच्या काळांत कोंकणी भाशेंत पुस्कळ बदल जाल्यात. हाका लागून तांतुतलीं बरींचशीं उतरां आयज घोळणुकेंतल्यान भायर पडल्यांत. हीं उतरां त्या काळार तयार केल्ल्या उतरावळींनी, खास करून दियोगु रिबैराच्या कोशांत, कोंकणी उतरां म्हणून मेळटात. हाचो अर्थ असो जाता की त्या काळावेल्या साश्टीकार क्रिस्तांवांक हो ग्रंथ पुरायपणीं समजला आसतलो. म्हणजे थॉमस स्टीफन्सान बाळगिल्ली मोख पुराय सफळ जाली आसतली, हातूंत शंका ना.

त्याच कारणांक लागून मराठी भास शिकिल्ल्या आयच्या महाराष्ट्री मनशांक हो ग्रंथ समजूंक बरेंच कठीण वता जाल्यार हातूंत अजाप जावंची गरज ना. दोनूय भासांनी साबार अशीं उतरां आसात जांचे अर्थ परस्पर भासांनी वेगळे आसात. ह्या ग्रंथांत साबार कोंकणी उतरां आसात जीं मराठी भाशेंत मेळनांत. शिवाय कांय सम दिसपी, पूण वेगळ्या अर्थाचीं, उतरां हो गोंदळ वाडयतात. हाका लागून कांय ओवींचे बाबतींत मराठी शिकिल्ल्या एका महाराष्ट्री क्रिस्तांव मनशाचो लेगीत गैरसमज जाता. क ांय देखी :

(क) I.1.14.3 : दुखियांचा बुजवणारु. खरो अर्थ : दुखेस्तांचो बुजवणार, सांत्वन करणार. फलकाव[6] हांणी दिल्लो अर्थ : सर्व दुःख दूर करणारा. हाचें कारण म्हळ्यार मराठींत बुजवणे हें उतर आसा पूण ताचो अर्थ सांत्वन करप असो जायना, तर बंद करप, पयसावप असोच जाता.

(ख) I.2.41 : चोउं भुतां वरुतें काय केलें। तेया सोभवंतें आकास रचिलें। चंद्रयाचे परी विस्तारिलें। विसाळ बरवें॥ खरो अर्थ : च्यारूय भुतां वयर कितें केलें? तांचे सभोंवतें आकाश (मळब) रचलें. तें चंद्राव्या परीं विशाळ बरें विस्तारायलें. फलक ाव हांणी दिल्लो अर्थ : चार महाभुतां नंतर काय केले? तर त्यांच्याभोवती आकाश रचले. ते चंद्रामा प्रमाणे विस्तारले. चांगले विशाल केले. हो अणकार तर्काक पटना. मळब तर धरतरेचें पाखें जाल्ल्यावरी पसरता जाल्यार चंद्र तातुंतलो एक गोलक मात्र. तो पसरूंक शकना. तर ''मळब चंद्रावरी पसरलें'' म्हणूंक जायत? एका माटवाचें सुंदर पाखे म्हळ्यार चांदवो. हाचे क डेन मळबाक सर करून स्टीफन्सान एक उत्कृष्ट उपमा दिल्या. प्राचीन कोंकणी भारतांत हें उतर कांय कडेन आयलां. देखीक , ऐशी सभा विचित्रि करुनु मखमलाचे चंद्राये त्यावरि बांदिले. [सप. क. 2].

(ग) I.8.114 : स्वामियाची अनुज्ञा न्हवे तरि। गिर्बुजी पण नपडे भुमि वरि। ऐशें मागां पवित्र पुराणा भितुरि। बोलिला जेजु स्वामी॥ अर्थ : स्वाम्याच्या हुकमा विरेत, एक गिर्बुजी सुद्दां भूंय पडना, अशें जेजू स्वाम्यान फाटीं पवित्र पुराणांत म्हणलां. (पळेयात मातेव 10:29). फलकाव : स्वामीच्या आज्ञेशिवाय विड्याच्या झाडाचे पान देखील भूमीवर पडत नाही. अशे मागे येशू ख्रिस्ताने पवित्र पुराणात सांगितले आहे. कारण : गिर्बुजी हें उतर मराठींत ना. ते खातीर चिमणी हें आसा. देखून पण हाचें मार्सडेन प्रतींत ''पान'' जालां तें पळेवन तें विड्याचें पान अशें धरलें जायत. हें अंतर मात फलकाव हांणी विसंगतींचे वळेरेंत (पाठभेदांचे सुचींत, परिशिश्ट 6) दिवंक ना.

(घ) I.10.33 : बोकडियांचे कळप घरीं। दास आणी दासरी। गर्धवें आणी करीं। अप्रमितें॥ अर्थ : (ताच्या) घरांत बोकड्यो, दास, दाशी, गाढवां आनी उंटां अपरमीत आसलीं. [उत्प. 30:43]. फलकाव : त्याचे घरीं मेंढ्यांचे कळप होते आणि नानापरीची कामे करण्यासाठी खूप दास व दासी होत्या. कारण : मार्सडन प्रतींत ''गर्धवे आणी करीं'' हाचे बदला, ''कितेक कामाचे नानापरी'' अशें बरयलां.

(ङ) I.11.50 : तुर्मी विस नार्णी दिधलीं रुपेयाचीं। मीं विस नार्णी सोनेयाचीं। आणी आगळीं घ्याल लाभाचीं। तरि मीं देइन॥ अर्थ : तुमी रुप्याचीं वीस नार्णी दिल्यांत. हांव तुमकां भांगराचीं वीस नार्णी, आनी कळंतराचीं आगळीं घेशात जाल्यार, तींय दीन. फलकाव : तुम्ही चांदीची वीस नाणी दिली आहेत. मी सोन्याची वीस नाणी देतो आणि तुम्हाला जर जास्ती पाहिजेत असेल, तर मी ते तुम्हाला देईन. कारण : लाभ हाका कोंकणींत कळंतर असो जो अर्थ आसा, तो मराठींत ना; फ ायदो इतलोच आसा.

(च) I.12.117 : ऐशें योज़ेन बोलिलें। तें उतर रायाशि मानलें। मंत्री प्रधान तोज पातले। सभा आदी करोनि॥ अर्थ : अशें जुज़ेन उलयल्लें उत्तर राजाक मानलें. सभेसयत मंत्री प्रधान अजाप जाले. फलकाव : योसेफ असे बोलला. ते उत्तर राजाने मानले. मंत्री आणि प्रधान, सभाजन व इतर लोक यांना बोलावले. कारण : तोज पातले हें उतर मराठींत ना, पूण ब्राग संहितें तले कोंकणींत मेळटा.

(छ) I.15.133.3-4 : तेणें आइकोनि आमंच्या चिता। अतोज जाहालें. अर्थ : तें आयकून आमच्या मनांत अजाप जालें. फ लकाव : ती ऐकून आमच्या मनाला खूप आनंद झाला. कारण : अतोज हें उतर आयचे मराठींत जावं कोंकणींत मेळना. पूण प्राचीन कोंकणी भारतांत हें उतर साबार कडेन अजाप ह्या अर्थान आयलां. देखीक, तो नवलावो देखुनु राजा (दुर्योधन) अतोज करूं लागलो. [सप. क.7]

(ज) I.29.26 : जैसा पिता पुत्रासि लावेया शिखा (शिक्षा)। करुनु ठेवी दंडकु निका। तैशें ते प्रजेशि शिखा लावेया आइका। देवें ता लोकु ठेविला॥ अर्थ : जसो बापूय (आपल्या) पुताक ख्यास्त लावंक एक बरोसो दांडुको (बडी) दवरता, तसोच ते प्रजेक ख्यास्त लावंक देवान तो लोक दवरलो. [इजा. 10.5-6]. फलकाव : जसे पिता पुत्राला शिकवण्यासाठी काही कायदे करून ठेवतो, तसे प्रजेला शिकवण्यासाठी देवाने 'देवलोक' ठेवला होता. कारण : ''शिक्षा'' ह्या उतराक ''ख्यास्त'' हो अर्थ घेनास्तना, शिक्षण असोच घेतला. शिवाय ''दंडकु निका'' हाचो अर्थ ''दंड संहिता'' असोच धरला काय दिसता. पूण हांगा जे प्रजेक ख्यास्त लायली ती म्हळ्यार इज्राएली प्रजा आनी ते खातीर ज्या लोकांक वापरले ते काल्देयी लोक. (काल्देय म्हणजे आसिरिया हो दक्षिण बाबिलोनीचो वाठार.) बायबलांत जितलेय कडेन ''देवलोक' उतर वापरलां तें इज्राएली प्रजे खातीरच. इजा.10:5-6 हातूंत अशें बरयल्लें मेळटा : ''..... म्हज्या रागाची बेतकाठी जो (आसिरियाचो राजा), ताच्या हातांत आसा म्हज्या क्रोधाचो दांडो.'' शिवाय त्याच अवेस्वराचे 23 वे ओवींत त्या काळावेल्या इज्राएली राजाचें नांव ओसेया अशें दिलां. हांगा वर्णिल्या ती घडणूक 2 राजा 17: 1-19. हातूंत आसा.

(झ) II.1.30 : तूं जेजू ख्रिस्ताचे कृपे सरी। गेनेसरे साघरा माजारीं। चालिनला उदका वरि। भावार्थाचेनि बळें॥ अर्थ : जेजू ख्रिस्ताचे कृपेन, भावार्थाच्या बळान गेनसरेत सागरा मर्दी तूं उदकाचेर चलून गेला. [मातेव 14:29]. फलकाव : येशु ख्रिस्ताच्या कृपेमुळे, तुझ्या श्रद्धेच्या बळावर गेनेसरेतच्या ज्ञानसागराच्या पाण्यामध्ये चाललास. कारण : ''माजारीं'' ह्या कोंक णी उतराचो अर्थ मध्ये असो केला; शिवाय गेनेसरेत म्हळ्यार एक खरेलो सरोवर आसून, तो काल्पनीक ज्ञानसागर न्हय.

(ञ) II.4.25 : येर लोक होंते समस्त। ते बाहिर उभे राहांत। स्वामियाचें चिंतन करित। प्रजा सकळी॥ अर्थ : हेर लोक जे आसले, ते भायर उबे रावून सगळी प्रजा स्वामियाचें चिंतन करताली. [लुकास 1:10]. फलकाव : तेथील इतर लोक बाहेर उभे राहिले. ते प्रात:काळी स्वामीचे चिंतन करीत होते. कारण ''सकळी'' (सगळी) हें कोंकणी उतर सकाळीं अशें वाचलें क ाय दिसता.

(ट) II.20.114 : मिरीं तिखी तेथोनि। येळ काराफूल घेउनि। आणिती तारुवें भरुनि। यां देशीं॥ अर्थ : थंयसून मिरयां, तिखी (दालचिनी), येळ, काराफुलां तारवां भरून हाडटात ह्या देसाक. फलकाव : तेथील मिरे, तिखट मिरची, वेलदोडे, लवंगा जहाजे भरून या देशात घेऊन येतात. कारण : ''काराफूल'' हें कोंकणी उतर लवंग म्हणून सारकें पारखिलां जाल्यार ''तिखी'' हें सारकें समजूंक ना. हीच चूक II.22.34 हातुंतूय केल्या; तिखी हाचो अर्थ मिरच्या असो केला.

(ठ) II.21.32.1 : सिमाउं तूं योनाचा कुमरु । अर्थ : शिमांव, तूं योनाचो पूत. [मातेव 16:17]. फलकाव : ''तू कोणाचा मुलगा?'' कारण : ही चूक मार्सडन प्रतींत जाल्या.

(ड) II.25.66.3-4 : येकांचीं पाउलें भिन होउनि। कुंटि काडिती॥ अर्थ : थोड्यांचीं पावलां फांटून, ते कुंट्टाले. फलकाव : एकाचे पाय उलटे सुलटे होते. कारण : मराठींत ''कुंटणे'' अशें उतर ना; आसा तें कुटणे = धाडावन चुरो करप. साश्टींतले कोंकणींत ''कुटप'' आनी ''कुंटप'' (लंगडप) हीं वेगळीं उतरां. हांगा ''कुंटि'' हें कुटील अशें धरलां काय दिसता. शिवाय प्राचीन कोंकणींत येक (भो. व.) हाचो अर्थ कांय असोच जाता.

(ण) II.31.19 : ते वेळीं हेरोदिची सुंवळी सुंधरि। जी कां फिलिपाची अंतौरी। हिरौनी नेली आपुलां घरीं। हेरोदी रायें॥ अर्थ : त्या वेळार हेरोदिची सुंदरि धाकटी भावज, जी आसली फिलिपाची पतीण, तिका राजा हेरोदीन हिरावन आपल्या घरा व्हेल्ली. [मातेव 14:3 - हेरोदियास म्हणलले, आपल्या भावा फिलिपाचे बायलेक लागून]. फलकाव : त्यावेळी हेरादाची गोड आवाज आसलेली पत्नी, जी फिलिपाची बायको होती तिला हेरोदने पळवून घरी नेले होते. कारण : ''सुंवळी'' हें कोंकणी उतर मराठींत ना. ताका ''गोड आवाजाची'' असो जो अर्थ लायला तो खंयच मेळना.

(त) II.35.9.1 : तेथ गरा घालि जळा आंतु। अर्थ : थंय उदकांत गरो घाल. [मातेव 17:27-दर्यांत वचून गरी घाल]. फ लकाव : तेथे पाण्यात जाळे टाक. कारण ''जळ'' (उदक) हें जाळें म्हूण वाचलें काय दिसता.

(थ) II.42.148 : तेचि वेळां साउं पेद्रुथें। बंदी घातला तेयाथें। तो सोडविला देवदुतें। बंदी पासोनि॥ अर्थ : त्याच वेळार सांव पेद्रूक बंदखणींत घाल्लो. ताका बंदखणींतल्यान देवदुतान सोडयलो. [ध.इ. 12:6-10]. फलकाव : त्याच वेळी भक्त पेत्राला तुरुंगात टाकले. त्याला देवाच्या पुत्राने तुरूंगातून सोडविले. कारण : फल्कावान दिल्ल्या मार्सडन उतान्यांत ''देवदूतें'' हाचे सुवातेर ''देवसुतें'' अशें आयलां, पूण हो फरक मात परिशिष्ट 6 हातूंत दाखोवंक ना.

(द) II.59.14 : लोहित वस्त्र लुळे भुजां वरि। करचरणीं आणी पासोळी सरी। पांच घाये केंपुंचे परी मिरवताति॥ अर्थ : तांबडें वस्त्र खांदांचेर लोळटा, हातां पांयां आनी कडवळार पांच घाये केंपूं भशेन मिरवतात. फलकाव : लाल वस्त्र हातांवर होते. हातापायांवर व कुशीत जखमा (कांचनाप्रमाणे) शोभत होत्या. कारण : साश्टींतले कोंकणींत खांदाच्या तोंकाक भूज म्हणटात. मराठींत (आनी ''कोंकणींतूय'') भूज म्हणजे बावळो. दोनूय भुजांचेर एक वस्त्र घालें जाल्यार तें खांदाचेरच आसचें पडटा, बावळ्यांचेर न्हय. पूण ''हात'' हो अर्थ सामकोच चुकता, खास करून हेच ओवींत हाताचोय उल्लेख जाल्ल्या क ारणान. मराठी ''भुजा'' हाचो इंग्लिश अर्थ arm असो मेळटा. हाचेवेल्यान ''हात'' हो अर्थ काडला जायत. ''केंपु'' हें उतर मराठींत ना. ह्याच खड्याक कोंकणींत ''माणीक'' म्हणटात आनी हें उतर मराठींत आसा. हें वापरी नासताना ''क ांचन'' (भांगर) कित्याक वापरलें म्हूण समजना.

हांगा एक गजाल विचारांत घेवंक जाय. डॉ. फादर नेल्सन फलकाव हो एक सामान्य व्यक्ती न्हय. एक मराठी भाशीक अभ्यासू आनी व्यासंगी पाद्री आसून तांणी इशज्ञानांत पिएच.डी. पदवी जोडल्या आनी तत्वज्ञान तशेंच ईशज्ञान ह्या विशयांचे प्रोफेसर आसात. शिवाय कातोल्क धार्मीक विशयांचेर साबार पुस्तकां आनी सोदप्रबंध बरयल्यात. हाचे वेल्यान तांचें बायबल गिन्यान अदमासूंक जाता. तरूय आसताना तांकां जर ख्रिस्तपुराण पुरायेन समजूंक ना जाल्यार सामान्य मराठी भाशीक वाचप्याक तो ग्रंथ बरोच कठीण वता हातूंत दुभाव उरना.

प्राचीन कोंकणी भारतांतलीं पर्वां : (कंसात दिल्ले संक्षेप) अरप = अरण्यपर्व; अश्वप = अश्वमेधपर्व; आप.= आदिपर्व; कप= कर्णपर्व; गप= गदापर्व; द्रूप = द्रूण पर्व; भिप= भिष्मपर्व; वैप.= वैराट पर्व; सप. = सभापर्व.

आधारग्रंथ :

1. **कृष्णदास शामा आनी सांगाती –** Codex nos. 771, 772, 773. अप्रकाशीत. मूळ बाडां मिञु विद्यापीठ ग्रंथालय, पुर्तुगाल हांगा उपलब्ध आसात. झेरॉक्स प्रती कृष्णदास शामा केंद्रीय ग्रंथालय, पणजी हांगा उपलब्ध आसात.

2. (अ) Diogo Ribeiro - **Vocabulario Concani Portugues, Portugues-Concani.** (1526) अप्रकाशीत.

(आ) Padres da Companhia : **Vocabulario Concani Portugues; Portugues-Concani** अप्रकाशीत. चारूय ग्रंथ कृ ष्णदास शामा केंद्रीय ग्रंथालय, पणजी हांगा उपलब्ध आसात.

3. Rocky V. Miranda - **The Old Konkani Bharata. Vol I.** (2011). Central Institute of Indian Languages Mysore. Vol. II. and III ready for Publication.

4. P.B. Janardhan - **A Higher Konkani Grammar.** (1991). Madras

5. G.S.S. Ghantkar - **History of Goa Through Goykannadi script.** (1993). Rajhans Vitaran, Panaji

6. डॉ. फादर नेल्सन फलकाव - **फादर थॉमस स्टीफन्सकृत ख्रिस्तपुराण.** (२००९). ख्रिस्तु ज्योती पब्लिकेशन्स, बेंगलुरू.

Pratap Naik S.J. was the director of the Thomas Stephens Konknni Kendr, Porvorim which houses a collection of old Konkani material. His publications include Zudas-Ekanki Nattok, *an account of Judas's perfective of the Christ story.* Machi Mogi, *2007, a translation of* Isopacheo kannio, *co-translated with Shilpa Salvi, Dalgado Konknni Akademi, 2012, lyrics for* Bhakti Sobhann, *Konkani songs recorded with Eric Ozario, by Mandd Sobhann, and various language learning texts. His essay 'Bhashantharachim Thathvamani Kala' (Principles of translation and art) was published in* Amar Konkani.

His essay addresses the position of translation in literature, its definition, types of translations, and principles of translation. He ends with a note on the need for translations into Konkani.

Translated literature is a third category of literature according to him, folklore being the first and creative literature being the second. Different words are used to indicate the word 'translation' in Konkani such as tharjumo, tharjann, anuvaad, annkaar, rupanthar, bhashanthar *which mean summarise, examine, repetition by way of explanation, copying, adaptation and translation respectively. The different types of translations include* shabdanuvaad *or literal translation,* anukarannvaad *or imitation and* rupanthar *or adaptation.*

ಭಾಷಾಂತರಾಚಿಂ ತತ್ವಾಂ ಆನಿ ಕಲಾ

ಪ್ರತಾಪ್ ನಾಯ್ಕ್, ಜೆ.ಸ. ತೊಮಾಸ್ ಸ್ಟೀವನ್ಸ್ ಕೊಂಕ್ಣಿ ಕೇಂದ್ರ್ ಆಲ್ತ್ ಪರ್ವರಿ, ಗೊಂಯ್

ಪ್ರಸ್ತಾವನ್

ಸಂಸಾರಾಂತ್ಲಿ ಖಂಯ್ಚಿಯ್ ಭಾಸ್ ಆಮಿ ಘೆತ್ಲಿ ಜಾಲ್ಯಾರ್ ತಿ ಭಾಸ್ ಪಯ್ಲಿ ಮನ್ಶ್ಯಾಂ ಉಲಯ್ತಾತ್ ಆನಿ ಉಪ್ರಾಂತ್ ಗರ್ಜ್ ಮ್ಹಣುನ್ ದಿಸ್ಲ್ಯಾರ್ ತಿ ಬರಯ್ತಾತ್. ಭಾಸ್ ಉಲಯ್ತಾನಾ ಧ್ವನಿಂಚೊ (speech sounds) ವಾಪರ್ ಜಾತಾ. ಬರಯ್ತಾನಾ ಕುರ್ಹಾಂಚೊ ವಾಪರ್ ಜಾತಾ. ಭಾಸ್ ಎಕಾ ಸಮಾಜಾಚೊ, ಸಂಸ್ಕೃತೆಚೊ ಗರ್ಜೆಚೊ ವಾಂಟೊ. ಮನಿಸ್ ಜೆದ್ನಾಂ ಹೆರಾಂ ವಿಶಿಂ ಸಮ್ಜುನ್ ಘೆಂವ್ಕ್ ಸೊಧ್ತಾ ತೆದ್ನಾಂ ತಾಕಾ ತ್ಯಾ ಲೊಕಾಚಿ ಭಾಸ್ ಯೆಂವ್ಚಿ ಪಡ್ತಾ. ಜರ್ ತಾಕಾ ತಿ ಭಾಸ್ ಯೆನಾ ತೆದ್ನಾಂ ತೆ ಭಾಶೆಚಿ ಮಾಹಿತಿ ಭಾಷಾಂತರ್ ಕರುನ್ ಕೊಣೆಂ ತರ್‌ಯಿ ದಿಂವ್ಚಿ ಪಡ್ತಾ. ಹೆರ್ ಭಾಸಾಂಚಿ ಮಾಹಿತಿ ಆಪ್ಲೆ ಭಾಶೆಂತ್ ಮೆಳುಂಕ್ ಭಾಷಾಂತರ್ ಹೆಂ ಏಕ್ ಉಪಯುಕ್ತ್ ಮಾಧ್ಯಮ್. ಭಾಷಾಂತರ್ ತೊಂಡಿ (oral) ವಾ ಲಿಖಿತ್ (written) ಆಸುಂ ಯೆತಾ.

0.1 ಭಾಷಾಂತರಾಚೆಂ ಸ್ಥಾನ್

ಎಕೆ ಭಾಶೆಚ್ಯಾ ಸಾಹಿತ್ಯಾಚೆ ವಾಡಾವಳಿಕ್ ತೀನ್ ಮುಖೆಲ್ ಪ್ರಕಾರಾಂಚ್ಯಾ ಸಾಹಿತ್ಯಾಚಿ ಚಡ್ ಗರ್ಜ್ ಆಸಾ.

ಪಯ್ಲೊ ಪ್ರಕಾರ್: ಲೋಕ್‌ವೇದ್ (folklore). ಹಾಂತುಂ ಲೊಕಾಚ್ಯೊ ಕಾಣಿಯೊ, ಸಾಂಗ್ಣ್ಯೊ, ಮ್ಹಣಿ, ಹುಮಾಣಿಂ, ಮಾಗ್ಣಿಂ, ಗಿತಾಂ ಇತ್ಯಾದಿ ಆಟಾಪ್ತಾತ್. ಸರ್ವ್ ಭಾಸಾಂನಿ ಲೋಕ್‌ವೇದ್ ಆಸಾ ಆನಿ ತೊ ಲೊಕಾಚ್ಯಾ ತೊಂಡಾರ್ ಚಡ್ ಘೊಳ್ತಾ. ಹೆಂ ಸಾಹಿತ್ಯ್ ಲೊಕಾಚಿ ಸಂಸ್ಕೃತಿ, ತಾಂಚೆ ಭಾಶೆಚೆಂ ಖಾಶೆಲೆಪಣ್ (uniqueness),

ತಾಂಚ್ಯಾ ಚಿಂತ್ಪಾಚಿ ರೀತ್, ಭೊಗ್ಣಾಂಚಿ–ಭಾವನಾಂ ರೀತ್ ಆನಿ ತಿಂ ಉಗ್ತಾವ್ಪಾಚಿ ತರಿ ಹಾಂಚೆರ್ ಉಜ್ವಾಡ್ ಘಾಲ್ತಾ.

ದುಸ್ರೊ ಪ್ರಕಾರ್: ಸರ್ಜನಾತ್ಮಕ್ ಸಾಹಿತ್ಯ್ (Creative literature) ಭಾಶೆಚ್ಯಾ ಬರೊವ್ಪ್ಯಾಂನಿ ನಿರ್ಮಾಣ್ ಕೆಲ್ಲ್ಯಾ ಹ್ಯಾ ಪ್ರಕಾರಾಂತ್ ಕಥಾ, ಕಾದಂಬರಿ, ಕವಿತಾ, ನಾಟಕ್, ಆತ್ಮ್‌ಕಥಾ, ಜಿವಿತ್‌ಕಥಾ, ಪ್ರವಾಸ್ ವರ್ಣನ್ ಇತ್ಯಾದಿ ಆಸ್ಪಾವ್ತಾತ್.

ತಿಸ್ರೊ ಪ್ರಕಾರ್: ಭಾಷಾಂತರ್ ಸಾಹಿತ್ಯ್. ಹೆರ್ ಭಾಸಾಂ ಥಾವ್ನ್ ಭಾಷಾಂತರ್ ಜಾಲ್ಲೆಂ ಸಾಹಿತ್ಯ್. ಸಂಸಾರಾಂತ್ಲ್ಯಾ ಸುಧಾರಿತ್ ಭಾಸಾಂನಿ ಭಾಷಾಂತರ್ ಸಾಹಿತ್ಯಾಚೊ ವಾಂಟೊ ಸರ್ಜನಾತ್ಮಕ್ ಸಾಹಿತ್ಯಾ ತಿತ್ಲೊಚ್ ಆಸಾ. ಘಡಿಯೆ ಭಾಷಾಂತರ್ ಸಾಹಿತ್ಯಾಕ್ ಲಾಗುನ್ ತ್ಯಾ ಭಾಸಾಂಚ್ಯಾ ಸಾಹಿತ್ಯಾಚೊ ಪಾಂವ್ಡೊ (quality) ಆನಿ ಆಂಕ್ಡೊ (quantity) ವಾಡ್ಲೊ ಆಸುಂ ಯೆತಾ. ಭಾಷಾಂತರ್ ಸಾಹಿತ್ಯಾಕ್ ಲಾಗುನ್ ಸಾಹಿತ್ಯಾಚೆ ದುಸ್ರೆ ದುಸ್ರೆ ಪ್ರಕಾರ್ ತ್ಯಾ ಭಾಸಾಂನಿ ಆಯ್ಲೆ ಆಸ್ತಿತ್.

ಪಾರಿಭಾಷಿಕ್ ಉತ್ರಾವಳ್

ಇಂಗ್ಲಿಷ್ ಹ್ಯಾ Translation ಉತ್ರಾಕ್ ಕೊಂಕ್ಣಿಂತ್ ವಿವಿಧ್ ಉತ್ರಾಂ ವಾಪರ್ಲ್ಯಾಂತ್. ತರ್ಜುಮೊ, ತರ್ಜಣ್, ಅನುವಾದ್, ಅಣ್ಕಾರ್, ರುಪಾಂತರ್, ಭಾಷಾಂತರ್. ತರ್ಜುಮೊ ಆನಿ ತರ್ಜಣ್ ಹಿಂ ಉತ್ರಾಂ ಆರೆಬಿಕ್ ಭಾಸಾಂ ಥಾವ್ನ್ ಆಯ್ಲ್ಯಾಂತ್. ತರ್ಜುಮೊ = summary ತರ್ಜಣ್ = examine ಅನುವಾದ್ ಆನಿ ರುಪಾಂತರ್ ಸಂಸ್ಕೃತ್ ಭಾಶೆಚಿಂ ಉತ್ರಾಂ. ಅನುವಾದ್ = repetition by way of explanation or free translation. ರುಪಾಂತರ್ = Adaptation. ಗೊಯಾಂತ್ ಅಣ್ಕಾರ್ ಹೆಂ ಉತರ್ ಘೊಲ್ತಾ. ಹೆಂ ಉತರ್ ಮರಾಠಿ 'ಅನುಕಾರ್' = (copying) ಉತ್ರಾಂತ್ಲ್ಯಾನ್ ಆಯ್ಲಾಂ. ದೆಕುನ್ 'ಭಾಷಾಂತರ್' ಹೆಂಚ್ ಉತರ್ translation ಹ್ಯಾ ಅರ್ಥಾನ್ ಹಾಂವೆಂ ವಾಪರ್ಲಾಂ. ಆರ್ಯನ್ ಭಾಸಾಂನಿ ಹೆಂಚ್ ಉತರ್ ಚಡ್ ವಾಪರ್ತಾತ್.

1.1 ಭಾಷಾಂತರ್ ಮ್ಹಣ್ಜೆ ಕಿತೆಂ?

ಎಕೆ ಭಾಶೆಚೆಂ ಉಲೊವ್ಪ್ ವಾ ಪಾಠ್ (texts) ಅಚುಕ್‌ಪಣಾನ್ (accurately) ದುಸ್ರೆ ಭಾಶೆಂತ್ ಹಾಡಪ್ ಹಾಕಾ ಭಾಷಾಂತರ್ ಮ್ಹಣ್ತಾತ್. ಭಾಷಾಂತರ್ ಕರ್ಚೆ ಪ್ರಕ್ರಿಯೆಂತ್ (process) ತೀನ್ ಘಟಕ್ (components) ಆಸಾತ್.

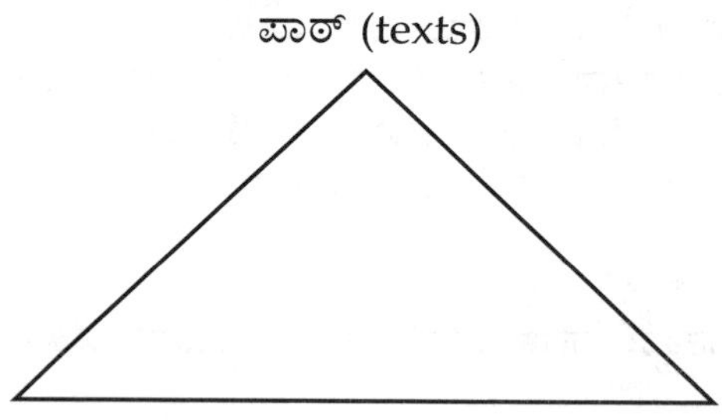

ಜೆ ಭಾಶೆಂತ್ಲೊ ಪಾಠ್ ಭಾಷಾಂತರ್ ಕರುಂಕ್ ಆಸಾ ತೆ ಭಾಶೆಕ್ ಮೂಳ್ ಭಾಸ್ ಮ್ಹಣ್ತಾತ್. ಜೆ ಭಾಶೆಂತ್ ತೊ ಪಾಠ್ ಭಾಷಾಂತರ್ ಕರ್ತಾತ್ ತೆ ಭಾಶೆಕ್ ಶೆವಟ್ ಭಾಸ್ ಮ್ಹಣ್ತಾತ್. ದಾಖ್ಲ್ಯಾಕ್: ಶಿವರಾಮ ಕಾರಂತಾಚಿ 'ಮೂಕಜ್ಜಿಯ ಕನಸುಗಳು" ಹಿ ಕಾದಂಬರಿ

ಘೆಯಾತ್. ಹಿ ಕಾದಂಬರಿ = ಪಾಠ್. ಕನ್ನಡ್ ಭಾಶೆಂತ್ ಆಸಾ. ದೆಕುನ್ ಕನ್ನಡ್ ಹಿ ಮೂಳ್ ಭಾಸ್. ತಿ ಕಾದಂಬರಿ ಜರ್ ಕೊಂಕ್ಣಿ ಭಾಶೆಂತ್ ಭಾಷಾಂತರ್ ಜಾತಾ ತರ್ ಕೊಂಕ್ಣಿ ಶೆವಟ್ ಭಾಸ್ ಜಾತಾ. ಪುಂಡಲಿಕ್ ನಾಯ್ಕಾಚಿ 'ಅಚ್ಛೇವ್' ಕೊಂಕ್ಣಿ ಕಾದಂಬರಿ ಇಂಗ್ಲಿಷ್ ಭಾಶೆಂತ್ ಭಾಶಾಂತರ್ ಜಾಲ್ಯಾ. ಥಂಯ್ ಕೊಂಕ್ಣಿ ಮೂಳ್ ಭಾಸ್ ಆನಿ ಇಂಗ್ಲಿಷ್ ಶೆವಟ್ ಭಾಸ್.

2. ಭಾಷಾಂತರಾಚೆ ಪ್ರಕಾರ್

ಭಾಷಾಂತರ್ ವಿವಿಧ್ ಪ್ರಕಾರಾಂನಿ ಕೆಲ್ಲೆಂ ಪಳಂವ್ಕ್ ಮೆಳ್ತಾ. ತಾಂತ್ಲೆ ಕಾಂಯ್ ಮುಖೆಲ್ ಪ್ರಕಾರ್ ಅಶೆ ಆಸಾತ್

2.1 ಶಬ್ದಾನುವಾದ್ (Literal translation): ಹಾಂತುಂ ಮೂಳ್‌ಪಾಠಾಂತ್ ವಾಪರ್‌ಲ್ಲ್ಯಾ ಉತ್ರಾಂಕ್, ವಾಕ್ಯ್ ರಚನೆಕ್, ಶೈಲಿಕ್ ಚಡ್ ಮಹತ್ವ್ ಆಸಾ. ಕಾಯ್ದ್ಯಾಚೆ ಪಾಠ್ (Legal texts) ಭಾಷಾಂತರ್ ಕರ್ತಾನಾ ಶಬ್ದಾನುವಾದ್ ಚಡ್‌ಸೊ ವಾಪರ್ತಾತ್. ಸಾಹಿತ್ಯಾಚೆಂ ಭಾಷಾಂತರ್ ಕರ್ತಾನಾ ಹಿ ಪದ್ಧತ್ ತಿತ್ಲಿ ಉಪ್ಕಾರ್ನಾ. ಭಾಷಾಂತರಾಚಿ ಕಲಾ ಆನಿ ತತ್ವಾಂ ಸಾರ್ಕಿಂ ನೆಣಾ ಆಸ್‌ಲ್ಲೆ ಶಬ್ದಾನುವಾದಾಕ್ ಚಡ್ ಮಹತ್ವ್ ದಿತಾತ್. ಮಂಗ್ಳುರ್ ಧರ್ಮ್‌ಪ್ರಾಂತಾಂತ್ ಮಾಗ್ಣ್ಯಾಂಚೆಂ ಕೊಂಕ್ಣಿ ಭಾಷಾಂತರ್ ಕರ್ತಾನಾ ಕೊಂಕ್ಣಿ ಭಾಶೆಚೆಂ ಖಾಶೆಲೆಪಣ್, ತಿಚ್ಯಾ ವ್ಯಾಕರಣಾಚಿ ಬಾಂದಾವಳ್ ಮತಿಂತ್ ಧರಿನಾಸ್ತಾನಾ ಶಬ್ದಾನುವಾದ್ ವಾಪರ್ಲಾ. ಹಾಕಾ ಲಾಗುನ್ ಮಾಗ್ಣ್ಯಾಂಚೆಂ ಉತ್ರಾಂ ಕೊಂಕ್ಣಿ ಪೂಣ್ ವ್ಯಾಕರಣ್ ಇಂಗ್ಲಿಷ್ ಜಾಲಾಂ. ದಾಖ್ಲ್ಯಾಕ್:

i. Hear our prayer O Lord ಹಾಚೆಂ ಕೊಂಕ್ಣಿ ಭಾಷಾಂತರ್ ಉತ್ರಾಕ್ ಉತರ್ ಧರುನ್ ಅಶೆಂ ಕೆಲಾಂ. "ಆಯ್ಕ್ ಆಮ್ಚೆಂ ಮಾಗ್ಣೆಂ ಏ ಸೊಮ್ಯಾ". ಹಿ ಚೂಕ್ ಹಾಂವೆಂ ದಾಕೊವ್ನ್ ದಿತಚ್, ಕೊಂಕ್ಣಿ ಭಾಶೆಚೆ ಬಾಂದಾವಳಿ ಪ್ರಮಾಣೆಂ "ಏ ಸೊಮ್ಯಾ, ಆಮ್ಚೆಂ ಮಾಗ್ಣೆಂ ಆಯ್ಕ್" ಹೆಂ ಭಾಷಾಂತರ್ ವಾಪರುಂಕ್ ಸುರು ಕೆಲಾಂ.

ii. Jesus, meek and humble of heart
Make my heart like unto thine

"ಜೆಜು ಭೊಳ್ಯಾ ಆನಿ ಖಾಲ್ತ್ಯಾ ಕಾಳ್ಜಾಚ್ಯಾ
ಕರ್ ಕಾಳಿಜ್ ಮ್ಹಜೆಂ ತುಜ್ಯಾ ಕಾಳ್ಜಾ ಸಾರ್ಕೆಂ" ಅಶೆಂ ಭಾಷಾಂತರ್ ಕೆಲ್ಲೆಂ ಲೋಕ್ ವಾಪರ್ತಾ. ಹೆಂ ಭಾಷಾಂತರ್ ಅಶೆಂ ಕೆಲ್ಯಾರ್ ಬರೆಂ: "ಜೆಜು ಭೊಳ್ಯಾ ಆನಿ ಖಾಲ್ತ್ಯಾ ಕಾಳ್ಜಾಚ್ಯಾ ಮ್ಹಜೆಂ ಕಾಳಿಜ್ ತುಜ್ಯಾ ಕಾಳ್ಜಾ ಸಾರ್ಕೆಂ ಕರ್"

iii. Pray for us, O Holy Mother of God
That we may be made worthy of the promises of Christ

ಭಾಷಾಂತರ್ ಅಶೆಂ ಕೆಲಾಂ:
"ಭಾಗೆವಂತಿ ದೆವಾಚೆ ಮಾಯೆ, ಆಮಾ ಪಾಸುನ್ ವಿನತಿ ಕರ್
ಕ್ರಿಸ್ತಾಚ್ಯಾ ಭಾಸಾವ್ಣ್ಯಾಂಕ್ ಆಮಿ ಫಾವೊ ಜಾಂವ್ಚೆ ಖಾತಿರ್"
ಹೆಂ ಭಾಷಾಂತರ್ ಸಾರ್ಕೆಂ ಕರ್ಚೆಂ ಜಾಲ್ಯಾರ್ ಅಶೆಂ ಜಾತಲೆಂ:
"ಭಾಗೆವಂತ್ ದೆವಾಚೆ ಮಾಯೆ, ಆಮ್ಚೆ ಪಾಸುನ್ ವಿನತಿ ಕರ್
ಕ್ರಿಸ್ತಾಚ್ಯೊ ಭಾಸಾವ್ಣ್ಯೊ ಆಮ್ಕಾಂ ಫಾವೊ ಜಾಂವ್ದಿತ್"
ಗೊಂಯಾಂತ್ ಮರಾಠಿಚ್ಯಾ ಪ್ರಭಾವಾನ್ ಇಂಗ್ಲಿಷ್ ವಾಕ್ಯಾಂ ಕೊಂಕ್ಣಿಂತ್ ಭಾಷಾಂತರ್ ಕರ್ತಾನಾ ಮರಾಠಿ ವ್ಯಾಕರಣಾಚೊ ಪ್ರಭಾವ್ ದಿಷ್ಟಿಕ್ ಪಡ್ತಾ. ದಾಖ್ಲ್ಯಾಕ್

i. Terrorists killed ten people
"ಆಕಾಂತ್‌ವಾದಿ ಕಡ್ಲ್ಯಾನ್ ಧಾ ಜಣ್ ಮಾರ್ಲೆ ಗೆಲೆ"
"ಆಕಾಂತ್‌ವಾದ್ಯಾಂನಿ ಧಾ ಜಣಾಂಕ್ ಮಾರ್ಲೆ" ಹೆಂ ಭಾಷಾಂತರ್ ಕೊಂಕ್ಣಿ ಭಾಶೆಚ್ಯಾ ವ್ಯಾಕರಣಾ ಪ್ರಮಾಣೆಂ ಆಸಾ.

ii. Divorce ಹಾಕಾ ಮರಾಠಿಂತ್ 'ಘಟಸ್ಫೋಟ್' ಉತರ್ ಆಸಾ. ಗೊಯಾಂತ್ ಶಿಕಪ್ ಆಸ್‌ಲ್ಲೊ ಹಿಂದು ಲೋಕ್ ಕೊಂಕ್ಣಿ ಉಲಯ್ತಾನಾ ಹೆಂ ಉತರ್ ವಾಪರ್ತಾತ್. ಆಯ್ಲೆವಾರ್ 'ಘಟಸ್ಫೋಟ್' ಹ್ಯಾ ಉತ್ರಾಚೊ ಶಬ್ದಾನುವಾದ್ ಕರುನ್ 'ಬುಡ್ಕುಲ್ಯಾಕ್ ಫಾರ್', 'ಬುಡ್ಕುಲೊ ಫುಟಪ್' ಅಸಲಿ ಹಾಸ್ಯಾಸ್ಪದ್ ಉತ್ರಾವಳ್ ಗೊಂಯಾಂತ್ ವಾಚುಂಕ್ ಮೆಳ್ತಾ. ಕ್ರಿಸ್ತಾಂವ್ ಲೋಕ್ divorce ಹ್ಯಾ ಉತ್ರಾಕ್ 'ಲಗ್ನ್ ಮೊಡಪ್' ವಾ 'ಕಾಜಾರ್ ಮೊಡಪ್' ಹೆಂ ಸಾದೆಂ ಸೊಂಪೆಂ ಕೊಂಕ್ಣಿ ಉತರ್ ವಾಪರ್ತಾತ್.

iii. Many great people were born in our country. "ಆಮ್ಚ್ಯಾ ದೇಶಾಂತ್ ಜಾಯ್ತೆ ಮ್ಹಾಪುರುಷ್ ಜಾವ್ನ್ ಗೆಲೆ" ಹಾಚೆ ಬದ್ಲಾಕ್ "ಆಮ್ಚ್ಯಾ ದೇಶಾಂತ್ ಜಾಯ್ತೆ ಮ್ಹಾಪುರುಷ್ ಜಲ್ಮಾಲ್ಲೆ" ಹೆಂ ಭಾಶಾಂತರ್ ಸಾರ್ಕೆಂ ಆಸಾ.

2.2 ಅನುಕರಣ್‌ವಾದ್ (Imitation): ಗೊಯಾಂತ್ ಚಡ್‌ಸೊ ಹಿಂದು ಲೋಕ್ ಆಪ್ಲೆಂ ಮುಳಾವೆಂ ಶಿಕಪ್ (primary education) ಮರಾಠಿಂತ್ ಕರ್ತಾಲೊ ಆನಿ ಆತಾಂಯ್ ಕರ್ತಾತ್. ಶಿಕ್ಪಾಕ್ ಲಾಗುನ್, ಸಾಂಸ್ಕೃತಿಕ್, ಧಾರ್ಮಿಕ್ ಆನಿ ಐತಿಹಾಸಿಕ್ ಕಾರಣಾಂಕ್ ಲಾಗುನ್ ತಾಂಚ್ಯಾ ಚಿಂತ್ಪಾಚೆರ್, ಉಲೊವ್ಪಾಚೆರ್, ಬರೊವ್ಪಾಚೆರ್, ಚಾಲಿ ರಿತಿಂಚೆರ್ ಮರಾಠಿ ಭಾಶೆಚೊ ಆನಿ ಸಂಸ್ಕೃತೆಚೊ ಬರೊಚ್ ಪ್ರಭಾವ್ ಪಡ್ಲಾ. ಮರಾಠಿ ಭಾಶೆಚೆಂ ಆನಿ ಸಂಸ್ಕೃತೆಚೆಂ ಅನುಕರಣ್ ಕೆಲ್ಲ್ಯಾನ್ ಅಶೆಂ ಜಾಲಾಂ. ಹಾಚಿ ತಾಂಕಾಂ ಕೆದ್ನಾಂ ಕೆದ್ನಾಂ ಜಾಣಿವ್ ಸಯ್ತ್ ನಾ. ದಾಖ್ಲ್ಯಾಕ್: ಗೊಂಯ್ಚ್ಯಾ ಹಿಂದು ಲೊಕಾಚಿಂ ಆಡ್‌ನಾಂವಾಂ ಘೆಯಾತ್. 'ಭೆಂಬ್ರೊ', 'ಗಾಯ್‌ತೊಂಡೊ', 'ಬುಡ್ಕುಲೊ', 'ಭೊಂಸ್ಲೊ', 'ಹೆದೊ', 'ಸೊಂದೊ', 'ಕೆಳೆಕಾರ್', 'ಕೆರ್‌ಕಾರ್'. 'ಪ್ರಿಯೊಳ್‌ಕಾರ್', 'ಮಡ್ಗಾಂವ್‌ಕಾರ್'... ಮರಾಠಿಚ್ಯಾ ಪ್ರಭಾವಾನ್ ಹಿಂ ಆಡ್‌ನಾಂವಾಂ ಅಶಿಂ ಬರಯ್ತಾತ್: 'ಭೆಂಬ್ರೆ', 'ಗಾಯ್‌ತೊಂಡೆ', 'ಬುಡ್ಕುಲೆ', 'ಭೊಂಸ್ಲೆ', 'ಹೆದೆ', 'ಸೊಂದೆ', 'ಕೆಳೆಕರ್', 'ಕೆರ್‌ಕಾರ್', 'ಪ್ರಿಯೊಳ್‌ಕಾರ್', 'ಮಡ್ಗಾಂವ್‌ಕಾರ್'... ಕಾಂಯ್ ಜಣ್ ಮಾತ್ರ್ ಕೊಂಕ್ಣಿ ರೂಪ್ 'ಕೆಳೆಕಾರ್', 'ಕೆರ್‌ಕಾರ್', 'ಪ್ರಿಯೊಳ್‌ಕಾರ್', 'ಮಡ್ಗಾಂವ್‌ಕಾರ್' ವಾಪರ್ತಾತ್. ಪೂಣ್ ಹಿ ಪ್ರಕ್ರಿಯಾ 'ಭೆಂಬ್ರೊ', 'ಗಾಯ್‌ತೊಂಡೊ' ಅಸಲ್ಯಾ ಆಡ್‌ನಾಂವಾಂನಿ ಜಾಂವ್ಕ್ ನಾ. ಹ್ಯಾ ಅನುಕರಣ್‌ವಾದಾಚ್ಯಾ ಪ್ರಭಾವಾನ್ ಆದಿಂ ಗೊಂಯ್ಚ್ಯಾ ಹಿಂದು ಲೊಕಾ ಮದ್ಲೆ ಬರೆಚ್ ಜಣ್ ಕೊಂಕ್ಣಿ ಮರಾಠಿಚಿ ಬೊಲಿ (dialect) ಮ್ಹಣ್ತಾಲೆ. ಆತಾಂಯ್ ಕಾಂಯ್ ಜಣ್ ಮರಾಠಿ ಗೊಂಯ್ಚ್ಯಾ ಹಿಂದು ಲೊಕಾಚಿ ಸಾಂಸ್ಕೃತಿಕ್ ಭಾಸ್ (Cultural language) ಮ್ಹಣ್ತಾತ್. ದೆಕುನ್ ಗೊಂಯಾಂತ್ ಕೊಂಕ್ಣಿ ಸಾಂಗಾತಾ ಮರಾಠಿಕ್ ರಾಜ್‌ಭಾಶೆಚೊ ದರ್ಜೊ ಮೆಳುಂಕ್ ಜಾಯ್ ಹೊ ತಾಂಚೊ ವಾದ್ ಅಜೂನ್ ಚಾಲು ಆಸಾ.

2.3 ರುಪಾಂತರ್ (Adaptation): ಮೂಳ್ ಭಾಶೆಚ್ಯಾ ಪಾಠಾಚೊ ಆಶಯ್ (essence), ಸಾಂಬಾಳುನ್ ರುಪಾಂತ್ (form), ಶೈಲಿಂತ್ (style), ಸಾದರಿಕರಣಾಂತ್ (Presentation) ಬದಲ್ ಕರುನ್ ಸರ್ಜನಾತ್ಮಕ್ (creative), ರಿತಿನ್ ಕೆಲ್ಲ್ಯಾ ಭಾಷಾಂತರಾಕ್ ರುಪಾಂತರ್ ವಾ ಅನುಸರ್ಜನ್ ಮ್ಹಣ್ತಾತ್. ರುಪಾಂತರ್ ಕರ್ತಾನಾ ಕಾಲ್ಪನಿಕತೆಕ್ ಚಡ್ ಮೆಕ್ಳಿಕ್ ಆಸ್ತಾ. ರುಪಾಂತರ್ ಕರ್ಪಿ, ಭಾಷಾಂತರ್‌ಕಾರಾ ಪ್ರಾಸ್ ಚಡ್ ತಾಕತ್ ಆನಿ ದೆಣಿಂ ಆಸ್‌ಲ್ಲೊ ಬರೊವ್ಪಿ. ದಾಖ್ಲ್ಯಾಕ್: ಯು. ಆರ್. ಅನಂತಮೂರ್ತಿಚಿ ಕನ್ನಡ್ ಕಾದಂಬರಿ 'ಸಂಸ್ಕಾರ' ಗೊಂಯಾಂತ್ ದತ್ತಾರಾಮ್ ಕಾಮತ್ ಬಾಂಬೊಳ್ಕಾರಾನ್ ನಾಟಕಾಚ್ಯಾ ಸ್ವರೂಪಾನ್ ರುಪಾಂತರ್ ಕೆಲ್ಯಾ. ತ್ಯಾ ನಾಟಕಾಕ್ ಪುರಸ್ಕಾರ್ ಮೆಳ್ಳ್ಯಾತ್ ಆನಿ ತೆಂ ನಾಟಕ್ ಲೊಕಾಕ್ ರುಚ್ಲಾಂ.

ಭಾಷಾಂತರ್‌ಕಾರಾಕ್ ಆಸ್‌ಲ್ಲಿಂ ಬಂದನಾಂ ರುಪಾಂತರ್ ಕರ್‍ತೆಲ್ಯಾಕ್ ನಾಂತ್. ಹಾಕಾ ಲಾಗುನ್ ರುಪಾಂತರ್ ಕೆಲ್ಲೊ ಪಾಠ್ ಶೆವಟ್ ಭಾಶೆಚೊಚ್ ಅಸೊ ದಿಸ್ತಾ.

3. ಭಾಷಾಂತರಾಚಿಂ ತತ್ವಾಂ

ಸಾಹಿತ್ಯಾಚೆಂ ಭಾಷಾಂತರ್ ಕರ್‍ಚೆಂ ಕಾಮ್ ಕಠಿಣ್. ತಿ ಏಕ್ ಕಲಾ. ಭಾಷಾಂತರ್‌ಕಾರ್ ಸ್ವತಾ ಏಕ್ ಬರೊ ಬರೊವ್ಪಿ ಆಸ್ಚೊ ಪಡ್ತಾ. ಸರ್ಜನಾತ್ಮಕ್ ಸಾಹಿತ್ಯ್ ಬರೊಂವ್ಕ್ ಕಿತ್ಲಿ ತಾಕತ್ ಜಾಯ್ ತಾಚೆ ಪ್ರಾಸ್ ಚಡ್ ತಾಕತ್ ಭಾಷಾಂತರ್‌ಕಾರಾಕ್ ಗರ್ಜ್ ಆಸಾ. ಬರೊ ಬರೊವ್ಪಿ ಮಾತ್ರ್ ಮೂಳ್ ಭಾಶೆಚ್ಯಾ ಬರೊವ್ಪ್ಯಾಕ್, ಮೂಳ್ ಭಾಶೆಂತ್ಲ್ಯಾ ಪಾಠಾಕ್ ಆನಿ ಭಾಷಾಂತರ್ ಕೆಲ್ಲ್ಯಾ ಪಾಠಾಕ್ ನೀತ್ ಆನಿ ಪಾಂವ್ಡೊ ದಿಂವ್ಕ್ ಸಕ್ತಾ. ಹೆಂ ಜಾಂವ್ಕ್ ಜಾಯ್ ಜಾಲ್ಯಾರ್ ಭಾಷಾಂತರ್‌ಕಾರಾನ್ ಕಾಂಯ್ ತತ್ವಾಂ ಆನಿ ವಿಷಯ್ ಮತಿಂತ್ ದವರುಂಕ್ ಆಸಾತ್.

3.1 ಭಾಷಾಂತರಾಚೆ ಉದ್ದೇಶ್ (objectives) ಆನಿ ಧ್ಯೇಯ್ (goals): ಭಾಷಾಂತರಾಚೆ ಉದ್ಧೇಶ್ ಖಂಯ್ಚೆ? ತಾಚೊ ಧ್ಯೇಯ್ ಕಿತೆಂ? ಭಾಷಾಂತರ್ ಕೊಣಾ ಖಾತಿರ್, ಕಿತ್ಯಾಕ್ ಖಾತಿರ್? ಹಾಂಚೆರ್ ಭಾಷಾಂತರ್‌ಕಾರಾನ್ ಭಾಷಾಂತರ್ ವಾವ್ರ್ ಸುರು ಕರ್‍ಚೆ ಪಯ್ಲೆಂ ಬಾರಿಕ್ಸಾಣೆನ್ ಚಿಂತುಂಕ್ ಆಸಾ. ಭಾಷಾಂತರಾಚೆ ವಾಚ್ಪಿ ಕೋಣ್ ಹಾಚೆರ್ ಆಧಾರುನ್ ಭಾಷಾಂತರಾಚೆಂ ಸ್ವರೂಪ್ ಬದಲ್ತಾ.

ಭುಗ್ರ್ಯಾಂ ಖಾತಿರ್ ಭಾಷಾಂತರ್ ಕರ್‍ತಾನಾ ಭಾಶೆಚಿ ಉತ್ರಾವಳ್, ವಾಕ್ಯ್ ರಚನಾ, ಶೈಲಿ ಆನಿ ಮಾಂಡಾವಳ್ ಭುಗ್ರ್ಯಾಂಕ್ ಸಮ್ಜಾತಾ ಆನಿ ಬರಿ ಲಾಗ್ತಾ ತಸಲಿ ಆಸ್ತಲಿ. ಸಾದ್ಯಾ ವಾಚ್ಪ್ಯಾಂ ಖಾತಿರ್ ಕೆಲ್ಲೆಂ ಭಾಷಾಂತರ್ ಆನಿ ಜಾಣ್ಕಾರಾಂ ಖಾತಿರ್ ಕೆಲ್ಲೆಂ ಭಾಷಾಂತರ್ ಹಾಂತುಂ ಜಾಯ್ತೊ ಫರಕ್ ಆಸಾ. ದಾಖ್ಲ್ಯಾಕ್: ಸಾದ್ಯಾ ವಾಚ್ಪ್ಯಾಂ ಖಾತಿರ್ ಇಂಗ್ಲಿಷ್ ಭಾಶೆಂತ್ Good News Bible: Today's English Version ಭಾಷಾಂತರ್ ಆಸಾ. ಪೂಣ್ ಹೆಂ ಭಾಷಾಂತರ್ ಬಾಯ್ಬಲಾಚೆರ್ ಅಭ್ಯಾಸ್ ಕರ್‍ತಲ್ಯಾಂಕ್ ಉಪ್ಕಾರ್‍ನಾ. ತಾಂಚೆ ಖಾತಿರ್ The Holy Bible. The New Revised Standard Version ವಾ New Jerusalem Bible ಹಿಂ ಭಾಷಾಂತರಾಂ ಆಸಾತ್. ತಾಂತ್ರಿಕ್ ಪುಸ್ತಕಾಂ (Technical Books), ಕಾಯ್ದ್ಯಾಚಿಂ ಪುಸ್ತಕಾಂ (Law Books) ಆನಿ ಅಧಿಕೃತ್ ಬರ್‍ಪಾವಳ್ (Official Literature) ಭಾಷಾಂತರ್ ಕರ್‍ಚಿ ರೀತ್ ವೆಗ್ಳಿ. ಥಂಯ್ ಪಾಠಾಚ್ಯಾ ಅಚುಕ್‌ಪಣಾಕ್ (accuracy) ಚಡ್ ಮಹತ್ವ್ ದಿಂವ್ಚೆಂ ಪಡ್ತಾ.

ಭಾಷಾಂತರ್‌ಕಾರಾಕ್ ಭಾಸಾಂಚೆಂ ಗಿನ್ಯಾನ್: ಭಾಷಾಂತರ್‌ಕಾರಾಕ್ ಮೂಳ್ ಭಾಸ್ ಆನಿ ಶೆವಟ್ ಭಾಸ್ ಹಾಂಚೆಂ ಬರೆಂ ಗಿನ್ಯಾನ್ ಜಾಯ್. ತ್ಯಾ ಭಾಸಾಂಚೆರ್ ತಾಕಾ ಧನಿಪಣ್ (mastery) ಆಸ್‌ಲ್ಲೆಂ ತಿತ್ಲೆಂ ಬರೆಂ. ದೆಕುನ್ ಭಾಷಾಂತರ್‌ಕಾರ್ ದ್ವಿಭಾಷಿಕ್ (bilingual). ದೋನ್‌ಯಿ ಭಾಸಾಂಚಿ ಆನಿ ತಾಂಚ್ಯಾ ಸಂಸ್ಕೃತಾಯಾಂಚಿ (culture) ಬಾರಿಕ್ಸಾಣೆಚಿ ಮಾಹಿತಿ ತಾಕಾ ಖಬರ್ ಆಸುಂಕ್ ಜಾಯ್. ದೋನ್ ಭಾಸೊ ದೋನ್ ಸಮಾಜಾಂಚೆಂ ಪ್ರತಿನಿಧಿತ್ವ್ ಕರ್‍ತಾತ್. ದೆಕುನ್ ದೋನ್ ಭಾಸಾಂಚಿ ವಿಶ್ವ್‌ನದರ್ (world-view) ವೆವೆಗ್ಳಿ ಆಸ್ತಾ. ವಿಶ್ವ್ ನದರ್ ಮ್ಹಣ್ಲ್ಯಾರ್ ಏಕೆ ಭಾಶೆಚ್ಯಾ ಲೊಕಾನ್ ಚಿಂತ್ಚಿ ಆನಿ ಉಲೊಂವ್ಚಿ ರೀತ್, ತಾಂಚಿಂ ಚಿಂತ್ನಾಂ ಆನಿ ಭೊಗ್ನಾಂ ಉಚಾರ್‍ಚಿ ರೀತ್, ಚಾಲಿರಿತಿ, ಫೆಸ್ತಾಂ ಪರ್‍ಬೊ, ಖಾಣ್ ಜೆವಣ್, ನ್ಹೆಸಣ್‌ಪಾಂಗ್ರುಣ್, ಆಚಾರ್ ವಿಚಾರ್ ಆನಿ ಸಂಸ್ಕೃತಾಯ್ ದುಸ್ರೆ ಭಾಶೆಚ್ಯಾ ಲೊಕಾ ಪ್ರಾಸ್ ವೆಗ್ಳಿ ಆಸ್ತಾ. ಹರೆಕಾ ಸಮಾಜಾಕ್ ಆಪ್ಲೆಂ ಮ್ಹಳ್ಳೆಂ ಖಾಶೆಲೆಪಣ್ ಆನಿ ವೆಗ್ಳೆಪಣ್ (separateness) ಆಸಾ ಆನಿ ತೆಂ ತ್ಯಾ ಸಮಾಜಾಚೆ ಭಾಶೆಂತ್ ಆನಿ ಸಂಸ್ಕೃತಾಯೆಂತ್ ಆಟಾಪ್ಲಾಂ. ಜರ್ ಮೂಳ್‌ಭಾಸ್ ಆನಿ ಶೆವಟ್ ಭಾಸ್ ಎಕಾಚ್ ಭಾಷಿಕ್ ಘರಾಣ್ಯಾಂತ್ಲ್ಯೊ (Language family) ವಾ ಸೆಜಾರ್‍ಚ್ಯೊ ಭಾಸೊ (neighbour languages) ವಾ ಥಳಾವ್ಯೊ ಭಾಸೊ (local languages) ಜಾಲ್ಯಾರ್ ಹೆಂ ಅಂತರ್ ಉಣೆಂ ಆಸುಂ ಯೆತಾ. ದಾಖ್ಲ್ಯಾಕ್: ಮರಾಠಿ ಆನಿ ಕೊಂಕ್ಣಿ ಎಕಾಚ್ ಘರಾಣ್ಯಾಂತ್ಲ್ಯೊ

ಭಾಸೊ. ಮಹಾರಾಷ್ಟ್ರ ಆನಿ ಕರ್ನಾಟಕ್ ಎಕಾಮೆಕಾಕ್ ಸೆಜಾರ್ಚಿಂ ರಾಜ್ಯಾಂ ದೆಕುನ್ ಮರಾಠಿ ಆನಿ ಕನ್ನಡ್ ಸೆಜಾರ್ಚ್ಯೊ ಭಾಸೊ. ಕರ್ನಾಟಕಾಚ್ಯಾ ಉಡುಪಿ ಆನಿ ದಕ್ಷಿಣ್ ಕನ್ನಡ್ ಜಿಲ್ಲ್ಯಾಂನಿ ಕನ್ನಡ್, ತುಳು ಆನಿ ಕೊಂಕ್ಣಿ ಥಳಾವ್ಯೊ ಭಾಸೊ. ಅಸಲೆ ಪರಿಸ್ಥಿತೆಂತ್ ಪ್ರಭಾವಿ ಭಾಸ್ (dominant language) ಹೆರ್ ಭಾಸಾಂಚೆರ್ ಆಪ್ಲೊ ಪ್ರಭಾವ್ ಘಾಲ್ತಾ.

ಜರ್ ಮೂಳ್ ಭಾಸ್ ಆನಿ ಶೆವಟ್ ಭಾಸ್ ದುಸ್ರ್ಯಾ ದುಸ್ರ್ಯಾ ಘರಾಣ್ಯಾಂತ್ಲ್ಯೊ ವಾ ವತಾರಾಂತ್ಲ್ಯೊ ಜಾಲ್ಯಾರ್ ತಾಂಚೆ ಮಧೆಂ ಚಡ್ ಫರಕ್ ಆಸ್ತಾ. ದಾಖ್ಲ್ಯಾಕ್ ತೆಲುಗು ಆನಿ ಕೊಂಕ್ಣಿ ಭಾಷಾಂತರ್‌ಕಾರ್ ದೋನ್ ಭಾಸಾಂಚಿ ವಿಶ್ವ್ ನದರ್ ಸಮ್ಜುನ್ ಘೆತಾ ಆನಿ ಮೂಳ್ ಭಾಶೆಚೊ ಪಾಠ್ ಶೆವಟ್ ಭಾಶೆಚೆ ವಿಶ್ವ್‌ನದ್ರೆಂತ್ ಬಸಾಸೊ ಕರ್ತಾ. ಹೆಂ ಕಾಮ್ ಬರೆಂಚ್ ಕಠಿಣ್. ದಾಖ್ಲ್ಯಾಕ್ ಗೌಡ್ ಸಾರಸ್ವತಾಂಚೆ ಕೊಂಕ್ಣಿ ಬೊಲಿಯೆಂತ್ಲೆಂ ಏಕ್ ವಾಕ್ಯ್ ಘೆಯಾತ್: "ತುವೆಂ ತುಗ್ಗೆಲಿ ಗಾಡಿ ಪೆಟೊವ್ನ್ ದಿವ್ಕಾ" ಗೊಂಯಾಂತ್ ಕೊಂಕ್ಣಿ ಉಲಯ್ತಲ್ಯಾಂಕ್ ಹ್ಯಾ ವಾಕ್ಯಾಚೆಂ ಇಂಗ್ಲಿಷ್ ಭಾಷಾಂತರ್ ಕರುಂಕ್ ಸಾಂಗ್ಲ್ಯಾರ್ ತಾಂಚೆಂ ಭಾಷಾಂತರ್ ಅಶೆಂ ಜಾಂವ್ಚಿ ಶಕ್ಯತಾಯ್ ಆಸಾ you must burn your vehicle. ಜಾಂಕಾಂ ಗೌಡ್ ಸಾರಸ್ವತಾಂಚಿ ಕೊಂಕ್ಣಿ ಬೊಲಿ ಖಬರ್ ಆಸಾ ತಾಂಚೆಂ ಭಾಷಾಂತರ್ you must send your vehicle ಅಶೆಂ ಜಾತಲೆಂ.

ಶೆವಟ್ ಭಾಸ್ ಭಾಷಾಂತರ್‌ಕಾರಾಚಿ ಆವಯ್ ಭಾಸ್ ಆಸಾ ಜಾಲ್ಯಾರ್ ಭಾಷಾಂತರ್ ವಾವ್ರ್ ಸೊಂಪೊ ಜಾತಾ ಆನಿ ಭಾಷಾಂತರ್ ಬರೆಂ ಜಾಂವ್ ಯೆತಾ. ಮೂಳ್ ಭಾಶೆಚ್ಯಾ ಪಾಠಾಂತ್ ಪ್ರಮಾಣ್ ಲಿಖಿತ್ ಭಾಸ್ (Standard written variety) ಆನಿ ಥಳಾವ್ಯೊ ಉಲೊವ್ಪಾಚ್ಯೊ ಬೊಲಿಯೊ (local spoken dialects) ಮಿಸಳ್ ಆಸ್ಲ್ಯಾರ್ ಭಾಷಾಂತರ್‌ಕಾರಾಕ್ ಹಾಂಚಿಯ್ ಬರಿ ವಳಕ್ ಗರ್ಜೆಚಿ.

ಭಾಷಾಂತರ್ ಕರ್ತಾನಾ ಮೂಳ್ ಭಾಶೆಚ್ಯಾ ಪಾಠಾಚೊ ಆಶಯ್ (essence): ಚಡ್ ಮಹತ್ವಾಚೊ, ಆಕಾರ್ (form) ಆನಿ ಶೈಲಿ ತಿತ್ಲಿ ಮಹತ್ವಾಚಿ ನ್ಹಯ್. ಮ್ಹಣಿ (proverbs), ವಾಕ್ ಪ್ರಚಾರ್ (idioms), ಕವಿತಾ ಹಾಂಚೆಂ ಭಾಷಾಂತರ್ ಕರ್ತಾನಾ ಆಶಯ್ ಸಮ್ಜುನ್ ಘೆಂವ್ಚೊ ಪಡ್ತಾ. ನಾ ಜಾಲ್ಯಾರ್ ಅರ್ಥಾಚೊ ಅನರ್ಥ್ (wrong sense) ಜಾತಾ. ಭಾಷಾಂತರ್ ಕೆಲ್ಲೊ ಪಾಠ್ ವಾಚ್ಪಿ ಸಾರ್ಕೆ ಸಮ್ಜತಾತ್ ಅಶೆಂ ಚಿಂತ್ಚೆ ಪ್ರಾಸ್ ತೆ ತ್ಯಾ ಪಾಠಾಚೊ ಚುಕಿಚೊ ಅರ್ಥ್ ಕರ್ತಿತ್ ಹಾಚೆರ್ ಲಕ್ಷ್ ದಿಲ್ಲೆಂ ಬರೆಂ. ಜೆದ್ನಾಂ ಚಡಾಂತ್ ಚಡ್ ಲೋಕ್ ಭಾಷಾಂತರ್ ಕೆಲ್ಲೊ ಏಕ್ ಉತಾರೊ (passage) ಚುಕಿಚ್ಯಾ ಅರ್ಥಾನ್ ಸಮ್ಜುನ್ ಘೆತಾ ತೆದ್ನಾಂ ತೊ ಉತಾರೊ ಸಾರ್ಕೊ ಭಾಷಾಂತರ್ ಕೆಲಾ ಮ್ಹಣುಂಕ್ ಜಾಯ್ನಾ. ದಾಖ್ಲ್ಯಾಕ್:

i. Cain knew his wife and she conceived and bore Enoch (Genesis 1:17). The New RSV ಬಾಯ್ಬಲಾಂತ್ ಹೆಂ ವಾಕ್ಯ್ ಆಸಾ. ಹಿಬ್ರೂ ಭಾಶೆಂತ್ಲ್ಯಾ ಉತಾರ್ಯಾಚೊ ಶಬ್ದಾನುವಾದ್ ಇಂಗ್ಲಿಷ್ ಭಾಶೆಂತ್ ಹಾಂಗಾ ಕೆಲಾ, ಹ್ಯಾ ಇಂಗ್ಲಿಷ್ ಭಾಷಾಂತರಾಚೆರ್ ಆಧಾರುನ್ ಕೊಣೆಂ ತರ್‌ಯಿ ಅಶೆಂ ಭಾಷಾಂತರ್ ಕರುಂಕ್ ಜಾತಾ. "ಕಾಯ್ನ್ ಆಪ್ಲೆ ಬಾಯ್ಲೆಕ್ ವಳ್ಖಾತಾಲೊ ಆನಿ ತಿ ಗರ್ಭೆಸ್ತ್ ಜಾಲಿ ಆನಿ ಎನೊಕಾಕ್ ಜಲ್ಮ್ ದಿಲೊ". ಕಾಂಯ್ ವಾಚ್ಪ್ಯಾಂಕ್ "ಕಾಯ್ನ್ ಆಪ್ಲೆ ಬಾಯ್ಲೆಕ್ ವಳ್ಖಾತಾಲೊ" ಹ್ಯಾ ವಾಕ್ಯಾಚೊ ಸಾರ್ಕೊ ಅರ್ಥ್ ಜಾತಲೊ ಹಾಚಿ ಖಾತ್ರಿ ನಾ. ದೆಕುನ್ "ಕಾಯ್ನಾನ್ ಆಪ್ಲೆ ಬಾಯ್ಲೆಕಡೆ ಎಕ್ವಟ್ ಕೆಲೊ ಆನಿ ತಿ ಗರ್ಭೆಸ್ತ್ ಜಾಲಿ ಆನಿ ಎನೊಕಾಕ್ ಜಲ್ಮ್ ದಿಲೊ" ಅಶೆಂ ಭಾಷಾಂತರ್ ಕೆಲ್ಯಾರ್ ಅರ್ಥಾಂತ್ ಸ್ಪಷ್ಟತಾಯ್ ಯೆತಾ.

ii. दाल में कुछ काला है ಹೆಂ ಹಿಂದಿ ವಾಕ್ಯ್ "ದಾಳಿಂತ್ ಕಿತೆಂ ತರ್‌ಯಿ ಕಾಳೆಂ ಆಸಾ" ಅಶೆಂ ಭಾಷಾಂತರ್ ಕರುಂಕ್ ಜಾಂವ್ಚೆಂ ನಾ. "ಹಾಂಗಾ ಕಿತೆಂ ತರ್‌ಯಿ ಶಿಜ್ತಾ" ವಾ "ಹಾಚೊ ದುಬಾವ್ ಮಾರ್ತಾ" ಅಶೆಂ ಭಾಷಾಂತರ್ ಕರ್ಚೆಂ ಪಡ್ತಾ.

ಆಶಯ್ ಸಾಂಬಾಳುನ್ ಇಂಗ್ಲಿಷ್ ಮ್ಹಣಿ ಕೊಂಕ್ಣಿಂತ್ ಭಾಷಾಂತರ್ ಕೆಲ್ಲೆ ಕಾಂಯ್ ದಾಖ್ಲೆ ಪಳೆಯಾತ್.

a. Bad workman quarrels with his tools.
"ನಾಚುಂಕ್ ಯೆನಾ ತಾಕಾ ಆಂಗಣ್ ವಾಂಕ್ಡೆಂ".

b. The cat would eat fish but would not wet her feet.
"ಕಾಷ್ಟಿ ಭಿಜಯ್‌ನಾಸ್ತಾನಾ ತಿಗುರ್ ಧರುಂಕ್ ಸೊಧ್ತಾ".

c. Give him an inch and he will take an ell.
"ಭಟಾಕ್ ದಿಲಿ ಆಸ್ರಿ, ಭಟ್ ಹಾತ್‌ಪಾಂಯ್ ಪಸ್ರಿ".

d. Bad habits die hard.
"ಸುಂಬ್ ಲಾಸ್ಲ್ಯಾರ್ ವಳ್ ವೆತಾ?"

e. Counting chickens before they are hatched
"ದರ್ಯಾಂತ್ ಆಸಾ ಮಾಸೊ, ಮೊಲ್ ಕರ್ತಾ ಪಿಸೊ".

3.4. ಭಾಷಾಂತರ್‌ಕಾರಾನ್ ಮೂಳ್‌ಭಾಶೆಚ್ಯಾ ಪಾಠಾಚೊ ಆಧಾರ್ ಜಾವ್ನ್ ಶೆವಟ್ ಭಾಶೆಂತ್ ಭಾಷಾಂತರ್ ಕೆಲ್ಯಾರ್ ಮಾತ್ರ ಭಾಷಾಂತರ್ ಕೆಲ್ಲೊ ಪಾಠ್ ಮೂಳ್ ಭಾಶೆಚ್ಯಾ ಪಾಠಾಕ್ ಪ್ರಾಮಾಣಿಕ್ ಉರತ್ ಆನಿ ಭಾಷಾಂತರ್ ಸಾರ್ಕೆಂ ಜಾಯ್ತ್. ಖಲಿಲ್ ಜಿಬ್ರಾನಾಚೆಂ 'ಅಲ್ ರುಸುಲ್' ನಾಂವಾಚೆಂ ನಾಂವಾಜ್ತೆಂ (famous) ಪುಸ್ತಕ್ ಅರೆಬಿಕ್ ಭಾಶೆಂತ್ ಆಸಾ. ಸಂಸಾರಾಚ್ಯಾ ಜಾಯ್ತ್ಯಾ ಭಾಸಾಂನಿ ತೆಂ ಭಾಷಾಂತರ್ ಜಾಲಾಂ. ಕೊಂಕ್ಣಿಂತ್ ತ್ಯಾ ಪುಸ್ತಕಾಚೆಂ ಭಾಶಾಂತರ್ ಕರ್ತಲ್ಯಾಕ್ ಅರೆಬಿಕ್ ಭಾಸ್ ಬರಿ ಯೆಂವ್ಕ್ ಜಾಯ್. ಇಂಗ್ಲಿಷ್ ವಾ ಹೆರ್ ಭಾಸಾಂಚ್ಯಾ ಭಾಷಾಂತರಾಚೊ ಆಧಾರ್ ಘೆಂವ್ಕ್ ಜಾತಾ. ಪೂಣ್ ತೊ ಆಧಾರ್ ಮೂಳ್ ಭಾಶೆಚೊ ಪಾಠ್ ಸಮ್ಜುನ್ ಘೆವ್ಪಾ ಪುರ್ತೊಚ್ ಆಸುಂಕ್ ಜಾಯ್. ಮೂಳ್ ಭಾಸ್ ಯೆನಾಸ್ತಾನಾ ಹೆರ್ ಭಾಸಾಂಚ್ಯಾ ಭಾಷಾಂತರಾಚೆರ್ ಆಧಾರುನ್ ಕೊಂಕ್ಣಿ ಭಾಷಾಂತರ್ ಕೆಲ್ಯಾರ್ 'ಭಾಷಾಂತರಾಚೆಂ ಭಾಷಾಂತರ್' ಜಾತಾ. ಹಾಕಾ ಲಾಗುನ್ ಭಾಷಾಂತರಾಚೊ ಪಾಂವ್ಡೊ ದೆಂವ್ತಾ. ಮೂಳ್ ಸಾಹಿತ್ಯಾಕ್ ಆನಿ ತಾಚ್ಯಾ ಬರೊವ್ಪ್ಯಾಕ್ ನೀತ್ ಮೆಳಾನಾ. ಮೂಳ್ ಭಾಶೆಚ್ಯಾ ಪಾಠಾಂತ್ ನಾಸ್‌ಲ್ಲೆ ವಿಷಯ್ ಭಾಷಾಂತರಾಂತ್ ಯೆಂವ್ಚಿ ಶಕ್ಯತಾಯ್ ಆಸಾ. ದಾಖ್ಲ್ಯಾಕ್: ಕನ್ನಡಾಂತ್ ಯು. ಆರ್. ಅನಂತಮೂರ್ತಿನ್ 'ಸಂಸ್ಕಾರ' ಕಾದಂಬರಿ ಬರಯ್ಲ್ಯಾ. ಎ. ಕೆ. ರಾಮಾನುಜಾನ್ ತೆ ಕಾದಂಬರೆಂಚೆ ಇಂಗ್ಲಿಷ್ ಭಾಷಾಂತರ್ ಕೆಲಾಂ. ಪ್ರಕಾಶ್ ಥಳಿನ್ ಇಂಗ್ಲಿಷ್ ಭಾಷಾಂತರಾಚೆರ್ ಆಧಾರುನ್ ತಿ ಕಾದಂಬರಿ ಕೊಂಕ್ಣಿಂತ್ ಭಾಷಾಂತರ್ ಕೆಲ್ಯಾ. ಅಶೆಂ ಕರ್ತಾನಾ ಮೂಳ್ ಪಾಠಾಂತ್ ನಾಸ್‌ಲ್ಲಿಂ ವಾಕ್ಯಾಂ ಭಾಷಾಂತರಾಂತ್ ಆಯ್ಲ್ಯಾಂತ್. ಕನ್ನಡ್ ಮೂಳ್ ಪಾಠ್:

"ಊಟಕ್ಕೆ ಕೂರುವ ಮುಂಚೆ ಗೋಗ್ರಾಸವನ್ನು ಬಾಳೆಲೆಯಲ್ಲಿ ಎತ್ತಿ ಹಿತ್ತಲಿನಲ್ಲಿ ಮೇಯುತ್ತಿದ್ದ ಗೌರಿಯ ಎದುರು ಇಟ್ಟು, ಹಸುವಿನ ರೋಮಾಂಚಿತ ಮೈಯನ್ನು ಒರೆಸಿ ಕಣ್ಣಿಗೊತ್ತಿಕೊಂಡು ಒಳಗೆ ಬರುತ್ತಿದ್ದಂತೆ 'ಆಚಾರ್ಯರೆ, ಆಚಾರ್ಯರೆ' ಎಂದು ಕರೆಯುವ ಹೆಣ್ಣಿನ ಸ್ವರ ಕೇಳಿಸಿತು. ಆಲಿಸಿದರೆ ನಾರಣಪ್ಪನ ಸೂಳೆ ಚಂದ್ರಿಯ ಸ್ವರದಂತಿದೆ. ಅವಳ ಹತ್ತಿರ ಮಾತನಾಡಿದರೆ ಮತ್ತೆ ಸ್ನಾನ ಮಾಡಿ ಊಟ ಮಾಡಬೇಕು. ಆದರೆ ಹೆಣ್ಣು ಹೆಂಗಸೊಬ್ಬಳನ್ನು ಅಂಗಳದಲ್ಲಿ ಕಾಯಿಸಿದರೆ ತುತ್ತು ಗಂಟಲಲ್ಲಿಳಿಯುವುದು ಶಕ್ಯವೇ?"

ಥಳಿಚಿಂ ಕೊಂಕ್ಣಿ ಭಾಷಾಂತರ್:

"ಜೆಂವ್ಕ್ ಬಸ್ಚೆಂ ಪಯ್ಲಿಂ ತಾಣೆಂ ಗೌರಿ ಹೆ ಆಪ್ಣಾಲೆ ಗಾಯೆ ಖಾತಿರ್ ಎಕಾ ಕೆಳಿ ಪಾನಾರ್ ಖಾವಡ್ ಘಾಲಿ ಆನಿ ತಿ ಪಾಟ್ಲ್ಯಾ ದಾರಾ ಚರ್ತಲೆ ಗಾಯೆ ಮುಕಾರ್ ವ್ಹರುನ್ ದವರ್‍ಲಿ. ಆಪುರ್ಬಾಯೆನ್ ಆನಿ ಭಕ್ತಿಭಾವಾನ್ ತಿಚಿ ಪಾಟ್ ಸಾಂಸ್ಪಿಲಿ. ತಿಚ್ಯಾ ಆಂಗಾರ್ ಕಾಂಟೊ ಫುಲ್ಲೊ ಆನಿ ಲ್ಹಂವ್ ಉಬಿ ಜಾಲಿ. ಜ್ಯಾ ಹಾತಾನ್ ತ್ಯಾ ಪವಿತ್ರ್ ಜಾನ್ವಾರಾಕ್ ಸಾಂಸ್ಪಿಲೆಂ ತೊಚ್ ಹಾತ್ ಶ್ರದ್ಧೆನ್ ದೊಳ್ಯಾಂಕ್ ಲಾಯ್ಲೊ. ಘರಾಂತ್ ಭಿತರ್ ಸರ್ತಾನಾಂ

ತಾಣೆಂ ಎಕೆ ಬಾಯ್ಲ್ ಮನ್ನೆಚೊ ತಾಳೊ ಆಯ್ಕಾಲೊ: 'ಆಚಾರ್ಯ್, ಆಚಾರ್ಯ್!' ತೊ ಉಲೊ ತಾಕಾ ನಾರಾಯಣಪ್ಪಾಚಿ ನಾಯ್ಕಿಣ್ ಚಂದ್ರಿಚೊಸೊ ದಿಸ್ಲೊ. ತಾಣೆಂ ಯೆವ್ವಿಲೆಂ: ಆತಾಂ ಹ್ಯಾ ವೆಳಾರ್ ಹಿಚೆ ಕಡೆನ್ ಉಲಯ್ನ್ ಜಾಲ್ಯಾರ್ ಹಾಂವ್ ಭಶ್ಟತಲೊಂ. ಜೆಂವ್ಚೆ ಪಯ್ಲೆಂ ಪರ್ತೆಂಯ್ ನ್ಹಾಂವ್ಚೆಂ ಪಡ್ತಲೆಂ. ಪೂಣ್ ಏಕ್ ಬಾಯ್ಲ್ ಮನಿಸ್ ದಾರಾಂತ್ ವಾಟ್ ಪಳಯ್ತ್ ಉಬಿ ಆಸ್ತಾನಾ ತಾಳ್ಯಾ ಸಕಯ್ಲ್ ಉಂಡಿ ಕಶಿ ವತ್ಲಿ?"

ಹ್ಯಾ ಭಾಷಾಂತರಾಂತ್ ಬರೊವ್ಪಾಚ್ಯೊ ಆನಿ ವ್ಯಾಕರಣಾಚ್ಯೊ ಚುಕಿ ಆಸಾತ್. ತಿ ಗಜಾಲ್ ಆಸುಂ. ಥಳಿಚ್ಯಾ ಭಾಷಾಂತರಾಂತ್ ಮೂಳ್ ಪಾಠಾಂತ್ ನಾಸ್‌ಲ್ಲೆ ಕಾಂಯ್ ವಿಷಯ್ ಭಿತರ್ ರಿಗ್ಲ್ಯಾತ್.

i. ಆಪ್ಣಾಲೆ ಗಾಯೆ ಖಾತಿರ್
ii. ಪಾಟ್ಲ್ಯಾ ದಾರಾ
iii. ಆಪುರ್ಬಾಯೆನ್ ಆನಿ ಭಕ್ತಿಭಾವಾನ್
iv. ತಿಚ್ಯಾ ಆಂಗಾರ್ ಕಾಂಟೊ ಫುಲ್ಲೊ
v. ಜ್ಯಾ ಹಾತಾನ್ ತ್ಯಾ ಪವಿತ್ರ್ ಜಾನ್ವಾರಾಕ್ ಸಾಂಸ್ಪಿಲೆಂ ತೊಚ್ ಹಾತ್ ಶ್ರದ್ಧೆನ್
vi. ಹಾಂವ್ ಭಶ್ಟತಲೊಂ

ಕೊಂಕ್ಣಿಂತ್ ಖಲಿಲ್ ಜಿಬ್ರಾನಾಚಿಂ ಅರೆಬಿಕ್ ಭಾಶೆಚಿಂ ಪುಸ್ತಕಾಂ, ರವೀಂದ್ರ್‌ನಾಥ್ ಟಾಗೊರಾಚಿಂ ಬಂಗಾಳಿ ಪುಸ್ತಕಾಂ, ಗಿರಿಶ್ ಕಾರ್ನಾಡಾಚಿಂ ಕನ್ನಡ್ ನಾಟಕಾಂ, ಹಿಬ್ರು ಆನಿ ಗ್ರೀಕ್ ಭಾಸಾಂಚೊ ಬಾಯ್ಬಲ್, ಸಂಸ್ಕೃತಾಂತ್ಲೆಂ ಮಹಾಭಾರತ್ ಭಾಷಾಂತರ್ ಜಾಲ್ಯಾಂತ್. ಪೂಣ್ ಹಿಂ ಭಾಷಾಂತರಾಂ ಮೂಳ್ ಭಾಶೆ ಥಾವ್ನ್ ಕೆಲ್ಲಿಂ ನ್ಹಯ್. ಭಾಷಾಂತರಾಚಿಂ ಭಾಷಾಂತರಾಂ. ಕೊಂಕ್ಣಿಂತ್ ಜಾಲ್ಲಿಂ ಕಾಂಯ್ ಭಾಷಾಂತರಾಂ ಖರ್‍ಯಾ ಅರ್ಥಾನ್ ರುಪಾಂತರಾಂ. ದಾಖ್ಲ್ಯಾಕ್ ಖಲಿಲ್ ಜಿಬ್ರಾನಾಚೆಂ 'ಅಲ್ ರುಸುಲ್' ಪುಸ್ತಕ್ ಬಾಕಿಬಾಬ್ ಬೊರ್ಕಾರಾನ್ ಇಂಗ್ಲಿಷ್ ಭಾಷಾಂತರ್ Prophet ಹಾಚ್ಯಾ ಆಧಾರಾನ್ ಕೊಂಕ್ಣಿಂತ್ 'ಪೈಗಂಬರ್' ನಾಂವಾನ್ ಕೆಲಾಂ. ರುಪಾಂತರಾಕ್ ಸಾಹಿತ್ಯಾಂತ್ ಸ್ಥಾನ್ ಆಸಾ. ಪೂಣ್ ತೆಂ ಭಾಷಾಂತರಾಚೊ ಜಾಗೊ ಘೆಂವ್ಕ್ ಸಕಾನಾ.

3.5. ಭಾಸಾಂಚಿ ಬಾಂದಾವಳ್: ಹರೆಕೆ ಭಾಶೆಕ್ ಆಪ್ಲೆಂ ಮ್ಹಣ್‌ಲ್ಲೆಂ ಖಾಶೆಲೆಪಣ್ ಆನಿ ವೆಗ್ಳೆಪಣ್ ಆಸಾ. ದೆಕುನ್ ಕನ್ನಡ್ ಭಾಶೆ ಪ್ರಾಸ್ ಕೊಂಕ್ಣಿ ವೆಗ್ಳಿ. ಇಂಗ್ಲಿಷ್ ಭಾಶೆಚ್ಯಾ ಗದ್ಯಾಚೆ ವಾಕ್ಯರಚನೆಂತ್ ಕರ್ತೊ (subjects) + ಕ್ರಿಯಾ (verb) + ಕರ್ಮ್ (objects) ಹೊ ಕ್ರಮ್ ಆಸಾ. ದಾಖ್ಲ್ಯಾಕ್:

The boy ate a mango.

ಕೊಂಕ್ಣಿಂತ್ ಹೊ ಕ್ರಮ್ ವೆಗ್ಳೊ ಆಸಾ. ಕರ್ತೊ+ಕ್ರಮ್+ಕ್ರಿಯಾ ದೆಕುನ್ ವಯ್ಲೆಂ ಇಂಗ್ಲಿಷ್ ವಾಕ್ಯ್ ಕೊಂಕ್ಣಿಂತ್ "ಭುರ್ಗ್ಯಾನ್ ಆಂಬೊ ಖೆಲೊ (ಖಾಲೊ)" ಅಶೆಂ ಜಾತಾ.

ಇಂಗ್ಲಿಷ್ ಆನಿ ಹಿಂದಿ ಭಾಸಾಂಚ್ಯಾ ಪ್ರಭಾವಾನ್ ಕೊಂಕ್ಣಿ ಬರೊವ್ಪಿ 'ಕಿ' ಹ್ಯಾ ಉತ್ರಾಚೊ that ಹ್ಯಾ ಅರ್ಥಾನ್ ವಾಪರ್ ಕರ್ತಾತ್. ದಾಖ್ಲ್ಯಾಕ್: Gopal said that the story was true.

"ಗೋಪಾಲಾನ್ ಸಾಂಗ್ಲೆಂ ಕಿ ತಿ ಕಾಣಿ ಖರಿ"

'ಕಿ' ಉತರ್ ಕೊಂಕ್ಣಿ ಉಲೊವ್ಪಿ ಸಾದಿಂ ಮನ್ಶಾಂ ವಾಪರಿನಾಂತ್. ಕಿತ್ಯಾಕ್ 'ಕಿ' that ಹ್ಯಾ ಅರ್ಥಾನ್ ಕೊಂಕ್ಣಿಂತ್ ನಾ. ದೆಕುನ್ "ಗೋಪಾಲಾನ್ ಸಾಂಗ್ಲೆಂ, ತಿ ಕಾಣಿ ಖರಿ" ಹೆಂ ವಾಕ್ಯ್ ಕೊಂಕ್ಣಿಚ್ಯಾ ಬಾಂದಾವಳಿ ಪ್ರಕಾರ್ ಆಸಾ. ಭಾಷಾಂತರ್‌ಕಾರಾಕ್ ಮೂಳ್ ಭಾಶೆಚೆಂ ವ್ಯಾಕರಣ್ ಆನಿ ಶೆವಟ್ ಭಾಶೆಚೆಂ ವ್ಯಾಕರಣ್ ಹಾಂಚೆ ಮಧ್ಲೊ ಫರಕ್ ಖಬರ್ ಆಸುಂಕ್ ಜಾಯ್.

3.6. ಮೂಳ್ ಪಾಠಾಚ್ಯಾ ಆಶಯಾಕ್ ಲಾಗಿಂ ಲಾಗಿಂ ಯೆತಾ ತಸಲೆಂ ಸಮನಾರ್ಥಿ ಉತರ್ (equivalent word) ಭಾಷಾಂತರಾಕ್ ಗರ್ಜೆಚೆಂ. ಸರ್ವ್‌ಸಮ್ ಉತರ್

(identical word) ಗರ್ಜ್ ನಾ. ದಾಖ್ಲ್ಯಾಕ್: Good morning ಹಾಚೆಂ ಸಮನಾರ್ಥಿ ಭಾಷಾಂತರ್ "ದೇವ್ ಬರೊ ದೀಸ್ ದೀಂವ್". "ಬರಿ ಸಕಾಳ್" ಹೆಂ ಸರ್ವ್‌ಸಮ್ ಭಾಷಾಂತರ್ ಅಡೆಚೆಂ (artificial) ಜಾತಾ.

Cousin ಹ್ಯಾ ಉತ್ರಾಕ್ ಕೊಂಕ್ಣಿಂತ್ ಜಾಯ್ತಿಂ ಉತ್ರಾಂ ಆಸಾತ್. ದಾಖ್ಲ್ಯಾಕ್: ಮಾವ್ಶೆ ಭಾವ್, ಮಾವ್ಶೆ ಭಯ್ಣ್, ಬಾಪುಲ್ ಭಾವ್, ಬಾಪುಲ್ ಭಯ್ಣ್, ಮಾಮೆ ಭಾವ್, ಮಾಮೆ ಭಯ್ಣ್...

ಇಂಗ್ಲಿಷ್ ಥಾವ್ ಕೊಂಕ್ಣಿಕ್ ಭಾಷಾಂತರ್ ಕರ್ತಾನಾ Cousin ಖಂಯ್ಚ್ಯಾ ಅರ್ಥಾನ್ ವಾಪರ್ಲಾಂ. ತ್ಯಾ ಅರ್ಥಾಚೆಂ ಕೊಂಕ್ಣಿ ಉತರ್ ದಿಂವ್ಚೆಂ ಪಡ್ತಾ. ಹಿಚ್ ಪದ್ಧತ್ ಸೊಯ್ರಿಕ್ ದಾಕೊವ್ಪಿ, uncle, aunty, nephew, niece ಹ್ಯಾ ಉತ್ರಾಂಕ್ ಲಾಗು ಜಾತಾ.

3.7. ಭಾಷಾಂತರ್‌ಕಾರಾನ್ ಮೂಳ್ ಭಾಶೆಚ್ಯಾ ಪಾಠಾಕ್ ಜಾತಾ ತಿತ್ಲೆಂ ಲಾಗಿಂ ರಾವುಂಕ್ ಆಸಾ. ಪೂಣ್ ಮೂಳ್ ಭಾಶೆಚಿ ಶೈಲಿ, ವ್ಯಾಕರಣಾಚಿ ಬಾಂದಾವಳ್, ಸಾಂಸ್ಕೃತಿಕ್ ಸಂದರ್ಭ್, ಅಲಂಕಾರ್, ಪ್ರಾಸ್ ಇತ್ಯಾದಿ ಪಾಳ್ಚಿ ಗರ್ಜ್ ನಾ. ತರ್‌ಯಿ ಕವಿತೆಚೊ ಪಾಠ್ ಗದ್ಯಾಂತ್ ಭಾಷಾಂತರ್ ಕರ್ಚೊ ನ್ಹಯ್. ಮೂಳ್ ಪಾಠಾಚ್ಯಾ ವಿಷಯಾ ಪ್ರಮಾಣೆಂ ಆನಿ ಭಾಷಾಂತರಾಚ್ಯಾ ಉದ್ದೇಶಾ ಪ್ರಮಾಣೆಂ ಭಾಷಾಂತರಾಚಿ ಶೈಲಿ ವಿಂಚ್ಚಿ ಪಡ್ತಾ. ಭಾಷಾಂತರ್ ಕರ್ಚೆಂ ಕಾಮ್ ಉಲಯ್ತಾ ತಿತ್ಲೆಂ ಸೊಂಪೆಂ ನ್ಹಯ್. ದೆಕುನ್ ಎಕ್ಲೊ ಇಟೆಲಿಯನ್ ಬರೊವ್ಪಿ ಮ್ಹಣ್ತಾ: **"ಭಾಷಾಂತರ್ ಎಕೆ ಬಾಯ್ಲೆ ಪರಿಂ. ಸೊಬಾಯ್ ಆಸ್ಲ್ಯಾರ್ ಪ್ರಾಮಾಣಿಕ್ಪಣ್ ನಾ. ಪ್ರಾಮಾಣಿಕ್ಪಣ್ ಆಸ್ಲ್ಯಾರ್ ಸೊಬಾಯ್ ನಾ."**

ಭಗವದ್ಗೀತೆಚೆಂ ಭಾಷಾಂತರ್ ಶೆಣೈ ಗೊಂಯ್‌ಬಾಬಾನ್ ಕೊಂಕ್ಣಿ ಗದ್ಯಾಂತ್ ಕೆಲಾಂ. ಭಗವದ್ಗೀತೆಚೊ ಸಾರ್ (content) ತಾಣೆಂ ಕೊಂಕ್ಣಿಂತ್ ದಿಲಾ. ಪೂಣ್ ಜಶಿ ಭಗವದ್ಗೀತಾ ಸಂಸ್ಕೃತಾಂತ್ ಗಾಂವ್ಕ್ ಜಾತಾ ತಶೆಂ ಶೆಣೈ ಗೊಂಯ್‌ಬಾಬಾಚೆಂ ಭಾಷಾಂತರ್ ಗಾವ್ಪಾಕ್ ಉಪ್ಕಾರ್ನಾ.

ಇಂಗ್ಲಿಷ್ ಭಾಶೆಚೆಂ Maiden Mother ನಾಂವಾಚೆಂ ಧಾರ್ಮಿಕ್ ಗೀತ್ ಆಸಾ. ತ್ಯಾ ಗಿತಾಚೊ ನಾದ್ (melody) ಸಾಂಬಾಳುನ್ ಮಂಗ್ಳುರಾಂತ್ ಕೊಂಕ್ಣಿ ಭಾಷಾಂತರ್ ಬರೆಂ ಕೆಲಾಂ. ಭಾಷಾಂತರ್ ಎಕುಣಿಸಾವ್ಯಾ ಶೆಕ್ಡ್ಯಾಚೆ ಆಖೆರಿಕ್ ವಾ ವಿಸಾವ್ಯಾ ಶೆಕ್ಡ್ಯಾಚೆ ಸುರ್ವಾತೆಕ್ ಕೊಣೆಂ ತರ್‌ಯಿ ಕೆಲಾಂ.

ಇಂಗ್ಲಿಷ್ ಮೂಳ್ ಗೀತ್

MAIDEN MOTHER
Maiden Mother, meek and mild
Take, Oh, take me for thy child;
All my life, Oh, let it be
My best joy to think of thee

Ch: When my eyes are closed in sleep
Through the night my slumbers keep;
Make my latest thought to be
How to love thy son and thee

Teach me, when the sunbeam bright
Calls me with its golden light,
How my waking thoughts may be
Turned to Jesus and to thee.

And, oh teach me through the day
Oft to raise my heart, and say:
Maiden mother, meek and mild,
Guard, Oh! Guard thy faithful child."

ಕೊಂಕ್ಣಿ ಭಾಷಾಂತರ್:

1. ಮಾಯೆ ಮ್ಹಜೆ ಭೋವ್ ಮೊಗಾಳ್
ಕರ್‍ನ್ ಘೆ ಮ್ಹಾಕಾ ತುಜೆಂ ಬಾಳ್
ಜಾಂವ್ ಮಾಯೆ ಉಡಾಸ್ ತುಜೊ
ಸಂತೊಸ್ ಮ್ಹಜ್ಯಾ (ಮ್ಹಜೆ) ಜಿಣ್ಯೆಚೊ.

ಸಕ್ಕಡ್: ಹಾಂವ್ ನಿದೊನ್ ಧಾಂಪ್ತಚ್ ದೊಳೆ
ಕಾಂಯ್ ಪೂಣ್ ವಿಘ್ನ್ ಯೆತ್‌ಗಿ ಪಳೆ;
ನಿದೆಂತ್‌ಯಿ ಹುಸ್ಕೊ ಮ್ಹಜೊ
ಕಸೊ ಕರುಂ ಮೋಗ್ ತುಜೊ.

ಸಕಾಳಿಂಚಿ ಜಾಗ್ ಜಾತಚ್
ತೊಂಡಾರ್ ಮ್ಹಜ್ಯಾ ದೀಸ್ ಫಾಂಕ್ತಚ್
ಪಯ್ಲಿ ಹಾ! ಚಿಂತ್ನಾಂ ಮ್ಹಜಿಂ,
ಜೆಜುಚಿ ಆನಿ ತುಜಿ.

ಸರ್ವ್ಂ ವಸ್ತುಂತ್ ಮ್ಹಣುಂಕ್ ಶಿಕಯ್
ಸೊಧುನ್ ಯೇವ್ನ್ ತುಜಿ ಸಸಾಯ್
"ಮಾಯೆ ಮ್ಹಜೆ, ಭೋವ್ ಮೊಗಾಳ್
ರಾಕ್ ಮ್ಹಾಕಾ ಹಾಂವ್ ತುಜೆಂ ಬಾಳ್."

3.8. ಭಾಷಾಂತರ್ ಕೆಲ್ಲೊ ಪಾಠ್ ಭಾಷಾಂತರ್ ಕೆಲ್ಲೆ ಪರಿಂ ದಿಸುಂಕ್ ಜಾಯ್ನಾ. ತೊ ಶೆವಟ್ ಭಾಶೆಂತ್ಲೊಚ್ ಪಾಠ್ ಅಸೊ ದಿಸುಂಕ್ ಜಾಯ್. ಅಶೆಂ ಜಾಂವ್ಕ್ ಜಾಯ್ ಜಾಲ್ಯಾರ್ ಭಾಷಾಂತರಾಚಿ ಭಾಸ್ ವ್ಹಾಳುಂಕ್ ಜಾಯ್. ಅಸ್ಪಷ್ಟತಾಯ್ (ambiguity), ಲಾಂಬ್ ವಾಕ್ಯಾಂ ನಾಸ್ತಾನಾ ಸೊಂಪಿ, ಸುಢಾಳ್, ಆಕರ್ಷಿಕ್ ಭಾಸ್ ವಾಪರ್ಚಿ ಗರ್ಜ್. ದಾಖ್ಲ್ಯಾಕ್ ಯಶವಂತ್ ಚಿತ್ತಾಲಾಚಿ ಕನ್ನಡ್ ಕಥಾ "ಆಬೊಲಿನ" ಘೆಯಾತ್. ಮೆಲ್ವಿನ್ ರುದ್ರಿಗಿಶಾನ್ ತಿ 'ಆಬೊಲಿನ್' ನಾಂವಾನ್ ಕೊಂಕ್ಣಿಂತ್ ಭಾಷಾಂತರ್ ಕೆಲ್ಯಾ. ತಾಂತ್ಲೊ ಏಕ್ ಉತಾರೊ ವಾಚಾತ್.

"ಆಮ್ಗೆರ್ ಸದಾಂಯ್ ಫುಲಾಂ ಹಾಡ್ಚ್ಯಾ ಚೆಡ್ವಾನ್ ತ್ಯಾ ದೀಸ್ ಆಬೊಲಿಂ ಹಾಡ್‌ಲ್ಲ್ಯಾ ವೆಳಾರ್ ಕಿತೆಂ ಎಕಾಚ್‌ಫರಾ ಮ್ಹಾಕಾ ಆಬೊಲಿನಾಚೊ ಉಗ್ಡಾಸ್ ಆಯ್ಲೊ. ಆಬೊಲಿಂ ಮ್ಹಳ್ಯಾರ್ ಜೀವ್; ಹಾಡ್‌ಲ್ಲಿಂ ಕಾಣ್ಘೆಜೆ ಮ್ಹಣ್ ಮ್ಹಾಕಾ ಭೊಗ್ಲೆಂ. ಪೂಣ್ ದುಸ್ರೆ ಘಡಿಯೆ, ಹಿಂ ಫುಲಾಂ ಆಪ್ಣ ಬರಾಬರ್ ಹಾಡ್‌ಲ್ಲೆ ಆನಿ ಕಿತ್ಲೆಶಾ ತೆಂಪಾ ಆದಿಂ ಆಮ್ಕಾಂ ಸಾಂಡುನ್ ಗೆಲ್ಲೆ ಮ್ಹಜೆ ಮೊಗಾಚೆ ಇಷ್ಟಿಣಿಚೊ ಆಬೊಲಿನಾಚೊ ಉಗ್ಡಾಸ್ ಯೇವ್ನ್ ಮ್ಹಜೊ ಜೀವ್ ಕಳ್ವಳ್ಳೊ. ಮ್ಹಜ್ಯಾ ತೊಂಡಾರ್ ತೆದಾಳಾ ಕಸಲಿಂ ಭೊಗ್ಣಾಂ ರುಪೆಲ್ಲಿಂ ಕೊಣ್ ಜಾಣಾ? ಲಾಗ್ಸಾರ್‌ಚ್ ಉಬೊ ರಾವೊನ್ ಆಸ್‌ಲ್ಲ್ಯಾ ಆಮ್ಗೆಲ್ಯಾನ್ ವಿಚಾರ್ಲೆಂ: "ಕಿತೆಂ ಜಾಲೆಂ, ಸುಮತಿ? ಫುಲಾಂ ಕಾಣ್ಘೆವ್ನ್ ಸೊಡಿನಾಂಯ್? ತುಜ್ಯಾ ಜಿವಾಚಿ ಗಾಂಟ್ ತಿಂ" ಮ್ಹಣ್ ಒತ್ತಾಯ್ ಕೆಲೊ.

ಬರ್ಯಾ ಭಾಷಾಂತರಾಚೆ ಸರ್ವ್ ಗೂಣ್ ಹ್ಯಾ ಭಾಷಾಂತರಾಂತ್ ಆಸಾತ್.

ಮೂಳ್ ಭಾಸ್ ಜ್ಯಾ ವಾಚ್ಪ್ಯಾಂಕ್ ಯೆನಾ ತಾಂಚೆ ಭಿತರ್ ತೆ ಭಾಶೆಂತ್ಲೆಂ ಮೊಲಾಚೆಂ ಸಾಹಿತ್ಯ್ ವಾಚ್ಪ್ಯಾಂಚೆ ಭಾಶೆಂತ್ ತಾಂಕಾಂ ವಾಚುಂಕ್ ಮೆಳ್ಚೆಂ ಹೊ ಭಾಷಾಂತರಾಚೊ ಮುಳಾವೊ ಉದ್ದೇಶ್. ಅಶೆಂ ಆಸ್ತಾನಾ ಭಾಷಾಂತರ್ ಕೆಲ್ಲೊ ಪಾಠ್ ಮೂಳ್ ಭಾಶೆಚ್ಯಾ ಪಾಠಾ ತಿತ್ಲೊಚ್ ವಾ ಚಡ್ ಕಠಿಣ್ ಜರ್ ಜಾಲೊ ತರ್ ಭಾಷಾಂತರಾಚೊ ಉದ್ಧೇಶ್ ನಿರ್ಫಳ್ ಜಾತಲೊ. ದಾಖ್ಲ್ಯಾಕ್ ಭಗವದ್ಗೀತೆಚೊ 9:18 ಶ್ಲೋಕ್ ಘೆಯಾತ್:

गतिर्भता प्रभु: साक्षी निवास: शरणं सुहृत ।
प्रभवः प्रलयः स्थानं निधानं वीजव्ययम् ।।

ಹಾಚೆಂ ಭಾಷಾಂತರ್ ದೆವಾದಿನ್ ಬಾಕಿಬಾಬ್ ಬೊರ್ಕಾರಾನ್ ಅಶೆಂ ಕೆಲಾಂ: "ಪುಸ್ತಿವಂತ್, ಸಗೊ, ಸ್ವಾಮಿ, ಸಾಕ್ಷಿ, ಥಾರ್, ದಿಗಿ, ಗತಿ ಉತ್ಪತ್ತಿ – ಸ್ಥಿತಿ ಲಯಯ್ ಹಾಂವ್ ಮುದಲ್ ವೀಜ್ ಅವ್ಯಯ್." ಹೆಂ ಭಾಷಾಂತರ್ ಸಾದ್ಯಾ ವಾಚ್ಪ್ಯಾಂಕ್ ಸೊಡಾತ್. ಶಿಕ್‌ಲ್ಲ್ಯಾ ಮನ್ಶ್ಯಾಂಕ್ ಸಮ್ಜನಾ. ವಯ್ಲ್ಯಾ ಶ್ಲೊಕಾಚೆಂ ಭಾಷಾಂತರ್ ಅಶೆಂ ಕರುಂಕ್ ಜಾತಾ: "ಸರ್ವಾಂಕ್ ಹಾಲ್‌ಚಾಲ್, ಪೊಸ್ಚಿ, ಧನಿ, ಸಾಕ್ಷಿ, ಥಾರೊ, ಆಸ್ರೊ, ಇಷ್ಟ್ ಹಾಂವ್ ಸರ್ವಾಂಚೊ ರಚ್ಪಿ, ನಾಸ್ ಕರ್ಪಿ, ಥಳ್, ಸಂಪತ್ತಿ, ಅವಿನಾಶಿ ಬಿಂ ಹಾಂವ್‌ಚ್"

4. ಸಾಹಿತ್ಯಾಚ್ಯಾ ಮಳಾರ್ ಕೊಂಕ್ಣಿ ಉದೆವ್ನ್ ಯೆಂವ್ಚಿ ಭಾಸ್. ಕೊಂಕ್ಣಿ ಸಾಹಿತ್ಯಾಚ್ಯಾ ವಿಕಾಸಾಕ್ ಭಾಷಾಂತರ್ ಸಾಹಿತ್ಯ್ ಏಕ್ ಸಾಧನ್ (means) ವಾ ದೆಣೆಂ ಜಾಂವ್ ಯೆತಾ. ಹಾಂತುಂ ದುಸ್ರೊ ವಾದ್ ಆಸಾಸೊ ದಿಸನಾ.

ಖಂಯ್ಚೆಯ್ ಭಾಶೆಚ್ಯಾ ಸಾಹಿತ್ಯಾಚೊ ದರ್ಜೊ ಫಕತ್ ಸರ್ಜನಾತ್ಮಕ್ ಸಾಹಿತ್ಯಾಚೆರ್ ಮಾತ್ರ್ ಆಧಾರುನ್ ನಾ. ಭಾಷಾಂತರ್ ಸಾಹಿತ್ಯಾಕ್ ಲಾಗುನ್ ತೊ ವಾಡೊಂವ್ಕ್ ಜಾತಾ. ಸೊಳಾವ್ಯಾ ಶೆಕ್ಡ್ಯಾಂತ್ ಜರ್ಮನ್ ಭಾಶೆಂತ್ ಬಾಯ್ಬಲ್ ಭಾಷಾಂತರ್ ಜಾತಚ್ ಜರ್ಮನ್ ಸಾಹಿತ್ಯಾಚೊ ಪಾಂವ್ಡೊ ವಾಡೊಂಕ್ ಸುರು ಜಾಲೊ. ಬಾಯ್ಬಲಾಚೆಂ King James Version ಭಾಷಾಂತರ್ 1611 ವರ್ಸಾ ಇಂಗ್ಲಿಷಾಂತ್ ಉಜ್ವಾಡಾಕ್ ಆಯ್ಲೆಂ. ಇಂಗ್ಲಿಷ್ ಸಾಹಿತ್ಯಾಂತ್ ಹ್ಯಾ ಭಾಷಾಂತರಾಕ್ ಚಡ್ ಮಹತ್ವ್ ಆಸಾ.

ಸಂಸಾರಾಂತ್ಲ್ಯಾ ಆನಿ ಭಾರತಾಂತ್ಲ್ಯಾ ಭಾಸಾಂಚೆಂ ಉಂಚ್ಲೆಂ ಸಾಹಿತ್ಯ್ ಆನಿ ವಿಚಾರ್‌ವಂತ್ ಬರೊವ್ಪ್ಯಾಂಚಿ ಬರ್ಪಾವಳ್ ಕೊಂಕ್ಣಿ ಲೊಕಾಕ್ ಆಪ್ಲೆ ಭಾಶೆಂತ್ ಮೆಳುಂಕ್ ಭಾಷಾಂತರ್ ಏಕ್ ಬರಿ ವಾಟ್. ಜೆದ್ನಾಂ ದೇಶಿ ಆನಿ ವಿದೇಶಿ ಭಾಸಾಂತ್ಲೆಂ ಉಂಚ್ಲೆಂ ಸಾಹಿತ್ಯ್ ಕೊಂಕ್ಣಿಂತ್ ಭಾಷಾಂತರ್ ಜಾತಲೆಂ ತೆದ್ನಾಂ ಕೊಂಕ್ಣಿ ಸಾಹಿತ್ಯಾಚೆರ್, ಬರೊವ್ಪ್ಯಾಚೆರ್ ಆನಿ ವಾಚ್ಪ್ಯಾಂಚೆರ್ ಪ್ರಭಾವ್ ಪಡ್ತಲೊ. ಹಾಕಾ ಲಾಗುನ್ ಕೊಂಕ್ಣಿ ಸಾಹಿತ್ಯಾಚಿ ದಿಶಾ, ನದರ್ ಆನಿ ವ್ಯಾಪ್ (scope) ಬದ್ಲುಂಕ್ ಸಕ್ತಾ. ಭಾಷಾಂತರ್ ಸಾಹಿತ್ಯಾಕ್ ಲಾಗುನ್ ಕೊಂಕ್ಣಿಂತ್ ನವಿ ಉತ್ರಾವಳ್, ವಾಕ್ ಪ್ರಚಾರ್, ಅಲಂಕಾರ್ ಯೆತಲೆ. ಹಾಕಾ ಲಾಗುನ್ ಭಾಶೆಚೊಯ್ ವಿಕಾಸ್ ಜಾತಲೊ.

ಕೊಂಕ್ಣಿ ಲೋಕ್ ಆಸ್ಚೊ ಪೊಸೊಭರ್ ಆನಿ ತೊ ಚಾರ್ ರಾಜ್ಯಾಂನಿ ಶಿಂಪ್ಡೊನ್ ಆಸಾ. ತಾಂತುಂ ವಾಚ್ಪಿ ಮೂಟ್‌ಭರ್. ಬರೊವ್ಪಿ ಚಿಮ್ಟಿಭರ್. ಭಾಷಾಂತರ್‌ಕಾರ್ ಬೊಟಾಂಚೆರ್ ಮೆಜುಂಕ್ ಮೆಳನಾಂತ್ ತಿತ್ಲೆ ಉಣೆ ಕೊಂಕ್ಣಿ ಸಾಹಿತ್ಯ್ ಕನ್ನಡ್, ದೇವನಾಗರಿ ಆನಿ ರೊಮಿ ಲಿಪಿಯಾಂನಿ ವಾಂಟುನ್ ಗೆಲಾಂ. ತೀನ್‌ಯಿ ಲಿಪಿಯಾಂತ್ಲೆಂ ಸಾಹಿತ್ಯ್ ದೊಳ್ಯಾಂ ಮುಕಾರ್ ದವರ್ಲ್ಯಾರ್ ಸಯ್ತ್ ಕೊಂಕ್ಣಿಂತ್ ಭಾಷಾಂತರ್ ಸಾಹಿತ್ಯಾಚೆಂ ಪ್ರಮಾಣ್ ಉಣೆಂ ಆಸಾ. ದೆಕುನ್ ಭಾಷಾಂತರ್ ಮಳ್ಯಾಂತ್ ಕಾಮ್ ಕರುಂಕ್ ಫಾವೊತಿಂ ಪಾವ್ಲಾಂ ಕಾಡುಂಕ್ ಆಸಾತ್.

4.1 ದೋನ್ ಪ್ರಕಾರಾಚ್ಯಾ ಭಾಷಾಂತರ್ ವಾವ್ರಾಚೆರ್ ಆಮಿ ಲಕ್ಷ್ ಘಾಲ್ಚೆಂ ಪಡ್ತಲೆಂ.

i. ಹೆರ್ ಭಾಸಾಂಚೆಂ ಉಂಚ್ಲೆಂ ಸಾಹಿತ್ಯ್ ಕೊಂಕ್ಣಿಂತ್ ಭಾಷಾಂತರ್ ಕರ್ಚೆಂ. ಕೊಂಕ್ಣಿ ಮನಿಸ್ ದ್ವಿಭಾಷಿಕ್. ಗುಜರಾತಿ, ಹಿಂದಿ, ತಮಿಳ್, ತೆಲುಗು, ಮಲಯಾಳಂ, ಕನ್ನಡ್, ಉರ್ದು, ಜರ್ಮನ್, ಫ್ರೆಂಚ್, ಸಂಸ್ಕೃತ್ ಇಟೆಲಿಯನ್, ಸ್ಪೆನಿಷ್, ಲಾತಿನ್, ಗ್ರೀಕ್, ಹಿಬ್ರು. ಇತ್ಯಾದಿ ಭಾಸೊ ಯೆವ್ಪಿ ಕೊಂಕಣಿ ಮನಿಸ್ ಆಸಾತ್. ಹ್ಯಾ ಭಾಸಾಂತ್ಲೆಂ ಸಾಹಿತ್ಯ್ ಕೊಂಕ್ಣಿಂತ್ ಭಾಷಾಂತರ್ ಕರುಂಕ್ ತಾಣಿಂ ಹಾತ್‌ಭಾರ್ ಲಾಂವ್ಕ್ ಜಾತಾ.

ii. ಕೊಂಕ್ಣಿಂತ್ಲೆಂ ಉಂಚ್ಲೆಂ ಸಾಹಿತ್ಯ್ ಹೆರ್ ಭಾಸಾಂನಿ ಭಾಷಾಂತರ್ ಕರ್ಚೆಂ. ಹೆಂಯ್ ಕಾಮ್ ತಿತ್ಲೆಂಚ್ ಮಹತ್ವಾಚೆಂ ಆನಿ ಗರ್ಜೆಚೆಂ. ಹಾಕಾ ಲಾಗುನ್ ಕೊಂಕ್ಣಿ ಸಾಹಿತ್ಯಾಚೊ ಪಾಂವ್ಡೊ ಖಂಯ್ ಆಸಾ ಹೆಂ ಹೆರ್ ಭಾಸಾಂಚ್ಯಾ ಲೊಕಾಕ್ ಕಳ್ತಲೆಂ. ಕೊಂಕ್ಣಿಕ್ ರಾಷ್ಟ್ರೀಯ್ ಮಾನ್ಯತಾಯ್ ಮೆಳ್ಳಿ, ರಾಜ್‌ಭಾಶೆಚೊ ಮಾನ್ ಮೆಳ್ಳೊ ವಾ ಕೊಂಕ್ಣಿ ಸಾಹಿತ್ಯಾಕ್ ಪುರಸ್ಕಾರ್ ಮೆಳ್ಳೆ ಮ್ಹಣುನ್ ಆಮ್ಚೆಂ ಸಾಹಿತ್ಯ್ ಹೆರ್ ಭಾಸಾಂಚ್ಯಾ ಪಾಂವ್ಡ್ಯಾಕ್ ಪಾವ್ಲಾಂ ಮ್ಹಣುಂಕ್ ಜಾಯ್ನಾ. ಜೆದ್ನಾಂ ಹೆರ್ ಭಾಸಾಂಚೆಂ ಲೋಕ್ ಭಾಷಾಂತರ್ ಕೆಲ್ಲೆಂ ಕೊಂಕ್ಣಿ ಸಾಹಿತ್ಯ್ ತಾಂಚ್ಯಾ ಭಾಸಾಂನಿ ವಾಚ್ತಲೆ ತೆದ್ನಾಂಚ್ ಕೊಂಕ್ಣಿ ಸಾಹಿತ್ಯಾಚ್ಯಾ ಪಾಂವ್ಡ್ಯಾಚಿ ಖರಿ ಪರಿಕ್ಷಾ ಜಾತಲಿ. ಬಾಂಯ್ತ್ಲೆ ಮಾಣ್ಕೆ ಬಾಂಯ್ತ್ ಬೊಬೊ ಫಾಲ್ತಾತ್ ಆನಿ ಆಪ್ಲಿ ಬಾಂಯ್ ಸಂಸಾರಾ ತೆದಿ ಆಸಾ ಅಶೆಂ ಚಿಂತ್ತಾತ್. ತಿ ಗತ್ ಕೊಂಕ್ಣಿಚಿ (ಕೊಂಕ್ಣಿ ಭಾಶೆಚಿ ಆನಿ ಮನ್ಶಾಂಚಿ) ಜಾಂವ್ಚಿ ನ್ಹಯ್.

ಆಧಾರಾವಳ್ (BIBLIOGRAPHY):

NIDA, Eugene A. 1982. The Theory and Practice of Translation. Leiden, E.J. Brill.

Snell-Hornby, Mary 1988 Translation Studies: An Integrated Approach. Amsterdam, John Benjamins Publishing Company.

नौटियाल, जयन्ती प्र. २००२ अनुवाद: सिद्धांत एवं व्यवहार
नई दिल्ली, राधाकृष्ण प्रकाशन

आमोणकर, सुरेश गु २००१ अणकार: कांय विचार
जाग २७:९ पानां १३-१५

ನಾಯ್ಕ್, ಪ್ರತಾಪ್ 1996. ಅಣ್ಕಾರ್ ಸಾಹಿತ್ಯ್ ಆನಿ ಕೊಂಕ್ಣಿ ಭಾಸ್ ಉಮಾಳೊ, ಎಪ್ರಿಲ್ 1996. ಪಾನಾಂ 9–10.

Conclusion

As Walter Ong's work emphasises, the history of oral languages is often represented at the moment it diverges from the norm set by dominant language history. This does not sufficiently capture the life of a language, as the following paragraphs suggest. In 1866, a foreword to a journal containing Portuguese and Konkani songs made the surprising suggestion that Konkani songs needed to be salvaged before they were forgotten. The short-lived journal, the *Ramalhetinho de alguns hymnos e canções,* which appeared in 1866, was one of three publications containing Konkani songs and hymns published between 1855 and 1866 in Goa.[1]

Though it never used the term 'folk', the *Ramalhetinho,* which contained both Portuguese and Konkani songs, represented Konkani music in a manner that approximated the portrayal of folk forms in later years.[2] Unlike its representation of formal and popular Portuguese songs, for instance, generic Konkani songs were footnoted with explanations of social context and ritual, placing them within the realm of social history and ethnography.[3]

---

[1] Miguel Vicente de Abreu, ed., *Ramalhetinho de alguns Hymnos e Canções profanas em Portuguez e Concani* (Nova Goa: Imprensa Nacional, 1866); Miguel Vicente de Abreu, *Stabat Mater e outras Orações em Concanim* (Nova Goa: Imprensa Nacional, 1855); *Miguel Vicente de Abreu, Cantigas Pias ou Orações, em Versos, da Virgem Maria Nossa Senhora e da Senhora Sant'Anna, em Língua Concani, Portuguesa e Latina* (Nova Goa: Imprensa Nacional, 1859). While the first issue announced that it would be a monthly, the second and third appeared only after four years in 1870 as the author was preoccupied with other writing.

[2] For an account of the demarcation of folk music from other forms and the implications of these terms in nineteenth-century Goa, see Susana Sardo, "Hospedeiros do Oriente – o Lugar do Oriente na Literatura Goesa sobre Folclore e Música em Século XX," in *ACT 27 - Goa Portuguesa e Pós-Colonial: Literatura, Cultura e Sociedade* (Lisboa: Húmus/CEC, 2014), 137–53.

[3] ibid.

One of the songs however, disrupted this representation of a society in which Portuguese was the norm and Konkani music a practice that was receding into the past. The song *Amiga Janona* contained some pidgin Portuguese, some standard Portuguese, Konkani terms for food, and some usages that were neither recognizably Portuguese nor Konkani. Diverse opinions were offered about the provenance and authorship of the song,which was republished twice in the twentieth century.[4] The linguist Hugo Cardoso states that theories proposing that these were creole usages, or that a domestic slave was one of the authors of the song are not persuasive. However, the fact that African or Brazilian usages were considered within the realm of possibility broadens the range of languages we imagine Konkani to be in interaction with.[5] The ambiguity over the provenance of words in *Amiga Janona* serves as a reminder that the representation of Konkani songs falling out of practice was pertinent only to a small readership.

In fact, this depiction of Konkani practices as though they were receding into the past was an effect of the standardisation of Portuguese writing in nineteenth-century Goa, which enlarged the distance envisioned between the realms of the oral and the written. The *Ramalhetinho* and the two other songbooks by the same author appeared in the decade between 1855 and 1866, as did the often-cited historical essay by J. H. da Cunha Rivara calling for the recovery of Konkani. In a context in which the language was said to be in need of recognition, it is not surprising that a songbook spoke of the imminent disappearance of its traditions. The relegation of Konkani to the space of the almost forgotten is also ironical as Konkani simultaneously began to appear in popular print in the form of vocabularies and dictionaries.

However, the *Ramalhetinho* is one among a range of texts that indicate that while oral practices were contained by print, they also disturbed self-representations of the ubiquity of the Portuguese language, though it had become the primary language of the elite. In Portuguese literary writing in particular, Konkani appeared as an eruption of the colloquial within formal speech, or as a parallel

---

[4] Sebastião Rodolfo Dalgado, *Berço duma cantiga em Indo-Portugues (à memoria de Ismael Gracias)* (Porto: Tipografia Sequeira, Limitade, 1921). The song was reproduced in the *O Heraldo* in 1904, and then by Ismael Gracias in the *Oriente Português* of 1918.

[5] Hugo C. Cardoso, "The African Slave Population of Portuguese India - Demographics and Impact on Indo-Portuguese," *Journal of Pidgin and Creole Languages* 25, no. 1 (2010): 100.

language of political commentary, but always, expectedly, as a marginal presence. At the end of the century, in the satire, *Jacob e Dulce*, Konkani was the earthy primary language into which the insufficiently educated elite slipped with their inadequate grasp of Portuguese.[6] It represented the world of bawdy witticisms that revealed the underbelly of polite society. The novel appeared in 1896, at approximately the same time as Valaulikar's valorisation of Konkani as a primal poetic reserve of folk culture, and his parodic depiction of the Hindu elite's attempt to claim Marathi as their high culture. Konkani orality was therefore configured differently in each linguistic context.

These contexts are visible if the binaries that underpin modern national linguistic models are made apparent. Thus, against the idea of language as a territorialised, historicised, written, individualised, classical and standardised entity, its existence as a contact language that appeared in conjunction with pidgins and other standard forms, or its spread outside of national boundaries in a discontinuous history recovers dimensions of its use. In contemporary times, in contrast to exclusive literary histories of the languages of the western coast, the fields of musicology and linguistics reveal the assumptions about language that underpin most studies of print and writing, when their objects of study tend to transgress the boundaries of literary study.[7]

In contrast to the quandary over how Konkani in Roman could be prepared to be an appropriate vehicle of high culture and language of state, the question of whether the Devanagari script in Konkani had a popular readership at all never had to be raised, since the idea of a natural affiliation between script and language legitimised Devanagari. Nor has there been a historical quest for the first Konkani text in Devanagari since it is the use of the script in other languages, and the belief in a continuous indigenous culture that secures its past. Thus the Devanagari script, infused already with the temporal and abstract cultural value attached to Sanskrit, antiquity, and the national movement, ensured a link with the past, and secured a foothold in the present. Konkani in comparison seemed to have a constitutively discontinuous history and a dispersed spatial existence defined by informal contact with a range of languages.

[6] Francisco João da Costa, *Jacob e Dulce: scenas da vida indiana* (Margão: Typographia do "Ultramar," 1896).

[7] Hugo C. Cardoso, "Oral Traditions of the Luso-Asian Communities: Local, Regional, and Continental," *Portuguese and Luso-Asian Legacies*, 1511-2011 2 (2012): 143–66.

It acquired an objective formal status through grammars and was accommodated to the temporal patterns of church narratives because of the convergence of caste structures, devotional practices and the impulses of the ecumenical Catholic Church on the west coast of India. It was this moment, rather than its other itinerant histories that were of most interest centuries later, in the context of modern state formation. Konkani could be groomed into being a modern language if divested of exactly those elements that had made its formalisation possible; the roman script and association with the colonial mission enterprise. The appearance of a translated/transliterated text in Devanagari in the mid-twentieth century was received as the point of arrival for a language, a text, and for its readers.

Acknowledgements

This project has extended over several years, in the course of which I drew on the goodwill of many whose kindness I count on once more if I have forgotten to mention them in this acknowledgement of help received.

For their generosity in responding to frequent calls on their time, I am grateful to Pratap Naik, S. J., Dr. William R. da Silva, Dr. Rocky V. Miranda, Leonard Fernandes, Frederick Noronha, Lourdes Bravo da Costa, Nithin Manayath and Ravi B.T., Sandra Ataíde Lobo, Mrs. Lilia Maria de Sousa, Paolo Aranha, Wei Jiang, Paul Melo e Castro, Shabnum Tejani, Avinash Jha (CSDS), K. P. Girija, Kaustubh Naik, Vivek Menezes, Hephzibah Israel, and Anil J. Pinto. For their support, I thank Rimli Bhattacharya, Asha Achuthan, Aparna Balachandran, Ravindra Karnena, Gitika De, Nuno Grancho, Manuel Magalhães and Sruti Chaganti. I particularly thank Lawrence Liang for his unstinting assistance at various difficult points in the project. I thank Dr. Nur Sobers-Khan for her help in sourcing a text in the collections of the British Library and meticulous attention to her translation of an excerpt. For their advice and help I am grateful to the late Dr. Suresh G. Amonkar, Gurunath Baliga, Prof. Valerian Rodrigues, Prof. Peter Ronald de Souza, S. M. Borges, Fatima da Silva Gracias, Tensing Rodrigues, Joachim Pinto, Ananya Chakravarti, Hansda Sowvendra Shekhar, Murali Ranganathan, Mr. Bhaskar Ramdas Shetty, Mr. Ramesh Pai, Prachi Deshpande, Annu Jalais and Pallavi Narayan.

This project owes much to Mr. Carlos Fernandes, curator at the State Central Library, Panjim, the library staff in the rare books section and especially Sr. Librarian Maria Ana Paiva for her frequent assistance and for creating a congenial workspace in Goa. All images, unless otherwise specified, are courtesy the State Central Library, Panjim. I am also grateful to Minakshi Khandolkar and the Director of the Thomas Stephens' Konkani Kendra, Porvorim for their assistance and to St. Aloysius College for access to historical material. I regret that the historian, Dr. Teotonio de Souza, whose essay is included in this volume, and whose work brought numerous sources for the history of Goa to the public eye, passed away earlier this year. I express my gratitude too late for the many times Edward Rodrigues and Alito Siqueira nurtured ideas through challenging and generous conversations. Their absence brings the realisation that they were a touchstone for us.

I especially thank Dale Luis Menezes for his involvement and dedicated work over an extended period of time and the many illuminating conversations about contemporary Goa. I am also grateful to Mabel Mascarenhas for contributing and editing the sections on Konkani in the Kannada script, and to Dr. Anil J. Pinto for his contributions and assistance at various points on the same sections. For their patience and contribution to this work I thank Fr. Victor Ferrão, Vidya Pai, and Melvyn Rodrigues, and Prof. Kiran Budkuley. For their help with translation I thank my parents, Rosario and Teofilda Pinto. I thank Aurelia Mendes for her care in Goa. For his constant support through all setbacks and for creating a home for us, I thank Vijay Rao.

I cannot thank Udaya Kumar enough for his encouragement and help at many stages through this work, and for his presence at the Department of English, Delhi University where I also benefited from the warmth and intellectual company of my colleagues. A fellowship at the Centre for the Study of Developing Societies, Delhi allowed me to rethink much of this work and I am grateful to its faculty and administration for sustaining a supportive and stimulating workspace. A congenial workspace during the term of my fellowship at the L'Institut d'Études Avancées at Nantes helped me complete this work. I thank Ketaki Bose of Orient BlackSwan for expressing an interest in this book and Aditi Jha for her detailed and meticulous work on it.

I thank the following for their assistance in securing permission to reprint the excerpts from their collections or from prior published work in this volume:

The late Dr. Teotonio de Souza, Adv. Uday L. Bhembre, Edwin J. F. D'souza, Dr. Rahul Tripathi, Sebastian Mariano Borges, Dr. Narayan B. Desai, Vidya Pai, Jason Keith Fernandes, Dale Luis Menezes, Jules Fausto Mendonca de Sa, Melvyn Rodrigues, Dr. William R. da Silva, Francis D'Cunha, Dr. Rocky Miranda, Ms. Maria Helena S. Godinho (for permission to reprint the work of Mariano Saldanha), and Mr. Joaquim Correia Afonso.

Upasana Majgonkar, Secretary, Goa Konkani Akademi, Kelwyn Monteiro, SJ, Thomas Stephens Konknni Kendra, Dr. B. D. Pai and Chandrahasa Rai B., Karnataka Konkani Sahitya Akademi, Dr. Melwyn Pinto, S. J., Institute of Konkani, St. Aloysius College, Prof. D. G. Rao of CIIL, Mysore, Br. Eusebio V. Miranda, sfx, *Vavraddeancho Ixtt*, Fr. Jocy D' Souza OCD, Chief Editor, *Naman Ballok Jesu*, Paulo Tremoceiro of the Arquivo Nacional da Torre do Tombo, Basti Vaman Shenoy, President, Konkani Bhas Ani Sanskriti Pratishtan, World Konkani Centre, Fr. Joaquim Loilola Pereira, Rev. Fr. Romeo Monteiro, Chancellor of the Archdiocese of Goa and Daman, and His Lordship, Peter Paul Saldanha, Bishop of Mangalore, Diocese of Mangalore.

The late Dr. Suresh G. Amonkar, Gautam Amonkar, and Mr. Sagun Velip, Director, Directorate of Art and Culture, Government of Goa, for permission to reproduce two essays by Mr. Sebastian Mariano Borges from *Goenchem Saunsarikikaran*. Mr. Sunil Sardessai, Mrs. Pramila Sardessai, Dr. Bhushan Bhave, Convenor, Language Advisory Board for Konkani, Dr. K. Sreenivasarao, Secretary, and Dr. S. Rajmohan, Deputy Secretary (Administration), Sahitya Akademi, Delhi, for permission to reproduce an excerpt from *A History of Konkani Literature*, by ManoharRai SarDessai.

Index